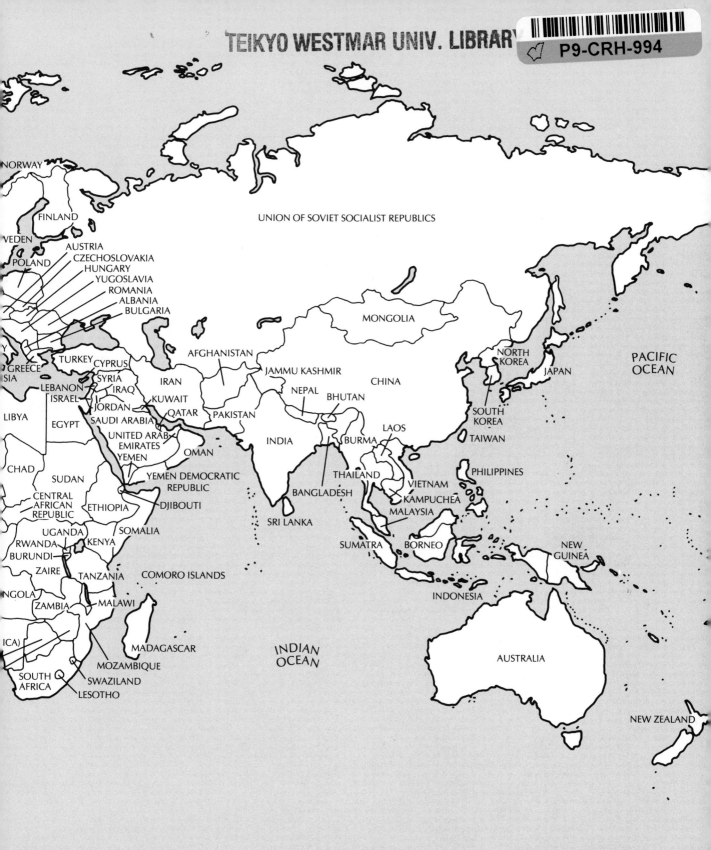

NORWAY

FINLAND

VEDEN

AUSTRIA
POLAND
CZECHOSLOVAKIA
HUNGARY
YUGOSLAVIA
ROMANIA
ALBANIA
BULGARIA

UNION OF SOVIET SOCIALIST REPUBLICS

MONGOLIA

Y
GREECE
SIA
TURKEY   CYPRUS
SYRIA
LEBANON   IRAQ
ISRAEL
JORDAN
SAUDI ARABIA
UNITED ARAB
EMIRATES
YEMEN

AFGHANISTAN

JAMMU KASHMIR

IRAN

NEPAL

KUWAIT
QATAR

PAKISTAN

CHINA

NORTH
KOREA

JAPAN

PACIFIC
OCEAN

SOUTH
KOREA

TAIWAN

LIBYA

EGYPT

OMAN

INDIA

BHUTAN

BURMA

LAOS

CHAD

SUDAN

YEMEN DEMOCRATIC
REPUBLIC

THAILAND

PHILIPPINES

CENTRAL
AFRICAN
REPUBLIC

ETHIOPIA

DJIBOUTI

BANGLADESH

VIETNAM

KAMPUCHEA
MALAYSIA

UGANDA

SOMALIA

SRI LANKA

RWANDA
BURUNDI
ZAIRE

KENYA

SUMATRA

BORNEO

NEW
GUINEA

NGOLA

ZAMBIA

TANZANIA

MALAWI

COMORO ISLANDS

INDONESIA

ICA)

MADAGASCAR

INDIAN
OCEAN

AUSTRALIA

SOUTH
AFRICA

MOZAMBIQUE

SWAZILAND

LESOTHO

NEW ZEALAND

THE
SACRED
PATHS

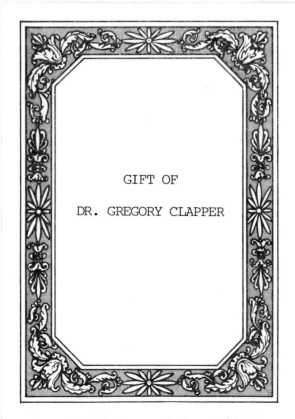

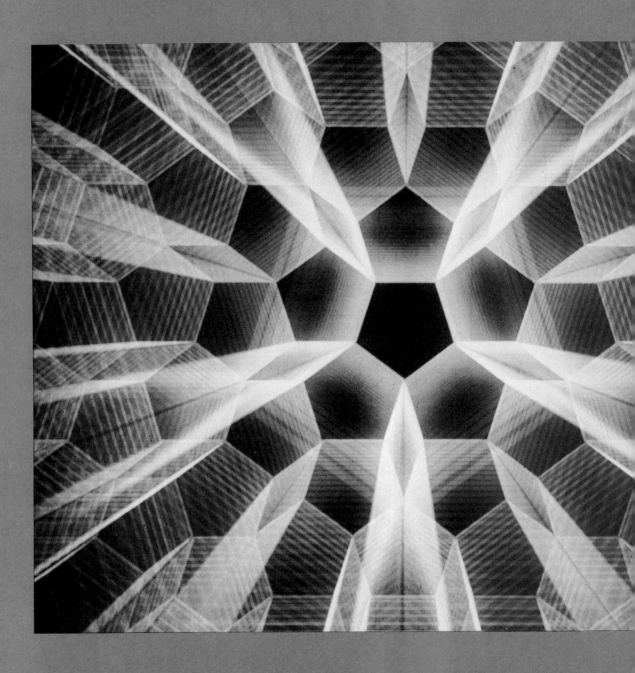

THEODORE M. LUDWIG
VALPARAISO UNIVERSITY

THE
SACRED
PATHS

Understanding the Religions of the World

90-291

MACMILLAN PUBLISHING COMPANY
NEW YORK

To my parents
Paul Walter Ludwig
Thekla Friedrich Ludwig

Macmillan Publishing Company
866 Third Avenue, New York, New York 10022

Collier Macmillan Canada, Inc.

LIBRARY OF CONGRESS CATALOGING-IN-PUBLICATION DATA

Ludwig, Theodore M.
    The sacred paths: understanding the religions of the world/
    Theodore Ludwig.
        p.   cm.
    Bibliography: p.
    Includes index.
    ISBN 0-02-372170-7
    1. Religions.   2. Religion.   I. Title.
BL80.2.L83 1989   88-22089
291-dc19   CIP

Printing: 1 2 3 4 5 6 7   Year: 9 0 1 2 3 4 5

PREFACE

A first step in understanding the religions of the world is to get a sense of what these religions mean for the people who live by them. Studying the historical development of each religious tradition—its origin, its development, its expansion into different sects or subgroups—is key to one's understanding, for each religion is a living, growing organism that cannot be understood apart from its historical and cultural environment. But, in addition to knowing the historical development of each religion, it is also essential to become conversant with the self-understanding of that community as expressed in their sacred stories, their basic ideas about life, and their ritual and ethical practices.

Given these considerations, how does one best begin to understand the religions of the world? This book combines discussion of the historical development of each religion with a thematic approach based on general questions of human existence that are of central concern in all religions. As explained in Chapter 1, these are questions about identity, about ultimate reality, about human nature, about the right way to live, and the like. These are questions with which the student can identify, and they open windows toward

understanding the meaning and guidance that people find in their religion. The master story (or stories) of the religion, its ideas and teachings, and its ritual and ethical practices are presented against the background provided by these thematic questions. By using this thematic approach and by taking up the same basic questions in looking at each religion, comparisons and contrasts among them can easily be noted. And the way is opened for understanding the main motifs and concerns of the general dimension of religion in human culture.

Further, this book takes up the major world religions in "family" groupings—the Abrahamic religions, the religions arising from India, and the religions of China and Japan. These groupings represent religions that have grown up together historically and also share many basic ideas and practices. Studying a family of religions together makes the comparison of basic themes appropriate and conducive to deeper understanding.

Each religious tradition is highly complex, with various movements, sects, or groupings at different points in history. In keeping with this book's purpose, the general mainstream of each religion is presented, with some of the major alternatives given where appropriate. This work is a basic introduction for students who are beginning their exploration of the religions; it does not attempt to be a complete catalogue of each religious tradition. For more thorough descriptions of the various movements that make up each religion, the student can consult the works on each religion listed in the Bibliography.

Again, since the purpose of this book is to help students become conversant with basic religious issues and with the major world religions, discussion of the more technical topics has been minimized, for example, the history of the academic study of religion, the various scholarly approaches to studying the religions, and scholarly reconstructions of prehistoric and ancient religions. Further, simplified spellings rather than scholarly transliterations of terms from the different languages have been used. For example, the Hindu god's name "Krishna" is written here rather than "Kṛsna," a more scholarly transliteration from the Sanskrit. And the name of the Muslim ancestor is given in this book as "Abraham" rather than " 'Ibrāhīm," a literal transliteration of the name in the Quran. These more technical aspects are important, of course, and advanced students are encouraged to consult the *Encyclopedia of Religion* and other works listed in the Bibliography.

Concerning the spelling of religious terms used in this book, it might be mentioned that simplified Sanskrit spellings have generally been used for Buddhist terms, except where the Pali term is noted. The older Wade-Giles spellings have been followed in the chapters on Chinese religions, with the *pin-yin* spelling (adopted in the People's Republic of China) given in parentheses in the glossary for some important terms. For Hebrew and Arabic terms, the consonant ' ('ayn) has been included in spelling, as in "Ka'bah," since this consonant is an obvious factor in pronunciation.

A number of study features have been included in this volume to assist the student in attaining familiarity with the religions. There are lists of important dates in each religion, maps to help visualize the geographical siting of each religion and of families of religions, and a glossary of important terms in the religions. Discussion questions at the end of each chapter are intended to encourage reflection on the meanings people find in their religion. And the Bibliography lists selected works that would be helpful as students probe deeper into religion and the religions, including both general works on each religion and some specialized studies that provide more depth in certain areas.

Appreciation is in order to many who have helped along the way toward the completion of this volume. The influence of my mentors at the Divinity School of The University of Chicago, especially Joseph M. Kitagawa with his careful insistence on an integral understanding of the religions, has been very important in my own approach to the religions. The stimulation and encouragement provided by my departmental colleagues at Valparaiso University have been most helpful; a special word of appreciation goes to Edgar Senne, my colleague in teaching the history of religions for the past two decades and my mentor in how to communicate this material to undergraduate students. Many scholars have read this manuscript at various stages of development and have made critical suggestions, including Michael Barnes, University of Dayton; Fred Clothey, University of Pittsburgh; John Corrigan, University of Virginia; Andrew O. Fort, Texas Christian University; Luke Timothy Johnson, Indiana University; Shigeo H. Kanda, California State University, Chico; Robert C. Lester, University of Colorado, Boulder; William K. Mahony, Davidson College; Robert N. Minor, University of Kansas, Lawrence; Ronald Modras, Saint Louis University; Charles S. Prebish, Pennsylvania State University; Franklin Proaño, Ohio State University, Marion; C. Allyn Russell, Boston University; Daniel P. Sheridan, Loyola University, New Orleans; Merlin Swartz, Boston University; David Terrell, Northwestern Michigan University; Karen Voss, San Jose State University; and Dewey D. Wallace, Jr., George Washington University. Their critical suggestions have been most helpful. My thanks to them does not, of course, imply their approval of what I have written, for which I must take the final responsibility. Finally, I want to express my appreciation to Helen McInnis, Executive Editor at Macmillan Publishing Company, whose enthusiasm, helpfulness, and quest for excellence sustained the long process of bringing this book to publication.

BRIEF CONTENTS

DETAILED CONTENTS

Understanding the Sacred Paths

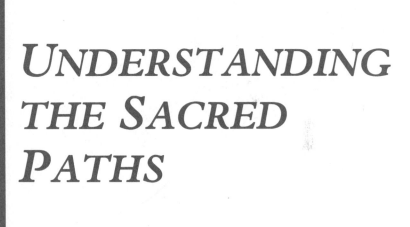

CHAPTER 1

BASIC DIMENSIONS OF RELIGION

"Who am I?" "What sense is there in life?" "How can I find *real* life?" Questions such as these are not mere philosophical problems for academic debate. They reach to the depths of life concerns that are felt, vaguely or forcefully, by all human beings. They deal with the fundamental concern of the *meaning* of human existence. Does life really have any meaning—any *real* meaning—or do we just live and die in a small frame of a pointless, accidental cycle of the universe? In such concerns we are dealing with the religious dimension of our human consciousness.

Of course, there are many dimensions of being human, many concerns that are not directly religious ones. We are concerned about our physical makeup, our biological structure, our reasoning capacities, our languages and forms of communication, our historical memories, our forms of society, our psychological makeup, and much more. We can investigate these dimensions of human existence, attempting to understand and even alter them. Such investigation and understanding comprise the disciplines of humanistic study: biology, philosophy, language and literature, history, political science, sociology, psychology, and so forth.

All these aspects of human existence are closely interrelated, for to be human is to be an integrated whole, not just a composite of many parts. Further, no matter what aspect of human existence we happen to look at, the question of meaning and purpose is close at hand: Why do we happen to function biologically the way we do? What is the meaning of sex? Why have we evolved into reasoning animals? Is there any sense or direction in our history? What responsibility do we have for fellow humans? In other words, the question of the *meaning* of human existence is met. And wrestling with that question of meaning in its deeper aspects involves us in religious thinking and experiencing.

Religion is not limited to one dimension of human existence, nor is it confined to established norms of logic and scientific methodology. Religion has to do with the overall meaning of human existence: Why is *everything* the way it is? What is the rhyme or reason behind all this? What is our purpose in living? Behind all such questions is a fundamental one: Where can we look for that which is ultimately real, that unlimited source from which we derive life and meaning?

It is to that which they feel is ultimately real, the unlimited source, that people within the various religions direct themselves in their many different ways. We designate this focal point of the religions as the "sacred," the ground of ultimate vitality, value, and meaning. The modes of experiencing the sacred, and the responses to this experience, are the forms and expressions that make up the religions of the world.

DIMENSIONS OF RELIGIOUS EXPERIENCE

It would be well at this point to suggest a working definition of what we mean by "religion." Here is a four-part description:

1. Religion is human involvement with what is considered to be the realm of the sacred.
2. It is expressed in thought, action, and social forms.
3. It constitutes a total system of symbols with deep meaning.
4. It provides a path of ultimate transformation.

Human Involvement with the Realm of the Sacred

The first part of the definition of religion suggests a relationship between two levels of experience: the limited human level and the level of that which is felt to be the sacred. Of course, we cannot examine the sacred as if it were an objective realm of reality; the sacred is not something to be proved or disproved. We must be clear that we are not attempting to define ultimate reality as an objective fact; we are simply investigating how people of different cultures have described their experiences of whatever it is that they consider the ultimate sacred. Still, it is the common experience of many people past and present that there is a sacred realm of reality with ultimate significance, and, further, that the ultimate good in human life has to do with relating to the sacred.

Although the idea of the sacred is distinctive in each particular religious tradition, it is possible to discern some general outlines that resonate across religious boundaries. After all, if there is a shared humanness throughout the different cultures of the world, we should expect some general similarities in the way people describe their experiences of what they consider to be the sacred. Rudolph Otto drew various religious experiences together in an influential study, *The Idea of the Holy*,[1] putting forth the view that basic to religious experience is a deep sense of the "numinous." This is a term he coined from the Latin *numen* (holy, sacred) to express our basic response to the experience of the sacred even before we develop rational and moral notions about it. Experiencing the numinous as ultimate mystery, people feel a strong sense of awe and reverence, at the same time being fascinated and drawn to the mysterious Other.

Drawing on Otto's perspective, let us make some observations about the experience of the sacred. First of all, bound up with the numinous is an unlimited, primordial, overpowering quality. The sacred is ultimate, the basis of everything else, and nothing can supercede or encompass it. It accounts for everything, and it holds everything together—but it is its own basis without depending on anything else. The sacred, whether expressed as God (Islam), Brahman (Hinduism), emptiness (Mahayana Buddhism), or some other formulation, is felt to be the universal foundation of all truth, reality, goodness, and value.

Experience of the sacred takes countless forms in the religions of the world. Here a Hindu woman makes an offering at the River Ganges.

We encounter the sacred as Mystery, as the Wholly Other that remains completely "other" even when experienced within the human world. It cannot be completely held by humans, either with their hands or with their reason. Words can attempt to describe the sacred, but it is understood that words can only point to the mystery in a symbolic way. Every word refers to a conditioned human reality, but the sacred both encompasses and transcends human realities. For this reason, religions express the experience of the sacred not only by words but also by a variety of other symbolic forms, such as sculpture, ritual actions, meditation, music, dance, silence, and so forth. On the Jewish festival of Simhat Torah, for example, dancing with the Torah scrolls expresses the experience of the sacred more than words can say. Bathing in "Mother Ganges" provides a direct, nonverbal sacred experience for Hindus. After the reception of the Eucharist in a Christian church, a moment of silence is often the most appropriate way of responding to the mystery. The stillness of Buddhist meditation brings one into direct touch with the ultimate truth in a way that words can never do.

The experience of the sacred is accompanied with awe and reverence. The sacred cannot be controlled by human design; it bursts the bounds of human understanding and overwhelms with energy and demand. The proper human response is awe, respect, and submission. For Muslims, for example, washing the body and prostrating oneself in prayer expresses the right human relationship to the sacred. Rudolph Otto called this quality of the sacred the *mysterium tremendum* (terrifying mystery). For the ancient Israelites, the mountain of Sinai was the awesome presence of the sacred; touching it could mean destruction. The image of a god or goddess in Hinduism is full of power so that one should not, for example, take pictures of it.

The experience of the sacred at the same time involves fascination and love; we are compelled and drawn to the ultimate origin of all that is good and true and beautiful, the source of meaning and purpose in life, the fountain of vitality and strength. The sacred is wondrous, marvelous, and compelling. Encounter with the sacred leads to the highest joy, rapture, and love. Buddhists who have experienced awakening describe it as ultimate bliss and rapture. The Muslim pilgrim is drawn to Mecca and the experience of the sacred there as by a powerful magnet. The Hindu worshiper lovingly performs *puja* to the image of the beloved god or goddess. A Christian writer, Augustine, said that the soul is restless until it finds rest in God.

Since the sacred is the source of ultimate value, the deepest need of human life is to have an on-going relationship with the sacred. It is this need that is the foundation of the various religions of humankind. Each religion has its own way of providing the context so that the sacred is present to the human community, with the power, value structures, meaning, and purpose that fulfill the religious needs of human beings.

Expression in Thought, Action, and Social Forms

The second part of our definition of religion suggests what goes into the making of that human involvement with the sacred. Since religion is, obviously, a human affair, it necessarily involves human forms or modes of expression. Joachim Wach, in his *Sociology of Religion*,[2] suggests there are three such modes of expression: theoretical (thinking, speaking), practical (doing, acting), and social (fellowship, community). These are the building blocks of religion and they fit together to form a complex, unique universe of meaning, that is, a religion.

The *theoretical* mode of expression comprises the verbal aspect of religion, what is told and described. Religions say things about the most important, basic issues of life: how the sacred is experienced, where the world came from and where it is going, what the goal of human life is, and how we can achieve that. These things are talked about in two basic ways: narrative or story (myth) and theoretical statements about reality (doctrine). All religions have stories or myths that put forth in narrative form the worldview and the important experiences of the sacred on which that religion is founded. Leading thinkers of a religion also express their basic perceptions in doctrines that generalize from the sacred stories to present the fundamental truths of the religion, providing intellectual guidance to the participants in that religion.

The *practical* level of expression in religion has to do with its visible and performed side: rituals, worship, meditation, ethical conduct, and so forth. Religion is not just mental but also physical, and the acting out, the performance, of the involvement with the sacred is just as important as the stories and the doctrines. Prostrating oneself before the sacred presence, sharing in a sacred meal, chanting texts and prayers, wearing colorful robes and swinging an incense burner, observing moral rules, and hundreds of other religious rituals and types of behavior represent the acting out or performance of the religious experience.

Religion is never simply an individual affair but always a group or communal experience involving *social forms*. It is the religious community that carries on the tradition, even before the individual was born and after he or she dies. And it is in identifying with the religious community that the individual finds personal identity. There are different structures of community depending on the type of religious experience, in family or clan, congregations, religious societies, and whole nations. And there are various types of religious leadership, such as queens, kings, priests, prophets, masters, shamans, and many more. Participation in the social forms of the religious community is what gives continuity to religious experience.

A Total System of Symbols

Taken together, these modes of religious expression form a total world view, a "map" of human involvement with the sacred, and this brings us to the third part of our definition. Religion guides and gives meaning by presenting a view of the whole order of existence. This religious map of human existence is made up of "symbols"—words, ideas, rituals, pictures, gestures, sounds, social groupings—which evoke the deepest feelings and most important meanings in our lives. These are the means by which a group of people express their perception of what life is all about. To live as part of this community is to share a whole way of knowing the world and one's place in it, a whole way of looking at life and death, and a whole set of assumptions about what is real and true and good. The system of symbols upholds deep-seated attitudes and motivations, providing a complete system of values for human life.

Let us consider a few examples of such symbols. In a Buddhist monastery an ordinary bowl for food becomes a "begging bowl," an important symbol of the spiritual status of the monk or nun on the path toward the ultimate goal of all people in the community. The words *blood* and *lamb* are words with ordinary, straightforward meanings. But for a Christian to say, "The blood of the lamb has saved me," arouses deep religious feeling and motivation. The act of eating a meal is one of the most common human activities and is often done without any particularly deep meaning. But a Jew sitting at the table celebrating the Passover seder with her family experiences deep religious meaning in that human activity. Similarly, washing oneself is an everyday human activity; but all religions have rituals that express sacred meaning in washing.

We can envision the world view of each religion as a circle with a center. The circle suggests the totality of what the people understand as their existence in the world. It contains their universe of symbols that provides the pattern of life that is their religious path. Within the circle, then, we see the most important symbols of that religion. The meanings that these symbols supply have been told in stories, painted and sculpted in art, sung and played by musicians, expressed in poems and dramas, acted out in rituals and worship, and argued and systematized by theologians and philosophers for centuries.

The various symbols fit together in a circle, for they are all related to each other in such a way as to present a comprehensive and persuasive outlook on life. Above all, the circle of symbols is centered, that is, there is a *central vision* that colors and permeates the whole circle in a pervasive way. We might suggest, for example, that for Muslims the center is the Holy Book, the Quran, whereas for Christians it is Christ. Buddhism centers on the path to nirvana, whereas the center for Shinto is the exhaustless life of the kami. The symbols closest to the center could be considered the *primary symbols*, those that are most essential to those of that religion. Toward the outside of the circle appear somewhat more *secondary symbols*, those that are more

inclined to change when new experiences and challenges arise, those that respond to the needs of the religious communities in different times and places. Of course, people do not always agree on whether a particular symbol is primary or secondary; diverse religious experiences lead to different emphases even within one religious tradition.

We should therefore keep in mind that a religion is not a static, unchanging affair but rather a dynamic organism. Changes and transformations do occur in response to new experiences, new stories, and new challenges. Sometimes what appeared to be a primary symbol to some at one time becomes less important in later ages, whereas a secondary symbol introduced by some new religious experience shifts into a primary position. For example, the idea of bodily resurrection was at one time primary to traditional Jews, but in recent times it has become of secondary importance to some modern Jewish thinkers. But the Land of Israel, which for much of the Middle Ages was simply a spiritual idea, has become for many modern Jews a very primary symbol in concrete form. In spite of changes in the circle of symbols, however, there is an ongoing basic continuity, flowing outward from the central vision and maintaining the fundamental pattern of faith and life.

As we look at the issues of human life and focus on specific symbols from the religions, we must keep in mind that a particular symbol must always be viewed in its total context. Some of the symbols will, of course, appear quite similar in a family of religions, and rightly so, given the shared history and culture. But our most important task is to see each symbol, each teaching, idea, story, ritual, practice, or community structure, in the light that is reflected from the central vision and from the total pattern of that system of symbols. For example, we want to see Muslims not just as monotheists (as are Jews and Christians) but as they experience their own comprehensive and unified view of life; and in the same way we need to see the uniqueness of the religious vision held by Hindus, Taoists, and all the others.

A Path of Ultimate Transformation
The fourth part of our definition points out that a religion is not only a system of beliefs and expressions

Chanting the scriptures—symbolic of the ultimate truth—is a very active ritual for these Japanese Buddhist monks.

about the relation to the sacred; it is also a path, a way of life. Each religion offers something that many humans find essential to human existence: a path to ultimate meaning and transformation.

An important part of religious experience is the realization of the broken or fractured nature of human involvement with the sacred, for from this arises the fundamental troubles and anxieties of existence. This awareness of the human problem is coupled with knowledge of the ideal, ultimate relationship to the sacred. One's religion provides a way of overcoming this fracture, of restoring the bridge to the sacred, of transforming oneself to attain the goal of life as expressed in that particular religion. The path continues throughout one's lifetime, through rituals, symbols, disciplines, study, social relationships, and states of consciousness. Buddhists, for example, follow the Eightfold Path toward the ultimate attainment of nirvana. Christians follow the path of Christ to overcome sin and attain eternal life. For Hindus the paths of action, worship, and knowledge lead toward spiritual realization and liberation from the cycle of birth and death. Following the life of Torah for Jews is the path toward spiritual perfection. The path is a way of life, a praxis designed to restore wholeness and ultimate meaning to human ex-

istence by involvement with the source of life, the sacred. We look at the path toward transformation in more detail later in this chapter.

FAMILIES OF RELIGIONS

It is almost bewildering to look at the great variety of religions in the world, past and present. Each tribal group has its own distinctive way of life, which is its religion. And even the highly developed, major religions of the world are quite numerous, each with its unique symbol system. We need a perspective on the religions of the world so that we do not get lost in the overwhelming variety of symbols and practices found in each. Whereas each religion is unique in the way it puts everything together, it is possible to make some family groupings.

One loose grouping of religions contains the tribal, nonliterate peoples who exist today (or existed until the recent past) in areas of Africa, Melanesia, the Americas, and other places. These peoples often have a strong sense of the presence of the sacred in various forms, sometimes as spirits, ancestors, and gods, sometimes as a diffuse, impersonal power. Their myths and rituals are closely related to their life in hunting, farming, or herding, having to do with the fertility and vitality of the animals or plants that are necessary for existence. The tribe itself is the central social reality, and no distinction is made between "religion" and the traditional way of life in the tribe. Another general grouping of religions contains the cosmic, nature-oriented religions of ancient civilizations. These were often city-state religions whose kings and priests served the great gods and goddesses of the universe. For these religions, the whole world is conceived as a divine organism, with the events of nature controlled by various divine wills. The highest importance for humans is to serve these divine powers and live in harmony with their will.

The three "Abraham" religions—Judaism, Christianity, and Islam—constitute a family of religions whose central perspective is monotheistic, that is, they envision one God who created everything. To them, monotheism is the heart of religion, with the other beliefs and practices stemming from it. Since there is one God, this God must be almighty and in charge of everything in the created world. The highest good for the creation is to fulfill the will and design of this almighty creator, and to do this, humans need revelation from God through prophets. These three religions are closely related historically, arising successively from the same Semitic society of the Near East, each tracing its roots in some manner to the patriarch Abraham.

Religions arising in India, sharing a historical development in the first millennium B.C.E. and a set of common perspectives on the world and the path to follow, constitute another grouping. These religions include the traditions known as Hinduism, Buddhism, and Jainism (Sikhism developed much later but shares some of the same perspectives). They tend to have a nondualistic (or monistic) worldview, the idea that somehow behind or within all the multiplicity of forms and forces in this universe there is one unified sacred reality. These religions do have gods that are important, but many thinkers in these religions go beyond the idea of a personal creator God, holding to the vision, for example, that the inner soul of reality or the truth of all reality itself is the sacred ultimate. They agree that human existence is part of the process of *samsara*, that

is, birth and death over and over in an endless cycle. According to this perspective, the highest good for humans is to achieve awareness of ultimate reality through practices of meditation or devotion and to find liberation from the cycle of rebirths. Whereas Sikhism arose in India and contains many of these ideas, this religion also accepts some basic monotheistic perspectives.

The religions of East Asia, particularly of China and Japan, form a loose family grouping. There are many gods here, in Japanese Shinto and in the Chinese religions, Taoism and Confucianism, but at their center is an emphasis on harmony with the divine flow of nature and reverence for the ancestors and family. Within that harmony, human existence is valued as positive and good. Chinese culture and religion have been influential throughout the lands of East Asia. In particular, the Mahayana form of Buddhism has adapted the Buddhist outlook to the East Asian perspective and thus plays a unifying role in the cultural grouping that makes up this East Asian family of religions.

We must keep in mind that this scheme represents only a general grouping of the perspectives found in the various religions, with emphasis on the historical and cultural connections within a family of religions. It is true that different perspectives can be found in the same religion in varying degrees. Nondualistic Hinduism, for example, knows a great deal about worshiping the great God who created and sustains everything, with teachings and practices that resemble monotheism. Islam, for all its fierce monotheism, has long harbored the Sufi mystical movement, which has cultivated language that sounds much like the Hindu and Buddhist nondualist thinkers. Yet it is helpful to group families of religions according to the dominant experience in each, the perspective that the people of that religion have put forth as their central way of looking at the world. Within each family, we take up the individual religions, attempting to see the distinct flavor of that perspective and thus to understand its particular meaning.

Comparison and Understanding

Since understanding also arises from comparison, it is part of our task to see how the perspective of different religions do have common presuppositions in their vision of human existence. In fact, seeing that which is common sets the stage for reflecting on the unique characteristics of each of the approaches.

A word needs to be added about looking at religion as we are doing here, studying it from the outside, as it were. Whereas many of us are Hindus, Muslims, Christians, Buddhists, Jews, or Confucianists, none of us belongs to all the religions. Therefore we necessarily find ourselves in the position of being on the outside looking in at the intimate practice of someone else. In looking from the outside, we miss the inner compulsion of commitment and the special meaning that the religion provides for the insider. Further, our view cannot be completely "objective," for our own personal religious beliefs and presuppositions stand in the way and color our perspective.

It is important, then, that we consciously make a deep effort to *understand* these religious traditions of others. To "under-stand" is to stand under that which gives meaning to the other. It means to stand in her or his religious stance, to look at the universe of religious symbols from the perspective of being on the inside. This is not an easy task, and it is always an incomplete accomplishment. One cannot fully understand Jewish religious experience unless one is a Jew, and the same is true of Buddhist and Shinto religious experience, as well as all the others.

It is possible to understand at least in an incomplete way, however, if a number of important measures are taken. First, an attitude of respect and openness is necessary, a recognition of the value and importance that the religion has for the other person. Second, a conscious effort must be made to become aware of our own religious presuppositions that color our own views of the religions of others. By becoming aware of our presuppositions, it is possible to "bracket" them to some extent so that they do not hinder us from entering into the worldview of the other religion. Third, it is necessary to refrain, at first, from the important theological task of evaluation, that is, of asking the question of the "truth" of a particular religious idea. Each religion by its very nature makes claims to truth and in doing so also passes an evaluation on the truth of other religions.

There is a time and place for responsible theological investigation, evaluation, and challenge to other religions in dialogue. But it is important first of all to understand, and a rush to evaluate and debate truth can stand in the way of understanding. Fourth, a willingness to learn from the other religions and even to grow in one's own understanding is an important component of the process of understanding the religion of others.

There is also a certain value in being able to look at several religions from the outside, as it were, if this is done sensitively and with understanding. By comparing various aspects in different religions, and especially by comparing that which is unfamiliar to elements familiar from one's own religion, it is possible to see universal structures of religion more clearly. We can see recurrent questions and concerns about life and death, and we can survey the persistent themes in the answers provided by the different religions. We can see common practices that give structure to life and society and thus develop deeper understanding of the common human needs that give rise to the various religious traditions of humankind. By confronting the religious beliefs and practices of others, we see our own beliefs and practices in a broader and deeper context.

BASIC HUMAN CONCERNS AND RELIGIOUS RESPONSES

Our ground plan in this book is to take up a number of universal questions and concerns about human existence in relation to the sacred and use them as windows into the fundamental views and practices of each family of religions. The goal is not to produce a synthesis of answers from all religions, for each is unique and distinctive. We must be especially careful not to impose outside ideas on a particular religion. Rather, we must try sensitively to hear how each religion frames it own concerns and responses. Still, looking at universal human questions provides opportunities to compare the religions while seeing clearly the unique characteristics of each.

Here is a preliminary listing of the main questions and religious responses to think about as we find our way into the basic dimensions of religion. The questions and responses fall into three general areas:

1. The Sacred Story and Its Historical Context (historical development)
   "Who am I?" The Sacred Story.
2. The Worlds of Meaning (the main theoretical teachings)
   "What's it *all* about?" The Sacred Reality.
   "What sense is there in life?" Creation and Human Existence.
   "How can I start living *real* life?" The Path of Transformation.
3. Worship and the Good Life (the practical and social aspects)
   "How can I find new power for life?" Sacred Time, Ritual, and Art.
   "How should I live?" Social Structure and the Good Life.

A brief discussion of these basic dimensions of religion will set the stage for our look at each of the religions in the following chapters.

The Sacred Story and Its Historical Context

One basic human concern is the question of identity: "Who am I?" When a person tries to answer that question, she starts by telling the story of her life. Although there are many parts of her life story she might emphasize, one important aspect would be her religious identity: "I'm a Hindu." "I'm Jewish." "My family is Buddhist." "I'm a Christian." "I'm Muslim." But what does that mean? It means that a person connects his or her own story with the sacred story of his or her religious tradition—with those crucial events or realities of the founding of the religion. To express his identity as a Buddhist, a person tells the story of the Buddha and the founding of Buddhism. To renew his Christian identity, a person looks to the sacred story of Christ, for that is the story—the sacred story—of his life. The story of the founding or the revealing of the religion is of particular concern, because it provides the divine authority for one's religious identity. In this study of the religions we devote considerable attention to the story and

also the historical transformation of each religion. Understanding this question of identity is crucial to developing a sensitive understanding of the ideas and practices of the religion.

Myth and Sacred Story

All religions have sacred stories telling of decisive events and leaders through which the new truths and practices were inaugurated as the basis of the new way of life. These birth-giving events and leaders are told about in their stories, written about in their scriptures, sung about in their songs, depicted in their art, and remembered in their rituals. They form the central focus, the paradigm, by which the people of that religion express their self-identity.

These sacred stories, or "myths," have a very important function in religion, for they establish the basic outlook and the way of life of the people of that religion. They tell of the central encounters of the people with the sacred, those clear episodes that illumine all aspects of life. Thus these stories, even though they may seem in some cases to refer to distant mythological ages, are understood to be real and true, for they reveal the bridge to the sacred that is essential for human existence. Although they are presented in story form, they provide a kind of map for human life, a model that can be followed so that life can be lived in the fullest way according to the design established by the sacred power. Knowing these stories means that the people know how human life is to be lived in a meaningful way; not knowing the stories or forgetting them would be to live a chaotic, subhuman existence.

But knowing and remembering the sacred story are not just intellectual exercises. To perform the stories—repeating them in words and acting them out in rituals—is actually to become participants in the founding events. It is to reactualize the central happenings so that they become real and powerful in human life today just as they were in the special time told about in the sacred stories.

In sum, the story provides an answer to the question of identity—Who am I?—by making it possible to identify with those events and beings that exemplify in a clear and powerful way the relationship with the

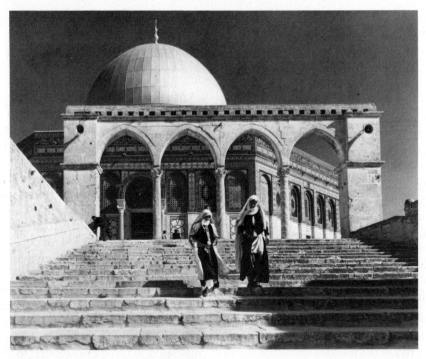

The Dome of the Rock in Jerusalem marks the spot from which Muhammad was taken on a journey to heaven. The mosque stands above the foundations of the Jewish temple.

sacred that undergirds human life. The stories tell about the beginnings, the origins, of the real, authentic way of human life. And thus they tell us who we really are.

Some of the religions are "founded" religions in the sense that their sacred history points to specific persons who created the origins of the religion. Judaism, Christianity, Islam, Zoroastrianism, and Buddhism are examples of founded religions. Since these religions focus on founders who lived in a particular age amid crucial events of human history, the stories tend to dwell more on actual historical events and human personalities than do the religions that do not have central founding events and leaders. Of course, Buddhism, with its particular distrust of the cycles of human life, tends to emphasize the eternal truth (Dharma) revealed by the Buddha, although the Buddhist stories

do present the events of the Buddha's life as having special significance as a model for all to follow.

Peoples of nonliterate societies, even though they often do not remember a particular "founder," have their myths about the sacred beings and ancestors of the "time of the beginnings" who performed the crucial actions to create life the way it is. These myths are repeated in festivals so that the power and vitality they tell about can become real once more for the people. Also, religions like Hinduism and Shinto, even though they have no particular founding events or leaders, have their stories about the gods and the cultural heroes, stories that provide the foundation of the authentic way of life.

In presenting and interpreting the stories of these communities, we rely on scholarly work that has clarified the origins and early history of each of the religions, providing a historical context for the stories. It is our intention, however, to present each story primarily as it is told and interpreted by that religious community. We are, after all, not dealing with history strictly speaking but with *sacred* history. And that sacred history is not expressed by archaeological finds or ancient history books but in the stories told in the worshiping communities.

Change and Transformation in the Religious Tradition

The history of the religious tradition does not end with the sacred story of the beginnings. Each religion is a living organism that changes and develops in new situations and experiences. Understanding this dynamic quality of religious tradition is important, for it is the "passing on" (*traditio*) of the story that finally shapes our religious identity. We receive and interact with the story through the tradition that has brought it to us.

For example, one cannot understand Buddhism in the world today without taking some account of the Mahayana developments and also the various developments in Southeast Asia and in East Asia. Judaism has been transformed by the teachings of the rabbis, the medieval persecutions, the emancipation, and most recently by the Holocaust. It would be most difficult to understand modern Christianity without taking account of the transformations brought about, for example, by the Christological disputes of the patristic age, the medieval synthesis of doctrine and life, or the new emphases of the Reformation and the Counterreformation. And so it is with each religious tradition. Although in this book we cannot focus extensively on the historical development of each religion, it is important to become aware of the major transformations and the effect they have had on the understanding and practice of the religion.

Worlds of Meaning: Theoretical Teachings

The Sacred Reality

"What's it *all* about?" Confronted with the maze of human life in a mind-boggling universe, we wonder how we can make sense of everything that is. How does it all hold together? The answer presented in each religion is the sacred, the ultimate reality. Each religion has appropriate terms for this ultimate reality: gods, goddesses, kami, God, Brahman, nirvana, Dharmakaya, Tao, and many more. Without such a vision of sacred reality, religious people feel there would be no center, no order, only a chaos of things and events occurring haphazardly without rhyme or reason. And so since the beginning of human life on this planet, people have always sought after sacred reality as the source and support for this world and human existence within it.

What are some of the ways people think about the sacred? In our definition of religion, we described the experience of the sacred as the awe-inspiring and fascinating mystery. Here we simply sketch some of the dominant ways in which the various religions describe their view of the sacred.

Some religions, especially in the ancient world and among nonliterate peoples of today, have understood the sacred to be experienced in numerous forms and powers. Some speak of an impersonal sacred power that penetrates and interacts with everything. Wherever we turn, in nature and in society, we encounter Power. Often the sacred is personified as gods and spirits, who are immanent in the various aspects of the world: one god shows power in the rain and storm, another in the healing and creating power of the sun, another in pregnancy and childbirth, and so forth. This view, often called polytheism, means power is shared, with no one sacred being having unlimited sway. Many of these religions do have a supreme god who is the primordial creator and has ultimate authority, but this god delegates the functions of the world to other gods and goddesses. This general vision of the sacred can also be found widespread within the religions of Asia, such as Hinduism, Buddhism, Taoism, and Shinto. It is generally understood, of course, that such divine beings are not ultimate in power or status.

Another view of the sacred is monotheism, the view that there is one sacred reality, a personal God who created and supports this world and everything in it, with no alternates, no competitors. There is one God and one world, the creation. However, God is not a part of this world. God is transcendent, that is, above and beyond the created world, holy and eternal. At the same time God is present in a personal way to the created world. God encounters us especially in historical events, giving us guidance and challenging us to fulfill the divine will. The three Abrahamic religions are strong advocates of this perspective on the sacred, but it can be found in modified forms in religions like Zoroastrianism, Sikhism, and even special groups within Hinduism and Buddhism.

Still another conception of the sacred is sometimes called nondualism or monism, a broad category of thought and experience with an emphasis placed on the unity of all reality. Nondualism means that there is no real difference between the ultimate reality and the phenomenal world. Monism is the view that all reality is one unified divine reality. There may still be many personal gods, but they may all be understood as facets of the one sacred reality. Within these traditions, it may be emphasized that the sacred is our inner true self; it may be the suchness of reality; it may be the state of ultimate consciousness; it may be the principle that is found in all reality. This kind of perspective on the sacred ultimate is present in some forms of Hinduism, Buddhism, philosophical Taoism, and Neo-Confucianism. Tendencies toward monism can also be found in certain mystical movements in Judaism, Christianity, and Islam, as well as in some philosophical thinkers in the Western tradition, such as Plotinus, Spinoza, and Hegel.

So the sacred can be experienced as many in nature, or one beyond nature, or one and many both in and beyond nature, and more. Depending on which vision is dominant, the religious path to the sacred has distinctive features in each particular religion. The crucial question is, how do we encounter the sacred? Is the sacred found in the forces of nature and society? Is the sacred encountered in history and events? Is the sacred met within as one's real self? Is the sacred experienced as a personal being or as impersonal reality? Is the sacred known as the ultimate truth about reality? In each of the religions, people have opted for a particular vision of the sacred and thus each has a distinctive religious path. Yet people in each religion often explore the other possible perspectives as well to add depth to their own vision and experience.

In ancient times it was a common assumption of almost all peoples that this world and human life are supported by divine power or powers, although various peoples differed in their conception of the divine realm. In modern times, however, far-reaching questions have been raised in people's minds about the traditional beliefs concerning the sacred. As science and technology have increased all around the globe, notions of sacred reality have gradually been eased out of the picture. We live our lives in a very secular way, that is, without paying attention to the sacred in most aspects of our existence. Is there really a God? Are the kami really powerful forces? Do Vishnu and Shiva actually control the forces of the world? Is nirvana real? Is it true that there is an underlying principle of all reality? These are pressing questions especially for those religions most associated with Western culture—Judaism, Christianity, and Islam—but increasingly all religions are facing the challenge that modernity and secularity pose for the traditional concepts of the sacred.

In spite of these developments, adherents of the religions today still find meaning in the depth dimension of the sacred. There are, of course, questions and problems that have to be dealt with, and as modern people we cannot easily go back to conceptions of the sacred reality as a heavenly grandfather who watches lovingly over all his children, for example, or as gods, goddesses, and demons who cause all good and bad things to happen. It is the experience of many people of the different religions today that the best resource for retrieving the sense of the presence of the sacred is to be found in the tradition and practice of one's religion. How can we find again a way to experience the sacred present and powerful in our lives? Take up the path and see, they would answer.

Creation and Human Existence

"What sense is there in life?" "And why are we here?" "Why does my life feel so uncertain?" "Why is there so much evil and suffering in the world?"

Questions like these are at the heart of all religions,

for they pertain to the deepest needs of human life—the need to understand our own existence within the world and society, the need to feel a purpose or destiny, and the need to integrate evil and death into our view of life without despairing.

The religions deal with questions like these especially in their cosmogonic stories, that is, their stories about the creation and maintenance of the world and of humans within it. For it is in knowing the origins of the world that we know its real essence and character.

In the creation stories of the peoples of the world, the origin of the world is attributed to many causes. Often a variety of gods and divine helpers create the world, remaining as ongoing powers within the world. Sometimes the creation of the world is seen as a battle between the various divine forces, and humans get caught up in the conflict. The monotheistic religions insist that the one God is creator of all. Again, the origin and the operation of the world may be viewed as an eternal recurring process, like waves on an ocean, emanating from the sacred reality.

The cosmogonic myths or stories telling of origins also provide important views about the nature of the world and the role of humans within it. Some of the religions of nonliterate peoples teach that the world is controlled by many divine forces, expressing their wills in the functioning of nature; therefore the most important role of humans is to serve and propitiate these gods. The Abrahamic religions teach that because there is one God, the creator and preserver of all things, this world makes sense as a good and purposeful creation. And humans are to assist God to care for this world, fulfilling God's design. Other religions, such as Hinduism and Buddhism, teach that the world as we experience it is somewhat illusory. The most important thing for humans to do is to get in touch with the ultimate reality rather than the illusory world. Again, it is sometimes taught, as in the Chinese religions and in Hinduism, that there is a universal world order or harmony into which everything fits, and humans do best by living their lives according to this order.

It seems that all religions have some view of human failure and imperfection. This follows from their vision of what the ideal is. The ideal human existence is sometimes expressed in creation stories, in descriptions of the origins of the world and of humans. There was an age of innocence, for example, a paradisaical state when people lived peacefully and in harmony. The original human state is looked to as a kind of standard of what we ought to be. And corresponding to that is the realistic view of how things actually are: fractured and estranged because of human imperfection and failure. Of course, the extent to which we are thought to be alienated from the good, ideal state differs in the various religions. But it is commonly accepted throughout the religions of the world that humans are not what they can or ought to be. Of course, much evil happens without our choice. But in our experience we know that people sometimes do things that are destructive and violent. In our own lives we recognize that we sometimes do things that are hateful and ugly, and we fail to do the things we ought to do—why? There is a big shadow of failure and imperfection and sin cast over human existence.

The religions of the world give differing reasons for human sin and evil. Some African tribal religions, for example, have myths of origin in which the first humans live in a paradisaical state with the supreme god, represented by the heavens, close to them on earth. Because of some fault in the humans—like being too greedy for food—the supreme god moves far away, with the result that human life becomes full of pain, death, and evil. The three Abrahamic religions teach that God, although making humans as the crown of creation, also gave them of all creatures a dimension of freedom. And within that freedom comes the possibility and the reality of rebellion, unbelief, and fracturing of the loving relationship with God.

Another way of looking at the human problem is found in Hinduism and Buddhism, where human existence is often seen as a kind of trap. Because of the fire of desire that leads us to cling to false ideas of self, we are trapped in an infinite cycle of material existences full of pain and suffering. We cling to the sensual ego-centered illusions, and by doing so we fall under the causal law of karma: we reap exactly what we sow, experiencing the fruits of our clinging actions. The general view in Confucianism, Taoism, and Shinto is that the highest human good is to be in harmony with the universal order of the cosmos and the flow of sacred powers of the world. When we act in ways to cause disharmony, whether in society or in nature, we experience the resulting fractures and discords as evil and suffering.

Sometimes the problem is put in the form of a question: Is human nature fundamentally good or evil? If human nature is through and through evil, then what else could we expect except violence and destructive behavior any time that humans are free to act unchecked? But some would say that humans are basically ·good and peaceful by nature. Then the violence and evil must be the result of other forces, such as possession by evil spirits, the corrupting influence of society, or oppression by tyrants. Or human evil may arise from our human tendency to forgetfulness and ignorance.

Is human nature fundamentally good or evil? To put the question thus is certainly an oversimplification, for most religions emphasize human moral responsibility. Somehow humans must be free to make their own choices in decisions of behavior, or they would not be responsible for anything they do. The realities of human existence lead most people to conclude that there is within us a struggle concerning choices about good and evil. Outside forces perhaps influence us; perhaps there are inner inclinations toward good or evil. But finally—in the view of most religions—the choice is authored by the person herself or himself, who bears the final responsibility for it.

What this unsettling state of conflict, ignorance, discord, or sin does, when realized against the standard of sacred design and law for human existence, is to impel us toward some change: repentance, seeking help from sacred powers, following a new path to counter and transform our fractured human existence.

The Path of Transformation and Salvation

"How can I start living *real* life?" "How can I find some way out of this mess?" "Where are meaning and peace to be found?" "How can I be saved?"

Questions such as these arise when we come face to face with the existence of fracture, failure, and sin in our lives, knowing at the same time that this is not the way things should be. These are questions about the possibility of transformation and salvation. "Salvation" in all religions means wholeness and health—a transformation away from the fragmentation, alienation, sin, and ignorance we feel in our lives, a movement toward peace, health, and perfection. Transformation as taught in a particular religion responds to the way in which the human problem is understood and experienced. For example, sin must be transformed by forgiveness, pollution by purification, ignorance by knowledge, fracture by healing, and wandering by guidance on the straight path. All religions offer some means by which salvation or transformation can be possible.

Functioning as a means of transformation, a religion provides methods of interaction with the realm of the sacred. This is the ultimate source of life and meaning, and the basic human problem arises when this source is cut off for one reason or another. The first need is some kind of restoration of this contact so that sacred power can transform life.

Although people of all religions agree that it is the power of the sacred that transforms humans, there are different visions as to how this power arises and operates in restoring the relationship. Some religions emphasize human depravity and helplessness; therefore all power and salvation must come from a source outside oneself. A good example of such an approach is Japanese Pure Land Buddhism, which stresses the notion of complete human degeneracy and helplessnesss in this "age of the end of the Buddhist law." This means that the only hope for humans to escape an endless series of rebirths in the suffering realms is to rely totally on help from the compassionate Buddha, Amida. On the other hand, some religions emphasize an approach to the means of transformation that relies on power within oneself. Also in Japanese Buddhism, Zen adherents say there is no need to look to Amida Buddha for help or salvation. Each person has the transcendent Buddha nature in her/himself and through the practice of meditation each person can awaken to that Buddha reality and reach enlightenment.

These two opposite extremes are from the same religious tradition, namely, Japanese Buddhism. This would suggest that even within one religion we might

A young boy's initiation ceremony among the Parsis in India, a remnant of the ancient Zoroastrians of Persia.

salvation comes totally from the sacred power, still humans receive it and live it out in human religious structures. And even if the whole emphasis seems to be on one's own power in terms of performing disciplines, still these disciplines draw on deep sources of sacred power. One of the distinctive characteristics of each religion, in fact, is its particular vision of the interaction between human practice and sacred gift.

The means of transformation or salvation that a religion offers will involve all three levels of human expression: theoretical, practical, and social. On the theoretical level, the myth and doctrines of the religion are to be understood and accepted by faith and/or reason, so that the person's whole outlook on life can be transformed. On the practical level, ritual, discipline, and practice are means of transformation. Such activities would include things like praying, baptism, acts of repentance, sitting in meditation, studying, keeping rules of purity, acts of self-discipline, and the like. Means of transformation on the social level would include participating in social structures such as families, congregations, sacred peoples, priesthoods, monasteries, and the like, so that the new way of life can be lived fully as a life-long practice.

Together these various means of transformation make up a path to follow. This path of transformation is a dynamic process that goes on throughout life in greater and smaller rhythms. It continually involves a double movement: a distancing and separating from the situation that is fractured and wrong; and a restoration and renewal of the state of wholeness and harmony with the sacred. There will be repentance of sins, vows of abstinence, withdrawing of thoughts from outer things, and rituals of washing and purifying oneself. There will be retelling of the revelation that comes from the sacred, teaching about sins being forgiven, and the awakening of the mind in enlightenment.

Further, the path of transformation is both a *means* and an *end* in itself. As a means it is a praxis, a method of moving toward a goal: transformation or salvation, restoration of the relationship with the sacred. In one sense, that goal is never fully reached within human life, for the problems of human failure and sin remain until death. For that reason many religions have ideas of the future human state in which the ideal goal is

expect to find both the "outside power" and the "self power" emphases. And this is the case. In Hinduism, for example, one finds both a tradition of worshiping the gods and relying on their grace, and also a tradition of passing beyond the gods to pure realization of the sacred through discipline and meditation. It is true that some religions speak of themselves more as religions of "grace" (outside power), such as Christianity; and other religions, such as Islam, place more emphasis on human responsibility for action (self power). But the relation to the sacred is always a two-way relation. Even if perfectly and completely consummated. There may be some model person who achieves that goal now, such as a saviour, saint, prophet, buddha, arhat, or sannyasin. But for the rest of us, the path is a means toward a goal of salvation or transformation that will be a complete, perfect reality only in a transcendent state or a world or lifetime to come.

However, seen from another point of view, the path of transformation is itself the experience of transformation. There is an "already, even though not yet" quality to the experience in following the path. The path is itself the means we have of experiencing contact with the sacred. Zen Buddhism expresses this most strikingly. Master Dogen insisted that practice (sitting in meditation) and enlightenment (experiencing the Buddha nature) are the same thing, with no difference at all. Other religious teachers would perhaps not identify the path so closely with the transformation it brings. But all would agree that following the path is not just a means to reward in another world to come; the goal of transformation is already at least partially present right now as we follow the path.

Worship and the Good Life

Religion by its very nature is practical and social. Theoretical teachings about the sacred and about life need to be lived, not just believed. And the path provides a structure of life within a religious community. It is never just an individual affair but always involves the person in a larger community of people going on that religious path. The religious community provides daily life with a structure including both sacred time and sacred life. That is, the ordinary time of one's existence is punctuated by special times of worship and festival. And the ordinary living of one's daily existence becomes the arena of the good life in fulfillment of the sacred design for the whole community.

Making Time Sacred through Worship, Ritual, and Art

"Where can I find new power for life?" "Where can I find meaning in the humdrum of existing day by day?" "How can I live more in touch with what is *real*?" These questions and many more like them have to do with our need regularly to renew the meaning and purpose of our lives, day by day, year by year, in family and in community, through worship and ritual.

Mircea Eliade[3] has shown that, looked at in a completely profane or secular way, human life would be a self-contained, closed system with intervention by sacred power logically excluded. There would be no "breaks" to the sacred, no special or strong (sacred) times that can provide centers of meaning and thus give structure and order to life.

Since humans cannot tolerate such a meaningless chaos of existing, we seek out special or strong times. In traditional religions, these are the sacred celebrations, the festivals, holy days, and rituals that periodically punctuate and renew the ordinary day-by-day passage of our existing. Even modern, secularized people who have little use for traditional religious rituals have not transcended the need to have sacred times. Breaks in time, centers of meaning and renewal, are widely sought after in such forms as vacations, national holidays, parties, sports, entertainment, and the like. The purpose of such sacred times is "re-creation," that is, the renewal and enlivening of our otherwise humdrum routine of existing.

Religious communities have found that the power that motivates life needs constantly to be renewed. Life-power tends to run down, to become exhausted and weak. There is need regularly to move into sacred time, the time in which the realities of the sacred story are experienced as new and present once again. Ordinary time is transcended, and the people of *now* become contemporary with the gods and the founders and heroes of the Beginning Time. The rituals and festivals provide a rhythm of periodic renewal.

Rituals and festivals are also sources of orientation for life, centers around which all else makes sense. They establish a pattern of living, derived from the sacred story, that can extend out and sanctify the ordinary hours and days of existing. They make real again the identity shared by the community and the incorporation of the individual within it.

Ritual worship connects the sacred with the common elements of human life. Fundamental to religious ritual is the sense of sacred presence in the most vital areas of human experience: eating, sexuality, birth, death, working, play, family, community, water, earth, sun, and so forth. The materials for ritual celebration stem from these basic elements of the human context. A meal is a most universal form of religious ritual, for example. So also is washing by water, or burying in the earth, or dancing and singing, or offering products of one's labor—the list of religious rituals is as long and diverse as are the vital aspects of human life.

Ritual worship not only incorporates the vital human aspects, but it also "returns" them, now sanctified, to life. By the offering of the first fruits of the harvest, all the harvest is sacred. Through the ritual uniting of a woman and a man, all their sexual life is consecrated. By means of the rites of puberty initiation, boys and girls are incorporated as men and women of the community. Ritual washing means all the body is pure and sanctified. Ritual worship thus transforms human life by lifting it up, connecting it with the sacred, and returning it, now sanctified and empowered, to daily existence.

Ritual celebration of sacred time, as an activity on the path of transformation, has a movement or structure for renewal. First of all there needs to be a *kenosis*, an "emptying out."[4] With the recognition that power has run down and become exhausted comes the need for an emptying out of the old situation, a distancing so that the renewal can take place. This kenosis takes many different forms in religious practice. Among the most common rituals would be those that symbolize washing or cleansing, removal of impurity, confession and repentance, separation from the usual state, returning to a condition of chaos or disorder, and dying.

Once the emptying out has been established, the *plerosis*, or "filling up," follows. Having been brought back to the original state, emptied of all exhausted powers, the renewing power of the sacred can be experienced. Rebirth and new life are symbolized by rituals such as emerging from the waters, putting on new clothes, sharing in a meal, receiving a new name, incorporation into a community, singing and dancing, and the like.

Very often the two movements of kenosis and plerosis are connected by an inbetween liminal state (from *limen*, "threshold"). This liminal state can be seen, for example, in puberty initiations. Young boys and girls may be separated from their mothers and removed to the bush (kenosis) before being incorporated back into the community as young men and women (plerosis). During that time in the bush they experience a liminal, threshold state; they are "betwixt-and-between," having died to their childhood existence but not yet been reborn as adults. In this liminal state they return in a sense to a prebirth existence. Everything may be stripped from them; they may experience ritual death and receive sacred revelations. After this critical threshold experience, they are reincorporated into the community as new, reborn people.

Such a liminal experience can be observed in many rituals and festivals. The New Year festivals of many cultures, for example, typically have a time of cleansing and purifying (kenosis), which leads into a liminal condition of "antistructure" or chaos; finally renewed structure and order are created (plerosis). The Christian ritual of baptism involves a distancing from evil (renouncing the works of the devil), a liminal passage of symbolic death in the waters, and a renewal ritualized by a new name, white garment, and a burning candle. The Muslim ritual of pilgrimage to Mecca includes symbols of distancing through a long journey, vows, and a special garment. The liminal period covers several days full of intense rituals and experiences. And the pilgrim has a new spiritual and social status upon completion of the pilgimage, symbolized by the title *hajji* (one who has done the Pilgrimage).

Festivals and Rituals of Passage

Among the most common rituals are those that occur periodically, such as seasonal festivals. They follow the rhythm of the year and celebrate different aspects of involvement with sacred power. Many of these seasonal festivals have some connection with the cycle of sacred power in nature: spring renewal festivals, fall harvest festivals, and the like. In some religions the seasonal festivals are associated with events in the sacred story. For example, the spring festival of Passover celebrates the deliverance of Israel from slavery in Egypt, and the spring festival of Easter celebrates the resurrection of Jesus from the dead. Both of these festivals, although they emphasize events in human history, retain symbolism of liberation of nature's forces from the captivity of winter.

Another very common type of festival occurring periodically is the holy day, a particular day singled out for commemorating and celebrating some aspect of sacred power. These may be lucky or unlucky days determined by the astrological calendar; they may commemorate the birth or death of some great saints or religious founders; they may be critical points in the transitions of the annual seasons, such as the winter solstice; or they may follow a repeating pattern, such as every seven days (Jews, Christians, and Muslims), every nineteen days (Baha'is), or bimonthly on the lunar pattern (Buddhists). Some rituals recur every day, such as morning devotions for Brahmin Hindus, or even periodically throughout every day, such as the five daily periods of prayer in Islam.

Seasonal festivals and periodic holy days and rituals offer a plentitude of sacred centers in the living of human life, a rhythm of recurring renewal to sustain the identity of the community and of the individual within the community.

Another major type of ritual celebration is that associated with the vital passages of human life, especially birth, puberty, marriage, and death. These "rites of passage"[5] are focused on the individual within the context of the community, serving to transform the person into the new stage of life and to integrate her or him into the community at that new spiritual level. Each of these passages of life is liminal—that is, it involves crossing a threshold from one state of existence to another. Each passage is critical to the full human development of the person and to the welfare of the community, and therefore religious rituals accompany and actualize the passage.

To move from one stage of life to another means first of all to put an end to the old stage. Thus rituals of separation, distancing, or dying are most appropriately used as the first movement in the celebration of passage. The end of an infant's prebirth state may be ritualized by burying the afterbirth, or washing the infant for the first time. Children to be initiated into adulthood are typically separated from their homes and parents as the beginning of their initiation. Carrying a bride-to-be away from her home to the marriage hall shows the end of her state of maidenhood. Funeral rituals typically include the removal of the body from the normal life surroundings.

Separated from the old stage, which is now completed and thus done away with, the person enters into a state of liminality, "betwixt and between." Having moved back to the precreation state, rituals of liminality bring the person into direct contact with sacred power. These include rituals of death and burial, suspension of time and identity, encounter with the ancestors, and so forth. Mother and newborn baby are often confined for a period of time during which various birth ceremonies take place. Children in nonliterate societies die symbolic deaths during their initiation rituals, have their sexual organs cut, or engage in battles with mythical monsters. Marriage passage rites often include a period of betrothal during which the man and woman are neither single nor yet joined as one. In funeral rituals, the newly dead person is often felt to be in an inbetween state, and the family and community observe a "wake" or sometimes a lengthy mourning period before the dead one is fully incorporated as an ancestor.

Finally, rituals of rebirth, filling up, empowering, and reincorporation into the community complete the passage. The person has left the previous state, passed over the threshold, and now is recognized and welcomed at the new level of life. The infant is named and thus incorporated into the community. The young people now speak a new language and take their places as adults. The marriage is consummated and rituals of establishing a new home take place. The dead one is welcomed back as an ancestor and is enshrined on the family altar.

Other rituals of passage have to do with spiritual rebirth; they follow the pattern of rites of passage but are not necessarily connected with the physical development of human life. Christian baptism, for example, is not simply a birth ritual but a ritualization of the death of the "old man" and the resurrection of the new spiritual being in whom Christ lives. In some societies initiation into secret religious societies follows the pattern of the rites of passage. Religious specialists such as shamans, yogins, priests, or monks and nuns enter into their new spiritual level of existence through passage rituals of ordination or consecration.

Artistic Expression and the Sacred

In our discussion of sacred time and ritual, we need to include some consideration of the arts. In the broad sense we can consider the arts as all human activities and creations that express the aesthetic sense of beauty and meaning, especially the visual, literary, and performing arts. Art is closely tied to celebration and ritual. Religious experience is expressed largely through aesthetic media, for our contact with the sacred must be grounded in our perception (*aesthesis*) of reality. People of the different religions have always known that the sacred is experienced through the things of the world and of human existence. Although interior, direct contact with the sacred is also known, the outer forms through which the sacred is experienced have been lovingly cultivated into artistic forms.

As used in the religions, art forms symbolize the sacred. That is, they point beyond themselves to some dimension of the sacred or of human relationship with the sacred. They are not mere signs or pointers, however. To symbolize the sacred means to share somehow in the sacred reality, to convey the power and the presence of the sacred. A statue of the Buddha on the altar is not itself, wood or stone, that to which Buddhists direct worship. But it conveys the presence of the Buddha to the worshipers and thus participates in the reality to which it points.

Some art is designed mainly to represent the sacred; other art intends actually to "present" the sacred. Art that represents the sacred may be instructional, bringing the sacred to the attention of the people. A drama acting out the story might have the goal of instructing the people. Images and statues on Hindu temples and Christian cathedrals function as a kind of visual narrative of the story of the religion.

Other art more directly *presents* the sacred for a worshipful, transformative religious experience. Use of the arts in worship and ritual is often of this more presentational type, evoking and creating the experience of the sacred. In Hindu puja (worship), the god is

Expression of the sacred in art: woodcut of Christ on the cross, by Paul Gauguin.

invoked into the image and worshiped. The artful liturgical words, objects, and actions of the Christian Eucharist convey the real presence of Christ to the worshipers. Of course, art can combine both types. The dramatic Jewish Passover meal (seder), for example, educates by narrating the story, but it also creates the religious experience of being present at the great deliverance of the exodus from Egypt.

From the religious point of view, all aspects of human existence have the possibility of being open to the sacred. Therefore religion, especially in worship and ritual, seeks to involve all possible human arts. Since the arts are highly expressive, they can evoke experiences of the sacred at deeper levels than the rational and logical. For example, the various literary arts do, of course, make use of the logical, rational structure of language. But there is a difference between a precise philosophical proposition of faith that attempts to define (and thus limit) the sacred, and a liturgical poetic expression that makes the sacred powerfully present. The great power that people find in the scriptures of their religion is related to the artistic quality of the sacred literature. The aesthetic sound of mantras (sacred formulas) in Hinduism and Buddhism conveys power even if the literal meaning of the words is not even understood.

Visual presentations of the sacred and of the sacred story are used in many religions, although there is also reluctance in some religions to portray divine realities in representational visual form. Iconography (representational art) presents essential aspects of the sacred, but it also imbues the sacred with sensuous form—and thus limitations. Paintings, sculptures, small figurines, and symbolic abstract designs all serve to evoke senses of the sacred full of aesthetic power and beauty, with form, color, and texture.

The art of music has been found to be a powerful presenter of the sacred in almost all religions. The beautiful sounds of music—gripping rhythm, haunting melody, special qualities of different instruments, reach to deep levels of aesthetic sensibility and express many different aspects of the experience of the sacred. It is particularly powerful when words are wedded to music in sacred chants, mantras, hymns, and the like.

The art of music, whether a solitary flute or the ringing Hallelujah Chorus of Handel's *Messiah*, gathers and directs spiritual emotions and evokes the sacred presence like no other art does.

Another art form widely cultivated in the religions is dance, the aesthetic and spiritual expression of body movements. Closely associated with dance would be drama and liturgical rituals. The ritual actions of a Taoist priest very much involve arts of dance and drama, as also the kagura dance in Shinto, the Eucharistic liturgy in Christianity, and the art of ritual prayer in Islam.

The sense of sacred place is artistically expressed in religions by distinctive forms of architecture. Temples and shrines symbolize the *axis mundi*, the center of the world, providing a center of orientation for all the rest of space. The sacred building is often thought of as a microcosm of the cosmic world. The aesthetic quality of architectural forms expresses essential dimensions of the vision of the particular religion. Soaring Gothic cathedrals reaching toward heaven, Muslim mosques filled with openness and light, Hindu temples with their dark and mysterious inner room, simple wooden Shinto shrines in Japan—all give expression to particular spatial-local qualities of the experience of the sacred.

Since artistic forms can evoke deep feelings with powerful presentations of the sacred, occasionally they can be experienced as destructive or demonic. People can look to the art form itself as ultimate, a situation called idolatry ("worship of an idol") in some of the religions. People in all religions know, however, that the art forms, no matter how beautiful or powerful, are *symbols* of the sacred. They point beyond themselves to the sacred, they convey and present the sacred; but they are not themselves the ultimate sacred. Still, many art forms have been resisted or banned in the history of the different religions. Poetry has been considered the work of demons. Music of certain types raises dangerous emotions. Dance can become too sensuous and ecstatic. Iconography—imaging the sacred in visual form—has probably been the most controversial art, because people fear that it leads to idolatry or to seeking to gain control over the sacred.

Each religious tradition chooses special aesthetic forms as the most appropriate, sometimes resisting others as useless, misleading, or even dangerous. We might say that each religion or culture has its own distinctive aesthetic sense, closely related to the deep insights of that spiritual vision. To really understand a culture, we must look at its literature, poetry, dance, visual portrayals, architecture, music, and the rest. For example, the Hindu experience of countless gods within an ultimate unity opens the way for the cultivation of all the arts. And the Muslim reluctance to link God together with likenesses of any thing has led to a restriction on representational visual arts and a flowering of decorative and verbal arts. Arts of some religions are more conducive to meditation, others to celebration and ecstasy. In broad terms, the religions of South and East Asia have stressed intuitional, meditative aesthetic experiences, whereas the religions of the West have often emphasized an aesthetic sense connected with the word, intelligence, and logic. But these differences can easily be overstressed, for the shape of the aesthetic vision is often a matter of emphasis. Even within one religion significant differences can be found.

Sacred Life: Social Structure and the Good Life

"How should I live?" "Where do I belong?" "What is my responsibility to human society?" Religious experience carries with it an imperative to live in a way that conforms to one's religious identity. A person is always a part of a group, a community, and the good life is structured in that community context. Acting according to one's religious identity involves, in many religions, a sense of responsibility and mission to others in the world.

As we saw earlier, each religion has a story that gives identity and purpose to the religious community and the individual within it. The story tells about the original people, special and sacred. These people are set apart for special identity, for special life, and for a special role in the world. The Japanese Shinto myths, for example, tell how the Japanese islands and the Japanese people descended from the kami (the divine beings). The emperor descended from the most powerful kami, the sun kami Amaterasu. This mythology has supported the sense of the Japanese as a sacred people, with the emperor as the divine head of the nation.

Indians bathing in a religious ceremony at the Pushkar Fair in Rajasthan, India.

Buddhist stories tell how the Buddha after his enlightenment gathered a band of disciples into a monastic community of monks and nuns, the sangha. The lay people participate in this religious community by supporting and honoring the sangha. In traditional China, ancient teachings support the strong notion that the clan or extended family is the center of meaning for each individual, and beyond that there is the hierarchically organized village and state within which the individual finds religious identity.

The structure and organization of the religious community are grounded in the sacred history and traditions of the religion. Provision is made for some kind of religious leadership. Sometimes the religious leaders function by virtue of the power of their office, like kings and priests. In other cases, religious leaders are recognized by virtue of their personal charisma or power, such as prophets, shamans, medicine persons, and diviners. The community also has social structures involving clan relationships, congregations, lay groups, secret societies, masters and disciples, apprentices, and the like.

The perspective about authentic life for the people is often tied together with stories about a sacred land or territory: the sacred islands for the Japanese, the tribal land and burial grounds for the African tribes, Jerusalem for Jews, the pilgrimage sites and sacred rivers in India, and the like. Sacred space is established by the presence of the sacred, and therefore it is experienced as the center of the world (*axis mundi*), as Mircea Eliade has elucidated.[6] This center functions as the connecting point between the human realm and the divine realms. Once the center is established, it provides orientation and a sense of being at home in the world. Sacred space can be a whole land, or it may be a village, mountain, shrine, temple, altar, or even a house. This is the *real* space that provides meaning and identity. It gives a feeling of rootedness; cut off from it we feel lost in the chaos of foreign, meaningless space.

The Moral Pattern for Authentic Life

The moral pattern for the good life is usually presented in the sacred history, for there we learn what the gods did in the Time of the Beginning, or the rules laid down by the ancestors, or the examples provided by the founder.

It is the conviction of people of each religion that this pattern for life is "natural" in a deep sense. It is the way of life that most fits our original nature, as we were intended to be before we turned away or forgot that pattern. Whereas rewards may be promised for living the moral life and punishments threatened for neglecting it, the fundamental motivation for following the ethical guidance of the religion is deeper. This is the model for *authentic* human life, that which harmonizes with the greater spiritual forces and patterns of the cosmos. To many nonliterate peoples, real human life is to do what the gods did in the Time of the Beginning. According to Hinduism, living according to the Code of Manu corresponds to the eternal Dharma (cosmic order), and that is right and brings happiness. The Shari'ah law code, in Islamic thought, follows perfectly the universal pattern of God's creation, and thus it brings peace and harmony.

The ethical life has something to do with how we *should* be, and therefore it is based in the religion's vision of creation and human nature. The law of morality is often thought to be an authority outside oneself, usually recorded in scripture and tradition, to which one submits. But the religious teachers also talk about how that law becomes internalized, transformed into the inner motivation for right living, so that one naturally does what is right—thus there occurs a sanctification of life.

It takes practice to live as one ought. Confucius taught that to transform ourselves into people of humanity (*jen*), it is most helpful to take up the discipline and practice of the principles of propriety (*li*). Hindus believe that following the Path of Action, doing one's duty according to one's place in life without desire for reward, is a way of reaching higher spiritual perfection and better rebirths. The thing that makes Jews distinctive from others is their willingness to take up the discipline of the commandments (*mitzvot*)—not for the reward that this will bring, but because the very doing of the mitzvot is itself the good life. Even Christianity and Pure Land Buddhism, with their mistrust of good works or merit, know of the sanctification of life, of the good tree that bears good fruit.

The religious tradition provides guidance in all areas of life. In personal behavior often the stress falls on self-control and moderation. One should not be controlled by the passions and desires, but rather these passions and desires should be controlled and redirected toward transformation of self. The religious tradition also spells out the relation of the individual to others and indicates the right and wrong way of treating others in the various situations. The ethical life is lived for the welfare of the community. In following the code of life, strife and competition are avoided and healing and harmony are promoted. The religions usually teach motivations of compassion and sacrifice, giving oneself for the good of the community.

Technically speaking, "ethics" is the activity of thinking about moral decisions on the basis of the tradition. The religious tradition provides ethical guidance about many or most of the crucial questions in life. But the individual and the community, living in concrete situations with changing circumstances, also continually make ethical decisions about a variety of possible actions. In modern times the ethical decisions have become increasingly numerous and difficult: Should I have an abortion? Should I obey the law of the secular state requiring me to fight in the army? Should I as a Muslim student in America adopt Western customs of behavior? Should I leave the traditional role as housewife and get a job outside the home? Thousands of questions like these face people in all the religions today, and as they think about the possible decisions on the basis of the tradition, they are engaging in ethical thinking.

Some religions are tribal, and this means they have little opportunity to express solidarity with humans outside the tribe. People of tribal religious traditions do often have a sense of harmony with the natural world. They promote the welfare and continuation of the world that supports human society, made up of vegetation, animals, and the earth itself, in a kind of primal ecology. A feeling for the sacredness of all human life is also demonstrated among many nonliterate, tribal peoples. Still, a sense of oneness with other humans in the world transcending the boundaries of the tribe is hardly to be expected.

Within the world religions there has developed more awareness of the universality of the human race and of the common human welfare in the world. Thus all the world religions have some vision of the nature and purpose of all humankind and of their own role or mission in the world.

There are a wide variety of ideas about the role or mission of the individual religions within the world, ranging from a stance that sees the rest of humankind as enemies, to the attitude of sharing a common pursuit for the benefit of all peoples. Sometimes views differ sharply even within one religious tradition, between those who emphasize a radical difference with outsiders and those who accommodate to the larger context of human culture.

Religions that make up a whole culture in themselves tend to promote that culture by giving it religious legitimation. It was assumed in medieval Christendom, for example, that the whole cultured world was Christian. Likewise, Hinduism can only with difficulty be divorced from Indian culture. However, religions that are minority groups in a dominant culture sometimes take an antagonistic stance toward the values and goals of the major culture, perhaps even working to convert and thus transform that culture. Of course, in modern times secularization has been perceived as a new threat by almost all religious traditions. One important task felt within many religions today is combatting these forces of irreligion that have permeated modern Western cultures and threaten all non-Western cultures.

In the context of world society, the religions have developed a sense of responsibility for the good of the larger world, especially in areas like social justice, education, and relief for the poor and hungry. In recent times concern for reconciliation and peace-making has come to the fore in many religions. Between the religions, and even within some of the religions, attitudes toward war show considerable variety. Most have some criteria by which they distinguish between justifiable war and war that is totally illegitimate. Strong traditions of pacifism or nonresistance appear within some of the major religions. Today people in all religions see the need for peace and harmony between different cultures, especially in view of the drastic threat of modern warfare.

Inherent in every self-conscious religious tradition is

the claim to be the truth and thus the ideal way of life. Whereas tribal peoples generally do not attempt to spread their religious practices beyond the borders of their own tribe, all religions that have a sense of universality also have some feeling of responsibility to bring the truth to the rest of the world. This does not necessarily mean actively trying to convince others to convert to this religion. This responsibility may simply be having a special role within the world that is of benefit to all, as is expressed in the Jewish identity as "chosen people." Hindus have such a tolerant attitude toward truth embodied at different levels that they are usually not motivated to promote Hinduism for other cultures. Also, the notions of reincarnation through many lifetimes and the repetition of world cycles, found in both Hinduism and Buddhism, do not lend any urgency to changing the world's understanding of truth.

The concern that the truth must be shared with all peoples is especially strong in the so-called missionary religions: Christianity, Islam, and to some extent Buddhism, and also some newer branches of the older traditions, like Bahai, Nichiren Shoshu, and the International Society for Krishna Consciousness. People of these religions feel a mission, for example, to Christianize all peoples, Islamicize the world, spread the Dharma, and so on—for the ultimate welfare of all. For people of these religions, this mission is an important part of their self-understanding and identity.

Concern for the welfare of the world, and the realization that other religions also have visions for the world and claims to truth, have led to conversation and cooperation between the religions. Many people today recognize that religions and ideologies have contributed a great deal to the conflicts in the world. In recent years a new movement of dialogue between the religions has become a part of the religious happenings of the world. At the very least, there has developed a widespread sense that peoples of different religions need to work together against the forces of exploitation and violence that threaten human society today in an unprecedented way.

DISCUSSION QUESTIONS

1. Do you think questions such as "Who am I?" and "What is the purpose of life?" are universal human concerns, or are they the product of modern Western thought?
2. What are some aspects of the experience of the sacred that seem to be shared by people of different cultures and religious traditions?
3. Give some examples of how symbol systems change over time.
4. What is implied in calling religious practices a "path"?
5. How can a story or myth from ancient times still provide identity for people today? Give some examples.
6. What do cosmogonic stories reveal about the way a particular people look at the world and human existence?
7. What is meant by speaking of "salvation" or "transformation" in the various religions?
8. How can participation in sacred times or festivals bring renewal of human life? What do the terms *kenosis*, *liminal*, and *plerosis* mean?
9. How does art represent and present the sacred? Why are some artistic forms considered dangerous in some religions?
10. Is the good ethical life something natural or unnatural?
11. Do you think a sense of universal truth and mission is something essential to a religion?

CHAPTER 2

RELIGIONS OF ANCIENT PEOPLES

In this book we are studying primarily the so-called world religions of today, looking at their roots in the past but concentrating on their present forms and practices. Among the families of humankind these world religions, highly developed and encompassing large populations, are relatively modern phenomena. All of them have reached their classical form within the past three thousand years, even though their roots may reach earlier. That means that we humans lived for hundreds of thousands and even millions of years—perhaps 99.9 percent of our human story in length of time—by religious visions and practices prior to the development of these world religions. Further, up to the present century at least, a large percentage of humankind in various parts of the world have remained outside the domain of our present world religions. Surely all of this accumulated religious experience is an important part of our human story. Our identity today as human beings is deeply indebted to these sacred experiences from other times and places.

It is far too much to suggest that all these religions of the past and present that fall outside the "world religions" form one great family of religions. There is great diversity among them, and within their vast domains it is possible to find almost all symbols and forms of religion that come to expression also in the world religions. However, perhaps we can classify these religions into three broad groupings. Many are *prehistorical*, existing before there were written records or existing in an ancient culture that had not yet developed writing, and thus we know only a small fraction of them through archaeological research. Other religions of the past are the *ancient classical religions*; these people did produce written records and texts so that, even though they no longer live, we can know about them through their literature and other artifacts. A third grouping contains the *religions of contemporary nonliterate peoples*, those who have lived to the present day at a premodern level of tribal economy and society, having continued their archaic traditions for countless generations. Sometimes this last group is called primitive religions, but that can be a misleading designation because of the word *primitive*.

Perhaps one common characteristic among these religions of prehistorical, ancient, and nonliterate peoples is their tribal or ethnic character. The people do not envision their religious practices as universal but as the mark of themselves as a particular people. However, some thinkers in some of the ancient traditions, such as Greece and Rome, did push toward a kind of intellectual universality. Another common element is the general acceptance of the plurality of sacred powers emanating from the cosmos—that vision that we sometimes call "polytheism." Yet again we must qualify that statement. Some Greek and Roman thinkers articulated a vision of sacred unity encompassing all of nature (pantheism); there were stirrings of monotheism in ancient Egypt and Persia; and many nonliterate peoples today have ways of speaking of the "One" behind all the plurality of sacred forces.

Ancient and nonliterate peoples tend to have a very natural involvement with the sacred in their ordinary lives. They are open to the interweaving of the sacred within their social life, government, food-producing activities, birth, sickness, death, and all the rest. Mostly these peoples do not even have a word for "religion," since it is identical with their traditional way of life. This is not to say that archaic and nonliterate peoples are naive and subrational, for they are capable of sophisticated intellectual activity and often excel in practical wisdom. But they, unlike many of us who are drenched in modernity and secularity, are open to experiencing the sacred in the vital dimensions of life.

Unfortunately, it is not possible in this one volume to study these religions of ancient and nonliterate peoples in extensive detail, culture by culture. The interested reader can consult the many excellent studies of the ancient classical religions and the anthropological investigations of the nonliterate cultures of more recent times. Here we provide a brief history of humankind's religious adventure and a look at representative

Ancient stone colossus at Nemrud Dagi (mountain of the gods) in southeast Anatolia.

ancient religions. Then, in the next chapter we focus on how the religions of nonliterate peoples exemplify the basic patterns and themes of religion.

THE STORY OF HUMANKIND

With each of the major world religions we begin by looking at the sacred story that gives identity to the people of the religion. Here at the beginning it is appropriate to sketch out a story of humankind, not as any religion tells it, of course, but as scholars have reconstructed the religious history of humanity. This is not really a sacred story, for we do not tell it through myth and ritual as the basis for our identity; but still we can feel respect and indebtedness to our human forebears who transmitted the spirit of life and whose religious visions have somehow over millennia contributed to our own humanity.

The Origin of Religion: Theories

Scholars of religion have long been interested in the question of the "origin" of religion—how did religion begin and where did it come from? If we could answer the question of origins, they have felt, we would have some notion of the "original form" of religion. In the late nineteenth and early twentieth centuries, many theories of the origin of religion were proposed, trying to explain why it would be that humans would somehow start having religious ideas and practices.

One of the founders of the discipline of anthropology, E. B. Tylor, argued that religion originated in "animism" (from *anima*, "spirit"), from the experiences primitive peoples had of death and of dreams. They reflected on where life goes when a person dies and how deceased people can still be seen in dreams, and they came up with the notion that people and things have spirits that can leave their respective bodies and carry on a separate existence. People started worshiping the more powerful spirits, and religion was born. Sir James Frazer collected massive materials from the various ancient and nonliterate cultures and argued that the earliest human response to the world was magic, the attempt to control and manipulate the forces of nature. Finding that magic did not deal effectively with the sacred forces, humans developed

religious beliefs and rituals directed to personal gods. And Sigmund Freud constructed psychoanalytic theories about the origin and nature of religion, including the view that belief in God is a psychological projection of our father figure, growing out of the human need to feel protected and secure.

These theories, and many more, answer the question of where religion came from. Whereas this is a very interesting and thought-provoking issue, many scholars today think it is a misleading question. It arose in the heyday of evolutionary theories of culture and it suggests that we might find some particular point in human development at which religion began. The data necessary for such an investigation are simply not available. Further, since religious values and practices seem to form an essential human dimension, it may be supposed that religion has been present as long as there have been human beings. So the really interesting question of origins is: How long have there been human beings to express themselves through religious experience?

The Origin of Religion: Prehistorical Developments

The answer to how long human beings have expressed themselves through religion depends on the consensus of paleontologists about the latest discoveries. Many scholars feel that a distinct human species existed three million years ago or earlier, walking erect, with fully developed hands and stone tools, sharing food in a group. Certainly full humanity becomes recognizable with the species called Homo Erectus, about 500,000 years ago, when fire was domesticated and people lived in cave communities with common speech, using stone tools, and cooperating in big hunts of elephants together. They had a brain size nearly like that of humans today. Unfortunately, the archaeological remains are too scanty to provide much firm evidence of spiritual ideas and practices.

The first clear archaeological evidence of religious ideas comes with the Neanderthal species, living around 100,000–35,000 years ago in parts of Europe, China, and Iraq. Neanderthal humans, contrary to popular prejudice, had developed a sensitive, complex culture with many tools and some forms of art. A number of finds in their burials suggest that they had religious ideas associated with death. For example, at one burial site flint tools had been placed near the hands of the dead; at another, a skull was surrounded with a ring of stones; and in another burial a group of skulls had been immersed in red ochre, perhaps a symbol of blood and life. There is evidence here that death was looked upon as a passage to another kind of life—a basic religious belief.

It is unclear whether Neanderthal is directly related to the line of descent of later humans or was a separate offshoot of the human species. In any case, in the next cultural era, the late Paleolithic period (beginning around 50,000 B.C.E.), the modern human species of homo sapiens developed, and now there is much evidence of religious beliefs and practices. Many burials show careful treatment of the bodies: red ochre is sprinkled on the bones, probably symbolizing life-power; necklaces and other implements are buried with the body, showing that the dead live on in some way; some corpses are buried in a huddled-up position, symbolizing returning to the womb for rebirth; often bodies are lined up together in the same direction; and special treatment of the skulls is indicated. All of these things point toward the religious conception of death as a passage to new life and to ritual practices associated with death.

Other items from the late Paleolithic period show the fullness of religious concerns and practices. Many female figurines are found, depicting some sort of religious beliefs about the Great Mother, the source of all life-power. These finds show that worship of the mother goddess was one of the earliest and most widespread forms of religious practice. And in dark caves of France and Spain, there are impressive artistic paintings on the walls, many having to do with animals and the hunt. Included are certain animal-human figures, which appear to be shamans or mythological figures such as the Master of Animals known from nonliterate hunting cultures of today. It seems clear that there were rituals connected both with the female figurines and with the cave art paintings, promoting the continuance of life-power and the activity of hunting the animals. From these archaeological remains, we can conclude

The Great Goddess from late Paleolithic times; the so-called Willendorf Venus.

that these paleolithic peoples, as early as perhaps 35,000 years ago, had religious ideas and practices not unlike the hunters among the nonliterate peoples of today.

For hundreds of thousands and perhaps millions of years of human history to very recent times, our human ancestors lived as hunters and gatherers, with religious experience shaped by that kind of focus. But in the Neolithic period, beginning after the last Ice Age, around 8000 B.C.E. in certain parts of the world, people began to discover how to produce food for themselves, changing the shape of human life and religion forever. The great agricultural revolution meant that people could settle down, build villages and cities, and develop a society in which some people produce the food while others create arts and industry. This development provided the incentive and the leisure to invent writing and promote learning. Religious interest focused more directly on Mother Earth and the cyclical death and rebirth of the vegetation, with appropriate rituals for the continuance of sacred life.

After the agricultural revolution, the changes in human culture began to come much more rapidly, into the Bronze Age (ca. 3200–1200 B.C.E. in the eastern Mediterranean areas) and the Iron Age (starting ca. 1200 B.C.E.), and the great empires developed with their ancient classical religions. And in the midst of these come the beginnings of the present-day world religions. In terms of total human history, the agricultural revolution, with the religious developments that have accompanied it, is a very recent event, one that still permeates our world view today. Whether the present-day technological revolution will have an equally drastic effect on our culture and religion remains to be seen.

THE ANCIENT CLASSICAL RELIGIONS

The depth and richness of humankind's story can be seen in the great religious systems of the ancient peoples of the world, associated with some of the classical civilizations. There are the ancient Egyptians, for example, and the peoples of Mesopotamia. Many religions stemmed from that original group of peoples called Indo-European, including the Iranians (Persians), Aryans (of India), Greeks, Romans, Celts, Germanic peoples, and more. The classical civilizations generally are agriculture-based societies, most of whom evolved complex city-state societies. They are characterized by belief in many great gods of nature, sacred kingship, strong priesthoods, and in many cases written texts. Most characteristic of these religions is the strong ritual component, for it is through the highly complex rituals that the society, the state, and even the cosmos are upheld.

Even though most of these religions did not survive, they made deep contributions to the human religious adventure. We see examples of ancient religions as we investigate the beginnings of some of the world religions: the ancient Hebrews, the Indus Valley civilization and the Aryans in India, and the religions of the Shang and early Chou eras in China. Here—to make our story of humankind more complete—are brief sketches of several of these important ancient religions. The interested reader can consult many useful studies of these religions for further information.

Ancient Egyptian Religion

For three millennia, from the first dynasty around 3200 B.C.E. to the first centuries of the Common Era, when Egypt converted to Christianity, the rich and diverse elements of Egyptian religion were practiced. With settled agricultural life in tune with the regular inundations of the Nile River, the Egyptians developed city-states, each with its own religious traditions. During much of their history these city-states were unified under a succession of dynasties. Their religion is one of cosmic integration, the whole world of nature filled with sacred power in the form of gods and goddesses, working together harmoniously through the mediation of the king and priests. Since they developed hieroglyphic writing at an early period, important sacred texts were written down on papyrus and on temple and tomb walls. The Egyptians had a large sacred literature, including myths, directions for souls of the dead, prayers and hymns, and philosophical wisdom texts.

The gods and goddesses of ancient Egypt were very numerous, and with the amalgamation of city-states different gods were identified with one another or took over one another's functions. One system of myths puts forth an original group of nine gods (the Ennead, revered especially at Heliopolis). Atum, the creator, rose from the primal ocean and, perched on the primeval hillock, created Shu, god of air, and Tefnut, goddess of moisture. They produced Geb, the earth god, and Nut, the sky goddess, who in turn became parents of Osiris and Isis, forces of life and regeneration. Further, Geb and Nut produced Set, the destroyer of life, and Nephthys, a protector of the dead. Osiris and Isis, for their part, became the parents of Horus, with whom the human kings of Egypt are identified in their divine status.

Throughout most of Egyptian history there was a

notion of the supreme god associated with the sun, called Re, Atum, Amun, or a combination of these names, as city-states fused their myths. For one brief period, under Akhnaton (r. ca. 1360–1344 B.C.E.), the "heretic" king, a form of monotheism was established by royal decree: only Aton, the sun-god, was to be worshiped as king of the entire world, embodying all the attribute of the other gods. This policy ended with the death of Akhnaton, but it shows the tendency in Egyptian religion to fuse the gods and elevate the sun-god to supremacy.

What is the real nature of the world? One widespread view of the cosmos pictured the sky as a giant cow whose four legs are supported by four gods, while other gods (stars) sail on small boats on her belly. The sun-god crosses the goddess's body during the day but is swallowed by her at night, passing through her body to be born anew in the morning, dispelling the darkness of chaos once again. Humans are created in the image of the gods and can enjoy success and happiness; yet death inevitably comes, when the soul leaves the body and journeys through the underworld. Therefore humans need to give attention to preparing for the afterlife and to preserve their bodies to live again.

So the path of transformation, including the worship of the gods and other duties of life, focused especially on the afterlife. In early times the idea of continued life after death seems to have been reserved for the royal family, but eventually all Egyptians became fascinated with the cult of the dead, associated with the god Osiris. Osiris was the god of the Nile and embodies the power of death and resurrection. A myth tells how he, as king of Egypt, was murdered by Set and his body scattered. His sorrowing Queen Isis found the pieces of his body and revived him sufficiently to conceive a son, Horus, by him. Osiris became the king of the underworld, and his son Horus became king of Egypt in his place. And so humans need to direct much attention to ensuring the safe passage of the soul through the judgments to the eternal kingdom of Osiris.

A key to Egyptian society was the divine king. Identified with Horus, in this life he was thought to be a "good god," to become a "great god" in the afterlife. He is the mediator between the realm of the gods and the human realm, acting as the high priest in carrying out the essential rituals to keep the world functioning. He is the one who causes *ma'at* (justice) to continue on earth. In addition there were many priests and priest-

The Sphinx and the Great Pyramid of Egypt.

esses, a high percentage of the total population, to assist the king in worshiping the gods.

Worship at the great temples was very elaborate and required many functionaries, aiming to maintain the world order by strengthening the gods. The temple was considered the mansion of the god, with the statue of the god kept in an innermost chamber, and daily rituals at the temple included washing and clothing the god and making meal offerings. At festival times the god would be taken out of the temple and carried in procession for all to see. Other important rituals were those associated with the cult of the dead, including prayers, incantations, and rituals of the "opening of the mouth," to bring life back into mummies and other representations of people.

The culture of Egypt attained high developments in religious ideas and also in the arts and sciences. Many texts lay out a pious, moral vision of how to live the good life; passing successfully to the next world requires making a "negative confession" before Osiris's tribunal, vouching for the good life one has lived. The ideal life is to uphold ma'at, justice and order, and thus live happily in this life. But always the reality of death is present. A fine literary composition gives a dialogue between a man and his soul about the man's wish to commit suicide. The soul can give no satisfactory argument against it, although it tries to persuade him to forget his cares and seek sensual enjoyment. Over against the unrewarding and weary life of seeking pleasure and facing the evils of society, death can be contemplated as a blessed release, as the man argues:

> Death is in my sight today
>> (Like) the recovery of a sick man,
>> Like going out into the open after a confinement. . . .
> Death is in my sight today
>> Like the longing of a man to see his house (again),
>> After he has spent many years held in captivity.[1]

Not all Egyptian thought is that pessimistic, but this dialogue shows the depth in which ancient Egyptians reflected on the questions of life and death. The wisdom of Egypt influenced the Israelite religion as well as Greek philosophers.

Religion in Ancient Mesopotamia

Civilization in ancient Mesopotamia (roughly the territory of present-day Iraq) developed at about the same time as in Egypt, starting around the middle of the fourth millennium B.C.E. First the Sumerians created a great city-state empire based in the delta of the Tigris and Euphrates rivers. By around 1800 B.C.E., Semitic peoples north of Sumeria moved to the ascendency and unified most of the whole region as the Babylonian Empire, followed around 1100 B.C.E. by the rise of the Assyrians in northern Mesopotamia. After a brief Babylonian revival, traditional Mesopotamian civilization faded when the Persians took over about 540 B.C.E.

Despite these shifts, Mesopotamian religion remained remarkably constant in the interplay between Sumerian and Semitic cultural traditions. The whole area was dependent on agriculture, with irrigation already used in ancient times, and the society was centered on a number of city-states. Cuneiform writing on clay tablets was invented by the Sumerians around 3500 B.C.E., and a large sacred literature of myths, ritual directions, prayers, hymns, and wisdom texts developed, first in Sumerian and then in Akkadian (the Semitic language of Babylon). Two especially important stories are the Enuma Elish creation story and the epic of Gilgamesh, which includes a well-known story of the gods attempting to destroy humankind by a flood. Fortunately, a goodly number of these texts, written on clay tablets, have been discovered in the ruins of ancient libraries.

In contrast to Egypt with its regular rhythms of Nile River inundations, life in ancient Mesopotamia was more unpredictable, with droughts and floods and invasions of peoples from the surrounding plateaus, and perhaps for that reason the religion of Mesopotamia is less trusting of the cosmic order. Order and fertility are not given through the regular operation of sacred powers, but they continually need to be achieved by integrating and harmonizing the many powerful sacred beings. The universe is rather like a cosmic state with a hierarchy of individual powers that are often in conflict and thus need to be controlled and integrated into a functioning cosmos.

These sacred powers are immanent within the forces

of nature—sky, storm, sun, moon, waters, earth, and the rest; all these natural phenomena have within themselves a will and power. And all together make up the divine cosmic state, governed by the great gods of the universe. The leader of the divine assembly is the sky god Anu, father of the gods and the one who maintains order in the cosmos through his command. Other leading gods are Enlil, god of the storm, exercising force for the gods; Enki (Ea), god of earth-waters and of wisdom; Ninhursaga, the earth mother-goddess; the moon-god Nanna (Sin); the sun-god Utu (Shamash); and many more. The "Great List of the Gods" from Assurbanipal's library (ca. 650 B.C.E.) includes no less than 2,000 names of gods! A widely popular goddess is Inanna (Ishtar), a sky goddess who functions as both the goddess of warfare and the goddess of love and fertility. The husband of Inanna is the fertility god Dumuzi (Tammuz), who dies and descends to the underworld, to be brought back to life in the spring. Marduk, the god of the city-state Babylon, reached supremacy among the Babylonians, ruling as king of the cosmos.

According to the Mesopotamian creation myths, the gods themselves arose out of the divine chaos forces and, defeating these forces in conflict, shaped the cosmos out of them. In the Babylonian version of the creation myth, the great god Marduk enters into battle with Tiamat, the dragon of chaos, kills her, splits her body into two, and from it makes the whole cosmos. The cosmos functions because all the gods are placed at their stations, immanent in the forces of nature. Humans are created to be the servants of the gods, to sacrifice to them and fulfil their needs. The cosmic forces need to be maintained, otherwise conflict and disaster may erupt, as when the gods decided to destroy humankind by sending a great flood. Humans long for immortality, but finally they are limited and helpless in the cosmos. The human plight is epitomized by Gilgamesh's heroic adventures in his search for immortality; he discovers the plant of immortality but when he pauses to bathe, a snake steals it and obtains immortality instead.

So the path for humans is to serve the gods, determine their will through divination, and assist in maintaining cosmic order through rituals and festivals.

These human responsibilities rested especially on the king of the city-state, who was the special servant of the city-god and a vessel of sacred power. In important rituals the king would play the part of the great god, and it was his rule that maintained order, fertility, and well-being for the people. One important ritual, for example, was the sacred marriage in which the king and a temple priestess would have sexual union, playing the parts of the fertility god and goddess so that the fertility of plants and animals would be restored. Many priests and priestesses assisted in the worship of the gods and the performance of the sacrifices, rituals, incantations, and divinations.

In Babylon the new year's festival (*akitu*) was a particularly significant festival, lasting nearly two weeks with many important ritual events. On the fourth day of the festival, the epic of creation, Enuma Elish, was read, telling how the city-god Marduk defeated the dragon Tiamat and created the world. On the fifth day, the temple of Marduk was purified, and the king of Babylon was divested of his royal insignia and slapped by the priest; then he made a confession as he knelt before the statue of Marduk and was reinvested with his insignia. Gods from the other city-states (represented by their statues) arrived on the sixth day, and on the eighth day the king "took Marduk by the hand" and led him to the Shrine of Destinies, where Marduk was proclaimed king over the assembled gods. Then the king led Marduk and the gods in a great victory procession along the street to the River Euphrates, where they all boarded boats and proceeded to the Akitu house. There a great banquet of the gods took place, and perhaps there also was a reenactment of the battle between Marduk and Tiamat and a sacred marriage between Marduk and his spouse. On the eleventh day the gods returned to Babylon and held a solemn assembly to fix the destinies of the land, and the new year's festival ended with another great banquet.

The ancient Mesopotamians did a lot of reflecting about the good and ethical life. A famous attempt to create a just society is found in the law-code promulgated by King Hammurabi of Babylon (fl. 1792–1750 B.C.E.) and inscribed on a stele. The preface to the code says that Hammurabi was called by the gods "to cause justice to prevail in the land, to destroy the

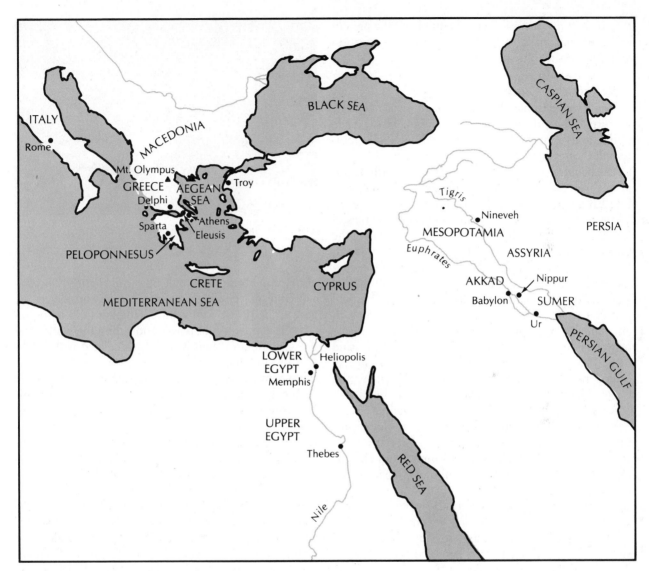

Ancient Civilizations.

wicked and the evil, that the strong might not oppress the weak."[2] Many prayers addressed to the gods, recorded on clay tablets, included confessions of sins and statements of repentance. Questions about why the gods sent suffering and death were discussed, as in the remarkable hymn called "I Will Praise the Lord of Wisdom." The author, like Job of the Hebrew Bible, is an official of high rank who, in spite of his piety, suffers misfortune and disease and raises questions about the moral governance of the world. "What is good in one's sight is evil for a god. What is bad in one's own mind is good for his god. Who can understand the counsel of the gods in the midst of heaven?"[3] There was no conception of reward in the gloomy world of the dead, so the good ethical life was focused entirely on the present existence, in serving the gods and maintaining justness and rightness in human society.

Religion in Classical Greece

As a third example of the ancient classical religions, we turn to the culture of classical Greece, which made tremendous contributions to the world in religion, philosophy, literature, politics, science, and art. The Greek peoples, like the Romans and other early Europeans, were heirs of the Indo-Europeans who migrated into Europe in the second millennium B.C.E., assimilating many of the traits of the indigenous peoples of the Aegean area. Living by agriculture, eventually the Greeks created various city-states, governed by kings, tyrants, powerful nobles, or democracies. Two city-states came to have special power, Athens and Sparta, and under Athenian leadership a brilliant classical period (ca. 500–338 B.C.E.) saw rich developments in art, philosophy, politics, and science. But the struggle between Athens and Sparta weakened the country, and in 338 B.C.E. Philip of Macedonia (north of Greece) gained rulership, followed by his son Alexander the Great. Alexander conquered far and wide in the eastern Mediterranean and the Near East, spreading Greek culture in an international form known as Hellenism. Finally, in the second century B.C.E., Greece was incorporated into the rising Roman Empire, and Hellenism continued to be a powerful cultural force for many centuries.

Although the Greeks did not have sacred scriptures as such, they did have a rich repertoire of myths (*muthoi*) about the gods, and these were passed on and added to by countless bards, singers, and poets, forming the basis of the broad Greek way of understanding the world. In the ninth and eighth centuries B.C.E., several literary works were composed, providing a grand view of the gods: Homer's *Illiad* and *Odyssey*, and Hesiod's *Theogony* (Birth of the Gods). Most of the myths presented in these works had already become literary tales, no longer living myths associated with rituals, but they provide us a vast panorama of the Greek sacred vision.

An outstanding feature of the Greek gods is their humanity. They are like humans in many ways—but

The Greek amphitheatre at Ephesus.

at the same time immortal, powerful, perfectly beautiful, and above suffering. The Greeks considered the gods to be of two kinds: the Olympian gods living on Mt. Olympus, full of power and ruling the world; and the Chthonian ("earthly") gods associated with earth-fertility and the realm of death. Among the twelve Olympians, Zeus (Jupiter to the Romans) is the father of the gods and the ruler of the universe, and his jealous wife is Hera (Roman Juno), goddess of women, marriage, and childbirth. Apollo, son of Zeus and a mortal woman, is the god of archery, prophecy, and music. And Hermes (Roman Mercury) is the messenger of Zeus and patron of travelers and thiefs, as well as the god of animals. Other Olympian gods are Poseidon (Neptune), god of the sea; Artemis (Diana), the virgin goddess and mistress of wild animals; Athena (Minerva), goddess of wisdom; Demeter (Ceres), goddess of grain; Ares (Mars), god of war; Aphrodite (Venus), goddess of love and beauty; Hephaestus (Vulcan), god of fire; and Hestia (Vesta), goddess of the hearth. Not included among the Olympians but still of great significance is Dionysus, god of fertility and ecstatic rapture. Dionysus represents the mystical and ecstatic aspect of Greek religion, whereas Apollo represents the rational and orderly aspect. Important among the Chthonic gods are the Heroes, such as Heracles, a man who achieved divinity by his great labors; and gods of the underworld such as Hades.

Greek mythology tells how Gaia (earth) sprang from

chaos and then gave birth to Uranus (sky); Uranus and Gaia gave birth to the Titans, among them Kronus who castrated his father Uranus and became sovereign. Kronus was a cruel father who swallowed his offspring, but Zeus, the sixth child, escaped this fate and overthrew Kronus and the Titans, himself to become sovereign over the gods.

According to Hesiod, the Greeks believed that there have been four ages of the world, each one more degenerate than the previous. The humans Zeus created to live in our present world are burdened with cares and troubles; but still Zeus and the other gods watch over them, observing their just and unjust deeds. The gods intervene in human life, even taking different sides in wars and fighting among themselves. Still, humans live at a great distance from the gods; we are mortal, destined to journey to Hades to exist as vague shadows. A major sin bringing severe punishment is *hubris* (pride), being unwilling to bow to the gods and what they have ordained, not accepting the lot of mortal humans. The path to follow for the blessed life, accordingly, is to give the gods their due through worship and respect, and to live human life in moderation and justice.

Public worship of the gods took place for the welfare of the whole community, led by ruling officials, priests, and priestesses, at official temples and shrines. Sacrifices were made of animals and other foods, to be consumed both by the gods and the worshipers. There were many great festivals throughout the year. For example, in Athens a major festival took place almost every month, such as a festival in honor of Demeter at the time of the sowing of corn, a celebration of the sacred marriage of Zeus and Athena, a wine festival in honor of Dionysus, a harvest festival in honor of Apollo, and many more.

Key to the Greek notion of the good ethical life is the acceptance of one's place with regard to the gods, and with that the practice of moderation. In a play by Sophocles, Odysseus is warned:

> Look well at this, and speak no towering word
> Yourself against the gods, nor walk too grandly
> Because your hand is weightier than another's,
> Or your great wealth deeper founded. One short day

> Inclines the balance of all human things
> To sink or rise again. Know that the gods
> Love men of steady sense and hate the proud.[4]

A characteristic development in Greek religion was the opportunity for individuals to practice forms of mystical union with the gods. This took place in a number of movements usually called "mysteries," since the rituals were done secretly by initiates. In the Dionysus cult, the divine forces hidden in nature and in humans were roused by rituals that led into frenzied ecstasy, wild dancing, and drunkenness, the experience of being possessed by Dionysus. Again, people could be initiated into the mysteries at Eleusis, associated with Demeter, goddess of vegetation, and her daughter Kore, resurrected from Hades. In highly secretive rituals enacting the rebirth of life, the initiates experienced union with Demeter and the promise of a happy life after death. Another movement was Orphism, also based on a myth about revival from the underworld that can be shared by the worshipers. Orphism taught that by purification and a strict moral code, such as abstaining from eating the flesh of living creatures, one can so purify the soul that it will live a blessed life in Elysium after death. These ideas about personal salvation and immortality continued to develop in the Hellenistic Roman period, as, for example, in the mysteries associated with Isis, the great goddess who resurrected Osiris and can thus give new life.

Of great significance for Western civilization was the development of humanistic and philosophical thinking among the ancient Greeks. The early philosophical schools were devoted to studying the nature of the universe, and they developed naturalistic, rational theories. The philosophers came to question the old mythologies about the gods and their immoral actions, and a new era of thinking began that directed itself to human, secular concerns on the basis of rational thought rather than mythology. Socrates (ca. 470–399 B.C.E.) quoted an inscription on the Apollo temple at Delphi, "Know yourself," and taught the young people of Athens to think critically about everything—and was condemned to death as one who spoke against religion and corrupted youth. Socrates' disciple Plato (427–347 B.C.E.) taught that reality consists of universal ideas or forms; human reason can discover or "remember" the ultimate principles of reality from which human reason is derived. And Plato's disciple Aristotle (384–322 B.C.E.) carried philosophy far into the investigation of the natural world, setting forth some of the basic categories of philosophy and science that guided the development of Western thought for many centuries.

DISCUSSION QUESTIONS

1. What is the nature of evidence for religious practices from the prehistorical periods?
2. What kinds of changes in religious ideas and practices were occasioned by the Neolithic food-producing revolution?
3. Discuss the ancient Egyptian concern about the afterlife and the role of the cult of Osiris.
4. What are some basic contrasts between ancient Egyptian and Mesopotamian perspectives on the world and human existence?
5. Explain the suggestion that the gods of ancient Mesopotamia form a "cosmic state."
6. What was the ancient Babylonian perspective on creation and the role and purpose of humans?
7. What is the ancient Greek notion of *hubris*? How is this related to their view of the nature and role of humans?
8. What do you think was the relation between ancient Greek religion and the development of philosophical thought?

CHAPTER 3

RELIGIONS OF NONLITERATE PEOPLES

Among the religions of the nonliterate peoples, both today and in the recent past, are a number of cultural types that correspond to food-producing techniques. First of all, there are hunters and gatherers, demonstrating the life-style of all our ancestors from the beginning of human history until the agricultural revolution. Included in this category are the gatherers and small game hunters, the peoples who carry on hunts of big game herds of animals, and those who live by fishing. Their religious ideas tend to focus on the sacred powers of the sky and on the gods associated with the life-power of the animals, such as the Animal Master. Important roles are played by shamans, people who can transcend their human limitations and communicate with the various spiritual beings; and much attention is directed toward the sacred relationship with the animals. Among the many hunters and gatherers of modern times are, for example, the Native Americans of the Plains with their buffalo hunt; the Eskimo (Inuit) of Greenland and North America and the Ainu of northern Japan who live by hunting the bear and by fishing; the Bushmen of southern Africa who gather plants and hunt small animals; and some groups of Aborigines of Australia's Western Desert who move about periodically in their hunting and gathering.

A second group includes planters, those who cultivate the earth to raise food as did our ancestors in the Neolithic period. Their religious interests are directed toward Mother Earth as the life-producing source. The sense of close kinship with vegetation is expressed in planting and harvesting rituals. And there is emphasis on rituals symbolizing the necessity of death so that there can be new life and on sexual rituals to enhance the life-giving powers. Different types of planting, of course, provide the context for somewhat different religious emphases. But, broadly speaking, most planting peoples place their main attention either on tuberous root-crop plants, such as the yam and taro, or on cereal and grain plants, such as wheat, rice, millet, and maize (corn). Root-crop planters include many of the peoples of Melanesia and Polynesia, such as the Marind-anim and the Kiwai of New Guinea, the Ceramese Islanders in Indonesia, and the Maori of New Zealand. Cereal-grain planting peoples have been numerous in many parts of the world, including maize-growing Native Americans; the rice-growing Ngaju of Borneo; and many peoples of Africa who grow millet and wheat, such as the Dogon, the Yoruba, and the Ashanti. Of course, many of these planters raise a number of other plant foods in addition to what has traditionally been their staple food.

A third category of nonliterate peoples is the pastoralist group, those who raise their own cattle or sheep. Pastoralists also often do some planting of food. Domestication of animals began as early as agriculture, and a number of important ancient civilizations were pastoralist, such as the Indo-Europeans and the ancient Hebrews. Religious ideas of pastoralists are often focused on sky gods and on the life-power of their herds of animals, expressed in rituals of sacrifice. Examples of pastoralists today can be found among African peoples, such as the Nuer, the Dinka, and the Zulu.

SACRED STORIES FOR NONLITERATE PEOPLES

"Who am I?" Sometimes we suppose anxiety about identity is one of the marks of modern human life, and we likely do not think of an African Bushman or a housewife in ancient Babylonia sitting around worrying about who he or she really is. But at the deepest levels the question of "Who am I?" reflects an existential concern about how our little space of life fits into the greater life of the world, the ancestors, the family, and the sacred powers. The most drastic punishment imaginable in many nonliterate cultures is to make a wrongdoer an outcast, to withdraw name and social support so that the person loses identity and becomes a nobody—no longer human, no longer a part of the sacred rhythms of life.

In order to provide the necessary context for human identity, each nonliterate people has some kind of sacred history told in the form of stories. Some of these stories are very elaborate and sacred to everyone in the society, memorized by mythtellers as a kind of oral sacred literature. Other stories are local and disconnected, passed on family by family. But one mark of these stories is that they tell a sacred history about origins and foundings and developments that made the people what they are. "Where did we come from?" "How did our ancestors learn from the sacred powers the real way of life?" "How did our rituals and social structures come about?" By knowing this sacred history, the people know who they really are.

Nonliterate peoples, with their openness to the involvement of sacred powers in all events and with their closeness to the rhythms of nature, are not as concerned in their stories about historical consciousness as are peoples of some of the world religions of today. This does not mean, as some have supposed, that they have no sense of history, for they do certainly remember important events even long past. But purely "historical" events are not particularly significant apart from the involvement of sacred power in those events. The real story about who they are comes not from wars and disasters and victories and whatever else makes up "history," but from the action of the sacred powers and the ancestors in founding a way of life according to the sacred pattern. So the sacred history often takes the form of myths and stories about the sacred beings who created human existence and established the patterns that are still followed to live in the fullest human way. This is oral literature, expressed in many different forms, formulated by gifted shamans and storytellers, memorized and passed on by elders and bards. This is a living history, so the stories change over time and incorporate new happenings within the sacred pattern.

Identity through the Sacred History

The myths and other texts have to do with encounters with sacred power. The setting is often the time of the beginnings or at least has some connection with that sacred time, as experienced in ritual and festival. It is in these eruptions of sacred power into the world, as told in the myths, that the vital aspects of existence were created and still are sustained. Myths sometimes tell about the creation of the whole world and of humans, of course. But myths also tell of the creation of vital realities like animals and hunting, plants and planting, fishing, eating, sex and reproduction, death and ancestors, social structure, sacred land, rituals and festivals, medicine, and all the rest—all that makes our existence fully human according to the sacred pattern.

In modern usage, the word *myth* usually connotes something that is not true or real. But when used to designate the sacred stories of the religions, *myth* means that which is *really* the Truth, that which people live by, that which provides ultimate meaning for their existence. Myth tells the truth, the real Truth. "It is so because it is said that it is so," the Netsilik Eskimoes say about their sacred stories. It is the Truth because it links us with the source of life and power, the Time of the Beginnings. "It was thus that the Nemu [mythical ancestors] did, and we do likewise," according to the Kai of New Guinea.[1]

One reason that the myths, epics, and songs are so important is that they provide models and paradigms to follow in living the fully human life, that is, the life shaped by the sacred beings and ancestors. These oral traditions permeate every corner of life, whether having to do with ritual or festival, diet or marriage, work or play, war or art. They provide orientation to the world, define culture, and maintain basic values, molding people into the sacred patterns by instructing them and defining their activities and goals.

Perhaps it is important to note that nonliterate peoples do not consider their oral traditions to be lacking or inferior simply because they are not written. A Carrier Indian in British Columbia is reported to have said, "The white man writes everything down in a book so that it might not be forgotten; but our ancestors married the animals, learned their ways, and passed on the knowledge from one generation to another."[2] In fact, the very orality of the myths, epics, and songs is what carries the power—passing them by word of mouth from one generation to the next, performing them in ritual and festival, transforming them, and adding to them as new experiences of the sacred are encountered. Let us consider several examples.

The Hopi, living on the desert mesas of southwestern North America, think of themselves as the first inhabitants of America. Their village of Oraibi may be the

Zuni ceremonial dancers at night. The Zuni are pueblo Indians of southwestern North America.

oldest continuously occupied settlement on the continent. Their sacred history about their emergence, wanderings, and settlement provides a sense of continuity and identity. The Hopi tell how this is the fourth world that humans have inhabited, the first three lower worlds having been destroyed. The first world was created very good and people were created wise, but gradually they forgot their origin and misused nature, so that conflict and war arose. The creator hid the people safe in an anthill while he destroyed the first world and created a second world for the people to live in. But eventually the people created conflict again, so the second world was destroyed, and then also the third world, and finally the fourth world, this present world, was created.

As they emerged into the fourth world, Masaw, guardian of the earth, told the people that to fulfill the creation the different clans should go separate ways and wander until they would settle together in the right place. Each clan should make four migrations—in the four directions—to the ends of the land, before coming back to the center again. So for many years the clans wandered about, leaving rock carvings, mounds, and broken pottery to record their migrations. Some peoples among them forgot the command of Masaw and settled in tempting places before finishing their migrations, building cities and civilizations that were to crumble. Some of the clans, however, finished the migrations properly and settled in the center of the world, the arid plateau between the Colorado and Rio Grande rivers, becoming the Hopi peoples. In their wanderings they all had sacred experiences, and when they settled in their permanent villages each clan contributed its special rituals and ceremonies to form the great ceremonial cycle of the year. Still today after major ceremonies are concluded, the men relate the history of their clans and their migrations, "so that we will always keep them deeply in our hearts. For the telling of our journeys is as much religious as the ceremonies themselves!"[3]

The Navajo, also from southwestern North America, have a sacred history with an emergence story similar to that of the Hopi, and this is followed by a world era of heroic adventures of the first Navajo people. As these heroes journey about, they get into difficulty and suffer because they violate regulations or enter forbidden territory. But when they are trapped in their predicament, they are helped by the Holy People (sacred beings) who perform ceremonies that restore them and also initiate these heroes into the ceremonial ways. The heroes then teach the ceremonies to the Navajo people as the pattern for their life. One example from this sacred history has to do with a young man on a hunting trip who had sexual relations with a beautiful young woman without realizing she was the wife of White Thunder. As he unwittingly continued hunting, White Thunder tricked him into setting his arrows aside so that, bereft of this magical protection, he could be shattered by lightning. Since he did not return, his family went out to search and were helped by Gila Monster, who showed his powers of restoration by cutting himself up and scattering the parts, which were then reassembled and restored according to his powers. Gila Monster then restored the hunter to life in the same kind of ceremonial, initiating the hunter into the knowledge and powers of Gila Monster. From this arose the Flintway ceremonial, by which Navajo can bring restoration in a situation of chaos, disease, and death.[4]

Such stories in the sacred history define the character, the purpose, and the boundaries of Navajo life. They provide a special identity for the people, linking them to the ancestral heroes of the beginning times and providing a model for life in this world. They show how to hunt, how to relate to other people and to the ancestors, how to marry and have a family, and above all how to relate to the Holy People and perform the ceremonials they have established. This history becomes real again every time the ceremonials are celebrated.

The sacred history of the Lugbara of eastern Africa provides identity for these people by telling how their society and clan relationships came about.[5] In the beginning phase the world was the inverse of what it is now; there was no society, and the people were nonhumans living through magical means and practicing incest. Then a transitional phase began with the birth of the two Lugbara heroes, who had both nonhuman and human characteristics. At first they lived as nonhumans, begetting offspring incestuously, even eating their own children. But they moved to Lugbaraland, and now they began to establish the social laws to be followed by their children, who are the founders of the present clans and the beginning of real human society in this present phase of the ordered, human Lugbara world.

This history shows how the Lugbara clans are the real people, living at the center as normal upright people. Outside this center is a second large circle of related tribes in which the peoples are not entirely normal and practice sorcery. Beyond this is the third area entirely outside the bounds of humanity. These peoples (including the first Europeans the Lugbara met) are entirely inverted, walking on their heads, eating rotten meat, practicing cannibalism and sorcery. Thus the Lugbara land and people form a sacred cosmos surrounded by progressively more chaotic and nonhuman spheres. Through remembering the sacred history, the order of the cosmos and the identity of the people as the real humans can be maintained.

The Link to the Culture Heroes

The sacred histories of the Hopi, Navajo, and Lugbara mentioned here all put forth an important role for the first ancestors and culture heroes of the people. It is by identifying with these first people in mythic times, by experiencing them as present in the telling of the stories and in the rituals that the people know their own place and role.

The story of the culture heroes is so important because they originated the real way of life. Aborigines of Australia have sacred histories about the heroes in the Dreaming Time, that time of the beginnings that overarches also the present time. These ancestor-heroes arose at the beginning of the world and traveled all over the surface of the land, shaping it and making it ready for humans. They are responsible for all natural growth, the seasons, the replenishment of animal species, and the land's fertility. Their power and presence remain as "Dreaming" in the physical aspects of the world—rocks and stones, hills, tracks, tools, paintings, and much more. People today know and feel their presence in their sacred sites and in the stories and rituals.

There are a great number of these ancestor-heroes,

and they are often linked to specific clans and to individuals. When a person is born it is felt that the life-power comes from a particular ancestor-hero, so that person remains linked to that hero in a special way. The ancestor-heroes reside at various places, so the stories and rituals take on a larger, interlinked pattern, as different individuals and different clans cooperate in the necessary ceremonies and rituals for the renewal of the seasons and the land. An important function of the history about the heroes is to set the rules for behavior in the clan, providing the model for how to live in the full human way.

As another example of sacred history about culture heroes, we turn to the islanders of Ceram (Indonesia), just west of New Guinea. The Wemale of western Ceram are tropical yam cultivators much like peoples throughout Melanesia. Within their sacred history about the time of the beginnings is a myth about their first ancestors and about Maiden Hainuwele, a being full of extraordinary power. This myth, recorded by Adolf Jensen,[6] tells how the nine families of humankind emerged at Mt. Nunusaku and migrated to the Nine Dance Grounds. Among them was Ameta, who chased a wild pig into the water and when he pulled it out found a coconut on its tusk (though there were no cocopalms in the world). He put the coconut in his house, covered with a cloth, and in a dream a man told him, "The coconut which you have covered with a sarong there on the shelf, you must plant in the earth, for it is already starting to sprout."

So Ameta planted the coconut, and it quickly grew tall and carried blossoms. He cut some blossoms from the palm, but in doing so he cut his finger, and his blood dripped on the blossoms. Later he discovered that where his blood had mingled with the sap of the blossoms a little girl was developing. In his dream the man told him to wrap the girl in the cloth and bring her home, and so he did, calling her Hainuwele (Branch of the Cocopalm). Maiden Hainuwele grew up quickly and had extraordinary powers: when she relieved herself her excrement consisted of precious articles such as Chinese plates and bells!

The nine families of humankind held a great Maro Dance in the Nine Dance Grounds, the men dancing the large ninefold spiral, and the women handing out betel-nut for them to chew on. In place of betel-nut, Hainuwele handed out precious items such as coral, Chinese plates, bush knives, betel boxes, golden earrings, and beautiful bells, the value of the items increasing each night of the dance. The people got very envious of Hainuwele and decided to kill her. So on the ninth night of the great Maro Dance, they dug a deep pit and, in the slowly circling dance movement of the spiral, they pressed Maiden Hainuwele into the pit and trampled earth over her.

When she did not come home, her father Ameta performed divination to locate her body. Then he dug up her body and cut it up into many pieces, planting the pieces throughout the dance grounds. These pieces were transformed into things that had never existed before, above all, the tuberous fruit that has been the main food of the people ever since.

Ameta carried Hainuwele's two arms to Maiden Satene, who at that time still ruled over the people. Maiden Satene was angry at the people because they had killed. She built a large gate and, holding Hainuwele's two arms, summoned all humankind, saying to them: "I do not wish to live here any longer, since you have killed. Today I am going away from you. Now all of you must come to me by passing through the gate. Whoever makes it through the gate will remain people; whoever does not pass all the way through will experience something different." So whoever of the people did not pass all the way through was transformed into an animal or spirit—that is how there came to be pigs, deer, birds, fish, and many spirits in the world. Those who passed through the gate to Hainuwele went on both sides; those on the left had to leap over five stalks of bamboo, and from these stem the Fivers; those going on the right had to leap over nine stalks, and from these stem the Niners. Then Satene left the people and went to dwell on the Mountain of the Dead, and whoever wants to go to her must first die.

This story tells of the first ancestors, the nine families of humankind, from whom the Wemale are descended. The actions of these ancestors shaped human life into the way it is now. The story relates the origin of many essential aspects of life: the cocopalm tree, the mystery of planting, the great Maro dance ceremony, death, rituals of divination, ritual killing and planting parts of the body, the journey to the realm of death, animals and spirits, and the main social divisions of the Wemale. Most important, the death of the powerful Maiden Hainuwele brings the great gift of yams that grow from her body. By telling and ritualizing the sacred story, the Wemale know who they are, how to live their lives, and how to relate to the culture heroes who are still present as they reenact the myths and rituals.

Modern Transformations in the Stories of Nonliterate Societies

The modern century has brought great stress and change to the nonliterate peoples of the world, to the extent that for many of them the traditional way of life is a thing of the past. Education into Western ways, exploitation and suppression, being uprooted from their sacred lands and forced to live in urban areas, conversion to one of the world religions—these factors and others have caused the religious vision of nonliterate peoples to fade along with the way of life that supported it, bringing about a profound identity crisis for these peoples.

But there is still a vitality among the traditional religions, as shown by certain creative responses to European encroachment and modernization. Even the story of Hainuwele, though it echoes from the past, responds to modern civilization. For what makes Hainuwele's powers so special that the people conspire to kill her is that she is able to produce fabulous *foreign* items—knives, earrings, bells. In fact, one modern scholar has argued that the real point of the Hainuwele story as recorded in 1937 was to respond to Western colonization, which had suppressed tradition and imposed taxes. This disrupted the traditional system of values based on equivalence, where prestige depends on giving and receiving in equal proportion. So the story deals with this incongruity in traditional terms, through killing and cannibalism.[7] Even if this interpretation is accepted, the modern version of the story certainly has deep roots in Wemale tradition, and it is an example of the vitality that oral stories have in meeting current issues through traditional modes of thought.

Of course, groups of archaic, nonliterate peoples do still exist in the world today, protected from outside forces of modernization either by governments or by remote location. The numbers of these peoples, however, have shrunk rapidly and will continue to shrink, probably eventually to disappear. But that does not mean the end of their religious visions. Among the traditional religious groups that have responded in vital, creative ways to the challenge of the modern secular world, two important directions of response can be seen. One response is to graft elements of Western culture and religion onto the traditional base and thus create new religious movements. The other response is to reaffirm the traditional identity and vision as an authentic and viable posture even within the modern world.

Religions of the Oppressed: Blending of the New and the Old

One particular response of the nonliterate peoples of Melanesia to the invasion of modern Western forces was the development of Cargo Cults. During the twentieth century these societies were forced out of the Neolithic period directly into the world of great cargo

The Americas and the Pacific.

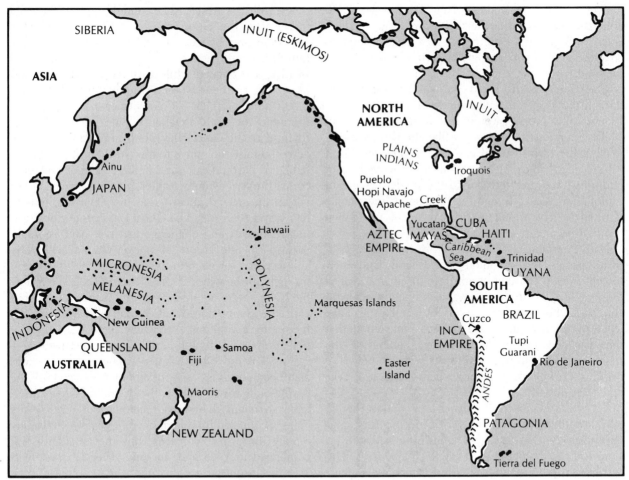

ships, cash, radios, beer, and all the rest, as Australian and Dutch colonizers, and American troops during World War II, arrived with their bizarre new culture. A significant response to this was a series of millenarian movements, looking for a new age in which the ancestors from the other world would come on great white ships laden with cash and goods of the Western world. The arrival of ships from the white world evoked memories of their own traditions about the ancestors living in the land of the dead across the sea, returning annually to visit at the end of the harvest season. These modern ships were really gifts from the ancestors that had been stolen by the whites; but now the ancestors would liberate them and a great age of prosperity would begin. After seeing airplanes land for the first time, the natives of the highlands of New Guinea began to anticipate the arrival of their ancestors in an airplane laden with gifts. In some places they even cleared an area for the planes to land and built storehouses to store the food.

The Cargo Cults could not survive, of course, though they kept surfacing off and on into the 1950s. Prophet after prophet would arise in different parts of Melanesia and fan the hopes of liberation and prosperity, but the revival would end in disappointment and despair. These movements symbolize the wrenching of traditional societies forced into the modern world of exploitation and cash, and they also show how people respond to new situations by drawing on their own spiritual resources.

Native Americans, devastated by the advance of white people through their sacred lands and their forced moves to reservations, produced a series of prophetic leaders in the late eighteenth and nineteenth centuries. For example, in 1799 Handsome Lake received new revelations and founded a movement that spread widely among the Iroquois, combining the traditional belief in the Great Spirit with the beliefs of the Christian Quakers, among whom Handsome Lake had been raised.

But the crisis in Native American identity boiled over toward the end of the nineteenth century, and starting around 1870 a series of antiwhite, Native revival movements swept the West and the Plains areas. The best known of these was the Ghost Dance movement, which reached a climax with the Sioux uprising and the tragic massacre by the United States Army of several hundred men, women, and children at Wounded Knee in 1890. One of the leaders of the Ghost Dance movement was a prophetic figure called Wovoka, preaching something new in the Native American vision: the cataclysmic end of this world age and the creation of a new age in which Native American culture and religion would be restored. All whites would be carried away by high winds, leaving their possessions to the Native Americans. The ancestors would return from the dead, the buffalo herds would be restored, and sickness and death would be eliminated.

In his visions Wovoka was told by God that the people should work hard, love one another, and live in peace with the whites. They should replace their old rituals with the Ghost Dance, a ritual of collective exaltation and trance. The dance would usually last four or five days, with people painting their bodies and wearing a decorated white garment called the Ghost Shirt. The men and women would arrange themselves in concentric circles, the arms of each resting on the shoulders of both neighbors, and in the vibrant rhythms of the dance they would sing laments for the dead and raise their arms to the Great Spirit. In ecstatic trance they would call out, "Father, I come! Mother, I come! Brother, I come! Father, give me arrows!,"[8] and fall on the ground unconscious in exhaustion, only to revive and continue. The Ghost Dance movement was in part protest and challenge to white oppression, in part apocalyptic vision taken over from Christianity, and in part a revival of tradition and identity. It spread through all the tribes of the Plains and the West; only the Navajo were not drawn into this Native revival. But with the Sioux tragedy at Wounded Knee and deteriorating conditions everywhere, active agitation for liberation and restoration could not be sustained.

Some of the Ghost Dance energy and vision was channeled into the rise of another movement, the peyote cult, which reflects the desire of Native Americans to retain their own religious roots even while being assimilated into modern white society. Spreading rapidly through most tribes, this movement was incorporated in 1918 and, in spite of legal harassments over the use of peyote in early years, continues to be influential today as the Native American Church. The leaders follow a course of peaceful coexistence with white people and have adopted many elements from Christianity while reasserting Native American values and traditions. For example, God the Father is the Great Spirit, Jesus is the Guardian Spirit of the Natives, and the Holy Spirit is enveloped in the peyote. Many Native traditions are maintained, centering on visions, spirits, and healing. The peyote cactus button, with its quality of producing visual and auditory hallucinations, had earlier been used ritually for healing, but in the Native American Church it becomes a communal sacrament eaten in a nighttime ceremony complete with prayers, drums, and visions. The movement follows a strict code of morality, and it offers to some Native Americans a religion that maintains their traditional identity within a modern setting.

The exploitation of Africans by Western nations and industrialists beginning with the slave trade, the advance of modern education and urban industry, and the missionary growth of Christianity and Islam have combined to fracture drastically and in many cases destroy the traditional African societies and their way of life. One response has been new religious movements that combine Christianity (or Islam) with native African ideas and practices. An example from outside Africa is Haiti, where the slaves brought from Africa retained many of their traditions. Today many Haitians still practice Voodoo, consisting of various beliefs and rituals of African origin under a veneer of Christianity. In Muslim parts of Africa, the people often retain most of their traditions and practices while adopting Islam. And many Christianized Africans have broken away from the mainline mission church bodies to join separatist or independent churches that have revived traditional African practices. In general these groups emphasize freedom from white control, possession by the Holy Spirit, experience of visions and dreams, and healing.

As an example of these many movements that mix Christian and traditional practices, consider the Zionist groups of South Africa. Zionism started at the beginning of the twentieth century, influenced by the American Zionist movement centered at Zion City, Illinois. This Christian-African movement provides a community identity for uprooted and oppressed people. Zionists sing hymns and chants with melodies from the Bantu and Zulu traditions, practice washing of feet, and focus attention on healing. Worshipers come forward to be vigorously shaken and stroked to expel demons from the body and bring wellness. Many rules govern life, especially prohibitions against eating pork or taking European medicines.

Many of the independent churches were founded by charismatic prophets who received new revelations, and among the Zionists the prophet Isaiah Shembe (1870–1935) stands out. Influenced by Christian ideas in his youth, he received a series of remarkable visions through lightning and thunder, and in obedience he gave up his wives and became a wandering prophet and faith-healer, eventually ordained in the African Native Baptist Church. In 1911 he founded his own Zionist church, the Nazarites. Shembe drew ideas and practices from the Bible and wedded them with Zulu customs—holy places in Zululand to go to for festivals, rituals with the people arrayed in traditional Zulu dress, hymns and melodies that echo traditional Zulu songs, and Shembe himself considered as a new Moses and Jesus for the Zulu nation in his role as prophet and healer. Still today Nazarites find meaning in the story of Isaiah Shembe, the servant sent by God to the Zulu nation.

The Revival of Traditional Religious Identity

The traditional religion of nonliterate peoples of today has faded largely because these peoples have suddenly been forced to become modernized, and these revivalistic movements have attempted to combine the two factors of tradition and westernization, creating something new in the process. Another sort of response, still small and uncertain but potentially powerful, is the attempt to recover the authentic traditional identity and live it in a viable way in the modern world. So there are groups today in many of the North American tribes who are taking a new pride in their tradition, seeking to restore the rituals and ceremonies and to live by the spiritual disciplines of their heritage. Some Plains Indians, for example, have renewed the ritual of sweat lodge purification and go on vision quests, and some tribes cooperate in staging the great Sun Dance each year.

Among the Australian Aborigines there is also an upsurge of interest in the unique Aborigine heritage and in their religious linkage to their traditional land, with some success in creating a Pan-Aborigine sense of identity. Polynesians and Melanesians are taking renewed interest and pride in their "Pacific Way." And modern Africans and Afro-Americans have for some time been experimenting with ways to retrieve their rich spiritual heritage as a resource for life in today's changing world. What will come of these new movements and revivals is difficult to predict, but the story of religion in our world today will be enlivened by the new adventures of these fellow humans who are renewing their traditional religious heritage.

NONLITERATE WORLDS OF MEANING

Religions of nonliterate peoples do not have systematized doctrines or written scriptures. But that does not mean that these peoples have ignored the theoretical side of religion. They reflect on the issues of life and express their ideas in a great variety of forms—in myths, epics, legends, songs, prayers, dirges, even dance, music, and art. All of these forms convey the perceptions and responses of these peoples to the deep questions of life, about knowing the truth, about ultimate reality, about the nature of this world and humans, about the path toward living real life. If we know how to hear and "read" them, these myths, sacred stories, art forms, and the rest will help us see inside their worlds of meaning.

The Sacred Reality in Sky and Earth

"What's it *all* about?" "What is the source of sacred power?" Since the beginnings of humankind people have wondered about questions like these, expressed in their own way. And the answers among the nonliterate peoples are extremely diverse and complex. These people speak from their own cultural experience, telling through their myths, rituals, and art how they envision that which is ultimately real. What is typical of non-literate peoples is that they understand the modalities of the sacred reality in association with the structures of our world—sky, earth, storm, animals, vegetation, water, humans, and more. They live in a sacred cosmos, and they expect to encounter sacred power through the functioning of this cosmos.

Some years back many scholars took an evolutionary view of religion, holding that very primitive peoples have only a vague conception of sacred power (dynamism) or spirits (animism). As their ideas advance they begin to believe in the great spirits and gods of nature (polytheism), and finally some peoples reach the point of seeing that one supreme God is in charge of all (monotheism). But field studies among nonliterate peoples of today have clearly shown the error of such a view. Hunters and gatherers living at the most archaic level of subsistence often have a well-defined view of a supreme creator god. On the other hand, highly developed agricultural peoples with great gods of nature may also have a sense of impersonal forces within animals and trees and even inanimate objects. Overall, it has become clear that nonliterate peoples have rather sophisticated and complex visions of sacred reality. Let us look first at the idea of supreme gods and then fill in the vast canvas of sacred reality with some of the other typical forms.

The Supreme God

For all the variety of religious systems, the ideas of supreme gods found in them have surprisingly similar features. Generally such gods stand uniquely alone, transcending the other sacred beings and supreme over them. Very often the supreme god is associated with the sky, so that many of the qualities of the sky become expressions of the unique power of the supreme god. It is not that one should think of the sky itself as god; rather, the god's power and qualities are manifested especially in the sky.

What are the special qualities of the sky? The sky is above all; it is without beginning and end; it is present everywhere; and it is seemingly beyond and unaffected by the rest of this changing world. And so the god of the sky, the "high god," is above all and supreme, the final authority. The supreme god is primordial and eternal, existing from the earliest beginning and thus the source of all power and creation. The supreme god is present everywhere (omnipresent) and therefore is all-seeing and all-knowing (omniscient). But also the supreme god is often remote and inaccessible (like the sky), and therefore this god appears to be passive and indifferent in the daily affairs of human existence. This remoteness is compensated for by divine helpers, the gods and goddesses of nature that are much more involved in human existence.

The nomadic hunters of Tierra del Fuego have a supreme god called Temaukel, although they do not pronounce this holy name and call him instead "Dweller in the Sky." He is eternal, all-knowing, all-powerful, and the primordial creator—but he withdrew beyond the stars after creating the original ancestors, who then accomplished the rest of creation. There are no priests who worship this supreme god and no images of him, although in times of great drought or sickness people may make special prayers to him, for he is the judge and ultimately the master of all destinies.

The Zulu of South Africa look to Inkosi Yezulu (Chief of the Sky) as the supreme source of power. He shows himself especially in storms and rain, and the Zulu have specialists known as "heaven-herders" who shepherd the thunderstorms sent by the god of the sky. Ordinarily people look to their ancestors for the various needs of daily life, but in times of dire need they will go to the hills to pray to the Chief of the Sky for help.

Although supreme gods of the sky are usually thought of as male, that is not always so. The Khasis people of Assam believe in a supreme goddess who is creator of all, who dwells in heaven and sees and hears all that happens on earth. And occasionally there are other gods and goddesses not necessarily associated with the sky whom we can recognize as supreme creator gods. The Koghi of Colombia, for example, have a supreme goddess who gives birth to all creation, ruling the cycles of life, death, and rebirth for all creatures. She is present everywhere; human existence takes place in her womb.

Gods and Goddesses of Nature

Since the supreme god is usually quite remote from daily affairs, nonliterate peoples look to a variety of closer sacred beings, generally associated with forces

Detail of the Aztec Sun God Tonatiuh, from the Codex Borbonicus.

of nature, for the ongoing needs of life. There are gods of the heavenly bodies and atmosphere, a great variety of gods of the earth, and gods and ancestors having to do with the social and cultural order. Each people has its own unique configuration of such sacred beings, all fitting together into a sophisticated vision of ultimate reality.

The great gods associated with the sun, moon, stars, and atmosphere are often considered to be manifestations or helpers of the supreme sky god. The characteristics of the natural phenomena are seen as qualities of the divine beings. For example, the sun-god epitomizes creativity, wisdom, omniscience, and constancy. Often considered a supreme god, the sun-god receives regular worship because of his crucial role in causing vegetation to grow. The god of the moon symbolizes mysterious power, death and rebirth, fertility and regeneration. Often considered female, she rules over the rhythms of life associated with water, vegetation, and fertility. Gods of storm and wind manifest strength and vitality, bursting open the clouds for rain and sending fertility to the fields, also sometimes causing destruction as well as bringing life-power.

First to list among gods of the earth is Terra Mater, the Earth Mother or Great Goddess known in some form in Upper Paleolithic times, long before the discovery of agriculture. The earth is the primary source and nurturer of all life, and it also receives all life back again, so all human cultures know the special qualities of sacred power through the earth. The Igbo of Africa, for example, worship Ala, the source of fertility for the land and the family, the abode of the ancestors, and the guardian of laws; barren women pray to her for children and men ask her help for increase in livestock. Closely related to the earth are the waters, experienced as the source of life but also as destructive. Sedna, the sea goddess of the Inuit (Eskimos), is the source of life from the sea and the mother of sea animals; but when humans violate taboos, she sends famine and destruction. Gods associated with mountains are also examples of powerful earth gods.

In promoting fertility and prosperity, the gods of the earth play important roles, for it is perhaps in securing and producing food that humans experience most deeply their close relationship with sacred powers. In hunting cultures it is expected that sacred beings will manifest themselves in animal form. To the Ainu of northern Japan, for example, the bear is really a "visitor" from the divine world. Many hunting cultures experience sacred power in the form of a master (or mistress) of animals, a god who protects the life of the herd, but who also provides boons to the humans by providing them the sacred life of the animals. The Northern Saulteaux of eastern Canada feel that the bear have a king or chief who watches over the bear and sends them into the people's traps; after killing a bear they dress it in fine clothing as an offering to the bear chief, who receives it back and regenerates its life again the next season.

Agricultural peoples learn the work of planting and harvesting from the gods and goddesses of vegetation, and it is the life-power of these sacred beings that humans receive by eating the plants. A Cherokee story tells of Corn Woman who produces food by rubbing her body and is killed because the people think this is witchcraft. But before she dies, she instructs them to drag her bleeding body over a field seven times, and corn sprouts wherever the blood of Corn Woman moistens the soil.

Cultural Heroes, Ancestors, and Spirits

Beyond the vast domain of gods of nature, sacred reality for nonliterate peoples includes other spiritual powers. There are culture heroes, conceived in human or animal form, who were active in the Time of the Beginning to make the world fit for human habitation, give gifts of food, fire, and speech, and establish order and creativity in human life. Corn Woman of the Cherokee story would be this type of culture hero, as would Hainuwele of the Ceram islanders. The Dogon of West Africa have twin culture heroes who are credited with bringing the first millet seeds from heaven to earth and with teaching the arts of blacksmithing and pottery. Typically a culture hero disappears after setting the world in order for humankind, returning to the sky, disappearing into the earth at a particular place, or being transformed into animals or plants.

For many nonliterate peoples, human ancestors possess power and thus participate in sacred reality. Even though they inhabit the world of spirits, they are still present in the human community as guardians of the family traditions, providers of good fortune, and punishers of those who break accepted mores. They, unlike the supreme god, are closely involved in the details of daily life, powerful agents for blessing or punishment. Especially among peoples of Africa, the "Living Dead" are crucially important for the continued welfare of the family and the community.

The notion of sacred reality broadens out to include still other kinds of spiritual forces. There are nameless spirits that inhabit certain localities. And even inanimate objects can possess spiritual power. For some peoples, for example, objects of "medicine" are particularly potent sacred powers that can be used for good—or, in the wrong hands, for evil.

In this context we can mention the concept of *mana*, a Polynesian word referring to the state in which certain places, people, and objects are especially strong and noble because they are filled with sacred power. For example, it may be believed that a particular noble family had great achievements and became the ruling family because of their intense mana. A related Polynesian concept is that of tabu. Places, people, and objects that are full of sacred power in a contagious, volatile way are felt to be tabu, and contact with them is governed by strict rules and prohibitions. A festival takes place under a state of tabu, for example, when profane activities could disrupt sacred power with disastrous effects on the community.

Like the Polynesians and their concepts of mana and tabu, most nonliterate poeples have the general notion that the world is full of power and that power can be confronted in special places, people, and things. But we should not consider notions like mana and tabu to be lower or more "primitive" forms of belief than the idea of a supreme god. Both mana and the supreme god—and all else in between—fit together in the complex world view that sees all reality grounded in sacred power and open to various manifestations of that power.

The Yoruba Vision of Sacred Reality

We must remember that beliefs about sacred reality arise out of the living experience of a particular people, answering such questions as "What's it *all* about?" So each religious system makes sense in its own integral, complete way. As an example of one such religious system, let us look briefly at the view of sacred reality found among the Yoruba of Nigeria in Africa.[9]

Quite a bit of diversity exists in religious ideas among the five to ten million Yoruba, but the major gods and spirits are generally known among all Yoruba. There are three main sources of power: the supreme god called Olorun, the great divinities called orisa, and the ancestors. In addition, there are multitudes of spirits associated with natural phenomena.

The main source of power is the high god, Olorun, the owner of the sky, the originating power in the universe. All other powers, including the orisa and the ancestors, owe their being to him. Olorun is everliving, omnipotent, and omniscient, the king and judge of all. Since he is unique and unlike anything else, the people make no images of him. Although Olorun is far away and has delegated many functions to the orisa and the ancestors, he is still approachable;

people can call on him at any time without needing priests or shrines.

Most religious action and worship is directed to the orisa, for these are nearer gods that have more direct effect on day-to-day life. There are a great many orisa—perhaps as many as 1,700—but several important ones are mentioned here as examples. Orisa-nla was one of the first gods created by Olorun, and he was delegated to fashion the earth and to bring the first sixteen humans created by Olorun to earth. Orisa-nla then sculpted additional humans, including deformed people who are specially sacred to him. He is known for giving children to barren women and for molding children in the womb.

Orunmila is a god closely associated with divination, for he was present at the creation of the human race and knows their destinies. Now he can be consulted about the future through rituals of divination. A rather complex god is Esu, who tests people to determine their character and even incites people to give offense to the other gods by failing to sacrifice to them. Since he contains both good and evil qualities in himself, he is a special mediator between divine and human power.

Yet another important god is Ogun, said to have been the first king of the holy city of Ife. He killed himself with his own sword and now is the god of metals, toolmaking, and war. He gives special guidance to hunters, blacksmiths, barbers, butchers, and (in modern times) mechanics and taxidrivers.

The Yoruba have two kinds of ancestors with power. Some are deified ancestors who in effect have become orisa and are worshiped widely. There is Sango, a tyrannical king with magical powers who after his death became associated with thunder and lightning, dealing out justice to the wicked. He is thus a guardian of social morality who punishes lying, stealing, and witchcraft. Oriso-oko was a leper who with his wife discovered agriculture, cured his leprosy, and taught others how to farm. So people worship Oriso-oko as the patron god of farmers. A popular goddess is Ayelala, a slave girl who was sacrificed in place of a man who had committed a wrong, as part of a covenant between two clans. Before she died she vowed that she would punish those disregarding the covenant, and so she became the goddess who punishes all immorality and wickedness. These

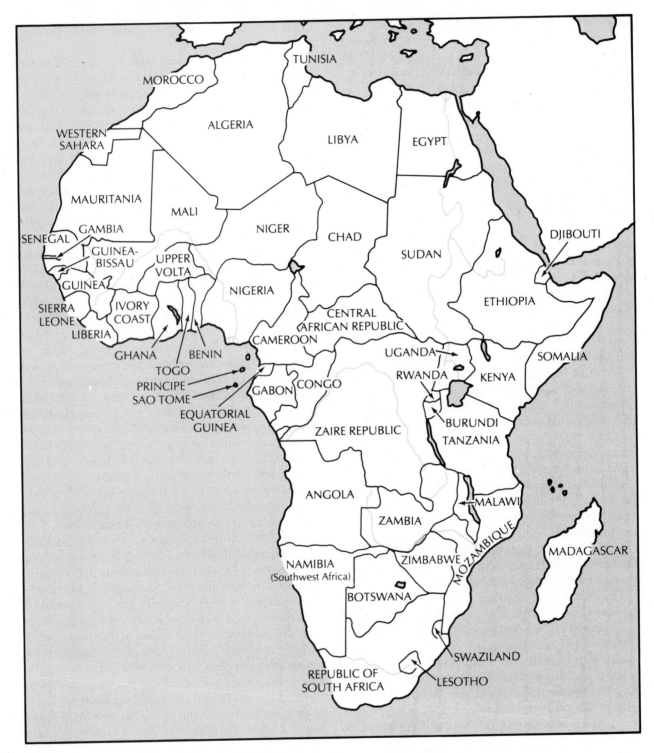

Africa.

gods were once humans, but now everyone knows their divine powers and worships them.

The sacred beings who are nearest are the family ancestors, and these play an important part in Yoruba family life. Not all people who die become ancestors, only those who lived good moral lives and died well, who now are in closer contact with Olorun and the orisa. These ancestors are the guardians of family life and traditions, seeing all that happens; they bless well-doing and they punish those who break the family rules. They are the nearest intermediaries to the world of sacred reality.

Filling out the vision of the Yoruba, there are many more spirits associated with natural phenomena like the earth, rivers, mountains, trees, and wind. The spirit of the earth, for example, receives special sacrifices at the time of planting and harvesting. And the Yoruba feel there is a sacred energy (*ase*) directed toward generation and regeneration, experienced in the presence of the gods and the ancestors. All these sacred powers fit together in the dynamic spiritual universe of the Yoruba.

The World and Human Existence

"What sense is there in life?" "Why are we here?" "Why is there so much evil and suffering in the world?"

These rather modern-sounding questions have actually been asked by humans for thousands of years, and nonliterate peoples of today are quite familiar with them. In fact, many of the myths are direct responses to questions like these, telling of the origin of the world and of humans, including stories that describe the nature and role of humans. These peoples accept life the way it is given, including the rhythms of growth and death. Yet they also know of failure and wrong-doing, and such conditions form the background for the paths of transformation.

Cosmogonic myths of nonliterate peoples provide a broad panorama of creative, imaginative perspectives on the origin of the world and of the basic conditions of life. Often the ultimate origin is a supreme god, but ideas of the world originating in chaos are also common. Even if there is a supreme creator god, typically other gods, goddesses, and culture heroes are involved in making the world the way it is today, fit for human

habitation, but also full of the tensions and conflicts that characterize existence.

The Navajo Emergence Myth

One type of origin myth is the emergence myth, telling how living beings inhabited various worlds deep down in mother earth, eventually emerging to this world. Like other peoples of southwestern North America, the Navajo trace their origins from far beneath the present earth surface. They tell of four or more previous worlds stacked one on top of the other, each populated with animal and insect people that were eventually to evolve into the animals and people of this world. Already in the lowest world, First Man and First Woman were born, together with Coyote and other Holy People. But these lower worlds were small and dark, and the peoples grew numerous and fell into conflict and committed evil acts, so that each world was ruined and they had to climb upward to emerge into the next world.

Finally the people emerged to the present world. First Man and First Woman began to whisper to each other, planning out how this world should be ordered for the people to live here. Then they performed ritual acts in a ceremonial hogan, a microcosmic building at the center of the world. First Man, using his medicine bundle, created the "inner forms" of all the natural phenomena. Pieces of jewel from the medicine bundle were put on the floor, forming a kind of painting of the life-forms that would be the sun, moon, mountains, plants, animals, and other physical features of this world. With prayers, creation songs, and smoke, these representations were then transported to their corresponding places on the earth's surface. The life-forms of dawn and evening twilight went on a tour of the new world, and they found everything in place, very beautiful. First Man and First Woman planned things carefully, but because Coyote and others interfered in their plans, things like unpredictable weather, sickness, and old age also became part of the order of things.

Finally Changing Woman was born, the Holy Person who grows old and then becomes young again, embodying the power of creation and sustenance. She gave birth to a set of twin sons, who prepared the earth for human habitation by slaying the monsters that had been produced by unnatural sex acts. To carry on the creative process, Changing Woman was given First Man's medicine bundle and created corn with it. She mixed cornmeal with balls of epidermal waste rubbed from her body and created the first Navajo people. After everything was created, the Holy People departed from the earth surface, some living in lower worlds, others in mountains and other objects. Now they cannot be seen or heard with our ordinary senses, but through rituals, festivals, and prayer acts, their presence is known. [10]

The myth of the emergence provides the center of the world and the center of life for the Navajo. Most of their ceremonials are based on the era of emergence and reenact these powerful events, tapping into the creative power of Changing Woman and the other Holy People so that life can continue to be sustained. The myth reflects their attitudes about the world and their place in it. The beautiful, orderly world is filled with sacred beings that form the inner life of everything. All life thus is interconnected, and humans are part of the same life-power, brother and sister to the animals, the plants, the mountains, and all the rest. There is conflict and evil, but this is a good world, full of the restorative power of the Holy People, if humans know how to live in harmony with them.

The Earth-Diver and the Twins: an Iroquois Creation Myth

Widespread among Native Americans is the earth-diver cosmogonic myth, and it is often associated with the myth of antagonistic divine beings who created the world the way it is today. Typically an animal dives into the primordial waters and brings up the first particles of earth, which then grow into the whole world. But then antagonism between divine beings who fashion the various aspects of the world results in the world as we know it, with its good and evil features. Whereas this type of cosmogonic myth is known in many parts of the world, it is especially popular among the Iroquois and other peoples of North America's eastern woodlands.

According to the Seneca version of the myth, in the beginning there was no earth, only a wide sea peopled by animals. But there was a world in the sky with a giant tree that radiated life. The sky-world people were told in a dream that the tree was to be pulled up so that a new world could be created below. A hole resulted when the tree was pulled up, and a woman sitting at the rim of the hole was impregnated by wind from below and fell through the hole, to be mother for the new world below. A flock of birds broke her fall with their wings and placed her on the back of a turtle. The animals dived to the bottom of the water to find earth, and one of them brought back a small portion of earth, which was placed on the back of the turtle and soon greatly expanded to its present size.

The woman gave birth to a daughter, who in turn was impregnated with twins while playing in the water. They fought in the womb, and at birth the one brother was born in the normal way but the other boisterously burst out his mother's side, killing her. When she was buried, corn and the other food plants grew from her body. When the twins were grown, the one called Good Spirit created human beings from dust and breathed life into them; he also made the good plants and animals of the world, lakes, and rivers with streams that run both ways to make travel easy. But his brother, Bad Spirit (who had burst his mother's side), created monstrous animals, pests, plant blight, disease, and death. He turned the currents in the streams so they would run only one way, and even once stole the sun. Finally the twins met in a duel in which Good Spirit won. Bad Spirit pleaded not to be killed and his wish was granted, but on the condition that he would henceforth help take care of humans. Another Iroquois version of the story tells that Bad Spirit was banished under the earth, but he still has helpers, half-human and half-beast, that he sends out to do his evil work. [11]

From this myth we learn of the origin of the earth from the waters, the coming of life-power from the world in the sky, and the animals' helpfulness in forming and supporting this world. And we see that the evil ways of Bad Spirit, just as the good ways of Good Spirit, shaped the world the way it is in its goodness and badness. Not only Good Spirit but also Bad Spirit continue to provide models for human behavior. The Seneca have a Society of Faces that uses masks to impersonate the many forms of Bad Spirit; they embrace those life-negating forces in order to cure disease, fight witch-craft, and remove disorder.

Creation in the Dreaming Time

The role of the ancestors and the culture heroes in creating human existence is paramount in many myths of origins, as we saw earlier in the myth of Hainuwele, from the people of West Ceram in Indonesia. The Aborigines of Australia have a particularly strong feeling of relation to their culture heroes of the Dreaming Time, when humans and the present conditions of life were created. The Wulamba people of northeastern Arnhem land tell stories about the wondrous exploits of the Djanggawul, a brother and his two sisters, all of them bursting with fertility and creativity, who wandered all over creating plants, animals, and the ancestors of the Aborigines.

From a sacred island out to sea came the Djanggawul, their bark canoe loaded with Dreamings (sacred drawings and emblems) kept in a sacred mat. The Djanggawul brother had an elongated penis, and the sisters had elongated clitorises; these were so long that they dragged on the ground as they walked, leaving grooves that can be seen still today. Later they shortened the penis and clitorises, and the parts they cut off were transformed into poles. As they wandered about, they left Dreamings everywhere. For example, the brother left his hairbelt as a sandhill, and they made waterholes by inserting a sacred pole in the ground. Throughout the country they left trees, springs, plants, and special drawings.

When they came to Arnhem land, the brother said to the older sister, "I want to copulate with you." "Why?" said the shy sister. "I want to put a few people in this place," he said, and so they had intercourse. After she was pregnant, the brother sat before his sister and placed his index finger in her vagina, and when he pulled it out a baby boy came out. She was careful to open her legs only a little, for if she spread them out, children would have flowed from her, for she kept many people stored in her uterus. She gave birth to many more male and female children. Then the Djanggawul brother and sisters left this place. The children they produced grew up and married and became the ancestors of the Aborigine people.[12]

The life-giving fertility of the culture heroes is celebrated in the rituals of the people, which reenact the major events during the wandering of the Djanggawul.

On the sacred ground, a special hut representing a uterus is erected, and in it are stored sacred poles representing those used by the Djanggawul. In ritual dancing these poles are removed from the hut and used to revitalize nature as in the myth. Women and children are covered with mats, representing the womb, and they emerge like the ancestors did from the wombs of the sisters. Human life comes from the sacred beings, their presence is felt all over the land, and by communing with them and repeating what they did, humans restore the world.

Myths of Origin in Africa

African peoples have a great variety of myths about the creation of the world and of humans. In one way or another, the theme of primordial separation between the creator god and the world of humans plays a part in many of them, explaining the origin of suffering, evil, and death, but also showing humankind's responsibility for restoring order and life for the earth.

The Dogon of Mali have a very sophisticated and complex myth of origins.[13] In the beginning, Amma, the supreme god, existed alone in the shape of an oval egg, which encompassed the whole universe by containing the four elements and the four directions. He designed the universe within himself and, after an initial unsuccessful attempt to create the world, transformed the world egg into a double placenta, each containing a pair of androgynous twins. But Ogo, one of the twins gestating in the egg, revolted and descended into the primordial darkness, taking a piece of the placenta, which became the earth. However, in copulating with the earth he committed incest (the placenta was his "mother"), and so the earth became defiled and sterile. Unable to restore complete order to his universe, Amma sacrificed the other twin, Nommo, scattering his body in the four directions to purify the universe, and the blood gave birth to various heavenly bodies, edible plants, and animals.

Now Amma restored Nommo to life and sent him and his other children, four pairs of heterosexual twins who are the ancestors of the human race, down to earth. They descended in a great ark lowered from the heavens by means of a copper chain; the ark contained everything needed to restore the earth and maintain

Dogon of Mali in ceremonial dress.

human life, including all species of animals and plants and all elements of human culture. The first rains came, the sun rose for the first time, and the ancestors settled on the spot where they had landed. The people began to cultivate the land, and they were taught speech, weaving, blacksmithing, dance, and music. The rebellious twin, Ogo, was transformed into Pale Fox who wanders the earth, by his tracks revealing mysteries that can be interpreted by diviners.

We know from the myth that this whole cosmos and everything in it emanates from the creator in the form of the cosmic egg. But the earth was created imperfect

and fallen, only partially restored by the supreme god's sacrifice of one of his twin sons. The world still contains the elements of darkness and sterility resulting from the revolt and defilement of the other son of the supreme god. Humans, descended from Nommo who restored the world, are caught up in this tension, having the responsibility to promote order and creativity through their life and rituals in which they repeat the creative signs and words of the creator god.

A very common theme in African myths associates imperfection and evil in the world with a separation between earth and sky, the realm of the supreme god. Originally earth and sky were very close together, and life was paradisiacal, with sufficient food and no sickness, sexuality, or death. But some wrongdoing on the part of the people, or some chance misfortune through no one's fault, caused the supreme god to move far away and resulted in the origin of sickness, deprivation, and death in this world. Since that time human life has been full of conflict, struggle, and failure.

The Ashanti, for example, say that the supreme god originally lived in the sky close to earth. The mother of humans constantly went on knocking against him with her pestle while pounding out the traditional grain food, so the god moved high in the sky to get away from the constant knocking. The Mende tell how the first people used to go to the supreme god to ask for things so often that in irritation he finally moved away. The Yao tell that when the people first learned to make fire, they set everything alight, causing the supreme god to withdraw to heaven. Some peoples tell of rules that were broken, such as being forbidden to look at the supreme god, or to eat animals, or to disguise the fact of death, and breaking these rules resulted in the god moving far away.[14] Whatever the reason, the separation brought tragic consequences for humankind: conflict, famine, sickness, death, and all the other stark realities of human existence.

Human Existence in the World

With this large variety of cosmogonic myths, it is difficult to sum up the nonliterate peoples' view of the nature of human existence, but a very general pattern is clear. The springs of life come from the sacred powers of the cosmos, the supreme god, the culture heroes, the ancestors. Human life is one with the animals, the plants, and the rest of the world. And the highest good is to live in harmony with all these sacred forces, fulfilling the responsibility of maintaining order and bringing renewal to the earth by repeating the myths and rituals of the beginnings.

Humans are neither good nor evil by nature, but are from the same sacred reality as the whole cosmos. Evil and failure are built into our world, intertwined in the creative events of the Time of the Beginnings. On the human level, evil shows itself in many forms, especially in sickness—physical, mental, spiritual, and social sickness. What causes this? Magic, sorcery, evil spirits, and like causes play into the picture. But finally it is a human question, and a human answer is needed. Humans need to take responsibility for living as they ought and fulfilling their role as humans.

The Path of Healing and Transformation

"How can I start living *real* life?" "Where are healing and wholeness to be found?" These are questions about the solution to life's failures and problems, as felt by all, including the nonliterate, tribal peoples. The answers are embodied in the way of life learned from the myths and traditions. The path of transformation is a practical pursuit involving individual and community, worship, disciplines, and all the rest. Here we are interested in the theoretical basis of the path: How can the various rituals and practices *transform* exhausted life into real life, sickness into wholeness?

Restoring the Exhausted Sacred Power

Nonliterate peoples do not seem to be primarily preoccupied with the afterlife, the destiny of the soul or life-force after death. Of course, death and what happens after are concerns, like other concerns, and they do have ideas about that. But they do not generally share the view of some world religions that only in a different state of life—heaven or paradise or nirvana—will there come the full authentic existence. Rather, the primary concern is with fullness and wholeness in human existence as it is given from the sacred powers

and from the ancestors. And that means a life in harmony with these forces—a life in which the buffalo are plentiful and intimate with humans, the corn and yams come forth in abundance from mother earth, and the family lives in health and peace under the blessing of the ancestors.

As we have seen, visions of the human problem are manifold and complex. An underlying common theme among many of the nonliterate peoples is the exhaustion of sacred power. In this world of good and evil, perfection and imperfection, the power that originated everything eventually gets used up. In the process arise sickness, disintegration, dry seasons, famines, death, and so forth. So the path of transformation is a way of life designed continually to retrieve and restore the sacred source of life. It is a path of healing and renewal. And that is possible through reestablishing contact and communion with the sacred beings, the ancestors, and the other sources of power. The primary way to do that is by repeating the myths, ceremonies, songs, and disciplines that have been given from the Time of the Beginnings. Through them it is possible to share again in the transforming events, and real life is restored.

The path is generally very concrete. It focuses on specific needs and concerns—someone is sick and needs healing; it is corn-planting time and good growth is needed; a wife is barren and children are needed. But the healing and renewal that come are of larger benefit than the immediate concern. Through the healing ritual or the corn-planting festival or the fertility producing ceremony, the people of the community learn anew the traditions, they reestablish communion with the sacred powers, the bonds of the community are renewed, and personal life is more complete.

Some people in these societies pursue the path with great vigor and discipline and experience deep transformation in their lives. For example, there are religious specialists, like diviners or shamans, who may undergo long training and pass through an elaborate initiation in which they experience a spiritual rebirth. But even ordinary individuals may feel the need for deeper communion with the sacred powers and pursue special practices, as in the vision quest among Native Americans.

The Navajo Blessingway Transformation Ceremonies

As an example of community practices on the path of transformation, we can look at the Navajo prayer ceremonials, especially the set that is called Blessingway. These Blessingway ceremonials were, according to Navajo tradition, first used at the beginning of time, when First Man built a hogan at the place of emergence and created the life-forms of this new world. Now Blessingway is used in ceremonial acts for many specific needs, such as blessing a new house, a girl's puberty rite, rain ceremonies, seed blessings, weddings, rituals for expectant mothers, and the like.[15] The overall effect of the Blessingway ceremonials is to make the primordial creative actions meaningful to specific life situations of today, so that the life of the community can be transformed and continue according to the sacred pattern.

At the emergence place, First Man and First Woman constructed a ceremonial hogan, and so Blessingway begins with purifying and blessing the hogan. This hogan becomes sacred space, a microcosm of the world and the center of the world where the Holy People who created the earth may again communicate with earth people and renew their acts of creation. A litany prayer follows by a singer with responses by the person for whom the ceremony is being held, who carries a mountain soil bundle representing the medicine bundle of Changing Woman who first created humans. The bundle is pressed to various parts of the body, identifying the person with the creative powers of the bundle.

Next, the person sleeps in the hogan, performing a ritual bath the next day, reenacting the ritual bath performed by Changing Woman. The body is dried by ritual application of corn meal. Then the whole night is spent singing Blessingway songs in a "no-sleep" ceremony. The night concludes with dawn songs and the person leaves the hogan and moves toward the east, "breathing in the dawn"—representing the final acts of creation in which the inner life-forms were transformed into the actual forms. The person thus departs from the sacred time of creation and returns to ordinary Navajo life—but now things are renewed and transformed.

A medicine man among the Navajo.

When Changing Woman taught these Blessingway songs to the people, she said,

> These will direct you as you live on in the future, and they will direct your mode of living. And should there be any mishap in things on which life depends, which enable you to live, all will be put in proper shape again by means of them, the body will be restored again by means of them.[16]

So, in reciting these prayers the original acts of creation are repeated, the world is recreated, and the person praying is made an integral part of that world by close association with the Holy People on whom all life depends. The creation put everything in its proper order, and that way is reinstated and maintained through the ritual. The source of life-power is directed to very specific needs, but the benefit is more general—the whole community participates in the renewal.

The Native American Vision Quest

As an example of individuals pursuing a path of discipline and heightened spiritual awareness, widely known among Native Americans is the vision quest. It was customary in some tribes that young boys—and sometimes girls also—as part of their puberty initiation began at a very young age to practice fasting and spending time in isolation pursuing the experience of a vision, receiving the power of a spiritual being. But the vision quest has been used more broadly also, in connection with special preparations at times of mourning, warfare, making important vows, meeting special needs, and acquiring a guardian spirit. Among some peoples it is felt that the visions come more or less spontaneously, without formal quests, but in most communities there is a need for special searching for spiritual vision and power.

It could be said that the vision quest stands at the core of the Native American religious path, for the basic idea is attaining spiritual powers essential to the successful fulfillment of human life. Through the vision quest the individual finds identity, direction, guidance, protection, and destiny joined to the traditional way of life. People may go on vision quests a number of times, and the meaning of the experience is not always understood completely at first. After the vision experience they examine it again and again, perhaps with the help of experienced holy men, reflect on it, consult it in different life situations, and live by its guidance.

Among the Plains Indians, for example, the Sioux, the vision quest attained important form and status, and today some Sioux people still try to restore their heritage and identity by following this path. Typically the vision quest begins by visiting an elder holy man and offering a sacred pipe, declaring one's intention to perform the "lamenting for a vision" for a number of days. Under the holy man's guidance, careful preparations are made. First comes an extensive purification in the sweat lodge, when the pipe is prepared to be used in the vision quest. The holy man offers many prayers to the spiritual powers to assist in the quest, such as this prayer directed to the supreme god: "O Wakan-Tanka, my Father and Grandfather, You are first, and always have been! Behold this young man here who has a troubled mind. He wishes to travel upon the sacred path; he will offer this pipe to You. Be merciful to him and help him!"[17]

After the purification ritual, the vision seeker is taken to a place on a mountain or hill where a sacred space is created by erecting four poles at the west, north, east, and south points. A bed of sage is placed in the center, and the sacred area may be enclosed with a tobacco rosary, a line with tiny tobacco pouches tied onto it. The seeker removes his clothes and remains in the sacred area for several days, offering his pipe to the spiritual powers, praying and communing with them, attentive to communication from them in the form of animals, storms, wind, and visions. The person performs many rounds of prayer, offering the pipe toward the powers of the west, the north, the east, the south, the sky, and the earth again and again. A modern Sioux, Arthur Amiotte, reports a small portion of his vision prayers this way:

> Facing the east, I asked these powers to hear me, and that the light which is the day that comes from the east should enter me and light my mind to its fullest power. I asked for the light of wisdom to see and understand what I must do and become so that my people may live. I asked for enlightenment for all the people, that they may discover the wisdom and peace of our religion as a light to guide them and bring day where there is so much

darkness. I asked for the new life of spring to come to the people so that they may meet life with hope, as the earth greets spring in regeneration. . . .

Pointing my pipe to the sky, I asked that the mystery of creation, reaching into infinity, bring together all of life in peace. I asked for wisdom to know and understand my part and place on this earth with other people. I asked to know humility and to become a better man so that my people may live better through my efforts and my work as a teacher. I asked for mercy and to be worthy to know the Spirit as it makes itself known to man.[18]

Fasting and praying for several days, the seeker hears communication from the various animals and objects and perhaps experiences deeply moving visions. At the end of the quest he returns to the sweat lodge and relates the experiences to the holy man, who interprets them so that the person can understand their meaning and their import for his life. Among the Sioux it is customary for the person to seek further clarification and guidance by going on a number of additional vision quests.

The vision quest exemplifies the path of transformation on the individual level. Through it a person restores communication with the sacred beings, receives spiritual powers, renews his or her identity with the tradition and the community, and attains understanding and guidance on life's path.

The Shaman's Path of Transformation

Nonliterate societies have a great variety of religious specialists, set apart because they are following the path in a deeper or more focused way than are the ordinary people. Through training, disciplines, rituals, and visionary experiences their personal existence has been transformed, and so they not only show special power in their lives but are able to use that power for the benefit of the rest of the community. Let us look briefly at the way a person's life is transformed by following the shaman's path.

The word *shaman* comes from Siberia and refers to the religious specialist well known throughout Asia who can go into ecstatic trances to communicate with spiritual powers for healing and helping others. Scholars have used the word *shaman* to refer more broadly to all similar types of religious specialists found in the different cultures of the world, including some of those more commonly known as medicine men and healers. Mircea Eliade[19] has shown that the most basic definition of a shaman is one who has mastered techniques of ecstasy. That is, a shaman is able, through rituals, songs, dances, meditation, drugs, or other techniques, to enter a state of ecstasy ("standing outside" oneself), break beyond normal human limitations, and communicate with sacred powers in the other realms. The shaman attains knowledge and power through this and is able to use that knowledge and power to heal sicknesses, cause beneficial things to happen, lead the souls of the dead, provide guidance for hunting or planting, and much more.

How does a person get on the shaman's path? Typically persons become shamans either through hereditary transmission of the role or through a special sense of calling. Often shamans-to-be experience deep physical or mental crises that set them off from the other "normal" people. They have an overpowering sense of being called or possessed by sacred powers, a call that they cannot refuse, often experienced in dreams or visions. A Siberian shaman, for example, relates how he was made ill by the family spirits for many years and then, in a dream, was taken to the ancestral spirit at the center of the cosmic tree:

In my dreams I had been taken to the ancestor and cut into pieces on a black table. They chopped me up and then threw me into the kettle and I was boiled. . . . While the pieces of my body were boiled, they found a bone around the ribs, which had a hole in the middle. This was the excess bone. This brought about my becoming a shaman. Because, only those men can become shamans in whose body such a bone can be found. One looks across the hole of this bone and begins to see all, to know all and, that is when one becomes a shaman.[20]

The person is chosen by the ancestors to be a shaman, and he or she experiences death and dismemberment, followed by a restoration in which special shamanic powers are received.

After the shaman has experienced a call of some

kind, often there is a period of training in which master shamans provide instruction in the shamanic techniques and initiate the neophyte. During this period the new shaman might withdraw to solitude to learn the techniques and the traditions, the structure of the cosmos, the paths leading to the other worlds, ways of communicating with the gods, guardian spirits, demons of disease, and the dead, and so on.

The final stage in becoming a shaman would be public emergence and demonstration of the shamanic path. Among the Buriats in Siberia, for example, after many years of apprenticeship there will be a public demonstration and consecration of the candidate. A strong birch tree is set up in the tent projecting through the smoke hole, and the candidate climbs to the top and shouts to summon the aid of the gods. Then the master shaman, the apprentice, and all the other shamans go to a sacred place where a goat is sacrificed and its blood is placed on the head, eyes, and ears of the candidate. The master shaman climbs a birch tree and cuts nine notches in the top of the trunk. Then the candidate and the other shamans all climb the birch and fall into ecstasy. Climbing the tree is a symbolic ascent into heaven; the new shaman is now recognized as one who is transformed and has the ability to communicate with the sacred beings and receive special power from them.[21]

The shamanic path typically lasts for one's whole lifetime. It is understood to be a special calling, in which a person sacrifices him- or herself for the greater spiritual realities. A Sioux holy man put it this way:

> You must know that a medicine man among our people is in possession of a special office. He is a servant of the people and of the gods. He enters upon a way that is sometimes not of his choosing, sometimes because he chose. . . . I did not ask for my office. My work was made for me and given to me by the other world, by the Thunder Beings. I am compelled to live this way that is not of my own choosing, because they chose me. I am a poor man; see how I dress and the house I live in. My whole life is to do the bidding of the Thunder Beings and of my people and to pay heed to what the Grandfathers tell me.[22]

WORSHIP AND THE GOOD LIFE

Sacred Time, Ritual, and Art

"Where can I find new power for life?" "How can I live more in touch with what is *real*?" Peoples of nonliterate cultures, like all peoples, find the answers to concerns like these in experiences of sacred time, through worship, ritual, festivals, and sacred art.

As we have seen, nonliterate peoples are open to sacred power and depend on it for meaningful and full human existence. One of the basic realities about power is that it runs down and becomes exhausted and therefore must continually be renewed. That renewal takes place in sacred time, when the ordinary run of time toward exhaustion and death is reversed and the sacred powers that created existence are made present once more in telling the myths and enacting the rituals. Since power runs down, there is need to establish a rhythm of periodic festivals and rituals, following the seasons and the life cycle, for regular and continual renewal of life.

So a major characteristic of sacred time, as nonliterate peoples experience it, is that it is *reversible*.[23] Ordinary profane time is not reversible; once something is done, it cannot be done over again. For many people in the modern Western world, this relentless irreversibility of time is compensated for by a heavy stress on progress toward the future. We are working toward a future age that will be different from, and better than, the past. To nonliterate peoples, this kind of abstract future is of little interest, for the source of being is the Time of the Beginnings, that is, sacred time, which does not slip relentlessly away but can be made present again in celebrating festivals and rituals. In that sense, sacred time is cyclical, not linear. In rituals and festivals, the people can go back and become contemporary with the sacred beings of the Time of the Beginnings.

Performance of the Myth in Ritual

Since the myths tell about the origins of the vital aspects of existence, in repeating them and using them in ritual the people are reactualizing the mythic events and thus recreating and renewing those vital aspects of existence. Telling the myths and stories "performs" them. When it is time for the rice to sprout, for example, someone who knows the myths of the origin of rice may spend the night on the rice field, reciting the myths so that the rice will come up as it appeared for the first time. In the deserts of southern Arizona, the Papago Indians, who depended for their survival on the growing of corn and squash during the short rainy season, would meet regularly at the council house during the summer to "sing up the corn." An old man who knew the myths of corn and squash would recite the story and the people would sing the songs. One version of the story tells how Corn was a man who seduced a Papago woman, and she lived with him a long time. When she returned to her husband she sang the songs Corn had taught her, passing on this important knowledge to the rest of the people. The song for when corn first appears goes like this:

Songs begin.
At the west they begin.
Thereby the corn comes up.
Upward its heart [the ear] is stretching.
At the west they begin. . . .
Songs are ending.
At the east they are ending.
Thereby squash come up.
In a row its hearts [fruits] are standing
At the east they are ending.

The Papago continue throughout the growing season to "sing up the corn" with the songs Corn taught the woman, as, for example, when the corn is one foot high:

At the west, the red corn.
See me!
I come forth and grow tall.
Yonder on the moist ground
I come forth.
At the east the white corn.
See me! I come forth and grow tall.
Yonder on the moist ground
I come forth.[24]

The performative power of the sacred words sung by the people renews both the crops and the life of the people.

New Year's Festival: The Ngaju of Borneo

Obviously there are countless ceremonies, rituals, and festivals among the nonliterate peoples of the world, and we must be careful not to overgeneralize their common features and patterns. But certainly a prototype of renewal ceremonies is the new year's festival that can be identified in many cultures—the time of the renewing of the crucial life-powers for the whole year. As an agricultural people of south Borneo (Indonesia), the Ngaju Dayak[25] spend most the year cultivating rice as their main sustenance, clearing places in the forests for their rice fields, planting the rice, and tending it until it is harvested. When the harvest is complete, they celebrate the new year's festival for an extended period.

This sacred time is called the "time between the years," and thus it is a period outside ordinary time; the year has run its course and been exhausted, and now there must be a return to sacred time to regenerate life-power. In the center of the village a staff and banner are erected representing male and female powers, together making up the tree of life, which in the myths is the source of all life in the cosmos. The ordinary social divisions of the people are dissolved, social or moral rules are thrown out, and mass sexual intercourse occurs outside the normal relationships. The whole society returns to chaos and disorder. Toward the conclusion of the festival there is a great ritual battle in which the tree of life is destroyed. And a human slave is sacrificed, with all the people participating in the ritual dance around the victim, stabbing him with spears and daggers, being smeared with his blood, and stamping dirt on the grave outside the village limits. In recent years small animals have been used in place of slaves for this sacrificial ritual.

What does all this mean with its elements of disorder and chaos, breaking down of social structures, mass sexuality, and human sacrifice? We should note first that this festival is a liminal period, betwixt and between ordinary times. Separation from ordinary life is marked by the destruction of normal social forms; and at the conclusion of the festival a renewed social order is put into place again. But in this time and space inbetween, time is reversed and the people move back into the precreation chaos of mythical times. For in the beginning, according to the Ngaju myth of origins, Mahatala, the god of the upperworld, and Jata, the goddess of the underworld, made the earth, rivers, and first humans. The headdress of Mahatala became the tree of life, and from its leaves and fruit were made a rice tree, the source of rice. But the goddess's female hornbill and the god's male hornbill, feeding on the tree of life, got into a terrible fight and destroyed the tree of life and finally themselves. From the tree of life came forth various aspects of the world, like rivers and lakes. A maiden was born from the tree, and from the slain female hornbill came a youth; eventually they married and from them descended the humans of our world.

So the festival reactualizes the mythic events of the creation of the world, the origin of all plant and human life within the tree of life, the destruction of the tree so that creation can be renewed, and the marriage of the ancestors. The people of the village become contemporary with those events, and in repeating them make their power effective again in establishing a new year, renewed social order, new fields, and new crops.

Rituals of Food Renewal: Hunters and Planters

Many of the important festivals and rituals of non-literate peoples have to do with the seasonal or annual renewal of the food supply, as in the Ngaju example just cited, in the process, of course, renewing the whole

Hupa Indian White Deerskin dancers (photograph from the late nineteenth century). Each dancer carries a pole around which a whole deerskin is draped.

life of the society. Two examples make this clear, one from a hunting people and the other from a planting people.

Spread across the arctic and subarctic regions of Asia and America are bear-hunting societies, and, like other hunters, they have rituals by which they maintain a sacred relationship with the animals they hunt. By performing these rituals they take responsibility for the maintenance and renewal of animal as well as human life. For example, the Ainu of Hokkaido and the other islands north of Japan have rich mythologies and rituals relating to the sacred life they share with the animals of their mountainous world, especially the bear.[26] They consider bears, like other animals, to be "visitors" from the world of the kamui (sacred beings) who have taken animal bodies to visit the Ainu world. By hunting them and using their bodies as food, the Ainu accept the gifts they have brought and return them to the kamui world.

The most important festival for an Ainu community is the Bear Festival, called Iyomante (sending-off). To hold a Bear Festival, an Ainu family or community captures a bear cub alive and rears it with care and affection; it is fed fish, millet, and even human milk, with groups of women giving their breasts to the cub in turns. When the cub is grown, the people of the village are invited for the Bear Ceremony. They arrive in ceremonial dress, offering sacred wine, dances, and prayers to "entertain" the divine visitor, singing, "To-day we worship you as a god, therefore eat what we offer, and enjoy yourself." The people fast and abstain from sexual relations that night, in preparation for the main ceremony on the second day. After prayers, sing-ing, and dancing, the bear is roped and led on a farewell walk, with the people making it run around to show its lusty and ferocious happiness. After it is strang-led, the neck is cut and its blood drunk. Then it is skinned, and the carcass is carried into the hut through the special "kamui window" and set in the place of honor on a mat. Now the bear is the chief guest at the feast, and more entertainment and prayers are offered, such as this one recorded by John Batchelor:

> My beloved cub, pray listen to me. I have cared for thee for a long time and now present thee with wands and dumplings. . . . Ride thou upon these wands and carry with thee the good things presented to thee. Go to thy father and mother. Be happy. Cause them to rejoice. Upon arrival, call together multitudes of divine guests and make a great feast. Come again unto us that we may once more rear thee and enjoy another festival with thee.[27]

All parts of the bear's carcass are used for food and other items, and the skull is taken out and placed on a pole in the center of the sacred wands outside the house. After farewell prayers, the skull of the "departing kamui" is turned toward the east and the "arrow of sending away" is shot toward the eastern sky, after which the skull is quickly turned away from the east. The festival con-tinues until all the flesh of the bear is eaten, and the skull of the bear is venerated as a guardian kamui.

So the Ainu celebrate their common life with the bear and renew that life-power—and in the process they tell the traditional myths, sing the songs, perform the dances, and in doing so bring about a renewal of the whole community.

Native American peoples of the North American eastern woodlands, such as the Creek, celebrate their most important annual festival, the busk (fasting), at the time of the first ripening of the corn in July or August, considering this the beginning of the year. No one is to eat the newly ripened green corn before this festival. The festival, lasting four days or so, takes place at a specially sanctified ceremonial ground outside the village. In prep-aration, the people clean their houses, repair their friendships, pardon sentenced criminals, and extinguish all their fires. Four logs are placed in the center of the ceremonial ground, pointing to the cardinal directions, and a new fire is lit by using a fire drill.

During the first three days of the festival, the men spend much time at the ceremonial grounds, fasting and purging themselves by drinking a purgative black drink. The whole community avoids certain foods, such as eating new corn or salt, and sexual relations are prohibited. Offerings of green corn and other items are made to the new fire, medicine specialists prepare new infusions of medicine on the fire, and women also come to receive the new fire for use in their homes. During these days many ritual events take place. For example, special dance rituals are performed, the men go to the river to perform a purification ritual, and young men and boys have their legs scraped so that the blood flows. On the last day the fast is broken with the eating of the new corn, and there are many joyous dances.[28]

So the ripening of the corn is a special time when the sacred forces are present in a powerful way. The festival is referred to as "peace time"—peace within the community and peace with the sacred powers. In this period of crucial cosmic process, it is important for people to fast and purify themselves of used-up life-force, so that they can participate in the renewal of life—the renewal of food, medicine, family, and social relations.

Rituals of the Passages of Life

Like the rhythms of nature, the rhythms of human life present special times for the individual and the community to renew power. In the critical passages of life—especially birth, puberty, marriage, and death—it is important to ritualize the separation from the previous state, the encounter with sacred power in the transitional liminal period, and the reincorporation into the community at the next level of human life. These rites of passage are exceedingly diverse and rich in symbolism among the nonliterate peoples of the world, and much study has been devoted to them. Let us look briefly at the rites of initiation into adulthood.

The puberty ceremony for a girl who has experienced her first menstruation is the most elaborate ritual of the Apaches of North America.[29] Preparations for the four-day ceremony begin well in advance, planning and rehearsing the ceremony and preparing the ritual costumes and huge amounts of food for the hundreds of people who will come. The girl's main ritual implement is a wooden staff or cane, painted yellow and decorated, which she will keep all her life; and a small pendant of abalone shell is tied to her hair to identify her with Changing Woman, the creatress. During the four days of the ceremony, the power of Changing Woman will reside in her.

The first morning as the sun begins to rise, she walks in ceremonial dress to the dancing ground, carrying the sacred cane, and, facing the rising sun, dances to songs that tell the story of Changing Woman. She prays, "Long life, no trouble, Changing Woman," as she

receives the powers of Changing Woman and is transformed from a girl into an Apache woman. A second set of songs recalls how Changing Woman was impregnated by the sun to give birth to Slayer of Monsters, the foremost Western Apache culture hero. So the initiate kneels and faces the sun, raising her hands and swaying from side to side, to ritualize receiving the fertilizing rays of the sun as Changing Woman did. In another ritual, her sponsor massages the girl as she lies on a buckskin, giving her the shape of a woman. A medicine man explains, "Changing Woman's power is in the girl and makes her soft, like a lump of wet clay. Like clay, she can be put into different shapes. [Her sponsor] puts her in the right shape and Changing Woman's power in the girl makes her grow up that way, in that same shape." Then the girl runs to the east, encircles her cane, and runs back again, four times, symbolizing health and long life through the stages of life.

The ceremonies continue for three more days, as the ways of womanhood are revealed to her and she takes on the power and creativity of Changing Woman, able to cure the sick and bring rain. Some ceremonies occur to disseminate this special power for the benefit of the whole Apache community. For example, basketfuls of candy are poured over her head, and because of contact with her these candies can bring healing, a good crop, and other benefits to the people who receive them. The girl has now become a woman, she is ready for marriage and a fruitful life—and the whole community has been renewed through the powerful presence of Changing Woman in myth and ritual.

Initiation rituals for boys are very widespread and tend more often to take place for groups of boys rather than individually. Among the Ndembu of Zambia in central Africa,[30] when a group of boys from a cluster of villages is approaching puberty, the leaders of the villages decide to hold a rite of circumcision. Without being circumcised, a man is considered polluting and cannot marry and have normal social relations with the people. A senior circumciser is chosen, and other recognized circumcisers are invited. A camp is set up where the parents of the boys will live during the ceremonies, and a fire is lit that will burn for the length of the rituals and on which the mothers will prepare all food for the novices during their seclusion. After dark, drums start to beat, and a wild dance follows in which the boys have to be carried so that they do not touch the earth. Suddenly the circumcisers enter in the procession with their apparatus and lead the wild dancing, which continues on and off throughout most of the night, the sleepy boys being roused to take part. Next morning the boys are fed a big meal, each mother feeding her son by hand as though he were an infant. Suddenly the drums begin to beat frantically, and the fathers and guardians of the boys grab them, strip off their clothes, and dash off into the woods down a newly cut path to the site of the circumcision, known as "the place of dying." The mothers are chased back to the camp, wailing as at the announcement of a death. The boys are carried off to the circumcisers for the brief operation, then herbal medicine is applied so that healing occurs. The men feed the boys and give them beer, and then the men go back to the camp and dance in a circle with the women.

There follows a period of several months in which the boys live secluded in a hastily erected lodge. During this whole period, until the wounds are healed, their parents must refrain from sexual intercourse or eating salt. The boys are forbidden to speak while eating and have to refrain from certain foods. During this period of seclusion in the lodge, they are taught the various things they need to know as adults in the society. When their circumcision wounds are healed, masked dancers come to beat the boys with sticks, and they are washed in a stream and sent into the bush to trap animals. The masked dancers go to the camp and dance for the women, also bringing salt for them to use. That night the parents of the boys, and also the circumcisers and their wives, are expected to have sexual intercourse. Not long afterward the boys are painted and dressed up and brought back to the parents' camp, so decorated that their mothers are not supposed to recognize them as the same children as before. There follows a joyful night dance with a huge crowd participating, climaxing in the burning of the seclusion lodge. The next morning closing rituals put an end to the rite of circumcision, and the boys return to their villages to continue to grow up and begin to participate in adult life.

Art Among Nonliterate Peoples

Most museums have sections devoted to "primitive art," and the strange statues, masks, and other artifacts seem to grow out of a vision from another world. Modern Western people puzzle over what kind of reflection of reality is expressed in these art objects, what symbolic statements these are about the meaning of life.

But to nonliterate peoples, art is not a matter of art objects. Rather, art is a living process, very much a part of life, vitally connected with the myths, rituals, and festivals of the people. Much of the art is presentational, that is, it presents sacred reality in living, creative events. Art is performed, and the objects that remain may only be the by-products and leftovers of these creative events. Nonliterate peoples tend not to set their religious beliefs and feelings into systematized doctrines or even in enduring art objects; rather they sing out and paint out and dance out their religious vision.

In almost all nonliterate cultures, sound is paramount, for through spoken or sung words the myths are presented, prayers are offered, incantations chanted. Through the vibrations of human words—and the words of birds, thunder beings, bullroarers, and drums—the sacred powers are present to create life again. The art of words is especially creative when wedded with music and dance, for it is not the informational content of the words but the *performative* quality that is important—spoken, sung, and danced, the words bring about the renewal of life according to the sacred pattern.

Widespread throughout nonliterate cultures is the carving of images, statues, symbols, and masks that present the sacred beings or powers. The process of making these sacred objects often is considered a religious process, with appropriate rituals of purification and dedication. These images, masks, and so forth are important insofar as they are alive with the power they present. Outside of that living ritual context, these objects are of little use or interest to the people. Among the Yoruba, the masked dancers (*egungun*) that perform at festivals and rituals wear special masks that have been handed down for generations in their families. These masks possess great power, and special rites must

An elaborate mask from the Yoruba of Nigeria.

for the purpose of curing illnesses. They depict Holy Persons according to a pattern known only in the memory of the painter, and these Holy Persons become present when corn pollen is sprinkled on the painting and on the sick person. In the ritual, the sick person then sits in the middle of the painting, and by taking sands from the figures on the painting and pressing them onto the body of the person, he or she is identified with the Holy Persons and their power serves to set the world in order again. The singer then completes the destruction of the painting and the sands are returned to nature. Here religion and art are one and the same; the paintings are created to make the Holy People present, and apart from that process they have no separate function. The destruction of the picture shows that these realities have become one with the sick person, to bring renewed life and health.

be performed by the men who wear them—for in wearing them the dancers actually become the embodiment of the family ancestors, present among the people in living form.

Other visual creations, such as drawing and painting, also serve to present the sacred for particular rituals and events. Aborigines of Kimberley in western Australia believe in ancestors of the beginning time called Wandjina, whose power is present in paintings on walls of caves. These spectacular paintings are larger than human size, with figures painted in red ochre and black charcoal against a whitened background. Rituals performed in connection with these paintings make these beings present to send life-spirits for humans and bring fertilizing rain for the land.

The Wandjina paintings are retouched and maintained over generations, but often drawings and paintings are not considered to have a long duration; a painting may, for example, be painted over for each new ceremonial use. Sandpainting is a well-known art among the Navajo of North America, and art appreciators bemoan the fact that each sandpainting must be destroyed on the day it was made. Made on the floor of a ceremonial hogan, sandpaintings are done in the context of various Navajo ceremonial ways, explicitly

Society and the Good Life

"How should I live?" "What is my responsibility to the world and to society?" Far from being untamed savages, as early explorers thought, nonliterate tribal peoples often have highly structured societies and complex codes of behavior and rules for living the right kind of life. And within their limited world they feel a responsibility for the continued peace, order, and health of their society and their environment.

The Sacred People: Communal Identity

John Mbiti reports an African saying that reflects the relation between the individual and the community: "I am, because we are; and since we are, therefore I am."[31] Of course, nonliterate peoples have a conception of the individual person, and there are many religious rituals designed to enhance individual well-being and personhood, as, for example, the vision quest noted earlier. But the individual is always rooted in a social nexus, consisting of the family, the clan, the village, and the larger community. Apart from that social nexus, the individual loses meaning and identity, thus becoming a nonperson, less than a human being. The real fulfillment of personhood comes within the network of communal relations grounded in the traditions of the people.

Tribal societies often have very complicated social structures. Typically there are a number of clans or extended families that together make up the whole people, but the relationships between these clans take different forms. There may, for example, be a moiety arrangement between two clans that make up a tribe, as is common among Australian Aborigines. In these cases marriages are usually exogamous (outside of one's own clan), and the two clans have different ritual responsibilities and duties. Within clans the relationships may also be complicated. The kinship system extends very broadly horizontally and means that, in one way or another, everyone is related to everyone else. In some African tribes it is possible that an individual has literally hundreds of "uncles," "brothers," or "sons and daughters."

Sacred leadership within nonliterate societies shows great diversity, of course, but some common types and functions can be recognized. Among leaders that have an official or "given" status are the head of the family or clan, the headman of the village, the chief or king of the tribe, and sometimes the priests who perform the official rituals. These are leaders who have power simply because of their position, and either their position is hereditary or they are chosen in some way by the people. But most leaders have their functions by virtue of personal power that is simply recognized by the people. There are shamans of various types, including medicine men who use shamanic trances. There are other healers who practice herbal medicine, diviners (who interpret communications from the sacred powers), and mediums (people through whom the spirits communicate). Some societies also have prophets who speak for the gods and lead the people according to the divine will. There may be rainmakers, singers, and more. And, of course, many societies have those who use power for evil purposes, namely, sorcerers, who may be much like shamans or diviners but use their power to hurt others.

Let us look at a typical example of social structure and religious leadership among nonliterate peoples. The Yoruba[32] of West Africa (Nigeria) are a farming people divided into a number of social groups, each with a specific urban center. A fundamental social unit is the family, where the family head performs the important religious functions, supervising the family ancestral shrine, giving names to the children, leading funerals, and so on. But at the level of the town or city, the oba (chief) assumes responsibility for ritual leadership. In the Yoruba view the chiefs rule their subjects on behalf of Olorun, the supreme god, and so the chiefs are below only the gods in power and respect. Because of their status, their bodies are sacred; an assault on a chief is regarded as an act of sacrilege. The chief of the holy city of Ife has superior position, for the gods established the world and the first kingship there.

Another important group of Yoruba religious leaders are the priests, associated with the many shrines throughout Yorubaland. The Yoruba have many gods (orisa), as discussed above, and each god is attended by a special priesthood. These priests are guardians of the shrines and of the objects of worship. They act as intermediaries, offering sacrifice, leading devotion, and declaring the god's will. One priesthood stands out with special importance for all Yoruba: the babalawo (father of secrets), who are priests of Orunmila, the god who knows the future and communicates through a special system of divination called Ifa. These priests, who go through long years of training, perform divination rituals and draw on a rich oral tradition of poems and legends to interpret the will of Orunmila. By this means they are able to give advice on what can be done to secure the most favorable outcome with regard to the basic concerns and needs of life.

In addition to the priests, there are mediums, people who become possessed by sacred powers during worship. In the ecstasy of possession, the person acts and speaks in a strange fashion, making utterances that the other worshipers understand as communications from the god that is possessing the person. Another recognized group of religious leaders are the medicine specialists, who are experts in identifying the causes for various illnesses and prescribing cures. Medicine specialists may use divination or work with a babalawo divination priest, but they have thorough knowledge of the incantations and the various traditional medicines, such as herbs, plants, leaves, roots, barks, animals, skins, bones, brooms, needles, minerals, and much more. Their medicine has power that comes from the gods.

The Yoruba recognize that specialists in power can also use that power for evil, and so there are sorcerers who use their powers to help people gain advantage over others or do harm to them. And few doubt that witches exist. These are mostly women but also a few men who meet regularly at night in spiritual form (their physical bodies are at home on their beds). At these meetings they contribute their human victims whose life-blood they have sucked out. Witchcraft is done secretly, yet many Yoruba believe there are such evil people, and they take measures to protect themselves.

Sacred Land and Sacred Space

The good life includes not only a sense of belonging to a community but also of belonging to a place, and nonliterate peoples have a strong sense of spatial orientation in their world. The myths tell of the creation of the world and the original ancestors starting right here on the sacred land. This Navajoland is the place of emergence, where First Man and Changing Woman created the world and the people. These mountains and valleys of Cherokeeland originated when the earth was first brought up from the bottom of the water and was still soft; Great Buzzard flew close to the land, and where his wings struck the ground and turned up again the valleys and mountains were formed. For almost all nonliterate peoples, the sacred history that gives identity for the people is tied up with their sacred land, and once they are torn away from their traditional land (as has happened very frequently in modern times) they experience great trauma.

There are, of course, many dimensions of sacred space—land, village, shrines, burial grounds, home. An important characteristic of sacred space, differentiating it from other "profane" space, is that it is founded around a center where manifestations of the sacred powers are experienced. The Achilpa of Australia are nomadic gatherers and small game hunters who move about from place to place. They believe that when Numbakula created the world and the ancestors, he lived with them for a while to establish their way of life. Then he made a sacred pole, anointed it with blood, and climbed it to disappear in the sky. The Achilpa have kept the pole as their most sacred possession, using it to direct their movements from one place

to the next. At their new camp they set it up once again so that they can again live in a meaningful world of sacred space. The pole is the center point of their world, the *axis mundi*, through which they can communicate with Numbakula in the sky. It is reported that once when the sacred pole was broken they were extremely disturbed, wandered about aimlessly, and lay down on the ground to await the death they thought was to come.[33] Without this center, their sacred world had become chaos again.

Another element in sacred space is the sense that the small space is a microcosm of the entire sacred world (the macrocosm). Houses, shrines, temples, and ceremonial halls are often built as symbolic miniatures of the world, to connect with those greater sacred forces.

For example, the sweat lodge constructed for Native American purification ceremonies is full of symbolic representations of the cosmos, as explained by Black Elk, a Sioux holy man.[34] The frame of the lodge, made from young willows, is set up so as to mark the four quarters of the universe, and the round altar at the center of the lodge is considered the center of the universe, full of the power of Wakan-Tanka, the supreme god. The door is to the east, from which wisdom comes, and the path leading to the east is covered with dirt taken from the center of the lodge. The fireplace, used to heat the rocks, is at the end of the path outside to the east, the fire representing power from the sun. Heated rocks are brought in to be placed in the round altar, one in the center, one at each of the directions, and then the hole is filled up with the rest of the rocks to represent everything in the universe.

In the ritual, the water poured on the hot rocks to make the steam represents the thunder beings. Tobacco and smoke are used, and also sage and sweet grass, representing fruits of mother earth. The sacred pipe is placed with its stem pointing toward the west, and the power of the west is invoked, then the powers of the north, east, and south, as prayers are said to all the sacred powers of the universe. A portion of these prayers, as reported by Black Elk, says:

> We shall burn the sweet grass as an offering to *Wakan-Tanka*, and the fragrance of this will spread throughout heaven and earth; it will make the four-leggeds, the

wingeds, the star peoples of the heavens, and all things as relatives. From you, O Grandmother earth, who are lowly, and who support us as does a mother, this fragrance will go forth; may its power be felt throughout the universe, and may it purify the feet and hands of the two-leggeds, that they may walk forward upon the sacred earth, raising their heads to *Wakan-Tanka*![35]

In the small confines of the sweat lodge, this small world is felt to be one with the sacred universe.

Morality and the Ancestors

There are many spiritual agents in the world that can cause suffering and evil. Even the supreme god sends natural calamities, destruction, and death. But at the bottom of it all, it is humans who initiate evil happenings, out of greed, ignorance, or vengeance on someone else. It is humans who use the spiritual powers toward bad ends. On the other hand, it is the responsibility of humans to maintain order and peace in the family and the community, and this is promoted by right, harmonious relationship with the spiritual powers. So morality is really human-centered, though it has links to the sacred powers, to the ancestors, and to nature.

Of course, the ultimate sanction for morality resides in sacred authority, and this is generally conceived in a hierarchical pattern. The supreme god or gods have ultimate authority over all morality, executing justice with impartiality, and when punishment for evil comes from this divine source, nothing can be done to change it. However, the supreme gods or sacred powers or culture heroes generally do not interfere in the ordinary life of the people; here morality is governed by the family ancestors and the family and community elders.

The standards of morality governing offenses generally are not absolute and universal but are situational, related to the results of the action. It is not actions in themselves that are considered good or evil, but the beneficial or damaging results that flow from them. A sin committed in secret does damage to no one and therefore is not "evil," for example, but if that action becomes public and results in shame and retribution, then it is evil. There are, of course, many laws, rules, customs, set forms of behaviors, and prohibitions that constitute the moral code of any given community, and

The Maasai of east Africa (Kenya and Tanzania) have a proud warrior tradition.

often these are thought to be ordained in the events of the Time of the Beginnings. Breeching this code constitutes a threat to established order and welfare of the community, and thus it must be punished in some way.

So what is the good life? It is to recognize one's place in the order of things, in family and community, and to live according to the traditions that promote the welfare of all. It means to honor the ancestors, consult them about important decisions, and not offend them. It means to worship the gods and spirits and to see to it that the important rituals and festivals are observed. The moral code obliges each person to avoid anything that upsets the sacred balances and causes harm to family and community, and on the other hand to work at mediating and reconciling whenever there is division within the community.

All of this calls for ethical reflection, for even in a nonliterate tribal community there are constantly changing patterns of relationship and obligation, and situational decisions have to be made. Such ethical decisions come about through consensus, for the most part, arrived at through a complex web of consultation and advice, through elders, priests, headmen, diviners, friends, relatives, and especially the ancestors.

Responsibility for Society and World

Almost by definition "tribal" societies are family- and clan-centered, and individuals find their highest good in promoting the welfare of their immediate group. This does not mean that nonliterate peoples have no sense of a greater human environment in nature and in society. First of all, most origin myths recognize that all other humans were created along with the tribal ancestors, and so there is a notion of common humanity even across tribal lines.

Further, responsibility for the environment of nature is keenly felt by nonliterate peoples. There is an ecological balance, created by the sacred powers of the beginning. Human life can be sustained only within the larger womb of the natural environment. And it is particularly the human responsibility—since humans know the myths and rituals that renew power—to ensure the continuance of nature's life and harmony. The good life means living in communion and peace with all the "peoples" of the earth—the animal, bird, plant, and other peoples. Perhaps this sense of responsibility toward the whole environment can be caught in the words of Smohalla, a holy man from the Wanapum tribe in the present-day state of Washington. He led a Native revival movement called the Dreamers in the second part of the nineteenth century, resisting attempts by government authorities to make his people become homesteaders.

> [God] commanded that the lands and fisheries should be common to all who lived upon them. That they were never to be marked off or divided, but that the people should enjoy the fruits that God planted in the land and the animals that lived upon it, and the fishes in the water. God said he was the father, and the earth was the mother of mankind; that nature was the law; that the animals and fish and plants obeyed nature, and that man only was sinful. This is the old law. . . .

> It is a bad word that comes from Washington. It is not a good law that would take my people away from me to make them sin against the laws of God. You ask me to plow the ground! Shall I take a knife and tear my mother's bosom? Then when I die she will not take me into her bosom to rest.

> You ask me to dig for stone! Shall I dig under her skin for her bones? Then when I die I can not enter her body to be born again.

> You ask me to cut grass and make hay and sell it, and be rich like white men, but how dare I cut off my mother's hair?

> It is a bad law, and my people can not obey it. I want my people to stay with me here. All the dead men will come to life again; their spirits will come to their bodies again. We must wait here, in the homes of our fathers, and be ready to meet them in the bosom of our mother. [36]

Many tribal societies have traditions of warfare, for the preservation and continuation of one's own people is of paramount importance. And in situations of limited space and resources, there necessarily will come conflict with other tribes and the need to preserve one's people through warfare. But most tribal societies, in emphasizing loyalty and bravery, do not inculcate violence and aggressiveness toward other humans. There is a contentment to live according to the patterns and level of life inherited from the ancestors, without the drive of modern westernized people to make "progress" and achieve ever greater wealth and luxuries.

In the modern world, as peoples of nonliterate tribal heritage have become aware of the international dimension of human life today, some of them have drawn from their own traditions to offer hope and encouragement to their own people and to the others in the world willing to listen to them. Lame Deer, a modern-day holy man of the Sioux, tells how White Buffalo Woman gave the sacred pipe to her people, the pipe that contains the whole universe, that binds all, even enemies, together in peace. Lame Deer looks to the day when those sacred pipes will again be used in purification and prayer, for peace in the whole world:

> We Indians hold the pipe of peace, but the white man's religious book speaks of war, and we have stood by while the white man supposedly improved the world. Now we Indians must show how to live with our brothers, not use them, kill them or maim them. With the pipe, which is a living part of us, we shall be praying for peace, peace in Vietnam and in our own country. We Indians say "our country" because it is still ours even if all other races are now in physical possession of it, for land does not belong to any single man but to all people and to the future generations.
>
> We must try to use the pipe for mankind, which is on the road to self-destruction. We must try to get back on the red road of the pipe, the road of life. We must try to save the white man from himself. This can be done only if all of us, Indians and non-Indians alike, can again see ourselves as part of this earth, not as an enemy from the outside who tries to impose its will on it. Because we, who know the meaning of the pipe, also know that, being a living part of the earth, we cannot harm any part of her without hurting ourselves. Maybe through this sacred pipe we can teach each other again to see through that cloud of pollution which politicians, industrialists and technical experts hold up to us as "reality." Through this pipe, maybe, we can make peace with our greatest enemy who dwells deep within ourselves. With this pipe we could all form again the circle without end.[37]

Perhaps the message that nonliterate peoples have for the rest of today's world will prove more important than has generally been thought!

DISCUSSION QUESTIONS

1. What are some basic characteristics of the myths of nonliterate peoples? In what sense can we say that myths tell that which is *really* the truth?

2. What does the myth about Hainuwele reveal to the Wemale about their existence?

3. What are two directions of response to modern Western civilization among traditional nonliterate peoples? Which do you think will prove more effective?

4. If they believe in a supreme god, why do nonliterate peoples often find greater significance in gods of the atmosphere and the earth?

5. What perspective on sacred reality is denoted by the terms *mana* and *tabu*?

6. Why do nonliterate peoples generally not place great emphasis on a better state of life after death? Do they have any ideas of "salvation" or "transformation"?

7. What connections are there between the healing of an individual and the wholeness of the community?

8. In what sense is the Vision Quest a path of transformation?

9. What does it mean to say sacred time is "reversible"? Contrast this with modern secular conceptions of time.

10. Interpret the religious significance of the breaking down of social structure, mass sexual activity, and human sacrifice in new year rituals.

11. What elements of "death" and "rebirth" are there in the Ndembu boys' initiation rituals?

12. How are religion and art united in Navajo sandpainting? Why is the painting destroyed in the process of the ritual?

13. In ideas about the moral life among nonliterate peoples, why is the role of the ancestors particularly important?

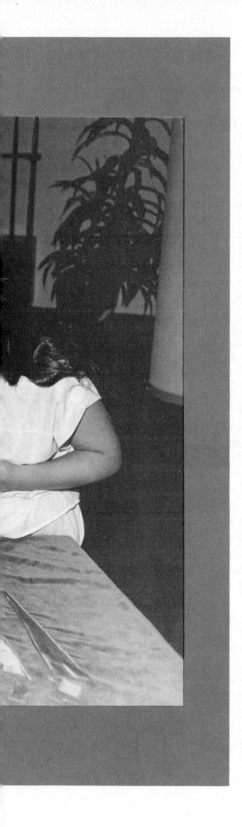

PART II

FAMILIES OF ABRAHAM:
Jews, Christians, and Muslims

INTRODUCTION

What is that common vision that makes it appropriate to speak of these three different (and at times, hostile) religions—Judaism, Christianity, Islam—as a family of religions, particularly as the "Families of Abraham"? To mention Abraham is to set our discussion in a certain historical and cultural context related to the Abraham who is mentioned in the sacred writings of all three religions. Abraham presumably lived around 2000 B.C.E. in Syria and Palestine, representing one of the numerous bedouin clans of the semidesert regions. In what sense could such a legendary character be a unifying figure for religions as separate in time and place as Judaism, Christianity, and Islam?

The common relationship of the three religions is twofold, both an historical-cultural continuity and a religious relationship. In the sacred history, Abraham is understood to be the ancestor of the Hebrews who escaped from Egypt and constituted themselves as the people Israel. Judaism, rising from the roots of Israel after the Babylonian exile, continues the line of Abraham. Christianity, though it arose 2,000 years after Abraham, grew out of the stock of Judaism, as Jesus himself and all his early followers were Jews. Even though Christianity rapidly spread to non-Jews throughout the Roman world, so that Christians, of course, can no longer claim to be physical descendants of Abraham, they represent a continuation of the history and culture of the Hebrews. Their way of thinking and their outlook on the world were highly influenced and shaped by the tradition of Judaism. Islam arose six hundred years after Christianity. Yet the bedouin/Semitic culture of Arabia was related in a general way to that culture represented by the Jewish people. Further, Muhammad and his companions were strongly influenced by the history and culture both of the Jews and the Christians through their sacred writings and their presence in Mecca and Medina.

Thus in terms of historical traditions and cultural continuities, it might be said that Christianity grew out of Judaism, and Islam grew out of both Judaism and Christianity. Without Judaism there would not have been either a Christianity or an Islam. And laying aside the question of how the earlier religions influenced and shaped the later ones, a general unity of culture can be postulated in the Semitic tradition of the Syro-Palestino-Arabian area during the formation of these three religions. They do make up one family of religions, based on a continuity of historical and cultural traditions.

But even apart from considerations of history and culture, each of the three religions looks to Abraham as "our father" in a religious way. For Jews to call Abraham "father" is to repeat the biblical assertions that God, seeking to carry out the divine will for the world, called Abraham and covenanted with him, promising that his descendants would be great and bring a blessing to the world. The covenant of God with Israel that forms the basis of the Jewish religion was seen as the fulfillment of the promises made to father Abraham. Similarly, the Christian scriptures call Abraham "our father," making it clear that this fatherhood is not "according to the flesh" by natural descent, but "according to the spirit"; God's promise to Abraham and God's plan for the world are being carried on by the followers of Jesus the Christ. The Muslim scriptures also look to Abraham as one of the great prophets of God, and further claim that

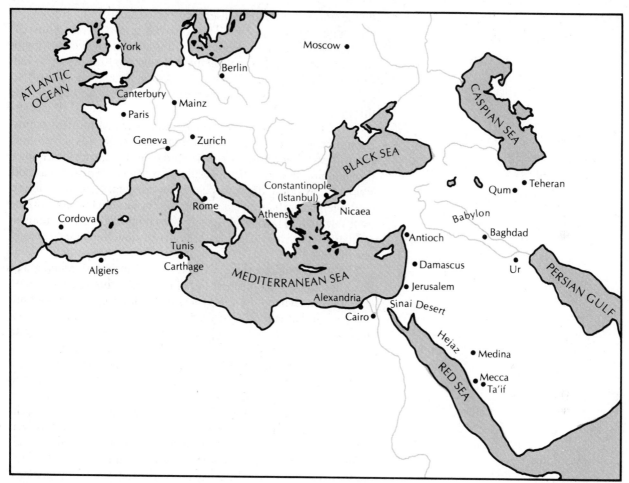

The Mediterranean World: Judaism, Christianity, and Islam.

Abraham is the father of all faithful Muslims. Tradition holds that the Meccans are descendants of Abraham through his son Ishmael, and that Abraham even built the great shrine in Mecca, the Ka'bah. Thus the religious experience of Jews, Christians, and Muslims can be expressed in a symbolic way by pointing to the relationship with father Abraham.

But what is that common vision that can be appealed to by reference to father Abraham? One of the most central ideas is the insistence on monotheism. There is one God, the creator of all that exists. In rejecting all forms of polytheism or plurality of gods that control this world, these three religions share a common vision both of God and of the world. God is the almighty creator, for no other divine power controls any aspect of the created world. But God is also transcendent, beyond creation, not a part of it. Thus the perspective of monism or nondualism is also rejected: everything is not God; the world is not divine but the good creation of God. Further, God is personal, acting in relation to humans as a partner working through people and events to carry out the sacred design for the world.

The three religions share the common view that humans are the highest creation of God and that their greatest good is in fulfilling the will of the creator. For their guidance the creator has spoken through prophets, and that revelation has been written down as holy scripture, providing the truth that is necessary for humans to live as God intends for them. This revelation is not in the form of timeless myths or secret knowledge, but it is based on God's own actions in human history, and it guides humans in how they are to live in obedience.

The three religions share a vision of human history moving in a linear fashion from a creation out of nothing at the beginning to an end of history when God will bring the divine design to completion. Involved in that end of history is God's evaluation in judgment and the appropriate reward or punishment in the life of the world to come. Thus in contrast to some of the other religions of the world, Judaism, Christianity, and Islam share a sense of movement toward the future, when God's design will be vindicated and creation will be brought to its fulfillment.

Jews, Christians, and Muslims will read the previous paragraphs about the common vision they all share and say, "Yes, but there is more. . . ." And there is more to each religion's vision of the world, more distinctive and vital assertions and commitments. To sketch out the common vision shared by the three religions is only to set the stage, the general plan onto which each weaves its own characteristic experiences and understandings of God and human existence. Each of these religions has had its own particular experiences and history, out of which it has developed insights and practices that are attuned to those experiences. Each has its own distinctive worldview and its own system of symbols that makes complete sense of human existence.

In the following chapters we attend to the various facets of the worldview of each of these religions. We see that, even though many of the symbols are similar, they reflect the truth of the religious vision in distinctive ways because of the configuration of symbols of which they are a part. One God, three distinctive modes of experiencing that one God—so it is with all the symbols, beliefs, and practices that make up those paths of life we call Judaism, Christianity, and Islam.

CHAPTER 4

Judaism: Sacred Story and Historical Context

"**W**ho am I?" To be Jewish means in some way to belong to the People of the Covenant.

The religion of Judaism has a long and complex history. Unlike both Christianity and Islam, which became full-formed religions within the generation of their founders, Judaism reached its classical form more than a millennium after the foundational sacred history associated with Moses and the covenant at Sinai. Through many vicissitudes during its long history, Judaism has developed and been transformed. Yet Judaism today still retains the essential characteristics that it acquired as it was shaped during the Rabbinic period—it still is the "Way of the Torah."

THE JEWISH STORY

To simplify the complex history of Judaism, we may speak of two foundings: the founding of the Israelite religion under the leadership of Moses, and the founding of Judaism after the Babylonian exile, beginning under the leadership of Ezra and culminating in what is known as "Rabbinic Judaism." The religion of *Israel* is that known from the pages of the Hebrew bible, the Tanakh. The religion of *Judaism*, grown from the Israelite religion, reached final form in the teaching of the rabbis as set down in the Talmud. However, to Jewish thinking, the Israelite religion and the Jewish religion are not two religions but one and the same. And the full sacred writings of this one religion of the descendants of Abraham are contained in both the Tanakh and the Talmud.

Thanks to an enormous amount of scholarly investigation, both in archaeology and in the ancient texts, the history of the people of Israel within the world of the ancient Near East can be seen with a certain amount of clarity. That history, beginning with the ancestors of the Israelites as seminomads on the fringes of the Arabian desert around 2000 B.C.E., is a remarkable story of an obscure tribe experiencing a moment of royal glory before fading from the world scene once more. Whereas the political history of Israel may have been relatively insignificant, its sacred history has been of momentous consequence for a good part of the human race. We can use the scholarly reconstruction of Israel's history to help in understanding, but most important is seeing the Jewish story as Jews themselves interpreted it.

Beginnings: Israel, People of the Covenant

According to the story, the people of Israel were created when Yahweh (the special name of Israel's God), the God of their fathers, heard their cries in slavery in Egypt and brought them out, taking them as a special people by making a covenant with them and giving them the Torah (law). This is the founding of the religion of Israel. But this is not the beginning of the sacred history.

Prologue: All Humankind and Abraham

The story of the Jews reaches back to the story of creation and the early history of universal humankind. According to the first chapters of Genesis, God created a good world and created humankind within it to take care of it and live the good life of serving God. But people turned away from God, following the evil inclination of their hearts. The first man and woman disobeyed God and were expelled from God's special garden; one of their sons (Cain) murdered the other (Abel) and was cursed to become a wanderer on the earth. Evil and violence filled the earth. When humans sought to glorify themselves by building a great tower to heaven, God confounded their languages and scattered them throughout the earth—and human history as we know it began.

This failure and scattering of humankind on earth, in spite of God's good intentions for them, set the stage for God's great plan of intervention in human history. The story introduces the family of Abraham. We know from archaeological material from ancient Mesopotamia that the stories about the clans of Abraham, Isaac, and Jacob fit into the general cultural milieu around the beginning of the second millennium B.C.E. These clans were seminomadic herders on the fringes of the Arabian desert, caught up in the general movement of similar Semitic people from southern Mesopotamia toward Syria and the land of Palestine. But, according to the story, this particular movement was more than a mere land-seeking migration of clans; it was directed by "Yahweh," the God of the later Israelites.

> Now Yahweh said to Abram, "Go forth from your own land, your kindred, and your father's house, to a land that I will show you, for I will make you into a great nation. I will bless you and make your name so great that there will be a blessing. Those who bless you I will bless, but I will curse those who curse you. And in you all the families of the earth will be blessed."
>
> (GEN. 12:1–3)

In this story, God took steps to initiate in human history a new design, focused on Abraham and his descendants as a great nation with a land given to them by God, who would bring a blessing to all the families of the earth through them.

Abraham and the clans associated with him were pastoralists, wandering from pastureland to pastureland. Worship focused on the clan God, called "the God of Abraham." And they also built altars to the supreme God El who was worshiped in different places under names such as El 'Elyon (Exalted God), El Roi (Seeing God), and El Shaddai (Mighty God). But in the view of the Israelite story, the God the ancestors worshiped was none other than Yahweh, the personal God of the Israelites (even though, according to the story, Yahweh revealed that name for the first time to Moses). God made a covenant with Abraham, giving him children in his old age. First Hagar, servant of his wife Sarah, bore him Ishmael, and then Isaac was born from Sarah, the ancestress of the people of Israel. As the sign of the covenant, God instituted the ritual of circumcision for Abraham and his descendants. Showing faithfulness, God continually renewed the promises to Abraham even when Abraham faltered in his faith, as when he passed off his wife Sarah as his sister so that the Egyptians would not kill him to possess her (Gen. 12:10–20).

In the end Abraham stood the test of faithfulness. When God commanded him to sacrifice his beloved son Isaac, Abraham obeyed, and God spoke through an angel: "Do not lay your hand against the boy or do anything to him, for now I know that you are God-fearing, because you have not withheld your son, your only son, from me" (Gen. 22:12). God provided a ram to be sacrificed in place of Isaac. Since then Abraham has been the model of Jewish faithfulness to God in all situations.

The story traces God's covenant through Abraham's son Isaac and his wife Rebekah, to Jacob, Isaac's younger son. The sacred history does not present these ancestors as perfect heroes. Jacob, for example, cheated his brother, and by his cunning he established himself as a wealthy man with twelve sons. A key story tells how Jacob wrestled with God one whole night, refusing to let go until he received God's blessing. With the blessing Jacob also received a new name: "No longer shall your name be called Jacob, but Israel, because you have striven with God and with men, and you have prevailed" (Gen. 32:28). The name *Israel* means, "he strives with God," and it became the name of Jacob's descendants in a very expressive way: they are God's people who always struggle with God.

The story reaches the end of the prologue by describing how Jacob (Israel) and his family found their way down into Egypt during a drastic famine and how Joseph (one of the sons, who had been sold into slavery by his brothers) rose to great power in Egypt. This took place during the time that lower Egypt was ruled by the Hyksos, Asiatic people who wrested control from the Egyptians for a time (ca. 1750–1550 B.C.E.). During this period the Hebrews, as Jacob's descendants were called, prospered in Egypt. But eventually the Hyksos were driven out by the Egyptians, and the Hebrews consequently fell upon bad times under Egyptian domination. The story tells how there arose a king of Egypt "who knew not Joseph" (Exod. 1:8), who enslaved and oppressed the Hebrews. Here was the deepest crisis of all: the children of Abraham were in bondage, with the God of their fathers and the covenant with Abraham forgotten.

Exodus from Egypt

The people cried out in their slavery, and "God heard their groaning, and God remembered his covenant with Abraham, with Isaac, and with Jacob"

Obeying God's command, Abraham prepares to sacrifice his son Isaac, but an angel of the Lord stops him. Painting by Giovanni Domenico Tiepolo.

(Exod. 2:24). Now the great drama of redemption begins, as God called Moses to deliver this people.

As told in the book of Exodus, the birth of Moses took place under foreboding circumstances, for the Egyptians were killing all Hebrew infant boys to control the Hebrew population. But Moses' mother placed her infant son in a basket among the reeds at the brink of the river Nile, and he was found and adopted by a daughter of the king. Given an Egyptian name, Moses was brought up at the Egyptian court, but he became a fugitive because he murdered an Egyptian who was beating a Hebrew. He fled to the desert east of Egypt, where he lived with Jethro, the priest of the Midianites, a clan related to the Hebrews. He stayed there for years and even married the daughter of the Midianite priest.

While Moses was tending the sheep of his father-in-law on the holy mountain of Midian, God encountered him, manifested in a burning bush, and told him to go to the pharoah of Egypt and demand that he let the Hebrews go free. When Moses asked who this God was, God revealed the special name, "Yahweh," interpreting it to mean, "I Am"—associating the name Yahweh with the verb *hayah*, "to be." At the same time Yahweh identified with the God worshiped by the

Moses in awe before God's presence in the burning bush. Painting by J. S. von Carolsfeld.

ancestors of the Hebrews:

> You shall speak thus to the people of Israel, "Yahweh, the God of your fathers, the God of Abraham, the God of Isaac, and the God of Jacob, has sent me to you." This is my name for ever, my memorial throughout all generations.   (EXOD. 3:15)

Then Yahweh commanded Moses, with his brother Aaron, to deliver the Hebrews from Egypt and to bring them back to worship at this wilderness mountain after they escaped from Egypt.

When the pharoah resisted Moses' demands, God brought a series of terrible plagues, ending with the destruction of all the firstborn of the Egyptians, after which the pharoah and the Egyptians finally relented. This "night of watching," described in Exodus 12, has ever since been celebrated in the Passover festival. Each Israelite family was to slaughter an unblemished lamb, paint the doorposts with its blood, and roast and eat it with unleavened cakes and bitter herbs. They were to eat it with belt fastened, sandals on their feet, and staff in hand, in a posture of haste. This was to be a day of remembrance, a festival to be kept generation to generation for all time—so that all future generations could reexperience the great deliverance of the Exodus.

When finally the Hebrews, brought together under the leadership of Moses, escaped from Egypt, the Egyptians pursued. But God safely brought the Hebrews through the Red Sea (literally, the sea of reeds), but then routed and utterly destroyed the army of the Egyptians in that same sea. God led them through the wilderness with signs and wonders, finally bringing them back to the holy mountain in the wilderness, Mt. Sinai.

Torah and Covenant at Mt. Sinai

Here at Mt. Sinai, according to the Jewish story, the greatest miracle of all took place:

> Moses brought the people out from the camp to meet God, and they took their stand at the foot of the mountain. Because Yahweh descended upon it in fire, all of Mt. Sinai was smoking.... And Yahweh came down

upon the top of Mt. Sinai, and he summoned Moses to the mountain-top. Then Moses went up. . . . And God spoke all these words: "I am Yahweh your God who brought you out of Egypt, out of the house of slavery. You shall have no other gods before me." (EXOD. 19:17–20:3)

Thus God spoke to Moses, and through Moses to the people of Israel, the whole Torah, the laws and commandments that would form the basis of life for the people.

The revelation of the Torah on Mt. Sinai climaxed with the making of the covenant with the people of Israel. The covenant God made with them was a two-way contract: God would be their God, bringing them to the promised land, protecting them; they would be a holy people, serving only Yahweh of all gods and obeying the commandments. After Moses told the people all the words of God and wrote them down, they sacrificed bulls as offerings. Moses took half the blood in basins and threw it against the altar; then he read the book of the covenant to the people. They said, "We will do all that Yahweh has spoken, and we will obey." And Moses flung the blood over the people, ratifying the covenant God had made with them on the basis of the Torah (Exod. 24:3–8). Here on Mt. Sinai came the self-revelation of God, and by it God created both Torah (the law) and Israel (the covenant people).

To understand the centrality and the uniqueness of this covenant relationship between Yahweh and the people Israel, it is helpful to see how the story contrasts it with the religions of the other peoples of the ancient Near East. Among the agricultural city-states of Egypt, Mesopotamia, and Palestine, a cosmic type of religion prevailed, with many gods in charge of the different forces of nature. It was the power of these gods that made the cosmos a functioning world, and the role of humans was to serve the gods, responding to their will, entreating them to act favorably, and empowering their vitality by periodic rituals and festivals. In this organic or biological view of the functioning of the universe, humans played an important role. When the vitality of the gods would run down (as, for example, when vegetation dies in the winter), it was necessary for the people by ritual means to expunge the used-up forces and restore the life-power of the gods.

Among the Canaanites, Israel's neighbors in Palestine, particular importance was attached to the storm-fertility god, Ba'al, and the fertility goddess, Asherah. To the Canaanite farmers the powers of these gods of vegetation were of vital importance. Rituals of awakening them so that the crops would grow included sexual rituals at the local shrines in which all the people had the duty to participate. The people felt bound to the gods in the recurring cycles of the forces of nature, and serving the gods meant participating in those natural fertility cycles so that the power of the gods would continually be replenished.

Contrasting the religion of Israel to this cosmic type of religion, which characterized the great civilizations of neighboring peoples, the Israelite story emphasizes over and again that the people of Israel are bound to their God Yahweh in a covenant relationship, based on law given by God. A covenant (*brit*) is a contract, a treaty between two parties, which binds them together with mutual promises and obligations. Rather than a cosmic or biological relationship, the Israelites were related to God in a political contract, with Yahweh as a personal partner who responded to them in the give-and-take of personal decisions and actions. Rather than focusing on the rhythm of the seasons of nature, their religion focused on encounters with Yahweh in the events of their historical life. Rather than being bound by the laws of the natural processes of death and life, they were bound by the mutual obligations of the covenant, based on the covenant law mediated to them by Moses.

Israel's covenant law was communal law, containing stipulations both in relation to God and to fellow Israelites. Yahweh alone was to be worshiped, not with graven images and fertility rituals like the Canaanite gods, but with prayer and praise, with repentance and sacrificial gifts. Fellow Israelites were to be treated with equality and justice, to be loved as oneself. Israel's whole life, whether concerned with worship of God or with human conduct in society, was structured by Yahweh's covenant demand: "You shall be holy, for I Yahweh your God am holy" (Lev. 19:2).

It was by the keeping of the covenant that they retained their identity as "Israel, the people of Yahweh."

The Promised Land and the Kingdom

After the exodus and the making of the covenant at Mt. Sinai, Israel's story continues with a movement toward the fulfillment of their destiny as Yahweh's people: the possession of the Holy Land and the establishing of the Kingdom of Israel. Characteristically intertwined in the story is the tension of the covenant, the "tug of war" between God and Israel symbolically portrayed by Jacob wrestling with God. God promises and demands and pushes Israel onward. Israel responds sometimes faithfully, sometimes unfaithfully. Yahweh punishes but restores in love. And the covenant relationship goes on between the two partners.

After setting out from Mt. Sinai to possess the promised land, according to the story, there were frequent murmurings and rebellions of the people against Yahweh. They even accused Moses and Yahweh of dragging them out to the desert to die. Yahweh punished—a whole generation died in the wilderness, including even Moses—but Yahweh also fulfilled the promise by bringing their children into the land of Canaan and giving them victory and possession under the leadership of Joshua. The actual conquest was, as we know, a long process of infiltrating, conquering, and assimilating. It is described in the sacred history as a "holy war," with Yahweh at their head conquering the enemies with a divine terror. They would move onward with the portable shrine called the "Ark of Yahweh's Covenant" leading the way. When the ark began to move, Moses chanted, "Arise, O Yahweh, and may your enemies be scattered." And when the ark stopped, he intoned, "Rest, O Yahweh of the ten thousand thousands of Israel" (Num. 10:35–36). These wars of conquest had religious meaning in that taking the land of Canaan was a covenant duty. The Holy Land was their promised inheritance, and by taking possession of it they were glorifying Yahweh's name before the nations. In retelling this story, then, the identity of the people of Israel has always been bound up with the Holy Land.

The people of Israel established themselves in Palestine by about 1200 B.C.E., and for the next two centuries they maintained a loose tribal confederation, adapting themselves to an agricultural rather than pastoral way of life, and rallying around tribal leaders (judges) to fight off hostile peoples. Eventually they reached two very important transformations of their destiny: they settled down as farmers, building cities to dwell in; and they became a kingdom, the Kingdom of David. Both these developments have central significance in the telling of the story, for both involved the relation of Israel to their covenant God.

Struggle with Canaanite Culture

The first transformation involved the relationship of the newly arrived Israelites to the agricultural religion of the Canaanites, which centered on the fertility god Ba'al, together with the goddess Asherah and other gods and goddesses. The Israelites had been seminomadic pastoralists, wandering with the herds in the semiarid regions of the area. They had met their God Yahweh in the desert, and as they wandered Yahweh went with them, the divine presence symbolized by the portable shrine, the Ark of the Covenant.

But now that they settled down, their way of life changed drastically. They became farmers, and, influenced by their Canaanite agriculturalist neighbors, the attraction of the gods of the land was strong. To some Israelites, Yahweh seemed to be the god only of the desert; but Ba'al's powers were important for the vitality of the land, so they became Ba'al worshipers. Many Israelites tried to remain faithful to Yahweh, but they introduced fertility rituals and ideas into their worship of Yahweh. According to the prophet Jeremiah, upon every high hill and under every green tree the people were sprawling like harlots, participating in fertility rituals at Ba'al shrines (Jer. 2:20).

This struggle between faithfulness to Yahweh and the need to worship the gods of the land went on for many centuries, providing much of the drama of the Hebrew scriptures. The key question was powerfully articulated by the early prophet Elijah, in a day when the queen of Israel was none other than Jezebel, a Ba'al worshiper from Tyre and a fierce persecutor of the worshipers of Yahweh. The story tells how Elijah challenged the people, "How long will you keep on limping on two different opinions? If Yahweh is God, follow him; but if Ba'al, follow him." So Elijah challenged the four hundred and fifty prophets of Ba'al to a contest, to see which god would answer their invocations by sending fire to consume the sacrifice. The prophets of Ba'al danced wildly, prophesying and crying out to Ba'al to no avail all day. Elijah indulged in ridicule: "Cry louder, for he is a god. Perhaps he is musing or engaged, or he is on a journey, or maybe he is sleeping and must be awakened." Finally it was Elijah's turn, and he prayed: "O Yahweh, God of Abraham, Isaac, and Israel, today may it be known that you are God in Israel and that I am your servant." The fire of Yahweh fell, consuming the offering and the whole altar; and the people fell on their faces and cried, "Yahweh is God! Yahweh is God!" As a final emphatic gesture, Elijah seized the prophets of Ba'al and slaughtered them all (I Kgs. 18:17–40).

Such stories tell how the Israelites, struggling and faltering, finally came to know Yahweh as the one God of all, even of the rain and the land and the crops. The upshot of the whole dramatic struggle of Israel with

Canaanite culture is the overwhelming monotheistic commitment emphasized in the psalms and prayers and prophetic writings of the Hebrew scriptures, echoed in the rabbinic writings and the liturgies of the Jewish synagogues.

The Kingdom of Israel

The other great transformation that the story brings to center stage is the creation of the Kingdom of Israel. The story delights in the struggle between Israel and Yahweh. The initial impulse toward kingship in Israel was the desire to have "a king to rule over us, like all the nations" (I Sam. 8:5), and this was understood by the tribal leader Samuel to be a rejection of Yahweh who had always been their king in the covenant relationship.

In the characteristic double action of warning and promise, Yahweh warned them of the tragedies and failures that lay ahead in becoming a kingdom ruled by a powerful king, warnings that are abundantly illustrated in the stories of the sins and rebellions of the

The world of early Judaism.

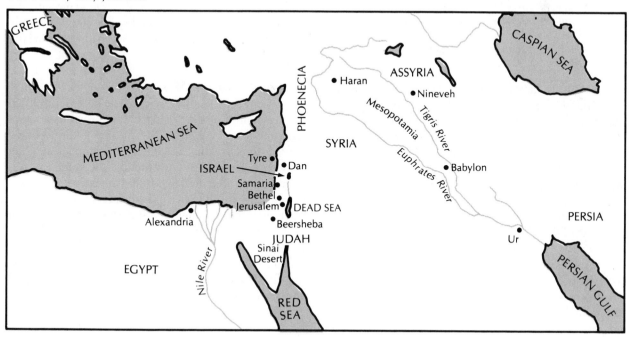

kings over the next five hundred years in Israel. But Yahweh also responded positively to the request for a king, and the symbol of Yahweh ruling through the agency of the king of Israel became a primary element of the religion of Israel. First Saul was anointed as a tribal king, but it was really David who consolidated all the tribes into the Kingdom of Israel and established the religious model of the king, adopted son of Yahweh, with whom Yahweh has made an everlasting covenant to rule over the sacred people. The Davidic kingship thus was integrated into the covenant relationship between Yahweh and the chosen people. This was celebrated in one of the psalms:

Your love, O Yahweh, I will sing forever! . . .
Of old you declared in a vision
    and spoke to your faithful one:
"I have endowed a warrior with strength,
    I have exalted a chosen one from the people.
I have found David my servant,
    with my holy oil I have anointed him . . . .
He will cry to me, 'You are my father,
    my God, my saving rock.'
And I will make him first-born,
    highest among the kings of the earth.
Forever I will maintain for him my love,
    and my covenant will stand firm for him.
I will establish his posterity forever,
    and his throne as the duration of the heavens."
(PS. 89:1, 19–29)

A king must have a royal city, according to the divine kingship ideology of Israel's surrounding cultures, with the god of the kingdom dwelling in the royal temple. Therefore in Israel also there was established the holy city of Jerusalem and the temple on Mt. Zion—extremely important symbols in the Jewish religious tradition. David was originally king only over the tribe of Judah, ruling from the Judean city of Hebron. But when the elders of all the tribes of Israel made a covenant with David before Yahweh and anointed him king of Israel, David needed a new capital city outside tribal territory to symbolize the unity of all the tribes. So he and his personal army attacked the Canaanite city of Jerusalem and took it. David took up residence in the stronghold of Zion, now renamed the City of David, and built his palace there. Prior to this time the Ark of Yahweh's Covenant had been moved around to different sanctuaries among the tribes, but now David wanted to bring this shrine of Yahweh's presence to his royal city to symbolize the religious unity of the new kingdom. So in a great festive procession, the ark was brought up to Zion, the City of David, and placed in a tent sanctuary there (2 Sam. 6). Now Yahweh was present in Zion, the holy city.

But this new interpretation of Israel's relation to their God was not accomplished without the characteristic struggle symbolized by the name of "Israel." When David decided to build a temple for Yahweh in place of the tent on Zion, the prophet Nathan brought word from Yahweh that the tradition of Yahweh dwelling in a tent should be maintained. From the religions of the surrounding peoples, the Israelites knew that the god of the land, Ba'al, was housed in temples rooted in the earth; to build a temple for Yahweh seemed to some a rejection of their God who had delivered them from Egypt and dwelt among them in the holy tent.

Yet David's son Solomon, in a time of peace and prosperity, accomplished what had been denied to David. With the help of Canaanite architects and workers, he constructed a magnificent temple, thirteen years in the building. In a great festival the priests brought the Ark of the Covenant to the inner shrine, the Most Holy Place of the temple, and "the glory of Yahweh filled the house of Yahweh" (I Kgs. 8:11).

The Idea of the Messiah

It is from the role of the king as the deliverer of Israel that the notion of the "messiah" arose in Israel. Originally the term *messiah*, which means "anointed one," applied to the king as the one anointed to lead Yahweh's people. But eventually the kingship was swept away in the destructions from foreign invasions. Yet the kingship had become an important part of the religious vision of Israel, and the expectation arose that God would not abandon the promises to King David, that one day the Kingdom of David would be restored and made great in the earth once more. Thus when the kingship fell on bad times, the hope arose that God would sometime in the future send a new son of David, a messiah, to restore the house of David. The idea of the messiah has undergone many developments in Jewish thought, but the basis of this important expectation was established when Israel chose, and Yahweh accepted, a king over the people Israel.

With the establishment of the Kingdom of Israel, the king ruling over Yahweh's people, and the temple as Yahweh's presence in the holy city of Jerusalem, the promised destiny of the people of Israel might seem to have been reached. And in a certain sense that is true, for most of the primary symbols of the Jewish tradition had by now been created: Abraham, Exodus, covenant and Torah, Yahweh as Lord of all the earth, the king, the messiah, and the holy city of Jerusalem with its temple. But the religion of Israel was based on a continuing covenantal tug of war with Yahweh, and that struggle went on in episodes of faithfulness and unfaithfulness, punishment and restoration.

Decline of the Kingdom: The Prophets

The story presents the history of kingship in Israel in dark colors. Even the glorious reigns of David and Solomon were marred by sin and serving other gods. The story reports that David's lust for the woman Bathsheba led him to have her husband murdered so he could have her. Solomon loved women so much that he had seven hundred wives, all princesses, and three hundred concubines; these foreign women enticed him to worship other gods. Finally as punishment God tore the kingdom from Solomon's son's hand, leaving only the tribe of Judah as the Kingdom of David, the other tribes breaking away to form the northern Kingdom of Israel.

The judgment passed on many of the kings of Judah and of North Israel is scathing. The great majority of them, according to the story, turned away to serve other gods, oppressed the poor, and generally broke covenant with Yahweh, all this leading to the destruction and exile of both North Israel and Judah. The northern Kingdom of Israel was destroyed and the population scattered by the Assyrians in 721 B.C.E. And the final night descended with the destruction of the Kingdom of Judah in 587 B.C.E. by the Babylonians and the exile of the few Jewish survivors in Babylon—the sole remaining heirs of the briefly glorious history of the covenant people of Yahweh. But in this struggle with darkness, a remarkable new religious phenomenon appeared—the prophets of Israel, providing yet another important element in the making of the Jewish religious tradition.

The early prophets in Israel were groups of seers who entered into visionary, ecstatic trances, like shamans, and gave out the word of Yahweh for a particular situation. Both Kings Saul and David, for example, were caught up in the ecstatic contagion of these bands of prophets (I Sam. 10:5–13; 19:18–24). Somewhat later individual prophets began to speak forth God's word, as when the prophet Nathan brought God's judgment against King David for having taken Bathsheba. Elijah and Elisha thundered God's words against the Ba'al worshipers of their day.

Beginning with the prophet Amos in the middle of the eighth century B.C.E., there arose a series of individuals known as the "classical" prophets, those whose words were recorded in the scrolls of the prophets. The prophets were spokespersons for Yahweh. They received a word from Yahweh for a particular situation, and they proclaimed and interpreted it to the king and the people, no matter what the consequences, be it a word of promise and hope or a word of warning and judgment. Sometimes they acted out the "word" of Yahweh, as when Hosea married a sacred prostitute from one of the fertility shrines to demonstrate how God kept loving Israel even as they went after other gods (Hos. 1–3). Again, Isaiah walked naked through the streets of Jerusalem for three years as a visual warning that the Israelites would be led away naked as prisoners of war (Isa. 20:1–4).

The prophets interpreted the word of Yahweh for the people, showing them how Yahweh had acted in the history of Israel and would continue to act in the future. They proclaimed that Yahweh had a plan, a design for the covenant people. The unfaithfulness of the people would lead Yahweh to punish and destroy them. But God would continue to love the people even in destroying them; eventually, the prophets envisioned, God would restore them anew as the covenant people.

The prophets strongly brought out the ethical consequences of being the people of Yahweh, proclaiming the wrath of Yahweh when they did not live up to the covenant. Amos, for example, lashed out against the women of the nobility: "Listen to this word, you cows of Bashan who are on Mt. Samaria, you who oppress the poor, who crush the destitute" (Amos 4:1). He uttered unthinkable words against the official religion, which masked the covenant demand for justice and morality. Through Amos the word of Yahweh sounded forth:

> I hate, I despise your pilgrim-festivals,
>> and I do not delight in your sacred assemblies.
> Even if you offer me your burnt offerings and cereal offerings,
>> I will not accept them,
>> nor will I look on the peace offerings of your fatted animals.
> Remove the noise of your songs from me;
>> the music of your harps I will not hear,
> Rather, let justice roll on like the waters,
>> and righteousness like an everflowing river.
>
> (AMOS 5:21–24)

To be the chosen people of Yahweh, the creator of the world, meant, according to the prophets, both a great rejoicing and a heavy responsibility to glorify God's name by demonstrating justice and righteousness in the world. And when they did not live up to their covenant commitment, they would receive special punishment from God. God's word came through Amos: "Hear this word that Yahweh speaks against you, O Israelites, against the whole family which he brought up from Egypt: 'Only you have I known among all the families of the earth; therefore will I punish you for all your iniquities'" (Amos 3:1–2). Echoing the words of the prophets, Jews of all ages have agreed that it is a "joyful burden" to be a Jew, one of the chosen people.

In their prediction of doom and destruction, the prophets insisted that it was Yahweh, the God of Israel, who was bringing the destruction, not the various powers of the world. When the Assyrians came against Israel, the prophet Isaiah said the Assyrians, in spite of their arrogance, were merely the tool of Yahweh, the rod of God's anger (Isa. 10:5). And Jeremiah interpreted the destruction of Jerusalem by the Babylonians as part of God's plan. He spoke the word of Yahweh: "I am the one who made the earth, humankind, and animals on the earth with my great power and my outstretched arm, and I give it to whomever I will. Now I give all these lands into the hand of Nebuchadnezzar, king of Babylon, my servant" (Jer. 27:5–6).

But precisely because the prophets saw the invasion and destruction of Israel by foreign foes as God's own doings, they had hope, for they knew that God would never abandon the divine plan and the promises to the chosen people. Through this same Jeremiah God spoke again,

> I will gather them from all the lands to which I banished them in my anger, wrath, and great fury, and I will return them to this place and cause them to dwell in safety. Then they will be my people and I will be their God. And I will give them one heart and one way of life, to fear me forever, for their good and their children's good after them. I will make an eternal covenant with them, not to turn away from doing them good. And I will place the fear of me in their hearts so they will not turn away from me. I will rejoice over them to do them good, and I will plant them in this land in faithfulness with my whole heart and soul. (JER. 32:37–41)

Yahweh would not let the people go, the prophets said. God would make a new covenant with them and restore them to their land, so that they could go on living as the sacred people.

So what would seem to be merely a tragic fate in the cruel movement of world history—a tiny nation perishing like countless others—becomes in the eyes of the prophets a part of God's own design. God is involved in human history through the chosen servant, Israel; as they suffer punishment, God suffers with them (Isa. 63:9). A deeply moving image in the prophetic writings is that of the Suffering Servant. The great prophet who wrote the words contained in the second part of the scroll of Isaiah (Isa. 40ff.) lived in Babylonian exile. To answer the question of why Israel was suffering so much, this prophet, whom we call Second Isaiah, spoke of God's plan to lay all the sins and burdens of the world on the chosen servant Israel (Isa. 53). To Jews, this picture of Israel as God's Suffering Servant, bringing justice and righteousness into the world even as they suffer with God the pains and the rejections of the world, has been a sustaining force in times of suffering and persecution.

The Founding of Judaism

The Babylonian exile (beginning in 587 B.C.E.) brought a drastic crisis in the sacred history of the Jews. In a sense the story of Israelite religion came to an end, for the Kingdom of Israel was no more, and the Kingdom of Judah was destroyed never to reappear as a kingdom, with its survivors as exiles in a strange land far from Jerusalem. The story relates that God intervened again to deliver the chosen people from Babylon through the work of King Cyrus of Persia, who conquered the Babylonians and established the Persian Empire. As part of his enlightened policy, in about 538 B.C.E. Cyrus permitted and even assisted Jewish exiles to return to Jerusalem (2 Chr. 36:22–23; Ezra 1:1–4). But the few exiles who returned found Jerusalem devastated and the surrounding population hostile. The glorious Kingdom of David was forever gone. Something new had to be created, a Jewish community that could remain faithful to the covenant under these difficult circumstances. Here Ezra the scribe enters the story with what we may call the second founding of Judaism.

Ezra and the Early Jewish Community

Ezra was a priest and scribe among the Jewish exiles still living in Babylon a century after the first groups of exiles returned to Jerusalem. The religious life of the Jews in Jerusalem was in disarray. The temple was used for secular purposes, intermarriage was producing children who could not even speak Hebrew (even the high priest had married a non-Jewish Samaritan), and businesses ran as usual on the Sabbath. Ezra arrived in Jerusalem from Babylon with an unusual commission from the Persian king giving him religious authority over all Jews in and around Judea. His official title was Secretary for the Law of the God of Heaven (Ezra 7:12). Ezra was learned in the Torah of Moses, and apparently he brought with him a copy of the Torah that had been edited by Jewish scholars in Babylon (Neh. 8:1).

Ezra's great task was to make the whole Jewish people renew their covenant obligations to their God; he argued that it was because they had broken the covenant that the disastrous destructions had occurred. He read the Torah publicly to the assembled people from early morning until noon. The reading and study of the Torah continued day after day, and the Jews renewed the covenant by swearing to obey all the law given by God through Moses. The purification of the people called for drastic action, for the reality of mixed marriages (Jews with non-Jews) had become such a deep problem that it threatened the very identity of the Jewish community. Ezra stood before Yahweh, weeping and confessing the sin of the people in marrying foreign wives and thus turning away from God. Drawn by this public display of emotional repentance, a great crowd gathered round and became convinced that the only hope lay in divorcing their foreign wives. A commission was set up to see that all mixed marriages were dissolved, and three months later the Jewish people were again pure (Ez. 9–10).

An important part of Ezra's purpose was to transform the lives of the people so that they would keep the covenant in all aspects of their daily lives, and this went beyond the dissolving of mixed marriages. He brought the people together day by day to study the Torah— and in the process Judaism was transformed into a religion centered on the study of the Torah. Ezra probably drew on his own experience in Babylon. Since there was no temple there, the Jews met at the abode of religious leaders on the Sabbath, and there they read the Torah, studied it, and applied it to their lives. It is from these kinds of meetings that over the course of the next centuries the important institution of the synagogue stemmed. Whereas the word synagogue came to mean a building, the Greek word originally referred to a religious meeting. Since these meetings took place apart from the temple, the focus was not on priestly sacrifice but on prayer and study of the Torah. To lead in studying the Torah, there developed a group of scribes capable of reading, interpreting, and applying the Torah—the teachers of Torah who later were called rabbis.

With these developments Judaism, while remaining faithful to the ideals of Israel, the people of God, took on a new look. A transition had been made from a royal nation to a community based on the Law of Moses. Now Judaism could exist with or without statehood, even scattered throughout the world. Central to life in

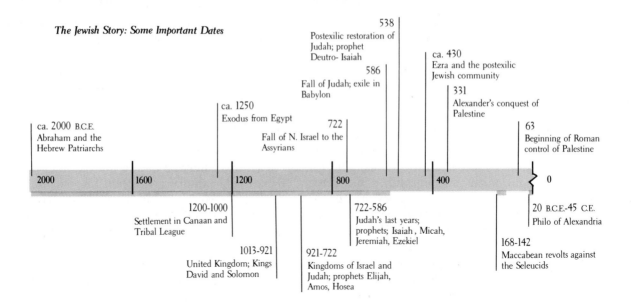

The Jewish Story: Some Important Dates

ca. 2000 B.C.E.
Abraham and the
Hebrew Patriarchs

ca. 1250
Exodus from Egypt

722
Fall of N. Israel to the
Assyrians

586
Fall of Judah; exile in
Babylon

538
Postexilic restoration of
Judah; prophet
Deutro- Isaiah

ca. 430
Ezra and the postexilic
Jewish community

331
Alexander's conquest of
Palestine

63
Beginning of Roman
control of Palestine

| 2000 | 1600 | 1200 | 800 | 400 | 0 |

1200-1000
Settlement in Canaan and
Tribal League

1013-921
United Kingdom; Kings
David and Solomon

921-722
Kingdoms of Israel and
Judah; prophets Elijah,
Amos, Hosea

722-586
Judah's last years;
prophets; Isaiah , Micah,
Jeremiah, Ezekiel

168-142
Maccabean revolts against
the Seleucids

20 B.C.E.-45 C.E.
Philo of Alexandria

the Jewish community was study of the Torah, and synagogues eventually developed wherever Jewish communities lived. Teachers of Torah became the key religious leaders, even though official religious and political power remained with the priests for a number of centuries.

The Maccabean Revolt and Roman Dominance

The next centuries were stormy years for the Jews. Great events took place, such as the war of independence against the Seleucids of Syria. Climaxing long years of Seleucid rule over Palestine, Antiochus IV, who called himself Epiphanes (The Manifest [God]), tried to Hellenize the Jews—make them accept Greek culture and religion—and thus break and destroy the Jewish religion. Around 167 B.C.E, he set up an altar of Zeus in the temple and issued laws prohibiting the distinctive Jewish practices. Led in revolution by the Maccabean family, Jewish fighters managed to drive out the Seleucids and create an independent state that lasted for the next century. Their victory culminated in

the cleansing of the desecrated temple in 165 B.C.E., an event celebrated in the festival of Hanukkah. But the Romans took over Palestine in 63 B.C.E., and Jewish national independence came to an end until about two thousand years later.

In spite of the Maccabean resistance, Hellenization did affect the Jews, especially those large numbers who lived in cities like Alexandria in Egypt, speaking Greek and following Hellenistic culture. For Jews such as these, a translation of the Hebrew scriptures into Greek was made, called the Septuagint (because seventy Jewish scholars were said to have made the translation).

A central figure among Hellenistic Jews was Philo of Alexandria (ca. 20 B.C.E.–ca. 45 C.E.). Committed to the Jewish faith, he attempted to show its correlation with the major teachings of Hellenistic philosophy. He accepted Greek philosophical ideas such as the dualism of material and spirit, and he taught that through reason the soul can be illumined by God. In order to reconcile biblical ideas with Greek philosophy, Philo made use of allegory in interpreting the Bible; the biblical stories showed the human path in overcoming the passions and seeking spiritual illumination. Abra-

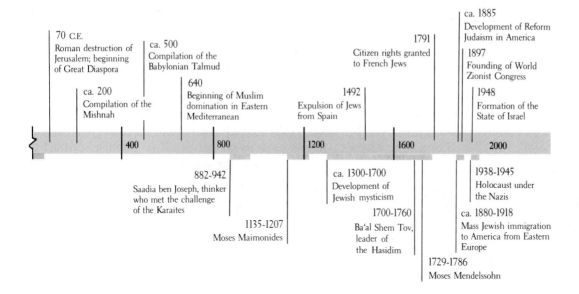

70 C.E.
Roman destruction of
Jerusalem; beginning
of Great Diaspora

ca. 200
Compilation of the
Mishnah

ca. 500
Compilation of the
Babylonian Talmud

640
Beginning of Muslim
domination in Eastern
Mediterranean

1492
Expulsion of Jews
from Spain

1791
Citizen rights granted
to French Jews

ca. 1885
Development of Reform
Judaism in America

1897
Founding of World
Zionist Congress

1948
Formation of the
State of Israel

400   800   1200   1600   2000

882-942
Saadia ben Joseph, thinker
who met the challenge
of the Karaites

1135-1207
Moses Maimonides

ca. 1300-1700
Development of
Jewish mysticism

1700-1760
Ba'al Shem Tov,
leader of
the Hasidim

1729-1786
Moses Mendelssohn

1938-1945
Holocaust under
the Nazis

ca. 1880-1918
Mass Jewish immigration
to America from Eastern
Europe

ham's journey to Palestine, for example, is an allegory of the soul's journey toward God.

During the Roman period in Palestine, Jewish groups developed that pursued different ways to live according to the Law of Moses. There were the Sadducees who made up the ruling class, the priests, and the nobility, who cooperated with the Romans and lived conservatively according to the Law. Activists called Zealots agitated for the violent overthrow of Roman dominion and the establishing of a new independent Jewish state. Separatists called Essenes withdrew from Jewish society because they considered it too corrupt; they lived in the desert near the Dead Sea and attempted to practice a "pure" Judaism. There was a group known as the Pharisees, including many scribes and teachers (rabbis), who reinterpreted the Torah in such a way as to apply it to all aspects of Jewish life. It was these Pharisees who were the forerunners of what is known as Rabbinic Judaism. And some Jews looked to Jesus of Nazareth as the messiah (the Christ) and called themselves "Christians"; these messianists eventually parted company with Judaism.

The Development of Rabbinic Judaism

An important event for the development of Rabbinic Judaism was the destruction of Jerusalem and the temple by the Romans in 70 C.E. and the scattering of the

The Western (Wailing) Wall, a most sacred site for Jews, is part of the foundation of the ancient temple. Above on the temple mount is the Muslim Dome of the Rock mosque.

Jews. This event initiated what is known as the Great Diaspora, or "scattering" of the Jews. It destroyed what had been the heart of Judaism: the temple and the Jewish community in Jerusalem. The establishment represented by the Sadducees, centered on the temple and its institutions, came to a final end. The Zealots held out at the mountain fortress Masada, near the Dead Sea, for several years; finally the whole group committed suicide rather than submit to the Romans, providing for all Jews a symbol of bravery and zeal. But this was the end of the Zealot aspiration. The Essenes were destroyed in the general upheaval. But the Pharisees scattered to other places, taking their Torah scrolls with them, setting up synagogues and schools to study the Torah. It is the rabbis of the Pharisees who continued the religion of Judaism in Palestine and beyond, structuring it as we know it today.

And so the sacred history of the Jewish people includes stories about the rabbis. A story about an important rabbi, Yohanan ben Zakkai, and his disciple, Joshua ben Hananiah, takes this view of the destruction of the temple:

> Once as Rabban Johanan ben Zakkai was coming forth from Jerusalem, Rabbi Joshua followed after him and beheld the Temple in ruins. "Woe unto us!," Rabbi Joshua cried, "that this, the place where the iniquities of Israel were atoned for, is laid waste!" "My son," Rabban Johanan said to him, "be not grieved: we have another atonement as effective as this. And what is it? It is acts of loving-kindness, as it is said, 'For I desire mercy and not sacrifice.'" (Hos. 6:6)   (AVOT DE RABBI NATAN, CH. 6)[1]

The rabbis taught that the temple was everywhere, in the home and in the heart; Jewish life has sacrifices greater than those of the temple. The Torah had commanded, "You shall be a kingdom of priests and a holy nation" (Ex. 19:6). Therefore the laws of the Torah about purity, thought by some to apply only to the temple, were to be extended to the life of every Jew in the home. The other realities of the life of Israel, God's people, were gone—the kingship, the Holy Land, and the temple. But the Torah remained. And in keeping the Torah, the Jewish community, wherever it might be, was fulfilling all the hopes and dreams of Israel, the people of God.

The Making of the Talmud

But how can the obscure, arcane, and difficult rules and commandments scattered throughout the Hebrew Torah, given in an ancient age for use in temple rituals, be "kept" by Jews living in a totally removed age and place? We can end our brief look at the essentials of the story of the founding of Judaism by hearing the rabbis on that: God has given the "oral Torah," which interprets the written Torah. According to the rabbis, at Sinai God handed down a two-part revelation: the part Moses wrote down and passed on publicly in Israel as the Torah; and the oral part, preserved by the great heroes and prophets of the past and handed on to the rabbis who finally wrote it down as the Mishnah and the Talmud. The *whole* Torah thus consists of both parts. And by studying and living according to the whole Torah, one is conforming to the very will and the way of God.

A striking Jewish notion is that the oral Torah is open-ended; new things can be discovered in the Torah. Whatever the most recent rabbi learns through proper study of the Torah can be considered as much a part of the Torah revealed to Moses as is a sentence of the Hebrew scripture itself. In that sense, learned Jews actually participate with God in the giving of the Torah. For Rabbinic Judaism, keeping the Torah becomes the key element in God's plan of salvation for the world. It is said, for example, that if all Israel would properly keep a single Sabbath, the messiah would come. If Israel would fully and completely keep Torah, all pagan rule would end.

Because of this central importance of keeping the Torah, the Jewish sacred history tells also about the great rabbis who participated in the creation and writing down of the "oral Torah" (the Talmud) as the essential guide to keeping Torah. There are, for example, the famous rabbis Hillel and Shammai in the early days of Herod's rule, who founded two houses that debated the law. Rabbi Akiba ben Joseph, tortured and martyred under the Romans for teaching the Torah, gathered much of this rabbinic material, and his disciple, Rabbi Meir, elaborated it. Eventually the material was classified and written down under the direction of the Patriarch Judah I (135–217 C.E.) and was called the Mishnah (repetition).

But the rabbinic teaching and discussion went on among rabbis in Babylon and in Palestine. These additional discussions produced many further teachings and commentaries on the Mishnah known collectively as the Gemara (completion) or Talmud (instruction). By the end of the fifth century C.E., the Gemara was also written down and added to the Mishnah. Eventually the whole set of writings became known as the Talmud (existing in both a Babylonian and a Palestinean version). We can close this brief look at the Jewish story by noting that the creation of the Talmud, the "oral Torah," is one of the essential elements in the story that provides identity for Jews.

SOME HISTORICAL TRANSFORMATIONS OF JUDAISM

Not long after the Babylonian Talmud was completed, providing a complete structure for Jewish life, the Islamic revolution burst onto the scene. For quite a few centuries the centers of Jewish life were in Muslim lands: Baghdad (in Babylonia), Egypt, North Africa, and Spain. The Middle Ages were full of suffering and persecution, although Jewish life continued to develop and flourish. With the Enlightenment came the beginnings of Jewish emancipation, and Judaism developed in new ways to meet the challenges of the modern age.

Jewish Life and Thought in Islamic Contexts

Muhammad respected the Jews as a "people of the book," seeing himself as the last of the line of prophets. Few Jews followed Muhammad's new revelation, but generally Muslims allowed Jews to live peacefully within the vast territories taken over by the rapid Islamic expansion. As Muhammad and his successors were establishing dominion over all of western Asia, North Africa, and Spain, Jews in these lands continued to look to the Jewish academies in Babylonia for leadership. As new situations arose, they submitted questions to the rabbinic leaders (Geonim) of these academies, who provided answers (*responsa*) with new interpretations of the Talmud. Through their *responsa*, these scholars fixed the pattern of Jewish worship and life.

During this time, Islamic scholars held the intellectual leadership of the world, translating the whole corpus of Greek scientific and philosophical thought into Arabic. A number of Jewish thinkers were attracted to this new learning, but there were also reactions against it. For several centuries Jewish thinkers struggled with the problem of faith and reason: is truth acquired by one's own reason and judgment, or simply from the authoritative revelation of the Torah?

The Challenge of the Karaites

A crisis appeared in the eighth century when a group arose to challenge the whole conception of the Talmud as the oral Torah. The Karaites (scripturalists) demanded that scripture alone be the guide for life, rejecting the centuries of accumulated rabbinic interpretation. In part the Karaites were rebelling against the authority of the Geonim, reflecting the feeling of some that the rabbinic scholars had grown distant and unresponsive. Operating in Arabic rather than Aramaic (the Talmudic language), they also were influenced by groups in the Islamic community that emphasized reason rather than established authority.

The Karaites appealed to the individual's reasoned interpretation rather than to rabbinic authority, offering simple, direct understandings of the injunctions of the Torah. For example, since Exodus 35:3 prohibited the kindling of fires on the Sabbath, the Karaites held that Jews should spend the whole Sabbath in the cold and darkness—against the rabbinic interpretation that fires can be used (although not kindled) on the Sabbath. They rejected ritual objects such as phylacteries and festivals such as Hanukkah, because they were not mentioned in scripture but rather constructed by the rabbis. Trying to break away from the Talmudic rabbis, they set up a community in Jerusalem, and their influence spread throughout the Jewish communities, posing a threat to rabbinic Judaism.

The challenge of the Karaites was met by thinkers like Saadia ben Joseph (882–942), head of the Sura academy in Babylonia. Trained in Hebrew and Arabic learning, he provided an Arabic translation of the Hebrew Bible. He was also learned in philosophy and was able to assure Jews that there was no conflict between revelation and the kind of reasoning used by the rabbis. God has endowed humans with the ability to reach truth through reason, he taught, although revelation contained a higher, uncorrupted form of truth. Saadia's counterattack was successful; the influence of the Karaites waned rapidly, and the Talmudic tradition held sway.

Jewish Philosophy: Maimonides

Troubled times came to the Muslim lands in Asia, and when some Muslims conquered Spain and established the Umayyad dynasty of Cordoba, the center of Jewish life gravitated westward from Babylon to Spain. There a brilliant Jewish culture developed under a tolerant Muslim rule. The golden age of Spanish Jewry, from about the ninth to the eleventh centuries, included substantial contact with the Arab philosophical schools, and Jewish thinkers took up philosophical questions seriously for the first time since Philo. There was considerable resistance in some quarters to the use of such Greek philosophical rationalism, for the work of the Talmudic thinkers had always been considered the highest form of reasoning. The great writer Judah Halevi (1075–1141), for example, used his considerable literary powers to provide a lyrical defense of traditional Jewish piety. He insisted that Aristotle's speculative God is not the same as the God of Abraham; religious truth is to be found in the words of those who stood at Mt. Sinai rather than in speculative philosophy.

Moses Maimonides (Moses ben Maimon, 1135–1204) was born in Spain as times were becoming more troubled for Jews there. Muslims were rousing themselves to meet the challenge of the Christian crusades, and Jews were being forced to convert to Islam. So Maimonides's family migrated to Morocco, then to Palestine, and eventually to Egypt, where he became a brilliant Talmudic scholar and also physician to the Egyptian ruler. His great work was to attempt to reconcile the revealed scriptures of Judaism and the intellectual basis of Aristotelian philosophy. In fact, he felt that philosophical reason could provide the key to understanding the revealed scripture.

His influential book, *Guide for the Perplexed*, written in Arabic, gave a rational definition of the essential faith of Judaism, unlike the traditional rabbinic teachings that emphasized conduct rather than rationalized doctrines. His famous thirteen principles of the Jewish faith, although not attaining the status of a creed in

After public school classes each day, this Jewish boy studies at a Torah school in Jerusalem.

Judaism, have been enormously influential and are included in the standard prayer books. They are:

1. The existence of God, the creator.
2. God's unity.
3. God's incorporeality.
4. God's eternity.
5. The obligation to worship God alone.
6. The truth of the words of the prophets.
7. The superiority of the prophecy of Moses.
8. The Torah as God's revelation to Moses.
9. The immutability of the Torah.
10. God's omniscience.
11. Retribution in this world and the next.
12. The coming of the Messiah.
13. The resurrection of the dead.

In his view of the relationship between reason and revelation, Maimonides held that the scriptural prophecy consisted of a harmonious flow of reason and inspiration from God to the human mind. The prophecy of Moses was different in kind from the rest, for it was a perfect expression of God's will. Maimonides accepted Aristotle's proof for the existence of God, and he was particularly interested to show God's incorporeality; God could not be one if he occupied a body. He dealt with the problem of biblical anthropomorphisms (descriptions of God in human form) by allegorizing them; for example, God's "voice" is not to be taken literally but as a symbol of rational prophetic understanding. But he rejected Aristotle's idea of the eternity of the world, for that went against the biblical idea of creation.

As to the various laws of the Torah, Maimonides saw much practical benefit in them. The laws prescribing animal sacrifice weaned the Jews away from worshiping pagan gods; the dietary laws kept people from gluttony; and circumcision was a way of keeping sexual desire under control. Keeping the Torah, for Maimonides, contributed toward a decent, humane society. He thought of the messianic age as a time when humans could devote themselves to philosophical study, drawing closer to the knowledge of God.

Maimonides was very influential in his own times and ever since, even though his kind of rationalism did not win wide acceptance. His God of the philosophers was too rational for intimate relationship, and he was criticized for not including the idea of love in his philosophical system. A different kind of Jewish response to the increasingly rigid Talmudic structures and the challenge of rationalism had been building up for some time, with emphasis on the religious experience of the heart, and this burst forth in the form of Jewish mysticism.

Mysticism and the Kabbalah

Close communion with God based on inner experience was integral to Judaism from the beginning. Moses on Mt. Sinai, face to face with God as he received the Torah, is a primary example of the inner, mystical experience of closeness to God. Further, there are poets like David in psalmic ecstasy and prophets like Jeremiah caught up in intimate communion with God's will. Ezekiel's vision of the chariot on which was enthroned the "appearance of the likeness of the glory of the Lord" (Ezek. 1:4–29) was especially considered the paradigm of the mystical, inner experience of God.

In the medieval period, Jewish mysticism spread and took the form of the Kabbalah (tradition). Mysticism had developed together with the Talmud, in the form of popular oral traditions, and it held an important place in Judaism from the twelfth to the seventeenth centuries. Advocates of the Kabbalah considered it equal to the Torah, but its meaning was open only to initiates. The Kabbalah was an esoteric (inner) form of biblical interpretation that looked for the inner, secretive meaning of the text. Based on the notion that the Hebrew scriptures contained all divine truth, it found every word, letter, number, and accent of the Hebrew text to have some inner significance.

The central work of the Kabbalah was called the *Zohar* (splendor), written as a mystical commentary on the Torah. Using an esoteric method of interpretation, the Zohar portrays a grand vision of God's relation to the world. God as the ultimate reality is En Sof, completely transcendent and beyond all human thought. But from the En Sof come ten emanations (*sefirot*), and these represent God's presence within the created spheres. Something of God is in every human, and therefore by living pious lives according to the Torah, Jews can assist in restoring the fullness of God and of the whole universe. Such a vision, which took a variety of forms, fascinated many Jewish mystics and left an important print on Judaism. It also had a strong influence on certain medieval Christian thinkers. The mystics dealt with the same issues as the philosophers: the nature of God, creation, exile and restoration, good and evil. Their vision had a wide appeal, and they stimulated expectation of the restoration through the messiah, providing meaning and hope to many who lived in difficult circumstances.

Tragedy and Response in Christian Medieval Europe

At the same time that Jewish culture flourished under Muslim rule, Jewish settlements were slowly spreading into Christian Europe. Already in the Roman period Jews were brought to Italy and Greece and other parts. With the triumph of Christianity Jews came under certain restrictions, but Charlemagne (crowned emperor of the Holy Roman Empire in 800 C.E.) saw the important contribution that Jews could make to the economic and scholarly life of the empire and encouraged their immigration. These Jews of Germany and France eventually became known as Ashkenazim, whereas the Jews of Spain and the Mediterranean areas became known as Sephardim.

Crusades and Persecutions

Jewish life and scholarship flourished in France and Germany. But a fateful day, November 26, 1095, brought a change that colored Jewish life indelibly. On that day Pope Urban II preached a sermon calling on Christians to recover the Holy Land from the infidel (the Muslim Turks). For the next two centuries a series of crusades aroused Christian religious passions and nearly always led to attacks on and massacres of Jews in communities throughout Europe—initiating a long, tragic period of Jewish persecution that went on for many centuries and was revived even in the twentieth century.

Aroused by the crusades, popular religious passions enflamed against the Jews under a variety of pretexts. They were frequently accused of the ritual murder of a Christian, using the blood to bake unleavened bread for Passover—this blood-libel charge continued into the twentieth century. Another accusation was that of desecrating the sacred host (the consecrated bread, which was understood to be transformed into the body of Christ in the celebration of the Mass); Jews were often charged with stealing the sacred bread and tormenting Christ by piercing and pounding it. In times of plague, Jews were accused of poisoning wells of Christians or performing other forms of evil sorcery. If there were no other pretext, people could always be aroused against the Jews by the reminder that they were the killers of Christ. Beginning with Pope Inocent III and the Fourth Lateran Council in 1215, Jews were forced to wear distinctive badges and endure many other indignities. From the fourteenth through the sixteenth centuries, Jews were expelled from almost every European nation, sometimes a number of times.

The Story of the Marranos

The story of Spanish Jewry is especially tragic. When massacres broke out in 1391, many Spanish Jews, unlike Jews throughout the rest of Europe, accepted Christian baptism and thus became equals of the Christian people. These "New Christians," called Marranos (pigs), remained Jewish at heart and kept Jewish practices secretly as much as possible. As they thrived amid their Christian neighbors, new outbreaks of hostility occurred, and Queen Isabella set up the special tribunal for hunting out and punishing heretic Christians—the dreaded Inquisition. The first *auto da fe* (Act of Faith) in 1481 burned six men and women of Jewish extraction, and many thousands more were tortured and executed over the next few decades. Professing non-Christian Jews still lived in Spain—but in 1492 Isabella and Ferdinand signed a decree expelling all Jews from Spain, a crowning tragedy for Spanish Jewry. Many went to neighboring Portugal, where again they were forced to become Christian by the brutal means of their children being seized and baptized. Great massacres occurred, such as the killing of 2,000 New Christians in Lisbon in April 1506.

The Marranos and other Spanish Jews, fleeing these persecutions, made their way to many parts of the world, taking their special Jewish culture with them, including their language Ladino (Hebraeo-Spanish). They went to Italy, England, France, the Netherlands, and Germany. Some migrated to the New World—to Brazil, Mexico, and Peru (followed even there by the Inquisition). In 1654 some Marranos from Brazil became the first Jews to immigrate to the area of the future United States. Other Marranos went to Turkey, Palestine, and Syria.

Renaissance and Ghetto

The Renaissance in Germany and Italy included the active participation of many Jews as scientists and scholars. There was a Hebrew renaissance that strongly influenced Christian thinkers such as Pico della Mirandola, Martin Luther, and John Calvin. As the leader of the Christian Reformation in its initial stage, Luther was at first attracted to the Jews, but twenty years later he turned against them with savage verbal attacks, just as he also castigated the Turks and the Papists.

The counterreformation of the Roman Catholic Church, with the church on the defensive, revived the old anti-Jewish laws, including the wearing of the badge. In 1555 Pope Paul IV forced Jews to live in Jewish quarters on certain streets, surrounded by high walls with the gates closed at night. These quarters were called ghettos, named after the Jewish quarter in Venice, the Ghetto Nuovo (new foundry). Of course, living in the ghetto afforded some protection to Jews from hostile people outside. And the ghetto acted as a conserver of Jewish solidarity and culture.

There was hardly any limit to the indignities the Jews were forced to bear. Their costume was regulated and their children were snatched away for baptism. They were forbidden to ride in carriages or employ Christian servants, and they were often denied the right to marry. They were forced to pay special tolls, take degrading oaths in court, attend conversionist sermons, and run stripped nearly naked in carnival races. But in the midst of this demeaning ghetto life, Jewish culture was shaped and even flourished.

Jewish Life in Eastern Europe

Jews had been living in eastern Europe for many centuries, but with the expansion of German communities into Poland came many more Jews. In the late Middle Ages, the persecutions in Germany and western Europe brought hundreds of thousands of Ashkenazic Jews to Poland and the surrounding Slavonic territories. It was there in eastern Europe that the heart of Jewish civilization was nurtured for a number of centuries up to the modern age. The Jewish community usually lived in towns or villages (shetls), complete with synagogues, rabbis, holy days and festivals, weddings and funerals—everything that makes up the complete Jewish way of life. Self-governing, autonomous, with uneasy arrangements with peasant neighbors, Jews were able to preserve their own values, language (Yiddish), institutions, and culture in full vigor, without being integrated into the Polish or Russian community at large. Jewish learning and scholarship were vigorously cultivated, especially the method of Talmudic interpretation called *pilpul*—special mental gynastics centered on the text. Every town had an academy and distinguished scholars, and the town prided itself on the number of young men devoted to the study of the Torah and the Talmud.

But tragedy followed the Jews of eastern Europe also. Beginning with the Cossack rebellion of 1648–1651, when some 200,000 Jews were slaughtered, Jews of Poland and the Ukraine underwent centuries of persecution, leading up to the pogroms of the 1880s and finally the Nazi Holocaust. The tide of refugees began to swell again, this time westward into the German states—and finally also to Palestine and to America.

A significant response to life in eastern Europe was the popular mystical revivalist movement of the Hasidim, founded by Israel ben Eliezer (1700–1760), known as the BESHT or Ba'al Shem Tov (Master of the Good Name). He taught that religious feeling and piety were more important than scholarship, and that each individual, no matter how poor or ignorant, could commune with God by spiritual exaltation and abandonment of self. There are certain Zaddikim (Righteous Ones), he taught, who are very close to God and carry on the leadership of the Hasidim (pious ones), as the disciples of the BESHT called themselves. They held large gatherings devoted to song and ecstatic dancing and feasting, spreading this revivalist movement throughout the Jewish communities of eastern Europe, attracting many Jews who were disillusioned with the rigid intellectualism of the Talmudic rabbis. In reaction, the traditional rabbinic leaders tried to expel those of the Hasidic movement. But gradually both sides became more moderate and tolerant, and the Hasidim, now numbered by the hundreds of thousands, took their place as a legitimate part of the Jewish way of life. Through the Hasidim, the emotional, poetic, and mystical dimension of religion was reinforced within Judaism and has strongly influenced many down to the present day.

Emancipation, Enlightenment, and the Modern Age

The emancipation of the Jews throughout Europe was the great development of the early modern age, ushered in by the Enlightenment of the eighteenth century. Enlightenment thinkers considered differences of race and religion to be mere accidents, thus opening the way to emancipation of the Jews and their full participation in society. Of course, age-old prejudices could not be swept away by mere ideas. It took drastic changes like the French Revolution of 1789 to make the decisive breach and bring down the walls of the ghetto.

Jewish Involvement in the Enlightenment

The Enlightenment (Haskalah) form of Judaism emerged in the eighteenth century, alongside traditional Talmudic Judaism and Hasidism, and it is well represented by Moses Mendelssohn (1729–1786). Born at Dessau in Germany in a medieval Jewish ghetto, he paid the special Jewish toll to enter the gate of Berlin and thus symbolically brought the Jewish community into the modern world. After studying in Berlin, he won a prize from the Prussian Academy of Sciences for the best philosophical essay, and immediately he was accepted and courted by the enlightened intellectuals of Prussian society. The writer Gotthold Ephraim Lessing, for example, was a close friend and modeled his *Nathan der Weise* after Mendelssohn. This enlightened, modern Jewish thinker brought together two strands that had heretofore been totally separate: traditional Jewish life and ritual, on the one hand, and enlightened scientific thought, on the other. Mendels-

sohn attempted to build a bridge between Judaism and Christian Germany by providing an interpretation of Judaism as a rational system of ethics thoroughly compatible with modern scientific thought. Moving away from Yiddish, he made a translation of the Torah in excellent German, with a commentary in pure Hebrew. Thus he provided an impetus for Jews to pursue both Germanic studies and modern Herbrew letters, transcending the ghetto boundaries of Yiddish (Hebraeo-German).

The Jews of the Enlightenment, like Mendelssohn, had to perform a balancing act. Mendelssohn remained a loyal Jew practicing his religion, but he also participated fully in the intellectual life of the Enlightenment. His fellow Jews wondered about his rationalism and rejection of everything mystical, and his philosophical colleagues wondered about his continued practice of Jewish tradition. As the age of the Enlightenment ended with pressures of reaction and nationalism, Jews increasingly had to come down more decisively on one basis or the other, as exemplified by Mendelssohn's own children—either as Jews, or baptized as Christians, or as free thinkers.

Many Jews of the nineteenth century participated in the revolutionary movements sweeping Europe, which established constitutional governments, and with this they were granted full emancipation as citizens. This, however, was accompanied by ever more vicious reactions and new outbreaks of hostility from their fellow citizens. Now that the religious basis of persecution became less persuasive, the prejudices were transferred to other grounds—national, ethnic, or "racial"—culminating in the anti-Semitism of the late nineteenth and twentieth centuries with its tragic, shattering consequences.

Reform, Orthodox, Conservative, Reconstructionist

Many Jews, especially in eastern Europe, retained the traditional Jewish life with little substantial change or question. But in western Europe and later in America leading Jewish thinkers responded to the Enlightenment, the scientific progress, and the industrial revolution, with new proposals for change in the traditional Jewish way of life—or impassioned defenses of that life. Their proposals and responses created the main forms of Judaism today.

The movement called Reform Judaism started in Germany as Jewish thinkers, influenced by Mendelssohn, attempted to modify traditional Jewish practice in keeping with the ideas and realities of modern scientific, secular life. With Abraham Geiger (1810–1874) taking the lead, these Jews advocated changes such as using German in the synagogue, men and women sitting together, organ music, and modification of dietary restrictions to better fit the modern age. By dropping or modifying practices that had ancient roots but did not fit the sensitivities of the modern age, the eternal meaning and message of Judaism could shine through for modern people. Geiger argued that Judaism changes with each age, reflecting God's progressive revelation in history. What was appropriate for one age might no longer fit in another. These Reform Jews emphasized the ethical dimensions of Judaism more than the ritualistic aspects, and they rejected the idea that the messianic age would mean a return to Zion. Rather, the goal of peace and harmony should be pursued in the European nations to which these emancipated Jews had dedicated themselves.

As German immigrants to America swelled in the midnineteenth century, Reform Judaism was firmly established. An early Reform document, the Pittsburgh Platform of 1885, stated that only the moral laws of Judaism were binding, and only such ceremonies that elevate life in modern civilization should be retained. Thus most dietary laws went out, and the traditional prayer shawl and head covering became obsolete. In recent decades Reform Judaism has moved to recover more of the traditional Jewish liturgies and practices, in keeping with the need of Jews today to establish their Jewish identity in our thoroughly secularized society.

Some Jews in Europe were uneasy with the radical changes brought about in Reform Judaism and the arguments based on enlightened, rational grounds. This moderate movement, later known in America as Conservative Judaism, was led especially by Zecharias Frankel (1801–1875) in Germany and later in America by Solomon Schechter (1847–1915). Judaism has indeed changed over the centuries, they acknowledged, but such changes have always developed from the liv-

A Jewish woman reading the Torah in New York City.

ing experience of the Jewish people as they centered their lives on the traditional rituals, which, Frankel argued, form the very soul of Judaism.

In America the Conservative movement was swelled by the arrival of a large wave of immigrants from Russia at the end of the nineteenth century. These immigrants shied away from the modernized Reform synagogues and were attracted to the Conservative congregations, which kept many of the traditional rituals but opened doors for the newly arrived Jews to begin the move into American society.

A Jewish movement born in America grew from Conservative Judaism. From the distinctive teachings of Mordecai Kaplan, professor at Conservative

Judaism's Jewish Theological Seminary, came Reconstructionist Judaism. Kaplan construed Judaism as a civilization that evolved to serve the needs of the Jewish people. The rituals, laws, literature, art, folkways, values, and ideals of Judaism should be "reconstructed" to provide the highest degree of Jewish self-realization. Whereas the Reconstructionist movement is small, its ideals have influenced Reform and Conservative Jews considerably.

The challenge of modern, enlightened Judaism both in its Reform and Conservative forms called forth a strong reaction in Europe and America in the form of the Orthodox movement, led especially by Rabbi Samson Raphael Hirsch (1808–1888) in Germany, who believed that Jews had to retain their total adherence to Jewish law even as they participated in the life of secular society. Hirsch and the other Orthodox leaders attempted to interpret the tradition so that it would be more attractive to enlightened modern people, but they insisted on the divine authority of the entire Torah and the necessity of observing all the traditional rituals. This, Hirsch argued, was the way God had revealed for the training of the authentic Jewish person, and abandoning any part of the traditional practices amounted to a betrayal of Judaism.

In America the arrival of hundreds of thousands of Jewish immigrants from eastern Europe at the beginning of the twentieth century, with whole communities in New York speaking Yiddish and carrying on the traditional Jewish way of life, augmented the Orthodox movement. Small communities of Hasidic Jews are also considered part of Orthodoxy in America. Orthodox Judaism is especially strong in the state of Israel.

Zionism, Holocaust, and State of Israel

Toward the end of the nineteenth century, the modern movement of Zionism arose with the goal of Jewish national liberation. The pogroms of Russia caused many Jews to look for respite in a Jewish homeland, and in western Europe emancipated Jews became disillusioned with the continuation of persecutions and discrimination. One sobering event was the Dreyfus trial in 1894. Alfred Dreyfus, a Jew in the French Army, was falsely convicted of treason in a blatantly anti-Semitic court proceeding, showing dramatically the precarious position of Jews even in a modern European society. Theodore Herzl (1860–1904) of Vienna provided an impetus for Zionism by writing an influential book, *The Jewish State*, and organizing the World Zionist Congress (1897). He and others felt that only in a state with Jewish sovereignty could Jews finally end their homelessness and shape their own destiny.

Some Jews (like Herzl himself) were indifferent to the location of the Jewish state. But many Jews especially from eastern Europe began to advocate Palestine as the only place for the Jewish homeland, where the historic Jewish way of life, steeped in the biblical values and ethos, could be preserved and cultivated. Jews began immigrating to Palestine, helped by the Jewish National Fund with contributions from Zionist Jews through the world. Not all Jews at this time were Zionists. Reform Jews tended to prefer assimilation within the national societies, and some Orthodox groups felt the restoration of Zion could take place only with the coming of the Messiah. But history itself gave the answer to the problem, with the Nazi Holocaust destroying European Jewry and providing the definitive answer for almost all Jews of today: the Jewish homeland is essential so that this will never again happen to the Jewish people.

The Holocaust, as the great modern example of humanity gone amuck, has evoked a number of responses among Jews of today. Some have spoken of the eclipse of God, the hiding of God's face in these tragic events. More radical thinkers speak of the death of God and hold that it is no longer possible to believe in God "after Auschwitz" (one of the Nazi death camps). Still others attempt to reinterpret divine providence in the face of this modern outburst of evil. One survivor of the Holocaust, Elie Wiesel, says that it is better to keep silent than to try to explain the unexplainable; he simply tells the story so that humankind will not forget. For many, both Jews and non-Jews, the Holocaust has become a symbol for the unthinkable inhumanity that can be unleashed by humans, a portent of the holocaust being prepared in the nuclear arms race.

One immediate effect of the Holocaust was the impetus given to the creation of the state of Israel. Jewish refugees fled the devastation of Europe and migrated in increasing numbers to Palestine, joining Jewish communities established there in the earlier phases of the Zionist movement. Supported by Jews all over the world, these Jews declared Israel to be an independent state in 1948, a Jewish state that would forever be a homeland for all Jews. The Jewish state has had a troubled history since that time with many clashes with the Palestinians and surrounding Arab states. But here in the biblical land Jewish identity has been forged anew. The biblical language of Hebrew is heard again, now as a modern language. The age-old festivals are celebrated, and the full Talmudic way of life is made possible once again. Of course, many Jews have become secularized, and many live elsewhere in the world. But for all of them the state of Israel helps provide a link with the traditions of Judaism and a guarantee that the Jewish people have survived and will continue to exist as the people of God in the eternal covenant.

DISCUSSION QUESTIONS

1. How do events of long ago—the Exodus and the covenant at Mt. Sinai—still provide identity for Jews today?

2. How was the covenant relationship between Israel and their God different from the way other peoples of the ancient Near East understood their relationship to their gods?

3. In what ways does the history of ancient Israel reflect the sense of a covenant "struggle" between Israel and God?

4. Why may Ezra be called the "founder" of Judaism?

5. What is the origin of the oral Torah (the Mishnah and Talmud), and what is its significance in Judaism?

6. Do you think there is any relationship between Christian treatment of the Jews in the medieval period and the Holocaust in the Nazi era? What is it?

7. What are the strong points of each of the modern American Jewish movements for presenting a viable and strong Judaism for the modern age?

8. Do you think preserving the state of Israel is an essential mission for Judaism today?

CHAPTER 5

Jewish Worlds of Meaning

ULTIMATE REALITY: ONE GOD AS CREATOR, REVEALER, AND REDEEMER

"What's it *all* about?" Modern historical study of the Tanakh has outlined the development of monotheism in the religion of ancient Israel. Jewish tradition, of course, accepts monotheism as a basic tenet of the Torah. The religion of Abraham and the ancestors of Israel was not monotheistic, according to the stories in Genesis, but a distinctive practice was the worship of the clan God, the "God of the Father"; later Yahweh, the God of Israel, was identified with "the God of the Fathers."

But even Yahweh, discussed in Chapter 4, was not at first known as the only God of all. Other gods of the land were also important for life and growth, so Israelite devotion was split between Yahweh and the fertility gods, Ba'al and Asherah. From another perspective, the religion of many early Israelites was henotheistic: Yahweh was their God to whom they must be loyal, avoiding the gods of other peoples. Since other nations had their own gods, at first the Israelites did not think of Yahweh as powerful over all peoples; those other peoples with their gods were hostile to Yahweh and Yahweh's people.

The Development of Monotheism

Through this struggle with other peoples and their gods, and through their own conflict over worshiping Yahweh and the fertility gods, the people of Israel came to understand the extent of Yahweh's power and presence in the world. They ultimately came to the conviction that their covenant God, Yahweh, was the one God of all nature and of all peoples.

Yahweh vs. Ba'al

The stories of the prophet Elijah (I Kgs. 17–22), who lived in the northern kingdom of Israel in the ninth century B.C.E., highlight the struggle between allegiance to Yahweh and worship of Ba'al, the god of the land. Since Ba'al was believed to be the god in charge of life-giving rain, Elijah issued a challenge right on Ba'al's front doorstep: "As Yahweh the God of Israel lives, whose servant I am, I swear that there will be neither dew nor rain these years unless I give the word" (I Kgs. 17:1). The drought lasted three years, until finally Elijah showed Ba'al up to be powerless in his great contest with the prophets of Ba'al on Mt. Carmel—and only then did Yahweh send rain. The story tells dramatically that Yahweh, not Ba'al, has the power to withhold rain and to grant it for the growth of the crops.

The prophet Hosea provides another viewing of the struggle between Yahweh and Ba'al in Israel's religious practices. From Hosea we learn that many Israelites participated in worship at Ba'al shrines, involving sexual religious rituals, offering raisin cakes to images of Ba'al, and the like—fertility rituals to promote the

growth of the crops and the well-being of the people. Hosea himself, on orders from Yahweh, married a cult prostitute and had children by her to dramatize the relation between Yahweh and the covenant people. Through him it was forcefully demonstrated that Israel had broken the covenant with Yahweh, saying instead, "Let me go after my lovers, who provide me my bread and my water, my wool and my flax, my oil and my drink" (Hos. 2:5). Hosea portrays Yahweh lamenting like a rejected lover: "She does not know that I am the one who gave her the grain, the new wine, and the oil, that I lavished silver upon her and gold which they used for Ba'al" (2:8). But Yahweh does not give up on Israel, planning to punish them in order to turn them back:

> I will punish her for the days of the Ba'als,
>> in which she burned incense to them,
>> and decked herself with her rings and her jewelry.
> For she ran after her lovers,
>> but she forgot me, says Yahweh.
> But now, listen, I will alure her,
>> I will go into the wilderness with her
>> and speak lovingly to her.
> And I will give vineyards to her there,
>> the Valley of Achor becoming a gateway of hope.
> Then she will respond there as in the time of her youth,
>> as when she went up out of Egypt.
> And on that day, says Yahweh, you shall call me "My Husband";
>> you will no more call me "My Ba'al."   (2:10–16)

Through the prophets, by such poignant images and actions as these, a new, deeper understanding of Yahweh grew in Israel. The realm of nature, fertility, and growth was not controlled by the Ba'als, or even shared by Yahweh and other gods of nature. Rather, the exclusive power and presence of Yahweh, Israel's covenant God, was felt in all areas of their existence. It was Yahweh who sent the corn at the harvest, the wine at the vintage; the Ba'als should be forgotten and never mentioned again.

Yahweh, God of All the Nations

As Israel began to understand that Yahweh has power over all aspects of human existence, so also they struggled to overcome the limitations of a henotheistic view. At one time it was accepted that one could not worship Yahweh outside the land of Israel: "How can we sing the song of Yahweh in a foreign land?" asks one of the psalms used among the exiles in Babylon (Ps. 137:4). As late as the Babylonian exile, some Jewish exiles lost heart because they believed this catastrophe had proved that Marduk, the god of Babylon, was more powerful and had defeated Yahweh. But the prophets drew out the implications of their faith, extending the sphere of Yahweh's power to all nations. Amos insisted that Yahweh had brought not only Israel from Egypt, but also the Philistines from Caphtor and the Aramaeans from Kir; and when any of these peoples commit crimes, it is Yahweh who punishes them (Amos 9:7; 1:3–2:3). The prophet Isaiah saw the invading armies of the Assyrians as Yahweh's "rod of anger" sent against the Israelites (Isa. 10:5). And Second Isaiah, the prophet of the Babylonian exile, went so far as to describe mighty King Cyrus of the Persians as "the anointed one of Yahweh," whom Yahweh had taken by the hand to subdue nations before him (Isa. 45:1).

In the vision of these prophets, Yahweh is no tribal God sharing power with other divine beings. The God of the covenant has universal power as the only God. Second Isaiah in particular stated eloquently the vision of a full-blown monotheism, ridiculing images of the gods that are powerless, insisting over and over that Yahweh is the one God, the creator and director of all:

> To whom can you liken God,
> > or what sort of likeness can you compare to him?
> . . .
> He is the one who sits throned on the vault of earth,
> > with its inhabitants like grasshoppers.
> He is the one who stretches out the heavens like a curtain,
> > and he spreads them out like a tent to live in.
> He is the one who reduces the princes to nothing,
> > he makes the earth's rulers as nought.
> > > > > (ISA. 40:18, 22–23)
> Thus says Yahweh, the king of Israel,
> > their redeemer, Yahweh of hosts:
> I am the first, and I am the last,
> > and beside me there is no God! (ISA. 44:6)

Not only Jews but also Christians and Muslims draw from this fundamental ancient Israelite vision of the Lord of Israel as the one God of all the earth, as expressed in the stories of the Tanakh.

The Jewish Vision of the One God

For over 2,000 years devout Jews have recited the Shema twice daily: "Hear, O Israel! The Lord our God, the Lord is One" (Deut. 6:4). Nothing in Jewish life is more hallowed than the saying of these words. These are the last words to come from the lips of the dying Jew and from the lips of those Jews who are present at that moment. This short credal statement shows that it is the *unity* of God that is the fundamental theological assertion of Judaism. By and large Jews have not tended to develop systematic theology, that is, rational doctrines about God. Rather than defining God, they relate to God through worship and through life. But they know that the most important doctrine about God is that God is One.

God as One and Unique

The Shema means, first of all, that God is not many. All forms of polytheism are rejected, for that tears God apart and thus also tears the world and humankind apart. Since God is one, all of reality is also a unified order, and there can be one universal law of righteousness that holds sway over all. No one is excluded from the rule of God, for there are no other gods.

The Shema also means that God is one, not two or three. At the time Rabbinic Judaism was developing, the Persian religion of Zoroastrianism was powerful, with a somewhat dualistic conception of reality: Ahura Mazda (Ohrmazd) is the God of goodness and light, but the realm of evil and darkness is controlled by the spirit Angra Mainyu (Ahriman). Such a theory is a handy explanation for the existence of evil in the world, and it was attractive also to some Jews and Christians. But the rabbis insisted that any thought of a divine power in competition to God had to be squelched. Further, of course, Jews cannot accept the Christian idea that God is triune, Father, Son, and Spirit. The problem is not so much different aspects of the one God, but the Christian insistence on the incarnation of God in the man Jesus.

It is true that Jews have some sense of different aspects or modes of operation of God. The Tanakh often speaks of God's "spirit," "presence," "angel," or "glory" being present with the people. In the Middle Ages Jewish mystics worked out a vision of God that contained both unity and diversity. God purely in God-self is *En Sof*, absolute and without limit. But the pure Godhead cannot be known to humans, so God is manifested in ten emanations known as the sefirot; God emerges from concealment in such a way that creatures can experience the divine reality. Many Jews have been uncomfortable with this Kabbalistic idea of God, but it does show that humans experience the one hidden God through various modes of God's self-revelation.

But saying that God is one is not just a matter of arithmetic. The Hebrew word for "one" (*ehad*) also means "unique," the one who is unlike any other. God is different from anything humans might name as gods or create as gods. From this sense of God's uniqueness arose the strict prohibition in Judaism against making any images or likenesses of God—for God is not like anything else. All else is made; God is not. All else changes; God does not. All else has rivals and comparables; God does not.

God as Transcendent and as Immanent

Another way of putting this is to say that God is *transcendent*, that is, far above and beyond the created world. In total contrast to everything that has been created in time and space, God is eternal with no beginning or end. God has no limitations of space or knowledge or power, being present everywhere, all-knowing, and all-powerful. Using terms like these, Jews point to the complete *other*-ness of God.

But to say that God is transcendent is only half the story. Jews also hold firmly to the conviction that God is not just a God far off, but a God near as well. God is *immanent*, near and present to all creatures. The Tanakh tells how God's "spirit" or "presence" went with the people on their wanderings. Though the highest heaven cannot contain God, still the Israelites concretely felt the presence of God dwelling in their midst in the temple at Jerusalem. The rabbis spoke especially of God's Shekhinah (from the root *shakhan*, to dwell), that is, the divine Presence that filled the Israelite tent of meeting and that fills all the world as well.

Thus God, the almighty creator, is immanent and at work within the processes of creation. The ongoing creator and sustainer of all continues at work, knowing when even a sparrow falls, giving food to each and every living thing. As creator, God is also the lawgiver, the source of natural law to which the world conforms and also of the moral law that guides human life. God is the director of history, unfolding the eternal will in the drama of the history of the sacred people and the whole world.

But God is also present in a *personal* way, according to Jews. Whereas the human idea of person in inadequate to describe God, we have no better word to designate the experience of meeting God as a helper, a redeemer, and a friend. God is one who loves the chosen people, as taught in countless ways by the rabbis. One of the favorite names for God that Jews use is "Our Father" (*abenu*). A Talmudic passage emphasizes the personal presence of God:

> Come and see how beloved Israel is before God; for wherever they went into exile the Shekhinah went with them. When they were exiled to Egypt, the Shekhinah went with them; in Babylon the Shekhinah was with them; and in the future, when Israel will be redeemed, the Shekhinah will be with them. (MEG. 29a)[1]

God and the Puzzle of Evil

The puzzle of evil casts a long shadow in the world, and Jews have known a large share of persecution and suffering. If there is one God, and God is both the almighty creator and a present loving father, what sense can be made of evil and suffering?

Since the times of Israel of old, Jews have struggled with this question, refusing to give up these beliefs that God is one, almighty, and loving. A variety of partial solutions to the problem of evil have been offered by Jews of different eras. For example, in some ways evil can be seen as the result of a previous sin of an individual or the community. Or it may be discipline or testing from God so that humans will learn to choose the good. If it seems too much now, it may be compensated in the life to come. What seems to be evil may result from a partial view of things, or it can be understood as the absence of good. But another kind of answer in Judaism is that of Job: "I lay my hand on my

The Yad Vashem Holocaust Memorial, honoring the millions of Jews and others who perished under the Nazis.

CREATION AND HUMAN EXISTENCE

"What sense is there in life?" "Why is there so much evil and suffering?" A sixteenth-century Jewish creed gives as the first principle of the Jewish faith: "I believe with perfect faith that the Creator, blessed be His name, is the Author and Guide of everything that has been created, and that He alone has made, does make, and will make all things."[3] Jews see creation from the point at the center: God's giving of the Torah to the covenant people. According to a well-known rabbinic teaching, God first looked into the Torah and then created the world, following the design spelled out in the Torah.

Creation and Preservation of the World

Judaism, as the root of the Abrahamic tradition, first contributed the fundamental idea of God as the one creator, with the world as God's good creation. At the very beginning of the Torah the ancient scribes placed a priestly liturgy about cosmic creation (Gen. 1:1–2:4). According to this hymn, God first of all called forth the world from a dark, watery chaos, and by divine command made it a good, purposeful world. God, completely separate and sovereign, created the world as an orderly, functioning cosmos. The creator separated the light from the darkness, created a firmament to hold back the waters of chaos above, and placed lights in the heavens to rule the day and night and the seasons. God gave the earth the power to bring forth plants, each according to its kind, and creative powers were also given to earth and sea to bring forth every kind of animal and fish. Day by day, the creation liturgy goes on, God created and then rejoiced in what was made: "It is good!" Finally the poem has all of nature in place, from the seas and the dry land to the stars and plants and animals. Then God said, "Let us make 'adam (humankind) in our image, after our likeness, and let them rule over the fish in the sea, the birds of the heavens, the cattle, over all the earth, and all reptiles that crawl upon the earth" (1:26). After creating humankind male and female in the divine image, finally God completed creation and rejoiced, "It is very good!" Resting on the seventh day, God

mouth," Job said. "I have uttered things that I do not understand, things too wonderful for me to know" (Job 40:4; 42:3). In discussions of the perplexities of evil and suffering, the rabbis like to quote a text from the Torah: "And Aaron was silent" (Lev. 10:3). Once, according to a rabbinic story, Moses was transported to Rabbi Akiba's lecture hall and was granted a vision of Akiba's martyrdom—his flesh being weighed in the meat market. Moses protested, "Such is his knowledge of the Law, and such is his reward?" But God said, "Silence, so it has seemed good to me" (Men. 29b).[2] Theologizing about God is after all not the central focus of Judaism. To be a Jew is to experience God by living the life of Torah, not by talking about God.

Since the Nazi Holocaust, however, there has been a great deal of discussion about God and evil among some Jewish thinkers. Some go so far as to say that it is impossible to believe in a God of the covenant after Auschwitz. Others hold that, whereas the Holocaust destroys all traditional categories of thinking about God, the experience of the covenant people with God goes on. Some feel that the main task of Jews today is to keep remembering the Holocaust; others say it cannot be spoken of today. In all, recognizing the breech in our thinking caused by this great outpouring of evil, Jews, like Israel of old, continue to struggle with God and refuse to let go.

instituted the Sabbath day as a day of rest and rejoicing in the good creation.

The Genesis story emphasizes the prior existence of God, transcendent and apart from the world. God has a design, a purpose for the world. But God is in no way mingled together with the creation; with a divine command all is called to be and to function. Later Jewish thinkers said that God created everything out of nothing, to emphasize that only God is eternal. The creation reflects the glory of God, but God is not within the creation. The world is God's creature, functioning according to the divine will and command.

God the creator is the ongoing preserver and guide of all creation. A Jewish morning prayer says,

> Praised are You, O Lord our God, King of the universe.
> You fix the cycles of light and darkness;
> > You ordain the order of all creation.
> You cause light to shine over the earth;
> > Your radiant mercy is upon its inhabitants.
> In Your goodness the world of creation
> > is continually renewed day by day.[4]

God is the personal, merciful creator who continually preserves and watches over the world, giving life and breath and food to all, returning living beings to the dust in their term, sending forth the divine spirit to replenish the earth. There is no place to flee from God's presence, no time or place of life when God is absent.

The Nature and Role of Humans

The role of humans within God's orderly and purposeful creation is to serve the creator and fulfill God's will in the world. The creation story says humans are created "in the image" of God, and that is explained to mean serving as God's representative in ruling over creation. A hymn from ancient Israel puts it in lyrical terms:

> O Lord our Lord, how majestic is your name in all the earth! . . .
> When I look at your heavens, the work of your hands,
> > moon and stars which you established—
> What is humankind that you should remember him,
> > humanity that you should care for him?
> Still you have made him but little less than God,
> > crowning him with glory and honour.
> You give him rule over all the works of your hands;
> > all things you have put under his feet. (PS. 8)

The power of this vision of the nature and role of humans can be seen by comparing this Jewish view with the commonly accepted notion of the role of humans in the ancient Near East. Creation texts from Babylon, for example, say that Marduk, the creator God, made humans from the blood of a demon, mixed with clay, to be slaves to the demands and whims of the gods. But the Jewish view elevates humans to "little less than God," cared for and loved by God, and given the great responsibility of being master over all God's creatures. Humans are to serve God, but they are at the same time partners with God in the ongoing creating and preserving of the creation, working to fulfill the purpose and destiny of all. The rabbis taught that humans are copartners with God in the work of creation, by causing the earth to be inhabited and not desolate and by using human skills to further God's creative purpose. A judge who judges justly, for example, is given credit with being a partner with God in the work of creation (Sanh. 10a).

Whereas humans are the high point of creation, the

Blowing the shofar on Rosh Hashanah is a symbol of God the creator summoning the people to new life.

other creatures also have a role and purpose. In the traditional rabbinic scheme, humans are midway between the animals who have no moral sense, on the one hand, and the angels who cannot do evil and the demons who can do only evil, on the other. Animals are to be respected and treated fairly and humanely; afflicting unnecessary pain on animals is particularly to be avoided. One rabbi ruled that a person must not eat before he gives food to his animals (Ber. 40a).

Serving God means a life of wholeness, faithfulness, and obedience. To the Jews has been given the Torah so that God's whole design for the good life can be followed. But to all creatures God has provided guidance, through nature itself and through the human conscience. All humans know and can follow the basic principles of God's law, sometimes called "the seven commandments of the sons of Noah":

1. Not to worship idols,
2. Not to commit murder,
3. Not to commit adultery and incest,
4. Not to eat a limb torn from a living animal,
5. Not to blaspheme,
6. Not to steal, and
7. To have an adequate system of law and justice.

In the Jewish view, human reason is not necessarily in conflict with serving and obeying God. Reason can lead astray when followed blindly, but used in submission to God's Torah, human reason can assist in living the good life.

The Shadow of Sin

Judaism highly values humans, but it has no delusions about human nature. Stories at the beginning of the Torah provide a realistic assessment of the human capacity for evil. Within the first human family, Cain rose up and murdered his brother Abel out of anger and jealousy, and God warned him—and all humans— that "sin is couching at the door" (Gen. 4:7). Humankind became so evil that God sent a great flood to destroy them. But even righteous Noah's family and descendents· demonstrated the same inclinations. These stories of rebellion and violence among the peoples of God's earth have strongly influenced the view of human nature found in Christianity and Islam also.

Throughout the Jewish Tanakh there is abundant evidence of the human capacity for wickedness and for causing great suffering and destruction in God's good world.

In the teaching of the rabbis, human sin is *averah*, from *avar*, meaning "to pass over" or transgress God's will. Judaism has a definite idea of what the good life is: following the commandments of the Torah. And sin is to transgress all this. Milton Steinberg explains the rabbinic view: sin is "any act or attitude whether of omission or commission which nullifies God's will, obscures His glory, profanes His name, opposes His Kingdom, or transgresses the *Mitzvoth* [commandments] of the Torah."[5]

Struggle to Control the Evil Inclination

In Judaism there is no idea of an evil or "fallen" human nature that inevitably drives humans to sin. Rather, the rabbis taught that there are two basic inclinations or drives in everyone: the *yetzer hatov*, the good inclination, and the *yetzer hara‘*, the evil inclination. Sin results when a person lets the evil inclination get the upper hand.

But why did God create humans with the evil inclination? This is the inclination that drives humans to gratify their instincts and wants; it has to do with ambitions and appetites, including especially the sex drive. Thus this "evil inclination" is really essential in providing motivating power for life. Commenting on God's words in the creation story, "It was very good," Rabbi Nahman ben Samuel said, "That is the evil inclination. But is the evil inclination very good? Yes, for if it were not for the evil inclination, man would not build a house, or take a wife, or beget a child, or engage in business" (Gen. R., Bereshit, 9:7).[6] Another rabbinic story tells that Ezra and his associates once wanted to kill the evil inclination. But the evil inclination (personified in this story) warned them that the whole world would go down if they did this. They imprisoned the evil inclination, but then they found that throughout the world there could be found no newly laid egg. Finally they put out his eyes so he could not tempt men to incest (Yoma 69.b).

Thus Judaism has the realistic view that life is a continuing struggle, but we can control the evil inclination and even use it in a positive, life-affirming way. The most important help in mastering the evil inclination is, of course, the Torah. A well-known rabbinic parable tells of a king who inflicted a big wound on his son but then counseled his son to keep a plaster on the wound. As long as the wound was protected by the plaster, his son could eat and drink whatever he wanted without any ill effects; but if the plaster was removed, the wound would fester (Kidd. 30b). So also God has in a sense "wounded" humans by giving them the evil inclination; but he has also given them the Torah as the antidote, allowing them to live their lives without fearing that the evil within them will drag them down to ruin. Another rabbinic parable says the evil inclination is like iron that one holds in a flame in order to make a tool of it; so, too, the evil inclination is to be held in the fire of the Torah (Avot de Rabbi Natan, ch.16).

Sometimes it is said that, unlike Christianity, which holds that a person sins because of being a sinner, in the Jewish view a person is a sinner because he or she sins. That is, sin is an action of transgressing God's laws, not a state of being that is twisted and alienated from God. But this does not mean that Judaism is unduly optimistic about human nature. The scriptures describe bounteous human evil, and Jews have seen sufficient evidence of that in their long history as a people. Saints do struggle and master the evil inclination; but even Moses, our rabbi, sinned and was punished.

The Results of Sin

Sin has consequences. The rabbis point out that when Cain killed his brother Abel, he also killed all Abel's unborn children. So there is punishment for sin, just punishment because sin arises from the free will of humans. Traditional Judaism does know of the idea of Satan, the accuser who tests people and tries to lead them astray (Job 1–2). But Jews strongly affirm that we humans have free choice and do have the capability, with the help of the Torah, of mastering the evil inclination. Therefore we are justly punished as the recompense for our sin.

But there are different kinds of sin, and therefore different kinds of punishment, depending on whether the sin is against God or against one's fellow humans. In one sense, the rabbis say, the sin itself is the recompense of sin (Avot 4:2). The guilt and sorrow and alienation caused by doing a sin is surely retribution for the sin. Some recompense for sin comes in this life, both in terms of punishment by society and also punishment by God. Disease, war, and slavery can be divine punishment, as when God sent Assyrian armies against Israel or caused a plague to punish wrongdoers. But Jews are also aware of the problems involved in explaining misfortune and suffering as punishment for sin. The story of Job's innocent sufferings leads the rabbis to say that finally we do not know why the righteous suffer; even Moses did not know (Ber. 7a).

In traditional Judaism, it is emphasized that final recompense for sin is given by God in the life to come. The rabbis used this teaching to explain why the wicked could be prosperous in this life in seeming defiance of God's just laws; their recompense will come with torments and sufferings in Gehinnom. Some rabbis did teach that even those suffering in hell will rest every Sabbath, or that the punishment would last for only twelve months. Whereas many Jews today feel uncomfortable with traditional descriptions of punishments in the world to come, they emphasize the main point that sin is hateful in God's eyes. It is better to live the good life, and God has given sufficient guidance and help for that.

FOLLOWING THE PATH OF TORAH

"How can I start living *real* life?" Judaism recognizes the tension between what humans are supposed to do according to God's design of creation and what humans actually do in their daily lives. Humans inevitably fall short of what God asks of them. Jews know from the biblical history that time after time human failure brings forth divine punishment. So what can one do to find whole life, to transform this human situation?

God as Redeemer
Jews first of all look to God not only as the creator but also as the redeemer, who forgives and restores and thus

makes it possible for humans to turn back to the life God intended for them. In the traditional daily prayer, after praising God as the creator and the revealer of Torah, Jews call upon God as the redeemer, the one who saves and delivers them:

> You are our King and our father's King,
> our redeemer and our father's redeemer. . . .
> You, O Lord our God, rescued us from Egypt;
> You redeemed us from the house of bondage. . . .
> [God] humbles the proud and raises the lowly;
> He helps the needy and answers His people's call. . . .
> Fulfill Your promise to deliver Judah and Israel.
> Our redeemer is the Holy One of Israel.[7]

In this prayer, Jews look to the great redemption of Israel in the past, and they look ahead to the redemption in the time to come. But redemption also takes place in the present—whenever God humbles the proud and raises the lowly, whenever God helps the needy and hears the people's call. Redemption or salvation takes place in common, everyday events.

How does God redeem? Not through an intermediary who stands between God and humans to save them, as in Christianity. Between God and humans stands no one. As Steinberg writes, "As nothing comes between soul and body, father and child, potter and vessel, so nothing separates man from God, Soul of his soul, his Father and Fashioner."[8] God redeems and saves by being God for humans. That is, God continually searches and calls for humans to become partners as they were created to be.

In this search of God for humans, Jews identify a number of important movements on God's part. God intervenes in human history to redeem the sacred people by mighty acts. God reveals the Torah as the total design for the good life. And God answers humans when they repent by showing them mercy and forgiveness. Yet God does not take away human freedom and initiative. The searching and calling come from God, but ultimately each person must take the first step of responding to God's call.

The Jewish sacred story is full of God's mighty acts of salvation. God delivered them from slavery in Egypt with a mighty arm. God brought them to the holy mountain and entered into a covenant with them, giving them the Torah. God led them into the promised land and gave it to them as an inheritance, raising up the house of David to save Israel from their enemies. Even God's acts of punishment were intended as a means of redeeming the people from their sins and turning them back to the right path. In the midst of the great catastrophe of the Babylonian exile, the prophet known as Second Isaiah spoke these words about the destruction of Israel and God's intentions for them:

> Comfort, oh comfort my people, says your God.
> Speak tenderly to Jerusalem, and call to her
> > that her time of service is fulfilled,
> > that her iniquity is satisfied,
> > that she has received from the Lord double for all
> > her sins. . . .
> See, the Lord God comes with might,
> > with his arm ruling for him;
> indeed, his reward comes with him,
> > and his recompense is before him.
> Like a shepherd he will pasture his flock,
> > he will gather them in his arm;
> he will carry the lambs in his bosom,
> > and lead the ewes to water.   (ISA. 40:1–2, 10–11)

Through mighty deeds of salvation, God has always been the redeemer of the people, and will continue so in the present and in the future.

Judaism also stresses the guidance that God has given to make it possible for humans to turn and lead the good life. This is the Torah, the great gift of God's

Since the Torah is God's great gift for guiding the people, study of the Torah is a central activity for orthodox Jews.

grace for the welfare of humankind. In a sense, giving the Torah is the one great act of God's salvation for humankind. The Jewish daily prayer celebrates this blessing from God:

Deep is Your love for us, O Lord our God;
Bounteous is Your compassion and tenderness.
You taught our fathers the laws of life.
And they trusted in You, Father and King.
For their sake be gracious to us, and teach us,
That we may learn Your laws and trust in You.
Father, merciful Father, have compassion upon us;
Endow us with discernment and understanding.
Grant us the will to study Your Torah,
To heed its words and to teach its precepts. . . .
Enlighten our eyes to Your Torah,
Open our hearts to Your commandments. . . .
You have drawn us close to You.[9]

As God has taught and guided the people of old in the laws of life, so Jews believe God continues to teach and guide, giving the will to study the Torah, the mind to understand it, and the heart to follow it.

The Human Movement of Repentance
So far it does sound like salvation comes mainly from God's side. And in a sense it does, for God is the redeemer. But Jews also insist that the human partner in this relationship likewise has an active role in this process of salvation and transformation. God created humans with an important realm of free will within the various conditions of life over which we have no control. And in this realm of moral freedom the drama of faithfulness or faithlessness is played out. A rabbi taught that before a human is conceived in his mother's womb, God has already ordained concerning him whether he would be strong or weak, intelligent or dull, rich or poor. But God has not predetermined whether he will be wicked or virtuous, since everything is in the hand of Heaven except the fear of Heaven (Ber. 33b).[10] God is in search for humans; but it is up to humans to seek God. Jews believe that the initiative in seeking God must come from the human side. Abraham Heschel, quoting the saying, "Whoever sets out to purify himself is assisted from above" (Yoma 38b), comments

simply: "God concludes but we commence."[11] God gives grace, calls us, searches for us—but God expects us to take the first step in responding to the call.

Within the human life of imperfection and sin, that first step toward God has to be repentance. The Hebrew word for repentance, *teshuvah*, literally means to "turn around," to make a complete change in one's direction of life. To turn to God means to answer the call, to respond to God's search and set out on the path of the good life of Torah. Through the prophet Malachi comes God's call: "Since your fathers' days you have turned aside from my statutes and have not kept them. Return to me, and I will return to you" (Mal. 3:7).

Repentance is a human act, not a mysterious sacrament that works even without our efforts. This human undertaking of repentance involves four concrete steps. First comes the readiness to acknowledge a wrongdoing. Second, the person does acts of compensation for the injury inflicted on others by what she has done, when it is a sin against others. Third, the person makes a genuine resolve to avoid a repetition of the same sinful deed. Only then is the person ready to take the fourth and final step of praying for forgiveness from God, knowing that she will receive God's mercy.[12]

Repentance is the highest of the virtues in Judaism. The rabbis taught that when a person repents out of love, her sins are converted into merits, and that in the place where a repentant sinner stands, even the righteous who have never sinned cannot stand (Ber. 34b). Reflecting on this philosophical puzzle, Joseph Albo (d. 1444) pointed out that if justice were to be the determining factor there could be no repentance at all, for justice demands that once done a wrong cannot be righted and the sinner must be punished. But repentance is based on God's infinite grace. When a person sincerely repents and turns to God in love, he is really demonstrating that the sin was not committed voluntarily but in error, for the sinner would erase it if he could. This repentance out of love brings God's grace into play, which flows in love to him and converts his sins into merits.[13]

One of the most holy days in Judaism, the Day of Atonement (Yom Kippur) is set aside for repentance. The liturgy used on this day in the Jewish synagogue strikingly expresses the deep Jewish sense of sin, repentance, and forgiveness, as in these few excerpts:

> Our God and God of our fathers, hear our prayers; do not ignore our plea.
> We are neither so brazen nor so arrogant to claim that we are righteous, without sin, for indeed we have sinned.
> We abuse, we betray, we are cruel.
> We destroy, we embitter, we falsify.
> We gossip, we hate, we insult.
> We jeer, we kill, we lie.
> We mock, we neglect, we oppress.
> We pervert, we quarrel, we rebel.
> We steal, we transgress, we are unkind.
> We are violent, we are wicked, we are xenophobic.
> We yield to evil, we are zealots for bad causes. . . .
> We have sinned against You unwillingly and willingly.
> And we have sinned against You by misusing our minds.
> We have sinned against You through sexual immorality,
> And we have sinned against You knowingly and deceitfully. . . .
> For all these sins, forgiving God, forgive us, pardon us, grant us atonement. . . .
> May it be Your will, Lord my God and God of my fathers, to help me abstain from further sin. With Your great compassion wipe away the sins I have committed against You.[14]

To say this prayer with conviction and sincerity means turning back to God and following God's way; it is a prayer of transformation.

The Life of Halakhah

Repentance is only the first step. The path of transformation for Jews is really the whole life of Torah. This means following the *mitzvot* (commandments), which God has given through the Torah as the discipline by which to purify oneself and shape one's life ever more closely to God's design. There are many mitzvot, 613 of them by traditional count, made up of 365 negative commandments corresponding to the number of days in the year, and 248 positive commandments corresponding to the number of members of a person's body. How these mitzvot apply to life is set forth in the Jewish Halakhah, the "way," the code of life spelled out in the Talmud. The Halakhah determines the way a person lives, how one shapes the daily

Reading the Torah at the Western Wall. Some of the worshipers have phylacteries (small boxes containing words from the Torah) on their foreheads.

routine into a pattern of holiness. The Halakhah governs every aspect of daily life, all the way from birth to death. It includes prescriptions about how to relate to God in prayer and in worship, what foods to eat and how to prepare them, how to marry and have children and die and bury the dead, how to treat others, and all the rest. We will look more closely at some of the specifics of the Halakhah in the following chapter. Here it is important to see that the Halakhah makes up a path of transformation for Jews, a discipline that involves a practice of outward behavior that brings about an inner transformation of the heart.

It is a misunderstanding of outsiders to think that Judaism is interested only in the outward performance of all these mitzvot. Commenting on the rabbinic saying, "God asks for the heart," Heschel writes,

> The true goal for man is *to be* what he *does.* . . . A mitzvah, therefore, is not mere doing but an act that embraces both the doer and the deed. The means may be external, but the end is personal. . . . It is a distortion to say that Judaism consists exclusively of performing

ritual or moral deeds, and to forget that the goal of all performing is in *transforming* the soul. Even before Israel was told in the Ten Commandments what *to do* it was told what *to be*: *a holy people*. To perform deeds of holiness is to absorb the holiness of deeds. . . . Man is not for the sake of good deeds; the good deeds are for the sake of man. . . . The goal is not that a ceremony be *performed*; the goal is that man be *transformed*; to worship the Holy in order to be holy. The purpose of the mitzvot is *to sanctify* man.[15]

In this understanding of the Jewish performance of mitzvot, it is clear that this is indeed a path of spiritual transformation. Looked at from the outside, the observance of all the minutiae of the Jewish law might seem to be outer show with little real spiritual depth or meaning. Indeed, a traditional Christian understanding of Judaism sees it as a religion of "works," in which humans strive by their good deeds to be rewarded with salvation. To Jews, however, this is not a matter of "salvation by works." Rather, the Halakhah provides a structure of life divinely given for the benefit of humans, a discipline based in real human action that transforms the heart in love for God. By walking in the way of God, humans can become Godlike. So Jews take on the discipline of the mitzvot with thankfulness and with joy.

Of the various mitzvot, we should single out the study of the Torah as the supreme obligation for Jews on the path of transformation. The study of the Torah is not just an intellectual exercise but a means for perfecting the human spirit that has been made in the image of God. Rabbi Meir said,

> Whosoever labours in the Torah for its own sake merits many things; and not only so, but the whole world is indebted to him: he is called friend, beloved, a lover of the All-present, a lover of mankind; it clothes him in meekness and reverence: it fits him to become just, pious, upright and faithful; it keeps him far from sin, and brings him near to virtue. (ABOTH 6:1:2)[16]

The very act of study, memorization, and commentary on the Torah is a holy act and in fact the central ritual of Judaism. It is through study of the Torah that one comes to know God and therefore to love God with the whole heart. If the Torah reveals God's complete pattern for the sanctification of human life, the first and most important response is to study and learn the Torah so that it becomes a part of one's very nature.

Universal Blessing, Now and Hereafter

A striking factor in the Jewish path of transformation is its seemingly limited application within the whole human race. Unlike Christianity and Islam, which are missionary religions seeking to bring their respective paths of transformation to all people, Judaism has always considered the path of Torah to apply only to the Jewish people. There is, of course, a repeated rabbinic tradition that God did intend the Torah for all peoples, but only the Jews accepted it. The path of Torah is closely linked to the covenant that God made with Israel, the chosen people. Jews have never felt they have the mission of bringing other peoples of the world into Judaism. Rather, Jews hold that, whereas anyone who wants to can become a Jew, no one has to do so in order to be saved in this world or in the next. Rabbi Joshua said that the righteous of all nations will have a share in the world to come (Tosefta Sanh. 13:2). Non-Jews can turn and follow God's way simply by keeping the "seven commandments of the sons of Noah." But for Jews, who have taken on the responsibility and the joy of the covenant, the path of Torah is the fulfillment of human potential and the way of salvation.

Following the path of Torah brings blessing, in this world and in the world to come. In this life, keeping the Torah is itself its own reward. For it is the divine pattern of life, and to live it is to become Godlike—which is the highest possible reward and blessing. One who lives the life of Torah becomes a channel of blessing in the world; in that way he or she receives the reward of the good life.

It is obvious, however, that many times righteous people undergo many sufferings in this life—just as the wicked may have wealth and success. So the Jewish tradition also teaches recompense for the righteous in the world to come, when the immortal souls of the righteous will be rewarded in Gan Eden (paradise), sharing the joys of their closeness to the divine glory. Traditional Jews also believe in the resurrection of the body, when the body will be reunited with the soul in the joy and bliss of paradise. Many modern Jews have reinterpreted these traditional beliefs in recompense, immortality, and resurrection, so they are not understood in a literal sense. Yet even Jewish modernists generally believe that some essence of the person lives on after death, and that there is a setting right of the scales of justice in terms of blessing and reward for those who have followed the path of Torah. In any case, we should always connect the world to come with how we live in this world. Rabbi Jacob said,

> This world is like a vestibule before the world to come; prepare thyself in the vestibule, that thou mayest enter into the hall. He used to say, 'Better is one hour of repentance and good deeds in this world than the whole life of the world to come; and better is one hour of blissfulness of spirit in the world to come than the whole life of this world.' (ABOTH 4:21, 22)[17]

DISCUSSION QUESTIONS

1. In what ways was the religion of some of the ancient Israelites polytheistic and henotheistic? Outline the development of monotheism.

2. What are some responses to the problem of evil and suffering according to Jewish thought? What is the impact of the Holocaust on this question?

3. What does the creation liturgy of Genesis I reveal about the nature of the world and of humans?

4. Is the Torah universal truth? What is the traditional idea about the seven commandments of the sons of Noah?

5. What is the rabbinic tradition about the good and evil inclinations? What perspective does this place on the question of the sinfulness of humans?

6. In the Jewish path of transformation, what are the roles of God and of humans?

CHAPTER 6

JEWISH WORSHIP AND THE GOOD LIFE

JEWISH WORSHIP AND RITUALS

"How can I find new power for life?" For Jews, the Torah provides the basis for making human life sacred. There are mitzvot (commandments) dealing with both ritual-ceremonial actions and ethical behavior, creating sacred times and sacred living. Traditional Jews keep both types of mitzvot; modern Jews sometimes tend to keep the spirit of ethical directives but not all the ritual and ceremonial laws.

Only the basic mitzvot are mentioned in the written Torah. On the basis of the oral Torah, the Talmud, with its interpretations and applications of the written Torah, rabbis over many centuries have compiled the Halakhah, the "path" or code that provides the blueprint for everything about life, daily, seasonally, from cradle to grave. Since the Halakhah is so all-encompassing, it is difficult to make a sharp division between sacred time and sacred life. Jews have, however, made a general distinction between ritual-ceremonial laws, on the one hand, and ethical laws, on the other. First we focus on the rituals and ceremonies of Judaism.

Sabbaths for Rest, Festivals for Rejoicing

Jews have a rich tradition of sacred times. The rituals and festivals provide a rhythm of return to the source of sacred power, daily, weekly, and seasonally.

Queen Sabbath

At the very center of Jewish life is Shabbat (Sabbath), the only festival prescribed in the Ten Commandments. Sabbath has been extremely important to Jewish life and identity. The Sabbath, say Jews, has kept Israel more than Israel has kept the Sabbath. It is the supreme symbol of the covenant relationship with God.

The Torah provides two important interpretations of the Sabbath, in the two listings of the Ten Commandments. According to Exodus 20, Jews are commanded to rest on the Sabbath because God rested on the seventh day after finishing the creation. In Deuteronomy 5, resting on the Sabbath day is a reminder of the deliverance from slavery in Egypt. Thus the Sabbath means rejoicing with God in the creation; and it means celebrating freedom in human society. Because of this, Sabbath has always been considered a joyous time by the Jews, a time of worship, prayer, and study, but also a time of family gathering, festive meal, rest from labor and worry, and giving rest to animals also. It is a festival of worshiping God and respecting human values.

The Sabbath begins at sundown on Friday evening and ends at sundown on Saturday evening. Jews prepare for the Sabbath celebration by cleaning house and getting the meals ready—for such work is not permitted on the Sabbath. At sundown the mother of the family lights two candles, says the Sabbath prayer, and "Queen Shabbat" comes. Friday evening is the time for the Sabbath family meal, often with a special guest or two. During the meal the special Sabbath prayer (Kiddush) is said over a glass of wine. In modern times, Friday evening is the occasion for a communal Sabbath service at the synagogue. Jews traditionally spent Saturday morning at the synagogue worshiping and studying the Torah. Nowadays Saturday is spent in rest and quiet with family and friends. As the end of Sabbath approaches on Saturday evening, Jews use special prayers and rituals to bid farewell to Queen Sabbath.

The Days of Awe: Rosh Hashanah and Yom Kippur

The Jewish year begins with the Days of Awe, also called the High Holy Days. They start with Rosh Hashanah, New Year, on the first of Tishri, coming in early autumn in the modern calendar. These are considered the most solemn days of the year. They symbolize death and renewal—the old is swept away and the new is put into place. Sins are forgiven, relationships mended, and people are sealed in God's books of life. Jewish tradition has it that everything a person does is recorded in God's books, and these are opened for examination at the beginning of the New Year to be weighed and judged and the verdict inscribed. One book is for the just, and another book is for the hopeless sinners. But the third book—for those who are in between—is not sealed until Yom Kippur, giving people a chance to repent.

The solemn liturgy of the Rosh Hashanah synagogue service has the main theme of God as King, the one who created the world: "This is the day the world was born." God the King continues to renew the creation, and is also coming to judge all things. A special ritual is the blowing of the *shofar*, the ram's horn, a number of times in the service. The stirring sound is interpreted as a call to arouse our sleeping souls for war against sin. People are greeted, "Le-shanah tovah tikateivu" (May you be inscribed for a good year). At home with family and friends, apples are dipped in honey expressing the hope for a sweet year. In the afternoon it is customary to walk to a body of flowing water and throw bread crumbs in, symbolically casting sins away. Orthodox and Conservative Jews observe Rosh Hashanah for two days, repeating the rituals on the second day.

The ten days between Rosh Hashanah and Yom Kippur (on the tenth of Tishri) are days of repentance, preparing for the most solemn holy day of all: Yom Kippur, the Day of Atonement. Superceding even the Sabbath in importance, it is called "the Sabbath of Sabbaths." Traditional Jews spend almost the whole day at the synagogue, fasting and praying. The interior of the synagogue is decorated with white, symbolizing purity. The Yom Kippur eve service begins with the famous *Kol Nidre* prayer, set to a haunting melody that symbolizes the longing of the soul for God. During the day of Yom Kippur, Jews individually and communally confess sins to God and ask for forgiveness. This is the only time of the year (besides once on Rosh Hashanah) that Jews prostrate themselves, in memory of the ancient temple service. The concluding service on Yom Kippur is called Neilah (closing), referring to the closing of the gates of heaven, a reminder that time for repentance is running out. The ark holding the Torah scrolls is left open to the end of the service, and people stand throughout the service—heightening the sense of urgency of reaching God with prayers. The service concludes dramatically with a final blast of the shofar signaling passage from sin to forgiveness, from death to life.

Sukkot: The Festival of Booths

Just five days after Yom Kippur, on the fifteenth of Tishri, Sukkot represents a quick shift in mood to a holiday of celebration. The Festival of Booths lasts for seven days, during which Jews build a hut (*sukkah*) and make it their home, at least symbolically. Sukkot was the festival of ingathering of harvest, and appropriately the festival includes the ritual use of citron, palm branches, myrtle, and willow. The frail temporary hut in which the family dines reminds Jews of the wandering in the wilderness; it also reminds them that physical possessions are unreliable and the simple, natural life is desirable. Guests are invited to share meals in the hut, and the mood is one of rejoicing and thankfulness.

Following the last day of Sukkot is a holy day of assembly in the synagogue; Reform Jews combine this with the last day of Sukkot. The celebration on this day is called Simhat Torah (rejoicing in the Torah), for on this day the annual cycle of reading the Torah scroll is completed, followed immediately by reading the opening verses of the Torah. In this service the whole congregation processes and even dances seven times around the sanctuary with the Torah scrolls to express their joy over God's revelation. Children are especially encouraged to join in the rejoicing.

Minor Festivals: Hanukkah and Purim

Hanukkah, the Feast of Lights, is a popular minor festival occurring at the winter solstice. This eight-day festival recalls the victory of Judah Maccabeus and the Jews over the Seleucids in 165 B.C.E. The Seleucids under Antioches Epiphanes had humiliated the Jews, outlawing their religious practices and desecrating the temple with worship of Greek gods and pig sacrifices. When the Jews rededicated the temple, they found only a small cruse of oil, enough to last one day. But when they lit the temple menorah (candelabra) with it, it burned for eight days. Hanukkah celebrates this miracle of oil and the Jewish fight for independence. Jews light the eight candles successively on the eight nights of Hanukkah. It is a season of joy, games, special foods, and gift-giving. The festival symbolizes the sanctity of the individual's conscience and the right of everyone to choose his or her own religious practices.

Purim, coming in early spring, commemorates the survival of the Jewish people told in the story of Esther. The wicked Haman of the Persians masterminded the extermination of the Jews, but Mordecai and his grand-niece Esther risked their lives to save their people. Purim has a carnival atmosphere as the story of the wicked Haman and the heroes Mordecai and Esther is told and acted out. The festival includes plays, masquerades, and games of chance, and even some social drinking is permissible. Purim is also a time for acts of righteousness.

Pesach (Passover)

Passover is one of the high points of the Jewish year, coming at the beginning of spring (in March or April). Since it celebrates Israel's deliverance from slavery in

A Jewish family celebrates the Passover.

Egypt, it is "the festival of our freedom." It has elements that were originally connected with spring festivals of both pastoralists and agriculturalists, but most importantly it is the festival by which Jews are commanded to remember God's intervention in Egypt and the deliverance of the people from bondage. As a spring festival, it also symbolizes the deliverance of all nature from the bondage of winter. A major message of the festival is that the Jews were delivered from Egypt not just for their own sake but for the sake of promoting freedom for all enslaved peoples. There is thus a note of anticipation in the Passover celebration, looking to the future deliverance of Israel and all peoples.

Preparing for Passover involves a thorough cleaning and purifying of the house, getting rid of all traces of *hametz* (leaven) and storing all utensils used for the rest of the year. Only matzah (unleavened bread) and other unleavened food can be eaten for the seven-day festival, for the Israelites fled in haste from Egypt and ate unleavened bread for seven days.

Passover is primarily a family festival. The focus is on the ritual meal called the seder (order) celebrated in the evenings of the first two days, during which the story of the Exodus from Egypt is told in word, song, and ritual. The procedure for the seder is written in a guide called the Haggadah (story). The seder includes four cups of wine to remember the redemption of Israel, a special cup for Elijah the herald of the future redemption, salt water to remember the tears of the ancestors, drops of wine spilt in sorrow over the plagues the Egyptians experienced, and four questions to be asked by the youngest child present. Passover is a celebration of new life and freedom, a season of rebirth and renewal.

Shavuot, the Festival of Weeks (Pentecost)

The final major festival, Shavuot, seven weeks after Passover, originated as a celebration of abundant spring harvest. It remembers especially the giving of the Torah on Mt. Sinai, God's great gift to Israel, the heart of the covenant bond between God and people. Shavuot is a festival of reconsecration to the teaching of the Torah and to the covenant. A beautiful metaphor used on Shavuot is that of marriage between God and people: Passover is the time of courting, Shavuot celebrates the marriage, and Sukkot is the setting up of the household.

For Shavuot, Jews often decorate the synagogue and home with green plants, branches, and trees. The story about the giving of the Torah on Mt. Sinai is read. Some Jews stand at the reading of the Ten Commandments and even read them in a special chant. In Israel the recent custom of bringing the first fruits of the harvest in joyful processions is performed on Shavuot. And many synagogues, especially Reform and Conservative ones, have confirmation ceremonies on Shavuot, celebrating graduating from religious school and attesting to the covenant given at Sinai.

There are other Jewish holy days, fast days, and celebrations, of course. An important recent addition is Yom Hashoah, Holocaust Memorial Day, observed in April as a memorial to the six million Jewish martyrs of the Nazi era. Significantly, some Christian churches also observe Yom Hashoah.

Mitzvot of Worship and Ritual

The performance of the ritual duties is not limited to the holy days and festivals in Judaism. Since all of life is to be made holy, ceremonial observances in worship of God extend to all of life. They include worship and prayer, daily rituals at home, observance of dietary laws, and ceremonies associated with the passages of life.

Worship, Prayer, and Study

The duty of worshiping God is at the heart of Judaism, as it is also for Christianity and Islam. In ancient Judaism worship at the temple included prayer and rituals of sacrifice, but since the destruction of the temple the focus has been on prayer. The traditional Jew lives his life constantly aware of the presence of God, always ready to utter words of praise and blessing to God. Jewish prayer can be spontaneous, arising from the longings of the heart. But the rabbis, knowing that we can easily forget a parent who is absent, specified periods during the day for worship. They created a tradition of prayer that blends together a fixed liturgy and the spontaneous offerings of the heart.

Important to Jews is the prayer book, a composite of Jewish worship experience from ancient times up to the present. The prayer book specifies the exact times for prayer and even provides the prayers to use on all important occasions. In recent times, prayer books have translations into the vernacular languages. The Reform movement in particular has modernized the prayers and provided translations. Yet the general shape of liturgical prayer remains.

Jewish prayers presuppose a community. The plural form is used, and prayer ideally is said in a congregational setting where there is a *minyan*, a quorum of ten men. Each prays by himself but is fully aware of the community. Traditional congregational prayer would involve a group of men in a room, each standing by himself yet close to others, some swaying this way and that, whispering or speaking in a low tone to God. Standing before God the king, they do not shuffle their feet unseemingly. They bend their knees when they begin and when they end in honor of God's presence.

Respect for God also requires proper attire for worship. Orthodox and Conservative men wear a *kipah* (cap) during prayer. For festival worship, many wear a *tallith* (prayer shawl), and some very pious ones wear a special undergarment with fringes on the four corners. Observant Jewish men will also wear *t'fillin* (phylacteries), small black boxes containing words of the Torah, attached to forehead and arm.

Morning prayer at the Western Wall. One worshiper is wearing a tallith (prayer shawl) and on his forehead is a phylactery (box containing words of the Torah).

Important among these prayers are the Eighteen Benedictions, to be said in the morning, noon, and evening prayers. They have to do with themes of repentance, redemption, healing and blessing, gathering of the exiles, redemption of Jerusalem and Israel, thankfulness, and the like.

The act of studying the Torah is also a holy ritual for Jewish men—in fact, it could be argued that it is the central ritual of the Jewish tradition. Whereas Jews, of course, study the Torah to gain intellectual knowledge, the act itself of studying is a holy ritual in which one is united with the rabbis and even with God in studying Torah.

The Daily Regimen and the Dietary Laws

From awakening in the morning until sleeping at night, the traditional Jew speaks words of thankfulness to God. There are blessings to be said when dressing, washing, attending to bodily needs, eating, seeing lightning, tasting a new fruit of the season, hearing good or bad news, and for almost every conceivable occasion. The three formal prayer services during the day require considerable time, and one is further expected to devote a portion of each day to study of the Torah. Women are generally exempted from such obligations, for the reason that their role as homemaker does not allow the time required for these ceremonial observances.

The Jewish idea of "kosher" food is widely known. The dietary laws go under the term *kashrut* (ritual fitness), although this term also refers to other ritual objects as well. The basis for kashrut is the Torah's injunction about prohibited and permitted foods in Leviticus 11 and Deuteronomy 14. All vegetables and fruits are permitted, but the flesh of horses, pigs, and birds of prey is prohibited, as are all shellfish. The permitted foods must be slaughtered in a carefully prescribed manner by a *shochet* (ritual slaughterer), who drains the animal of blood. Further, meat products and dairy products may not be prepared or eaten together, and the utensils used for preparing each must be kept separate.

These dietary laws from ancient Israel, as has often been pointed out, show an early awareness of sanitation and cleanliness. Some of them also possibly relate to ancient tabus or cultic practices involving other gods. But to Jews the most important reason for observing these dietary laws is religious; they are divine laws, and for whatever reason God gave them, obeying them is a sign of keeping the covenant. They have preserved the uniqueness of the Jewish people throughout their tumultuous history, keeping them from being assimilated into other peoples. Keeping kashrut is a ritual that preserves the Jew's sense of communal identity with other Jews.

The question of the observance of the dietary laws is, of course, answered quite differently by various groups of Jews today. Traditional Jews observe all the laws without compromising and with rejoicing. Others observe kashrut at home but not outside. Some observe the laws selectively, avoiding pork and shellfish, for example. Still others argue that, whereas these laws may have applied in ancient times, they no longer have literal relevance today.

From Cradle to Grave

As all religions, Judaism has rituals that sanctify the important, critical moments in an individual's lifetime: birth, puberty, marriage, and death. These are passages from one stage of life to the next, and the rituals associated with them express the death-rebirth symbolism that establishes the ending of the old stage and the beginning of the new. Whereas the rituals pertain to individuals, they always involve the community of which the individual is a part.

The covenant between God and Israel is literally engraved on the flesh of all male Jewish infants through the covenant of circumcision, *brit milah*, done on the eighth day after birth. Circumcision is performed by a *mohel*, a circumcision specialist, in the presence of a quorum of ten men. An empty chair is left for Elijah, the guardian of the covenant. Over a cup of wine this blessing is said: "Praised are You, Lord our God, who sanctified the beloved from the womb and set a statute into his very flesh, and his parts sealed with the sign of the holy covenant."[1] Male infants are named at their circumcision, but traditionally female infants are named in the synagogue by the father when he is called up to read the Torah.

The passage through puberty is sanctified by the bar mitzvah (son of the commandment) ritual. The young Jewish boy is expected to progress in studying the Torah and Talmud up to his thirteenth birthday, and then he will be called up in the synagogue to recite blessings and lead part of the service, perhaps also giving a talk on the message of the Torah. A joyous social celebration follows the bar mitzvah ceremony, in recognition that the boy has now taken his place as a responsible adult in the Jewish people. Recently in Reform and Conservative congregations this puberty ritual has also been extended to girls, being called in this case bat mitzvah, daughter of the commandment.

The sacred duty of marriage in Judaism is spelled out in many passages of the Talmud, for it is a supreme mitzvah for the survival of the covenant people. Indeed the Talmud says that one who remains unmarried impairs the divine image (Yeb. 63b). One rabbi, when asked what God has been doing since the creation of the world, replied that God has been sitting on the divine throne and making matches, assigning this man to that woman, this woman to that man, and so on (Genesis Rabbah 68:4). The wedding ritual sanctifies the marriage, which is performed under a *huppah* (canopy). There are blessings over two goblets of wine, and the groom places a ring on the bride's finger with the words, "Be consecrated to me with this ring as my wife, according to the law of Moses and the faith of

A Jewish wedding, in the rain, under the huppah.

Israel." The marriage contract is read, seven wedding benedictions are chanted, and the bridegroom breaks a glass with his foot in memory of the destruction of Jerusalem—a reminder of sorrow on this occasion of joy. With shouts of "Mazel tov!" (good luck), the wedding celebration begins for this new household in Israel.

The rituals of death focus realistically on this common end of all mortal life, rejoicing in the life that God had granted and reflecting hope for the world to come. Orthodox Jews believe in the bodily resurrection of the dead in the world to come, whereas more modern Jews take an agnostic view of the life beyond. In any case, great importance is placed on the respectful burial of the dead. In traditional Jewish communities the burial society is a most highly respected group. Members sit with the dying person, offering prayers and reciting the Shema, the last mitzvah for a dying Jew. Jewish law forbids embalming the body; it should return quickly to the dust. The body is thoroughly washed and dressed in a white shroud. Before the burial service, the mourners tear their garments. The service concludes with the recitation of the Kaddish, a doxology sanctifying God's name. The initial period of mourning is the *shivah* (seven days), followed by another period of mourning until thirty days after the burial. Special prayers are also said on the annual anniversary of the death.

The Place of Art in Jewish Religious Life

The Jewish aesthetic sense was strongly influenced by the Torah's prohibition against making images of any living thing, a corollary of the oneness and uniqueness of God. Because of this, Jews have always avoided any representations of God and saintly personages, and traditionally they have given little attention to representational art in general. There is evidence of some Jewish pictorial art using human figures in certain periods, especially in the Hellenistic era and in manuscript illuminations during the medieval period. And, of course, there are many well-known modern painters who create art based on Jewish themes; Marc Chagall, for example, has expressed the spiritual themes of Judaism in his paintings and stained-glass windows. In Israel today a kind of Jewish national art has developed, reflecting in some sense the new Jewish identity in the holy land.

Although they generally steered away from representational art, the other arts have been fully developed in Judaism. Jews have devoted much artistic energy to what might very generally be called the aesthetics of the word: literature, poetry, prayers, psalms, liturgies, calligraphy, and manuscript decoration. An impressive Jewish literature has developed, in Hebrew and the Hebraeo dialects like Yiddish and Ladino, and also in the various other languages of the world. And in all historical ages Jewish artists devoted much time to making ritual objects such as candelabras and crowns for the Torah scrolls.

The Psalms say that everything that has breath should praise the Lord, and Jews have excelled in the arts of music, songs, dancing, and the like. It is true that, after the destruction of the temple, rabbinic custom excluded the use of musical instruments in synagogue worship, except for the shofar (ram's horn). The exclusion of musical instruments served to heighten the emphasis on the text, for which forms of chanting were developed. Dancing was also avoided in some periods, but in traditional places like Yemen, religious dancing is a part of festivals like Simhat Torah, circumcision, weddings, and the like. Modern choreographers have created dance and ballet inspired by Jewish history, ritual, and music.

The ancient temple in Jerusalem was a magnificient architectural creation, designed according to a heavenly divine model; its function was to be a sacred place of divine presence, a meeting point between God and humans. In Judaism, the architecture of the synagogue, the primary meeting place for prayer and study, has been cultivated in keeping with its meaning and function. Unlike temples of ancient times or in other religions, the synagogue is designed to contain all the worshipers, not just the priests. And the focus is not outward from the center of divine power toward the people, but inward toward the center of prayer and study. The synagogue took different forms in different parts of the world, but everywhere the architecture expresses the centrality of the bimah, the altar with the Torah scrolls—the center of Judaism.

THE LIFE OF TORAH: COMMUNITY AND ETHICS IN JUDAISM

"How should I live?" To the Jew this question has never been difficult to answer. A Jew should live as one who belongs to the *k'lal yisrael*, the total community of Israel, following the laws given by God in the Torah. The sense of Jewish peoplehood has remained strong since ancient times. Though difficult to define or explain, belonging to the Jewish people still provides deep identity and meaning today for traditional practicing Jews and modern secular Jews alike.

The Jewish People

How does one become a member of the Jewish people? Basically, one is a member of the Jewish people either by birth or by conversion. According to Jewish law, a person is a Jew by birth if her mother is Jewish. Recently, Reform Judaism has extended this provision to include either parent, so long as the family shows the intention to raise their children in the Jewish religion. One who is a Jew by birth can never be deprived of that identity, even if he or she completely abandons Jewish practices. The symbolic entry into the Jewish people for boys born in a Jewish home is the ritual of circumcision, performed on the eighth day after birth as the sign of the covenant.

Even though Judaism does not seek to gain converts, in every age there have been persons who by their own choice have become Jewish. Such a person, traditionally called a "proselyte," is welcomed into the Jewish community by rituals of circumcision (for males) and a ritual bath (*mikveh*). When a non-Jew becomes convinced that she or he wants to be Jewish and persists in doing so (Jewish tradition says the rabbi is to discourage potential proselytes and yield only if they persist), they become of equal rank and status as a Jew by birth.

It is not an easy matter, then, to answer the question, "Who is a Jew?" It does not depend on race, color, or nationality, for among Jews may be found people of all races, colors, and nationalities, and none is excluded. It may perhaps be said that a Jew is one who, whether by birth or by conversion, has taken on the identity of the covenant people of God, choosing to be different from all other peoples of the world by this unique role.

As a sacred people, Jews do not have any tight structure or organization. Rather, the people of God function as a kind of extended family, gathered into communities in various parts of the world, helping and encouraging one another to live the life of Torah. Wherever they live, Jews form congregations, gathering in local synagogues for study and worship. The congregation is governed by the people, especially those recognized as elders and scholars. Ever since the destruction of the temple in Jerusalem by the Romans in about 70 C.E., Jews have had no priests as religious leaders. Rather, religious leaders are those who are most learned in the Torah and Talmud, that is, the rabbis. Traditionally, a rabbi is one who has received ordination from other rabbis in recognition of his knowledge of the Law, qualifying him to be a leader and judge for a community of Jews.

There is no worldwide organization that governs the whole Jewish people. Rather, Jews in various lands tend to develop their own structures of organization, including both religious organizations and philanthropic groups. In the state of Israel the Ministry of Religious Affairs recognizes the Orthodox chief rabbinate as the authority in matters of Jewish religious law. In America, there are four organizations that set the standards for Jewish rabbis and the congregations they serve: the Reform, Conservative, Orthodox, and Reconstructionist groups. Orthodox Jews try as much as possible to maintain Jewish life and ritual according to the traditional Jewish Law, whereas Conservative Jews have adapted somewhat more to the demands of modern life. Reform and Reconstructionist Jews have changed or replaced certain elements of the Jewish Law to meet the needs of modern times, such as ordaining women as rabbis—a practice that Conservative Jews have also finally adopted.

The Way of Halakhah

"How should I live?" Jews use the term *halakhah* to designate that code of laws that prescribes how a Jew should live every aspect of life. Halakhah literally means "way," and it is a total way of life, drawn from the Torah and the Talmud. In traditional Jewish thinking, the Halakhah is the revealed will of God and therefore the ultimate criterion for all human conduct. A number of collections and systematizations of the Halakhah exist, but the most famous and influential is the *Shulhan Aruk* (The Set Table) made by Rabbi Joseph Caro (1488–1575). This brief four-part code of Jewish law has been expanded through commentaries and supercommentaries but still today is the place Jewish discussions of law begin. The opening sentence, elaborated by commentators, is famous:

> A man should make himself strong and brave as a lion to rise in the morning for the service of his Creator, so that he should "awake the dawn" (Psalm 57:9). . . . "I have set the Lord always before me" (Psalm 16:8). This is a cardinal principle in the Torah and in the perfect ways of the righteous who walk before God.[2]

That is, all our actions should be infused with the radical awareness that we are in every moment acting in the presence of God and therefore that every detail of our actions is important.

The Discipline of Halakhah

Judaism speaks of reward and punishment for deeds, but it would be a misunderstanding to see the performance of the mitzvot in this light. The commandments are to be performed for their own sake, not for the sake of reward. There are, of course, resulting benefits to self and others in doing the commandments, but fundamentally it is the act itself that carries value and goodness. Abraham Heschel has likened the Halakhah to artistic creation; works of piety are like works of art, serving a functional purpose but carrying the most important value intrinsically.[3]

A way of understanding the significance of performing the Halakhah is to see that, in Heschel's words, "the true goal for man is *to be* what he *does*."[4] We are what we do. The law provides a structure of life and a discipline, in harmony with God's design, and it is in following that structure and practicing that discipline, with its required rituals and actions, that people express their identity as Jews and as humans.

A basic idea of Jewish ethics is that what God has made is good—but not perfect. The distinction and obligation of humans are that they can improve what God has made. The divine image is in humans, and therefore they can, if they will, transform this world. For that they need the guidance and the discipline of the Halakhah.

The Halakhah is not understood to be a burden; rather, it is a great joy. To Jews, the mitzvot of God's law are gifts and a sign of God's great love. The law submits all human faculties and passions to God's will, but it supresses none. Even the passions are beneficial when controlled under God's law. In fact, God connects law with everything God loves—and the distinguishing mark of God's people Israel is that there is not a single thing in their lives that God through the Torah has not connected with a commandment.

Enjoy the Good, Struggle Against the Evil

The Halakhah is based on a positive, optimistic view of human life. Since God created all things good, humans have the obligation to enjoy and enhance life. Good food, wealth, and sexual pleasure are all gifts of God and should be enjoyed in the rightful way. It is a mitzvah, for example, to get married and raise children—Jewish law does not condone celibacy or asceticism. In general, we are commanded always to do what enhances life, for others and for ourselves, such as acts of kindness to others, keeping our body clean, feeding animals, and burying the dead—all these are acts of ethical distinction.

On the other hand, we are forbidden to do that which degrades life. Overindulgence in food and drink, lack of cleanliness, and the like degrade one's own life. Exploiting and using other people or humiliating them degrades their life together with one's own. The Halakhah contains many laws against theft, which includes underpaying the laborer, interrupting his work, deceiving by making something old look new, and the like. Further common sins against others, prohibited by the law, include things like taunting, insulting, misleading, slandering, hating or being angry, and nursing revenge.

Jewish law follows a middle way, advocating neither complete self-denial nor selfish indulgence. Even the so-called evil tendency, as we saw earlier, is a gift of

God for the promotion of human good; without the passions we would not eat, marry, or work toward success. Even selfishness and competitiveness, controlled under God's law, can be beneficial. It is good and right that one should desire good food and eat it with relish. But it should be for more than just assuaging hunger. It should be done with thankfulness to God, serving as the occasion for strengthening the bonds of family and friends.

Sexual pleasure, too, is a duty in Judaism, sanctified in a marriage marked by love. Marrying and having children is a duty, but marriage is not only for the purpose of producing children. Rather the sexual act between husband and wife is the culmination of the loving relationship between the two. Abstinence from marriage is a triple sin, against the health of the body, the fulfillment of the soul, and the welfare of society. Divorce is allowed in Jewish law when the partners no longer love or care for each other—though, of course, moral and social pressure is exerted against divorce. A wife can dissolve the marriage, for example, if it took place under false pretenses, if the husband is immoral, if his profession is intolerable to her, if they are sexually incompatible, if he has blemished her reputation, if he has embarrassed or insulted her, and so forth. The husband can dissolve the marriage for similar reasons. Marriage is holy, but it is not meant to be a lifetime of suffering.

Among the various principles of the Halakhah is the important principle of *tzedakah*. This is sometimes translated as "charity," since it has to do with the duty of giving to those in need. But the Hebrew word means "justice" or "righteousness"; giving to those in need is not just an emotional matter of compassion, but it is something that is just and right. It is on the basis of justice that the Torah commanded the ancient Israelites to leave a small portion of their fields unharvested for the poor to glean. An important aspect of *tzedakah* is to guarantee the dignity and honor of those in need, even to restore independence and an honorable living to them. And, the rabbis taught, the poor man really does more for the rich man than the rich man does for the poor man (Ruth Rabbah 5:9). Special concern should be shown for those who cannot help

themselves. A rabbinic exhortation says,

> In the future world, man will be asked, "What was your occupation?" If he reply, "I fed the hungry," then they reply, "This is the gate of the Lord; he who feeds the hungry, let him enter" (Ps. 118:20). So with giving drink to the thirsty, clothing the naked, with those who look after orphans, and with those, generally, who do deeds of loving kindness. All these are gates of the Lord, and those who do such deeds shall enter within them. (MIDR. PS. ON 118. 19)[5]

Another important principle is to seek and pursue peace among members of the community. Shalom, the Hebrew word for peace, is thought of as the highest ethical imperative. It is so important that a person may even lie or suffer humiliation to preserve it—something not permitted under other circumstances. Patriarch Judah I said, "Great is peace, for even if the Israelites worship idols and there is peace among them, God says, 'I have no power, as it were, over them, seeing that peace is among them' " (Gen. Rabbah, Noah, 38:6).[6] Astonishingly, shalom takes precedence even over the most basic of all the commandments.

Whereas the outsider may be overwhelmed with the number and complexity of the Jewish commandments, Jews have often pointed out that they all boil down to love: love for God and love for one's fellow humans. A famous story tells that a heathen once came to Rabbi Shammai and told him he would become a proselyte to Judaism if the rabbi could teach him the whole law while he stood on one foot. Rabbi Shammai drove him away. Then the heathen went to Rabbi Hillel, who received him and taught him, "What is hateful to you do not to your fellow: that is the whole Law; all the rest is explanation; go and learn" (Sab. 31a).[7] The Jewish path of Halakhah is an elaborate system embracing every aspect of human life, sanctifying it all and infusing it all with God's blessing, putting into concrete operation love for God and love for fellow humans.

The Missions of Peoplehood

The Chosen People of the Covenant

Ever since the ancient Israelites gathered at Sinai and concluded a covenant with their God there, the

At his Bar Mitzvah, a Jewish boy becomes an adult member of the Jewish people.

term "chosen people" has been central to Jewish identity. God entered into the covenant relationship with them and gave them the gift of the Torah.

God chose Israel. But Jews know that this can be easily misunderstood by others and even by Jews. The idea is not that of a tribal God protecting and blessing the chosen people no matter what. Nor is this the idea of one people chosen to rule all others, or a people superior to all others. Again, the idea of Jews as the chosen people does not mean Jews have special rank and privileges before God that other peoples do not have. The sacred scriptures emphasize several important things about Israel's election as God's people. First of all, Jews were not chosen because they are better than others:

> The Lord loved you and chose you not because you are more numerous than all the nations, for you are the smallest of all nations. It is because the Lord loved you and was keeping his oath which he swore to your forefathers, that the Lord brought you with a strong hand and redeemed you from the house of slavery.
>
> (DEUT. 7:7–8)

Second, this choice was a two-way affair: God chose Israel, but Israel chose to be chosen: "Moses came and related to the people all the words of the Lord, all his laws. And the whole people answered with one voice and said, 'All the things that the Lord told us, we will do' " (Ex. 24:3). The rabbis told how God offered the Torah to all the other nations, but all refused it. Then God gave it to Israel who accepted it joyfully (Sifre to Dt. 33:2). Israel thus became the chosen people not simply because God chose them, but because they themselves chose to be God's people through their readiness to accept the Torah and to struggle for its truths.

Third, being the chosen people of God means greater responsibility and higher standards of performance are demanded of the Jewish people compared to other peoples. The prophet Amos listed the punishments that will befall all the nations of the world for their particular transgressions, but he saved the harshest judgment for the chosen people: God says to Israel, "Only you have I known among all the families of the earth; therefore I will punish you for all your iniquities" (Amos 3:2). To be God's chosen people is not something lightly to boast about; it involves heavy responsibility. God expects much more from the chosen people than from the other peoples.

The term "chosen people" really means "treasured people" (*'am segullah*). Jews are God's treasure because their primary task is to be God's witness in the world, testifying that there is one God and that all people are God's children. The prophet called Second Isaiah put it this way:

> I am the Lord. I have called you in righteousness;
>> I have taken you by the hand and I have kept you.
> Now I have given you as a covenant to the people,
>> a light to the nations,
> to open the eyes of the blind,
>> to bring out the prisoners from the dungeons,
>> those who sit in darkness from the prison.
>
> (ISA. 42:6–7)

The Jewish people are to be God's instrument for activating the conscience of all humans to serve God in truth and justice. In Zecheriah 2:6 God says, "I have spread you abroad as the four winds of the heavens." One rabbi pointed out that this passage does not say that Israel is spread "upon" the four winds but rather "as" the four winds; this means that, just as no place in the world is without wind, so also the world cannot exist without the people of God present everywhere (Ta'an. 3b).

Holy Land and State of Israel

During their long history of being oppressed and scattered throughout the earth, Jews have retained a strong sense of "peoplehood." The unity and mutual responsibility of Jews is often expressed in the Talmud: "Israel's reconciliation with God can be achieved only when they are all one brotherhood" (Men. 27a).[8] In fact, the people of Israel form one unity through all generations; one rabbinic teaching said that when Moses summoned the people before God to make the covenant, all souls were present then, though their bodies were not yet created (Tanh. B., Nizzabim, 8,25b). Especially since the great Holocaust of World War II, during which more than six million Jews were deliberately exterminated by the Nazis while much of the rest of the world did very little to come to their aid, the centrality of peoplehood for Jews has taken on new and urgent significance. Only if they care for each other, Jews feel, and take responsibility for the survival of the Jewish people will they ensure that such a Holocaust will not happen again.

The recent experience of the Holocaust is part of the reason that Jews throughout the world feel such a strong commitment to the State of Israel today. The Holy Land has always been an important symbol in the Jewish identity, ever since the promises God made to Abraham and the gift of that land to the Israelite people of old. After World War II the dream of a Jewish homeland in the Holy Land became a reality with the establishing of the state of Israel. Today Jews in every land feel the mitzvah (commandment) to guard and protect the survival of the Jewish people by maintaining the existence of the state of Israel as a Jewish state in the Holy Land.

Responsibility to the World

Why should there be the Jewish people among the peoples of the world? Do Jews have any kind of responsibility toward the welfare of others? The distinctiveness and uniqueness of the Jews does not abolish the universality of God's love and design for the creation. Jews do not feel compelled to try to convert others to the Jewish religion. Yet they see the ethical life of the Torah as a design that reaches out also to the non-Jews of world society. The commandments about enhancing life rather than degrading it, for example, apply to all people, not just Jews. The moral principles of the Torah are to govern societies as well as individuals.

The personal mitzvah of *tzedekhah* is translated into philanthropy, devising creative ways to provide for the needs of the poor and help them regain independence and dignity. The resources of nature and of society make up a gift from God that should enhance the welfare of all people. This does not mean abolition of private property, for the law guarantees the individual the right to own what she or he has worked for and to enjoy its fruits. But no one, including governments, has the right to withhold wealth from use, to destroy it by wastefulness, or to use it selfishly against the communal interest.

Where evil rises in the society, Jews are required not only to avoid it passively but to defy and actively protest it. The rabbis taught that a person who can protest and prevent his household from committing a sin and does not is accountable for the sins of his household. Further, if he could protest and prevent his fellow citizens but fails to do so, he is accountable for the sins of the fellow citizens; and if he could keep the whole world from sinning but does not, he is accountable for the whole world (Sab. 54b). On the basis of their ethical principles, many Jews have been in the forefront of protesting slavery and injustice in society, rather advocating freedom and equality, compulsory education, rights of workers, improvement in the status of women, and other humanitarian moral changes for society.

The important mitzvah of pursuing peace is extended to conflict and warfare between peoples and nations. The Hebrew Scriptures' description of holy war in the early period, commanded by God, can perhaps be interpreted to mean that such warfare is in accordance with the divine will. But it should be remembered that those passages are balanced with other sections in the Scriptures that emphasize shalom. A famous passage in Isaiah 2 says that, in the messianic age, all nations will flow to Jerusalem and beat their swords into plowshares, learning war no more (Is. 2:4).

The rabbis pointed out that the command to "seek peace and pursue it" (Psalm 34:14), unlike many other commandments, does not begin with "if" or "when," to be fulfilled only on the appropriate occasion. Rather, you should seek peace wherever you happen to be, and you should run after it if it is elsewhere (Num. Rabbah, Hukkat, 19:27). Shalom does not just mean the absence of war, however; it expresses the health and wholeness of humans who experience equality and justice. Therefore the Jewish approach to war and conflict has emphasized the connection between peace and justice. Noting that God told Moses to make war on Sihon, but Moses sent messengers of peace instead (Dt. 2:24ff.), the Talmud says, "How great, then, must be words of peace, if Israel disobeyed God for peace's sake, and yet He was not wrath with them" (Tanh. B., Debarim, 3b).[9]

Judaism does not, however, advocate pacifism. The rabbis distinguished between optional war and obligatory war, which is a just war in defense against attack from outside. The right of a person to preserve his own life is paramount, and thus a war of self-defense is justified. However, the rabbis taught that destructive action should be avoided if a lesser action suffices. The theme of making peace, balanced with the requirement of justice, is still characteristic of the Jewish approach today. The massive atrocities of the twentieth century require an active resistance to evil. But the threat of nuclear destruction leads some modern Jewish thinkers to conclude that ancient ideas about justified warfare are, in the modern context, a contradiction in terms.

Basic to the Jewish ethical vision, though shaken a bit by the events of the Holocaust, is the optimistic idea of transforming the world. Only humans can transform and perfect the world that God has made. Particularly in Reform Judaism, the pursuit of social justice and human fulfillment has been made into a central emphasis; Judaism's mission is to be an irresistible force for freedom and human improvement in the world. Orthodox Jews resist this kind of focus, but they also hold to the traditional teaching that, when humans repent and perform righteousness, then the messiah will come and bring in the ideal age. There is a sense in Judaism that deeds of righteousness sustain the world and keep it from disaster. Rabbi Jonathan played with

the passage from Psalm 36:6, "Thy righteousness is like the mountains of God; thy judgments are a great deep," transposing it to read, "Thy righteousness is over thy judgments as the mountains of God are over the great deep"; then he explained, "As these mountains press down the deep, that it should not rise and engulf the world, so the deeds of the righteous force down the punishments that they should not come upon the world" (Pes.K. 73b).[10]

Bringing Truth to the World

As noted, the Jewish mission to the world is not conceived in terms of converting all others to Judaism. Jews certainly believe their way of Halakhah is supreme and God-given, but their mission is to work with God toward a transformation of the world, a purging and perfecting of human society.

One of the most characteristic Jewish ideas is that of the coming of the Messiah, sent by God to redeem Israel and usher in a new era in which all people will worship the one true God. Traditional Jews have always held that this will be a personal Messiah; others have thought more in terms of a messianic age of restoration that God will bring about sometime in the future. Here, we quote Louis Jacobs on this complicated topic, who writes that the basic affirmation of the expectation of the messiah is that human history will find its culmination and fulfillment here on earth. "Ultimately, the doctrine declares, God will not abandon His world to Moral chaos. Eventually He will intercede directly in order to call a halt to tyranny, oppression and the pursuit of evil so as to restore mankind to the state of bliss here on earth. ...." We must admit we simply do not know what will happen in the messianic age, Jacobs writes;

> we affirm our belief that God will one day intervene, that no good deed goes to waste, that the human drama will somehow find its fulfilment here on earth, that we do right to long and pray for God's direct intervention. More than this we cannot say. We must leave it to God who alone knows all secrets.[11]

Some modern Jews have found deep meaning in the teaching of the medieval Kabbalists about the "breaking of the vessels." Isaac Luria's (1534–1572) mystical vision of the creation of the world involved the idea that God withdrew into Godself to make room for the world, then sent out divine light into this space. The light was to be preserved in special "bowls" (*sefirot*), which had been emanated from God for this purpose. But the divine light was too much for the lower vessels; they burst and were hurled down with some of the divine light. From these shards the dark forces of gross matter took substance. Now all the worlds had sunk to lower levels. But immediately after the disaster the process of restoration (*tikkun*) began, which means the restitution and reintegration of the original whole. The restoration has been almost completed by the supernal lights, but certain concluding actions have been reserved for humans. It is the human historical process and particularly its innermost soul, the religious actions of the Jews, which prepare the way for the final restitution of all the scattered and exiled lights and sparks.

For all the intricacies and strangeness of this medieval vision, it does supply a mystic model for a Jewish mission in the world: to assist God in restoring this imperfect world into the transformed world of God's purpose.

DISCUSSION QUESTIONS

1. What is meant by the Jewish saying that the Sabbath has kept the Jews more than the Jews have kept the Sabbath?
2. What are the main themes of the High Holy Days (Rosh Hashanah and Yom Kippur)?
3. What freedoms does Pesach celebrate?
4. What sense do the dietary laws make for modern Jews?
5. How might one best answer the question "Who is a Jew?"
6. What is the "whole law" that Rabbi Hillel taught to a heathen man while he stood on one foot? What do you think is the significance of this story?
7. What are the central meanings of the Jews being called the "chosen people"?

CHAPTER 7

CHRISTIANITY: SACRED STORY AND HISTORICAL CONTEXT

THE STORY OF CHRISTIAN BEGINNINGS

"Who am I?" A Christian is one who is baptized in the name of Jesus Christ. The sacred story as told by Christians centers on the life of Jesus, as related in the Christian writings called the gospels. But it encompasses much more than just the story of Jesus' life. It reaches back to the sacred history of Israel as God's preparation for the fulfillment in Jesus; it includes the gathering of the Christian church after the death and resurrection of Christ; and it extends to the decisions and clarifications about Christian faith and life given in the New Testament writings and even in the decisions of the early councils of the Christian church.

The Jewish Foundations of Christianity

Jesus was a Jew. Born in a Jewish family, he lived his life practicing the Jewish way; he died and was buried a Jew. Those who followed him and formed the Christian church after his death were Jews. Thus the Christian story begins with Judaism, with those Jews living in Palestine in the Roman occupation and looking for the way to live according to God's covenant.

The times in which Jesus lived were confused and violent. The Jewish people under oppressive Roman rule feared for their religious identity, and they developed different forms of Jewish life under these circumstances. The party of the Zealots, agitating for a Jewish state independent of Rome, was causing uprisings. About the year 4 B.C.E., a certain Judas of Galilee led a bloody revolt against the puppet ruler Herod, king of Galilee, over the question of tribute money being paid to the Romans. The Zealots were defeated and some 2,000 savagely crucified, but their revolutionary sentiments continued to be felt widely throughout the Jewish people.

Other Jews felt differently. The Pharisees believed that a return to the full keeping of the whole Torah would purify the Jewish people, for the kingdom of God would come by keeping the Torah, not by violence and force. The Sadducees, made up of the establishment Jews, considered it essential to preserve the temple and traditional way of life, so they worked together with the Romans to maintain a degree of security and stability. The Essenes felt the majority of the Jews to be hopelessly impure and so withdrew to the shores of the Dead Sea to live a life of purity and await the coming of the messianic age. Many Jews felt a sense of expectancy, of a time soon when God would intervene to restore the sacred people and establish the kingdom of God. But the ideas about how that kingdom would be established differed from group to group.

Christians and the Jewish Sacred Story: the "Old Testament"

In this setting Jesus was born about 4 B.C.E. (the traditional dating is slightly incorrect) and grew up in Nazareth of Galilee, just a few miles from the city of Sepphoris where the Zealots revolted. He was born into a poor family, helped his father as a carpenter, became a wandering preacher and healer and teacher, claimed to present a new message about God and God's kingdom, presented a threat to the authorities, and was executed by crucifixion by the Romans when he was about thirty-three years of age. His was a short, tragic life. But the Christian story sees it differently. Christians see in this short, tragic life the presence of the messiah, the Son of God, the saviour of the world.

The Gospel of Matthew, standing first in the Christian collection of writings known as the New Testament, begins with a genealogy of Jesus: "A book of the descent of Jesus Christ, son of David, son of Abraham" (Matt. 1:1). Thus the Christian story begins by firmly linking Jesus with the history of God's covenant people Israel. As Jews, the first Christians read and interpreted the Torah in much the same way as did their fellow Jews—with one crucial difference: everything in the Torah and in the whole Hebrew Scriptures was understood to point symbolically to Jesus as the messiah.

According to the Christian story, then, God the loving parent created humans to live in fellowship and happiness with their creator. But humans fell into sin, rebelling against God and thus creating an estrangement from God that will continue for all generations. Because of this estrangement, humans live in evil and suffering and death, with eternal punishment the only prospect for the future. God, although a righteous judge, is also a loving parent. So God set about on a plan of salvation, a plan to overcome the sin and evil of humankind and reconcile them to God. For that purpose God called Abraham and his descendants, made a covenant with them, set up the Kingdom of David, and sent prophets to proclaim the divine word. In all of these events, people, and words, God was revealing the plan for the salvation of the world, promising Israel that one day this plan would be fulfilled in a complete and final way. The faithful people of Israel believed in God's promises, and it was counted to them as righteousness. Thus the Christian story looks upon the "Old Testament" (the Hebrew scriptures) as the gradual unfolding of God's plan of salvation, foreshadowing and preparing for the culmination of this salvation through God's work in Jesus Christ. In this sense everything in the Old Testament points ahead to Christ: the high priest foreshadows Christ's priestly role; the king points to Christ's royal office as Son of God; the blood shed at the covenant ceremony prefigures the shedding of Christ's blood to establish a new covenant; and so forth.

The Christian story stresses the incomplete character of the Old Testament. It is understood to be open-ended, revealing the nature of God and the plan of salvation but ending before that salvation has been accomplished. In the Old Testament there are key prophecies, in which God reveals the divine intentions, given to encourage the faithful people to trust the promises and look to the future salvation. In particular, the prophecies about the coming of the messiah and the establishing of the messianic age are important. For example, Isaiah 61:1–2 presents a vision of the messianic age, according to the Christian understanding:

> The spirit of the Lord God is upon me,
>   because the Lord has anointed me;
> he has sent me to proclaim good news to the poor,
>   to bind up the broken-hearted,
> to proclaim liberty to the captives
>   and release to those who are bound;
> to proclaim the year of the Lord's favor.

According to the Christian story, Jesus read this passage at a synagogue meeting, and as he explained it he said, "Today this scripture is fulfilled in your ears" (Luke 4:16–21).

Therefore, as the gospel writers introduce Jesus and describe his life and death, they carefully link him to God's plan of salvation as it has been unfolded in the story of the Old Testament. The expectation of the messiah is in the foreground, and the key question is that one asked by disciples of John the baptizer: "Are you the one who is coming, or do we look for another?" (Luke 7:20). The stories chosen and narrated about Jesus by the writers of the gospels answer that question with a clear, "Yes, this is the one!"

Life and Teachings of Jesus

The focal point of Jesus' story is his death on the cross and his resurrection, understood by Christians as the climax and fulfillment of God's plan of salvation. To the story of his death and resurrection, however, are affixed stories of Jesus' birth and youth, his teachings about God, and the deeds by which he was witness to God's power of salvation. These stories point to the identity of Jesus as the Christ, the one in whom God's presence comes into the human world.

The Birth and Baptism of Jesus

The birth of Jesus, as told in Matthew and Luke, came when God intervened once again in the course of human history to redeem the sacred people, as at the time of Moses. "The birth of Jesus Christ was in this way," wrote Matthew. "Mary his mother was betrothed to Joseph, but before they came together she was found with child by the Holy Spirit." When honorable Joseph was about to set aside the marriage, an angel of the Lord appeared to him and told him this child was conceived by the Holy Spirit. "She will bear a son, and you shall give him the name Jesus [saviour], for he will save his people from their sins" (Matt. 1:18–25). While Joseph and Mary were in Bethlehem to enroll in the census at their ancestral town, the baby Jesus was born, an event accompanied by hosts of angels singing the praises of God to shepherds in the fields. Wise men from the east came to offer gifts to the newborn king of the Jews. All these events symbolized the fulfilling of God's plan and prophecies of old.

When Jesus was a grown man, he began teaching and healing. The gospels first introduce John the baptizer, an ascetic Jew living in the wilderness and

Birth of Jesus. Woodcut by Ryusei Furukawa.

preaching repentance and baptism for the remission of sins. This is the man of whom the prophet Isaiah had written, "The voice of one crying in the wilderness, 'Prepare the way of the Lord'" (Mark 1:2). John pointed to Jesus as the one who was to come after him, the lamb of God; and Jesus went out to be baptized by John in the river Jordan. Again God intervened with a sign: as Jesus came up out of the water, he saw the heavens open and the Spirit descending like a dove on him; a voice spoke from heaven, "You are my beloved son, with you I am well pleased" (Mark 1:9–11). Then Jesus, now knowing that he was God's chosen one, went out to the wilderness to be tested for forty days, thus repeating in his own life the story of God's people Israel (who were tested forty years in the wilderness).

Preaching and Doing the Kingdom of God

Attested by divine signs as the messiah, the chosen one of God, Jesus began preaching in his home area of Galilee, proclaiming the "good news of God" and saying: "The time is fulfilled, and the kingdom of God is come near! Repent, and believe the good news!" (Mark 1:15). Jesus, in his own preaching as presented in the gospels, told that the decisive age had now come for human history. The long period of preparation was over, the "time" was fulfilled. What was bursting upon the people was the long-awaited kingdom of God, when God would intervene in human history to bring about a new age of divine rule. And the proper response to this astounding revelation was to repent and believe the good news.

Shortly after Jesus began preaching the coming of the kingdom of God, he started to gather a community of disciples around himself. Walking by the sea of Galilee he saw two fishermen who were brothers, Simon Peter and Andrew. The story reports that Jesus said to them, "Come with me, and I will make you to be fishers of men." At once they left their nets and followed him (Mark 1:16–17). He called two more fishermen who were brothers, James and John; eventually twelve disciples gathered around him. Although the number twelve seems important to the story, symbolizing as it does the twelve tribes of Israel, many more people also followed Jesus as he went about Galilee as a wandering preacher and healer: "He went

about the whole of Galilee, teaching in their synagogues, preaching the good news of the kingdom, and healing every disease and infirmity among the people. . . . And great crowds followed him" (Matt. 4:23–25). These disciples came from various social groups, although many appear to have been poor and uneducated. He associated with known sinners and tax collectors (whom many Jews condemned as collaborators with the Romans). And there were also women among his followers, including Mary Magdalen, thought to be a prostitute, and Mary and Martha of Bethany. The numbers of disciples and followers fluctuated, and many deserted him when times got bad. But here was the kernel of the new community, following Jesus as their master.

Jesus' work over the short period (traditionally thought to be three years) from the beginning of his preaching in Galilee to his trial in Jerusalem is rehearsed somewhat differently in each of the four gospels. But each describes a combination of teaching and deeds of helping and healing, all of which was to make the kingdom of God present among the people. Jesus' teaching about the kingdom of God described it as a new order in which the love of God and the love of the neighbor would be the ruling motivation. In contrast to nationalistic expectations of a revival of the grand kingdom of David, Jesus taught about an inner kingdom, shared by all those who do God's will.

Much of Jesus' teaching about the kingdom took the form of parables, that is, short stories from everyday life that suggest the reality and the quality of the kingdom. He taught that the kingdom of God is like a wedding feast to which people are invited. The kingdom is not political, nor is it just a future event. The kingdom is already at hand, working in a mysterious and quiet manner, having to do with the community of those who follow Jesus.

That the new era was breaking upon them was vividly demonstrated in Jesus' actions. At Capernaum, where Jesus was teaching in the synagogue, a man possessed by an unclean spirit shrieked: "What do you have to do with us, O Jesus of Nazareth? have you come to destroy us? I know who you are—the Holy One of God!" Jesus exorcised the unclean spirit with a command, and all the people said, "What is this? A new kind of teaching with authority! He commands even the unclean spirits, and they obey him" (Mark 1:21–28). The gospels recount many such incidents where Jesus performed deeds of healing, exorcism of evil spirits, multiplying food and wine, even raising the dead—as signs that the new age of God's kingdom had dawned.

A Radical New Way of Life

Corresponding to the new age of the kingdom, Jesus taught a new way of life. As a practicing Jew himself, he emphasized two main tenets of the Jewish Torah: to love God with all one's heart, soul, and mind; and to love one's neighbor as oneself (Matt. 22:35–40; cf. Deut. 6:5; Lev. 19:18). However, he taught a more radical approach to loving God and one's neighbor than most of his fellow Jewish teachers did. In the homily called the Sermon on the Mount, he contrasted his teaching with the accepted tradition:

> You have heard that it was said to our forefathers, "You shall not kill; anyone who kills will be liable to judgment." But I say to you, anyone who nurses anger against his brother will be liable to judgment. . . . You have heard that it was said, "Do not commit adultery." But I say to you that everyone who looks on a woman lustfully has already committed adultery with her in his heart.   (MATT. 5:21–28)

Much of Jesus' teaching overturned the usual notions of behavior and God's rewards for it. Again from the Sermon on the Mount:

> Blessed are those of gentle spirit, for they shall inherit the earth.
> Blessed are those who hunger and thirst for righteousness, for they shall be satisfied.
> Blessed are those who show mercy, for mercy shall be shown to them.
> Blessed are those whose hearts are pure, for they shall see God.
> Blessed are the peacemakers, for they shall be called children of God.
> Blessed are those persecuted for the cause of righteousness, for theirs is the kingdom of heaven.   (MATT. 5:3–10)

So radical is the demand for a new kind of life in the new age that Jesus said, "You have heard that it was said [to your fathers], 'Love your neighbor, and hate your enemy.' But I say to you, love your enemies and pray on behalf of your persecutors. . . . You therefore shall be perfect, as your heavenly father is perfect" (Matt 5:43–48).

Throughout these teachings and deeds there is the ring of a strong sense of authority, of speaking for God, of sensing God's presence in a powerful way. In his prayers to God, Jesus (who spoke Aramaic, the common language of Palestine at this time) used the Aramaic term *Abba*, a familiar and endearing word for "father." It is true that many of Jesus' sayings about his relationship with God are shot through with mystery and ambivalence. In the earliest gospel, that of Mark, Jesus is not reported to have claimed to be the messiah or the Son of God—though others speak of him that way. But the gospel writers, telling the story at least a generation after the time of Jesus, certainly knew the belief of the earliest Christians that Jesus in fact was the messiah. The Gospel of John, for example, has Jesus clearly revealing his identity as the Son of God through whom the Father is working. In any case, Jesus' actions and words were so radical and so full of the claim to God's authority that he was bound to come into conflict with the accepted Jewish interpretations.

The Conflict Over Authority

The gospels and epistles of the New Testament, the new Christian scriptures, were written some years after Jesus' death, and they reflect to some extent the conflicts that developed later between the Jewish and Christian communities. But the Christian story pinpoints the heart of the conflict especially in Jesus' new interpretations of the Jewish Torah. On the one hand, he made the requirements much more stringent and radical. But, on the other hand, he acted as if he were above the Torah. For example, when he and his disciples walked along the road on a sabbath, they picked grain in the fields to prepare some food. When confronted by the Pharisees over this unnecessary breaking of the sabbath law, Jesus stated: "The sabbath was made for the sake of humans and not humans for the sake of the sabbath; therefore the son of man is master even of the sabbath" (Mark 2:27–28). He healed people on the sabbath. He forgave sins in his own name, leaving some lawyers to say, "Blasphemy! Who but God alone can forgive sin?" (Mark 2:7).

Possibly the biggest scandal Jesus caused resulted from his attitude toward sinners, toward those who consistently broke the Torah. He associated with such people and became known as a "friend of sinners." He sat at table with them, extending the intimacy of table-fellowship to those who had put themselves outside the covenant people of God. And he taught that God forgives such people—in defiance of the traditional perception that God rewards those who do the divine will and punishes those who willingly break laws of the Torah and refuse to repent. Further, he suggested that even the presumed righteousness of the religious teachers was no real righteousness at all. In words reminiscent of the prophets of old, Jesus castigated them: "Woe to you, scribes and Pharisees, hypocrites! For while you give tithes of mint and dill and cummin, you have neglected the more important demands of the Law, namely, justice, mercy, and faith. These you should do while not neglecting the others. O blind guides, you strain the gnat out, but you drink down the camel!" (Matt. 23:13–24). The parable of the wedding feast summed up this upside-down view of God and the covenant people. Those good people invited to the wedding, who found various excuses not to come, will find themselves shut out, while the bridegroom will send out to the highways and hedges to bring in the poor, the maimed, the blind, and the lame (Luke 14:15–24).

What Jesus was teaching about the Torah and about God went beyond the covenant notion of the life of Torah as the highest good for humans and of God as a partner who rewards those who are faithful and punishes those who break the Torah. Jesus said that he came not to destroy the Torah but to fulfill it (Matt. 5:17); but he radicalized the demands of the Torah so that the most pious people in Israel fell far short of keeping the Torah in his eyes. And he taught that God is a friend to sinners, searching out the outcasts and rejected of the people. The whole notion of God as one who rewards and punishes based on covenant law was rejected in Jesus' teaching. Rather, God forgives and accepts sinners—even the woman caught in adultery, even the tax collector.

These teachings and acts of Jesus seemed to some to be extremely arrogant and boastful—after all, Jesus was putting himself above the Torah; he was presuming to give radical new interpretations of the commandments. He claimed to be "master of the sabbath." Above all, he claimed to have a special close relationship with God as "Abba," which gave him authority to teach things about God that seemed to contradict the Torah given through Moses. In the traditional view, such rash words and deeds were "blasphemy," that is, dishonoring God, putting oneself in place of God.

Crucifixion and Resurrection

The historical facts of Jesus' arrest, trial, and execution cannot be clearly and accurately reconstructed, for the Christian story is more interested in the theological meaning of this happening than in historical detail. Jesus certainly did antagonize some of the leaders of his Jewish community, and it is possible that they brought religious charges against him. But he also posed a political threat to the Roman occupational government; large groups of people acclaiming him as the messiah, the "king of the Jews," could easily turn into a violent, nationalistic uprising. So it was the Roman government that arrested him, condemned him hastily to death, and executed him by crucifixion. It is true that there are elements of anti-Jewish feeling in the stories of Jesus' trial as recorded in the gospels—probably reflecting the sour relations between Christians and Jews in a later generation when the gospels were written. It is also true that in later centuries Christians sometimes rashly charged Jews with the death of Jesus. But Christians today have come to realize that such anti-Jewish elements are not an authentic part of the story of Jesus. He did no doubt have conflicts with some Jewish teachers and leaders. But, as the Apostles' Creed insists, he "was crucified under Pontius Pilate," the Roman governor.

The Meaning of Jesus' Death

But the Christian story really is not interested in the question of who killed Jesus. Much more important is the question of why Jesus died. The gospels present his death as having a meaning and purpose, indeed of happening in accordance with God's will and design. From early in his public career, Jesus began to predict that he would have to follow God's plan and suffer and die at Jerusalem. The story says that, after Peter had just stated that he believed Jesus to be the Christ, the messiah, "he [Jesus] began to teach them that the son of man must suffer many things, be rejected by the elders, chief priests, and scribes, be put to death, and after three days rise again" (Mark 8:27–32). Why did this have to happen? Jesus taught that "the son of man goes as it is written of him" (Matt. 26:24)—that is, in the scriptures God's plan had been revealed, and by Jesus' suffering and death this plan of salvation would be accomplished.

The disciples, of course, did not understand such talk, and Peter rebuked Jesus for saying this. Their idea of the messiah was still that of a royal hero who would set up a great kingdom and place them at his right hand and his left in positions of power (Mark 10:37). Only after his death did his followers begin to understand that God's plan for the salvation of humankind involved taking all the sins and burdens of the world on Godself through the righteous servant. God's plan was to have a *suffering* messiah. They looked to the great prophetic passage from Isaiah 53 as the key to understanding why the son of man must be given up to suffer and die:

> He was despised and rejected by men,
> > a man of sorrows and acquainted with grief;
> and as one from whom people hide their faces
> > he was despised, and we had no esteem for him.
> Surely he himself has borne our griefs,
> > and our sorrows he carried;
> yet we counted him stricken,
> > smitten by God, and afflicted.
> But he was wounded for our transgressions,
> > tortured for our iniquities;
> the chastisement upon him made us whole,
> > and by his stripes we are healed.
> All of us strayed like sheep,
> > each of us turned to his own way.
> But the Lord laid upon him the iniquity of us all. . . .
> Therefore I will allot him a portion with the great,
> > and with the mighty he will share the spoil,

> because he poured out his soul to death,
> > and with the transgressors he was numbered.
> Yet he bore the sin of many,
> > and for the transgressors he interceded.
> > > (ISA. 55:3–6, 12)

Jesus' role as the messiah was to follow the path of the suffering servant. Telling his disciples to be servants of one another, Jesus said, "For even the son of man did not come to be served but to serve, and to give up his life a ransom for many" (Mark 10:45).

The Holy Week in Jerusalem

Because of this conviction that he was carrying out God's plan, Jesus turned with his disciples from Galilee and made his way up to Jerusalem to confront the religious leaders there. The gospels concentrate on this "passion story," the events from Jesus' triumphal entry into Jerusalem until his death. He rode into Jerusalem as a king, seated on a donkey, with great crowds before and after singing the old chant of tribute to the king: "Hosanna to the son of David! Blessed is the one who comes in the name of the Lord!" (Matt. 21:9). He confronted the authority of the religious leaders directly with his own charismatic authority. He went into the temple, the symbol of priestly authority, and overturned the tables of those who exchanged money and sold pigeons for sacrifices; and he healed blind men and cripples in the temple, refusing to answer the elders when they asked him, "By what authority are you doing these things?" (Matt. 21:23).

In Jerusalem, Jesus went to an upper room where he celebrated the Passover meal together with his community of disciples. Teaching them again about his coming death, Jesus used the wine and the bread of the Passover meal to symbolize his own body and blood, which would be sacrified, as reported by Matthew:

> During supper Jesus took bread, and, saying the blessing, broke it and gave it to the disciples with the words: "Take and eat; this is my body." Then, taking a cup and giving thanks, he gave it to them saying: "Drink from it, all of you, for this is my blood of the covenant, poured out for many for the forgiveness of sins."
> > (MATT. 26:26–28)

The early Christians understood this act as the institution of the sacred meal of the Christians, the Lord's Supper or Eucharist. Paul wrote that Jesus told them to "do this in remembrance of me," and then Paul added, "As often as you eat this bread and drink this cup, you proclaim the death of the Lord, until he comes" (I Cor. 11:23–26).

Later, after the Passover meal, Jesus and his disciples went out into the Garden of Gethsemane to pray. Jesus was in agony, and he prayed, "My father, if it is possible, let this cup pass from me. Yet not as I will, but as you will" (Matt. 26:39). One of his disciples, Judas, had betrayed his whereabouts to those looking to arrest him; when he was seized, all his disciples deserted him and fled. He was first brought to the house of the high priest, where various charges were brought against him. Finally the high priest put him under oath and demanded, "Tell us if you are the messiah, the son of God?" Jesus answered, "You have said. But I tell you this: hereafter you will see the son of man seated at the right hand of Power, coming on the clouds of heaven." At this, the high priest and council decided he was

Jesus' agony in the Garden of Gethsemane. Painting by El Greco.

indeed guilty of blasphemy, and they handed him over to Pilate, the Roman governor (Matt. 26:59–66). In the meantime, Peter was denying that he even knew Jesus, and Judas was in remorse for what he had done and hanged himself.

Jesus refused to answer Pilate's questions during the trial, and finally Pilate, washing his hands to signify his innocence in the matter, had Jesus flogged and handed him over to his soldiers to be crucified. Taking him to Golgotha, the hill of execution, they crucified him between two other criminals. Suffering on the cross, Jesus asked forgiveness for his tormentors and, in his torment of suffering, cried out the words of Psalm 22, "My God, my God, why have you forsaken me?" Finally, with the words, "It is finished!," he died. The gospels tell how his death was accompanied with divine signs: three hours of darkness came first; then, when he died, the curtain partitioning off the Holy of Holies in the temple was torn in two from top to bottom. And the Roman centurion watching this all was moved to say, "Truly this was a son of God" (Mark 15:39).

The Christian story tells how Jesus' body was taken and buried in a tomb by a respected Jew, Joseph of Arimathaea, and how a guard was set so Jesus' followers would not steal the body. The next day was the sabbath, so early on the day after the sabbath several women who were followers of Jesus came to the tomb to anoint his body with oils—but they found the tomb was empty, and a youth sitting there in a white robe told them, "Do not fear! You are looking for Jesus of Nazareth, who was crucified. He is risen, he is not here" (Mark 16:6).

Other disciples at first refused to believe this news, according to the gospel accounts; but Jesus, risen from the dead, appeared to them a number of times—while several of them were walking on the road, and again while the eleven disciples were sitting at table. He had told them to meet him on a mountain in Galilee, and they made their way there. Before he finally left them, he gave them a commission to go out into all the world and bring the good news of salvation to all. Luke reports that after Jesus had given them this commission, he was lifted up, and a cloud removed him out of their sight (Acts 1:9).

Thus ends the story of the earthly Jesus—and begins

the story of the risen Christ, Lord of the church, reigning at God's right hand and present in the world wherever his followers are. For this story of Jesus is a *sacred* story; in it Christians see revealed God's own son, the messiah, the saviour of the world. When Christians gather together they tell this story to one another as the Gospel, the Good News of God acting in Jesus Christ to bring salvation for all the world. Christians identify with this story, taking inspiration from it and modeling their lives on Jesus' own life.

Beginnings of the Christian Church

The four gospels are followed in the Christian scriptures by a writing called "The Acts of the Apostles," continuing the story of the risen Christ and the gathering of his followers into the "Christian church"—that is, the real founding of Christianity as a religion.

Pentecost and the Birth of the Church

The story tells how the disciples were confused and afraid after Jesus' death, and that only seeing the risen Christ kindled their courage. But before Jesus left them he told them to wait in Jerusalem to be baptized by the Holy Spirit. So on the Jewish festival of Shavuot (Pentecost) they were all together, when suddenly a great wind filled the house and tongues like flames of fire rested on each one. They were filled with the Spirit and began to speak in other tongues so that Jewish pilgrims from various parts of the world could understand them, each in his own language. Peter, assuming a leadership role, stood up and preached the first Christian sermon, explaining that this happening was the promised pouring out of God's Spirit (Joel 2:28–32), which was to take place on the great day of the Lord. The new age had come! Peter explained how this Jesus, who was crucified, had been chosen by God; in God's plan he had been killed, but God raised him to life. "Let all the house of Israel then know for certain that God has made him both Lord and messiah, this Jesus you crucified!" When the people asked what they should now do, Peter said, "Repent and be baptized, every one of you, in the name of Jesus Christ, for the forgiveness of your sins; then you will receive the gift of the Holy Spirit" (Acts 2:1–39).

Those who accepted Peter's words were baptized (some 3,000 that day, the story says), and the Christian church came into being. They continued to practice baptism, to meet together to hear the apostles teach, to celebrate the Lord's Supper, to pray, and to share the common life. At first they sold their property and had everything in common. When disagreements arose concerning distribution of food to widows, the whole group selected seven deacons to handle the needs of food and clothing of the community, while the apostles devoted themselves to prayer and the ministry of preaching the gospel. With that began the earliest forms of ministry in the church.

Trials and Persecutions of the First Christians

The Christian sacred story tells of the trials of the early church in Jerusalem. They still considered themselves Jews and attended the temple; but other Jews, considering them to be an erring sect worshiping a false messiah, persecuted them, scattering many of them to the country districts of Judea and Samaria, where they continued to convert and baptize many. The first martyr was Stephen, one of the deacons, whose testimony to Jesus enraged a crowd so that they stoned him.

A witness to the stoning was a young Jew named Saul, born as a Roman citizen in Tarsus of Asia Minor but who came to Jerusalem to learn better the Jewish way of life. Saul joined in the persecution of the Jewish Christians with great zeal until, on the road to Damascus, a light flashed from the sky and Saul heard a voice saying, "Saul, Saul, why do you persecute me?" It was the risen Jesus, who gave Saul the mission to proclaim his name before nations and kings (Acts 9:1–16). Saul, later known as Paul, became the great missionary for Christ, making trips throughout the Greek-speaking world—Asia Minor, Greece, and Italy—preaching the gospel of Christ and establishing Christian congregations wherever he went. Other apostles and leaders also went out in mission, to Samaria, Syria, Ethiopia, Arabia, and other places, and many people believed in the gospel about Jesus Christ and were baptized. Christians were carrying out the commission given by Jesus: "You shall be my witnesses in Jerusalem and in all Judea and Samaria and to the end of the earth" (Acts 1:8).

In this Christian story of the people of God gathered around Jesus Christ, two developments were particularly crucial on the way to the universal Christian church. One arose from the tension within the early Christian community between the Jewish heritage and the mission to bring the gospel to all the world. The other development arose from the need to translate the Jewish Christian gospel into language and concepts understandable to people in the Hellenistic (Greek-speaking) world of the Roman Empire. Both of these developments involved a great deal of thinking and struggling with the meaning of faith in Jesus as the Christ. This was the beginning of *theologizing*, that is, creating Christian doctrines of faith to guide people and preserve the good news about Jesus. These developments arose out of specific situations in the different Christian communities. It was in response to such situations that the gospels and the letters that make up the New Testament were written. Paul, whose letters responding to problems in different congregations are the earliest writings in the New Testament, had a particularly profound influence on the development of Christian theology. The Johannine writings (the Gospel of John and the letters of John), traditionally attributed to Jesus' disciple John but of uncertain authorship, have also had a deep impact on theological perspectives.

Jews and Gentiles in the Christian Church

After Paul's conversion, he returned to Tarsus, and then with his colleague Barnabas he set up work in Antioch. He felt himself called especially to bring the gospel to the gentiles (non-Jews), so with Antioch as a base he launched out into the Greek world. At first he regularly went to the Jewish synagogues to proclaim to the Jewish communities, scattered throughout the Roman world, that the fulfillment of their hopes was in Jesus as the messiah. Usually he had limited success among the Jewish people, so more and more he began to take the message about Christ to the non-Jewish population. Thus there arose many Christian con-

gregations that were made up of both Jewish and gentile Christians. And the question arose: should the non-Jewish Christians be compelled to follow the rules of the Torah, like circumcision and the dietary laws? Some Jewish Christians were insisting that they must, since these were laws given by God; others apparently advocated separating into two churches, one comprised of Torah-observing Christians and the other of gentiles who did not observe the laws of the Torah.

The basic question was discussed in a meeting of the apostles in Jerusalem. They decided to impose no "irksome burdens" on the gentile Christians, except for these essentials: to abstain from meat offered to idols, from blood, from anything strangled, and from fornication (Acts 15:6–29). It was their view, thus, that it is not necessary for Christians to observe all the Torah of Moses. The problem kept arising, however. In Galatia,

Christian monks in Jerusalem on the Via Dolorosa, the traditional route on which Jesus was led to the cross.

some Jewish Christians tried to insist that the gentiles must be circumcised and obey the dietary laws in addition to faith in Christ, and Paul responded with the Letter to the Galatians in which he wrote what became the classic defense of Christian liberty. He insisted that a person is right with God only by trust in the promise about Christ, not by any works or ritual observances. Here he articulated the central Christian doctrine of salvation simply by faith, and he further showed how this would lead Christians to live their lives freely motivated by the promptings of the Spirit of God. And in the Letter to the Ephesian congregations Paul showed how there can be but one Christian church. Although Christians come from various races and nationalities, they are one because they are part of the one "body of Christ." The Johannine writings likewise emphasize that, within the different communities, there is "one flock and one shepherd" (John 10:16).

Bringing the Gospel to the Hellenistic World

The other major development in the Christian sacred history of the earliest church was the translation and interpretation of the good news about Jesus for the peoples of the Hellenistic world. For the early Jewish Christian, the good news of Jesus could be told almost entirely in terms and concepts drawn from the Jewish scriptures, as Peter did in his first sermon on the day of Pentecost (Acts 2). Jesus was the fulfillment of God's promises through the Old Testament prophets; he was the messiah, the son of David, the suffering servant on whom God places sins, the sacrificial lamb of atonement; God chose him at the fullness of time, to establish the long-awaited kingdom of God through him. Jews who heard this message would understand it, even if they were not inclined to accept Jesus as the messiah. But gentiles of the Hellenistic world knew nothing of the Old Testament, of the expectation of the kingdom of God and the messiah. They looked at the world and human existence in a different way, in ideas shaped by Greek thinking, mystery religions, and a pervasive religious perspective known as Gnosticism. Thus it was the delicate task of early Christian theologians to translate the good news about Jesus into ideas that these people could understand and believe, without losing what the good news was all about.

In a general way the picture of the world in the Hellenistic religions was more vertical, without the Jewish sense of history moving horizontally toward a fulfillment in the new age of the kingdom of God. People pictured two realms, the divine realm of light above, and the material realm of darkness beneath, which was held by demonic forces. The human soul is a spark of light from above, whereas the body is a prison of material from which the soul has to be liberated. In the Hellenistic mystery religions this salvation took place by initiation into the worship of a personal divine redeemer through whom liberation could be experienced. In the Gnostic groups, it was felt that a divine redeemer from the world of light would impart secret knowledge to people, teaching them how their souls could be delivered from the prison of the world and their bodies.

Struggling with how to communicate the gospel of Christ to people with these kinds of ideas, Paul, the Johannine author, and other early theologians began to plumb the depths of the doctrine of *Christology*, that is, thinking about the nature of Christ. They argued that to call Jesus the messiah, the saviour on whom God laid the sins of the world, was to say at the same time that God was somehow present in a special and powerful way in Jesus the messiah. It was to say that God "came down" and became the redeemer of the world in Jesus. It was to say, then, that Jesus was God. One way of putting it was this:

> [Christ Jesus], being in the form of God, did not think to grasp at equality with God but emptied himself, taking the form of a slave, being born in human likeness. And being found in human shape, he humbled himself, being obedient even to death—death on a cross. Therefore God exalted him highly and gave to him the name which is above all names, that at the name of Jesus every knee should bow—in heaven, on earth, and under the earth—and every tongue confess, "Jesus Christ is Lord," to the glory of God the Father. (PHIL. 2:5-11)

Again, the early Christians confessed that "He [Jesus] is the image of the invisible God. . . . All the fulness of God was pleased to dwell in him, through him reconciling everything to himself, making peace through the blood of his cross" (Col. 1:15–20).

The early theologians rejected the Gnostic ideas about the material world and the body being an evil prison. Rather, they talked about the "incarnation" of God in Jesus Christ: God became flesh in the person of Jesus and thus was united with the flesh of all humanity (John 1:14). Further, they continued the Jewish belief in the resurrection of the body, rejecting the Greek idea that only the soul was immortal and would be delivered from the evil prison of the body.

In communicating the gospel to the Hellenistic world, the early Christian church came to incorporate in its story the ongoing encounter with God through the worship of the risen Christ, the Son of God who is present in a real way in his body, the church. The Christian story in the Hellenistic world also continued the Jewish perspective of history moving toward a consummation. Christ will come again, and then will be the resurrection and the judgment and the full establishing of the kingdom of this world as the kingdom of God.

In telling the story of Jesus and of his church, then, Christians are telling their own identity. For they are "little Christs," living as his body present in the world.

SOME HISTORICAL TRANSFORMATIONS OF THE CHRISTIAN WAY

At the close of the New Testament period, around the end of the first century c.e., the church had been established in many parts of the Roman world. But there were many challenges that it faced over the next several centuries, as Christians created a church that transcended the decline and fall of the Roman Empire. The medieval synthesis of culture produced Christendom, but that was shaken and torn apart in the Reformation and the Enlightenment. Much of the modern history of Christianity has been tied up with the rise of science and industralization, introducing problems that the Christian churches are still trying to meet. Christian identity today has been shaped by all these historical transformations.

The Early Christian Church in the Roman World

Because Christians had been closely tied to Judaism, severing that relationship was a painful process. Further, leaving the security of being a Jewish sect that was permitted by the Roman authorities, the Christian church found itself an illicit religion in the Roman Empire, and at times its members suffered persecution and had to practice their religion secretly and underground. This "church of the catacombs" continued to grow, however, and the blood of the martyrs became the seed of the church.

The Challenge of Gnosticism

Continuing challenges to faith and doctrine came in the form of Hellenistic cults and philosophies. Gnosticism especially proved to be a persistent influence in shaping beliefs of the Christians, providing as it did an answer to the question of evil and how one can be freed from it. The world of matter is evil and unreal, but humans are essentially spiritual, Gnosticism taught; salvation means escape from this worldly prison. These ideas led to new pictures of Jesus as the great Spirit descended from the world of light, spreading his secret teaching to liberate the souls of his followers from the prison of this material world.

A leading Christian thinker with Gnostic tendencies was Marcion (d. ca. 160). He taught that love is the central element in Christianity, and that Christ's salvation is of the spirit, not the body. Since the Old Testament is based on law and justice, Marcion concluded that the God of the Old Testament was an evil creator who had made physical sex the means of reproduction. Marcion rejected the Old Testament completely, and he carefully edited Christian writings to exclude anything contrary to his Gnostic ideas. He rejected marriage, wine, and anything to do with the body. Only celibates could be baptized.

Many Christian thinkers entered the lists to defend Christian faith against Gnosticism and Marcionism. For example, Irenaeus (ca. 130–202) defended the authority of the Old Testament, arguing that God created all matter and form. Humans are created in the image of God, even though they have become bogged down into sin. Christ, eternal with the Father, truly became man, exhibiting what humans should be in growing to their full stature; the divine entered this life to show us how to recover the image of God.

Canon, Creed, Clergy

In order to resolve the questions raised by Gnostics and others, the early church needed to do three things: declare what its authentic Scriptures were, formulate its beliefs clearly, and establish the continuity of a recognized leadership. The result was the canon (accepted sacred writings) of the New Testament, the Apostles' Creed, and the structure of clergy leadership.

Between the second and fourth centuries, Christian leaders came to agreement on which sacred writings should make up the Christian scriptures of the New Testament. Copies of various gospels and letters of the apostles had been circulating in the churches, but now an effort was made to determine which ones should be considered authoritative for all Christians. The major test was that they should have been authored by an apostle. Further, the content should correspond to the faith that was handed down by the apostles. By these tests, eventually the Gnostic and other questionable writings were excluded, and the New Testament was narrowed down to the generally accepted canon of twenty-seven writings.

The Apostles' Creed was the earliest confession of faith that widely circulated in the early church, having been composed around the year 150. It emphasized doctrines especially against Gnostic ideas, asserting the creation of the world by God, Christ as true man who suffered and died, the resurrection of the body, and the final judgment.

To combat the misguided teachings and maintain unity and order, the early church devised ecclesiastical leadership. The office of bishop (overseer) became the church's bulwark of unity and defense against heresy, the bishop standing in apostolic succession reaching back to Peter and Paul. To assist the bishop in leading communities of Christians, presbyters (elders) and deacons were also ordained, the presbyter to preside over worship and the deacon to minister to the people's needs.

Philosophy and Theology

As more and more educated people of the Roman world converted to Christianity, the fertile challenge of Greek philosophy became more pressing. Up to now Christian thinkers had responded to challenges on an ad hoc basis, with letters, specific defenses (apologies), sermons, and manuals of ethics. But the serious confrontation with philosophical world views called for more comprehensive theological systems. The big question increasingly raised itself: how does Christian belief about the world stand up to the systematic understanding of the philosophers and scientists of the Graeco-Roman tradition?

Some Christian thinkers, trained in philosophy but now convinced of the truth of Christianity, answered this by arguing the truth of Scripture and the apostolic tradition over against the uncertainties of human reason. Tertullian (ca. 145–220), for example, argued that God's revelation was found in the Scriptures and apostolic testimony, not in philosopical speculation: "What has Christ to do with Plato, Jerusalem with Athens?" Still, Tertullian began to devise a theological system explaining the Triune God as Father, Son, and Holy Spirit.

Others, like Justin Martyr (ca. 100–166) and Clement of Alexandria (150–215), saw Greek philosophy as an authentic expression of God's truth. Justin felt that the same Logos (Word, John 1:1) that had inspired the prophets of the Old Testament and that became manifest in Christ had also inspired the Greek philosophers. He did hold, however, that the truth of philosophy is incomplete apart from its completion in Christ. Clement also held that all truth comes from the universal Logos, and thus philosophical speculation and prophetic revelation are compatible. Clement even suggested theologians could look to the thinkers of ancient Persia, India, and other places to find truth that comes from the eternal Logos and that is fully expressed in the Christian scriptures and in Christ.

Emperor Constantine and Imperial Christianity

Christians steadily increased in the Roman Empire. But as an illicit religion, they continued to suffer periodic persecutions. The last persecution was

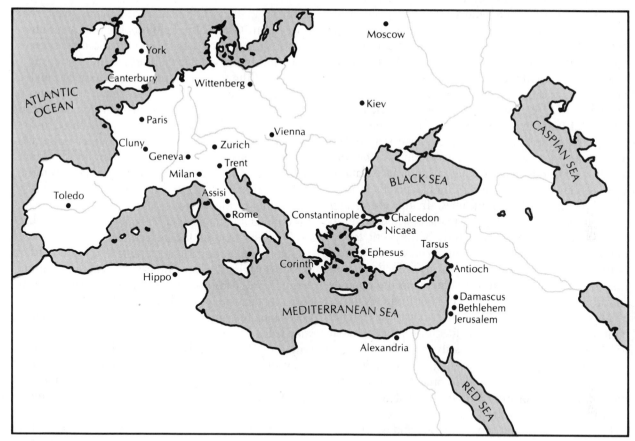

Christianity in Asia, Africa, and Europe.

the most vicious—that under Emperor Diocletian (r. 284–305). But in 312 one of his generals, Constantine, was victorious over the other generals in gaining control of Rome, and a new day began. Perhaps seeing the trends, Constantine began to side with the Christians (although he himself was not baptized as a Christian until he was on his death bed). In 313 the Edict of Milan granted toleration to Christianity, and Constantine did much to strengthen and unify the church. Although anti-Christian policies were briefly revived under Emperor Julian (the Apostate, r. 361–363), by 380 Emperor Theodosius I made Christianity the *only* religion allowed in the Roman Empire.

Now the situation of the Christian church changed— it was established, an integral part of Roman culture, joined with the political structures of the Roman Empire. Its destiny was for the time at least intertwined with Rome. Christianity clearly had become a world religion.

Counterculture: Monasticism
Judaism had placed little importance on asceticism, that is, withdrawal from the social and sensuous aspects of life. But from early on groups of Christians devoted themselves to fasting, prayer, contemplation, and a life of poverty. Many followed Paul in considering virginity and celibacy to be superior to marriage, and martyrdom was seen as the supreme way to heaven.

As the Christian church moved into partnership with the political structure and culture of the Roman state, the monastic movement created a kind of counterculture of withdrawal. And, whereas monasticism began as a rigorous discipline practiced in isolation, later the monasteries became important socializing forces in the development of Christendom, as most church leaders underwent training and discipline in the monasteries.

Already in the third century there appeared the two basic types of monasticism. The eremitical (hermit) monk was an individual seeking salvation in isolation, and the cenobitic (communal) monks practiced their disciplines in small communities. In the fourth and fifth centuries thousands of Christians withdrew from society and took to monasticism. Some went to extremes, doing things like living in caves or tombs, fasting frequently, not bathing, waking every three minutes to praise God, avoiding contact with the opposite sex, and generally outdoing each other in the extremes of physical deprivation. One well-known but extreme eremitic monk was Simeon Stylites (d. ca. 454) who sat for thirty-six years on top of a sixty-foot pillar!

Two important leaders of monasticism were Basil of Caesarea (ca. 330–379) and Jerome (ca. 347–420). Basil created a monastic Rule that provided structure for the monks within the larger church order. He set forth an ideal of perfect service to God and communal obedience, emphasizing poverty, chastity, prayer, study, and labor. Basil's Rule formed the basis of monasticism in the eastern section of the Christian church. In the western part of the Roman Empire, Jerome combined his scholarly pursuits (such as translating the Bible into Latin) with the promotion of monasticism. Under his influence even rich women of Rome joined monasteries or turned their homes into monasteries. One widow, Paula, traveled with Jerome to Syria and Palestine, founding monasteries and convents and a hospice for travelers.

Theological Controversies and Church Councils

As Christianity became a world religion, it spread through the Roman Empire and beyond it to the East—to Edessa, Armenia, Mesopotamia, Persia, Arabia, perhaps even to India and China. Growing and maturing in these different environments, with challenges from Gnosticism, philosophy, and a variety of eastern spiritual influences, some basic differences of belief and thought arose within the church.

Many of the major controversies concerned the doctrine of God, especially the Trinity and the person of Christ. These Trinitarian and Christological controversies took place in the fourth and fifth centuries, giving rise to a number of important ecumenical (worldwide) councils—gatherings of bishops from all over the church to debate and decide on orthodox doctrine. Through these debates and the resolutions decided by the councils, the catholic (universal) Christian faith was defined and the dissenting beliefs rejected as "heresies" (beliefs dividing the church).

The Arian controversy erupted in the eastern churches of the Roman Empire and caused a great rift. Arius, a priest from Egypt, put forth the view that the Son was created by the Father in time. This created Logos took the form of the earthly Jesus to bring saving knowledge. Thus, "there was when he was not," and only the Father is truly eternal God. This Arian view was widely accepted, for it was based on biblical statements, and it seemed to solve the problem of the Trinity appearing to be three Gods. Here appeared to be a simple, strong monotheism.

But Bishop Athanasius (ca. 296–373) and other Christian thinkers recognized a danger to the Christian faith in this popular Arian view. To worship Christ as a being created in time would be to worship a divine being other than the one God! Emperor Constantine, anxious to settle this dispute and unify his realm, convened an ecumenical council at Nicea in Asia Minor in 325. The council solved the problem by deciding that the Son is "true God from true God, begotten, not made, one in being with the Father." The catholic position was that there is one God who nevertheless consists of three "persons"—Father, Son, and Holy Spirit. Some years later the Council of Constantinople arrived at a final formulation for this Trinitarian view: the Trinity is an eternal unity, the Father eternally ingenerate, the Son eternally begotten of the Father, the Holy Spirit eternally proceeding from the Father.

Whereas these councils settled the issue of the Son as fully divine, another controversy arose concerning the nature of Christ himself: did he have a split personality? did his divine nature replace his human nature? what part of him was divine and what part human? Nestorius of Syria held that Christ was two persons, one divine and the other human; but only the human person was born from Mary's womb. Another group called Monophysites (single nature) took an opposite view, insisting that Christ has only a single divine nature. Finally the Council of Chalcedon in 451 formulated the orthodox position: the incarnated Christ has two natures, divine and human, united in a single person. He is

> one and the same Christ, Son, Lord, Only-begotten, recognized in two natures, without confusion, without change, without division, without separation; the distinction of natures being in no way annulled by the union, but rather the characteristics of each nature being preserved and coming together to form one person and subsistence.[1]

Augustine, Bishop of Hippo

Emperor Constantine moved his capital eastward to Constantinople, and the Greek-speaking Christians of the East began drifting away from the West. The northern barbarians were closing in on Rome. The church, now identified with the Roman Empire, was wracked with new controversies in place of those that had been settled. For example, Manicheism, a mixture of Zoroastrianism, Christianity, and Buddhism, presented a strong rival to Christianity. It taught a dualism of light and darkness and advocated a severe asceticism to liberate the divine particles of light. Within the Christian church, Pelagius was teaching that every person is free, as Adam was, to sin or not to sin; thus there was not a universal need for Christ's work of redemption.

In these intercrossings of history and controversy, Augustine (354–430) stood forth as one of the greatest theologians of the early church. In his *Confessions* (an autobiographical masterpiece of Latin literature), Augustine says that the soul is restless until it finds rest in God. He did much searching before he found his resting point. He lived with a mistress for fifteen years, had a son, and searched for the truth in Manicheism for many years. He reports his own prayer during this time: "Give me chastity and continence, but not yet."

Then he studied Neo-Platonism, heard the preaching of Ambrose, bishop of Milan, and found his way back to the Christian faith (the religion of his mother). While he still was struggling with his attachments to his sensual way of life, he heard a child's voice from over a garden wall crying, "Tolle lege, tolle lege" (Take up and read, take up and read). He opened at random a copy of Paul's Letter to the Romans and read: "Let us walk becomingly, as in daytime, not in rioting and drunkenness, not in lust and wantonness, not in strife and rivalry. Rather, arm yourself with the Lord Jesus Christ, and give no thought to the flesh for its desires" (Rom. 13:13–14). Feeling this was an oracle from God, Augustine's doubts were resolved, and he soon was baptized. He practiced the monastic life, became a priest, and finally was made bishop of Hippo in north Africa.

Arguing against Pelagius, Augustine insisted that the fall into sin caused a basic change in human nature. Sin lodges in the will, consisting of the attempt to usurp the place of God. We are not able not to sin, and hence we cannot help toward our salvation but must depend entirely on God's grace in Christ.

Augustine like others was deeply affected by the sack of Rome by Alaric and the pagan Goths in 410—eternal Rome had fallen! To show that this was not the fault of Christianity, Augustine wrote his monumental *City of God*, finishing it just four years before his death, when his city of Hippo was under siege by the Vandals. Augustine argued that there are two cities, the earthly city and the heavenly city. Those who belong to the city of God are the elect, although they are compelled to live in the earthly city. Because humans have fallen, God has provided governmental institutions to regulate sinful society. The two cities intermingle throughout history—but in the church the city of God has begun its fulfillment. Since the earthly city does give relative peace and order, Augustine argued Christians should participate and seek at least to mitigate violence and injustice in the world.

Medieval Christianity: The Age of Faith

With the invasions of the barbarians of northern Europe and the decline of the Roman Empire, the

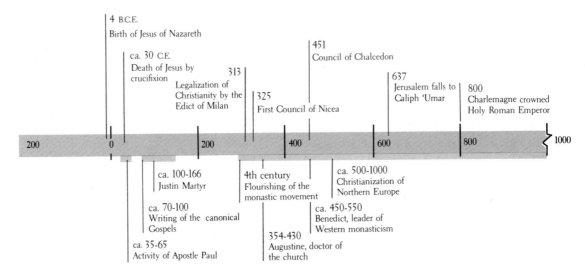

4 B.C.E.
Birth of Jesus of Nazareth

ca. 30 C.E.
Death of Jesus by crucifixion

313
Legalization of Christianity by the Edict of Milan

325
First Council of Nicea

451
Council of Chalcedon

637
Jerusalem falls to Caliph 'Umar

800
Charlemagne crowned Holy Roman Emperor

200 — 0 — 200 — 400 — 600 — 800 — 1000

ca. 100-166
Justin Martyr

4th century
Flourishing of the monastic movement

ca. 500-1000
Christianization of Northern Europe

ca. 70-100
Writing of the canonical Gospels

ca. 450-550
Benedict, leader of Western monasticism

354-430
Augustine, doctor of the church

ca. 35-65
Activity of Apostle Paul

Christian church faced an uncertain future. Having finally Christianized the Roman Empire and become established as its state religion, Christianity now faced hordes of non-Christian invaders and the threat of being swept away with the Roman Empire. The challenge was met; the invaders were Christianized and carried the new religion to new regions north and east. The period of Christendom was ushered in, to last for the next thousand years until the Renaissance.

Christendom

Germanic tribes repeatedly invaded the western part of the Roman Empire. But as the nature of the empire changed under their influence, they gradually adopted the culture and religion of the people they were conquering. A particularly significant event took place near the Rhine River in 496. Clovis, king of the Franks, was a worshiper of tribal gods; but, under the influence of his Christian wife, Clovis appealed to Christ in a battle against another Germanic tribe. Clovis won the battle, and afterward he and many of the Franks were baptized. Clovis remained a cruel tribal chieftain, and the Christianization of the morals and societal values of the Germanic peoples was a long process. But the result

was a new construction: Christendom, arising from the fusion of the religion of the Roman Empire with the culture of the northern barbarians.

As the power of the Roman political state declined, the church in the West especially cultivated the monastic life. Benedict (ca. 480–550) became the fountainhead of Western monasticism by establishing a Rule at Monte Cassino, which became the pattern followed widely. Promoting a moderate asceticism, the Rule called for the communal life to revolve around the Divine Office of prayer at fixed times throughout the day. Prayer was to be balanced by work and study, and these monasteries following Benedict's Rule became major centers of social work, evangelism, and scholarship during the Middle Ages.

Some of the monastic orders were especially devoted to missionary work among the barbarians. The old Celtic Christian church in Britain fell into disarray with the incursion of the Anglo-Saxons. But the Benedictine monk Augustine (d. 604) was sent as missionary to these pagan invaders and initiated a new era of Christian growth in England. Augustine followed a principle of accommodation as he evangelized the Anglo-Saxons: shrines and holy days dedicated to the

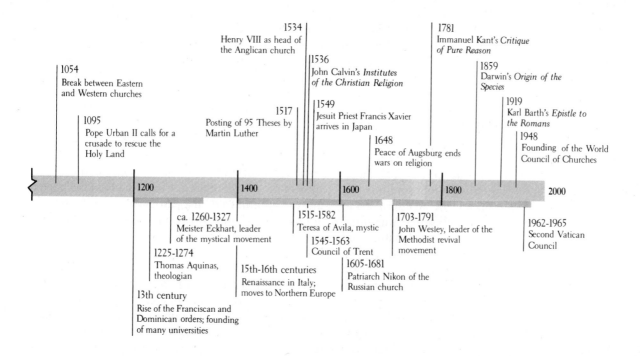

pagan gods could be taken over and Christianized, thus making the conversion of the pagans less traumatic and more enriching for Christianity. Before long, the monasteries of England were sending missionaries to Germany.

As the Germanic peoples were taken into the Christian fold, they often in turn became strong missionaries to other Germanic tribes. Frequently such "evangelizing" turned more to force than to persuasion, as in the Christian conquest of the north German Saxons or the exploits of King Olaf in Christianizing Norway. The great Charlemagne (ca. 742–814) led the way in converting the north German Saxons, as he established an empire stretching from northern Spain to Bavaria. Pope Leo III crowned him Holy Roman Emperor on Christmas Day, 800. The result was the creation of a more stable, unified Christendom including also the northern Germanic tribes.

In the East, two brothers, Cyril (826–869) and Methodius (ca. 815–885), were sent out as missionaries to the Slavs of Moravia. The conversion of Prince Vladimir of Kiev in the tenth century led to the "baptism of Russia," and the Eastern Orthodox church flourished there. After the fall of Constantinople to the Turkish Muslims, Moscow became the center of Eastern Orthodoxy and was considered the "Third Rome" of Christianity.

When the pope crowned Charlemagne as Holy Roman Emperor, the idea was born of a unified Christendom with even the secular rulers under the authority of the pope. The church was a part of Europe's feudal structure, with church officials serving as vassals of great nobles. Often the rulers and the popes came into conflict, especially when the German emperors interfered in church affairs. After a confrontation, Pope Gregory VII (r. 1073–1085) excommunicated Emperor Henry IV. Relenting, Henry stood barefoot in the snow for three days outside the castle of Canossa, in submission to the authority of the pope. But three years later, balking at a second excommunication, Henry marched on Rome and deposed Gregory. Thereafter a compromise of sorts was reached between the cross and the crown, as spelled out in the Concordat of Worms (1122). Secular rulers were to recognize the local bishops' loyalty to the pope, and the pope was supposed to appoint bishops acceptable to the emperor.

Eastern Orthodoxy: Split with the West

During the period of the early church councils, much of the theological leadership of the church had been in the eastern Greek-speaking regions. The theology and liturgy of the Eastern church continued to cultivate accents different from the Western Latin churches. The Western church, following Augustine, emphasized the utter sinfulness of human nature and Jesus' death as the key to God's redeeming activity. But the tendency in the East was to focus on the restoration of God's image in humans through the incarnation of Christ. Christ united the Godhead to human nature; by sharing in Christ's perfect humanity, humans could be raised up to God. The Eastern Church kept a "high" Christology, in which the divine nature of Christ was the focus, for this is what, in union with humankind, makes it possible for humans to rise to God.

Eastern Christianity was also developing the sacred liturgy as a solemn celebration recapitulating the whole drama of salvation, unifying worshipers on earth and in heaven. The solemn ritual, beautiful chanting, rich vestments, and colorful icons combined to provide a powerful expression of the Christian faith in ritual. The liturgy spread over into mystical practices in the monasteries, where cultivation of interior contemplation focused on illumination of the soul with the divine Light.

The invasions of the barbarians effectively cut the Eastern church off from the Western, and gradually they lost touch with each other. Often Rome and Constantinople found themselves in political conflict, and ecclesiastical rivalry also became more bitter, as the Roman popes pressed their claims to papal authority. The Eastern bishops were willing to recognize the Roman bishop as *primus unter pares* (first among equals) because of the tradition of Paul and Peter at Rome; but they refused to accept the universal jurisdiction claimed by the Roman popes.

A symbolic crowning touch to the East-West split was the little Latin word *filioque* (and the son). Already in the sixth century, some Western churches began adding to the Nicene Creed the phrase that the Holy Spirit proceeds from the Father "and the Son." Eastern theologians feared that this clause would impair the unity of the Trinity, for they saw the Father as the foundational source of the Trinity, with the Son eternally begotten of Him and the Spirit eternally proceeding from Him. The squabble was symptomatic of deeper rifts, and neither side would give in. An Eastern council condemned the Roman pope for heresy because of the *filioque* clause. Finally in 1054 the pope in turn excommunicated the patriarch of Constantinople, putting the finishing touch on a schism that had been developing over several centuries.

Islamic Pressure and the Crusades

Medieval Christendom gradually absorbed and Christianized such foreign invaders as the Vikings from Scandinavia and the Magyars (the later Hungarians) from Asia. But the eruption of Islam into the Christian world was a different story. Within fifteen years of the Prophet Muhammad's death, Jerusalem fell (637) to 'Umar, the second caliph. The new religious wave devastated Christian Palestine, Syria, Egypt and north Africa, as Muslim armies overthrew the Byzantine overlords and the peasant population happily accepted the new religion of equality and justice. The Muslim tide advanced into Spain and even across the Pyrenees into France, stopped finally by Charles Martel at Poitiers (732). Later, across Asia Minor (Turkey) the Muslims went, and finally in 1453 Constantinople fell to the Muslim Turks, putting an end to the Byzantine Empire.

Since the Muslims recognized Christians and Jews as monotheists, "people of the Book," they were not forced to become Muslim, although many did. Christian communities continued to live and thrive in Muslim lands, paying a special tribute tax to the rulers in return for security and autonomy. Christian pilgrims were still permitted to visit the holy places of Jerusalem. But when the more intolerant Seljuk Turks gained control of Jerusalem in the latter part of the eleventh century, Europeans feared they would suppress pilgrimage and destroy the Christian shrines. The Byzantine emperor was also under pressure from the Turks, and in 1095 he appealed to Pope Urban II for assistance.

Urban II preached a remarkable sermon at the Council of Clermont in France (1095). He described the desecration of Jerusalem, portrayed Christ himself as leading any army that went to the rescue, and promised cancellation of debts, exemption from taxes, possession of new lands, and a reward of eternal life to any who joined the holy war against the Muslims. Crying "Deus vult!" (God wills it!), knights from Germany, France, and Italy set out for the holy land. Many claimed new land for themselves and settled along the way, but in 1099 a small band reached Jerusalem. On Good Friday they breached the walls and instigated a great massacre, unmoved by the tears of women and children. Their victims included Christians who happened to look like their Muslim neighbors.

Despite the "success" of the first Christian crusade, the Muslims continued to fight back, and a series of crusades followed. The second crusade was promoted especially by the saintly, peace-loving man of God, Bernard of Clairvaux—but it failed miserably because of quarrels among the leaders. The third crusade also failed, and the fourth crusade (1201–1204) went out of control and attacked Christian Constantinople. There were other crusades, like the Children's Crusade of 1212 led by a shepherd boy, whose most tangible result was a host of slave boys for Mediterranean ship captains. The spiritual energy that had promoted this crusading effort cooled, and what was left was desire for booty and control of trade routes. Three new orders of knighthood to protect the Holy Land emerged: the Hospitalers, the Templars, and the Order of Teutonic Knights. But the Holy Land was not won, Islam was not driven back, and the church was not purified.

Reformers, Scholastics, and Mystics

Even preceding the crusades there was a growing desire for reform of the church and especially its monasteries and clerics who had become infected with worldly concerns. Two new monastic orders in particular brought new life to the church in the Middle Ages. Dominic (1170–1221) realized that to win the masses it was necessary to live simply and preach the Word

St. Francis in ecstasy. Detail from a painting by Giovanni Bellini.

clearly. In 1214 he founded the Dominican Order, dedicated exclusively to preaching and scholarship. They lived by begging and were called the Black Friars because of their simple black habit. One rule was that no one could preach without three years of theological training. The Dominicans established themselves in the fast-growing universities and produced one of the greatest Christian thinkers of the times, Thomas Aquinas, and also the great mystic Meister Eckhart.

Francis of Assisi (1182–1226) revolted against his own youthful indulgence in riches and sensuality to devote his life to the ideal of lady poverty. He begged for his livelihood, working only to serve, storing nothing and owning nothing. He wandered about preaching and tending lepers, and even made a trip to Egypt to preach to the Muslims. His followers were organized into the Franciscan Order.

The pressure for learning was mounting. Between 1200 and 1250, many new universities were started in Europe, with professors and students coming from all over western Europe, communicating in the Latin of the day. Scholars began to rediscover Greek philosophical thought, especially through the commentaries of Muslim scholars like Avicenna and Averoes. In the thirteenth century Christian scholasticism thrived especially through the work of Thomas Aquinas (1225/7–1274).

Aquinas, who taught at the universities of Paris and Naples, used a synthesis of Plato and Aristotle to create a systematized theology, which has remained widely influential down to the twentieth century. He held that philosophy examines the natural order by means of reason, whereas theology examines the supernatural by means of revelation. Philosophy cannot contradict theology because both are forms of truth. Theology perfects philosophy, taking it to realms it cannot penetrate on its own. Aquinas felt that humans can discover the existence of God through observation and reflection. Philosophy is available to all, even Jews and Muslims, and so it provides a universal basis for reflection and discussion. His magnum opus, written during the last two years of his life, is the *Summa Theologica* (left incomplete), a massive, systematized statement of the Christian faith.

An important movement, which was at one and the same time an expression of medieval spirituality and an alternative to the intermediary function of the church, was mysticism. The mystics sought direct contact with God rather than relying only on ecclesiastical machinery, sacraments, and satisfactions.

A leading mystic in Germany was Meister Eckhart (ca. 1260–1327), who chose to talk of God in essentially negative terms. Thinking in Neo-Platonic concepts, he felt God to be beyond being and nonbeing but also present as the divine spark in the world and in the soul. The mystical goal is complete union of the divine spark in us with God, which is the loss of individuality and immersion in God's reality. It is through negating the empirical self, leading a life of poverty and stillness and contemplation, that creatureliness can be transcended in union with God.

Eckhart's disciple Johann Tauler (ca. 1300–1361) emphasized the life of sacrifice and charity that the mystical experience of God enables. When the plague of the Black Death struck (1348), Tauler expended himself ministering to the sick and dying. Eckhart and Tauler inspired thousands of clergy and laypeople to practice this kind of simple mysticism, dedicated to the inner life of contemplation and piety. Another mystically inclined movement that emphasized practical love and included both clergy and laity was the Brethren of the Common Life. They lived in houses with a rule like monks but did not take permanent vows. Practicing the "new devotion" of a simple, undogmatic faith, they established schools and gave free instruction. One of them, Thomas a Kempis (ca. 1380–1471), produced Christianity's most widely used devotional book, *The Imitation of Christ*.

Thus mysticism moved beyond ecclesiastical structures and caught the imagination of common people who desired intense religious experience within their ordinary vocations. It appealed also to women, such as Catherine of Siena (1347–1380), who spoke of her mystic experience as a "spiritual marriage with God" and devoted herself to helping victims of the Black Death. Two centuries later another woman mystic, Teresa of Avila (1515–1582), graphically expressed the mystical experience in her writing, *The Interior Castle*. She pictured the human soul like a crystal castle with seven mansions; the innermost mansion was Jesus Christ, and the closer one moves to this inner mansion the stronger the light of union with Christ becomes.

The Period of Renaissance and Reformation

The need for continual reformation and renewal is felt in most world religions. As an established part of culture and society, religion can easily become fossilized or used for nonspiritual ends. From time to time movements of renewal arise, calling the religion back to the original experience and purpose.

Renewal and Renaissance

In the later Middle Ages, as the feudal structure of society was weakening and the grand system of the medieval church was starting to unravel, new voices for reform spoke out, leading to the Protestant Reformation and drastic changes in church and society. An English scholar, John Wycliffe (ca. 1329–1384), promoted translating the Bible into English and became a critic of many aspects of the medieval church, including the papacy. The availability of the Bible in the vernacular proved to be a revolutionary force. In

Czechoslovakia John Hus, rector of the University of Prague (ca. 1373–1415), led a religious rebellion, appealing to Scripture to attack abuses of the church that were out of line with the injunctions of the New Testament—and was burned at the stake in Constance as a heretic. The influence of Wycliffe, Hus, and other reformers reverberated across Europe, setting the stage for more widespread reformation and transformation of society.

Some of these reforming movements were influenced by the larger movement of cultural and social change known as the Renaissance, which contained the seeds of many aspects of modernity: individualism, secularism, rationalism, nationalism, urbanization, and industrialization. Interest in the culture of ancient Greece and Rome increased, and Christian scholars learned the biblical languages. The spread of printing presses made for the rapid dissemination of the new learning. The Renaissance scholars dedicated themselves to a humanistic philosophy not necessarily centered on religious concerns, sometimes even questioning the basis of religious beliefs and practices. Christian humanists, like Johannes Reuchlin (1455–1522) and Desiderius Erasmus (ca. 1466–1536), attempted to reconcile the new learning with traditional Christian faith. But the popes of the Renaissance were not up to the challenge of the times, giving themselves to corruption or consolidating their political power.

Martin Luther and the Reformation

The spark that ignited the Reformation was an ironic piece of the Renaissance. In the wave of enthusiasm for the new classicism in architecture, Pope Julius II developed some ambitious plans for a new and magnificent St. Peter's Basilica in Rome and laid the first stone in 1506. The project dragged on at enormous cost, and Pope Leo X (1475–1521) began to raise money through the traditional practice of selling indulgences. The church had long claimed the right to grant indulgences, that is, remission of punishment in purgatory due for sins, drawing on the great store of merit gained by Christ and the saints. Whereas it was the question of indulgences that first sparked Luther's protest, actually the whole medieval synthesis of Christendom was being called into question.

Martin Luther (1483–1546), of peasant stock, went to the University of Erfurt to get a law degree. A crisis in his life led him to join the Augustinian Order and study theology, after which he was assigned to teach at the new university of Wittenberg in Saxony. In 1510 his order sent him to Rome, but his experience of the ignorance and corruption of the Holy City left him with doubt and despair. He wrestled with his own sense of unworthiness and inability to find relief through the monastic practices. But a momentous experience changed his life: his so-called tower experience. Preparing for lectures on the Psalms, he was bothered by the references to God's righteousness. Turning to Romans 3:21–24, he read:

> Now God's righteousness is revealed apart from the law, testified to by the Law and the Prophets, God's righteousness which is through faith in Jesus Christ unto all who believe. For there is no difference; all have sinned and fall short of the glory of God, being justified as a gift by his grace through the redemption that is in Christ Jesus.

Raging at God over the impossibility of living up to the righteousness of God, Luther suddenly saw a totally different meaning: the righteousness of God is a *forgiving* righteousness, by which God makes us righteous through Christ. This theology of "justification through faith by grace" henceforth became the heart of Luther's theology, leading him ultimately to reject all ideas of justification through one's own monastic practices or through the works of the church: penance, the sacraments, absolution, and the like.

Confronted by the sale of indulgences, which many German priests and rulers found objectionable, by the pope's legate, John Tetzel, Luther was provoked into action. Following the custom of academic disputation, he composed ninety-five theses for discussion, setting forth a variety of arguments against the practice of indulgences. His protest hit especially at the papal claim to control the treasure of merits generated by the saints out of which credits could be drawn to cover sinners' debts. But the protest was really much broader, calling into question the whole structure of papal authority and the intermediary practice of the church. The ninety-five theses circulated rapidly, thanks to the

Martin Luther at Wartburg Castle, where he translated some of the scriptures into German.

newly invented printing press and the general discontent in Germany with papal rule.

Before long the pope condemned Luther for heresy, and Luther responded with additional protests and writings in which he rejected papal supremacy and the infallibility of the church councils. The pope finally excommunicated Luther. But in the rising tide of German nationalism, the Elector of Saxony took Luther under his protection, even when Luther was put under the Ban of the Empire in 1521.

Luther's doctrine of justification by faith through God's grace meant that humans can do nothing to merit salvation—thus undercuttng the ecclesiastical penitential system. It also called into question the monastic ideal—and thousands of men and women in Germany left the monasteries for secular life. Luther himself married a former nun, Katherine von Bora, and established the model of married clergy. A second important teaching, that Scripture is the sole authority, led Luther to translate the Bible into German and, with the help of the printing press, make it available to all people (in the process creating a standard for the German literary language). This principle undercut the authority of the pope and the bishops to decide on matters of faith. His third important principle, the priesthood of all believers, put laypeople on a par with monks and priests and elevated the worth of secular vocations for Christians.

The Reformation Spreads

Many others joined Luther in the protest (the Protestants), and the result was a drastic restructuring of the church throughout Christendom. Another important reformer was John Calvin (1509–1564), who provided a systematic presentation of Protestant thought in his landmark *Institutes of the Christian Religion.* Calvin started from the premise of the absolute sovereignty and glory of God, stressing also its corollary, the complete pervasiveness of sin in human nature. Salvation is by grace alone, although it is limited to those whom God has elected for salvation. Calvin carried the emphasis on God's sovereignty into the order of society, establishing a theocracy at Geneva in which the order of God governed all aspects of human society. Strict regulations were enforced: people could be punished for missing church or for adultery. Some holding unorthodox views, such as Michael Servetus, were burned at the stake for heresy. The Calvinist teachings spread to France, Germany, the Netherlands, England, and Scotland, where it became known as Presbyterianism. From these places Calvinism also spread to America and became an important force in American Protestantism.

A more radical form of reformation found a representative in the fiery Ulrich Zwingli (1484–1531) of Zurich in Switzerland. He abolished the mass completely and removed pictures and images from the churches. He later died in battle leading a Protestant army in a civil war against the Catholics. After his death some carried the movement to a still more radical phase, promoting a church based strictly on the New Testament and specifically denying the validity of infant baptism (hence their name, Anabaptists). Since they insisted that every Christian should believe and be baptized for him- or herself, they posed a threat to the union of church and state, which still existed even in Lutheran and Calvinist regions. So they were fiercely persecuted and nearly all the early leaders were put to death—an estimated 50,000 martyrs by 1535. With their radical emphasis on individual faith, they were the forerunners of Baptists and Congregationalists in England who wanted to separate church and state functions. A portion of the Anabaptists were committed to pacifism, following teachings of Jesus. From these have derived the Mennonites, the Hutterites, and the Society of Friends, all deeply committed to peace and works of service.

In England the ideas of the Reformation fanned the dissatisfaction with Rome that already existed. Henry VIII (r. 1509–1547) broke with Rome over the pope's refusal to annul his marriage, and in 1534 he declared himself supreme head of the Anglican church. He dissolved the monasteries, seized church property, and executed those who refused to recognize him as head of the church. Soon a new liturgical order, *The Book of Common Prayer*, was produced. There were also dissenters who wanted to completely purify the Anglican church from all rituals left over from the Catholic church. These Puritans, as they were called, followed Calvinistic teachings; the community was ruled by the elect saints and a strict moral code was enforced. Puritans achieved political power during the Cromwellian period, but with the Restoration and the reestablishing of the *Book of Common Prayer*, the Puritans joined the Baptists, Quakers, and other nonconformists outside the Church of England.

The Reformation movement also reached to the Roman Catholic church, with reforming popes who corrected abuses and corruptions in the Roman church. Scandals such as the sale of indulgences were checked, and great care was taken to appoint men of high caliber to posts of bishops and abbots. The impact of the Protestant Reformation was so great and raised so many questions about traditional doctrines and practices that a general church council was needed to clarify Catholic teaching and discipline. The Council of Trent met in three sessions between 1545 and 1563, carefully spelling out the Catholic teaching on a great number of questions. Although there were hopes of reconciliation with Protestant reformers, the Council basically held firm on all the traditional teachings regarding the authority of the popes, the celebration of the mass in Latin, reverence for the Virgin Mary and the saints, celibacy for the priests, and other such contested doctrines and practices. The pope was empowered to draw up an Index of Forbidden Books (to stop the spread of Protestant ideas). Positions on both sides of the Reformation were now solidified and all hope of reconciliation was gone.

With the Catholic Reformation went a great renewal of faith and piety among the Catholic Christians. New religious societies were founded, among them the influential Society of Jesus (the Jesuits). Ignatius Loyola (ca. 1491–1556), a former Spanish military officer, founded the Jesuits for the purpose of propagating the Catholic faith, both in far-flung mission fields and at home in resistance to Protestantism. It was foremost through the Jesuits, for example, that the Christian faith was planted in East Asia. Among them, Francis Xavier (1506–1552) first brought Christianity to Japan in 1549, and Matteo Ricci (1552–1610) had a remarkable career as a missionary in China. Other Catholic orders also sent out missionaries and planted the Catholic church firmly in India, the Philippines, and

Central and South America. What the Catholic church lost in Europe was gained in the mission fields.

State Churches and Denominations

With the Reformation, medieval Christendom came apart at the seams. Conflict erupted into open religious warfare. The Peace of Augsburg in 1555 brought temporary peace with an influential principle: *cuius regio, cuius religio*, that is, the religion of the ruler became the religion of the realm. After more religious wars, the Peace of Westphalia (1648) drew the religious map of Europe, setting up the state churches of Catholicism, Lutheranism, and Calvinism, which have remained substantially the same ever since.

In the Eastern churches, the Reformation changes did not have as much immediate effect as in the West. The Greek Orthodox church was still struggling to hold back the Muslim-Turkish expansion. A reformation did take place in the Russian church under the great Patriarch Nikon (1605–1681), who worked to develop an educated clergy and to simplify the elaborate liturgy. These reforms, however, led to state interference in church affairs, and later Peter the Great (1676–1725) had the state take over the administration of the church. A further repercussion of the reform was a faction of "Old Believers" who refused to accept the reforms and split off from the main church.

In the immigrations to the New World, all these state and dissenting churches were represented, so that a central characteristic of American Christianity is its multiplicity of "denominations." In the American development, groups from the different state churches of Europe have sometimes united, sometimes further subdivided, to add to the complexity of the denominational structure. Further, the American experience has created new denominations more on the fringes, such as the Church of the Latter Day Saints (Mormons), the Jehovah's Witnesses, the Seventh-Day Adventists, and the Christian Scientists.

An important development in the American Christian experiment is the practice of separation of church and state. The Pilgrims who came to America were from the dissenting Congregationalists of England, bringing the idea of separating church and state functions, both still under divine law. Eventually a separation of state and religion was written into the Constitution and has been a powerful influence in the development of American Christianity and of American law and politics.

The Christian Church in the Modern Period

Responses to the Scientific Revolution and the Enlightenment

Christendom, disrupted by the various Reformation movements, now was confronted with the scientific revolution and the Enlightenment. The discoveries of Galileo and Copernicus, scientists working in the heartland of Christianity, shook the traditional Christian views of God and the world. Questions were raised about the authority of the church and its tradition, humans no longer seemed at the center of things, and skepticism began to spread about miracles and supernatural events.

The Enlightenment brought in a new emphasis on reason and philosophy. Attempts to develop a rational religion independent of revelation resulted in Deism, a philosophy that held that religion could be based on certain innate rational principles, such as the existence of a God and the certainty of reward or punishment for ethical or unethical deeds. The philosopher Immanuel Kant (1724–1804) proved by the use of reason that the existence of God cannot be proved by reason; he did hold, however, that religion belongs in the realm of morality, not reason.

Reacting against the sterile rationalism that was developing even in the Reformation churches, a pietistic revival began among the Bohemians and Moravians. Influenced by them, John Wesley (1703–1791) began preaching a revival of religious experience in England, emphasizing the need for an inner experience of Christ and a feeling of certainty of salvation. His movement, called Methodism, appealed widely to peoples recently moved to the cities in the Industrial Revolution. In great open-air meetings, Wesley eloquently preached about the dominion of sin and the warmth of God's love. Once a person was born again through the experience of salvation, she was assured that she would never fall away and be dammed. The

Methodist movement spread rapidly, bringing a whole new repertoire of pietistic hymns and emotional experience across England and over to America.

Biblical Scholarship, Liberal Theology, and Fundamentalism

One fruit of the new scientific, enlightened view of the world was scientific biblical scholarship, giving rise to a dramatic intellectual crisis in Christianity. The Bible had always simply been accepted as the inspired Word of God, providing the source of God's direct revelation. But inevitably the methods of critical historical research were turned to the biblical literature, and the results threw up questions about many cherished beliefs: the literal truth of miracle accounts, the veracity of historical descriptions in the Bible, the Mosaic authorship of the Pentateuch, and even the reliability of the portrait of Jesus in the New Testament. Biblical scholars were investigating the holy writings just as they investigated other books, showing that the Bible contains legends, errors of fact, and later events read back into earlier periods.

Adding to the threat was another fruit of the scientific approach to human history: Charles Darwin's *Origin of Species* (1859). The new evolutionary theory of the development of the species seemed to reject the whole biblical account of creation and, moreover, suggest that humans were simply highly evolved beasts.

The force of this new scholarship and scientific perspective was powerful, and many Christian thinkers tried to deal with it positively. The Catholic Modernist movement attempted to reconcile biblical critical scholarship with traditional Catholic teaching. And Protestant thinkers constructed a liberal theology that advocated a humanitarian ethic built on progress and social concern, at the same time reviving a piety that centered on Jesus as the ideal human life.

But other Christians reacted strongly against the perceived threat, finding these products of science to be in deep conflict with their traditional faith. They insisted on holding firmly to their fundamental tenets. They interpreted the Bible literally, including all its supernatural elements. Christians of this persuasion were found in all denominations. In an encyclical in 1907,

Pope Pius X ruled against those who applied the new methods of research to the scriptures or theology, and among Protestants the Fundamentalist movement was dedicated to a literal interpretation of the Bible. The large and sometimes bitter gap between liberal Christians and Fundamentalists has been an important factor in modern Christian history and is still very real today, particularly in American Christianity.

Modern Theologies: Neo-Orthodoxy, Correlation, Aggiornamento

In the present century numerous challenges have confronted the Christian churches, focusing the direction of Christian thinking and action today. The rapid increase of industrialization, two catastrophic world wars, worldwide instant communication, the nuclear age, the growing disparity of rich and poor nations, liberation movements—such developments have set much of the church's agenda in modern times.

Liberal ideas of progress and humaneness were shattered by World War I, and Christian thinkers responded with neo-orthodox theologies centering on human sinful failure and the radical message of salvation, which comes from the transcendent God. Karl Barth (1886–1968), a Swiss Calvinistic theologian, used the methods of biblical scholarship to focus on the essential biblical message, which brings the self-revelation of God. Human reason is incapable of reaching out to God, but God through biblical self-revelation does the work of salvation for humans. All religions, including Christianity as a human institution, are man-made and stand under God's judgment. Only God's revelation in Christ brings renewal and salvation, Barth taught.

Paul Tillich (1886–1965), a German Protestant theologian, although agreeing with some of the concerns of Barth, taught that theology must practice a method of correlation: the modern world frames questions, and the theologian uses the resources of the Christian tradition to construct an "answering theology." Modern science, philosophy, art, and even the religions of the world become resources for Christian theology in this method of correlation.

Roman Catholic theologians like Karl Rahner likewise have constructed methods of relating Christian

Pope John XXIII at St. Peter's Basilica for the opening of the Second Vatican Council in 1962.

faith to the intellectual and social trends of the modern world. Pope John XXIII, sensing the moment of renewal, called the Second Vatican Council (1962–1965) to carry through a visionary program of *aggiornamento*—bringing Catholic tradition and practice up to date while retaining their vitality and commitment. Liturgical reforms brought the use of the vernacular into worship in place of Latin. The Council expressed concern and hope of peace in the world, asked for cooperation with other Christians, and spelled out a theology of respect for other religions.

Missions, Social Renewal, and the Ecumenical Movement

Whereas the Roman Catholic church, through its religious orders, was engaging in widespread missionary activity already in the sixteenth century, the nineteenth and twentieth centuries saw a surge of missionary activity also by Protestant denominations. Missionaries went out to India, China, Africa, and throughout the world in a great march onward of Christian soldiers. Mission societies were formed in Europe and America to support foreign missionaries. It is true that some of this earlier missionary activity carried a flavor of Western superiority and sometimes accompanied political and economical exploitation. But Western Christians have learned from Third World Christians, and today the mission outreach of the Christian churches is generally associated with service, partnership, and respect.

Christian awareness of oppression and poverty in the societies of the world today has grown in modern times. Today many Christians work for liberation: liberation of people from the tyranny of racism, liberation of women from roles of subjugation, liberation of oppressed and poverty-stricken peoples in countries throughout the world. Social concern is high on the agenda of many of today's Christian churches. Other Christian groups, of course, resist what they see as too much involvement of the church in worldly affairs.

Experiences in the missionary movement and in social concerns have led many Christians of today to promote Christian unity. The fragmentation of the church that occurred over the past several centuries is finally being reversed as Christians from many denominations work together in closer harmony. Growing out of this "ecumenical" (worldwide) concern was the World Council of Churches, founded in 1948 at Amsterdam, representing a degree of cooperation between most of the Protestant churches. And the Second Vatican Council of the Roman Catholic church also set up a Secretariat for the Promotion of Christian Unity.

As Christians work together more closely throughout the world, new attitudes have begun to prevail concerning the links that hold all humankind together. The peace movement, transcending national boundaries, is promoted by many Christians in the East and West. Christians work together with secular agencies and institutions to promote the welfare of human society. And a new attitude of respect and dialogue with peoples of other religions is evident, at least among many Christian groups.

DISCUSSION QUESTIONS

1. How does the Christian view of the scriptural story of God working through the people of Israel differ from the Jewish view?
2. What was the main content of Jesus' preaching of the coming of the Kingdom of God?
3. Outline some of the areas in which, according to the Gospels, Jesus differed from the understanding of the Jewish tradition held by his fellow Jewish teachers.
4. Why is the Christian story so interested in the question of *why* Jesus died?
5. What were some of the main contributions of Paul to the developing Christian story?
6. What were some of the basic issues in the theological controversies of the fourth and fifth centuries? What were some of the main doctrines settled on by the church councils, such as the ones at Nicea and Chalcedon?
7. Describe the differences in emphasis between the Eastern and Western churches.
8. What were the main issues involved in the Reformation movement in the sixteenth century?
9. What were some of the effects of the Enlightenment and the rise of science on Christianity?

CHAPTER 8

CHRISTIAN WORLDS OF MEANING

ONE GOD AS FATHER, SON, AND SPIRIT

Christianity, growing out of Judaism, has much the same view of God as that held by the Jews, up to a certain point. God is the one God of all peoples and ages, both transcendent and immanent, both lawgiver and merciful parent. Christains place a great deal of stress on the mercy and compassion of God: "God is love," according to a well-known text (I John 4:8). Jews also have this conception of God, so the difference is one of emphasis. Like Jews, Christians also see God as the judge who upholds standards of justice and punishes wrongdoings.

Seeing God's Face in Christ

The essential difference in the Christian vision comes at the point where the real heart and mind of God are revealed. For Jews, the way to really know God is in the covenant relationship, especially in the Torah given by God in love. For Christians, the way to really know what God is like is through the revelation in Jesus Christ; here God's divine face is shown for all to see. Apart from Christ, God remains the almighty, righteous creator beyond human knowledge or contact; in Christ, the mystery has come to dwell among humans, so that they can experience God's own glory and truth and love. Thus what is distinctive about the Christian vision of God is that the eternal brilliance of God's mystery is reflected through the "image" of God, Jesus Christ. The same Old Testament writings as used by the Jews now take on new meaning, for God's design and purpose can be seen in them in a new way.

Thus Christian thinking about God starts from Jesus' own experience of God as revealed in the New Testament. One of Jesus' favorite terms for God was "Abba," by which he showed both his closeness to God and also God's character as the near and loving "father." This does not take away from the transcendence of God or the demands of the divine law. God is still the judge and evaluator of all, and one of Jesus' parables paints a vivid picture of the final judgment when God rewards the righteous with the eternal joys of heaven but consigns the wicked to everlasting punishment (Matt. 25:31–46). God does uphold justice. But what Jesus reveals about "Abba" is that God's *real* intention for all creatures is mercy, and that God is involved in the dirt and grime of human existence to see to it that the design of mercy wins out.

God as the Loving Parent

Among Jesus' many stories telling about God's real nature, the parable of the prodigal son stands out. Once there was a man, Jesus told, who had two sons; on the younger son's insistence, he gave him his inheritance. The younger son left home and squandered all in reckless living. Finally, starving and wishing he could eat with the pigs he was tending, he came to his senses, resolving to return home and confess to his father his sins, begging to be treated like a servant.

> So he set off and came to his father. But while he was still at a distance, his father saw him, and his heart went out to him. Running out, he flung his arms around him and kissed him. Then the son said to him, "Father, I have sinned against Heaven and against you; no longer am I fit to be called your son." But the father said to his servants, "Quick! get the best robe and put it on him, and put a ring on his hand and shoes on his feet. Then bring the fatted calf, kill it, and let us feast and make merry."

The older son was angry that the younger son was rewarded for his riotous, sinful living whereas he himself got no special rewards for his years of dedicated service for his father. "Dear son, you are always with me," said the father, "and all my possessions are yours. It is fitting to celebrate and be glad, for your brother here was dead and has come alive, he was lost and is found" (Luke 15:11–32). This picture of God as a waiting father, standing on tiptoe, straining to see in the distance a glimpse of his wayward son returning, has colored the Christian view of God from beginning to end.

Christians therefore see God as the loving father/mother, wanting to create humans in order to be able to show love to them. They understand God as pained and hurt in the face of human rejection. As the righteous judge, God punishes them in anger, never, however, letting them go. As loving parent, God waits for the wayward children to return, sends warners and prophets, and finally goes out to bring them back, so that the divine love may be fulfilled. God, who was present in so many ways through the people of Israel, finally became concretely present in human history in Jesus Christ as the forgiving parent who welcomes even sinners. One time, as Luke tells, the tax collectors and other bad characters were all crowding in to listen to Jesus, and the Pharisees and scribes grumbled: "This fellow receives sinners and eats with them." And Jesus answered them with this parable:

> Which one of you having a hundred sheep and losing one of them, does not leave the ninety-nine in the wilderness and go after the lost one until he finds it? And finding it, he lifts it on to his shoulders rejoicing, and

coming home he calls together his friends and neighbors, saying, "Rejoice with me, for I have found my lost sheep." (LK. 15:1–7)

And that is what God is really like.

Because they see God present in Jesus, Christians understand the suffering and death of Jesus as God's way of becoming the "friend of sinners" in a complete way. Just as God has been present to the world through the servant people Israel, now God is present to the world in the new servant Jesus, through him receiving all the evil and sin of the world and absorbing it in Godself, so that finally both divine justice *and* mercy might prevail.

One God, Three Persons: The Trinity

Because Christians believe they have seen God's true nature revealed in Jesus Christ, they call Jesus the "Son of God." Since God was present in the world in a powerful and saving way in Jesus, Christians say God was "incarnated" in Jesus: God "became flesh and dwelt among us" (John 1:14). Whereas this teaching arose out of the early Christians' experience of Jesus' death and resurrection, it took several centuries of experiencing and reflecting for Christians to be able to explain what they meant by calling Jesus the "Son of God." It was not until the church councils of the fourth and fifth centuries C.E. that satisfactory formulations were devised to say what needed to be said to guard from error and misunderstanding, but at the same time not to say too much about the mystery of God. It was partly this need to understand and preserve the experience of God's presence in Christ that Christians, much more than Jews, started theologizing, thinking and reasoning about God and God's work. Out of this theologizing came the doctrine of the Trinity: God is one God in three persons.

In all of this thinking, Christians tried carefully to insist on the unity of God. But their experience had taught them that God, eternally unified in self, is present and works in the created world in a number of aspects or modes or "persons" (from the Latin *persona*, the masks worn by actors playing roles on the stage).

Using biblical terms, Christians called these aspects or persons by the names of Father, Son, and Holy Spirit. But what do these words designate about the one God? The words of the Nicene Creed, formulated in the early church councils, guide Christians in understanding the mystery of the Triune God.

The soaring gothic arches and vaults of Washington Cathedral draw attention heavenward, symbolizing the presence of God.

The Nicene Creed

The first statement in the Nicene Creed emphasizes the unity of God: "We believe in one God." Then the creed goes on to specify the several faces of God: first, "the Father, the Almighty, maker of heaven and earth, of all things seen and unseen." The Father is God's face as creator, almighty and transcendent, Lord of the whole universe. God created everything in the world, and God's purpose is justice and mercy for all.

The second article of the Nicene Creed goes on to specify the face of God as it is reflected in the Son:

> We believe in one Lord Jesus Christ, the only Son of God, begotten of his Father before all worlds, God from God, Light from Light, true God from true God, begotten, not made, one in being with the Father, through whom all things were made. For us humans and our salvation he came down from heaven and became incarnate from the Holy Spirit and the Virgin Mary, and was made man. He was crucified for us under Pontius Pilate; he suffered death and was buried. On the third day he rose again in accordance with the scriptures, and he ascended into heaven and is seated at the right hand of the Father. He will come again with glory to judge the living and the dead. His kingdom will have no end.

What is this statement saying about the one God? It insists very carefully that the Son of God is totally and completely one with God: he was not created at a certain time but has always been God, not of a different being from the Father. The Son is also, as was said of the Father, the creator of all. But in this face of God we see the incarnation: "for us" God came down and was born a human and died on the cross. God became the redeemer, not solely in the form of the transcendent God but in the person of humanity. In Christ, the Son of God, the divine nature and the human nature were united, so that God could redeem the human race. The Son rose in victory and now rules the world with the Father. With the Father, the Son will be the judge of all to fulfill justice and mercy completely.

But the Bible tells of another face of God's presence in the world, the "Spirit." So the third article of the Nicene Creed specifies:

> We believe in the Holy Spirit, the Lord and the giver of life, who proceeds from the Father (and the Son), who with the Father and the Son is worshipped and glorified, who has spoken through the prophets.

Whereas the Father represents God as the creator and sustainer, and the Son represents God as the redeemer, the Holy Spirit represents God's ongoing spiritual presence in the world and in humans. Through the Spirit comes life; through the Spirit comes revelation and guidance. This is the presence of God that prompts human longings and prayers, that sustains them in their doubts, that cleanses and renews them. And the Spirit is worshiped together with the Father and the Son—one God in three persons.

Christians do not find it easy to explain the meaning of the doctrine of the Triune God, for these terms, many of them derived from Greek philosophy, are limited in their appropriateness to describe the mystery of God's own being. But Christians have found this idea of one God in three persons a helpful and necessary one to express the way in which they have experienced the mystery of God—and that helpfulness is not so much in rational thought as in worship and praise of God.

The Problem of Evil in the World

As to the problem of how God could allow evil and suffering in this world, which God created and loves, Christians use many of the same responses as Jews. Out of love God disciplines, punishing so people will repent. God tests people to refine their faith. Evil is but the absence of good. The sufferings of the moment will cause the eternal rewards to shine more brilliantly. Evil comes as a result of the freedom that God has allowed. But there is one more specifically Christian response to pain and suffering: in all our suffering, God suffers. Through the cross of Christ, evil is overcome by God's own submission to the evil that works so much suffering and ruin in creation. This answer does not explain evil away or give a reason for its existence. But it does help Christians to bear it, trusting that even at this point God is with them as their loving father—and as their loving mother, we should say, as modern Christians are becoming more aware that God is beyond gender and that feminine images of God are as equally biblical as masculine ones.

CREATION AND HUMAN EXISTENCE

Christians, as they think about creation and the role of humans in the world, largely take over the Jewish view put forth in the Hebrew scriptures as in Genesis 1 and Psalm 8. That is, the one God created the universe in an orderly fashion, determined it all to be good, and placed humans as the crown of creation, to play the role of God's representative within this good world.

The Nature of Creation

The Christian view of creation is succinctly summed up by Paul when he writes, "From him [God] and through him and to him are all things; to him be glory forever" (Rom. 11:36). Creation had a beginning "from" God, out of nothing. God is the only being who is necessary, existing self-sufficiently; all other things are contingent and could easily not exist. This world is entirely God's creature, dependent on God for the gift of being and life. Creation is "through" God, continuing through God every day. Every instant the whole universe exists in the power of God's activity as the preserver. And creation is "to" God; it has a goal, a future that centers in God. There is a design or purpose to this universe inherent in the will of the creator who brought it into existence. But that means there is a demand, a law built into creation, which leads it to fulfill the design of the creator.

Creation in Christ

What is most distinctive about the Christian view of creation, as compared to the Jewish view with which it shares many points, is that Christians understand creation from the point at the center of their faith: the revelation of God's love and mercy in Christ. Why is there something and not nothing? What caused God to create? Love, Christians answer, the love that is seen in Jesus Christ. The Letter to the Colossians emphasizes this Christocentric view so strongly that it says, "Everything has been created through him [Christ] and for him. He exists before everything, and everything holds together in him" (Col. 1:16–17).

Therefore Christians read back from Christ to understand God's creation of the world and of humans. They understand the stories about creation in the book of Genesis from this point of view, emphasizing above all God's parental love. God wanted a world. God wanted humans as children to respond to the divine love in personal trust and fellowship. So God's great love overflowed in creativity, and the world and all that is in it came into being. All of God's creatures are special, but humans were made as very special creatures, so God could express love by entering into a close personal relationship with them. God lovingly created the first human, as told in Genesis 2, of the dust of the ground, breathing "spirit" or breath into him, making a woman as a fellow human, and thus choosing humans of all the creatures to be special partners in a loving relationship.

Since Christ is the focus of God's revelation and reveals God's deepest design and intention, Christians see all God's law or design summed up in Christ, who is the "end" or fulfillment of both God's love and justice. In answer to a lawyer's question about what the greatest commandment was, Jesus said, quoting the Torah, that loving God with one's whole being and loving one's neighbor as one's self sum up all the teaching of the law and the prophets (Matt. 22:35–40). This means that the law of creation is the law of love. For it is finally love that moves people to be fruitful, helpful, and creative, to invest themselves in their families, their work, and their art. Whatever is valuable and creative derives from such personal investment and love—and that is first and foremost true of God and the creation that was lovingly brought into existence.

A Good and Right Creation

God the creator has a design and purpose for creation, Christians believe, and humans play a central role in that design, as God works through human history to accomplish that purpose. That means that this is a moral universe, for it is fashioned according to

God's design. God's love is balanced with justice or rightness throughout creation. That law of creation is known and felt by humans in their natural experience, so that all have a knowledge of God's will. The good life according to God's design, then, includes both love and justice, as lived by humans in loving and serving God in faith and obedience.

Christians affirm with Genesis 1 the essential "all-rightness" of the world. God gives the world not only its existence but also its value. This universe is ultimately right and moral, not just accidental and neutral. God's creatures—especially humans—are intrinsically valuable. And life within this created, material world is meaningful and full of value and significance. "Glory be to God for dappled things," wrote Gerald Manley Hopkins, expressing the Christian's delight in all aspects of God's good creation. "God saw everything that he had made," Genesis 1 reports, "and it was very good." That includes matter, food, drink, play, and bodily appetites, including sex.

Humans are children of God. As creatures they are to love and serve God, fulfilling the design of creation in human fellowship and in harmony with all God's creatures. All this existence is valuable, because the creator has given it value. This means, for one thing, that there is no person, and no aspect of a person's life, that is insignificant or trivial. For another thing, it means that no earthly being or institution can claim absolute value—all persons are created equally valuable. Further, the world of nature has been given its own value, not to be tyrannized or ruinously exploited by humans.

Christians affirm that reason is a special gift from God. Since humans know from their own nature and conscience what God's basic design (law) is, they ought to be able reasonably to fulfill that design, living in love and justice with fellow creatures. But human reason is also driven by other factors, especially by the will that turns a person back upon oneself in pride and selfishness—the condition that Christians call sin. Therefore human reason is an ambiguous guide to living the good life and fulfilling God's real design in creation. A minimal kind of justice and order can perhaps be created by humans at their best, using their reason and effort—but the real meaning of creation, the whole-

ness of existence full of both justice *and* love in relation to the creator and also to the fellow creatures, is beyond the reach of human striving on the basis of reason. Something more is needed, and that must come as grace from God's side.

Sin and Separation From God

Why do people do evil and destructive things? In spite of the strong feeling that humans were created in the image of God, perfect and good as God wanted them to be, most Christians emphasize the sinfulness of human *nature* more forcefully than do Jews or Muslims. It is not just a matter of an evil tendency, which can be controlled or mastered by one who has the mind to do so. Rather, there is a deep, complete fracture in the very nature of humans, causing separation from God and inevitable sinfulness in human existence. Sin for Christians is not just an act done by a person; sin is the very being of humans, the state of alienation from God and God's design.

Paradise and the Fall into Sin

The story of origins in Genesis 2 and 3 is especially important for Christians, and they read it somewhat differently from Jews. God created humans to be partners, perfect and in full harmony with all of creation, serving God and taking care of creation. God provided all that is needed for a full, happy life: a garden of delight, work to fulfill human existence, animals to be named by humans, a fellow human for companionship—above all, close fellowship with God. God did give a command to the man and the woman in the garden: "You may freely eat from every tree in the garden, but from the tree of the knowledge of good and evil you may not eat" (Gen. 2:16–17). Why? God gave no reason. But clearly this is important in the human relation to God: a command sets a limit, and it requires a response on the humans' part. No longer can they maintain their dreaming innocence—God wants real partners. The command is the opening of the way for humans to transcend their own inner limits and relate to the power outside themselves. God stands over against us humans as "you," so that we can no longer only think incessantly of "me." Now, with God's command inserted into human life, the humans become aware both of God and of themselves as free agents making decisions, acting on them, and taking responsibility.

This story is told about the first man and the first woman, but in the Christian view it really is the story of all humans. God encounters them as personal Lord, and they are faced with a decision: to obey or to disobey the divine will. Humans are always confronted with this decision: whether to respond to God as personal Lord and Master in their role as creatures, or to turn to their own way in defiance of God's will. That they are free to decide shows that God has entered into a personal relationship with them. That they consistently turn to their own way shows their inevitable human sin and rebellion against the creator.

This inevitable human sin and rebellion is depicted in Genesis 3 in the well-known story of the "fall." Some Christians take this story literally as an account of the first human pair and their fall into a sinful state. Most understand it as a symbolic description of the natural state of humans: created to be partners of God but always choosing the selfish and rebellious course. Whether read literally or symbolically, the story in Genesis 3 presents a powerful portrait of human existence as seen in the Christian view.

The man and the woman were roused out of their dreaming innocence by the snake, the "wisest" of all the creatures God had made. Whereas the man and the woman had not done any thinking or deciding yet, just taking care of the garden, cleaving to each other unashamedly, and taking walks with God in the garden, the snake had been thinking: "Did God really say that you shall not eat from any tree of the garden?" (3:1). The snake exaggerates, and the woman exaggerates also in her answer. But the crucial step is made: the humans begin to think and to desire and to exercise their freedom—in rebellion against God's command.

This decision in rebellion against God disrupted the human situation with God in every area of human existence, since God is the basis of all that makes for human existence. If the relation to God the creator is disrupted, all else is also shattered. When God comes to walk in the garden in the cool of the day, the humans hide in their shame. Now enmity breaks out with the animals, nature no longer cooperates with the man in producing food, and the woman experiences great pain and risk of death in the natural function of childbirth. The man and the woman are alienated from each other: they cover themselves with clothes, they blame each other, and the man usurps the rule over the woman in this disrupted state. Finally the humans are driven from God's presence out into the ruptured world of human existence, with no way back to the garden.

Originating Sin

The Christian interpretation of this story sees in it the "fall" of humankind into a sinful state, blotting out or distorting the image of God in which they were created. Paul writes that "sin came into the world through one man"; now, however, "there is no difference, for all have sinned and come short of the glory of God" (Rom. 5:12; 3:23). Augustine interpreted this state of humankind as "original sin," the condition of all humans of not being able not to sin.

There has been considerable disagreement among Christians about the nature of "original sin." Some Christians have followed Augustine in thinking of original sin in terms of a fallen nature passed on physically through birth from one generation to the next, starting from the first human parents. Again, some Christians tend to say sin originates with the devil who tempted the first parents and who still goes about as a roaring lion seeking people to devour. Most Christians today try to find ways of thinking about sin that do not blame our sinfulness on Adam and Eve or on the devil—sin is something that belongs to our own nature and we must take responsibility for it.

One way to understand original sin would be as "originating" sin, that is, the fundamental tendency in all human nature to follow one's self-will, placing oneself as creature in the place of God the creator. The originating sin thus produces a kind of idolatry, worshiping oneself instead of God. The human will is in bondage, curved in upon itself.

The Christian idea of sin is not easy to understand, but it tries to uphold a number of important meanings. For one thing, to say that sin is original means that sin is inborn, a condition that all humans share without exception. There is no one who is perfect and sinless in this view.

This means, at the same time, that there are no persons who are worse sinners than others. Of course, there are some who do more hurtful, destructive actions than others; the sins people commit do have varying gravity and consequences. But all are equal in sharing the same sinful human nature. And therefore if one can be redeemed, all can equally be redeemed. There is no human, even the worst murderer and rapist, who is so despicable as to be nonredeemable. In fact, sometimes one who has obviously committed a lot of sins is more aware of his or her predicament and need for God's help than one who has lived a "good" life and feels confident of personal merit before God. Jesus told a story about a Pharisee and a tax collector, to give a lesson to some who trusted in themselves that they were righteous and despised others. Both went to the temple to pray. The Pharisee thanked God that he was not like evil men, especially this tax collector. But the tax collector stood far off, eyes cast down, beating his breast, and said, "O God, be merciful to me, a sinner." Jesus said, "I tell you, this man went home justified rather than the other" (Luke 18:9–14). Whereas there may be differences of sins in terms of evil effects, there is no difference in sinful nature: all have an equal share of original sin.

The idea of original sin also means that sin involves the whole person, originating from the center of one's being. It is not that sin comes from certain animal drives and lusts, or that it has to do mainly with one's lower members below the belt. All members, faculties, hearts, minds, wills, and whatever it is that makes humans what they are, all share in the sinful nature. There is nothing humans can do, then, no matter how noble or intellectual or creative, that is not at the same time contaminated by human sin.

The Christian view of sin sounds pessimistic and gloomy—and so it is, pointing to the condition of humans separated from God. But it should be noted that this idea places the big emphasis on humans' sinful nature, not so much on the various things humans do. Therefore this is a freeing and positive idea as well. It frees a person to live courageously in this world amid the ambiguities of human existence. Acknowledging one's sinful nature—and therefore the need to turn to God for help and mercy—a person can live with courage and hope in the ups and downs of human existence, knowing that pleasure and drink and sex and wealth and everything else are not bad in themselves. It is our sinful nature, Christians believe, that originates sin—and the only help for that comes from God.

The Wages of Sin

God does hate sin, however, demanding that humans be perfect as God is perfect. So the sin that humans share calls forth God's wrath and punishment. Every individual sin, of course, has its own consequences. But by tracing sins back to a sinful nature, it is possible for Christians to talk of consequences that all humans share equally. These consequences are spiritual "death" or separation from God, a fragmented and warped human life, and ultimately eternal death and punishment.

Paul writes that "through one man sin came into the world, and through sin came death, and so death spread to all people, because all have sinned." Again, he says that "the wage for sin is death" (Rom. 5:12; 6:23). This does not mean creaturely finitude is punishment for sin—only God is eternal, and all creatures are limited by beginning and end. But Christians use the image of "death" to refer to the separation and estrangement from God that sin causes. Adam and Eve had to leave the Garden; people, by worshiping themselves instead of God, separate themselves from the source of all life and love and wholeness. Cutting the lifeline to God—which is what sin does—means spiritual death.

And such spiritual death, in the Christian view, affects everything we are and do as humans. Cut off from God, our relations with each other become hurtful and hateful. People abuse and exploit the wonderful world of nature that God created good and gave over to them to take care of. They find no harmony and peace in their fragmented lives. Their creaturely limits, symbolized by death, cause great anxiety, suffering, and a feeling of hopelessness.

Christians believe that death is not the end of human existence, but that the consequences of sin will continue in the world to come. God is the judge of all, and God's evaluation of sinfulness will bring about the final

consequence: eternal death and punishment. Christians of earlier times depicted the horrors and everlasting torments of the damned in hell by graphic words and pictures (read Book 21 of Augustine's *City of God*). Many Christians today have problems with these grotesque portraits. But what they do show is the seriousness of sin in God's sight—and the need for humans to receive help and forgiveness from God.

THE PATH: SALVATION BY GRACE

The question of salvation is a central question for Christians, who see all human nature enslaved to sinfulness. God has a high design for humans; they are to be perfect in love and fellowship with the creator. But in the face of human rebellion and idolatry, this design becomes a demand that is beyond the human possibility. Humans are lost and helpless, cut off from God, without hope in the world. And so the most important question becomes, "How can I be saved from this sin and punishment?"

Saved by Jesus Christ

The story of the jailer at Philippi is a familiar one to Christians. With Paul and Silas bound in his prison at Philippi, the jailer experienced great terror when an earthquake occurred, which he thought had allowed his prisoners to escape. There was nothing left for him to do except to take his own life. But Paul and Silas stopped him, for none of them had tried to escape. Trembling with fear, the jailer fell down before them and asked, "Men, what must I do in order to be saved?" And they answered simply, "Believe on the Lord Jesus, and you will be saved, both you and your household." He believed, and he and all his family were baptized. Then he took them up to his house, washed their

The last judgment, as envisioned in this painting by Van Eyck.

wounds, set a meal before them, and rejoiced with all his household (Acts 16:25–34).

The starting point in the Christian vision of salvation is the recognition that ultimately humans cannot attain salvation by themselves; they cannot on their own restore the relationship with God that has been disrupted through sin. To say this is not to deny that there are good things that people can do, in the sense of righteousness and justice in relationship with fellow humans. God's law is sufficiently in our nature that we do by nature know justice from injustice, and even our self-interest will lead us to try and establish a society of order and fairness. But to be in the right relationship with God is the key to salvation, and this, most Christians believe, is beyond our human possibilities because of our fundamental sinful nature.

It is at this point that Christianity diverges significantly from both Judaism and Islam. For Jews, as we have seen, the divinely given path of Torah is the path of transformation; following it and performing its mitzvot bring blessing, joy, and salvation. For Muslims likewise, as discussed later, following God's law is the path of transformation that brings felicity in this world and the next. But in Christian understanding, the law (God's demands on humans, as revealed in the Torah) cannot be a path of salvation, for it demands of us what we cannot do. "You shall be holy, as I the Lord your God am holy" is the demand of God's law. But no human is or can be holy, and so following the way of the law cannot restore the relationship with God; it cannot bring salvation. In fact, Paul argued that the law becomes an accuser, showing us our sin every time we fail to keep a precept perfectly.

Most Christians believe that God's law does have the function of maintaining some form of order and justice in human society, curbing people's wickedness and guiding them toward God's design of justice. But more importantly with respect to the path of salvation, the law shows the depths of the estrangement from God. Whereas in Jesus' parable the Pharisee praying in the temple thought about his merits in keeping the Torah, the tax collector thought of that same divine law and could only beat his breast, saying, "God, be merciful to me a sinner." And Jesus says the tax collector is the one who went home justified by God—that is, recognition

of sinfulness is the first step in turning toward the redemption that comes from God. For as long as a person tries to justify herself—that is, tries to claim worth and merit before God on the basis of what she does—she remains trapped in a no-win situation. It is a tendency of human nature to try and claim worth in oneself, to justify one's existence—whether through work, determining self-worth by how much one earns, or through one's social standing among friends, or through some other accomplishment. God's law breaks through all this and shows us how futile it is to try and justify ourselves by our performance in life.

When we abandon our attempts at self-justification and turn to God, Christians believe, we find that we are justified and saved through Jesus Christ. But how does this happen? How does Jesus save us? To understand this mystery of salvation, Christians start from the testimony of the Scriptures. "God was in Christ, reconciling the world to himself" (2 Cor. 5:19). Just as Jews look back to many acts of salvation by which God delivered the sacred people, so Christians believe that God was also at work through Jesus Christ to bring salvation for all peoples.

This means first of all that whatever happened in Jesus Christ is the fulfillment of God's whole plan and design to restore humankind to the relationship of love

Christ's death on the cross, illustrated by Cuna Indians (of Panama and Colombia) who have become Christian.

and fellowship with God. Of all of the images in the Scriptures about God saving the people, the Jewish image of sacrificing a lamb to make atonement for the sins of the people has appeared to many Christians to set the pattern by which God brings salvation. Symbolically the sins of the people were placed on the lamb; the lamb became a substitute, bearing and thus abolishing the sins of the people. Christians look to the prophecy of Second Isaiah (ch. 53), telling of the suffering servant of God, on whom God will place the sins and the burdens of all to make atonement for them. This pattern of atonement reaches its fulfillment in Jesus Christ, atoning for the sins of all humankind by his sacrifice on the cross, and by this atonement bringing about the restoration of the loving relationship between God and humans.

But even this image of the atonement does not really explain *how* this salvation takes place. In trying to understand it further, Christians have used additional metaphors and images. For example, Christ can be envisioned as a victorious king, triumphing over the powers of hell by his cross. Or he can be viewed as the sinless one who paid the debt of sin that we all owe before God the judge, whose scales of justice must be balanced. Or, again, Jesus Christ can be understood as the mediator who reconciled the two parties at war with each other, God and humans. These and other images of the atonement are all attempts to explain the same reality, the experience of salvation and restoration through Jesus Christ.

Every metaphor or human analogy has its limitations when used to understand a divine mystery. Are we to think that in some magical way the sins that all people have authored are somehow heaped on Christ's shoulders as he died on the cross? Are we really to think there are evil powers of hell that the Son of God had to do battle with and defeat in order to free humans from their grasp? Are we really to think of God as an angry judge, insisting on someone paying the debt all people owe so the scales of justice can be balanced? Are we really to think of a war between God and humans that has to be settled by a mediator? Taking any one of these images in a strict literal fashion can lead to some less than Christian ideas about God and God's relation to humans. Yet such human images are helpful, and

Christians have found much meaning in all these images by which to understand the atonement.

God So Loved the World

The basic motif behind all these ways of understanding the atonement is God's love demonstrated concretely in Christ. God is holy and hates sin—for sin ruins God's good creation, and it destroys fellowship and love. It causes suffering, pain, and death, and that not just in this present existence but also in the world to come. Something has to be done from God's side, Christians believe. God has to intervene as God really is, as both holy judge and as lover of all creation. But to be a real lover of humankind, God becomes vulnerable, as all lovers do.

How does God, the transcendent creator, become a lover for humans? In the Christian experience, it is by God taking a body in the created world with which to bear the sin of the world. The demands of justice and judgment are met, according to the truth that sin has consequences. But the Christian good news is that God took these consequences on Godself in Jesus Christ, replacing the demand and punishment of the law with the power of love. That means God's love must be a suffering love; God suffers for the sins of the world in the servant, Jesus Christ. It is God's love that does not allow giving up humankind to judgment and condemnation, for

> God is love. In this the love of God was manifested to us, that God sent his only son into the world, so that we might have life through him. In this is love, not that we have loved God but that he has loved us and sent his son as an expiation for our sins. (I JN. 4:8–10)

Jesus Christ is thus the means through which God brings the divine love into the world for the salvation of humankind.

In the end, all the consequences of sin are summed up in death: "The wage of sin is death." So the atonement made by Christ also brings triumph over the fear of death. Jesus Christ is raised from the dead! In the perspective of the Bible, a resurrection from the dead is not utterly amazing, where God's power is concerned. There are scriptural stories of people who escaped death or were raised from the dead; Jesus himself raised people from the dead. But the resurrection of Jesus Christ is unique in that this is the first fruit, the foretaste of the world to come in which death is abolished. It is God's stamp of approval on the redemption worked out through the life, sufferings, and death of Jesus Christ.

Who is Christ?

So who was or is this Jesus Christ? Together with the doctrine of the atonement, Christian theology stresses the doctrine of the incarnation, with its classic expression in the Gospel of John: "And the Word became flesh and lived among us, and we have seen his glory, glory as of the only Son from the Father, full of grace and truth" (John 1:14). More than any other teaching of Christianity, this teaching of the incarnation of God in the human being Jesus has caused lines of defense and objection to be established by both Jews and Muslims. How can God become a human? How can God have a son? What does this teaching of the incarnation mean?

This is a question faced by the early Christians, and by Christians ever since. Is this Jesus Christ a human, or is he God, or is he a God-human mixture, or what? The answer to this question is the Christian doctrine of Christology, thinking about the nature of Christ. The important thing, in the Christian view, is to see this question in relation to the doctrine of soteriology, the belief in salvation through Jesus Christ. That is where Christians start in their religious experience; through Jesus Christ they experience the love of God in its fulness, meeting God present with saving power. And therefore they think of Jesus Christ as the Son of God, through whom God's love and salvation are experienced within creaturely existence in this world.

For several hundred years Christian thinkers struggled with the need—and the difficulty—of expressing clearly just who Jesus Christ is in both the divine and the human dimensions. The need was to keep the good news of salvation from becoming something else—another law or demand, a magical story, or the like. The difficulty was the uniqueness of this mystery: how does one even begin to talk about God taking human sin on Godself? Finally, Christians decided that in order to maintain the good news of salvation, it is necessary to teach that Jesus Christ is both fully and completely God and fully and completely human.

There were other options, of course. Some Christians (led by Arius and thus called Arians) were teaching that Jesus was really human, created to be God's son and saviour of the world. But Christians found that to restrict Jesus from being fully God causes problems for soteriology; how could the suffering and death of a mere human, no matter how noble, make atonement for the sin of the whole world? Only if God makes this atonement could it bring to all people the promise of forgiveness and salvation. Another group of Christians approached the question from the other side from the Arians; the Docetists (from the Greek word *dokeo*, meaning to "seem" or to "appear") taught that Jesus Christ was fully God but just "seemed" to be a human with the mask of flesh and blood. But Christians found that if this view were followed, the whole notion of Jesus Christ sharing human sufferings and bearing human burdens and sins would become meaningless. For only one who is truly human can experience the suffering and death that humans must experience.

So Christian thinkers decided that the only way to preserve the good news of salvation through Christ is to talk of Jesus Christ as fully God and fully human, two natures united in the one person. Most Christians do not pretend to be able to explain rationally how this can be so. But they believe it because it is the good news of salvation. Christ took human sin, suffering, and death on himself as the human brother, making atonement for the sin of the whole world as the divine Lord. And still today, Christians believe, Christ lives and rules as fully God and fully human. He sympathizes with human weaknesses because he knows human nature; and he intercedes for humans and declares them righteous by virtue of his divine power.

The Way of Faith

The path for salvation is necessarily a two-way affair, even in Christianity, and in the Christian vision the appropriate human response is faith, which is the accepting of the grace that comes from God in Christ. It is not a "work" in the sense of fulfilling God's law and demand, or justifying oneself by some worthwhile deeds. Rather, faith is saying yes to God's love, accepting the divine promise that we have been reconciled to God. Faith is not primarily an intellectual act, although it does involve mind and reason. It is the movement of the will in response to God's love, trusting that God has made all things whole again.

There is an objective, intellectual side to faith, having to do with ideas and doctrines about God and humans. But the primary meaning of having faith, Christians believe, is coming into a personal relationship with Jesus Christ as Lord. For Jesus said, "I am the Way, the Truth, and the Life; no one comes to the Father except through me." And again, he said, "If someone loves me, he will keep my word, and my Father will love him, and we will come to him and make our abode with him" (John 14:6, 23). When the good news of Jesus Christ is told, God is promising, "I love you, and I have saved you." Faith is accepting that promise and getting in on the story of Christ, making that story one's own story. As a person responds in faith and trust, Christ makes his home with her. Her life is filled with Christ's love, and her death is shared with

him, trusting Christ's promise that she will also share his resurrection and eternal life. This personal relation with Christ is the overcoming of the fracture of sin. It is reconciliation with God.

Salvation through faith is a lifelong process, and Christians, like Jews and Muslims, make use of prayer and worship as the means toward this transformation. Baptism is an important ritual for Christians, for it symbolizes the inclusion of the new person in the family of God. Through baptism the person dies to the sinful nature and is reborn with a Christlike nature, for Christ dwells in him. Throughout one's lifetime the knowledge that "I have been baptized" provides comfort and hope whenever doubts and anxieties arise. Hearing the word of the gospel is a reminder over and over of the story of Christ that has become each Christian's story. Sharing in the Eucharist (Lord's Supper) is a concrete experience of being united with Christ through this sacred meal. And prayer in the name of Christ keeps the new relationship with God alive and well. Christians speak of these practices as the "means of grace," believing that as one participates in them, the Holy Spirit is at work in her heart, continu-

Seventh-Day Adventists, a minority Christian denomination in predominately Roman Catholic Poland, are baptized in the Wisla River in southern Poland.

ally transforming her sinful nature so that her faith and love become more perfect.

The struggle of life continues, however. Christians realize that until the end of life a person will always be *both* a sinful human being *and* a redeemed human being. But though sin continues, God's forgiveness continues. So we can live courageously, Christians believe, not having constantly to prove our worth before God, and thus free to live in the world and show love to one another as God loved us.

It is at this point in the path of transformation that Christians talk of the value of work and actions. Works grow out of faith. People who have experienced God's love and grace will be inwardly motivated to demonstrate that kind of love and grace also in their lives— freely, not for sake of reward. Christians speak of the process of the "sanctification" or making holy of our lives. Through the power of the Holy Spirit, our faith and our experience of God's love shape and mold our hearts, minds, and wills, so that more and more we live Christlike lives in the world. "We become what we are," Christians might say: by faith we *are* saved, and now we go about becoming the kind of persons who demonstrate in their lives what that salvation means.

The Life of the World to Come

Like Jews and Muslims, Christians also believe in the world to come: resurrection, judgment, and eternal life in heaven. The eternal life that begins now through faith in Christ is not something that death can snuff out. Christ died, but he broke the power of death and rose again on the other side of death. Now he rules as the Lord over all. All who are united with him in faith also experience that resurrected life already in this world, through worship of the risen Lord. But Christ has promised that he will come again to judge all people. Christians understand this as a word of promise rather than of threat, for the judge is none other than the Saviour, the friend of sinners and our brother. And he has promised that he will say, "Come, you blessed ones of my Father, inherit the kingdom which has been prepared for you since the world was founded" (Matt. 25:34).

Traditional Christian piety has constructed many imaginative descriptions of paradise in heaven and the bliss of eternal life, descriptions that are still meaningful to modern Christians even though the cosmology underlying them is no longer held. Many modern Christians have problems with the notion of heaven as an exclusionary place, from which the vast majority of God's human race will forever be banned. They ask, could the loving parent of all peoples allow heaven for only that small part of humankind who had the good fortune to hear about Christ and believe in him, while consigning all other peoples who have lived on this earth to eternal punishment?

This is a difficult question. The attitude of many Christians is to leave these things up to God's eternal love and mercy. God will judge; and the judge will be none other than the Saviour. The important point remains that eternal life comes by God's grace, not on account of one's deserving merit. And this means that life in heaven, too, is a gift of grace, not a reward. The prospect of life in heaven is not to be the motivation for becoming a Christian. It is God's love that stirs one to the life of faith, and heaven is simply the last image in the process of salvation. Just as God at the beginning said the creation is "very good," so at the end the promise of eternal life in heaven is God's way of saying that the new creation of salvation is very good.

DISCUSSION QUESTIONS

1. What key aspects of God do Christians believe are revealed in Jesus Christ as the "image" of God?
2. Discuss what the Nicene Creed states about the three "persons" of God.
3. How can there be both a good world created by God, and a world full of sin and evil? Is God's love or God's justice predominant?
4. Explain the Christian doctrine of sin (called by some "original sin").
5. What are some of the things Christians mean when they talk about being "saved" by Christ?
6. What were the views of the Docetists and the Arians about the nature of Christ? What is the traditional orthodox doctrine?

CHAPTER 9

CHRISTIAN WORSHIP AND ETHICAL LIFE

CHRISTIAN WORSHIP AND RITUAL

"How can I find new power for life?" Christians, like Jews, believe that all life is to be worship of God. How Christians live is based on the teachings and the example of Jesus, focusing on love. God is to be worshiped and praised, both in acts of love toward God and in good deeds of love toward others. Jesus, quoting the Torah, said there are two great commandments: to love God with all one's heart, strength, and mind; and to love one's neighbor as oneself. Of course, God is worshiped not because this has been commanded, but out of love and gratitude. Christ lives within, and this provides the motivation and power to live a life in worship of God.

Breaking Bread and Praising God

We are told that the earliest Christians "day by day, both attending the temple together and breaking bread in their homes, partook of food with joyous and simple hearts, praising God and enjoying favor with all the people" (Acts 2:46–47). From the beginning Christians followed the Jewish tradition of assembling together to pray and praise God, also "breaking bread" in their homes, that is, observing the Lord's Supper, which Jesus instituted during his last Passover meal with his disciples. From these earliest practices evolved the distinctive Christian forms of communal worship, including the Sunday service of prayer and Eucharist and the cycle of holy days and festivals throughout the year.

It should be noted that Christian groups in the modern world differ significantly from one another in their attitudes and practices regarding worship and rituals. Christians do not have a commonly accepted pattern set down by divine law, as is the case in Judaism and Islam. Even those rituals and ceremonies of worship mentioned in the New Testament have been interpreted differently in the various Christian communions. Some groups do have "canon law," which governs the conduct of public worship. Other groups take an approach of freedom and spontaneity, following, of course, their own accepted pattern of worship. It is possible to speak of "liturgical" and "nonliturgical" church bodies. Those that are liturgical place a good deal of emphasis on the traditional liturgy (order of public worship), properly ordained clergy, and use of sacred rituals or sacraments. The nonliturgical denominations emphasize a free and spontaneous approach to prayer, reading the Bible, testifying to faith, and exhorting others in worship together. Liturgical denominations include the Roman Catholic, Eastern Orthodox, Anglican, and Lutheran churches; nonliturgical groups would be Baptists, Quakers, and the variety of free evangelical churches. Somewhat in between are such groups as the Methodists and the Calvinist (Presbyterian, Reformed) churches, who do not emphasize the traditional liturgies and sacraments but do follow commonly accepted forms of worship. Of course, there is variety even within one denomination, between those who are "high church" (more liturgical emphasis) and those who are "low."

In recent times the so-called liturgical renewal has affected most church groups, bringing a higher appreciation of the traditional forms of worship even in the nonliturgical churches. In the following description we look in a general way at the broadly based, traditional practice of Christian worship, noting significant variances where appropriate. It should also be said, of course, that many modern Christians, just like many modernists of other religions, participate only marginally in the sacred rituals of the church, though they still consider themselves Christian and live generally in keeping with Christian morality.

Sunday Worship

Just as Jews consider the Sabbath the heart and soul of Judaism, so also Christians observe the central practice of communal worship each week, the day being Sunday, the day of Christ's resurrection. Worship takes place on other days, too, but the Sunday worship service is the most distinctive Christian sacred time. The service itself developed from the Jewish synagogue service of praise, prayer, Scripture readings, and exposition of Scripture. To this service focused on God's word, the early Christians added the liturgy of the Eucharist (Thanksgiving), that is, the celebration of the Lord's Supper instituted by Christ. Thus the complete Sunday worship service in many liturgical churches consists of two parts, the Liturgy of the Word and the Liturgy of the Eucharist, although some may at times use only one part.

Often an Entrance Rite begins the service, with a call to worship, communal confession of sins, hymns, and prayers. The Liturgy of the Word includes readings of the Scriptures: Old Testament, Gospels, and Epistles. A minister expounds the Scripture in a sermon or homily, and the people respond with hymns, psalms, and the saying of the creed. They offer common prayer for all Christians and for all people according to their need. The Liturgy of the Eucharist may begin with the people greeting one another with peace and bringing offerings to God, including the bread and wine to be used in the Eucharist. There follows the Great Thanksgiving prayer narrating Christ's institution of the sacred

A Catholic nun leads singing during a mass in Idaho.

meal, asking for the Holy Spirit, and establishing unity with all Christians everywhere. After the bread is symbolically broken, the people commune with Christ and with each other by eating and drinking the bread and wine, believing that in this ritual Christ is present among them. At the conclusion of the service, the minister blesses the people and may say, "Go in peace, serve the Lord," an indication that the people carry the renewed spiritual blessings into their daily life. Nonliturgical churches, of course, have many variations of the Sunday worship service, with more emphasis on reading the Bible, preaching, songs, and prayer.

The Sacraments

The Eucharist is considered by many Christians to be a "sacrament," that is, a sacred ritual through which God's saving power comes to the believers. Most Christian denominations perform some sacraments, although they do not all use that term or agree on what it means. Some of the ceremonies were mentioned or authorized in the New Testament, and others were added. Ceremonies called sacraments include baptism, the Eucharist (Lord's Supper), confession and forgiveness, anointing the sick, confirmation of the baptized, ordination of clergy, and the rite of marriage. Roman Catholics and some Anglicans refer to all seven of these ceremonies as sacraments; Lutherans and some Reformed traditions retain most of these ceremonies but reserve the term sacrament for baptism, the Eucharist, and (sometimes) confession and forgiveness. Other denominations avoid sacramental language altogether, although virtually all Christian groups practice baptism. The important symbolism of the sacraments is that God's power and presence are connected with ordinary human activities like washing, eating, drinking, and so forth. Participating in the sacrament, people dedicate their total being to God and receive divine forgiveness and power, thus sanctifying all of life.

The Eucharist (also called the Lord's Supper, Holy Communion, the Mass, or the Divine Liturgy), has been the central sacrament of the Sunday service from the beginning, although Christians have not been unified in interpreting its meaning. One long-standing view, traditionally accepted by Roman Catholics, is the doctrine of "transubstantiation," a miraculous change of the bread and wine into the body and blood of Christ. In the Reformation, thinkers like Luther reacted against the idea that each mass was a new sacrifice of Christ, holding rather that Christ was "truly present" in, with, and under the bread and wine. More radical reformers like Zwingli held that the bread and wine only symbolize the body and blood of Christ. These basic interpretations are still held in the Christian denominations of today, so that the Christian church experiences division precisely in this sacrament of unity. Ecumenical discussions today are attempting to reach some kind of consensus or at least better mutual understanding of the alternate positions on the meaning of the Eucharist.

Festivals and Holy Days

Christians, like people of other religions, celebrate sacred times throughout the cycle of the year. Most Christians agree in setting aside as sacred time the spring celebration of Christ's death and resurrection on Good Friday and Easter, the winter celebration of his birth at Christmas, and also the coming of the Spirit and the beginning of the church on Pentecost. Many churches expand these with times of preparation and extended celebration, and many additional holy days are observed throughout the year.

Lent and Easter

The most obvious holy season from the very beginning was the Paschal (Passover) season when Christ's death and resurrection occurred. Eventually this Paschal season was extended by celebrating the events of Holy Week: Christ's entry into Jerusalem, the last supper, the crucifixion, and the entombment—all leading up to the climactic event of the resurrection. In further developments, the preparation for remembering Christ's death began six weeks earlier with the Lenten season, and the Easter celebration itself extended six weeks after Easter.

Starting from Ash Wednesday, when traditional Christians put ashes on their foreheads, the season of Lent is devoted to special disciplines of prayer, repentance, fasting, or voluntarily giving up certain pleasures. Holy Week begins with Palm Sunday, remembering the triumphal entry into Jerusalem and the beginning of Jesus' passion week. Maundy Thursday celebrates Christ's last supper with his disciples when he used the bread and the wine of the Passover meal to institute the Lord's Supper. Good Friday is an especially solemn day for Christians, remembering Christ's three hours of agony on the cross and his death and entombment. Saturday night may be given over to a service of vigil. And early Sunday morning, with the rising of the sun, Christians begin to celebrate the resurrection of the Lord in a joyous festival service. Such an Easter service may have a colorful procession of clergy and people, trumpets sounding, and choir singing. People greet one another, "Today Christ is risen!" "He is risen indeed!" This joyous mood continues for the next six weeks, including the celebration of Christ's ascension into heaven forty days later on Ascension Day.

Advent, Christmas, and Epiphany

Christmas, the Feast of the Nativity, began to be observed widely in Christian churches about the fourth century, when December 25 was set. Of course, the actual time of year when Jesus was born is not known. Many Christians observe the season of Advent for four weeks before Christmas and the season of Epiphany for some weeks after Christmas. This is the time of the celebration of God's love in the incarnation of Christ.

Advent is the beginning of the Christian year, commencing also the half-year cycle in which events from Christ's life are celebrated. Advent is a season of preparation, and the worship services bring Christians back to Old Testament times, hearing the voices of the prophets, preparing their hearts for the coming of the Messiah. Some Christians place an advent wreath with four candles in their homes, lighting one additional candle each week in preparation for the nativity of Christ.

Christmas is a highly joyous festival, with songs, plays, nativity scenes, and other rituals celebrating God's great love in becoming one with humanity as a baby born in a manger. It is a time especially dear to children, who are given special roles in telling of the Christ-child. Symbolic of God's great gift is the tradition of exchanging gifts and greeting cards at Christmas time, and decorating an evergreen tree with lights symbolizes Christ's light shining in the darkness of this world.

The Feast of the Epiphany (showing forth) comes on January 6. This feast originated in the East as a commemoration of Christ's baptism, and still today the Eastern churches have a ritual of blessing the baptismal waters. In the Western churches, Epiphany has become associated with the story of the wise men from the East coming to Bethlehem to present gifts to the new-born King.

Pentecost and the Season of the Church

Pentecost, some fifty days after the resurrection of Christ, is the celebration of the outpouring of the Spirit on Christ's disciples after his ascension into heaven. Its roots lie in the Jewish feastival of Shavuot, the celebration of the giving of the Torah on Mt. Sinai. In the Christian view, instead of the Torah God gave the Spirit to give guidance to the church, so Pentecost, the feast of the Holy Spirit, is also the birthday of the church.

Beginning with Pentecost, the next half-year is considered the season of the church, since it contains no major festivals from Christ's life. Feast days in this period observed by many Christians are All Saints' Day on November 1, set aside to commemorate the saints and heroes of the faith, and All Souls' Day (Commemoration of the Faithful Departed) on November 2, remembering all those who have kept the faith and gone on to their reward. In the more liturgical churches, holy days in honor of the apostles and saints are scattered throughout the whole year, devoted, for example, to St. Luke the Evangelist, St. Peter and St. Paul the Apostles, St. Michael and All Angels, St. Mary Mother of Our Lord, and many, many more.

Worship in Daily Life

How does one sanctify daily life? Christians, like Jews and Muslims, find the practice of daily prayer and study of the Scriptures to be important in keeping a close relationship to God in ordinary life. And there are Christian rituals surrounding the main events and passages of life.

Prayer and Meditation

The early Christians took over from Judaism the practice of daily prayers at certain times of the day. The apostles prayed at the third, sixth, and ninth hours (9:00 a.m., 12:00 noon, and 3:00 p.m.). Later the tradition of daily prayers developed into a cycle of public worship throughout the day, the "Daily Office," followed especially in the monastic setting with lay people also attending. Prime, mattins, lauds, terce, sext, none, vespers, and compline are names that have been used for these short services throughout the day, which included psalms, hymns, Scripture readings, and prayers. The churches of the Reformation simplified these services. Some churches abolished the daily office in favor of more informal devotions, whereas the Lutherans and Anglicans retained at least mattins (morning prayer) and vespers (evensong).

Apart from these daily services, which are little observed in modern hectic life, many Christian families have a time set aside daily, usually in the evening, for Scripture reading and prayer. Groups may meet together occasionally for Bible study. Some Christians make the sign of the cross on themselves with a brief prayer upon rising in the morning and going to bed at night. Prayers of thanksgiving at mealtime are custom-

ary, but there are no prescribed dietary laws to follow as in Judaism. In times of sickness there is intercession to God and perhaps a pastoral visit from a congregational leader who prays with the sick. In some denominations Christians periodically confess their daily sins to a priest and receive forgiveness—confession (or penance) is one of the sacraments in some of the liturgical churches.

Rituals of the Sacred Passages of Life

Whereas some Christians have taken over from the Jews the practice of circumcision of newborn male children, this does not have any special religious significance. The universally practiced rite of initiation into the Christian community is baptism, for male and female alike, and for most Christian denominations this occurs shortly after birth. Some Protestant denominations, especially those in the Baptist tradition, reserve baptism until the child is old enough to understand the meaning of this ritual. Baptism uses the universal water symbolism of cleansing and purifying. Most Christians believe the child is born with sin, like all humans, and the ritual of baptism signifies the washing away of sin through Christ's merit. The child is said to be "born again," having participated in the death and resurrection of Christ. Now the child is united with Christ and with Christ's body, the church, for the rest of life.

The ritual of washing in baptism may be done by complete immersion in water—a vivid experience of death and resurrection preferred by groups who practice adult baptism only—or by a symbolic washing with a small amount of water, the general custom for infant baptism. The baptizer reads about baptism from the New Testament and asks the child to profess the faith and vow to be faithful to Christ. In the case of infants, family and friends (godparents) speak on behalf of the infant, underscoring the communal character of this ritual. Administering the washing with water, the baptizer says, "I baptize you in the name of the Father, Son, and Holy Spirit." Some churches follow the early Christian practice of anointing with oil, and in the Eastern Orthodox churches the infant receives Holy Communion as a full member of the church.

The Western churches who baptize infants have

established the practice of confirmation for both boys and girls, at an age roughly corresponding to puberty. This ritual, a sacrament in some churches, is seen as a confirmation of the vows that were made at baptism and an entrance into full membership in the church. It is thus a kind of passage to adulthood in the religious community. Confirmation is performed in a group before the congregation. The bishop or minister may lay hands on the head of each candidate or give the right hand of fellowship to symbolize full incorporation into the church. Confirmation, like bar mitzvah, is a time for family and friends to celebrate the new spiritual status of the youth.

Some Christian churches see marriage as a sacrament, but virtually all groups provide a ritual to accompany this important passage of life. In the history of Christianity there has been some feeling that marriage is not as high a spiritual state as celibacy. But Christians are unanimous in considering marriage a great blessing from God, resulting in the family as the heart of the human community and the church. Marriage is considered a lifelong commitment of faithfulness to one's spouse, intended so by God.

The wedding ritual differs widely in the various churches. Usually performed in a church sanctuary, it is always a festive occasion for family and community. A traditional form of the ritual, followed by many (with modernizations), is that of the Anglican *Book of Common Prayer*. After Scripture readings, songs, and prayer, the priest asks each,

> Wilt thou have this woman [man] to thy wedded wife [husband], to live together after God's ordinance in the holy estate of Matrimony? Wilt thou love her, comfort her, honour, and keep her, in sickness and in health; and, forsaking all other, keep thee only unto her, so long as ye both shall live?

Answering, "I will," both now give their troth to each other, holding their right hands together:

> I, _____ , take thee, _____ , to my wedded wife [husband], to have and to hold from this day forward, for better for worse, for richer for poorer, in sickness and in health, to love and to cherish [and to obey], till death us do part, according to God's holy ordinance; and thereto I plight thee my troth.

Finally the minister says,

> Those whom God hath joined together let no man put asunder. Forasmuch as _____ and _____ have consented together in holy wedlock, and have witnessed the same before God and this company, and thereto have given and pledged their troth to each other, and have declared the same by giving and receiving of a ring, and by joining of hands; I pronounce that they be man and wife together, In the Name of the Father, and of the Son, and of the Holy Ghost. Amen.

These pledges and vows of lifelong faithfulness and love are considered the heart of the wedding ritual. Many

A Christian wedding, with the bride and groom receiving the sacrament of the Eucharist.

local customs attend the celebration, such as throwing rice on the newlyweds, giving gifts, and a joyous party in honor of the new family.

Death is considered by Christians as a passage to the life promised and won by Christ, so death rituals combine the sense of loss and sadness with the mood of joy and confidence. The reality of the saints—the faithful who have gone before—has always been strong in Christianity, and a funeral is a time to commend the departed one to the company of saints awaiting the resurrection and eternal life in heaven. A funeral is a time to reflect on the brevity of life and the destiny that awaits all. It is a time to renew hope and confidence in God's mercy and promises. Johannes Brahms' musical composition *German Requiem* combines these two moods in a sublime way: there is the funeral march with its driving drumbeat, and there is the vision of the heavenly dwellingplace.

Like weddings, death rituals differ widely in different parts of Christianity. For some, the sacrament of extreme unction—anointing the dying person with oil—is practiced; for others prayer accompanies the passage into death. The church bell tolls mournfully, informing the congregation of the death. Chosen mourners carry the body in a casket into the church for a service of Scripture reading and prayer. The procession then goes to the church cemetery, where the body is placed in the grave in the earth. Throwing earth upon the casket, the priest may say,

> Forasmuch as it hath pleased Almighty God of his great mercy to take unto himself the soul of our dear brother [sister] here departed: we therefore commit his body to the ground; earth to earth, ashes to ashes, dust to dust; in sure and certain hope of the Resurrection to eternal life, through our Lord Jesus Christ; who shall change our vile body, that it may be like unto his glorious body, according to the mighty working, whereby he is able to subdue all things to himself (*Book of Common Prayer*).

Whereas no specific periods of mourning are followed, most Christians remember the dead in various ways, such as lighting a candle or saying prayers on their behalf.

Art in Christian Worship and Ritual

Fundamental to Christian teaching, in contrast to Judaism and Islam, is the incarnation: God became human. Thus the Christian aesthetic sense has generally encouraged full use of all the arts in the worship of God: sculpture and paintings, architecture, music, literature, poetry, drama, and dance.

It is true that Christianity inherited Judaism's aesthetic sense, including the prohibition of images, and for the first centuries Christians continued the Jewish emphasis on the word rather than on pictorial art. As Christianity spread throughout the Roman Empire, however, the tradition of representational art developed, especially for portraying Jesus and the saints. Christian iconography was preoccupied with the person and role of Jesus and his followers, portraying Jesus both as the earthly founder of the church and as the heavenly saviour. Many symbolic expressions developed, such as portraying Jesus as the Good Shepherd. In the different cultural areas and times, portrayals of Jesus and the saints have taken many different styles. Whereas in the early centuries the crucifixion scene seems to have been avoided, later this became a central theme of Christian art, presenting both the victorious Christ on the cross and, especially in the medieval period, the suffering saviour.

In the eighth century there was a serious controversy regarding the use of icons—flat, two-dimensional paintings of the saints. Some felt these icons were receiving too much worship and miraculous powers were being attributed to them. But a theology of icons developed and won the day: since Christ consented to become a man, theologians argued, it is permissible to portray Christ in visible human form. Artists in the Middle Ages and the Renaissance created countless paintings and sculptures with Christian themes, some to be used on altars in churches. But in Reformation times an iconoclastic movement developed among the more radical reformers, who reacted against "papist" imagery and ritual, destroying iconographic imagery and liturgical furnishing. They established the tradition in Reformed and Baptist churches of little art, ornamentation, and liturgy. The liturgical churches have continued the tradition of using all the arts, with color, ornamentation, paintings, statues, poetic liturgies, music, and the like.

Religious drama in Christianity grew from the liturgical mass, which itself was presented as a kind of historical drama. Important for the education and edification of the common people were the mystery and morality plays put on in the Middle Ages. Music has played a great role in most parts of the Christian church. From plainsong chants to the rich musical compositions of Johann Sebastian Bach to modern folk masses, Christian artists have cultivated the possibilities of music as artistic expression of Christian theology and inspiration for faith and life.

Christian architecture, influenced by the synagogue, started with house churches and developed into the basilica, a structure that set aside sacred space with the altar, the symbol of Christ, as the center of action. In the medieval period cathedrals developed where bishops presided with many priests and monks. There would be rood screens fencing off the area for the monks to chant the daily offices, together with many altars for celebrating daily masses. Particularly expressive of Christian medieval ideas is the Gothic cathedral, soaring to heaven but planted on earth. With its pointed vaults and crisscrossing ribs, it expresses verticality with a sense of heavenward movement. The baroque cathedral became a kind of divine theater, giving the worshipers a sense of being in contact with heaven above. Eastern Orthodox Christians have favored the dome as a representation of heaven, with space radiating downward to the earth, giving architectural expression to the incarnation.

In the Protestant Reformation, the reformers destroyed the rood screens and brought the pulpit to the center, or they put the pulpit, altar, and baptismal font together at the east end, creating space in which all worshipers present could hear and see all that goes on, focused on the word of God.

THE LIFE OF LOVE: SOCIETY AND ETHICS

"How should I live?" To be a Christian means to live as befits a member of the Christian church, the new "people of God" gathered around the worship of Jesus Christ, living the life of love as Jesus lived.

The Society of the Church

The Greek word for church is *ekklesia*, from the word meaning "called out." The church is made up of the people "called out" by the Spirit of God to form the new people of God in fulfillment of God's plan of salvation. Christians think of the church as the continuation of the chosen people of God, gathered around the Christ who is the fulfillment of God's whole design. Peter uses many Old Testament images of the people of Israel to describe this new people of God:

> For you are a chosen family, a royal priesthood, a holy nation, and a people of God's possession, that you should proclaim the triumphs of the one who has called you out of darkness into his wonderous light. Once you were no people, but you are now the people of God. You were outside his mercy once, but now you have received his mercy. (I PET. 2:9–10)

According to the Christian perspective, once the people of God were the Jewish people with whom God covenanted, and the gentiles were on the outside. But now in Christ gentiles are also made a part of God's family, the church.

Who Makes Up the Church?

The church is not like other voluntary human societies that people choose to join or not to join. It is not a club or interest group. The church exists wherever there are believers in Christ who share their commitment to Christ and live Christian lives. Jesus said, "Wherever two or three are gathered together in my name, I am there in the midst of them" (Matt. 18:20). That means that the church is constituted by the worship of Christ.

How does one become a part of this new people of God? One does not become a Christian by birth. Rather, one chooses to belong by believing and being baptized. Of course, being born into a Christian family is an important way in which the family of God continues. Most Christians practice infant baptism as a sign that children as well as the rest of the family share in the family of God. A significant number of Christians prefer to wait until the children are old enough to choose for themselves to be baptized. In either case, the emphasis is on faith and choice. A person baptized as an infant chooses to remain in that baptismal identity. He or she is instructed and guided in faith and life and typically reaffirms the baptismal identity in the ritual of confirmation when grown up. An adult who has not been a part of the church may come to believe in Christ, and the profession of faith and reception of baptism testify that he or she has been called by the Spirit to be part of the new people of God.

Churches, Congregations, Ministry

The catholic (universal) church, like Christ, is incarnated; it is embodied in concrete form in Christian communities or "churches" everywhere on earth. Although there were periods in earlier church history when many Christians were under one ecclesiastical structure, in modern times there are numerous world churches, state churches, denominations, and sects that make up the body of Christ. The body of Christ, Christians believe, must be present in concrete form within the diverse cultures and ethnic groups of the world. In this real, living church of Christ, there sometimes appears to be little unity, and many Christians

A Sunday morning service at the Jesus Church, a rural congregation in China.

are troubled by these divisions. One of the most significant developments today is the ecumenical movement, in which Christians are trying to make real the unity of the whole *oikumene* (world) of diverse Christian communities.

On the local level, Christians typically gather together into communities called congregations, centering usually in a church building in which the believers assemble for worship on Sundays and other important times. Congregations in turn are usually associated together in larger structures, whether that is a worldwide organization like the Roman Catholic church, a state organization like the Anglican church of England, a demomination like the Methodist church in the United States, or the like. For all the trauma caused by competing associations of Christians, the various churches and denominations of the world do represent the concrete, human embodiment of the universal church, the body of Christ.

Christians as Christ's presence in the world share in common the responsibility for the ministry of the gospel and the worship of God. In order to provide for the ongoing function of the ministry of preaching the word and celebrating the rituals, most Christians believe that Christ instituted a "ministry" within the church to guide and carry out this work for the benefit of all. In the early Christian church a three-part ministry developed. A bishop was appointed for each Christian community, having responsibility for the ministry of worship and for serving the well-being of the believers. As the communities grew, the responsibility for worship was entrusted to presbyters (elders or priests) and the responsibility for service and caring for the family of believers was given over to deacons.

Today the various Christian communities have many versions of this ministry of bishop, priest, and deacon, ordained to lead and guide the family of believers in their worship of Christ and their ministry of the world. One of the stumbling blocks to the unification of the church is the great variety of understandings and practices related to the ordained ministry. Some churches, like the Roman Catholic and the Anglican church, have hierarchically structured church leadership, starting with the pope or the archbishop of Canterbury and moving down to the levels of parish priests. Other churches, like the Southern Baptists or the Quakers, operate with a church polity from below, with each congregation of believers responsible for designating leaders in the ministry of the church. Many of the denominations, such as Methodists, Presbyterians, Lutherans, and the United Church of Christ, have begun the practice of ordaining women to all the offices of the ministry. But other denominations, such as the Roman Catholic and Eastern Orthodox churches, have strongly resisted this inclusion of women within the ordained ministry.

The Sanctification of Life in Ethics

"How should I live?" Christians, like Jews and Muslims, believe that all of life should be worship of God, whether these are acts of love for God expressed in ritual and prayer or acts of love toward others. Jesus drew on the Torah to teach the two great commandments: You should love God with all your heart and all your soul and all your mind; and you should love your neighbor as yourself (Matt. 22:35–40). Although Jesus spoke of the great commandments, and whereas Christians look to the Ten Commandments and especially to Jesus' new commandment of love, Christians do not live the ethical life because it is "commanded." Rather, it is because of love and gratitude to God. Faith and the experience of forgiveness create a new being in place of the old. The new person lives in union with Christ. "It is no longer I who live but Christ who lives in me," Paul said (Gal. 2:20). Since the springs of motivation are touched by Christ, ethical behavior is not so much a discipline leading *to* transformation as an expression *of* transformation.

Love Fulfilling Law in Liberty

From earliest times in Christianity there has been considerable thinking about the basis of ethical actions. Certainly the early Christians agreed that the heart of Jesus' ethical teaching was love. But how does one put that love into action? The discussion was at first (and still is, for that matter) couched in terms of law versus liberty. Should we do the right, loving things in life because it is God's will (law)? Or, as forgiven and restored children of God, are we free to do what we ourselves find to be best and most loving (liberty)?

Since the first Christians were Jews, it was natural that they held the Jewish Torah in high esteem as the great gift of God. So, as they sought guidance in how to love God and their neighbors, they turned to the commandments given by God. Surely the Torah would provide the best definition of God's will of love, for God is the supreme evaluator of good and evil. Following God's law without question is the sure guide to the loving ethical life, without falling into rationalized, self-serving decisions about how to act.

Whereas this legalistic approach to ethics has much merit in terms of order and confidence, there are drawbacks, as Christians discovered. As new situations arise, it is not always clear what the law would have one do, especially since Christians look to the New Testament more directly than to the Old Testament for ethical guidance. Often a person has either to rely on the authority of the church to tell what one should do, or to resort to arbitrary interpretations of the law. God's law prohibits all killing, but what about state-ordered killing (war or capital punishment)? Are women permitted to be priests and ministers or not? Is homosexuality a sin? Christians disagree on what God's law actually says about such matters. But the biggest weakness in the legalistic approach is the feeling that, once one has done what the law stipulates, he has fulfilled God's will of love. We keep the Ten Commandments—so why should we worry about housing discrimination or the church's investments in companies doing business with South Africa's government?

In counteracting notions of Jewish Christians about the necessity for Christians to keep the Torah, Paul placed a great stress on freedom: "Christ has freed us for freedom; stand firm, then, and do not again submit to a yoke of slavery" (Gal. 5:1). Paul was concerned first of all about faith rather than works of the law as the basis for salvation. But Christians have applied this "freedom" approach to the ethics of love also. Christ has abolished the law. Love cannot be coerced, love must be freely given. Since we have been redeemed and made new creatures, with Christ living in us, we should rely on that motivation to love freely and truly. Those who stress the freedom of love often quote Augustine's saying, "Love, and do what you will. . . . Let love's root be within you, and from that root nothing but good can spring."[1] If one truly loves God, one's love will always find the best way to act toward others also.

This "freedom" ethical approach brings out important dimensions of Christian love, especially in contrast to the legalistic approach. But there are serious drawbacks here as well. In some early Christian congregations there arose "antinomians" (people against the law), who taught that, since Christ has abolished the law, Christians are free to do whatever they please. Some held that Christians have been perfected by Christ and thus can do no wrong; others held that, since God forgives all sins through Christ, it doesn't matter that one sins. In either view, freedom is the style and law is out as a guide to love. But it quickly became clear to Paul—and to Christians ever since—that total liberty as a moral principle easily degenerates into selfish license and some very unloving behavior toward others.

Paul said there is "a more excellent way" (I Cor. 12:31), the way of love as a transformation of both law and liberty. "Indeed, love is the fulfilling of the law," Paul wrote (Rom. 13:10), showing that God's will as revealed in the law is brought to fulfillment through the practice of love. The law of God is not just a written code, to be fulfilled by slavish adherence to all its details. It is a revelation of God's fundamental intention for humans. Paul wrote, "All the law is fulfilled in one word, in this: 'You shall love your neighbor as yourself'" (Gal. 5:14). This means freedom from the literal form of the law, but not freedom to do whatever one pleases. People need God's will for guidance—with the understanding that loving and caring for the neigbor is what God's will is all about. As to who the neighbor is, Jesus himself had much to say on that, identifying the neighbor as anyone in need: the sick, prisoners, those hungry and thirsty, strangers, and orphans. Whatever we do in caring for the least of these our brethern, Jesus tells us, we do for him (Matt. 25:40).

So law is transformed by love in freedom, and freedom is transformed by love in God's will (law) of caring for the neighbor. With the Corinthian congregation Paul took up a specific question of Christian freedom, namely, whether it is lawful for Christians to eat food that has been sacrificed to idols. His answer sums up

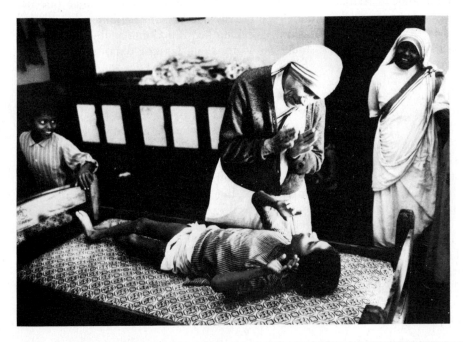

Mother Teresa, champion of the poor in India and winner of the Nobel Peace Prize, talks to a sick child in Calcutta.

the relation between law, liberty, and love: "All things are allowed, but not all things are beneficial. All things are allowed, but not all things build others up. No one should seek his own good but that of the other" (I Cor. 10:23–24). On the one hand Christians are free to follow their own consciences; on the other hand the welfare of their neighbors is dear to God. Christian love is the way to bring both together in an ethical Christian life.

One more word from Paul: "For you, brethren, were called to freedom; only do not use your freedom as an occasion for the flesh, but through love be servants of one another" (Gal. 5:13). In love Christians are truly free and truly servants. How can one be free and slave at the same time? It is through love. Of course, there are different kinds of love. What is meant here is God's kind of love shown in Christ, that is, *agape*, which is unconditional, nondiscriminatory, self-giving love. Other kinds of love—important for full human life—are based on mutual friendship (*philia*) or passionate attraction (*eros*). But agape is love with no strings attached, based in God's grace for all. Friendship and passionate love certainly have their place in Christian ethics; but it is in showing God's kind of love, agape, that Christians can both be free and be servants of all.

Justice and Mercy Toward the Neighbor

The ethic of love is not just a theory but a matter of practical action. How do I love my neighbor as myself? Does loving mean never punishing but always forgiving? In this imperfect world with evils in every choice, don't we always wind up doing some harm as we try to do the good? Questions like these abound as Christians attempt to live real life in love. Traditionally Christians have looked to the Ten Commandments of the Torah as an indication of how love works in action. Interpreting the Ten Commandments through the perspective of the New Testament, Christians see that these commandments provide the ideal combination of both God's justice and God's mercy. There must be justice in order for all God's creatures to live with integrity and value; there must be mercy in order that the failures of our human freedom might be transformed.

Taken from Ex. 20, in the traditional numbering used in some Christian churches (e.g., in the *Book of Common Prayer*), the Ten Commandments are:

1. You shall have no other gods before me.
2. You shall not make for yourselves any graven image.
3. You shall not take the name of the Lord your God in vain.
4. Remember the Sabbath day, to keep it holy.
5. Honor your father and your mother.
6. You shall not kill.
7. You shall not commit adultery.
8. You shall not steal.
9. You shall not bear false witness against your neighbor.
10. You shall not covet your neighbor's house; you shall not covet your neighbor's wife, or his manservant, or his maidservant, or his ox, or his ass, or anything that is his.

These Ten Commandments may be divided into two "tables": the first four have to do primarily with loving God, and the last six have to do with loving the neighbor. But, as has often been pointed out, keeping the first four requires loving the neighbor—for we live in human communities, not as solitary individuals. And, of course, keeping the last six requires loving God. Another important aspect of these Ten Commandments is that each has a positive as well as negative quality. To have God alone as the center and source of life (first commandment) means to treat all other people as creatures loved by God. Not to steal and not to kill require promoting the just wealth and the well-being of others. In this way the Ten Commandments become for Christians not just a law code but a basic guide to the freedom and service of Christian love.

In practice Christians do not always agree about personal ethical decisions. Christian love does not translate directly and unequivocally into positions on abortion, taxes, homosexuality, warfare, or capitalism, and faithful Christians often disagree on such questions. But some traditional Christian ethical positions might be briefly sketched out.

Christians have always viewed marriage—and thus human sexuality—as one of God's great gifts, and some Christians even consider marriage a sacrament.

There has been a certain tendency to view sexual passion itself as tainted by the fall into sin, and thus arose the Christian tradition of celibacy as a higher spiritual life. Most Christians feel, however, that sex within marriage is a healthful, positive human activity. It provides for procreation and thus creates the family, and it gives love and companionship. Some churches, it is true, have held that the only purpose of sex in marriage is for procreation.

One thing the great majority of Christians agree on is that marriage should be monogamous: God intends one woman and one man to be wed for life as the best way of fulfilling the divine loving design. As for the other questions, in modern times there tends to be a general division between "liberal" and "conservative" positions on questions of marital and sexual ethics. Such a division often exists even within the same denomination. One position would hold that premarital sex, abortion, divorce, and homosexuality, for example, are always absolutely wrong. The other position would find the same situations to be wrong or right depending on whether caring love is expressed within them.

Christians agree on the value and dignity of human life, labor, and happiness. Therefore private property and freedom to accumulate wealth and possessions have generally been supported by Christians. There is a certain suspicion about unbridled human greed and a concern to ensure fairness and equal opportunity for the downtrodden in the face of human selfish competition. Some have gone to vows of poverty; others have advocated a kind of socialism as the ideal type of society. There are indeed Christian Marxists as well as Christian capitalists.

The Christian ethic of love from the very first created an attitude of pacifism toward violence and war. Jesus' own example and teaching lent strong support for this: "If any one strikes you on the cheek, offer him the other one also" (Lk. 6:29), "love your enemies" (Lk. 6:35), and so forth. Christian pacifism was the rule for the first centuries, until the Roman Empire became Christian and the need arose for Christian political leaders to take responsibility for maintaining order and justice in society. At that point the doctrine of the "just war" was developed by theologians like Augustine. In this theory, Christian participation in violence or war is held to be justified if it meets certain requirements. The war must be entered into only as a last resort, for a just cause of defense or protection, declared by a lawful authority, and with a reasonable prospect of success. The war must be conducted justly without excess violence or harming of noncombatants, the means used must be proportional to the end result, and mercy must be shown to the vanquished. Throughout the medieval period and until recently most Christian denominations have supported the basic outline of the just war theory, although groups like the Mennonites and the Quakers developed a strong position of nonviolence and pacifism.

In the face of modern warfare, however, many Christians find the whole idea of a "just war" to be untenable, since the necessary requirements could never be met, certainly not in nuclear warfare. So Christian churches are struggling anew with the problem of the love ethic: how to establish both justice and mercy in the volatile world of today with the enormous problems of nation states and huge arsenals. Some still advocate a kind of just security ethic, reasoning that the welfare of the human race depends on a balance of terror between the super powers. Other Christians are finding new meaning in pacifism, not as a passive resignation but as active nonviolent pursuit of justice and peace. As a result, many Christians are active in peace movements in the East and in the West.

Responsibility and Mission in the World

The Christian church is made up of real communities of Christians throughout the world. But just as the Jewish people, so also these people of God transcend particular space and time. The church is "catholic," that is, universal, extended through all the world and all time, past, present, and future. It represents all humankind. At the same time Christians believe the church is one, just as Christ is one. In spite of various divisions, in spite of different races and nationalities, all believers in Christ are united in one family of God.

A favorite image used by the New Testament writers to refer to the church is "the body of Christ." This emphasizes the oneness of the church, even though it encompasses a great variety of Christians. Just as a

Defying a ban on rallies, Rev. Dr. Allan Boesak, Roman Catholic Archbishop Stephen Naido, and Anglican Archbishop Desmond Tutu (winner of the Nobel Peace Prize) join in a service in Cape Town to show support for South African detainees.

person's body has many members that work together for the good of the one body, so the diverse communities of Christians all live and work for the oneness and well-being of the body of Christ (Rom. 12:4–5).

To say the church is the body of Christ is also to evoke the idea that Christ is still present in the world in this "body." All those who make up the church are Christ's ongoing presence within the world. Jesus commissioned his disciples: "Peace be to you! As the Father has sent me, so send I you" (John 20:21). In this way the church is defined by its role or mission — to be about loving, healing, forgiving, and reconciling the peoples of the world by being the continuing presence of Jesus Christ in the midst of human society. Generally Christians speak of this mission both as a

social responsibility and as a saving mission: both seeking the welfare of the world and bringing the saving gospel of Christ to them so they can believe and share the Christian hope.

In the World but not of the World

The world is God's good world, but it is also a fallen world, and therefore participation in the life of the world is an ambiguous thing. Jesus left Christians with a rule of thumb: they should be *in* the world but not *of* the world (John 17:11, 16). Being of the world, in the language of the times, meant to have the fallen, lust-driven world as one's source of being. Christians, rather, are born of the Spirit. Yet they are to be in the world, for it is still the world that God has redeemed, and Christians are to continue the presence of Christ in the world for that purpose.

Christians agree on the mission to bring the gospel to the world. But what does this mean in relation to the cultural and societal existence of people? What about government, economics, art and literature, oppression, poverty, and all the rest? Christians have not completely agreed on what the church's responsibility is toward the concrete problems and possibilities of this world. For some Christians, the only possibility is total withdrawal and renunciation of the world as hopelessly evil. For others, the coming of God's kingdom is understood to be identical with social improvement and the perfecting of this world's potentials. Both these are radical positions: either Christianity is in total opposition to this world's culture or it is totally identical with the best of it. Most Christians have not accepted either of these radical positions but have sought some middle ground to live out the role of being in but not of the world.

Among these various approaches, a dualist view and a transformationist view have been particularly dominant. The dualist view would understand this world to be primarily a preparation for the next, with the conclusion that Christians have no special role to play in the social, political, economic, and cultural arenas. As human beings, of course, Christians should be good citizens and work to the extent of their abilities for the betterment of life. But Christ came, they say, not as a social worker but as the saviour. Therefore the church's mission is not primarily to change the effects of original sin (poverty, oppression, and violence) but to bring people to eternal salvation.

The transformationist approach sees things a bit differently. To be sent as Christ was sent means being involved in loving one's neighbors, easing people's sufferings, and actively seeking to transform the structures that control this world. This approach does not deny the fallenness of the world or the mission of spiritual salvation. But God is still active in the creation. If Jesus Christ is indeed the first fruits of the new creation, and Christians are his presence in the world, then it is a high priority for Christians to be involved in whatever it takes to transform human society and culture so that it more completely reflects God's will and design. Motivated by this vision, many Christians of today are actively involved in movements of liberation, peacemaking, betterment of education and the arts, enhancing the dignity of women and minorities, and the like.

Missionary Work

The identity of the Christian church has been deeply shaped by the charge that Christ gave to his disciples before his ascension into heaven:

> Go forth and make disciples of all the nations, baptizing them in the name of the Father and of the Son and of the Holy Spirit, teaching them to observe all that I have commanded you. And, lo, I am with you always, until the end of the age.   (MATT. 28:19–20)

The missionary emphasis in the "great commission" is not just on being in the world or bettering the world, but teaching and making disciples of all peoples. So evangelism, sharing the good news of Christ in order to bring others to faith in Christ, has always been a central activity of Christians.

Carrying out this mission of witnessing has had its high and low points in the history of the church. Many early Christians traveled widely, spent their lives learning new cultures, debated and argued, performed great works of love, and even sacrificed their lives in witnessing the good news of Christ. After Christianity became dominant in the Roman Empire, missionary activity tended to become tied to imperialistic goals, and that has been a special burden for the Christian mission down to the present century. The need to integrate Christian witnessing with an attitude that values and respects those of other religions has become much more urgent in the modern global village. Many Christians today are rediscovering that, in its origins, Christianity was a religion of humility and love. Being Christ's presence in the world means sharing one's deepest beliefs and hopes with others, but it also means listening to them and learning from them in dialogue.

DISCUSSION QUESTIONS

1. What are main elements of the Sunday worship service?
2. Describe the main movement of Christian festivals throughout the year.
3. Discuss the meaning of the "church." How can it be both universal and local, both one and many?
4. What is the relationship between law, freedom, and love in Christian ethics? How might these elements come into play in difficult ethical decisions today?
5. Pacifism has been an important tradition from earliest times in Christianity—why? What is meant by the "just war" doctrine? What is the stand of major church groups today?
6. What are some main Christian attitudes toward involvement in social concerns?

CHAPTER 10

ISLAM: SACRED STORY AND HISTORICAL CONTEXT

"Who am I?" To be a Muslim means to find one's identity in the sacred story of Islam. Like Jews and Christians, Muslims also look to a historical figure who is the founder of their religion. But Muhammad is the founder in a different way than either Moses or Jesus were founders. Moses transmitted God's Torah—but he died before entering the promised land and thus could not himself put the laws into practice in the life of the nation of Israel. Jesus transmitted God's revelation, but more importantly he himself became God's revelation; he died before there was a Christian church, and he is worshiped as the divine Lord. Muhammad

187

also transmitted God's revelation. But he himself also founded the Muslim community and put the laws of the revelation into total effect in the lives of the people. To Muslims, Muhammad is the final agent of God's revelation, the seal of the prophets. And the story of the Muslims is focused on the miracle of that revelation through Muhammad and the establishing of the community of Islam based on God's revelation.

THE MUSLIM STORY: THE PROPHET AND THE UMMAH

The Jewish scriptures and the Christian scriptures contain much material about Moses and Jesus, as well as narratives about the other important founders and events. In contrast, the Muslim scripture, the Holy Quran, is predominantly God's message to humans and thus contains very little narration about Muhammad and the events that led to the founding of Islam. Whereas some of the suras of the Quran can be placed in the context of events in Muhammad's life, for the most part the Muslim story of the founding of Islam relies on reports (*hadiths*) from Muhammad's companions, material that has become known as the Hadith. Based on material from the Hadith, there are many early Muslim biographies of Muhammad's life; the best known is by Ibn Ishaq[1] in the middle of the eighth century C. E., about 120 years after Muhammad's death.

The Times Before Muhammad

As in the case of Christianity, the Islamic sacred history links itself clearly with the religions that preceded it, Judaism and Christianity. Muhammad, of course, was not a Jew or a Christian, but Islam considers him to be the legitimate successor of and fulfillment of the founders of both previous religions. The Muslim story joins the Jewish and Christian stories in telling of God's work: God created the world and Adam and Eve, and from them all peoples. God sent prophets such as Abraham, Moses, and David to guide humankind. And God worked through Mary and made her son Jesus a great prophet. Of course, the Muslim story interprets these events and prophets somewhat differently than do the Jewish and Christian stories, but it is important that the link is made. The revelation in Islam is the fulfillment and the end of the revelations that God has been giving since Adam and the beginning of the human race.

The Prophet Abraham

One specific link with the past religious history is of particular significance for the Muslim story: Muslims are not Jewish, but Abraham is also their ancestor. Abraham, the Quran says, lived before there was a Jewish or Christian religion; he surrendered himself to God in practicing the pure religion, the same revelation that God gave to all the prophets and to Muhammad. Abraham was the father of both Isaac, who was the ancestor of the Jews, and Ishmael, who became the ancestor of the Muslims. Ishmael was actually the firstborn of Abraham; in her barrenness, Abraham's wife Sarah gave her maid Hagar to Abraham for a wife, and Abraham had Ishmael by her. When God asked Abraham to sacrifice his son Ishmael, he proved faithful; both he and his son submitted to God, and God blessed them (Quran 37:103). Abraham practiced the true religion of Islam (*islam* means "submission" to God) and thus he was a muslim (submitter).

Muslim tradition says that, when Sarah forced Abraham to send Hagar and Ishmael away, Abraham brought them to Mecca and later visited Ishmael there. According to the Quran, God commanded Abraham and Ishmael to purify God's house in Mecca, the Ka'bah, which had been destroyed by the flood; so Abraham and Ishmael submitted to God and rebuilt the house, purifying it and making it a refuge and a place of pilgrimage (2:124–127). The stone on which Abraham stood is still seen in the great mosque at Mecca, a constant reminder to pilgrims that Islam continues the pure religion of "Abraham the muslim." The Quran states that Abraham prayed, "My Lord, make this land secure, and turn me and my sons away from serving idols. . . . Our Lord, I have made some of my seed to dwell in a valley where is no sown land by Thy Holy House; Our Lord, let them perform the prayer" (14:35–37).[2] Abraham and Ishmael prayed

A traveler in the desert stops for a prayer to Allah.

that Allah would raise up a messenger in the midst of their descendents who will declare God's revelations to them and instruct them in the scriptures and in wisdom (2:129). Thus it was among the descendents of Abraham and Ishmael in Mecca that the pure worship of the one God was preserved, and, when it was forgotten, from their midst God raised up a new prophet and a new community of Muslims.

The Times of Ignorance

According to the Muslim story, the world of 1,500 years ago had become exceedingly black, and humanity was steeped in ignorance and superstition. The religions revealed through Moses and Jesus, though they had originally been pure Islam, had been distorted and reduced to hodgepodge by Jews and Christians. A religion was demanded that would be for the whole human race. At such a crucial stage of human civilization, God raised up a prophet in Arabia for the whole world. The religion God gave him to propagate was Islam, like all the prophets before; but now it was in the form of a complete and full-fledged system, covering all aspects of human life.

Arabia was the best-suited country for the birth of the much-needed world religion, according to the Muslim story. It was situated right between two great civilizations, the Byzantine and the Persian empires, and the Arabs were a fresh and energetic people, not affected by the artificial and decadent social systems of the great civilizations. And their language was the human language most suited to express the high ideals and subtle aspects of divine knowledge, the one that could most powerfully move humans to submit to God. The world was ready for the new religion to be born in its midst.

But the people of Arabia, because of their ignorance, were in deep spiritual darkness. Cut off from other civilizations, with no arts and sciences, their minds were filled with superstitions and barbarous thoughts. There was no government; each tribe was an independent unit and a law unto itself. Life was violent, murder and robbery were common, and the most trivial incidents often set off prolonged blood wars between the tribes. Their ignorance extended to morality; they reveled in adultery, gambling and drinking. Because daughters were considered a burden, they even practiced infanticide of infant daughters. This was "the age of ignorance" (al-jahiliyyah), according to the Muslim story.

The people of Arabia knew nothing about the teaching of the prophets of old, although they had a vague idea that Abraham and Ishmael were their forefathers. The Jews and Christians who lived in Arabia had passed on some of their teachings, but their ideas about the prophets were distorted and filled with figments of their own imagination. The Arabs worshiped many gods and divine forces. Trees and springs were venerated; sacred stones were rubbed or kissed to derive power from them; other spirits of the desert and the oasis played important roles. There was the high God called Al-Lah (the God) who was thought to be creator of the world. There were also three special goddesses spoken of as the daughters of Al-Lah: Al-Lat, a mother goddess associated with the moon; Al-'Uzza, the goddess of the planet Venus; and the mysterious goddess of fate called Manat (53:19–20). Al-'Uzza in particular was worshiped by sacrifice (perhaps human sacrifice), and she was associated with stone pillars, symbolic of generative power. There were shrines for these gods and goddesses in various places. The city of Mecca was a special sacred area, with its ancient shrine called the Ka'bah, which contained many images of gods, a sacred well called Zamzam, two holy mountains, and many sacred stones and pillars. During part of the year a truce from fighting was observed by the desert tribes so that they could make pilgrimages to Mecca to worship and participate in festivals. Rituals included circling around the Ka'bah (sometimes naked) and running back and forth between the two hills.

The Coming of the Final Prophet

By the time Muhammad was born in 570 C.E., Mecca had become a cosmopolitan city. Some of the desert tribes had given up bedouin life and settled in Mecca, tending the sacred sites and participating in the active caravan trade that crisscrossed the desert. There was some rivalry among the tribes that made up the Quraysh, as these tribes of Mecca were called. Muhammad's grandfather 'Abd al-Muttalib of the Banu Hashim family seems to have been prominent among the Quraysh about the time Muhammad was born, but soon the Umayyad family came to dominate and the Hashim fell on bad times. 'Abd al-Muttalib had a number of wives from different clans who gave him ten sons and six daughters (Muhammad's father and his uncles and aunts). For his son 'Abdallah he obtained as a bride Amina bint Wahb, and their first and only child was Muhammad.

'Abdallah died either during Amina's pregnancy or shortly thereafter, leaving his wife impoverished. According to custom, the infant Muhammad was given over to a nurse from a bedouin clan so that he might be filled with the culture of the desert. He was reunited with his mother Amina when he was about five, but she died soon after. Muhammad, orphaned from both parents, lived with his grandfather, who died when he was eight, and then with his uncle Abu Talib, who now was the head of the Hashim clan. Abu Talib brought Muhammad up, at least once taking him along on a caravan trip to Syria. As a young man Muhammad began to work for the caravan company of a wealthy widow named Khadija; she was impressed by him and soon they were married. He was twenty-five at the time, and she was fifteen years older; yet she still bore him six children, four daughters and two sons who died in infancy. Now Muhammad had become a secure, respected member of Meccan society.

The Light of Prophecy Rests on Muhammad

Such is the bare outline of the first part of Muhammad's life. But the Muslim sacred history makes it clear that, from the very beginning, God had designs for this man, and this is indicated by extraordinary events reported in the traditional biographies. For example, a story about Muhammad's conception relates that 'Abdallah had a white blaze between his eyes when he went in to Amina, but the light disappeared when Muhammad was conceived; the light of prophecy had been passed on in the conception of Muhammad. And while Amina was pregnant the light shone from her so that she could see as far as Syria. Another story tells that Muhammad saw two angels come to open his breast and clean his heart. Then they put him on scales, putting on the other side of the scales first ten of his people, then a hundred, then a thousand, and he outweighed them all. The one angel said, "Leave him alone, for by God, if you weighed him against all his people he would outweigh them." Yet another story is told about a trip to Syria with his uncle, where a Christian monk named Bahira recognized Muhammad as the envoy of God, in accordance with the Christian writings. Bahira then examined Muhammad's back and found the seal of prophecy between his shoulders.[3] Thus even a learned holy man of the Christians recognized that Muhammad was to be the prophet of God.

As a young man Muhammad showed himself to be honest, moral, and wise, even though he was unschooled and illiterate. He tended the sick and organized a movement to protect the weak and fight for the rights of the oppressed in the violent society of Mecca. He became known as Al-Amin, the trusted one. At one time the people of Mecca were rebuilding the Ka'bah, but leaders of the four main clans fell into a bitter dispute over who would have the honor of putting the revered Black Stone back in its position. They appealed to Muhammad as an arbitrator, and he placed the Black Stone in the middle of a cloak and had the clan leaders lift the stone by the corners of the cloak, himself putting it back into its place in the wall of the Ka'bah. During these years, the story holds, Muhammad held himself apart from the pagan religious practices of the Quraysh, even though he had not yet received the revelation of monotheism from God.

The Night of Power

Muhammad, now a respected man among the Quraysh, was not yet content. He felt the need to find solitude and meditate, so he started retiring for days at a time to a cave in the mountain of Hira nearby. One day, when he was about forty, he came home from the cave greatly agitated and cried out, "Cover me, Khadija, cover me!," as he lay prostrate on the floor. After a while he told her about a vision of the angel Gabriel in the cave:

> He came to me while I was asleep, with a coverlet of brocade whereon was some writing, and said, "Read!" I said, "What shall I read?" He pressed me with it so tightly that I thought it was death; then he let me go and said, "Read!" I said, "What shall I read?" He pressed me with it again so that I thought it was death; then he let me go and said "Read!" I said, "What shall I read?" He pressed me with it the third time so that I thought it was death and said "Read." I said, "What shall I read?"— and this I said only to deliver myself from him, lest he should do the same to me again. He said:
> Read in the name of thy Lord who created,
> Who created man of blood coagulated.
> Read! Thy Lord is the most beneficent,
> Who taught by the pen,
> Taught that which they knew not unto men.
> (QURAN 96:1–5)[4]

It is said that Muhammad in his panic over this visionary experience thought to throw himself over a precipice—but then he heard a voice from heaven hailing him: "O Muhammad, you are the Messenger of God!" In a vivid vision he saw a glorious being standing erect high up in the sky near the horizon; then the angel moved down until he was only two bow-shots from Muhammad and communicated to him a revelation from God (Quran 53:1–18).[5] Khadija comforted Muhammad and told him to rejoice, since God would not forsake him. She sent him to her cousin Waraqa, a monotheist who was versed in Jewish and Christian writings, and Waraqa told him this was truly a revelation from God. This night of the first revelation, believed by many to be the night of the 26th of Ramadan, was later to be called "the night of power," a night that was worth a thousand months (Quran 97:1–5). God had sent down divine revelation through the angel Gabriel upon Muhammad.

For many days after this the revelation did not come

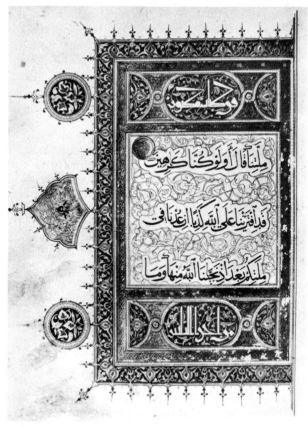

A page from a thirteenth-century manuscript of the Quran.

began the new religion that would be known as Islam. At first Muhammad preached quietly and secretively to people who would listen about the new revelations, and in three years there were about forty followers for this new faith, mostly young men and some outside the clan system. But after that three-year period revelations came from God telling him to preach openly to all the Meccans.

As Muhammad now began openly to proclaim the revelations he was receiving from God, more converts were made, but the vast majority of the Meccans became angry and grew hostile to him. The revelation from God warned them to give up their false gods and worship only the one God, to abstain from promiscuity and lust, to live in virtue, and to treat one another with kindness and equality. This was a message that they found threatening to their way of life. It would mean giving up their tribal gods and rituals, the way of life of their fathers; it would mean abandoning much of the luxury and pleasures of the kind of life they were accustomed to; it would mean reforming Meccan society and thus threatening the position of the wealthy merchants; it would mean giving up the lucrative pilgrimage trade.

Muhammad continued to proclaim his message whenever he could, at fairs, during the pilgrimages, in the marketplace. At first the opposing Meccans mocked and jeered at him, and even his uncle Abu Lahab called him a madman. The Meccans would throw dirt and excrement on him as he passed by. They demanded that he produce some sign to testify that he was a prophet or perform some miracle. Muhammad simply insisted that the only miracle was the revelation sent by God, and he challenged them to produce a writing like it—which they could not do.

Some of those who converted and became Muslims were treated violently by the Meccans. But Muhammad's own Hashimite clan, headed by his uncle Abu Talib, stood by its obligation to protect Muhammad as a member of the clan, even though Abu Talib and most of the Hashim refused to become Muslims. At one point the other Meccans sent a delegation to Abu Talib demanding that he withdraw his protection, but the uncle was resolute. Another time they offered to give Muhammad anything he wanted if he would stop

again, although Muhammad secluded himself in the cave, thirsting after the glorious vision he had seen. But then the revelations came again; the angel appeared again and spoke, "O thou wrapped in thy mantle, arise, and warn!" (74:1–2). And the revelations continued to come over the next years, now causing less surprise and terror, though these were still deep spiritual experiences for Muhammad.

Proclaiming the Revelation in Mecca

Khadija was the first one in Mecca to accept Muhammad's words as true revelation from God. Soon afterward Muhammad's friend Abu Bakr, his cousin 'Ali (son of Abu Talib), and Zayd, a slave freed by Muhammad, submitted to the new revelation. Thus his persistent preaching—money, honor, kingship, even a cure from the spirit possessing him. But Muhammad insisted that he wanted neither money, honor, nor power; God had simply sent him as a messenger, revealed a book to him, and commanded him to be an announcer and a warner. They challenged him to remove the mountains that shut Mecca in and open up rivers or to resurrect their fathers—then they would believe. Muhammad simply persisted: he had brought God's message to them, and they could either accept it or reject it and await God's judgment.

Since they could neither get Muhammad to give in nor get his clan to repudiate him, the other clans of the Quraysh tried a political move; they ordered a social and economic boycott of the Hashim clan: no one should have any dealings with them, sell food to them, visit or converse with them. The boycott lasted for several years, causing a good deal of suffering and hardship. But Abu Talib and the Hashim maintained the clan's obligation to protect Muhammad, and eventually the boycott was ended.

Crisis in Mecca

During these difficult years Muhammad continued to receive revelations from God. One night, the story relates, Muhammad was sleeping next to the Ka'bah, when suddenly he was miraculously transported to the site of the temple in Jerusalem, where he prayed with Abraham, Moses, and Jesus. Then, riding on a winged horse, Muhammad ascended through the celestial spheres to Allah's presence.

Conversions to Islam also continued during these years, in spite of the difficulties. One important convert was 'Umar ibn al-Khattab, who had been an active opponent and even struck his sister when she became a Muslim. But when he listened to the Quran being recited he was so moved that he professed submission to God. 'Umar, who later became the second caliph, was strong and active and contributed much to the growth of the Islamic community.

But the year 619 C.E. brought new trials for Muhammad and the Muslims. The death of his wife was a deep personal loss, for she had been a strong support for him. Soon after that, Abu Talib died, and he was succeeded as head of the Hashim clan by Abu Lahab,

another uncle of Muhammad's who had already been strongly antagonistic. At first Abu Lahab appeared reluctant to withdraw the traditional protection of the clan, but Muhammad's continued attacks on the clan as unbelievers provoked the uncle to look for some way to reject him. He asked Muhammad pointblank whether Abu Talib, who never became a Muslim, and his grandfather 'Abd al-Muttalib (who died when Muhammad was a young boy) were condemned to hell as unbelievers. When Muhammad answered that they were, Abu Lahab angrily considered this a grave insult to the leaders of the clan and withdrew his protection.

Immigration to Medina and the Beginning of the Ummah

Unable to preach safely in Mecca, Muhammad went to the neighboring city of Ta'if and preached for ten days, but the people there only ridiculed him. Back in Mecca the situation grew dangerous. However, about this time (620 C.E.) six men from Medina, an oasis settlement two hundred miles north of Mecca, came to Mecca to do the pilgrimage, and they were impressed with Muhammad's personality and his message. Medina was made up of about a dozen different tribes, including some Jewish tribes, and a long-standing blood feud was causing much difficulty. The next year these Medinans came back with others, representing most of the tribes; they made a promise to Muhammad to accept him as prophet. Muhammad sent a trusty Muslim back with them to instruct them, and by June of 622 a representative party of seventy-five people from Medina made the pilgrimage to Mecca. They met secretly with Muhammad and pledged to fight on behalf of God and God's messenger Muhammad.

Hijra: Immigration to Medina and Founding of the Ummah

In small groups over the next months, Muhammad's followers in Mecca began slipping out and migrating to Medina. Muhammad himself, together with Abu Bakr and 'Ali, remained until the last minute, to detract attention from this escape. The enemies of the prophet grew alarmed at the prospect of a power base for Muslims in Medina and decided to seize and kill him, with a member of each clan striking together so that all would share the responsibility for his blood. On the night they came, 'Ali lay in Muhammad's bed while Muhammad and Abu Bakr escaped and hid in a cave for three days. Finally they reached Medina on September 24, 622, to the great joy of the Muslims in Medina. Upon their offer of quarters, Muhammad loosened his camel, and when she stopped in an empty lot in the quarters of the Banu Najjar, Muhammad chose that as the site to build his house, which was also to be used as a mosque (hall for prayer). This immigration of the Muslim community from Mecca to Medina is called the Hijra; with it began a new age in the Islamic movement, and in honor of that Muslims date their calendar from the first day of this lunar year. The year 622 C.E. is Hijra year 1 in the Islamic calendar, for now for the first time the community of Muslims could put the whole Islamic system of life into full practice.

The Muslims from Mecca who migrated to Medina were known as the Emigrants (Muhajirun), and those people of Medina who received the Emigrants were known as the Helpers (Ansar). Together they made up the community of Islam, the ummah. The ummah is a community based on a common faith, a community of prayer and worship as well as a community with its own government, economy, and military force. The basis of this ummah is recorded in the Constitution of Medina, which states that any serious dispute between parties in Medina must be referred to God and the prophet Muhammad.

Whereas most of the tribes of Medina submitted to Muhammad's religious authority, the Jewish tribes refused to recognize him as the new prophet from God, and eventually most of these Jewish tribes were expelled from Medina. There were also tensions among the Muslims: the Helpers suspected they were being treated unfairly by the Emigrants; and some Medinans only superficially accepted Islam and subsequently became known as the Hypocrites. In spite of these tensions, the ummah thrived and grew, and Muhammad's role as both their religious leader and their political leader became stronger.

During these years at Medina, Muhammad continued to receive revelations from God, so that by the time of his death in 632 C.E. the entire content of the Quran had been revealed. The basic rituals and duties of Muslims were established: confessing the one God and Muhammad as God's prophet, ritual washing and prayer, giving alms, fasting, and pilgrimage. The regulations on matters of religious law were either revealed to Muhammad or stipulated by him on the basis of the revelation in the Quran. One important revelation was the change in direction in which the Muslims should face to say their prayers. Previously they had faced Jerusalem in prayer, but now God revealed that they should face the Ka'bah in Mecca (2:142–150).

Muhammad's own family played an important role in the formation of the community of Islam. After his wife Khadija died in 619, he married numerous other wives and established the model of an active, dedicated Muslim household. Almost all of these wives were widows of Muslims killed in battles with the Meccans and other hostile tribes. One wife who was not a widow was 'Aisha, the young daughter of Abu Bakr; she was especially lively and caught the interest of the community. She lived some fifty years after Muhammad's death and left more reports (*hadiths*) about Muhammad than anyone else did. Collectively the wives of the prophet were highly respected and known as the "Mothers of the Believers."

The Submission of Mecca

With the development of the ummah at Medina, the new religion was now fully in place, and the age of ignorance was over—except that the holy city of Mecca was still in the hands of unbelievers. In 624, two years after the Hijra, a Meccan army headed for Medina. Outnumbered three to one, the Muslims were uncertain whether God wanted them to defend themselves, that is, to fight in the name of their religion. God revealed to Muhammad in a sura, perhaps at this time:

> Assuredly God will defend those who believe; surely God loves not any ungrateful traitor. Leave is given to those who fight because they were wronged—surely God is able to help them—who were expelled from their habitations without right, except that they say "Our Lord is God." (22:38–40)

In this battle at Badr, God gave victory to the Muslims, the army "fighting in the way of God" (3:13). The victory was a turning point for the Muslim community, for it established the conviction that God would see to it that the divine will would be carried out in historical events. The Meccans made two more major assaults. In 625 they nearly killed Muhammad at the battle of Uhud. And in 627 a Jewish tribe and the Hypocrites joined the Meccans in an assault on Medina. This serious threat was met when the Muslims, on the advice of a Persian convert, dug a trench around the city, frustrating the tribal war tactics of the Meccans. After this, Muhammad consolidated the Muslim position in Medina and the surrounding area, and the time came to end the problem of Mecca.

Although Muhammad now had the strength to assault Mecca, he turned to conciliation instead. He made a ten-year peace truce with the Meccans, and in 629 (A.H. 7), Muhammad and a host of Muslims went on a pilgrimage to Mecca. In keeping with the peace truce, the city was vacated of its inhabitants during the Muslims' three-day visit. But soon the Meccans again instigated hostility, and on January 1, 630 (A.H. 8), Muhammad set off with a force of 10,000 men toward Mecca. While they were still a day's journey from the city, a delegation of Meccans met them and offered to submit to the new faith. Muhammad entered the city in peace, treating the Meccans with great magnanimity and gave them a general clemency. And he personally entered the Ka'bah and destroyed the 360 idols, proclaiming, "God is great! Truth has come. Falsehood

The Prophet Muhammad, from a miniature in the Royal Asiatic Society.

has vanished" (17:81).[6] Henceforth this was to be the shrine of Allah alone, and it should be tended and visited only by Muslims. And the former unbelievers of Mecca submitted to Allah and became Muslims.

Muhammad soon dispatched emissaries to all parts of Arabia to preach Islam to the tribes and tear down pagan temples. Several tribes had to be subdued by force, but in 631, the "year of delegations," many former pagan tribes of Arabia sent representatives to Mecca to offer their submission to God and their fighting men to Muhammad. Now they entered God's religion in crowds, as God said to the prophet: "When comes the help of God, and victory, and thou seest men entering God's religion in throngs, then proclaim the praise of thy Lord, and seek His forgiveness; for he turns again unto men" (sura 110). And Muhammad sent out teachers to teach the precepts of Islam to these tribes, telling them to deal gently with the people. Christian and Jewish tribes in Arabia reached agreements with Muhammad, paying a tax in return for protected status.

Muhammad had fulfilled his mission: much of Arabia had submitted, a land and a people that had never before been united under any set of ideals. Idolatry was destroyed; superstition and vice were replaced by faith and virtue. Blood kinship for the first time was subordinated to a community based on faith that offered equal rights and justice for all. Laws from Allah regarding charity, acting justly, observing peace, worshiping God, and the like were now commonly accepted by all even across tribal lines. In the short period of twenty years since his first revelation, Muhammad had realized a goal of Islam: the whole people of Arabia united in one brotherhood, fulfilling in their lives the total design of the one God.

Muhammad's Farewell Pilgrimage and Death

Once more Muhammad returned to Mecca with a large group of followers in March of 632 to make what turned out to be his "farewell pilgrimage." The city had been purified of all traces of idolatry, and now Muhammad established the model for the pilgrimage ritual (Hajj), which, he decreed, could only be performed by Muslims. He retained many of the earlier pilgrimage traditions, such as circling the Ka'bah seven times, kissing the Black Stone, running between the two hills, drinking water from the well of Zamzam, and throwing pebbles at stone pillars. But these rituals were now completely disassociated from polytheistic ideas and restored to their meaning as acts of submission to the one God. Ever since that final pilgrimage, Muslims have participated in Muhammad's story by retracing his steps and repeating the rituals of the pilgrimage as he did.

During the closing rituals of the pilgrimage, astride his camel atop Mt. Arafat, Muhammad spoke his "farewell" sermon to the assembled multitudes, saying:

> O men, listen to my words. I do not know whether I shall ever meet you in this place again after this year. Your blood and your property are sacrosanct until you meet your Lord, as this day and this month are holy. You will surely meet your Lord and He will ask you of your works. . . . I have left with you something which if you will hold fast to it you will never fall into error—a plain indication, the book of God and the practice of His prophet, so give good heed to what I say. Know that every Muslim is a Muslim's brother, and that the Muslims are brethren.

Muhammad's sermon ended with this statement: "O God, have I not told you?" And the assembled multitude echoed, "O God, yes!" And the prophet said, "O God, bear witness!"[7]

Not long afterward the prophet fell ill in Medina. Though weak and feeble, he continued to lead the faithful in public prayer up to the third day prior to his death. In his last exhortation to the faithful assembled at prayer he said, "O men, the fire is kindled, and rebellions come like the darkness of the night. By God, you can lay nothing to my charge. I allow only what the Quran allows and forbid only what the Quran forbids."[8] He died a few hours later in the arms of his young wife 'Aisha, in June 632 (A.H. 13). And he was buried in 'Aisha's home, on the spot where later a mosque was erected.

There was concern and confusion among the Muslims during the days of Muhammd's illness, and when he died there were some who claimed that the apostle of God was not dead but would return. But Abu Bakr went into the house and kissed Muhammad, saying, "You are dearer than my father and mother. You have tasted the death which God had decreed: a second death will never overtake you." Then he went out and cried to the people: "O men, if anyone worships Muhammad, Muhammad is dead; if anyone worships God, God is alive, immortal!" Then Abu Bakr recited this verse from the Quran, which the Muslims had forgotten: "Muhammad is nothing but an apostle. Apostles have passed away before him. Can it be that if he were to die or be killed you would turn back on your heels? He who turns back does no harm to God and God will reward the grateful" (sura 3:144). 'Umar, who had been saying Muhammad was not dead, now said, "By God, when I heard Abu Bakr recite these words I was dumbfounded so that my legs would not bear me and I fell to the ground knowing that the apostle was indeed dead."[9] Thus it was that an extremely important point was established in Islam: Muhammad is the prophet of God, but God alone is to be worshiped.

Because he was the prophet through whom God gave the Quran, however, Muhammad was looked to as the model for what a Muslim is to be, and therefore his own story became the central story for Muslims to model their own lives after. His words and his actions, passed on by his companions in the traditions of the Hadith, provided the paradigm for interpreting the stipulations of the Quran and applying them to the various situations of life. In this sense the story of Muhammad is the story of every Muslim.

A Religion for All Peoples: Expansion of Islam

The story goes on, for until this point Islam had become the religion of the peoples of Arabia but not yet a universal religion for all. Under the first four caliphs (deputies of Muhammad) the religion of Islam expanded to become a religion for all peoples. These first four successors of Muhammad are called the "rightly guided caliphs."

Successors to Muhammad: The Caliphs

Muhammad did not designate who should be his successor as leader of Islam, but after his death the Muslim leaders quickly decided that Abu Bakr,

Muhammad's trusted friend, father-in-law, and one of the first converts to Islam, should be caliph. The role of caliph combined the offices of chief executive, commander-in-chief, chief justice, and leader (imam) of public worship—but not that of prophet, since Muhammad was the final prophet. Abu Bakr (r. 632–634) was honest and deeply committed; it was said that he wept whenever he recited verses of the Quran. In the two years he was caliph before he died, he consolidated the unity of Islam among the tribes of Arabia, dealing resolutely with tribes that apostasized after the death of Muhammad, with those who refused to pay the alms tax, and with false prophets that arose. He also began the task of assembling and collating the scattered suras of the Quran, which were memorized and recited by many but not written down in one volume.

The next two caliphs, 'Umar (r. 634–644) and 'Uthman (r. 644–656), had also been early converts to Islam, and it was their contribution, in only about twenty years, to make Islam a world religion through great waves of Islamic expansion far beyond the Arabian peninsula: to Palestine (Jerusalem fell to 'Umar in 637), Syria, Persia, and Asia Minor, to Egypt and across north Africa. Whereas this expansion was accompanied by military battles in a "holy war" for Allah, many of these people willingly accepted Islam as a liberation from their former oppressive rulers and religions. 'Umar adopted fair means of treating the Jews and Christians who fell subject to Islamic rulers; they were "people of the Book" and were guaranteed basic rights and freedom of worship in exchange for the poll tax paid to the Muslims. 'Umar began the process of putting the guidance of the Quran into public law throughout the Muslim world, and 'Uthman had the official final recension of the Quran produced.

The fourth rightly guided caliph was 'Ali, Muhammad's cousin (son of Abu Talib), one of the first converts, who married Muhammad's daughter Fatima. 'Ali was a widely respected Muslim, a very close companion of the prophet. But a tragic period of internal fighting becomes part of the Muslim story at this point. The last part of 'Uthman's reign was marred by dissension between his own Umayyad family and the other Muslims, leading to 'Uthman's assassination. After 'Ali was chosen as the fourth caliph, Mu'awiya as leader of the Umayyad family disputed his leadership. After an indecisive battle, arbitration was decided in favor of Mu'awiya, and soon after that 'Ali was assassinated by fanatics (661). Mu'awiya then established the Umayyad Caliphate, which ruled the Islamic world from its capital at Damascus for the next century.

The Beginning of the Shi'ites

'Ali was Muhammad's cousin, and Hasan and Husayn, the sons of 'Ali and Muhammad's daughter Fatima, were the surviving male heirs of Muhammad. Because of special interest in the family of Muhammad, there had long been a "faction (shi'a) of 'Ali" that felt 'Ali was the obvious successor to Muhammad. 'Ali was tragically assassinated, as were his son Husayn and others of the family—but these martyrdoms only gave impetus to the feeling among his faction, the Shi'ites, that the family of Muhammad, through 'Ali, Hasan, Husayn, and their descendants, should be the real spiritual leaders of Islam. The Shi'ites call these leaders "imams" rather than caliphs, tracing them down through a number of generations from Imam 'Ali. Most Shi'ites hold that there were twelve imams before the final one disappeared to return sometime in the future. Shi'ites look to these imams for special guidance, since the light of Muhammad was passed on to Imam 'Ali and on to the rest of the imams. Thus the imams also have become part of the story for Shi'ites. In all the other important respects, however, the Shi'ites share the same story with the Sunnites, the majority group in Islam that looks to the four rightly guided caliphs as the proper successors to Muhammad.

The House of Islam

The story culminates, then, in the rule of Islam as a unified, worldwide ummah, whether that is called the caliphate or the imamate. This is, of course, an ideal that has never been completely achieved. But it is the goal set forth in the Muslim story: that the ummah become the ideal human society, in which Muslims as representatives of true humanity submit their lives totally in accordance with God's will as revealed through the prophet Muhammad. The best way to achieve this goal is in the establishment of the Islamic state, as Muhammad and the early caliphs did, in which all the laws that govern life, in both the public and the private domain, are based on God's revelation in the Quran.

To be a Muslim means to identify with this sacred story, seeing the revelation that God gave through Muhammad in the Quran as the final truth for all human society, and looking to the model of Muhammad and his companions for guidance in living the full human life.

THE ISLAMIC UMMAH IN HISTORY

After the founding period of the prophet and the four rightly guided caliphs, the Muslim movement settled down in its secure place in world history. The territory under control of Muslim rulers was called the Dar al-Islam, the "abode of Islam," in contrast to the Dar al-Harb, the "abode of war" controlled by unbelievers. In the Dar al-Islam it was possible to conduct all aspects of life, spiritual, political, cultural, and social, in accordance with the law of Islam, and this provided opportunities for great achievements in Islamic thought and culture. The classical period of Islam included the Umayyad and the Abbasid caliphates, up to the chaos caused by the invasion of the Mongols in the thirteenth century.

The Classical Period of Islam

The Umayyad Dynasty

With the assassination of 'Ali, the fourth caliph, in 661, Mu'awiya of the Umayyad family was able to gain consensus throughout the Muslim world for his caliphate centered in Damascus. There he established a family dynasty, the Umayyad dynasty ruling the House of Islam for the next century. There was a brief challenge to Umayyad rule in 680 posed by the revolt of Husayn, 'Ali's younger son, but this was put down ruthlessly in a great massacre at Karballah in Iraq. Although this gave the Shi'ites a rallying point and helped establish the permanent existence of the Shi'ite movement within Islam, effective political resistence to

rule by the Umayyad family was stopped for the time being.

Mu'awiya was a brilliant leader at Damascus, ruling consensually as the first shaykh among shaykhs. The Umayyad rulers called themselves caliphs, even though later Muslim historians sometimes refer to this dynasty as the "Arab kingdom," implying that the Umayyad dynasty was more like an oriental kingdom than deputies of Muhammad. Under the Umayyads, Islam continued its rapid expansion all the way across north Africa and up into Spain. The Islamic tide even crossed the Pyrenees into France, turned back finally by Charles Martel at Poitiers in 732. Expansion also continued eastward in central Asia up to the borders of India. Islamic art and architecture entered into a creative phase; an outstanding artistic achievement was the building of the Dome of the Rock mosque in Jerusalem by 'Abd al-Malik (691).

The Abbasids

As Islam expanded, the numbers of mawali (non-Arabs "adopted" into Islam) who joined the ummah rapidly increased. These mawali found themselves in a kind of second-class status under the Umayyads; for that reason, many of them were attracted toward the more egalitarian policies of the Shi'ites. Finally a group of Arabs from Khurasan in the northeast rallied the opposition to the Umayyads. Calling themselves Abbasids, after Muhammad's paternal uncle al-'Abbas, they proposed restoring rule to caliphs who were of the house of the prophet—thus attracting the support of the Shi'ites. The mawali also joined them, their army including many soldiers from Iran.

The Abbasid rulers brought Islam to its golden age. It was multicultural and international, and scholarship, literature, and the arts flourished as never before. Shortly after taking rule in about 750, the Abbasids removed the capital to a new Madinat al-Salam (City of Peace) on the Tigris River called Baghdad. There the caliphs ruled much in the style of Persian oriental kings, enjoying such titles as "the Presence" and "the Caliph of God." The fabulous culture of Baghdad under these caliphs is reflected in the stories of the *Arabian Nights*, telling the exploits of the famous

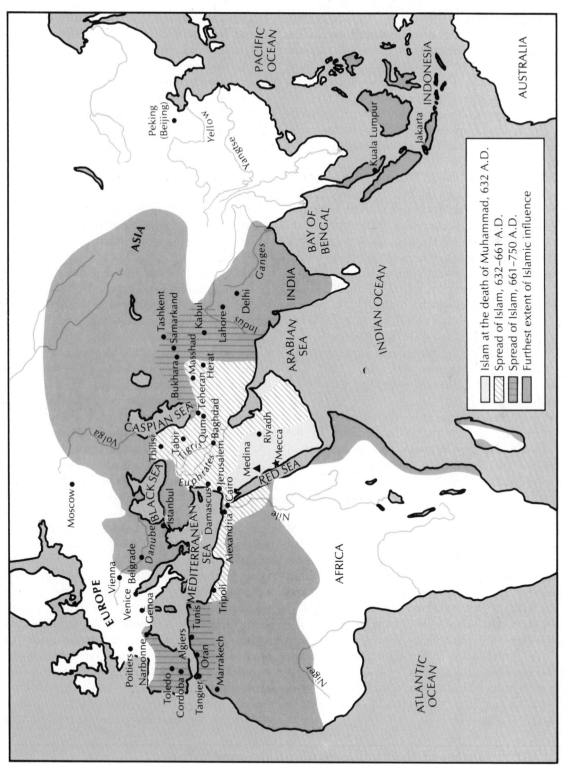

Expansion of Islam.

caliph Harun al-Rashid (786–809). Baghdad society here seems worlds away from the Arabic culture of the Quran. In Baghdad the caliph of God had absolute power of life and death. It is said that officials going into the inner rooms of the Presence routinely carried their shrouds on their arms in case they should displease the caliph and meet instantaneous execution. Here were viziers (ministers) with lavish palaces, poets, slaves, eunuchs and harems, exotic travel, and great wealth and luxury.

But important for Islamic history was the surge of scholarship that took place under the Abbasids. A great library was built in Baghdad, and scholars translated Greek and Syriac works into Arabic. Now Aristotle and Plato became known to Muslim scholars, and they turned their attention to questions of reason and revelation, and of divine power and human will. In Muslim Spain a rival caliphate ruled, a remnant of the Umayyad family, under which a brilliant Islamic scholarly culture was cultivated. And in Egypt a Shi'ite dynasty managed to establish itself as another rival to the Abbasids. Calling themselves Fatimids (after Fatima, daughter of Muhammad and wife of 'Ali), they founded the city of Cairo and established the famous university Al-Azhar.

But the classical golden age of Islam came to an end with the difficulties in the Abbasid realm in the eleventh and twelfth centuries. Turkish tribes from central Asia surged into Iran and Iraq and gradually assumed power. In Baghdad the new Turkish leader, the "Prince of Princes," took over real power and the caliph became merely a figurehead. When the Seljuk Turks became dominant in Palestine and threatened Christian pilgrimage access to Jerusalem, Christian leaders of Europe initiated the crusades to drive the Muslim infidels from the Holy Land. Jerusalem fell to the crusaders in 1099, although it was captured back in 1187 by Salah-al-Din (Saladin). The end of the classical period of Islam was signaled by the eruption of the Mongols into the Islamic lands in the thirteenth century. In 1258 the Mongols attacked Baghdad, burning it to the ground and executing the last caliph. For a couple of centuries Muslim rule was in disarray, until new dynasties established themselves in various parts of the Muslim world.

The Development of the Shari'ah (Law) and Rational Theology

This golden age of Islam under the Umayyads and the Abbasids proved very fruitful in religious and cultural expressions. It produced brilliant new discoveries of science and established the canons of Islamic art, as calligraphy, architecture, and poetry flourished. Most important developments came in the systematic working out of Islamic law, the Shari'ah, and in the creation of *kalam*, rational theology.

Since the Quran is understood as God's perfect and final guidance, from early on Muslims attended to the question of how to apply it to every aspect of life. The example (*sunnah*) of the Prophet himself, as reported in the Hadith, provided the primary sources for interpreting the law of the Quran. In the centuries following Muhammad, these *hadiths* were assembled and evaluated, and scholars were hard at work formulating the Islamic Law, striving (*ijtihad*) to work out applications to all areas of life.

Since this process took place in different localities, the shape of the Shari'ah differed slightly from place to place. Eventually four schools of law emerged among the Sunni Muslims: the Hanafi, Maliki, Shafi'i, and Hanbali schools. There are no fundamental differences between them, and each regards the others as fully orthodox. The Shi'ites developed three schools of their own, the most prominent one being the Ja'fari. Shi'ite law shares the main aspects with Sunnite law, differing principally in the conception of divine authority, which comes through the imam, the perfect leader and successor of Muhammad.

The development of the law in Islam was the culmination of the fundamental Quranic principle that all of life is governed by God's decrees. Whereas the law was organized and systematized by the legal scholars, it was not created by them. It grew out of the ummah's striving to bring all aspects of life into accordance with God's design. By the tenth century most of this legal design was fixed, at least in Sunnite Islam, and the principle function of the legal scholars changed from formulating law to passing on the decisions of the past. This fixation of the law was known as the "closing of the gate of *ijtihad*," and from then down to the modern era scholars have passed on the legal formulations of the past. Shi'ite scholars, with their conception of divine guidance from the imam, have generally not considered the gate of *ijtihad* to be closed.

At first disputes about faith in Islam were settled simply by appeal to the Quran itself or to the testimony of the Prophet's companions. Increasing contact with Greek philosophical thought during the classical period opened new possibilities of exploring the basic doctrines of faith and drawing further implications from them.

There were some early disputes about how to understand certain points of faith. The relation between believing in God and performing the required actions—between faith and works—was interpreted in a radical way by the Kharijites. They rejected the idea that a grave sinner could still be considered a believer. They taught a perfectionist ethic and ruthlessly purged their own community of those guilty of grave sins. It was some radical Kharijites who assassinated Caliph 'Ali because he did not take a firm stand in God's cause against Mu'awiya. The view that prevailed among Muslims, however, was that judgment about sinners should be suspended and left to God, thus avoiding the wrenching of the Muslim community that would be caused by the constant searching out and punishing of those guilty of sinning.

Another early doctrinal discussion concerned human freedom and divine predestination. Those who emphasized free will came to be known as Qadarites (those who discuss determination), holding that humans have the power and capability to act and thus should be held responsible for their actions. The Qadarites (like the earlier Kharijites) tended to oppose the Umayyad dynasty, which they held was not according to God's decree but a result of the misuse of human freedom. In reaction, the Umayyad supporters took a more deterministic stand, insisting that God had decreed the Umayyads to rule as caliphs. The prevailing view that matured in Islam stood strongly on divine predestination, putting more emphasis on the unity and almighty character of God than on human freedom.

In spite of these controversies, a spirit of tolerance developed concerning the boundaries of the ummah. Diverse and dissident groups generally were considered part of the ummah, as long as they believed in the oneness of God and the prophethood of Muhammad, performed the prayer, and fulfilled the requirement of sharing wealth.

Whereas the earlier controversies were settled in a kind of ad hoc fashion, with the overall welfare of the ummah in mind, the intellectual climate heightened during the Abbasid period. Now Muslims were spread across Asia, North Africa, and Spain, and they came into direct contact with Greek philosophical thought. The need became urgent for more rational, systematic expressions of the faith.

It was the Mu'tazilites who initiated Islamic rational theology (*kalam*). The Mu'tazilites (withdrawers) got their name by "withdrawing" to an intermediate position on the question of whether believers can commit grave sins. But they went on to apply rational speculation to questions about revelation, the nature of God, and divine justice.

In some respects the Mu'tazilites were conservative orthodox thinkers; they held firmly to two basic Islamic beliefs: the unity of God and absolute divine justice. With rigorous logic they attacked some questionable popular ideas. For example, most traditional Muslims interpreted the Quran literally even when it described God in anthropomorphic (humanlike) terms, such as God sitting on a throne, people seeing God's face in the resurrection, and so forth. The Mu'tazilites, holding strongly to the unity of God, insisted that such ideas were only metaphors—God cannot be described in human qualities.

Further, Muslims traditionally said that the Quran was eternal and uncreated. But the Mu'tazilites argued that this could not be so; such a view would amount to *shirk*, associating another eternal divine essence with God. The Quran, they said, is not divine and eternal but was created in time by God to give guidance to humans.

The Mu'tazilites also felt compelled to defend God's justice by declaring that God's predetermination is not absolute; humans have freedom to choose between good and evil. It would be accusing God of gross injustice to say that people are punished or rewarded for actions that God had predetermined!

Mu'tazilite thought flourished for a century before

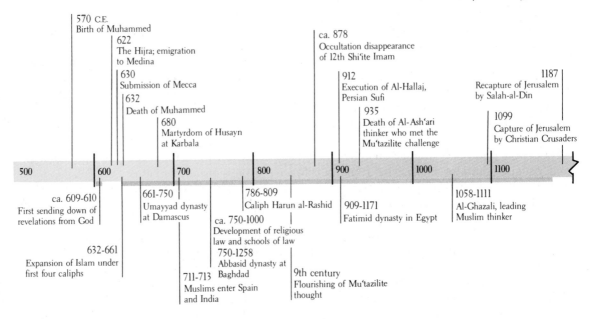

being pushed aside by more traditional positions, but in the process it stimulated the further development of rational theology. Orthodox Sunni thinkers worked with reason and logic to meet the Mu'tazilite challenge, up to the limits of human reason, while remaining in submission to the authority of revelation. The great theologian al-Ash'ari (d. ca. 935) combined reason and revelation in a way that has found acceptance by orthodox Muslims. He held that when the Quran speaks of God in human terms, such as describing God's hand, this was to be accepted as accurate, even though the mode in which God possesses this quality is unknown to humans. Believers accept this truth literally, "without asking how and without likening [to humans]."

The Quran, al-Ash'ari and other orthodox thinkers held, is eternal. But a set of distinctions exists between the eternal attributes of God's word and the physical written or recited Quran, which is created. As to divine determinism and human free will, they argued that God indeed causes all events in the universe; but not being limited by the divine law God is beyond ideas of

evil and injustice. Although God causes all things, humans through their actions "acquire" responsibility for them. By such argumentation the orthodox theologians used reason and turned it against the Mu'tazilites.

Even after the defeat of the Mu'tazilites, Muslim thinkers continued to try to square Islamic faith with Greek philosophy (*falsafa*). One such philosopher was Ibn Sina (d. 1037), widely known in the West as Avicenna. But the theologian-mystic al-Ghazali (1058–1111), one of the greatest thinkers in the history of Islam, blasted such dependence on reason with his book, *The Confusion of the Philosophers*. Some Muslim intellectuals continued to work with rational speculation, like Ibn Rushd (d. 1198), known in the West as Averroes. Against al-Ghazali's attack he defended rational theology with his book, *The Confusion of the Confusion*. But generally orthodox theology backed off from speculative philosophy, even while keeping the method of Aristotelean logic. In fact, the greatest impact of thinkers like Avicenna and Averroes was on Jewish and Christian thinkers such as Maimonides and Aquinas. Islamic theology, like Islamic law, solidified

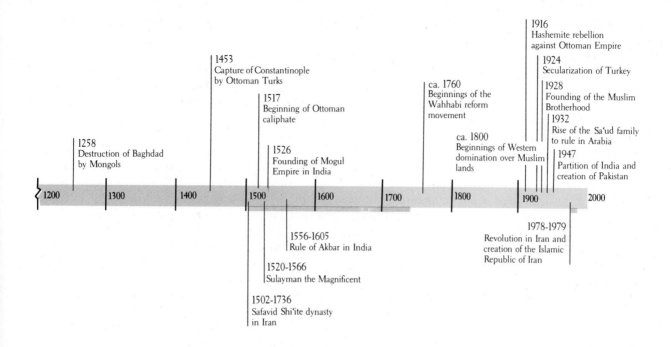

1258
Destruction of Baghdad
by Mongols

1453
Capture of Constantinople
by Ottoman Turks

1517
Beginning of Ottoman
caliphate

1526
Founding of Mogul
Empire in India

ca. 1760
Beginnings of the
Wahhabi reform
movement

ca. 1800
Beginnings of Western
domination over Muslim
lands

1916
Hashemite rebellion
against Ottoman Empire

1924
Secularization of Turkey

1928
Founding of the Muslim
Brotherhood

1932
Rise of the Sa'ud family
to rule in Arabia

1947
Partition of India and
creation of Pakistan

1200   1300   1400   1500   1600   1700   1800   1900   2000

1556-1605
Rule of Akbar in India

1520-1566
Sulayman the Magnificent

1502-1736
Safavid Shi'ite dynasty
in Iran

1978-1979
Revolution in Iran and
creation of the Islamic
Republic of Iran

in orthodox form, to remain largely unchanged until the modern era.

Islamic Mysticism: the Sufis

At the same time that Islamic legal scholars were solidifying the law and Greek philosophy was having strong influence on Muslim thinkers, other Muslims were being attracted to mysticism—the interior contemplation and experience of union with God. Like similar developments in Judaism and Christianity, the mystical movement in Islam came to clash with orthodox beliefs and practices.

Sufism, as the Islamic mystical movement is generally called, began as an ascetic movement. The Umayyad and Abbasid rulers had made the house of Islam into "the Arab Kingdom," with the lure of wealth and power too much for many to resist. In reaction, some Muslims went back to the model of Muhammad and the four rightly guided caliphs, who lived lives of honesty and simplicity in their devotion to God. In spite of his great authority, Muhammad had a very frugal life-style; 'Umar's shabby garments were legend-ary; and 'Ali gave away everything to the point of poverty for himself. The Muslim ascetics who distanced themselves from sensuous life and luxury took coarse woolen garments as their symbol, probably receiving the name Sufi from the Arabic word *suf* (wool). Since they aspired to a life of poverty, the term *fakir* (poor one) was also used to refer to them.

The Sufi movement soon incorporated additional elements. The legal discussions of the day focused on outer conformity to the Islamic law—but what about inner emotional submission to God in love? Love (*mahabbah*) became a central theme for the mystics. The rationalists strove for intellectual knowledge of God—what about interior, contemplative, experiential knowledge? Such interior knowledge of God (*ma'rifa*) likewise became a central theme for the Sufis.

The Sufis looked to evidences in the Quran and Hadith for their emphasis on love and inner union with God. God is our friend, who will have "a people He loves, and who love Him" (5:57–59). God is nearer to us than the jugular vein (50:16); and wherever we turn, "there is the Face of God" (2:115). Muhammad was the intimate friend of God, having his consciousness transformed through long vigils, contemplations, and direct revelations from God. His night journey to heaven and his face-to-face communion with God were seen as a mystical paradigm that could be repeated in the Sufi path. In their interpretation of the Quran, the Sufis used, in addition to the literal meaning, also an allegorical and symbolic meaning that guided their mystical practices.

The emphasis on love of God can be seen, for example, in the poetry of the great woman Sufi saint, Rabi'ah (d. 801), who lived a life of rapture and joy amid her austerities. She expressed her mystical thirst for God in a prayer: "O God, if I worship Thee for fear of Hell, burn me in Hell, and if I worship Thee in hope of Paradise, exclude me from Paradise; but if I worship Thee for Thy own sake, grudge me not Thy everlasting beauty."[10] A famous poem defines the kind of love she had for God:

> I have loved Thee with two loves, a selfish love and a love that is worthy (of Thee). As for the love that is selfish, I occupy myself therein with remembrance of Thee to the exclusion of all others. As for that which is worthy of Thee, therein Thou raisest the veil that I may see Thee. Yet there is no praise to me in this or that. But the praise is to Thee, whether in that or in this.[11]

Sufis felt that, whereas other Muslims follow the Shari'ah as the outer path to God, there was also an inner way beyond the outer path, and they called this the Tariqa. The Sufi path begins by following the outer path in order to break attachment to earthly things. But at its higher levels the Tariqa becomes a way of inner meditation, leading finally to freedom from attachment to self and a "passing away" (fana) into God. The method of the inner path involves techniques of dhikr, the "remembering" of God which the Quran says should be often done (33:41). By remembering God both aloud and silently in the heart, Sufis advanced on the inner path through the "stations" and "states" of spiritual attainment toward inner knowledge and experience of union with God.

Some Sufis became so intoxicated with the inner path that clashes with orthodox teaching set in. One group of Sufis felt themselves beyond the Shari'ah to the point where they could willfully reject and transgress the law. Some Sufis focused on achieving the intoxicating union with God at any cost. An early Sufi, Abu Yazid (d. 875), experienced God deeply in his soul and shocked orthodox Muslims by exclaiming, "Glory to Me! How great is My Majesty!" Another intoxicated mystic, still controversial among Muslims to this day, was al-Hallaj (d. 922). He had a deep knowledge of Christianity, in addition to Hinduism and Buddhism. Al-Hallaj described the mystical union with God by the famous allegory of a moth that circles ever closer to the candle's flame and is finally united with it by being consumed by it—an allegory of the soul and God. He bothered orthodox Muslims especially by his public pronouncements of his experience of union with God, such as his famous utterance, *ana al-Haqq* (I am the Truth, e.g., God). Refusing to take back such a blasphemous statement, al-Hallaj accepted death so as to be one with God. Taken to be crucified, al-Hallaj approached the gallows laughing, thanking God for showing him the mysterious vision of God's face. Perhaps knowing his resemblance to Jesus, al-Hallaj prayed:

> And these Thy servants who are gathered to slay me, in zeal for Thy Religion, longing to win Thy favor, forgive them, Lord. Have mercy on them. Surely if Thou hadst shown them what Thou hast shown me, they would never have done what they have done. . . . Whatsoever Thou dost will, I praise Thee![12]

In later centuries some Muslims have pointed out that al-Hallaj, in saying *ana al-Haqq*, was surrendering his own existence and testifying that God is all. Yet his public flaunting of his mystical experiences gave offense to many Muslims.

Al-Ghazali and the Acceptance of Sufism

In the radical mysticism of Sufis such as al-Hallaj, the Sufi Tariqa seemed to have become incompatible with the orthodox Shari'ah. But in the experience and teaching of the great Al-Ghazali (1058–1111), a reconciliation was effected between the Sufi way and the orthodox law, making it possible for Sufism to become thought of as the "heartbeat of Islam." Al-Ghazali lived as the Muslim ummah was approaching its five-hundredth anniversary (he died in the year 505 of the Hijrah), and his life of devotion and work of renewal have led many to consider him the second greatest Muslim after Muhammad. At thirty-three years of age he started teaching in the new Islamic institute in Baghdad, becoming a master of rational theology and philosophy. But a spiritual crisis affected him, as he realized he was mired in his comfortable and rewarding position. In his spiritual autobiography, *Deliverance from Error*, he wrote:

> I considered the circumstances of my life, and realized that I was caught in a veritable thicket of attachments. I also considered my activities, of which the best was my teaching and lecturing, and realized that in them I was dealing with sciences that were unimportant and contributed nothing to the attainment of eternal life. After that I examined my motive in my work of teaching, and realized that it was not a pure desire for the things of God, but that the impulse moving me was the desire for an influential position and public recognition. . . . One day I would form the resolution to quit Baghdad and get rid of these adverse circumstances; the next day I would abandon my resolution. I put one foot forward and drew the other back. . . . Worldly desires were striving to keep me by their chains just where I was, while the voice of faith was calling, "To the road! To the road!"[13]

Falling into a physical ailment in which he could barely eat and could not talk, al-Ghazali finally took to the road and lived as a Sufi for the next eleven years in Syria, Palestine, and Arabia. Eventually he returned to teaching for a while, and then he founded a Sufi retreat center in his native Persia. In his many works he was able to bring about a synthesis between Sufism and the orthodox tradition of law and theology. He lived by the law, but he provided for it a deep spiritual sensitivity. In his teaching and especially in his own example, he brought Sufism back into the orthodox Islamic path.

Sufi membership, which before al-Ghazali had been small, elite groups, now became more representative of all levels of society. Following al-Ghazali's example, other orders or brotherhoods were established. Each was based on a spiritual master (*shaykh*) who had perfected a distinctive path or Tariqa and gathered disciples around himself. The disciples (*faqirs*) lived with the master and practiced the path communally. Among

Sufi whirling dervishes doing their characteristic dance in Turkey.

the distinctive practices of the different brotherhoods were chanting of certain divine phrases, breath control while chanting, communal recitation, ecstatic dancing, and the like.

One particularly well-known Sufi brotherhood was founded by the great Sufi poet, Jalal al-Din al-Rumi (d. 1273). Rumi, born in Afghanistan, moved to Anatolia and became a master of Sufism. An intense friendship that ended in a tragic death inspired him to put his deep love for God into poetry—and the result is some of the most inspired Sufi poetry of all time. Rumi founded the order of the Mawlawiya, often called the "whirling dervishes" because of their distinctive ecstatic dance: with the shaykh in the center, the dancers with flowing robes spin and circle around to the accompaniment of plaintive music.

A Sufi thinker who went far beyond the bounds set by al-Ghazali but who had much influence on Islamic thinkers was Ibn 'Arabi of Spain (1165–1240). Trained in all the religious sciences, Ibn 'Arabi focused on the twin points of unity of being and love. Feeling his thinking led by an inner light from God, he taught that all created things are manifestations of God—external to God but having emanated from the divine mind. In stressing the unity of being, Ibn 'Arabi also exalted the feminine principle, declaring that to see God in woman is more perfect than seeing the divine one in any other forms. Love was at the heart of his vision of the universe, and on that basis he was tolerant of all religions as reflections of the unity of being.

Religious Ideas of the Shi'ites

During the classical period the one major division in the worldwide Islamic community developed: the Shi'a movement, which today comprises about fifteen percent of the world population of Muslims. The split between the Shi'ites and the Sunnites (the orthodox Muslims) began as a political division but later led to some divergent religious emphases.

From the time of Muhammad's death there had existed a shi'at 'Ali, a "faction of 'Ali" who thought Muhammad's cousin and son-in-law 'Ali was destined to be the successor of Muhammad. Although 'Ali was passed over in the choice of the first three caliphs and died tragically after his brief, frustrated time as fourth caliph, his followers continued to hold that he and his descendants were the proper successors to Muhammad in God's design. 'Ali had married Muhammad's daughter Fatima, and their sons Hasan and Husayn were the male descendants of Muhammad—and the Shi'ites felt that the successors of Muhammad should come from the "people of the house," that is, Muhammad's house. Shi'ites report hadiths that indicate that Muhammad did at various times indicate that 'Ali and the "people of the house" were to be his successors. A particularly significant incident took place at the pool of Ghadir al-Khumm as Muhammad was on his way back to Medina from his farewell pilgrimage. There, before the assembled Muslims, Muhammad publicly designated 'Ali as his successor, according to the Shi'ites, saying that whoever has Muhammad as his master has 'Ali as his master.[14] Whereas Sunnites hold that this incident simply shows the affection Muhammad had for 'Ali, Shi'ites see it as proof that 'Ali is the divinely designated imam or successor of Muhammad. Yet 'Ali, sensing the importance of maintaining the unity of the ummah, did not press the claim.

After 'Ali's death and Mu'awiya's takeover of the caliphate for the Umayyad family, 'Ali's son Hasan gave up any claim as successor of Muhammad. But in 680 'Ali's younger son Husayn put forth the claim to be the rightful successor. On his way to Iraq where he had many supporters, Husayn and his whole family were ambushed at Karballah; the men were massacred and the women taken in chains to Damascus. But what appeared to be a great defeat became a religious rallying point for the Shi'ites. They interpreted Husayn's death as a martyrdom in God's cause, showing that God provides blessing through the sufferings of the people of the prophet's house. Muhammad's own death, the death of his infant sons, the death of the youthful Fatima, 'Ali's assassination, Hasan's death by poisoning, Husayn's martydom at Karballah, plus the tragic deaths of succeeding imams, all show God's redemptive design. Annually on the tenth of Muharram, Shi'ites remember the massacre at Karballah with processions, passion plays, and intensified spiritual discipline.

Besides their view of the proper successors of Muhammad and their inclination to view the suffering and deaths of the imams as having deep spiritual meaning, the Shi'ites differed with the Sunnites in a number of ways. Sunnites viewed the caliphate in a contractual way, the caliph ruling by consensus as the deputy of Muhammad. But the Shi'ites developed a more vertical, intrinsicalist view of the imamate: the highest spiritual authority of Muhammad was passed on to 'Ali and then to each of the succeeding imams. Just as Muhammad was kept sinless and perfect, so also the imams, possessing the "light of Muhammad," are kept by God from error in interpreting God's revelation. All true interpretation therefore comes from the imam, not from the consensus of other scholars.

Further, Shi'ites held the idea of the "hidden imam." In particular, the twelfth imam Muhammad disappeared and went into a state of hiding or occultation (*ghaybah*), from which he will return one day to destroy evil and establish a new perfect age of Islam. Meanwhile, this hidden imam illumines and guides the religious scholars (*mujtahids*) as they interpret the Quran and establish law for Muslims. The largest group of Shi'ites accepts this idea about the twelfth imam, earning thereby the name Twelvers (*Ithna 'Ashariyah*). The Twelvers became dominant in Iran during the sixteenth century and still today make up the vast majority of Muslims in Iran, with large numbers also in Iraq.

A smaller group differs from the Twelvers on the identity of the fourth imam, holding him to be Zayd, a grandson of Husayn; the Zaydites, living in Yemen today, are very close to Sunnites in their practices. Still another group claims the proper seventh imam was Isma'il; since they consider him to be the last imam, the Isma'ilites are often called Seveners. From the Isma'ilites have come some splinter groups of a more radical nature, such as the order of the Assassins, who used the art of the dagger, combined with taking hashish, to accomplish their purposes. Small groups stemming from the Isma'ilites, such as the Druze of Lebanon and the 'Alawites of Syria, developed radical, secretive teachings and practices to the extent that many other Muslims no longer recognize them within Islam.

It should be emphasized that the Shi'ites agree with the Sunnites on all the major points of Islamic faith and practice, with the exceptions noted here. They have their own schools of law.

Medieval Empires: Stagnation and Flourishing Culture

After the disruptions caused by the Mongol invasions, eventually new Muslim empires were established in the sixteenth century to restore some order and stability in the Muslim world. Three empires were especially im-portant: the Safavid Empire in Iran, the Mogul Empire in India, and the Ottoman Turkish Empire bridging western Asia, northern Africa, and eastern Europe.

From the fifteenth century on, the West was moving into the Renaissance, followed by the great explorations and discoveries, the rise of science, and the Enlightenment. But most of this bypassed Islam. The Muslim world, having had its golden age earlier, entered into a period of stagnation and retreat. Although the disruption caused by the Mongols was overcome in the new Muslim empires, the scientific revolution and Enlightenment did not reach into Muslim society until the western powers began to encroach upon Muslim lands in the nineteenth century. Still, there was continued expansion of Muslim rule, both into eastern Europe and into all of India. And although modernity did not emerge, there was a great flourishing of traditional Muslim culture in the Middle East, India, and the Malaysian-Indonesian archipelago. In fact, areas under Muslim rule had never been greater than during the medieval empires.

From the time that the Persians first accepted Islam, they carried Persian influences into their new faith. One effect of this Persianizing of Islam was the ready acceptance of the Shi'ite tradition. The shahs who established the Safavid dynasty (1502–1736) claimed to be descendants of the seventh imam and established Shi'ism as the religion of the realm, and it has remained so in Iran up to the present. Among the great cultural achievements of Iran was the capital city Isfahan, created by Shah 'Abbas (r. 1586–1628), most famous of the Safavids. Full of beautiful gardens and Islamic schools, Isfahan attracted travelers and Muslim scholars from all over the world.

Already in the tenth century Muslim warriors invaded India, and the sultanate of Delhi was set up to control northern India. These first Muslim invaders looked upon Hindus and Buddhists as polytheists, with their elaborate temples and devotion to gods, Buddhas, and bodhisattvas. So they looted the temples and destroyed the monasteries.

The Mongols were converted to Islam, and early in the sixteenth century an army led by Babur (d. 1530), a descendant of Genghis Khan, invaded India and founded the Mogul Empire in northern India. The

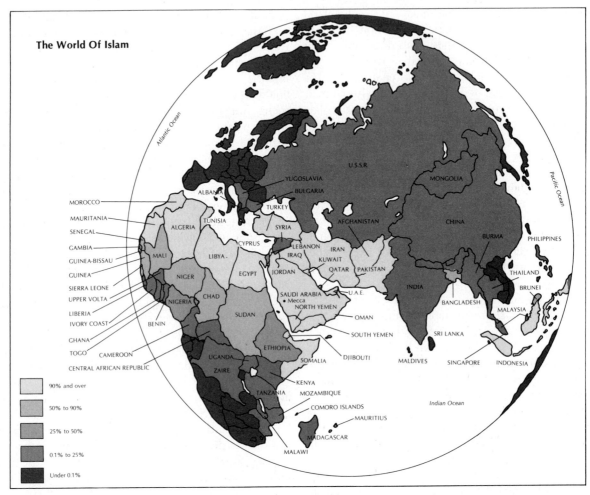

The World Of Islam

	90% and over
	50% to 90%
	25% to 50%
	0.1% to 25%
	Under 0.1%

The world of Islam. Estimated Muslim population as a percent of national total. The total number of Muslims in the world is at least 800 million.

famous ruler Akbar (r. 1556–1605), grandson of Babur, extended his rule to include most of India. Akbar was a Muslim, but he developed a very tolerant attitude toward Hindus, marrying a Hindu princess and revoking all Muslim laws that discriminated against them. He set up a policy of universal religious toleration and encouraged discussions at his court between Muslims, Hindus, Zoroastrians, Jains, and even Christians. Eventually, in the second half of his reign, Akbar tried to establish a new religion, the Divine Wisdom, a kind of synthesis of all these religions.

But Akbar's successors recognized that Akbar had gone beyond the boundaries of Islam, so they restored the Muslim faith. One of these successors, Shah Jahan (r. 1628–1658), achieved enduring fame by building the Taj Mahal as a crowning glory of Islamic art. But Mogul power disintegrated rapidly, and when British forces became dominant in the eighteenth century

The Taj Mahal, a grand Muslim building from the Mogul period in India.

Ottoman rule. The Ottoman caliphate was proclaimed in 1517 as the supposed head of the Muslim ummah, and it continued, with a long period of decline, until it was terminated by the Turkish people themselves in 1924.

Some have felt that the reign of Sulayman the Magnificent (1520–1566) was the most glorious in all the annals of Islam. He was a great warrior and statesman, effected a massive codification of law, built many architectural glories throughout Istanbul (formerly Constantinople), and promoted music, poetry, and the arts at his lavish court. Religious scholars ('ulama) played a very important role in the Sunnite Ottoman Empire with its close fusion of religion and state, but they lost their independent standing and became a clerical bureaucracy within the Ottoman system.

Reform Movements and the Modern World

Whereas Islamic society was standing still in comparison to the modernization of the West, a far-reaching premodern reform revitalized traditional society in the form of the Wahhabi movement. But soon the forces of Westernization were felt on all sides, and Islam was pushed and shoved into the modern era with all its religious problems and opportunities.

The Wahhabi Reform Movement

Just as the first rumblings of Western intervention were striking the Ottomans, a different kind of challenge erupted from central Arabia. Muhammad ibn 'Abd al-Wahhab (1703–1792) founded a reactionary movement that attempted to purify Islam of centuries-long accumulations of beliefs and practices, returning to the original purity of the Quran and the Sunnah of the Prophet. The reform movement was premodern in that it was not a protest against traditionalism in the name of modernity, nor was it a reaction against modernization. The Wahhabis were traditionalists who attacked innovations like those of the rationalistic and esoteric interpretations of the Quran, the Sufi blurring of the distinction between God and humans, the cult of saints that had developed, and the like. They held that the clear words of the Quran and the tradition of the

they took over effective administration of its remnants. At the time when political unity was disintegrating, a Sufi leader, Shah Wali Allah (1703–1762), founded a Muslim revival movement, which sought to unify the Muslim community and revitalize its religious practice. He attempted to revive early forms of Islamic belief and practice rather than simply relying on the four schools of law. He even translated the Quran into Persian to make it more available to the people. The legacy of the Mogul Empire in India is the largest single group of Muslims in the world—now divided in India, Pakistan, and Bangladesh.

Late in the thirteenth century, the Turk Osman (d. 1326) is said to have founded the Osmali or Ottoman dynasty in Asia Minor. The Ottomans reconquered most of the old area of the Islamic ummah, subjugating the smaller Muslim principalities and taking over guardianship of the holy cities of Mecca and Medina. They also made deep inroads into Christian Europe: in 1453 Constantinople fell to the Turks, and by 1550 they controlled the Balkans, most of Hungary, and parts of southern Russia. Some of the panic of European Christianity at the time of the Reformation reflects this surge of Islam. Yet Christian communities generally fared well in Turkish Muslim lands, and Jews fleeing persecution in Europe found safe haven under

Prophet should be literally understood as direct guidance for life. The Wahhabis destroyed tombs and shrines dedicated to saints, and they initiated religious education and enforced Islamic morality.

The Wahhabi movement spread rapidly and became a highly disciplined group of Muslims practicing a purified Islam. They struck up an alliance with the house of Sa'ud in Arabia and managed to gain control of the holy city of Mecca in 1806. Although the Ottomans eventually recaptured Mecca, a century later the Sa'ud family succeeded in reconquering Arabia, and they reinstituted the Wahhabi policies. Still today the Wahhabi influence is dominant in Saudi Arabia, where the ancient form of Islamic law remains in force as the law of the land. The Wahhabis also provided a strong stimulus to Muslim reform outside Arabia. At the beginning of the nineteenth century, Muslims in India and West Africa moved with the same zeal to purify the dominant Muslim establishments.

Challenge from Western Culture and Muslim Response

As the Western world moved gradually into the modern era, the Ottomans were overpowered by new Western advances in naval power, the steam engine, and other developments of the scientific age. The symbolic beginning of the modern period in the Islamic world was in about 1800, when Napolean and his forces came to Egypt and opened this Muslim land up to Western dominance and exploitation. The same pattern was followed in other Muslim lands throughout the nineteenth century and even up to the midtwentieth century. The Dutch took control of Indonesia, the British ruled Malaya, Russia moved into central Asia, Iran was divided between the British and the Russians, and north Africa became a group of European colonies. In 1876 the Christian Queen Victoria was proclaimed Empress of India!

Such events shook the Muslim world deeply, bringing both a loss of independence and a loss of confidence in the face of the modern achievements of the West. The pattern of Muslim rule in the various empires that had evolved in the medieval period no longer was viable. One of the first responses to the onslaught of the modern era was a new nationalism in some of the Muslim lands.

In the nineteenth and early twentieth centuries, the Ottoman Empire was in the process of disintegrating. People of the Balkans expelled their Muslim overlords and created independent nations. As the world lurched into World War I, the Ottomans took the side of the central powers. With British encouragement, this provided the chance for the Hashemite Arabs of the Hejaz, under the leadership of Husayn ibn 'Ali, to revolt against their hated Turkish overloads. The British guaranteed the Arabs autonomy once the war was ended, but after the war the British and French retained mandates over most of the Arab lands in the Middle East. Husayn's sons were appointed hereditary rulers of Iraq and Transjordan. But Britain reserved Palestine with the intent of creating a homeland for the Jews in accord with the secret Balfour Declaration of 1917—a policy that the Arabs considered a betrayal by the British. The Hashemite leader Husayn ibn 'Ali was driven out of the Hejaz by the Sa'udis, who established the kingdom of Saudi Arabia. Under pressure from the rapidly increasing Jewish immigration into Palestine, Arab nationalism rose to a high pitch. However, the divisions in the Arab world were such that Arab nationalism did not result in unified actions or goals. The complicated Arab-Israeli political conflicts have spilled over into tensions between Muslims and Jews.

Nationalism prevailed also in Turkey—but of a different sort. The last effective ruler of the Ottoman Empire, al-Hamid II (r. 1876–1909), had tried to reassert his role as true caliph for all the Muslim world. But the defeat suffered in World War I and the threatened dismemberment of the Turkish homeland itself created a nationalist revolution led by Mustafa Kemal (1881–1939). This revolution ushered in a modern Turkish state and a national identity based on distinctively Turkish culture, history, and language. Islam was included merely as one of the elements of this national identity, and the Ottoman caliphate was declared ended. To throw off the shackles of traditionalism, the Islamic scholars ('ulama) were excluded from any public role, and secular law replaced Islamic law. Religion became a personal, voluntary matter, and women were emanci-

Muslim women praying in a mosque in Edirne, Turkey.

pated from the traditional family codes. The Turkish leaders insisted that this was not an antireligious movement but rather a reform of religion; freed from the authority of the religious scholars, men and women could turn to the religion of the Quran to meet their religious needs.

In India, nationalism took the form of an Indo-Muslim movement. Thinkers like Muhammad Iqbal (1876–1938), seeing that Muslims in India were faced with being a perpetual minority within a secularized Hindu state, advocated the partitioning of India and the creation of a separate, independent Muslim state. A poet and philosopher of Islam, Iqbal saw Western secular influences as destructive because the West had no spiritual roots in service to God. In order for a Muslim to live life in submission to God, it was neces-

sary to have a Muslim state. At the same time, Iqbal advocated liberal values for society and the creation of an Islamic League of Nations. India was partitioned in 1947, with great suffering and displacement of populations, and the Muslim state of Pakistan was created. Later East Pakistan rebelled and established the separate state of Bangladesh. For many Indian Muslims, the creation of Pakistan was a great new day for Islam; others regretted it deeply and chose to remain in India.

Whereas the changes have not been so dramatic elsewhere in the world, in the last half-century most of the Muslim lands have been restored politically to Muslims. The British, French, and Dutch have gone, and Muslims generally have been free to choose their own method of self-rule. The price of this nationalism has been the breakup of the worldwide unity of Islam.

Now a Muslim is a "citizen" of a particular state rather than a "believer" within the ummah. There have been Muslim thinkers in the modern era who proposed and fought for a pan-Islamic unity that transcends nationalism, and there still exists a sense of worldwide Islamic brotherhood. But Islam needs to fulfill itself in concrete religious, social, and political forms; and in the modern world it has not been possible to transcend the political barriers of the nation state.

Modern Thinkers: Muhammad 'Abduh and Amir 'Ali

One important Muslim response to modernization influences has been to rethink the bases of Islam. Some Muslim thinkers have tried to show that Islam is compatible with modern science and progress; in fact, Islam has contributed a great deal to the modern spirit. Muhammad 'Abduh (1849–1905) of Egypt wanted to strengthen Islam and push out Western influences and power, but he saw no basic conflict between religion and modern science. He pointed out that Islam has always been an advocate of progress in science, researching and understanding the natural law that operates according to God's design. In Egypt 'Abduh supported educational reform and tried to modernize the curriculum of the famous university al-Azhar, so that Islamic scholars would become grounded in modern thought as well as in the religious sciences. In his view, Christianity as an other-worldly religion was less suited to the modern spirit than was Islam with its long tradition of scientific investigation.

Another influential modern thinker was Amir 'Ali (1849–1928), an Indian Shi'ite lawyer who advocated the goals of the brotherhood of all Muslims, respect for women, and government for the people. In his widely read book, *The Spirit of Islam*, Amir 'Ali portrayed Muhammad as a political liberator for the people of his day, and therefore Islam today should return to that kind of vision. Muhammad allowed plural marriage because in the society of his day it was the best way of protecting women from destitution and exploitation; and secluding them was the way of showing them respect. But it is only traditionalism that has rigidly perpetuated these practices in modern times. Amir 'Ali thus argued that Islam really offers modern people a liberating spiritual base. In the process, Amir 'Ali interpreted the Quran in the light of its historical context; the laws it prescribes are the best for its day but are not to be considered unchangeable edicts for all time. To many Muslims, however, this is an unacceptable form of modernization.

The Modern Resurgence of Islam

Whereas many Muslims today live in very secularized societies, the weight of Islamic tradition goes against accepting such secularization of life with all its accompanying effects on the individual and on society. In response to the ever-increasing pervasiveness of secular Western influences in every part of the world, the last few decades have seen new Islamic revival movements. One such militant revival is the Muslim Brotherhood, founded in Egypt in 1928 and spread to north Africa, Syria, and Iraq. The Brotherhood holds that all efforts toward modernization have to be purged of their Western influences and adjusted to the pure teachings of Islam. Even modern Islamic regimes should be swept away if they perpetuate a secular society or one that is imperfectly Islamic. The primary nation of Muslims is the ummah, and allegiance cannot be given to Western-style nation states that do not promote the ummah.

Another example of the revival of Islam to meet the threat of Westernization is the Islamic Republic of Iran. Shah Reza Pahlavi strongly promoted the modernization of Iran's economy, education, military, and culture. Western-style recreation, consumer goods, and social life prevailed. Women in the cities, for example, went about in short dresses without covering hair or arms. In addition to the shah's rejection of traditional Islamic values and customs, he enforced harsh repressive security measures against his opponents. Finally, in 1978–1979 the Shi'ite religious scholars, led by the exiled Ayatolla Khomeini, overthrew the shah and established an Islamic republic. The constitution of Iran makes it clear that, whereas this is a modern state with full protection and rights for all its citizens, the fundamental law of the state is the Islamic law, and the final authorities in the interpretation of that law are the religious scholars. Iran is perhaps the clearest example of the attempt to wed complete sub-

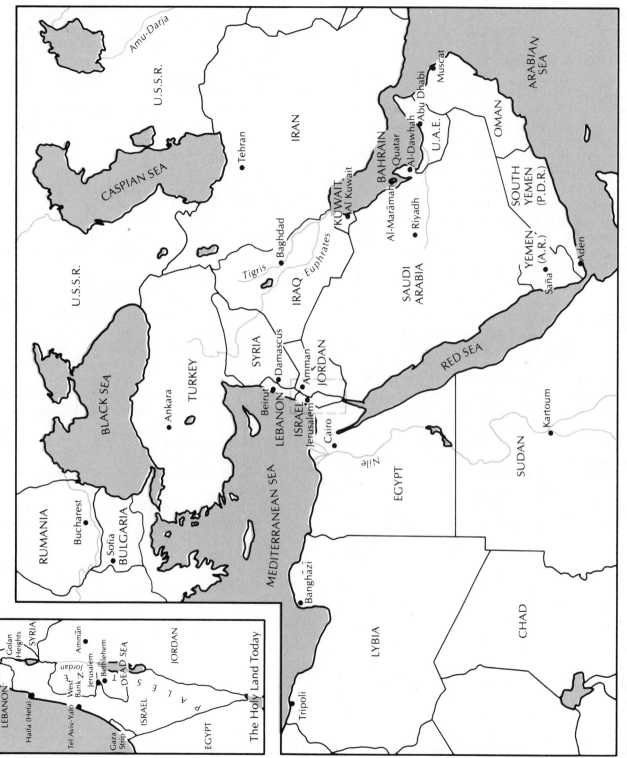

The Middle East today.

mission to God's law with the demands and opportunities of modern civilization.

Islam in the West

A new factor in modern Islam is the increasing numbers of Muslims living in Western societies. There are over six million Muslims in the European West, for example, and the numbers of Muslims who have immigrated to America or are studying in America have increased dramatically. The problems and opportunities of these Muslims living individually or in small communities in non-Muslim societies have been increasingly discussed by Islamic leaders.

In addition, the movement of Black Muslims in America has attracted many Afro-Americans. Headed by Elijah Muhammad (1897–1975), who was born in Georgia as Elijah Poole, the Black Muslim movement at first was based on a black racial mythology that excluded integration with whites. A leader who moved away from the racial mythology was Malcolm X, founder of the Organization of Afro-American Unity, which supported black nationalism but rejected black separatism. Malcolm X was assassinated, but eventually Elijah Muhammad's son, Wallace D. Muhammad, took over leadership of the main Black Muslim group and transformed it into a nonracist, authentic Islamic community in America. Continuing to serve Afro-Americans of the urban neighborhoods, these mosques are attempting to forge closer links with the other Muslim communities.

Because of the increasing presence of Muslims in the Western world, and also because of crucial situations involving Muslims and non-Muslims in parts of the world such as Palestine and India, in recent years some Muslims have shown an interest in establishing dialogue with people of other religions, particularly Christians and Jews. Whereas Christians and Jews have been engaging in dialogue for some years, these "trialogues" are fairly new developments. Muslims in the West are increasingly seeing the importance of imparting an authentic understanding of the Islamic religion to non-Muslims and creating strategies and opportunities for interfaith cooperation.

DISCUSSION QUESTIONS

1. Describe how Muhammad began receiving revelations from God. What kind of reaction was there among the Meccans to his first proclamation of the revelations?
2. Why was the Hijra such an important event that the Muslim calendar dates from it?
3. What was the role of the caliph? What was accomplished by the first four caliphs?
4. What did the Mu'tazilites argue for, and what was the response of al-Ash'ari and other orthodox thinkers?
5. Describe the main aspects of the Sufi movement. Why was al-Hallaj executed? What was the contribution of al-Ghazali?
6. What were the main Shi'ite religious ideas that differed from the Sunnites?
7. Describe the intent and results of the Wahhabi reform movement.
8. What have been the major forms of Muslim revival and renewal during the twentieth century?

CHAPTER 11

MUSLIM WORLDS OF MEANING

ALLAH, LORD OF THE WORLDS

"What's it *all* about?" To Muslims, the assertion of the oneness (*tawhid*) of God is the bedrock of all life and truth. The Muslim confession of faith is brief and focused: "There is no God but God, and Muhammad is the messenger of God." This is called the Shahadah (Confession), and it is the basic statement of faith for all Muslims. Reciting this confession with faith and true intention is what makes one a Muslim. These are the first words recited in a baby's ear at birth, and they are the last words on the lips of a dying Muslim. Recited in prayers many times each day, the confession epitomizes the spirit of Islam.

215

Life Centered in One God

"There is no God but Allah"—*la ilaha illa Allah.* There is no reluctance among Muslims to pronounce the divine term *Allah* (God) such as Jews feel about pronouncing the divine name of Yahweh. Rather, the feeling is that this confession, with its sonorous, liquid syllables, should perpetually be heard. Indeed, the very mention of Allah brings blessings, and so it is the most repeated word in the Muslim vocabulary. Friends are greeted with the name of Allah. After any favorable action a Muslim voices, "Praise be to Allah" (*alhamduli-llah*). Referring to intentions for the future, the Muslim adds, "If Allah wills" (*insha allah*). Every sura of the Quran (except sura 9) begins with the *bismillah*, "In the name of Allah." And in the call to prayers five times every day, and on countless other occasions, the cry goes out, *Allahu akbar*, "God is Greater!"

The Unity of God

When Muslims say, "There is no God but Allah," the emphasis is not particularly on the existence of a divine reality or on the name that one calls this divine reality. The Arab tribes of Muhammad's time did not doubt the existence of gods, and they also knew and believed in Allah as the supreme God, the creator. What Muhammad proclaimed that was new and radical was the sole existence of Allah, to the exclusion of any other divine beings. The word *Allah* in Arabic simply means "the God" (*al-ilah*). It is not a personal name known only by devotees of a particular religion, like the name Yahweh or Jesus Christ or Krishna. It is the word universally used in the Arabic language to designate "the God."

What the confession stresses above all is the unity of God, the doctrine of *tawhid.* God is one. Whereas this sounds deceptively simple, to Muslims the whole experience of God is concentrated in these words.

God is one. That means, first of all, that God completely fills up the divine realm to the total exclusion of any other divinity. God cannot be divided into many parts, or even three or two parts. It is not possible for there to be competitors to Allah in the divine realm. There are no associates, no divine helpers or enemies of God. Muslims do believe in the existence of angels,

including wicked angels with Satan (Iblis) at their head. But these angels are creatures of God, belonging to the created space-time world. Only God is God.

The unity of God further means that God is transcendent, that is, far beyond and separate from the created world. Emphasizing the transcendence of God in stronger tones than do Jews or Christians, Muslims insist on a total separation of the two realms, the divine and the created, with no overlapping and no mixing together. To mix God together with the created realm would be to compromise God's oneness and uniqueness. It would be to elevate something created to the status of divinity, thus positing a competitor to the one God. The greatest sin, according to the Quran, is *shirk*, associating something else with God. This is the great sin of polytheism, which looks on created things such as sun and moon, mountains and trees, spirits and angels, as fellow divinities with God. But this is also the sin of Christians, who say that God has a son, thus mixing God together with human flesh and imagining that there are thus two gods, the Father in the divine realm and the Son in the created realm. "It is not for God to take a son unto Him. Glory be to Him!" (19:35)

The oneness of God means, therefore, that all power belongs to God. There is no other source of power, since God has no competitors. It follows, then, since God is the only creator of the world, that everything that takes place in the created world results from God's will. The Quran says, "No female bears or brings forth, save with His knowledge; and none is given long life who is given long life neither is any diminished in his life, but it is in a Book" (35:11). Again, "No affliction befalls in the earth or in yourselves, but it is in a Book, before We create it" (57:22). God does, within the structure of almighty governance, allow a certain measure of freedom to creatures, thus giving them moral responsibility for their actions. But the fact that God is almighty means most importantly that no other divine power rules and directs our lives.

The Unity of the All Human Knowledge

Since God is one, it follows that the created world is also one. It is not enslaved to a variety of supernatural powers but is totally under the dominion of the one

---

God. In an eloquent passage the Quran celebrates the unity of God's power:

> What, is God better, or that they associate [gods with Him]? He who created the heavens and earth, and sent down for you out of heaven water; and We caused to grow therewith gardens full of loveliness whose trees you could never grow. Is there a god with God? Nay, but they are a people who assign to Him equals! He who made the earth a fixed place and set amidst it rivers and appointed for it firm mountains and placed a partition between the two seas. Is there a god with God? Nay, but the most of them have no knowledge. (27:60–61)

The Quran says that if there were in heaven and earth other gods besides God, surely the heaven and earth would dissolve into chaos (21:22). Thus belief in the oneness of God is an affirmation of the unity and dignity of the created world. The creature knows that God alone is the possessor of all power, and that none besides God can bless or harm, give or take away life. This belief thus frees humans from fearing any other power in the created world. It makes it possible to live life to the fullest as God intends, not overawed by the greatness of another, not putting oneself above another. Knowing that all power, blessing, and wealth come from God makes it possible to treat all other creatures fairly, to have a humble and modest attitude, and above all to strive in everything to obey and observe the law that God has given as the guide for all creatures. Associating God's power and authority with created beings would take away the dignity, unity, and value of God's creatures.

So God is not like anything, for anything else is part of the created realm, and God is beyond all this. To liken God to anything created raises the danger of compromising God's oneness. Therefore Islam strictly prohibits the use of pictures or images of God. Even words and verbal images that compare God with anything else are to be avoided. "God is Greater!"

So can we know or say anything at all about God? God has given self-revelation to humans, and it is that revelation that is the source of knowledge of God—the Quran. What the Quran says about God we are to believe and submit to, recognizing that words of hu-

Interior of a mosque in Turkey. In Islam, God is not depicted in representational forms; instead arabesque and geometric designs, with flowing Arabic calligraphy, express the sacred presence.

man language are limited in expressing the reality of God. But since God is the only divine power, all of the knowledge we derive from this created world is also, in essence, knowledge of God the one creator. Thus knowledge encompassed in the sciences and humanities, insofar as it is not contaminated by human error, leads to the same truth about God as that found in the Quran. There is no other divine power to be discovered with human reason, through science and humanities; all knowledge must lead to the one God. The unity of God thus means the unity of human knowledge.

God is Present and Merciful

Even while stressing God's transcendence and almighty power, Islam expresses a strong experience of the real presence of God, that is, God's immanence. God is not present as part of the created world, but the divine reality is present everywhere nonetheless. "To God belong the East and the West; whithersoever you turn, there is the Face of God," says the Quran (2:115). Or again, the Quran says that no three men meet together but God is their fourth; nor five men but God is their sixth; no matter how many, God is with them wherever they may be (58:7).

God as present to us is known by many names, which express the various divine attributes.

> He is God; there is no god but He. He is the King, the All-holy, the All-peaceable, the All-faithful, the All-preserver, the All-mighty, the All-compeller, the All-sublime. Glory be to God, above that they associate! He is God, the Creator, the Maker, the Shaper. To Him belong the Names Most Beautiful. All that is in the heavens and the earth magnifies Him; He is the All-mighty, the All-wise. (59:22–24)

One of the attributes of God most stressed in Islam is mercy. The *bismillah*, a statement that begins all but one sura of the Quran, emphasizes this with a double force: "In the name of Allah, the Most Merciful, the Most Compassionate." Thus Muslims know that God's ultimate design for creation is one of love and mercy.

Muslim Thinking About God and the Problem of Evil

The problem of evil and suffering in the world is understood by Muslims within the context of God's almighty power and mercy. In one sense, God is the cause behind everything, and therefore even what appears to be evil and suffering is also caused by God. At the same time, the Quran teaches that within the overall structure of the divine design God gives freedom and responsibility to all creatures, rewarding them for good and punishing them for disobeying. In this sense, we bring evil and suffering on ourselves by our unbelief and disobedience.

Beyond this explanation Muslims do not go. For it is not proper to inquire too inquisitively into the divine character; rather one should worship and submit to God. "God is our Enough," Muslims say when faced with a puzzle of life, for it is the reality of God rather than our understanding that comes first and foremost. Characteristically, Muslims end all inquiries about God and God's ways with the words, "God knows." And that is sufficient.

THE NATURE OF THE WORLD AND HUMANS

Muslim Ideas about Creation

The *Fatihah* or "Opening" of the Quran states, "In the name of God, the Merciful, the Compassionate. Praise belongs to God, the Master of the Worlds!" (*rabb al-'alamin*). And so God is, in Islam as in Judaism and Christianity, the master and designer of all that exists. Much that is said by Jews and Christians about the creator and about the world and humans as the creation has familiar echoes in the Islamic affirmations. But the Muslim view has its own distinctive colorations, for Muslims start from the center of their faith to understand creation—from the Quran, with its rhapsodic revelations about God as the creator and master, and the world as servant and sign of God's power and design. Moving out from the revelation of the Quran, Muslims believe they can see the signs of God the creator in everything, for all exists and operates according to God's design and purpose.

God as the Master Creator

God is the Master of the Worlds. This means two important things for Muslims: God is transcendent with no associates in the created realm; and creation fulfills its worth and dignity in serving God.

God is the Master (*rabb*). The Quran says, "That then is God your Lord; there is no god but He, the Creator of everything. So serve Him, for He is Guardian over everything" (6:102). God does not share creative power with anything; God has no associates in the created realm who assist in the divine powers. Unbelievers often mistake elements of the created world to be associates with God, such as forces of nature, angels, or divine-human beings. But this is *shirk*, the great sin of compromising the unity of God. Throughout the Quran the rhapsody goes on, changing color and tone but presenting the same essential message:

> In the Name of God, the Merciful, the Compassionate
> All that is in the heavens and the earth magnifies God;
> He is the All-mighty, the All-wise.
> To Him belongs the Kingdom of the heavens and the earth;
> He gives life, and He makes to die, and He is powerful over everything.
> He is the First and the Last, the Outward and the Inward; He has knowledge of everything.
> It is He that created the heavens and the earth in six days then seated Himself upon the Throne.
> He knows what penetrates into the earth, and what comes forth from it, what comes down from heaven, and what goes up unto it . . . .
> To Him belongs the Kingdom of the heavens and the earth; and unto Him all matters are returned.
> He makes the night to enter into the day and makes the day to enter into the night.
> He knows the thoughts within the breasts. (57:1–6)

The Quran speaks of God creating the world in six days, although there is no day-by-day narrative account as in Genesis 1. But as to how God created, there can be no compromising God's transcendence: creation comes through the mighty word: God simply commands, "Be," and it is (36:82). Even the idea that God rested on the seventh day is avoided. After the six days of creation, God sat on the throne, regulating the world (10:3). For God to rest might imply weariness, and therefore the Quran states emphatically that God was not wearied by the act of creation (50:15). For this reason, perhaps, the notion of a sabbath rest is not a part of Islamic worship; the communal day of prayer (Friday) is not considered to be a day of rest from work.

Dignity and Value of Creation

Since God is Master of the worlds, this means all creation has been given dignity and value as creature. Those who mix God's divinity with created things actually undermine and denigrate the worth of the created realm. All creation finds its worth in being servant ('abd) of the master creator. God created everything in the universe with a design. The Quran says,

"We have not created the heavens and earth, and what between them is, for vanity" (38:27), nor as "playing" (21:16). Rather, everything in the orderly universe is assigned a place in a grand scheme, all knit together by the Master of the Worlds to follow that design and purpose.

And it is in following that design and purpose that all things find their true value and dignity. God created everything for one overarching purpose: to serve God. "To Him has surrendered whoso is in the heavens and the earth, willingly or unwillingly " (3:83). All things by nature follow the cosmic law of creation—the law of the Master—and that means the whole of nature is in some sense "muslim." There is a natural, cosmic "islam," in which stars and rain, molecules and plants, minerals and animals all worship and serve God by conforming to the law of their being. Since all follow God's design, all things must have dignity and value, for God "has created all things well" (32:7).

Humankind: Caliph and Servant

Like the Torah, the Quran singles out humans as God's special creation, some passages bringing together both the original creation of humans from dust and clay, and God's continuing creation of humans in the womb:

> Surely We created you of dust,
>   then of a sperm-drop,
>   then of a blood clot,
> then of a lump of flesh, formed and unformed
>   that We may make clear to you.
>   And We establish in the wombs
>   what We will, till a stated term,
>   then We deliver you as infants,
>   then that you may come of age (22:5).

Whereas the Quran nowhere talks of humans made in the "image" of God (which might be misunderstood as being "like" God), it does state that God breathed the "spirit" into humans, providing the breath of life, the animating spirit. And humans were created male and female: "Mankind, fear your Lord, who created you of a single soul, and from it created its mate, and from the pair of them scattered abroad many men and women" (4:1).

Among all the created things, humans are singled out for a special role, designated as the *khalifa* (caliph) of God. The Quran states:

> And when Thy Lord said to the angels,
> "I am setting in the earth a viceroy (*khalifa*)."
> They said, "What, will you set therein one
> who will do corruption there, and shed blood,
> while We proclaim Thy praise and call Thee Holy?"
> He said, "Assuredly I know
>   that you know not."
> And He taught Adam the names, all of them;
> then He presented them unto the angels
> and said, "Now tell Me the names of these,
>   if you speak truly."
> They said, "Glory be to Thee! We know not
> save what Thou hast taught us. Surely Thou art
>   the All-knowing, the All-wise."
> He said, "Adam, tell them their names...."
> And when We said to the angels, "Bow yourselves to
> Adam."   (2:30–34)

The word *khalifa* means deputy or representative, indicating that humans have a preeminent status and role, to exercise dominion over the rest of creation as the caliph of God. God teaches humans the names—this establishes human competence in identifying, naming, and managing creation, and it is something even the angels cannot attain. In another dramatic passage the Quran reports that God offered the divine trust to the heavens and the earth and the mountains, but they refused to carry it, being afraid of it—but humankind carried it (33:72).

But just as humans are God's caliph over the rest of creation, the proper relation to God the Master is to be servant. "Praise belongs to God, the Lord of all Being.... Thee only we serve," states the opening sura of the Quran. Humans share this servanthood with all creation—indeed, human life largely submits to God's law by nature: genetic patterns, heartbeat and breathing, growth in youth and decline in old age, all this is "muslim." But humans differ from all other creatures in three divine qualities: an intelligence that can discern between the true and the false; a will freely to choose; and the power of speech to worship God.[1] God possesses these qualities perfectly, and God has given them in trust to humans. It is in this arena that the real

Prayer in a mosque in old Cairo. Being servants of God is well expressed in the five daily prayer rituals.

drama of humans serving the Master is played out. One who achieves completeness by using reason, free will, and speech to follow God's design is a perfect "muslim," with not only her body but also her reason, judgment, and speech submitted to God. Now she is at peace with the whole universe, serving the one whom the whole universe serves—and thus she is fit to be God's caliph within creation.

To be God's caliph and servant, humans need guidance. "Guide us in the straight path," says sura 1. And this is what is provided in the Quran and in the Law taken from it—a detailed blueprint of the Islamic order for human life. Such guidance does not contradict or demean human reason. In fact, Muslims feel that God endowed humans with the capacity to reason and acquire knowledge, and by using this correctly humans will choose the truth of the Master. Guidance comes from the Quran—but through human reason this same truth can be uncovered in all the human arts and sciences for the human welfare.

Negligence and Unbelief

Why do people do evil and destructive things? The Muslim answer is quite different from the Christian answer to that question. There is no idea of a fundamentally sinful human nature in Islam, as there is in Christianity. The Islamic view is more similar to the Jewish answer but still has a distinctive shape. What is perhaps most distinctive in the Muslim view is the idea that it is forgetfulness and negligence of what we really are that lie behind human sin and evil-doing.

By Nature Muslim, but Forgetful

All people are "muslim" by nature, according to the law of God's creation. Just as a stone falls and a tree grows and a fire burns in accordance with the law of nature, so humans involuntarily follow God's natural law in most of their various psychosomatic functions. But God created humans for a special role among all creation; God gave them the divine qualities of reason, free will, and speech and expects them to be God's viceroy on earth. Yet only God is perfect. Humans are limited and imperfect, and there are obstacles in the way of using intelligence, will, and speech in submission to God's law. Humans by nature are negligent, not paying attention to the true nature of things and to their own true nature. And they are forgetful, allowing the guidance given by prophets in the past gradually to slip out of active remembrance. Though humans were created as God's caliph and though they made a covenant with God to accept the divine trust, they are always forgetting who they really are and neglecting the natural law of submission to God as the way of fulfilling their true nature. Humans have the tendency to fall asleep, as it were, and live in a kind of dream world, unaware of who they are and what they should be doing in this world.

Thus, looked at in the ordinary human state, people are weak and negligent, subservient to their surroundings and prisoners of their own needs and passions. It is not that their needs and passions are evil. God created humans with passions and drives as part of the design for a full, useful human life. Without passions, humans would never be motivated to strive for success and well-being in family and society. Some Muslims, like Jews, talk of two inclinations that God created in humans: the spiritual inclination that directs the intelligence and will to follow God's law; and the inclination to fulfill the desires and passions with which God has endowed humans. Both inclinations are necessary and good, when followed in harmony with God's law for human nature and fulfillment. But one who is asleep to his true nature unknowingly becomes a slave to the inclination of the passions. And this means becoming a slave of the creaturely surroundings of human life—a slave of other humans needed to gratify one's lusts, and a slave of the material world needed to satisfy one's cravings for wealth and pleasure.

And that is why humans need revelation from God as guidance. Even though God has created humans in such a high status as *khalifa* and given them the divine trust, humans are usually not able to lift themselves up out of their stupor and dreaming state by their own devices. As part of the divine design for humans, God sends revelation to them as guidance. Starting with Adam as the first human, God has always and to all people been sending revelation, so that they will use their intellect and will and speech to submit to God, get themselves into harmony with the law of creation, and fulfill their role as God's caliph within creation.

Muslims emphasize that sin is not of the essence of human nature. There is no such thing as "original sin," which would mean that the human will is fatally warped and inevitably leads to evil deeds. Rather, sin arises from forgetting and neglecting what we really are, failing to use our intellect and will to recognize the Lord and Creator. This leads us to misuse our reason and our freedom of choice by choosing to deny God and surrendering to our needs and passions.

A Kafir: Concealing One's Muslim Nature

A person who out of forgetfulness and neglect denies God is called a *kafir*, an unbeliever. In Arabic, *kufr* means to cover or conceal. The one who denies God is really concealing what is real and true in the whole universe and in his own life and nature. He thinks he has true knowledge and understanding, having the illusion that he is following his reason and choosing that which is true. An unbeliever is really blinded by ignorance. For she sees the intricate working and design of the whole universe, but she is blind as to the Designer of it all. She experiences the marvelous working of her own body, but she understands nothing of the Maker of her body. Such a one participates in the human race, to whom God has given the divine trust and the divine qualities of intellect, will, and speech—yet she denies the Source of this all. Like a person who has rented a house but refuses to pay the rent, she as one of humankind has accepted the trust that God gave to humans but refuses to acknowledge the Creator or live up to her part of the bargain.

What an unbeliever does, really, is to rebel against the very course of nature, the law that God has ordained for all things. He sets up creaturely things as worthy of the love and reverence he should show only to God. Thus the *kafir* always becomes a *mushrik*, one who associates other things with God and thus commits the great sin of denying the unity of God (*shirk*). An unbeliever bows his head to other powers, whether these are sun and moon, angels, humans heroes or powerful tyrants, or the person's own wants and passions. Thus he commits the greatest injustice and treason possible: he uses God's bountiful gifts, at the same time denying and disobeying his real Lord and Master.

The Struggle with Sin

Since sin is not of the essence of humans, it is possible to live in total submission to God's law—that is, it is possible for humans to be perfect Muslims, since God does not require anything of us that is beyond our capabilities. The prophets through whom God has sent revelation have all been perfect humans, completely fulfilling God's will. However, Muslims recognize that prophets are rare individuals, and that most humans have the tendency of forgetfulness and neglect. Ikhwan al Safa has penned a striking description of the conflict within the heart of one who strug-

gles to be Muslim:

> Looking deep within myself, . . . I found my nature composed of various, mutually conflicting elements, of firebrand passions imbedded in sulphuric bodies . . . whose flames are inextinguishable—like the huge waves of the sea that sweep everything before them; hunger bestirs eternally to make me fall on its object like a starved wolf; the fire of my ambition and anger would fain consume the world, that of my pride regards myself as the best of all and mankind as my slaves and agents whose necessary and sole duty is to obey me. . . . Its desire to recreation makes of myself a mad, drunken god; its love of praise, the most virtuous and worthiest of all; its passion for vengeance weighs on it like a tremendous mountain. . . . Looking closer at this self of mine, I have found that it is all raging flames and inextinguishable fire, perpetual fighting and war between irreconcilable elements, incurable disease, unabatable anxiety, struggle incessant—except in death.[2]

Muslims do take sin seriously; to master one's forgetfulness and resultant unbelief is the great war or struggle (*jihad*) in human life.

In the Muslim view, any act of doing what God has prohibited or failing to do what is commanded is a sin. But there are some sins that are more serious and damaging than others. Here is a list of some of the acts that are major sins and thus liable for severe punishment:

1. To believe that there are partners of God.
2. To disbelieve in God, God's prophets, or God's books, or to deny any of the fundamental principles of Islam.
3. To lie.
4. To commit adultery or other illegal sex.
5. To steal.
6. To cheat or deceive anyone.
7. To bear false witness.
8. To bring false charge against anyone.
9. To backbite.
10. To do damage to anybody or injure anyone's feelings.

As in Judaism and Christianity, so also in Islam, unbelief and sin have consequences. Of course, the unbeliever cannot do harm to God, the Master of the worlds. But by *kufr*, humans bring about their own disgrace and failure, both in this life and in the world to come.

By going against the natural law given by God, unbelievers destroy all harmony and peace in their own lives, and in every part of the world they bring infection and abuse with their unbelief. So unbelievers will not find peace and well-being in life. Having destroyed the natural order, they will meet failure in everything they do. Their selfishness and treason against God will infect their family life, business, and relations to others. They will cause war and bloodshed in human society. And they will abuse and disrupt the harmony of nature. In one way or another, all the evils and troubles of the world have their origin in human unbelief.

On the day of judgment, God will make an accounting of what each person has done. Each person's deeds will be weighed in a balance, and in the case of an unbeliever the evil deeds will far outweigh the good deeds. Everything the unbeliever has done will testify against him or her. Then God will consign the traitor to the horrors of the eternal Fire. In this way the laws that had been so disrupted and twisted by the unbeliever will finally be set back in order.

> All this; but for the insolent awaits an ill resort,
> Gehenna, wherein they are roasted—an evil cradling!
> All this; so let them taste it—boiling water and pus,
> and other torments of the like kind coupled
> together. (QURAN 38:55–58)

In the Muslim view, there is no excuse for being an unbeliever. God's design in the world, and the gifts of intelligence and will, should lead all people to acknowledge and submit to the Creator. To awaken humans out of forgetfulness, God has always and to all peoples been sending prophets with reminders. So there is no excuse; all who sin in unbelief are justly punished by God.

The warning of the coming punishment for unbelief should lead us to repent, to ask God for mercy. In God's gracious design it is possible for us to repent, be forgiven, and turn our efforts anew to living our lives as God would have us.

GUIDANCE ON THE STRAIGHT PATH

"How can I start living *real* life?" "How can I be saved?" It should be noted from the outset that Islam has no word that is properly translated as "be saved" or "salvation." Muslims consider the idea of "salvation" to be appropriate to religions like Christianity, where the stress is on God's action while humans have a passive role. In the Muslim's view, as we have seen, humans have a divinely designed nature that has the capacity of

Muslims in long lines in the prayer ritual, in Pakistan.

realizing God's design. Rather than asking, "How can I be saved?," Muslims would rather ask, "How can I achieve the life of felicity?" The Muslim word "felicity" (*falah*) or the verb "to become felicitous" denote a thoroughly active concept of the human path toward the ideal life. There is action from God, the Merciful and Compassionate, of course. God guides, forgives, and inspires. But fundamentally the path is an active one of human self-transformation in harmony with God's design of felicity.

As we have seen, Islam sees humans as not essentially sinful or wicked. God created them good and endowed them with intelligence, free will, and speech, divine attributes by which humans can realize the divine trust. But humans are imperfect, and this shows itself especially in forgetfulness and negligence, from which derive all acts of sin and unbelief with their disastrous consequences. The path of transformation then is a "reminding" to counter human forgetfulness and an "inspiring" to counter negligence. And the practice of the path will be directed toward the divine qualities of intelligence, free will, and speech. The path fills one with knowledge, brings about willing submission, and provides the practice of prayer and worship.

Islam as a Path of Knowledge

The path of Islam is fundamentally a path of knowledge. Although the central concept is that of *islam* or submission, this is not where the path begins. As we have seen, there is a cosmic *islam* in which the whole creation submits to God's design in following the natural law, and to a large extent also in human life we share in this natural submission. But in the distinctly human realm, that constituted by the divine qualities of intelligence, free will, and speech, submission to God does not take place naturally according to the law of creation. For this is the realm in which humans are called upon to take up the divine qualities and fulfill the divine trust by submitting to God out of free will.

But what is it that leads to *islam*, submission to God, in the distinctively human realm? The Muslim answer is *iman*. This is the Muslim word for "faith," but its meaning is somewhat different from the Christian notion of faith. Muslims point out that Christians often see "faith" as a believing without knowing why, an accepting without rational certainty, a "leap of faith" even against the testimony of reason. But *iman* in the Muslim path is faith on the basis of rational certainty arrived at through the use of our intelligence. This is the highest form of knowledge. It goes beyond the pseudo-knowledge of rational thinking without God's guidance, on the one hand, and the superstition of believing without reason, on the other. It is this *iman*, which we can translate as "certain knowledge," which then leads one freely to *islam* or submission.

How do we arrive at this *iman* or certain knowledge? It is true that God's whole creation is like a book full of signs that speak to our intelligence and should bring about certain knowledge on our part. But because humans are forgetful and negligent, these signs alone are usually not sufficient to arouse us out of our dreaming. Therefore, God has sent reminders through the prophets for guidance on the path toward certain knowledge and submission. This is the role of all the revelations that God has sent to all peoples of all times and places, culminating in the Quran as the final, perfect reminder. God's revelation arouses our intellect from its dreaming state and challenges us to use our reason to ascertain the truth about existence.

> Recite: In the Name of thy Lord who created,
> created Man of a blood-clot.
> Recite: And thy Lord is the Most Generous,
> who taught by the Pen,
> taught Man that he knew not (96:1–5).

Although this guidance in the Quran comes from God, no one is compelled to accept and follow it. "No compulsion is there in religion," the Quran states (2:256). Rather, humans are to hear the revelation, study, examine, test, and inquire of it, until finally their reason leads them to *iman*, certain knowledge of the truth. This is possible because the same God both created human reason and sent down the Quran as guidance. If we truly and freely follow our intellect, Muslims believe, we will arrive at the certain knowledge that the truth presented in the Quran is the ultimate truth and highest knowledge. And—following our intellect further—we will find that everywhere in this universe the same truth is to be found, for everything is of one piece in God's design. Both from studying the Quran and from investigating the world itself, we become certain that the one essential truth is that there is no God but God. All the other truths are one with this, and they are clearly presented in the Quran and throughout God's creation, for our intellect to examine and become convinced. In this way, through using our intelligence in studying God's revelation and the world, we arrive at *iman*, certain knowledge, saying with the Quran: "The truth has come, and falsehood has vanished away" (17:81). In this sense, Muslims say, Islam is the natural religion.

Studying the Quran at a university in Egypt.

Because of the emphasis on each person following only the dictates of his or her own intelligence, Islam does not have any priesthood or religious magistracy that tells Muslims what must be believed. Every Muslim, of course, is duty bound to teach others what he knows; and Islam does have its teachers whom it venerates. But no Muslim is required to accept anything as true just because other Muslims have found it to be true. One must accept only what she herself finds rational, coherent, and corresponding to reality. Nothng is to be accepted by faith without being rationally convinced.

It has been the common experience of Muslims, however, that everything presented in the Quran is certain knowledge, for it corresponds with reality as we know it through our intellect. Further, since the Quran is the perfect guide to the truth, the total depth of its meaning can never be plumbed. Each time one studies a passage of the Quran, some new aspect of the truth can be understood. Even a whole lifetime of study of the Quran can never exhaust the meaning of its truth.

Submission in Free Will

Thus *iman*, certain knowledge, is the first step on the path, the intelligence actively searching and reaching certain knowledge. Then it is possible, in the arena of free will, for *islam*, submission, to take place. A choice has to be made on the basis of knowledge. Do we choose the true or the false? If we have not arrived at certain knowledge, if we have instead followed the pseudo-knowledge of reason blind to God's guidance or the superstition of irrational faith, than we cannot choose the good because our mind is trapped in falsehood. But if we have arrived at certain knowledge through our intelligence, then our will can choose the true and we can submit to God.

It is important that this *islam* take place by virtue of free choice, for that is the only way God's design can be fulfilled. It is said that the reason heaven and earth did not accept the divine trust when it was offered to them is because they have no free will. Humans only accepted this trust because they are free moral agents and can realize the design of God's creation. Knowledge achieved by intelligence, then submission chosen by free will—this is the path of Islam.

The attainment of certain knowledge and submission bring about a transformation in humans. This changes the heart and brings about a total transformation in human life. If one is a *kafir*, an unbeliever, one is out of harmony with the law of nature and brings disruption and bloodshed into the world. But if one achieves certain knowledge and therefore submits, then one is in harmony with God's will and design, being at peace with the creator and whole creation. Mawdudi describes this state of transformation:

> He has now consciously submitted to Him Whom he had already been unconsciously obeying. He has now willingly offered obedience to the Master Whom he already owed obedience to involuntarily. . . . Now his reason and judgement are set on an even keel—for he has rightly decided to obey the Being Who bestowed upon him the faculty of thinking and judging. His tongue is also truthful for it expresses its belief in the Lord Who gave it the faculty of speech. Now the whole of his existence is an embodiment of truth for, in all spheres of life, he voluntarily as well as involuntarily obeys the laws of One God—the Lord of the Universe. Now he is at peace with the whole universe for he worships Him Whom the whole universe worships.[3]

The practice of the path of Islam involves studying and learning, teaching, reciting, praying, thinking, and choosing. It is a life-long path, which continues from birth to death. This path of transformation is based on the Shari'ah, the law or code of behavior in Islam. This law, which is taken from the Quran and the Hadith, provides guidance for the regulation of all aspects of life in the best interests of humans and in accord with God's design. We look at some of the specifics of the Shari'ah later. But here we need to understand that performing the Shari'ah is the following of the path of Islam. It is the means by which the individual person molds and shapes his or her own life into the larger design intended by God. This discipline of following the law is a process of education in the highest sense, for the cultivation and perfection of Godlike qualities.

The Greater Jihad

The path of transformation is a continuous struggle. Whereas humans are not evil by nature, they are also not perfect by nature. So the path of submission is one that requires constant striving, repenting, studying, praying, and disciplining. One term for this spiritual struggle in Islam is *jihad*. This idea refers to the need for striving and struggling to establish God's design in the world. Sometimes it takes the form of outer struggle or holy war in defense of the law of God. But it also refers to the inner struggle of all Muslims, the life-long striving to shape one's own life into conformity with God's design—this is called the greater jihad. This is the path: a continual holy war against all God's enemies—unbelievers and evildoers, of course, but also all our own failings, sins, and unbeliefs.

Blessings Now and in the Life Hereafter

Following the straight path brings blessings and rewards. It brings felicity in this world and in the next. As in Judaism and Christianity, so also in Islam, one of the important blessings is simply the following of the path itself. For it is the way of life most in harmony with God and all creation, and therefore it brings peace and happiness to all who practice it. Those who know God's design will always be successful, respected, wealthy, and happy. For they will always choose the right way in all fields of knowledge and action. Since Islam is the natural religion, those who follow it will be blessed by the Creator and will be sources of blessing in the world.

All Muslims consider belief in life after death to be one of the essential truths of existence. This belief includes the ideas of judgment and reward or punishment based on one's deeds. If people follow the straight path, the Quran says, they will be rewarded with the joys and delights of paradise.

> So God has guarded them from the evil of that day, and has procured them radiancy and gladness,
> and recompensed them for their patience with a Garden, and silk;
> therein they shall recline upon couches,
> therein they shall see neither sun nor bitter cold;
> near them shall be its shades, and its clusters hung meekly down,
> and there shall be passed around them vessels of silver, and goblets of crystal,

crystal of silver that they measured very exactly. . . .
Immortal youths shall go about them;
when thou seest them, thou supposest them scattered pearls,
when thou seest them then thou seest bliss and a great kingdom.
Upon them shall be green garments of silk and brocade; they are adorned with bracelets of silver,
and their Lord shall give them to drink a pure draught.
"Behold, this is a recompense for you, and your striving is thanked."   (76:11–22)

DISCUSSION QUESTIONS

1. What are the implications, for thought, ethics, and art, of saying "There is no God but God"?

2. How does the unity of God mean that the creation has dignity and value?

3. In what sense is the whole world of nature "muslim"?

4. What is the nature and role of humankind, according to Islam?

5. Why do many people become unbelievers? Are they evil by nature?

6. What does the path of transformation in Islam involve? What goal does it lead to?

CHAPTER 12

MUSLIM WORSHIP AND THE GOOD LIFE

SACRED TIME AND WORSHIP

"How can I find new power for life?" Muslims believe that how God wants humans to live is totally structured in the Shari'ah, the Law. God is the Master (*rabb*) and our role is to be the servant (*'abd*). Therefore all of life is to be service (*'ibadat*), that is, worship of God. This includes both the ritual and the ethical duties of life, since nothing is excluded from God's perfect design. Let us first look at the ritual duties, and then the ethical part of worship.

The basic idea of worshiping God for Muslims is similar to Jewish and Christian views. As creatures, our primary goal is to submit to God and serve God faithfully. God deserves our praise, and remembering God constantly as we go about our life is our highest good. Like Jews, Muslims believe God has given direct guidance in *how* people should worship, providing specific rituals that are designed to meet their deepest needs as human beings and to bring harmony and well-being into their lives because, performing these rituals, they will be in harmony with God's design. There can be no separation of religion from the rest of life; all aspects of common everyday life are lifted up in the continued observances of the worship of God.

Muslim holy days and festivals differ somewhat from those in Judaism and Christianity in that they are not geared to the cycles of nature in the seasons of the year. There are, of course, religious observances in the different months of the Muslim calendar. But this calendar follows the lunar pattern (twelve months of twenty-eight or twenty-nine days each), meaning that each year is some eleven days shorter than the solar calendar. Thus, over a period of about thirty-two years, a particular Muslim festival will move through all the seasonal changes of the year—a sign of God's mercy, Muslims say. Another difference is that not as much stress is placed on one holy day of the week as the special day of rest and celebration. Whereas Friday is significant as the day for congregational noon prayers, that day does not carry the same importance as Sabbath for Jews or the Sunday worship for most Christians.

The Five Pillars

The Five Pillars are Confession, Prayer, Alms-giving, Fasting, and Pilgrimage to Mecca. As the minimum duties of Muslims in ritual worship of God, these Pillars are obligatory on all adult Muslims insofar as they are not excused because of sickness or other such reasons. Muslims believe these Five Pillars are perfectly fit to achieve complete human welfare in God's design. They are performed by each person individually, thus establishing a strong sense of individual personhood. At the same time they create the unity of the whole community, because they are done communally, even throughout the whole world. They combine physical activity with spiritual reflection, thus transforming the whole person. Simple to perform, they at the same time possess spiritual profundity. All these rituals center squarely on the unity of God and are practical rituals of submission to God. They also are designed to achieve social improvement and serve effectively in the Islamicization of society.

Saying the Confession (Shahadah)

To Muslims, the brief Confession is certainly one of the most important human vocal sounds, chanted out in sonorous Arabic syllables: *ashhadu an la ilaha illa Allah, ashhadu anna muhammad ar-rasulu Allah*, that is, "I testify that there is no God but God; I testify that Muhammad is the Messenger of God." The Confession is a testimony, a public witnessing to the unity of God and to the Quran as God's final revelation. Saying it, with conviction and intention, makes one a Muslim. The whole universe submits to God's will through the laws of nature. But humans have the great responsibility of testifying to the unity of God by utilizing the special human gifts of intelligence, free will, and speech—and this testimony comes first and foremost in saying the Shahadah.

The Confession is constantly on the lips of Muslims; as noted earlier it is the first thing spoken in an infant's ear and the last thing spoken and heard by a dying Muslim. It is incorporated into every call to prayer and into the prayers themselves, thus sounding forth many times every day in every Muslim community. The Confession frequently appears as a visual art form, used as calligraphic decoration on walls and ceilings of mosques, posters, banners, curtains, and the like.

The unity of God also means the unity of humankind. One Muslim thinker, Muhammad Lahbabi, calls the Confession "a perpetual crossroads between transcendance and immanence, between the Absolute and finitude."[1] Muslims speak this as a constant testimony and act of submission to God, demonstrating thereby also their solidarity with all other Muslims. Since Muslims live in all lands of the world and in all time zones, the Confession is literally a perpetual sound that never ceases.

The Ritual of Prayer (Salat)

According to most Muslims, the Pillar of Prayer is the heart and soul of Muslim life. Since the greatest evil would be forgetting God, it is gracious divine guidance that requires humans to remember God by submitting in Prayer five times a day, seven days a week. It is difficult to forget God when one's daily activities are so interpenetrated with the ritual of prayer.

Prayer is basically a public expression of praise and submission to God. It is not spontaneous conversing with God—Muslims do use that kind of prayer also, which they call *du'a*. But the required Prayer ritual follows set patterns and uses standard formulas—in Arabic—from the Quran and other prayers. According to Muslims, the ritual of Prayer is perfectly designed to sanctify all of life. It combines mental concentration with vocal expression. It is deeply spiritual but also puts the whole body physically into the service of God. An individual action, it provides a compelling sense of community with fellow Muslims. The vision of the Prayer is profound: Muslims in every land, representing the whole human race, facing the same center of the world, saying the same Arabic prayers throughout every day, in submission to the one God. That the unity of God means the unity of the human race is powerfully experienced in Prayer.

The Pillar of Prayer takes place five times every day, at early morning, noon, midafternoon, sunset, and evening. It is also required at funerals and recommended to be performed at certain other times. Muslims say prayers in a mosque, at home, or in any clean spot outdoors. It is best to say the Prayer in a group, although praying individually is also valid. When praying in a group, one person acts as the imam or prayer leader, standing in front, and the others follow the pattern of the imam, standing in straight lines. It is important to perform the Prayer correctly and in harmony. The signal for Prayer comes when the muezzin sings out the call to prayer from atop the minaret tower (nowadays often a loudspeaker system is used). In a haunting, compelling chant, the muezzin calls out in Arabic, repeating each phrase the required number of times: "God is most great! I testify that there is no God but God. I testify that Muhammad is the Messenger of God. Hurry to Prayer. Hurry to success. God is most great! There is no God but God." Muslims prepare to perform the Prayer first of all by purifying themselves,

The muezzin chants the call to prayer from the minaret. From a painting by Jerome.

washing the hands, arms, face, nostrils, hair, ears, and feet with water.

Mental, vocal, and physical actions are united in the Prayer. Standing and facing Mecca, having declared the intention to pray, the worshiper raises the hands to the sides of the head and says, *"Allahu akbar"* (God is most great!). With hands resting on the abdomen, he or she recites the first sura of the Quran together with other prayers and verses. Then the worshiper bows with hands on the knees saying "Glory to my great Lord" and, after praising God again in a standing position, swiftly descends to the prostrate position with knees, forehead, and palms on the floor or ground. In this physical attitude of total submission, he or she says "Glory to my Lord, the Most High!" Then the worshiper sits and finally does the prostration again before resuming the standing position. This completes one cycle of prayers; the cycle is repeated again a number of times, depending on which Prayer it is. There are two cycles of prayers in morning Prayer, four at noon, afternoon, and night Prayer, and three at sunset Prayer.

Near the close of the Prayer, the worshiper testifies the Confession, blesses the Prophet Muhammad and his family, and turning the head to both sides says, "Peace be upon you all and the mercy of God"—directed to all fellow Muslims and to all humankind in need of God's guidance.

At the Friday noon Prayer, Muslims are to assemble at the mosque as a congregation (women are not required to attend the mosque). The imam leads the prayer standing in front of the the *mihrab*, the niche in the wall showing the direction to Mecca, and the worshipers stand in long straight lines behind. An important feature of this congregational service is the sermon (*khutba*), given by the imam or another recognized scholar from a pulpit (*minbar*), providing guidance for the people.

The Pillar of Alms-giving (Zakat)

Wealth is not viewed as evil by Muslims—God blesses the faithful with prosperity. But all wealth belongs to God, who has directed us to share it with those who are less fortunate, as a sign that all are equal before God and deserve a just and fair livelihood. As a legal religious duty, Alms-giving is not the same as charity; Muslims should also be generous and provide for the needy in other ways. Alms-giving is more like an annual religious tax computed on various forms of wealth, such as money, cattle, and crops.

Alms-giving is required of Muslims who have reached their majority (usually sixteen) and who possess a minimum of each type of wealth. The general rate is two and one-half percent annually. It is to be given, according to the Quran, to those who are poor, the needy, those who collect alms, new converts, slaves for their ransom, debtors, those doing good works in God's way, and travelers (Quran 9:60). It should not be given to Jews and Christians who live in the Muslim community—they should be given other types of help where needed. It is also not to be used for things like building mosques, burying the dead, nor given to parents, children, or spouse—there are other ways to take care of such needs. Traditionally, Muslim governments collected and distributed this tax, but now in some lands it is a matter of individual responsibility.

Alms-giving—or wealth-sharing, as some modern Muslims prefer to call it—is definitely not to be regarded as doing a favor, either by the giver or the receiver. The wealth is God's, and it should not be given in a way that embarrasses the recipient or makes the giver proud.

The Pillar of Fasting (Sawm)

One important holy season that comes every year is the month of Fasting, the month of Ramadan. Ramadan is an especially sacred time for Muslims because during this month the first revelation descended on the Prophet. By fasting during the daylight hours, Muslims set apart this whole month as sacred time. It is a time of intense spiritual discipline, for Muslims abstain not only from food and drink but also from evil thoughts toward others. But it is also a joyous time, with opportunities to gather with family and friends at night. Fasting is not a means of punishing the body, as in some religions. The bodily needs and passions are not evil; they are good gifts of God and necessary for life. But people sometimes let themselves be controlled by their drives and passions, and Fasting is a time to break bad habits and regain control. By slowing down and withholding things, one learns a richer appreciation of material pleasures. There are physical benefits to Fasting as well, and it helps one feel a deeper sympathy for the deprived and hungry of the world. It strengthens the solidarity of the community, and, most importantly, it provides discipline for greater submission to God.

The practice of Fasting is simple: from first light in the morning until sundown at night, nothing is taken into the body. Forbidden are eating, drinking, smoking, sexual relations, even taking medicine. Breaking the fast intentionally carries penalties, such as extra days of fasting or giving meals to needy people. However, Fasting should not be permitted to impair one's health, and the sick, the elderly, pregnant women, and small children are excused from the requirement; those who are able should make it up later. During the nighttime hours eating and drinking are permitted, and Ramadan nights are joyful, communal times. But overall there is heightened spiritual atmosphere during Ramadan, with many giving special attention to studying the Quran and prayer. Restaurants and ordinary entertainments are closed during the day, and the Muslim community revitalizes its spiritual foundations.

The Pilgrimage (Hajj)

The highpoint of life for many Muslims is the Pilgrimage, required once in the lifetime of a Muslim. Muslims may undertake the Pilgrimage only if they are physically and financially capable. One cannot borrow money for this, since all debts must be paid before the Pilgrimage. Nor should one deprive the family in order to go on the Pilgrimage; money should be saved up for many years for this great duty. Women also are equal participants in the Pilgrimage, accompanied by husband or relatives.

The Pilgrimage epitomizes the ritual duty of Muslims. It is a dramatic connection to the sacred story, walking in the footsteps of Abraham, Ishmael, and Muhammad. It is an intensely individual spiritual experience, and at the same time a movingly communal experience. Testimony to the unity of God is constantly on the lips of everyone. The pilgrims come from all parts of the world, representing all nations and peoples, yet they come together at the center of the world as one—one human race standing together in submission

An engraving from times past showing Muslims heading across the desert for the pilgrimage at Mecca.

to the one God. It is a transforming experience of death and new life, and the transformed one returning home from the Hajj is appropriately given a new title, Hajji.

The rituals of the Pilgrimage, as determined by Muhammad in his final Pilgrimage, make use of some of the pre-Islamic practices, but these rituals are transformed in their meaning. For the pilgrim, leaving home is a kind of death. The Muslim enters into a special spiritual state (*ihram*), symbolized by special garments and vows. All men wear a two-piece white garment, showing that all are equal; women may wear a white garment or their ordinary clothes. All take vows to avoid sex, cutting one's hair, uprooting living things, wearing jewelry, arguing, and so forth.

After extensive identity checks by the Saudi government (only Muslims are allowed into the sacred area of Mecca), the pilgrims finally see the Ka'bah. For their whole life they have been saying the Prayer in this direction, and now finally it is right before their eyes. The Quran says that Abraham and his firstborn son Ishmael, commanded by God, built the Ka'bah, so the pilgrim feels a closeness to these great prophets of God. A sacred atmosphere is created with the pilgrims constantly chanting the Pilgrimage formula, "I am here, O God, I am here! I am here! You are without associate! I am here! Praise and riches belong to you, and sovereignty!"

The full Pilgrimage takes place during the month of Pilgrimage and includes many rituals over a period of several days. The first main ritual is the Circling (*tawaf*), walking and trotting around the Ka'bah seven times in a counterclockwise direction—thus putting the House of God, the center of the world, at the center of one's own life. Circling the Ka'bah, the pilgrims reach out to touch the Black Stone embedded in one corner. This Black Stone, tradition says, was given to Abraham by the angel Gabriel as a sign of God's pleasure, and Abraham and his son Ishmael built it into the Ka'bah. The next ritual is the Running (*sa'y*) between two hills seven times. This is in memory of Hagar and Ishmael. Because Abraham's wife Sarah was barren, she gave her servant Hagar as a wife for Abraham and he had Ishmael by her. After Hagar and Ishmael were expelled from Abraham's house because of Sarah's jealousy, they were dying of thirst in the desert at

Mecca. But God miraculously provided the well of Zamzam to save them. So the pilgrim acts out Hagar's frantic running in search of water and gratefully drinks from the well of Zamzam.

On the eighth day of the Pilgrimage month, the whole company of pilgrims moves out to the desert, to live in tents for the next several days. The climax of the Pilgrimage comes on the ninth day with the ritual of Standing (*wuquf*) at the Plain of Arafat and the Mount of Mercy. From noon until sunset all the pilgrims stand together as the representatives of the whole human race, praising and submitting to the one God of all.

In the next days come the rituals of Stoning and the Feast of Sacrifice (*'id al-adha*). The Quran and Hadith tell that Abraham, commanded by God, brought his son Ishmael here to sacrifice him. Satan tempted Ishmael to run away, but Ishmael threw stones at Satan to drive off this temptation. God, seeing Abraham and Ishmael's faithfulness, intervened through an angel and provided a ram for the sacrifice. To make this experience of their ancestors real again, each pilgrim performs the ritual of Stoning, throwing forty-nine pebbles at three stone "Satans" in a series of episodes over the next days. The Feast of Sacrifice requires the head of each household to ritually slaughter an animal and

The Holy Ka'bah in the Grand Mosque at Mecca (one of the important sites visited during the Pilgrimage, and the point toward which Muslims throughout the world face during daily prayers).

prepare a feast, giving some of the food to the needy. This Feast of Sacrifice is observed by Muslims throughout the world, providing a link between those on the Pilgrimage and the world Muslim community.

During these rituals in the desert the pilgrims make a return to Mecca for a second Circling of the Ka'bah, and the required rituals are completed. Pilgrims usually make one more "farewell" Circling of the Ka'bah, and many also go on to visit the holy places of Medina, where the Prophet first founded the ummah of Islam and where he and many early leaders are buried.

Other Festivals and Rituals

Holy Days and Commemorations

The Muslim calendar year does not have a lot of required festivals. There are two "feasts." One is the Feast of Sacrifice already noted. The other is the Feast of Fast–breaking (*'id al-fitr*), which comes on the first day of the month following the Ramadan Fasting, a celebration of thankfulness for having been able to complete the Fasting. After morning Prayer at the mosque and a visit to the cemetery, the feast celebrates the completion of the Fasting and the return to normal life with banquets and other events. In many places this joyous festival lasts for three days.

A widely celebrated holiday is the birthday of the Prophet Muhammad (*mawlid al-nabi*), on the twelfth day of the third month, Rabi' al-Awwal. In such places as Egypt, this is a major holiday with a festive mood. Reciters chant verses from the Quran and a narrative of the Prophet's life. Merchants sell candies in the shapes of knights on horses for boys and doll brides for girls to celebrate this holiday. Some Muslims, especially under the Wahhabi influence in Saudi Arabia, consider this holiday an innovation and do not celebrate it. For other Muslims, not only the Prophet but also other saints are remembered with celebrations on their birth anniversaries. Shi'ites especially celebrate the birthdays of Imam 'Ali and the members of his family.

The month of Muharram is the beginning of the Muslim calendar, associated with the Hijra of the Muslims from Mecca to Medina and therefore a significant sacred time. In early times the tenth of Muharram was a day of fasting called *'ashura* (ten), and it is still observed with voluntary fasting by some Sunnite Muslims. Shi'ites have attached another significant celebration to 'Ashura, for it is the traditional anniversary of the martyrdom of Imam Husayn, son of 'Ali. They spend the first nine days of Muharram remembering the tragic events at Karbalah in an atmosphere of mourning. On the climactic tenth day, the drama called Ta'ziyeh is presented. Actors represent Husayn and his family on one side, and the Umayyad forces on the other in the passion play. The theme is the redemptive value of the sufferings and martyrdoms of Husayn and others of the house of Muhammad.

Rituals of the Passages of Life

Although the Quran does not prescribe rituals for birth, Islamic tradition holds that soon after birth a man should pronounce the call to prayer in the baby's right ear and the summons to perform the prayer in the left ear. On the seventh day after birth the baby is usually named and a sacrifice may be performed. On the fortieth day the mother is purified and thus is able to resume the ritual duties.

Circumcision (*khitan*) is an important ritual of passage for boys. In some places, like Indonesia, it is performed at eleven or twelve years of age, thus functioning as a passage into adult spiritual status. In other places it commonly takes place soon after birth or a few years later. Although it is not mentioned in the Quran, Muslims everywhere regard it as an essential purification ritual. The circumcision is the occasion for much festivity, with many guests, special food, and music, and the boy is paraded around in honor and triumph as a little prince. In some localities a similar operation is performed for girls, cutting away or scarring the clitoris. Muslims disagree whether such female "circumcision" (clitoridectomy) should be performed, but those who practice it consider it a ritual of purification.

The whole Muslim tradition encourages a Muslim to marry as soon in life as possible and to have many children. Since marriage is one of God's good gifts, celibacy and marital abstinence are forbidden, except for exceptional reasons during certain periods of a person's life. Marrige is not a sacrament, as in Christianity, nor is it an unconditional binding together no matter what. The marriage is usually arranged by parents, since it brings two families together into a new relationship. No one may be married without his or her own consent, but in practice the girl is usually represented by a guardian, who interprets her silence as consent. A legal contract is written that spells out the rights and duties of both. Should one party fail to live up to the contract, the marriage can be annulled. One thing included in the contract is the bridal gift (*mahr*), which the groom must provide for his bride.

The marriage is legally completed by the ritual of signing the marriage contract, by the groom and the guardian of the bride. But after this ritual is completed, the great communal celebration commences, with many guests, special foods, music making, and dancing. The festivities reflect the traditional culture of the people and thus differ widely in the different parts of the Muslim world. In more traditional societies the men and the women celebrate separately.

The Islamic rituals surrounding death show a realistic acceptance of death as the end of life and a belief in the passage through the grave to resurrection, judgment, and reward. One should be ready at all times for one's own death. Al-Ghazali gave this spiritual advice:

> When you want to go to sleep, lay out your bed pointing to Mecca, and sleep on your right side, the side on which the corpse reclines in the tomb... Remember that in like manner you will lie in the tomb, completely alone; only your works will be with you, only the effort you have made will be rewarded.[2]

Feelings about the grave are also colored by the belief that interrogation by the angels begins as soon as one is buried and the body may undergo purgatorial punishments in the grave before the general resurrection. True believers, of course, can expect reward and happiness on Judgment Day.

At the onset of death, the dying person's face should be turned toward Mecca and the words, "There is no God but God," should be recited, and also sura *Ya Sin* (36), which deals with death and resurrection. The body should be given the full purificatory washing and perfumed, then wrapped in a simple cotton shroud resembling the Pilgrimage *ihram* garment. The Muslim is now commencing his or her final pilgrimage. It is required that Muslims perform the Pillar of Prayer in the presence of the deceased person, with the entire service performed standing. Special prayers are said on behalf of the deceased, like this one spoken by Muhammad:

> Allah, do forgive him and have mercy on him and make him secure and overlook his shortcomings, and bestow upon him an honoured place in Paradise, and make his place of entry spacious, and wash him clean with water and snow and ice, and cleanse him of all wrong as Thou dost clean a piece of white cloth of dirt, . . . and shield him from the torment of the grave and the torment of the Fire.[3]

After the procession to the cemetery, the body is placed in a grave with a niche carved out on one side; the body lies on its side directly on the ground, with the face in the direction of Mecca. As the mourners drop earth to cover the grave, they may recite the words of the Quran, "Out of the earth We created you, and We shall restore you into it, and bring you forth from it a second time" (20:55). The bereaved mourn for three days after the burial and thereafter remember the deceased periodically with prayer and reading of the Quran.

Art in Islamic Worship and Life

The Quran and the Hadith repeat the Jewish prohibition of making images and even strengthen it. The Quran insists that nothing in the created world is like God. Thus not only representational art but even metaphoric imaging of the divine in words is prohibited. Generally Islamic art has avoided not just representations of God but all forms of representational art. It is said that on Judgment Day God will command those who made images now to bring them alive; failing, they will be punished in the Fire. There, of course, has been some use of representational art in Islamic societies, particularly for secular purposes, such as decorative painting on ceramics or book illustrations. Illustrative painting has been most used in Iran and in India. A special branch of Islamic painting is the depiction of the Prophet Muhammad on his night journey through the heavens, mounted on the steed Buraq; on these paintings Muhammad's face is usually covered or left blank. The strong sense of avoiding representations

of the Prophet and the close companions was demonstrated in a recent film about the career of Muhammad, in which Muhammad and the close companions are represented only by voice, never by visible characters; the action is carried on by characters somewhat distant from the Prophet.

In place of representational art, Islamic culture has richly developed other art forms: decoration, calligraphy, architecture, poetry, and literature. One way to avoid representational art is to give prominence to abstract design, straight lines, angles, and intricate geometrical patterns on a flat plane. An important decorative form is arabesque, lines depicting an endless continuation of leaves, palmettes, and sometimes animallike motifs growing out of each other. Geometric patterns and arabesque are often combined with calligraphy, serving well to express spiritual reality rather than the material and concrete world, conveying the rationality of the Muslim faith.

Since Islam places high importance on the word of the Quran, the art of calligraphy has been richly cultivated, rendering the divine word visible in countless artistic variations of the Arabic script. Calligraphy is the central dictum of Muslim art, preserving and conveying the unchanging, eternal words of God given to humans. The divine words are woven in brocade,

An early example of Muslim architecture is the Dome of the Rock in Jerusalem.

carved in wood and stone, painted on ceramics, emerging from mosaics on mosque walls from Baghdad to Cordova. There are many styles of calligraphic scripts, and often the script is combined with arabesques and geometric designs to draw the eye and the mind to the divine word cradled within, calling for thoughtful reflection. For example, the bismillah (In the name of Allah) may be written in such a way as to convey the shape of a bird or a beast; and the ninety-nine names of God may form a calligraphic mosque on a poster.

The mosque is the crowning Islamic creation in the field of architecture. The ka'bah at Mecca, the first and primary sacred building, is a simple cubelike structure, and the mosque of the Prophet at Medina was also simple and practical, a gathering place for believers to pray and study. Mosques differ all over the world, but their grandeur expresses the glory of God and their openness and light symbolize the apprehension of God's truth. All mosques have certain common features: a mihrab, a niche in the wall indicating the direction toward Mecca; a minbar or pulpit for the sermon at congregational prayer on Friday; and a minaret, a tower or spire from which the call to prayer goes out to the community.

The arts of poetry and literature have been very heavily influenced by the Quran itself, the supreme example of the artistic word. Especially among Sufi mystics like Ibn al-Farid (1182-1235) and Jalal al-Din Rumi (1207-1273), the art of poetry has been highly developed as a form of spiritual expression, as in al-Farid's poetic description of the mystic vision:

> . . . the vision blest
> Was granted to my prayers . . .
> The while amazed between
> His beauty and His majesty
> I stood in silent ecstacy
> Revealing that which o'er my spirit came and went.
> Lo! in His face commingled
> Is every charm and grace:
> The whole of beauty singled
> Into a perfect face
> Beholding Him would cry:
> "There is no god but He and He is the most High."[4]

The use of the arts in Islam has given real aesthetic focus to the concepts of the faith and brought these rational ideas into the realm of the everyday life of the people. Overall the faith of Islam has created a distinctive style of art that is diverse around the world but still unified at its basic core.

THE LIFE OF SHARI'AH: SOCIETY AND ETHICS

"How should I live?" The Muslim answer is as simple and universal as the Jewish and Christian answer. The Muslim should live as one who belongs to the ummah, the worldwide community of Muslims, following the guidance of the Shari'ah, the Law.

Social Structure of Islam

The New, Universal Ummah

The word *ummah* is difficult to translate. It has elements of a community, a people, a nation, and a religion. According to the Quran, originally all people were one ummah, but then they fell into variance (10:19). Prophets were sent by God to the different ummahs. The ummah of each prophet received true revelation from God and thus they were muslims insofar as they submitted to that revelation and lived according to it. Most of these communities, however, forgot the true revelation and lapsed into unbelief and sin.

God gave to Muhammad, the final prophet, the mission of establishing a new ummah, which would be the social embodiment of God's design for all humankind and which eventually would reunite all humankind into one ummah. The peoples of Arabia were divided into tribal loyalties, and this greatly hindered Muhammad's work in Mecca. So the decisive moment in the creation of the ummah was the Hijra, the emigration to Medina, where for the first time there arose an ummah that was unified in worship and faith. In making the Hijra, Muhammad and the Muslims were moving against their own kin in Mecca to an alien center outside; faith-solidarity was now sharply pitted against blood-solidarity. The Emigrants had to rely upon the assistance of people outside their tribes, the Helpers of Medina. The Constitution of Medina clearly identified the new community as an ummah bound together by faith and submission to God and his prophet, showing that the bond of faith had replaced tribal loyalty.

In Medina, the political and social structure was totally Islamicized, and that set the pattern for the ummah. There is no separation between the secular and the religious in Islam, between the political and the spiritual, between state and church. The ummah is all-embracing, based on the foundation of the Quran and the Law drawn from the Quran.

As Islam expanded under the caliphs, a large territory came under the immediate jurisdiction of the ummah. This is called the Dar al-Islam, the Abode of Islam, inside of which infidels could not be tolerated. But the ummah is not limited to the area of the Dar al-Islam. The ummah is universal, and all who submit to God and recognize the Prophet are equally in this brotherhood and sisterhood of Islam. Equality and unity are of central importance. No one Muslim, no matter what position, has rights of precedence over another Muslim; all are equal before God. In the days of Caliph 'Umar, the powerful governor of Egypt had a son who, annoyed by an Egyptian commoner in a horse racing contest, struck him, saying, "Don't you know I am the son of the great man?" And the governor imprisoned the Egyptian youth for a time. But when he was released, the youth went to Medina and appealed to 'Umar. 'Umar recalled both the governor and his son, and after they confessed he ordered the Egyptian youth to beat them both. 'Umar spoke to the governor: "By what right do you tyrannize over men? Have they not emerged from their mothers' wombs as free citizens?"[5] Although there may be differences of position or wealth, all Muslims are equal with respect to justice under God's law.

Since God's unity is the bedrock of Islamic belief, the ummah also is an expression of that unity. Ideally the ummah demonstrates the fundamental unity of the human race. The Quran states, "O mankind, We have created you male and female, and appointed you races and tribes, that you may know one another" (49:13). The rituals of Islam provide dramatic experience of the oneness of the whole Islamic community. Five times a day Muslims everywhere on earth face the same center of the world and say the same prayers. And in the pilgrimage to Mecca, Muslims of both genders and of all races, nations, and language groups come together as one, representing the whole human race. The ummah is not called out to be a special people separate from the whole human race; it is the ideal form that all humankind is designed to be.

Social Structure and Leadership

The ummah is universal and worldwide. But it takes concrete form in the various Islamic nations and especially in the communities of Muslims all over who group themselves together as mosque assemblies. Although Muhammad and the first four caliphs were seen as leaders of the one ummah, down through the centuries Islam has linked together with a variety of nations and empires, so that today there is no one worldwide unified ruling authority. Muslims today live in a variety of political structures, from Islamic states like Pakistan and Iran to secular states like Turkey; and a significant number of Muslims live in small Muslim communities scattered throughout the Western nations. Yet there is a remarkable unity of Islamic belief and practice throughout the worldwide ummah. Most Muslims consider themselves to be Sunnites, following one of the four orthodox schools of law codified by the Islamic scholars in the generations following the time of Muhammad. The Shi'ites are a significant minority, making up about fifteen percent of the world population of Muslims and following their own schools of law. Yet for the most part Sunnites and Shi'ites recognize each other as equal and true practitioners of the Muslim way.

There is no clergy or priesthood in the ummah. The ruling family of Saudi Arabia has assumed responsibility for the holy places there, exercising some control over who is considered to be a Muslim in terms of who is allowed to enter Mecca on the pilgrimage. But there is no person or body who has authority over the whole ummah. Since Islam is a path of knowledge, the most respected leaders are the scholars, the 'ulama (sing., 'alim), who study the Quran and the Hadith and are responsible for determining the application of the law. Among the 'ulama the mufti is recognized as a legal expert who can be consulted for a formal legal opinion on a particular question pertaining to, for example, marriage, divorce, or inheritance. Another important figure is the qadi, the religious judge who is appointed by the political leader and carries out justice in matters of religious law. The Shi'ite religious scholars in Iran, called mullas, have an extraordinarily high level of respect and authority in all matters pertaining to religious law—which, in an Islamic republic like Iran, means authority over all matters of human society.

On the local level, most mosque communities contract with a learned Muslim to be the imam, the spiritual leader of worship and teaching in the mosque. Any Muslim has the right to lead prayers and to teach others. But it is helpful if the mosque has a recognized scholar as imam, to teach, preach at the Friday prayers, and give spiritual guidance to the people in a variety of matters.

The Way of Shari'ah

"How should I live?" Christianity turned away from the Jewish idea that God's law directly governs and guides all conduct; rather, faith in Christ means that love is the motivating power, following the law in freedom. In many ways Islam rejects the Christian view and returns closely to the Jewish view of Torah. The Shari'ah is divinely given, complete and perfect in all its details.

The highest human good is to follow the path outlined in the law, omitting no details no matter how small. Humans were created to fulfill the divine design, and that design finds its expression in the Shari'ah.

Basic Principles of the Shari'ah

The Quran, of course, comes from God, revealed through the Prophet Muhammad. But where does the Shari'ah, the massive religious legislation that governs all aspects of Muslim life, come from? This also comes from God, Muslims say, because it is drawn from the Holy Book. Since law is so important to Muslims, the great Islamic thinkers spent their creative energies elucidating the legal structure of Islam, while Christian thinkers were spending their time on theological issues.

There are actually two basic sources for the Shari'ah: the Quran and the Hadith (the collection of the sayings and doings of the Prophet Muhammad). Many duties of human life find direct, explicit expression in the Quran. But, whereas the Quran is God's perfect revelation and the "mother of all books," it is not large enough to state explicitly everything that humans should do in life in all situations. That which is implicit in the Quran, or that which is unclear in our limited

Afternoon prayers at the Attur Mosque on the Mount of Olives in Jerusalem.

understanding, is made explicit in the Hadith. Muhammad's close companions reported what he said and did in all circumstances, and these *hadiths* (reports) convey the example (sunnah) of Muhammad as the second source of law. To distinguish the reliable reports from those that are not so reliable, Muslim scholars elaborated a scientific, scholarly method of scrutinizing the "chain" (*isnad*) of people who passed on the report. If the chain can be linked securely back to a close companion of the Prophet, it is reliable and can be used as a basis for Shari'ah.

But even the Hadith does not specify what is to be done in all situations. As new situations arose, the law had to be searched and interpreted to meet the new needs. So Muslim scholars cultivated the method of "analogy" (*qiyas*), likening the new situation to one mentioned in the Quran or the Hadith and thus drawing legal conclusions. Analogy is a very creative undertaking, so finally it has to be checked, verified, and codified by the consensus (*ijma'*) of the recognized legal scholars—for Muhammad had said that his people will never agree on an error. In this way, from the Quran and the Hadith, by means of analogy and consensus, the whole body of Islamic law was formed and put in place as the divine pattern for human life.

We should not let the process of developing the Shari'ah obscure the fundamental truth that the Shari'ah represents God's total design for life. The Shari'ah has been revealed by the same God who made the whole world for the sake of humans. The guidance supplied in the law is therefore a regulation of life in the best interest of humans, showing us the best way to live to fulfill the highest potential. God has not given anything that is useless or unnecessary; and humans should use all their faculties, powers, and resources in such a way that they can reap the highest benefits from them. Abul A'la Mawdudi explains,

> The fundamental principle of the Law is that man has the right, and in some cases the bounden duty, to fulfil all his genuine needs and desires and make every conceivable effort to promote his interests and achieve success and happiness— but (and it is an important "but") he should do all this in such a way that not only are the interests of other people not jeopardised and no harm is caused to their strivings towards the fulfillment of their

rights and duties, but there should be all possible social cohesion, mutual assistance and cooperation among human beings in the achievement of their objectives.[6]

The Shari'ah, then, is the most humanizing force in the world. It is not in conflict with other true humanizing forces of religion and science, but it is the final, all-encompassing, perfect guide.

Because the Shari'ah was worked out by scholars in different parts of the Muslim world, a number of different schools of law developed with slight differences. The Hanafi school, dominant today in central and western Asia, northern Egypt, and India, is the most liberal and flexible. The Maliki school, prominent today in north Africa and southern Egypt, and the Shafi'i school, in Malaysia and east Africa, are generally considered middle of the road. The Hanbali school, dominant in Saudi Arabia, is the most conservative and strict one. But in practice there is no fundamental difference between these schools, and all are regarded by one another as fully orthodox. The Shi'ites have three schools of law, differing from the Sunnite schools mainly in the authority of the imam, the recognition of temporary marriage (a limited time of marriage specified in the marriage contract), a stricter divorce law, and more provision for female relatives in the inheritance law.

Muslim Ethics in Practice

Islamic law is learned, in its basics, by all Muslims so that they can live their lives properly. But how can there be definite divine rules about every aspect of human life? The Islamic answer is to classify all acts into five basic categories or principles that allow for a range of shading and flexibility. Some duties and acts are *required* (*fard*) of all Muslims; performing them brings reward and omitting them brings punishment. Again, some acts are strictly *forbidden* (*haram*), and doing them brings punishment. Some acts are *recommended* but not required, and performance of them is rewarded. Some acts are *disapproved* but not forbidden or punished. And, finally, some acts are *indifferent*, neither rewarded nor punished. The Pillar of Prayer, for example, is required; drinking alcohol is forbidden. Recommended acts would be, for example, saying extra prayers or visiting Medina after the pilgrimage. The categories of indifferent acts and disapproved acts allow for some disagreement between legal scholars and between the schools of law. An action may be held disapproved by one but indifferent by another; or something considered to be forbidden by one scholar might be thought of as merely disapproved by another.

There are other elements of flexibility in Islamic jurisprudence. The law only applies to those who are *rashid*, that is, free Muslims of legal age and sane. Non-Muslims have complete legal freedom provided they do not interfere with the religious interests of Muslims. Further, a fundamental principle of religious law is intent. Normally forbidden actions are permissible under duress. For example, drinking wine or having illegal intercourse under threat of death is permissible; refusal under these circumstances would be forbidden. Punishments for forbidden actions can only be carried out if very stringent requirements of proof of wrongdoing are met—for example, four eye witnesses are required in a charge of unlawful sexual intercourse.

A good part of Islamic law is focused on the family, for this is the broad arena in which the individual lives most of her life. In fact, for women in traditional Muslim societies social contacts outside the extended family are few. Marriage is a duty carried out on the basis of a legal contract consented to by both parties. Sexual expression is considered good and healthy, but it is strictly reserved for marriage, All other forms of sex are forbidden and punished: premarital and extramarital sex, homosexuality, prostitution, bestiality, and so forth. Even lustful consideration of another person is tantamount to fornication. For that reason Islamic law forbids intermingling of sexes (unless they are nonmarriageable relatives) in any social gathering or even in schools. Further, the law requires modesty in dress; the most conservative law school holds that no more than a woman's face and hands should be visible when she is outside the home. Men are also to clothe themselves modestly.

What is the position of women in Islamic law? Men and women are equal before God, according to the Quran (16:97). The woman like the man has standing as a legal individual, retaining her property to use as she sees fit. But women have a different role from men. Whereas the man's role is to work and support the family, the woman's place is in the home, providing care and stability for family life. If a woman must work outside the home, it should be in certain types of occupations appropriate for women, such as teaching or nursing. A Muslim man is permitted to marry four wives, whereas a Muslim woman may have only one husband. Muslims point out that one basic reason for polygamy is to ensure that all women can be married and thus fulfill themselves in family life. Further, in actuality very few Muslim men have more than one wife, for Islamic law dictates that a man must treat his wives equally both in sexual relationship and in financial support. There are other aspects of law in which women seem of lesser value than men. For example, certain legal proceedings require two male witnesses or one male and two female witnesses. Further, a Muslim man is permitted to marry a non-Muslim monotheistic woman, but this permission is not extended to a Muslim woman. Muslims explain these seeming inequalities on the basis of the particular role of women in society and in the family.

When the question of the status of women in Islam is brought up, Muslims point out that, whereas in Christendom and in most parts of the world until very recently women were considered little more than property with no legal rights, Islamic law instituted by Muhammad lifted the status of women and gave them equal rights with men. This does not mean, however, that they should have the same function as men in society, for in God's divine pattern women fulfill their high potential in maintaining the well-being of the family.

Divorce is permitted in Islam, although Muhammad said that God considers divorce to be the most detestable of permitted things. Traditionally the man could divorce his wife by the formula of repudiation, uttering "I divorce you" three times, usually with a prescribed waiting period between the utterances. Once the third repudiation is uttered, it is irrevocable and the man has no more claim on the woman. If they for some reason want to be married again, the woman must first be married to someone else and then divorced. The woman also has some rights to initiate divorce, especially if certain conditions written into the marriage contract have not been carried out. She may also obtain a divorce on grounds such as the husband's physical incapacity, desertion, failure to provide support, cruelty, and the like.

With respect to personal life, the Shari'ah forbids the use of things that are injurious to one's physical, mental, or moral life. Besides alcohol and drugs, there are forbidden foods, falling into four basic categories: carrion, blood, pork, and anything sacrificed to another god. By carrion is meant beasts of prey and anything that died without being slaughtered properly, such as by old age, illness, or being killed improperly (by another animal or by a hunter, for example). People are required to keep the body clean, and one should not wear excessively costly clothes or jewelry.

The rights of other people in society are especially guarded by the Shari'ah. Lying, cheating, theft, bribery, forgery, and other means of illegal gain at the expense of others are forbidden. And gambling and games of chance are forbidden because in them someone wins at the expense of others. Likewise forbidden are various forms of exploitation, such as monopoly, hoarding, blackmarketing, withholding land from cultivation, and the like. Usury, that is, charging interest on loans, is also considered a form of gain at the expense of others and thus is forbidden. Whereas this makes capitalistic endeavors difficult, it promotes solidarity and cooperation with respect to the use of financial resources. Another device by which Islam prevents the excessive accumulation of wealth by one party is inheritance law, which requires that the wealth be distributed to all eligible relatives rather than being kept in one estate. Muslims consider wealth as God's blessing, but it is not to be hoarded or squandered but rather used to the betterment of oneself and others.

Non-Muslims sometimes think of Islam as a religion of the sword, a religion of violence. It is true that certain Muslim political radicals have committed acts of terrorism—but no more so than certain political radicals of other religions in other places. The Shari'ah also has legislation on the justification and conduct of war. In general it may be said that the only permissible reason for warfare is striving in the cause of God—which is what the term *jihad* (often translated holy war) means. This means that wars for land, resources, pow-er, wealth, and all the rest are prohibited. Striving in the cause of God means enforcing God's law about equality and justice for all. Thus Islam has a kind of "just war" idea, in that Muslims are obligated to take up arms in self-defense or defense of others who are being oppressed and treated unjustly. Such warfare, however, is strictly regulated: negotiations must always be made first with the other side, booty may not be taken, and innocent people may not be injured.

Transformation of Human Society

Islam has a vision for society, and that vision is the life of Shari'ah. Since this law is God's final and perfect design, it is the responsibility of Muslims to implement it for all societies of the world. And since the Islamic principles of faith are the same universal principles that have been revealed by all God's prophets, it is the duty of Muslims to convince all other peoples to submit to this truth of Islam. In other words, Muslims have the duty to work for the Islamicization of the whole world, both in the laws of society and in the faith of all people.

Since the Shari'ah is the way of life designed by God to bring human society into full harmony with all of creation, fulfilling all human potential, Muslims have always felt the responsibility of spreading this way of life to all. But the Islamic vision of the good life under the law has one important difference from the Jewish or Christian vision. To live the Shari'ah in *all* its aspects requires that one live under a Muslim government. In fact, ideally there should be one Muslim ruler (the caliph) who rules over the whole Dar al-Islam. Since the Shari'ah contains provisions that can only be carried out by a government, it is not possible to follow the complete life of Islam while living under a non-Muslim ruler.

Thus the Islamicization of society means establishing an Islamic government. The notion of *jihad*, "striving" in the path of God, plays a part at this point. It refers to conquering all that opposes God's will, starting with one's own sins and unbelief. Since the realms of society not ruled by Muslim governments do not conform to God's law, in theory there is a perpetual state of jihad between the Dar al-Islam and the infidel society, the Dar al-Harb. Living by Islamic law has benefits even for non-Muslims, since it keeps them from forbidden acts. The Islamic ideal would be for the whole world to come under Islamic rule and Islamic law.

The Spiritual Mission of Islam

Spreading Islamic law does not mean religious coercion, which is expressly forbidden in the Quran (2:256). The Shari'ah permits some religions to continue even in the Dar al-Islam. Those who are monotheists and possess a sacred scripture are known as People of the Book—this includes Jews, Christians, and Zoroastrians; although their faith is faulty, they are nonetheless acceptable to God. They can live peacefully within Muslim domains by paying a special tax. But, at least according to traditional law, polytheists must either convert to monotheism or flee; otherwise they face imprisonment or execution.

The missionary impulse in Islam comes from the knowledge that this is the final religion with the final, perfect revelation of God. Whereas God gave revelation of the same faith through prophets in all other lands, the Arabic Quran is the last such revelation and is intended for all peoples universally. Submitting to the divine trust, Muslims feel compelled to share this revelation with all others.

But how should Muslims share this revelation with others? God's great gifts to humans are intelligence, free will, and speech. Speech is the means of sharing the Quran with others. God's gift of free will means no coercion or forcing people to accept Islam. Rather, God's truth should be spread in a rational way, appealing to human intelligence, allowing others to become convinced by their reason and submit to this final truth. If people really consider Islam in a rational, free way, Muslims believe, they will see that it is the highest truth of God and human existence. Mawdudi says,

> This is Islam, the natural religion of man, the religion which is not associated with any person, people, period or place. It is the way of nature, the religion of *man*. In every age, in every country and among every people, all God-knowing and truth-loving men have believed and lived this very religion. They were all Muslims, irrespective of whether they called that way Islam.[7]

DISCUSSION QUESTIONS

1. In what ways is the Prayer the heart of Muslim life? Describe the performance of the Pillar of Prayer.
2. Describe the Pilgrimage to Mecca and its meaning for Muslims.
3. What is the ummah? What kind of leadership is there in the ummah?
4. On what is the Shari'ah based? How do analogy (*qiyas*) and consensus (*ijma'*) fit in?
5. How is it possible for the Shari'ah to govern all aspects of life? Describe how it functions.
6. What are the basic aspects of Muslim law about the family and the relationship of men and women?

PART III

RELIGIONS ARISING FROM INDIA:

Hinduism, Buddhism, Jainism, and Sikhism

INTRODUCTION

Like the Middle East, India has been a fertile spawning ground for world religions. The story of these religions reaches back to the Indus Valley civilization in ancient times and the Aryans who came in from outside to establish Aryan religion and culture in

245

India. From these ancient streams have arisen Hinduism, Buddhism, Jainism, and—much later, after Muslim influence became strong in India—Sikhism. What is the common vision that this family of religions shares?

There is, of course, a close historical and geographical relationship among these religions. Hinduism, Buddhism, and Jainism all took classical shape at approximately the same time in north India. Hinduism does trace its sacred story to the earlier Aryans with their Vedic scriptures, and Jainism reaches back to Parshva (ninth century B.C.E.). But certainly one of the most formative periods for each religion was around the sixth century B.C.E. In Hinduism the Upanishads were being composed as the foundation of the Hindu perspective. Siddhartha Gautama was following the way to enlightenment and founding the first Buddhist community. And Mahavira also was walking the path to enlightenment as the leader of the Jains. There was some interaction among members of these three traditions, and they grappled with many of the same issues as they created three distinct paths. It was not until a thousand years later

South and East Asia.

that Sikhism was founded, but still it grew up in India and drew on the religious vision and practice of Hinduism, shaping that together with Muslim ideas into a distinctive way of life.

For all of them, India has been "Mother India," not only historically but also culturally and spiritually. Most of these religions have been content to stay within the bosom of Mother India, with little attempt to spread and translate their spiritual wisdom into other languages and cultures. Only Buddhism has become a missionary religion, losing its status in India but spreading the truth of the Buddha to South Asia, Southeast Asia, and East Asia. Even though Buddhism does not have a lot of adherents in India today, Buddhists still look to India as the sacred source, since their history happened there and almost all their scriptures were composed there.

In their religious thinking, the people of these religions tend to start from experience in the world. And their common perception of human existence is that it goes in cycles, lifetime after lifetime, world age after world age. The human individual stands now; but many existences before have brought about the present state of affairs, and many existences to come are being caused by this existence. Furthermore, the whole universe goes in cycles, without beginning or end, in recurrent evolutions and devolutions like the waves on the sea.

One of the big questions that one needs to ask, then, has to do with what is real and ultimately significant. It cannot be the passing phenomena, whether of the world or of myself. The vision of India says that the real is unified and absolute, forever beyond the changes and cycles of existence. The sacred is generally not seen in personal, historical terms—although, of course, the sacred can be revealed or reflected in such forms. The ultimate sacred reality is impersonal, transcending historical processes, not an individual creator God involved in the maintenance of the world.

The real essence of humans is not our life in this passing world, but rather what connects us with the sacred. Our true nature is somehow identical with the ultimate sacred, and the goal of religious practice is to bring this truth to realization. And so each religion teaches its adherents to discipline themselves to withdraw attachments to the passing world, blocking up the causes that will bring about future existences. There are religious practices, especially meditation, to help in seeing the sacred within, leading to spiritual fulfillment and liberation from the cycle.

But perhaps we have said too much already about the common vision, for Hindus, Buddhists, Jains, and Sikhs bring much more to their visions, interpreting these basic ideas in distinctive ways, developing their own worlds of symbols that guide and structure life. Many of these symbols look similar, of course, as we would expect among closely related religions. But in each religion the symbols reflect the truth of the religious vision in a characteristic way because of the total configuration of the world of symbols.

Buddhism spread widely throughout Sri Lanka, Southeast Asia, and East Asia, and in each of these areas it has developed distinctive forms. But all forms of Buddhism retain a basic continuity with the Buddhist community that first arose in India. In Part III, Buddhism in China and Japan will be discussed only briefly, since those forms of Buddhism will be further explored in Part IV, Religions of China and Japan.

CHAPTER 13

HINDUISM: SACRED STORY AND HISTORICAL CONTEXT

"**W**ho am I?" "I'm Indian, I'm Hindu."

Identity as a Hindu is a very broad affair, with few restrictions or exclusions. Indeed, it almost seems that being a Hindu is the same as being a person of India. As a matter of fact, *Hindu* is a Persian word meaning "Indian." To be Hindu implies accepting and respecting the ancient traditions of India, especially the ancient scriptures (the Vedas), and the social class structure with its special respect for brahmins (the priestly class). Thus, except for several dissenting Hindu groups, the only Indians who are really excluded from this Hindu identity are those who do not accept the authority of the Vedas and the special place of the brahmins—that is,

Buddhists, Jains, and Sikhs, together, of course, with Indian Muslims, Christians, and Parsis (the small community of Zoroastrians in India). The Vedas and the social class system—and the sacred realities of which they are a part—provide the center of the Hindu story.

FOUNDINGS: STREAMS INTO THE RIVER OF HINDUISM

Unlike the other religions arising from India and unlike the Abraham religions, Hinduism has no specific founders involved in historical events that gave rise to the religion. The Hindu sacred history places little emphasis on what we normally think of as historical events or persons, and it shows only slight interest in historical sequences. Most things happen in a transcendental kind of timeframe. For example, the events told in the Ramayana Epic take place in the *treta* age, several million years ago, whereas the Mahabharata Epic tells of events in the *dvapara* age, still hundreds of thousands of years ago. The sacred reality is reflected in all these ages and cycles, but it also transcends them. So the stories about the gods and goddesses, the heroes and heroines are not concerned about how they fit in the human history of our age. There is no particular interest in the "historical" Krishna, for example, in contrast to Christian interest in the historicity of Christ. The great kings, heroes, gods, and goddesses the stories tell about are important because they are models of eternal, mythological truth.

So the sacred history is not so much about the founding of Hinduism, but it is about the *foundation* of Hinduism—that is, the sacred realities that form the pattern for Hindu life and meaning. As we look at the Hindu story, we need to provide some historical orientation, which includes events like the migration of the Aryans into India around 1500 B.C.E., the composing of the Upanishads, the development of city-states and the Hindu social order, and the like. But we must take care not to confuse the historical orientation with what Hindu tradition considers to be the real sacred history: the ancient sages hearing and transmitting the eternal Vedas and the legendary and mythological events about gods and heroes described in the Epics.

We need the historical orientation, but we also need to understand that the real meaning of the sacred history, for Hindus, is in those events that transcend our historical age. After a look at the main elements of the Hindu story, we also note some of the major historical transformations that shaped Hindu identity in the medieval and modern periods.

The Formative Period of Hinduism

The Hindu sacred story highlights the Aryans and their sacred texts as the foundation of Hinduism. We know that the Aryans actually were Indo-European peoples who came into India and eventually became the Hindus. But we also know that there was a great civilization in India before the Aryans arrived, the Indus Valley civilization, which had reached its zenith around 2500 B.C.E. Around 1500 B.C.E. the Aryans, migrating into India from the northwest, superceded this civilization—but in the process some of the indigenous peoples and their religious ideas eventually were absorbed into Hinduism as it developed over a number of centuries. Here—as in the case of the ancient Israelites settling in Canaan—took place a fascinating encounter of two very different cultures: the Indus Valley people were basically agriculturalists, and the Aryans were pastoralists. We do not know much about the details of the encounter, unfortunately, but the resulting creation was the richly textured religion of Hinduism. It seems that other indigenous peoples in India outside the Indus Valley also influenced the development of Hindu religious ideas and practices.

The Indus Valley Civilization

Archaeologists working in the past sixty years have uncovered an amazingly advanced civilization stretching for a thousand miles along the valley of the Indus River, comparable in many ways with the two other great river valley civilizations that existed at this same time, ancient Egypt along the Nile and ancient Sumer along the Tigris and Euphrates rivers. Like them, the Indus Valley civilization lived by agriculture and domestic animals, had developed a system of writing (unfortunately, not enough remains to be deciphered), and built cities. Two of the cities, Mohenjo-Daro and Harappa, are quite large and appear to have been centers of political rule. There is a most striking uniformity of culture throughout the whole civilization, suggesting rigid control by powerful rulers. For example, the cities were all carefully laid out on the same plan, with major streets crossing each other at right angles. Each house was supplied with water and had a bathroom from which water drained out into covered sewers.

Archaeological investigations have turned up a number of things suggestive of the religious vision of these people. One striking point is that they had a great reverence for water and its purifying power. In addition to the bathrooms in individual houses, apparently for ritual purposes, a large bathing tank has been found in the citadel of Mohenjo-Daro, flanked by dressing rooms and arcades. It seems they considered water to have important purifying powers, an idea that we find also in later Hinduism.

As befits an agricultural civilization, there appears to have been emphasis on the fertility of mother earth. Many female figurines have been discovered, clearly associated with powers of fertility and the growth of

The Hindu goddess Durga. Goddesses were widely worshiped already in the Indus Valley civilization.

plants. For example, a drawing on a clay seal depicts a fertility goddess upside down, with a plant growing from her vulva—as clear a symbol of mother earth as can be imagined! Other seals show sacred trees as the focus of sacred power. On one seal there is a horned goddess amid the branches of a pipul tree (sacred in later India), worshiped by a figure on bended knee, assisted by seven priestesses lined up in a row. It may be assumed that later Hinduism's worship of the great goddesses and perhaps even its emphasis on the cyclical pattern of death and life was influenced by the fertility religion of these ancient people.

Another religious emphasis has to do with male creative powers. Many seals depict powerful male animals —bulls, tigers, rhinoceroses, antelopes, elephants, and a unicorn-type animal. A two-tiered incense stand is always set before the unicorn, showing that these male animals represented sacred power to be worshiped. A number of phalluses, models of the male sexual organ, have been found in the excavations, suggesting some ritual worship of male fertility power. A most fascinating symbol is depicted on several seals: a male person seated in a kind of yoga posture with legs drawn up and heels together, similar to the posture used in yoga meditation in later Hinduism. In one seal the god (we may presume he represents sacred power) is surrounded by an elephant, a tiger, a rhinoceros, and a buffalo, and beneath his stool are two deer. He wears a headdress of two horns, with a plant growing between them. The figure appears to be ithyphallic (with an erect penis). The combination of symbols is striking: fertility of plants and animals, yogic meditation, and male sexual energy. It has been suggested that this god is a prototype of the great god Shiva in later Hinduism, who is known as the great yogi and often symbolized by the *lingam* (phallic symbol).

No historical documentation exists to show the impact these religious ideas had on the development of Hinduism, and certainly Hindus do not usually count the Indus Valley people as part of their story. But we—looking now from the outside—may surmise that the Indus Valley civilization, along with other pre-Aryan peoples in India, contributed to some of the characteristic Hindu ideas and practices, especially those associated with water, the great goddesses, the cyclic pattern of existence, yogic meditation, and the god Shiva.

Aryan Religion: the Vedic Period

The group of people who migrated into the Indus Valley from the northwest around 1500 B.C.E. called themselves Aryans (noble ones). They were Indo-Europeans, related to all those peoples who migrated in various directions from the original Indo-European homeland, probably in the steppe land that stretches from Eastern Europe to Central Asia. Some of these original Indo-European peoples migrated westward into Europe and became the Greeks, the Romans, the Germanic peoples, the Slavs, the Balts, and so forth. Others of these peoples migrated eastward and became the Persians (Iranians) and the Aryans. The language spoken by the Aryans, Sanskrit, was closely related to the other Indo-European languages, as was their culture and religion. Wherever the Indo-Europeans went, of course, they interacted with indigenous peoples and created distinct cultures and religions.

The Aryans were pastoralists (cattle herders), grouped in a number of tribes each headed by a chieftain. Their society was divided into three classes: the warriors, the priests, and the herders or producers. They were fierce warriors, having domesticated the horse and invented the chariot, and they were skilled in metallurgy and weaponry. After settling in India and replacing the declining Indus Valley civilization, the Aryans continued to develop their own traditions for a number of centuries, gradually allowing local, non-Aryan beliefs and practices to enhance the fundamentally Aryan religion.

Although the Aryans did not have a writing system, from early times they composed hymns called *Veda* (knowledge). Hindus understand the Vedas to be timeless, eternal truths "heard" by the *rishis*, the seer-poets of old; they are the original foundation of Hinduism. Special place is accorded to the four Samhitas (collections), also simply called Vedas. The Rig Veda is the oldest and most important group of hymns. The Sama Veda contains verses arranged to be sung by the musical specialist during the sacrifice, and the Yajur Veda supplied short formulas spoken by the priest who performed the physical operations in the sacrificial ritual. The fourth collection, the Atharva Veda, contains incantations for priests to use for various needs like childbirth, illness, securing the affection of a lover, and much more. These Vedic hymns are to be recited, chanted, and performed as sacred liturgy.

The religion that is expressed in these Vedic hymns and formulas centers around worship of gods by means of sacrifice, petition, and praise. The gods are many, residing in the three realms (sky, atmosphere, and earth) and showing their powers in the various processes of nature. Among the most important Vedic gods are Varuna, Indra, Agni, and Soma.

Varuna is god of the vault of the sky, sometimes described as creating the world, whose function it is to guard the cosmic order. In that capacity Varuna is the god who sees humans in their wrongdoings and catches them in his noose, punishing them with disease. Thus he must be petitioned to remove those offenses.

> For the emperor [Varuna] I will sing a splendid, deep prayer, one that will be dear to the famous Varuna who struck apart the earth and spread it beneath the sun as the priest who performs the slaughter spreads out the victim's skin. He stretched out the middle realm of space in the trees; he laid victory in swift horses and milk in the dawn cows, intelligence in hearts and fire in the waters. Varuna placed the sun in the sky and Soma on the mountain.... If we have cheated like gamblers in a game, whether we know it or really do not know it, O god, cast all these offences away like loosened bonds. Let us be dear to you, Varuna.   (RG VEDA 5.85.1–2, 8)[1]

Indra is a god of the atmosphere, the storm god who shows himself in the lightning and thunder. Like Thor among the Scandinavians, Indra is a boisterous warrior god, drinking soma (a hallucinating, invigorating drink) and leading people in battle against their enemies. Many hymns tell of Indra's cosmic battle with the demon Vritra, who has shut up the waters and the sun; after a fierce battle Indra slays him and releases the life-giving forces.

> Let me now sing the heroic deeds of Indra, the first that the thunderbolt-wielder performed. He killed the dragon and pierced an opening for the waters; he split open the bellies of mountains. He killed the dragon who lay upon the mountain; Tvastr fashioned the roaring thunderbolt

for him. Like lowing cows, the flowing waters rushed straight down to the sea. Wildly excited like a bull, he took the Soma for himself and drank the extract from the three bowls in the three-day Soma ceremony. Indra the Generous seized his thunderbolt to hurl it as a weapon; he killed the firstborn of dragons.   (RG VEDA 1.32.1–3)[2]

Of the many gods of the third realm, earth, Agni (Fire) assumes special importance as the god of the sacrificial fire. The power of Agni is centered especially in the fire sacrifice, Agni being the sacred power that accepts the offerings and transports them to the realm of the gods. For that reason, Agni is addressed in nearly one-third of the Rig Vedic hymns.

> With praises we worship you, O Fire, king of sacrifices, long-tailed like a horse. May you, O son of strength, be propitious and bountiful to us in your great way. May you, who moves everywhere, O Fire, protect us from mortals far and near who seek to harm us. May you, O Fire, convey our offering of praise to the gods. . . . O Fire, invoked through praises, enter the sacrifice, favor it and complete it.   (FROM RG VEDA 1.27)[3]

Throughout all periods of Hinduism, special importance has been attached to the ritual of fire sacrifice — and thus to the god Agni. Another god of the earth realm who is prominent in the Vedic hymns is Soma, a god whose power is known in *soma*, an intoxicating drink offered to the gods in sacrifice and drunk by the worshipers. "We have drunk the Soma; we have become immortal; we have gone to the light; we have found the gods," a hymn celebrates (Rg Veda 8.48.3).[4] Soma symbolizes both ecstasy and the special power of consciousness experienced through this divine power.

In the early Vedic conception, then, power for running the world and human existence derives from the gods. How humans live and relate to the gods is important; properly serving the gods results in wealth, long life, many sons, and a happy life after death. The Aryans thought of human life as centered in the *atman* (breath, soul), which lived on after the death of the body. At death the atman, by means of the funeral fire sacrifice, with help from the person's meritorious deeds, is transported to the heavenly realm of the fathers to enjoy the continued blessings of life.

In the early Aryan system, the most important way of serving the gods was by sacrificing to them by means of the fire sacrifice ritual. Daily the head of the household performed domestic sacrifices to Agni and to the sun god, and periodically much more elaborate sacrifices were performed with the aid of the priestly class. The basic idea behind the sacrificial cult is the vision of the Vedic seers that humans need to participate in sacred power by sustaining and reinvigorating Agni and the other gods so that the gods will continue their work of creating and bringing blessing to the world and to human existence. Although this Vedic perspective on the centrality of sacrifice underwent development in the next periods, the fact that humans are partners with the gods in continuing the creative processes of the world by sacrifice is a basic presupposition of Hindu thought and ritual. And the Vedic hymns and daily sacrifices are yet today considered essential to the Hindu community.

Searching for the One Reality Behind All This

In the story of how Hinduism developed, there is an important speculative period leading from the early Vedic religion toward the classical flowering of Hinduism. We can see beginnings of this speculative period already by about 1000 B.C.E. with some late hymns that were added to the Rig Veda (in Rg Veda Book 10), followed by the Brahmanas, sacrificial manuals and interpretations (ca. 800 B.C.E.), and then finally the Upanishads (starting ca. 600 B.C.E.). In these texts we find important new ideas about sacred reality and human existence. Whereas there is no way of demonstrating the origin of these new ideas, it might be supposed that some of them came about in response to non-Aryan religious ideas and practices.

That something new is happening is evident by a new style used by the seers: they turn to questioning and speculation. "Which god should we worship with sacrifices?" is the refrain of one hymn that attempts to probe the origins of everything and find some one reality behind all the gods (Rg Veda 10.121). No longer satisfied with the traditions about the power of the various gods, the sage speculates that some power prior to the gods is the origin of everything. In a similar way,

India.

another hymn even questions the power and the knowledge of the traditional gods: "Who really knows? Who will here proclaim it? Whence was it produced? Whence is this creation? The gods came afterwards, with the creation of this universe. Who then knows whence it has arisen?" (Rg Veda 10.129.6).[5] What the sages are searching for is the sacred center of all, the unified One from which all derives. In their tentative speculations they give different names to this One and describe it in different ways. The poets say that this One is the one life of all the gods, the reality who encompasses all the worlds (Rg Veda 10.121.7, 10). One graphic description envisions the One as a gigantic person (*purusha*) who pervades the whole universe, from whom everything, including all space and all time, derives. Even the gods form part of the one Purusha (Rg Veda 10.90).

This last-mentioned hymn to Purusha shows that, along with the vision of the One, a number of related notions were coming to the fore. It is when Purusha is *sacrificed* that all of the universe comes into existence. The early Vedic idea of the sacrifice reinvigorating the gods is now extended to the whole universe. This primordial sacrifice of the One creates everything (including the gods); this means, by derivation, that each time a priest performs the ritual sacrifice he is repeating this primordial sacrifice and thus creating and sustaining the world.

It is significant that this hymn to Purusha includes the Hindu social order as part of the universe created in the primordial sacrifice. The mouth of Purusha became the brahmins (priestly class), his two arms were made into the kshatriyas (warriors), his two thighs became the vaishyas (merchants, workers), and from his two feet the shudras (servants) were born. This first mention of the basic Hindu social class system in the Hindu sacred texts is noteworthy in that, first of all, it considers these four classes to be part of the cosmic order initiated in the primordial creation. But it also shows that by now the warrior class has lost its superior standing and has been replaced as the top class by the brahmin class. The priests, after all, are the ones who know how to perform the sacrificial rituals that uphold the world and even the gods, and thus their authority is all-important.

Another tendency during this period is the increased emphasis on the importance of knowledge. Finally, the sages conclude, it is not so much the outward performance of the sacrifices that upholds the world and provides blessings, but it is the knowledge of the inner reality. One text from the Brahmanas explains the great public sacrifice known as the Building of the Fire Altar—made of materials collected over the course of a whole year. The text interprets the real meaning of the building in terms of the upholding of the whole universe:

> Indeed, the Fire Altar built here is this world. Its enclosing stones are the waters. Its Yajusmati bricks are the men. . . . The plants and trees are its cement. . . . Yet, verily, the Fire Altar is the air also. The horizon is its enclosing circle of bricks. . . . Yet, verily, the Fire Altar is the sky also, . . . the Sun also, . . . the stars also, . . . the year also. . . . Yet, verily, the Fire Altar is all beings and all gods.

But the interpretation of this ritual makes it clear that the important thing is not just the performance of the ritual; rather, the *inner knowledge* is the power that leads to the world of blessing: "They ascend through knowledge to the place where desires vanish. Neither sacrificial gifts go there, nor do the zealous performers of sacrifices without knowledge. He who is ignorant of this truth does not go to that world by sacrificial gifts and devout practices. It belongs to those with knowledge" (Satapada Brahmana 10.5.4).[6]

Searching for the One, raising the power of sacrifice to cosmic levels, developing the class system with the brahmins as supreme, and putting an emphasis on inner knowledge—with these developments some of the basic lines of Hinduism start to emerge. These ideas are worked out more fully in the Upanishads (composed ca. 600–200 B.C.E.) and still more ideas are added to form the foundation of thought for classical Hinduism.

Speculation and Knowledge: The Upanishads

There is no clear break between the Brahmanas and the Upanishads; some of the earlier Upanishads (called Aranyakas, Forest Treatises) were composed as part of the Brahmanas. Hindus consider the Upanishads to be revelation of the same truths as the Vedic hymns and the Brahmanas, and all of these texts are collectively called Veda. The earlier Vedic rituals and sacrifices were being continued by many people. The ritual manuals called Brahmanas had multiplied the sacrificial ceremonies and made them extremely complex and complicated—in keeping with the idea that the order of the whole world is upheld by the proper performing of the ritual sacrifices. But there were some teachers and disciples who continued searching and probing after the inner truth of all reality, the cause of human problems, and the possible solutions offered by knowledge and meditation. The Upanishads resulted from this search. The word *upanishad* refers to teaching passed from a teacher to a disciple, and the setting given in many of the Upanishads is just that: a teacher answering the disciple's questions, a father teaching his son, or a sage instructing an assembly.

Some of the Upanishads talk about ritual and sacrifice, but these acts are both cosmosized and internalized. The Brihad-aranyaka Upanishad, for example, begins with a description of the great horse sacrifice; but then it proceeds to show how this ritual is really an internal act of meditation by which the whole world is sacrificed. The worshiper is instructed to meditate on the dawn as the head of the sacrificial horse, the sun as his eye, the wind as his breath, the year as his body, the sky as his back, the atmosphere as his belly, the earth as the under part of his belly, and so forth. "He [who knows this] wards off repeated death, death obtains him not, death becomes his body, he becomes one of these deities" (Brihad-aranyaka Upanishad, 2.7).[7]

The motivation for this speculation seems to be a new conception that had been developing in some circles, perhaps influenced by the Buddhist and Jain movements. Now, instead of the early Vedic optimistic view of life in this world and the next, there is increasing concern about "repeated death"—that is, death ending not only this life but also the future life. Some way to escape this re-death needs to be found, and this is beyond the power of rituals and sacrifices to the gods. In the Upanishads this idea of re-death was broadened to a cyclical view of human existence: being born in this world is the result of dying in another life,

and on and on in a never ending wheel of existence. The way to understand the human problem, according to the Upanishads, is to see that it is *samsara*, an endless round of birth and death.

What causes samsara? Tied together with the notion of samsara is the discovery of *karma*, the law that every action has its effect. Karma literally means "action," and the sages knew from experience that what one does causes consequences to happen. The idea of karma already had religious implications, in the notion that the action of the sacrifice causes results for the gods and for humans. The teachers of the Upanishads related karma to samsara. It is because of the actions that I have done in my previous life that I am born again into this existence. Moreover, the type of karma I have done determines what kind of rebirth I have, whether relatively happy or miserable.

The sages are convinced that there must be a better way, a way to be liberated from the wheel of birth and death.

If all this world, including the gods, is caught up in samsara, where can we turn for that better way? The Upanishads continue the earlier speculation about the One, that which is truly real and the source of all, and the importance of knowledge more than ritual and sacrifice. Although many terms had been used, the Upanishads finally settle on *Brahman* as the designation of the One, the Real. Earlier, the term *brahman* had meant the sacred words used in the sacrificial rituals. Now Brahman is extended to identify that one power, the inner source of all, that which is absolute and eternal and prior to all that is known as samsara.

Further, the sages insist that my true self, the atman, is not what I usually think of as "myself" but is in fact identical with Brahman. If my atman is really the Brahman, it transcends limitation, decay, and death. It is because of my ignorance in thinking of myself as bound up with my body and senses, and because of my desire to perform actions on behalf of this illusory self, that I generate karma and bind myself to the cycle of birth and death. The way out of samsara, then, is a path of knowledge: knowing the real atman, and thus knowing the Brahman, means *moksha*, liberation from the cycle caused by ignorance, desire, and karma.

The means for attaining this liberating knowledge,

according to the teachers, is meditation on the atman and the Brahman. No longer the outer rituals and actions, but the inner knowledge leads to the source that brings the power of transformation and transcends the trap of samsara. The Upanishads, and the sages who continued to practice this way of knowledge, devised disciplines and techniques of meditation designed to bring about this transformation and thus final liberation (moksha) from samsara.

Whereas the vision of the Upanishads is complex and the goal practical only for those who are spiritually advanced, the basic ideas of the Upanishads have become the foundation for all aspects of Hinduism. The reality of Brahman and atman, the problem of karma and samsara, the goal of moksha—all Hindus recognize these as fundamental to the Hindu religion.

The texts of the Upanishads complete the sacred writings collectively called the Vedas. All of these texts—the Upanishads, together with the early Vedic hymns (Samhitas) and the Brahmanas, are known collectively as the Shruti (that which is "heard" by the sages), the eternal revelation of the truth. These writings may not be easily understood, but they are the eternal truth, and being a Hindu means respecting them as such and honoring those who study and recite them.

The Many Faces of Classical Hinduism

The Indo-Aryans gradually settled into towns and cities, and a city-state culture developed in north India. Starting in the sixth century B.C.E. the Persian Empire established a province in western India, and in the fourth century Alexander the Great invaded western India. Stimulated by these incursions, the Maurya family established a dynasty in north India that eventually grew to include most of central and south India as well. The Mauryan rulers were not especially devoted to the Vedic traditions, often giving their support to non-Vedic groups like Jainism and Buddhism, both of which developed into major movements during the fifth and fourth centuries. King Ashoka (ca. 269–232 B.C.E.), in fact, became a devout Buddhist and promoted Buddhism throughout his empire and beyond. After Ashoka, the Mauryan Empire broke up into disunity once again, but in the meantime the traditional system of Vedic sacrifices and priestly control lost ground among the people.

In response to the new situation, a variety of religious tendencies were being developed in the Brahmanical tradition, in this creative period from about 400 B.C.E. to 400 C.E., which we might designate the classical, epic era of Hinduism. Some of these tendencies go back to earlier ideas and practices; others probably represent non-Aryan forms surfacing in the Hindu synthesis. These included practical forms of meditation and seeking release from samsara, concern for the ongoing life of society, and a flourishing of interest in worship of the gods old and new.

During this time a great many new sacred writings were composed, expressing the new ideas and practices. To distinguish these new writings from the Shruti scriptures, they are usually referred to as the Smriti (remembered) writings, the Tradition. Whereas these scriptures thus have a lower status than the earlier ones and not all Hindus respect them all equally, to many Hindus these writings provide the most immediate guidance in the sacred story of Hinduism.

Development of Practices of Withdrawal and Yoga

The practice of withdrawing from the world and practicing asceticism and meditation is ancient in India, mentioned already in the Rig Veda (Rg Veda 10.136). The Upanishads talk about sages like Yajnavalkya who live a detached life as hermits in the forest to practice mental disciplines. These disciplines involve bodily discipline and controlling the mind to realize the true inner atman and reach moksha. A famous image is that of the chariot representing bodily life and the charioteer as the soul; as the charioteer controls the chariot to reach his destination, so the soul should control the various forces of the body, disengaging the atman from its temporary sojourn in a bodily existence (Katha Upanishad 1.3.3–9).

Another technique to reach liberation that developed was called yoga (from the same root as "yoke"). It is by controlling one's attachment to the outer world and withdrawing inward, withdrawing even from mental activity, that liberation can be attained. Classical Hinduism developed many forms of yoga. Indeed,

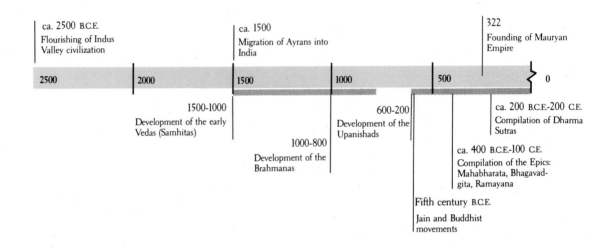

almost every movement has some form of yogic discipline; physical bodily control, mental discipline, ways of performing actions, even worshiping the gods can all be called yoga. The best-known form of classical yoga is described in the Yoga Sutras of Patanjali (ca. 200 B.C.E.), and these writings have the status of scripture for many. Patanjali devised an eight-step method of discipline and control leading to transformation and liberation. This "royal yoga" as set forth by Patanjali (discussed later) became the basis of one of the later schools of philosophy, and it has guided much of the development in yogic practice ever since.

Compilation of the Dharma Sutras

Another stream of Hindu thought and practice, also reaching back to ancient times, is the emphasis on the eternal order of everything and of human life within that order. In early Vedic times Varuna was looked to as the guardian of this eternal order. In the classical period the eternal order of everything was called Dharma, and sages were busy composing writings that spelled out what this order was all about, especially for society and for the individual within society. These Dharma sutras (Dharma texts) picture an idealized society that is in conformity with the eternal truths of the Vedas. In fact, what Westerners call "Hinduism" is to Hindus simply the "Eternal Dharma." It is true that some tension exists between the goal of moksha, liberation from the world of samsara, and the concern of Dharma, maintaining the good of the social order. But Hinduism is built on that tension, and most religious practices acknowledge the duty both to support the social order and to seek the goal of moksha.

Basic to this vision of Dharma is the idea of karma and rebirth, as taught by the Upanishads. Everyone is born into a particular place in society because of the karma accumulated in past existences. The role of the individual thus is determined by birth, and she or he is expected to perform the actions (karma) appropriate for that particular role. The best known of the Dharma sutras is the writing called the Law-code of Manu, traditionally thought to be given by Manu, the originator of man and the first lawgiver. This extremely influential writing spells out the Dharma especially in terms of class (*varna*, or color), giving detailed descriptions of

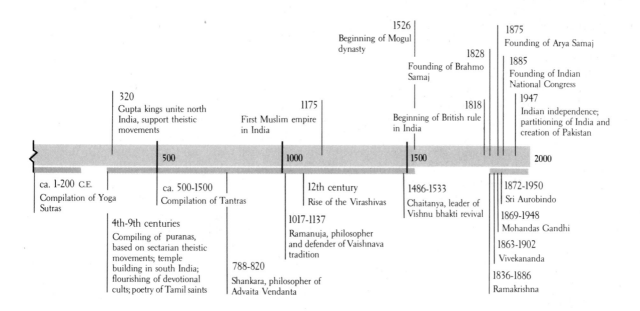

320
Gupta kings unite north India, support theistic movements

1526
Beginning of Mogul dynasty

1875
Founding of Arya Samaj

1828
Founding of Brahmo Samaj

1885
Founding of Indian National Congress

1175
First Muslim empire in India

1818
Beginning of British rule in India

1947
Indian independence; partitioning of India and creation of Pakistan

500   1000   1500   2000

ca. 1-200 C.E.
Compilation of Yoga Sutras

ca. 500-1500
Compilation of Tantras

12th century
Rise of the Virashivas

1486-1533
Chaitanya, leader of Vishnu bhakti revival

1872-1950
Sri Aurobindo

4th-9th centuries
Compiling of puranas, based on sectarian theistic movements; temple building in south India; flourishing of devotional cults; poetry of Tamil saints

1017-1137
Ramanuja, philosopher and defender of Vaishnava tradition

788-820
Shankara, philosopher of Advaita Vendanta

1869-1948
Mohandas Gandhi

1863-1902
Vivekananda

1836-1886
Ramakrishna

the duties of people born as brahmins, kshatriyas, vaishyas, and shudras. This idealized varna system later developed into the caste system in which there are hundreds of subcastes linked with these four classes, and it has continued to exercise great influence over Hindu society. To answer the question, "Who am I?" surely requires an identification of one's class and caste, that is, one's place in the Eternal Dharma.

The Ramayana and Mahabharata Epics

An important development in the story of Hinduism is the use of popular stories to convey religious meaning. In fact, for many Hindus, the part of the story they are most familiar with involves the great epics, the Mahabharata and the Ramayana, for these tell the stories of the gods and the heroes of old who provide models for the Hindu way of life. The epics combine interest in the path of knowledge and liberation with support for the values of Dharma and action in society. They also provide a broad foundation for bhakti, that is, worship of the gods. Probably the epics were composed or at least reached their final form between 200

B.C.E. and 200 C.E., although the Hindu tradition sets them in previous world ages, many years ago. The events described in these epics are not historical in the same sense as the rise and decline of the Mauryan dynasty, for example; rather they are legendary and mythological events. Yet the Hindu tradition considers these events, as ideal types and models of eternal truth, to be a more significant "history" than the confusing, fleeting realm of day-to-day historical events.

The story of the Ramayana epic is the cosmic battle between the great god Vishnu and the demonic forces of evil, and it establishes the paradigm for human conduct according to the notion of Dharma. The main hero of the story is Rama, a prince who is an *avatara* (incarnation) of the god Vishnu, and his opponent is Ravana, the demon king of the island of Lanka. Rama fought a great war to defeat Ravana and rescue his wife Sita who had been abducted, getting help from a race of monkeys, with the god Hanuman as their chief. In the process Rama set the model for honest and proper conduct, ruling as a righteous king. Even before he became king he showed high ethical qualities, accepting fourteen years of exile rather than question his father's rash promise that gave the kingship to his younger stepbrother. After he had finally established order and a righteous kingdom, he again demonstrated the highest ethical conduct by banishing his pure, beloved wife Sita from the kingdom because some subjects questioned her chastity while she had been under the demon's power. Besides providing a model of Hindu morality and self-control, this story also presents the god Rama as the divine hero to be worshiped. Throughout northern India the cult of Rama is very popular, with a great autumn festival called Ramlila, in which the story of Rama is recited and acted out.

Rama, divine hero of the Ramayana Epic.

The Mahabharata is an immensely long and complicated epic poem (nearly 100,000 verses long) dealing with conflicts between two related clans in north India in a previous world age. The issues have to do not with good and evil forces but with questions of the dharma of warriors, the goal of moksha, and the importance of devotion to the gods. The heroes of the epic are the five Pandava brothers, who have a conflict with their cousins over who will rule north India. In this rambling, fascinating story, the most famous section is a chapter called the Bhagavad Gita (song of the beloved one). As the two armies prepare to meet on the battlefield, Arjuna, the most renowned warrior of the Pandavas, sees that the ranks of the enemies include relatives, friends, teachers, and the like, and he is overcome with grief. He drops his weapons and says that it would be better to be killed than to inflict such suffering on others. His charioteer is Krishna, an avatara (incarnation) of the great god Vishnu, who proceeds to teach Arjuna—and all of us—the truth about existence, providing a synthesis of Hinduism that to this day remains the most popular scriptural presentation of the way of Hinduism.

Arjuna really is raising a fundamental question of human life: is it always best to do one's duty? His duty as a warrior is to fight, but wouldn't it be better for everyone if he did not fight? In answer, Krishna first teaches that, although the body is destroyed, the atman is imperishable and simply takes itself to a new body, much like a man discarding old clothes and putting on new ones—therefore one should not grieve over death. Secondly, Krishna explains, action done without desire for its fruits, that is, done simply because it is one's duty, is higher than nonaction. The key is to perform actions without attachment and desires: "When he renounces all desires and acts without craving, possessiveness, or individuality, he finds peace" (Bhagavad Gita 2.71).[8] In this way Krishna synthesizes both paths: seeking liberation and performing one's duty in society.

But the real focus of the Bhagavad Gita is *bhakti*, devotion to one's god. The highest path, Krishna teaches, is the path of selfless action and wisdom through loving and surrendering to Krishna as the supreme Lord. Krishna really is none other than the great god Vishnu, creator and preserver of the whole universe. But, Krishna teaches, from age to age as evil arises Vishnu sends himself forth as an avatara into the world, to destroy evil and establish righteousness (4.5–11). And those who worship him can find the highest liberation: "Keep me in your mind and devotion, sacrifice to me, bow to me, discipline your self toward me, and you will reach me!" (9.34).[9] Women and shudras were excluded from performing Vedic rituals; but everyone including women and shudras can worship Krishna and find salvation in him (9:32). Even those who are devotees of other gods and worship them are really worshiping Krishna! (9.23).

So the Gita presents a grand synthesis of Hinduism and opens the way for a great flourishing of bhakti, devotion to the gods. In this great poem, beloved by Hindus of all persuasions, we see most clearly the foundation for what it means to be Hindu.

The epics describe other gods also, besides Vishnu and his incarnations, Rama and Krishna. The Mahabharata tells of the other great god of classical Hinduism, Shiva, the divine mountain yogin. We saw earlier that perhaps a prototype of Shiva was worshiped in the Indus Valley civilization—a god seated in the yoga position. The epic also refers to the virgin goddess Durga who delights in wine and animal sacrifice and slays the buffalo demon. As Hinduism moves into the medieval period, the growing bhakti practice tends to cluster around these theistic traditions associated with Vishnu, Shiva, and the great goddess.

So with all these elements of the story—the Upanishads and the Yoga Sutras with their emphasis on meditation and release, the Dharma Sutras outlining the proper way of life in society, and the epics summing it all up and emphasizing devotion to the gods—we can see the general outline of Hindu identity.

TRANSFORMATIONS IN THE SACRED STORY

The master story of any religion is always somewhat open-ended; the creative events continue to have effect even to the present time. Often, however, there is a sense of closing the age of the sacred story. For example, Muslims consider the source of truth to be the revelation through Muhammad as the final prophet; and Christians determined the limits of the canon of scripture. What happens afterward is historical transformation of the story. In Hinduism, however, the sacred story merges into historical transformations without any clear break. Even after the great epics, sacred writings continue to come forth, expanding the stories of the gods and the possibilities of truth and ritual, at least throughout much of the medieval period (ca. 400–1800).

Medieval Hinduism: Shaping the Sacred Ways

The major developments in the medieval period, shaping the way Hindus think and act, centered around philosophical systems and theistic bhakti movements. A significant but limited movement was Tantrism, focusing on the great goddess and employing ritual techniques to achieve liberation. And a substantial impact came from the Muslim invasion and dominance over much of India during the medieval period.

Rethinking the Vedic Truth: Systematized Philosophical Views

In a dialogue between student and teacher, written by the great philosopher Shankara, the student asks these kinds of questions:

How can I be released from samsara?

Is this suffering indeed my own nature?

Or does it result from some cause, my own nature being indifferent?

What is that cause?

And what will remove it?

And what is my own nature?

What is ignorance?

What is its object?

And what is knowledge by which I can realize my own nature?[10]

Such questions have provided the grist for Hindu philosophy for over 2,000 years.

The intellectual underpinnings of Hinduism go back to the sages of the early Vedic hymns and the teachers of the Upanishads, and the quest for intellectual understanding never halted. Eventually six orthodox schools (*darshanas*, viewpoints) of philosophy came to be recognized (orthodox because they recognize the authority of the Vedas and Upanishads), in addition to unorthodox philosophies like Buddhism and Jainism. Two of these schools (Nyaya and Vaishesika) were concerned chiefly with cosmology and logic as a means to liberation, and one (Mimamsa) occupied itself with showing how the Vedas are eternal and the Vedic rituals are important for religious duty and attainment of salvation. The most influential schools have been the Samkhya-Yoga pair and the Vedanta school.

We mentioned the practice of yoga earlier, focused on the eight-stage path taught by Patanjali. The Yoga philosophical school with its path toward higher release developed in close relation to the Samkhya school's "map" of the cosmos and the causes of bondage. Samkhya taught a dualism of nature (*prakriti*), out of which develops the whole person with mind and senses, and pure spirit (*purusha*), which is the transcendent consciousness. The problem is that the embodied mind mistakes itself for purusha, which causes bondage in the samsara cycle. And so the goal of yogic practice is to disentangle purusha consciousness from the material self and mind and bring about liberation.

The Vedanta school has been very influential in Hindu intellectual developments, continuing to the present day (Mimamsa also continues today among a small number of Brahman ritualists). Philosophers of Vedanta (end of the Veda) were especially interested in the teaching of the Upanishads concerning the Brahman as the one ultimate reality and the self as identical with Brahman. Vedanta philosophers had disagreements on the nature of Brahman and how Brahman is related to the world—thus there is Nondualist (Advaita), Qualified Nondualist (Vishishtadvaita), and Dualist (Dvaita) Vedanta. But they all agree that knowledge of the Brahman and the atman is of primary importance for liberation. Many Hindus look to the brilliant philosopher Shankara (788–820), of the Nondualist Vedanta school, as an outstanding Hindu thinker. Shankara, from south India, became a sannyasin as a boy and died at an early age, but in those few years he wrote very influential commentaries on the Upanishads and the Bhagavad Gita.

Shankara starts with insistence on the nondual character of reality: there is only Brahman, the ground of being, without qualities, unchanging. Further, Brahman is identical with the eternal, unchanging atman (soul), which underlies all individuals. Moksha (liberation) means the knowledge that one's atman is the eternal Brahman itself. But our problem, according to Shankara, is that we commonly view the world as changing, full of different realities, persons, and things, including our own soul as an individual reality. The way out of this illusion, Shankara says, is not through rituals, actions, or worship, but through knowledge attained through meditation, knowledge that I and the Brahman are one.

This radical nondualism of Shankara has repercussions for traditional Hindu ideas and practices. One is forced to conclude that there really are no permanent individual selves, and that even the samsara cycle and release from it are ultimately illusions. Most radical, perhaps, is the implication that devotion to a god cannot bring liberation—for even the gods must be illusion! And what about the Vedas and Upanishads? Shankara was led to conclude that, in the state of highest knowledge, there are no scriptures. But—and this has been most influential in shaping Hinduism—Shankara allowed that there are different levels of truth, corresponding to one's spiritual development. At the lower levels of truth the scriptures and devotion to the gods can be of benefit for spiritual transformation. But one who reaches the highest knowledge realizes that there is only one Brahman; such a one transcends gods, rituals, Dharma, and scriptures.

Whereas most Hindus do not actively follow the path of knowledge set forth by Shankara, and later philosophers like Ramanuja disputed his radical nondualism by bringing devotion to God back to center stage, his vision exemplifies the intellectual foundation of the fascinating diversity of what we call Hinduism. How can both an atheistic philosopher and an ardent lover of Krishna—and everyone else in between—all be considered Hindus? Shankara's philosophy shows that there are many levels of spiritual development and each soul proceeds at its own pace toward the goal of liberation.

The Flowering of Bhakti: the Puranas and Ecstatic Devotion

Another important development during the medieval period is the great flowering of devotional cults, a movement that came to dominate all of Hinduism with its gods and goddesses, puja (worship of divine images), temples, festivals, and the like. The new line of kings that reunited northern India in 320 c.e., the Guptas, gave strong support to worshiping the gods, especially Vishnu, raising theism to the level of a state religion, supporting theistic groups and building temples. The gods had always been worshiped in India, but gradually some of the Vedic gods were eased out of prominence, whereas other gods—some perhaps non-Aryan in origin—came to dominate or were combined with Vedic gods. The great epics provided a broad foundation on which bhakti could flourish, and in the centuries following, from perhaps the fourth century to the ninth century c.e., a series of *puranas* (ancient stories) were composed describing the various gods and devotion to them. Many devotional cults sprang up, focused on Vishnu or Shiva or Durga and the gods associated with them, and poets and singers never tired of creating a wealth of joyous, ecstatic devotional literature.

In general, most Hindus see their identity intimately connected with these devotional traditions. Who am I? I'm a devotee of Vishnu, a Vaishnavite. Or I'm a Shaivite, a worshiper of Shiva. Whereas most Hindus follow one of these two great theistic traditions, others devote themselves to the great goddess Durga or, as she is also known, Shakti, Devi, or Kali. Many consider this goddess devotion as part of the Shaivite tradition. It is important to understand that, whereas bhakti seems to presuppose a great number of gods and goddesses, devotees tend to focus on one of the great gods as the source of ultimate sacred power. To a Vaishnavite, Vishnu is all, the creator, preserver, and destroyer of the universe. Shiva is everything to a Shaivite, and a devotee of the great goddess Durga likewise is "monotheistic" in outlook. At the same time, there generally is a tolerance for the other traditions of bhakti and a sense that God shows herself or himself in many forms.

The Vishnu Purana, the Harivamsa, and the Bhagavata Purana provide a wealth of material about worshiping Vishnu, his wife Lakshmi, goddess of beauty and wealth, and his delightful avatara, Krishna. Krishna of the Bhagavad Gita, as an avatara of Vishnu, taught Arjuna the essence of the way of Hinduism. The puranas elaborate the story of Krishna greatly, focusing on Krishna Gopala, the lovable baby and young man among the cowherd people of Vrindavana. In festivals devotees performed the stories of Krishna's love affairs with the cowherd girls and especially with Radha, his favorite—stories that demonstrate the highest form of loving God.

The delight of worshiping Krishna and Rama forms the theme of much religious poetry composed by saint-singers throughout the medieval period, as, for example, in Gitagovinda Jayadeva's Love Song of the Dark Lord (twelfth century), one of the world's most beautiful love poems. In the sixteenth century a great revival of Vishnu bhakti swept north India, especially Bengal, led by the famous saint Chaitanya (1486–1533). He introduced the practice of devotees parading around the streets publicly singing and chanting and dancing in praise of the lord. He and his followers established Krishna temples and systematized the theology of Krishna worship. Chaitanya himself was widely regarded as an incarnation of both Krishna and Radha (Krishna's lover) in one body. This tradition of ecstatic Krishna worship has continued to the present and even has been introduced into America through the International Society for Krishna Consciousness (popularly known as the Hare Krishnas).

The story of Shiva in the puranas has quite a different mood from that of Vishnu. There is no connected life story for Shiva, as there is for Krishna and Rama, but there are abundant stories revealing one aspect or another of this great god. Shiva combines all dualities in himself, so the stories tell about his powers of life and death, his passionate pursuits and his ascetic withdrawal, his love and his anger. He is sometimes pictured in images as half-male and half-female, uniting the cosmic generative forces; and his most typical symbol is the lingam (phallic symbol) placed in a yoni (symbol of the female organ). He is the creator and nourisher of existence, but at the same time he is the great destroyer.

Throughout the medieval period, Shaivite movements cultivated the bhakti of this great god in his various aspects. Since Shiva is the great divine yogin, among those devoted to him were a variety of ascetics (sadhus) and yogins. Worship of Shiva became especially dominant in south India, and poets sang praises of him in Tamil. The largest group of Shaivites, the Shaiva Siddhanta, collected their ritual texts in the scriptures called Agamas, holding them to be equal in value to the Vedas. Another important group, Virashaiva, developed in the twelfth century as a kind of countercultural movement, its founder refusing to go through the sacred thread initiation ceremony. Known as the Lingayats because they wear a small stone lingam on a chain around the neck, they protested against the caste system, worship of images, and many other Hindu beliefs and customs. In their poems in praise of Shiva, written in Kannada, they insist on a Shiva monotheism.

Associated with the Shaivite tradition is the worship of Shiva's female aspect called his *shakti*, for Shiva perfectly embodies the divine powers both male and female. This Shakti can be seen as Shiva's energy and power, or Shakti can be personified as the wife of Shiva, under names like Parvati, Devi, and Uma. Or this Shakti can become the focus of worship in her own right as the great goddess, usually under the names of Durga and Kali. The relationships of these goddesses to each other and to Shiva is by no means clear in the puranas. What is clear is that both Durga and Kali are ferocious, terrifying goddesses, expressions of the terrible energy and destructiveness of the sacred. The central sacred story about Durga relates how she delivered the world from the vicious attack of the buffalo-demon Mahisha. She is worshiped by her devotees, the Shaktas, as the Divine Mother who brought forth the world and is the divine power closest to humans.

Perhaps the part of the sacred story most strange to non-Hindus deals with the dark goddess Kali. When battling demon armies, the story goes, Durga became furious and her face turned black as ink; from between her brows emerged the terrible Kali, brandishing a sword and carrying a noose. She wears a garland of human heads and a girdle of severed arms, causing the world to tremble with her bloodthirsty cries and frantic dancing. Yet this terrifying goddess became the focus of bhakti for some groups in Hinduism, especially in

An image of the goddess Kali, taken out in festival procession.

Bengal, who find ecstasy and fulfillment in worshiping God also in her destructive aspects. The worship of Kali, the terrifying, destroying mother, forms an important though difficult to understand strand of bhakti Hinduism.

The Development of Tantrism

Closely related to the worship of the great goddess is a small but significant movement called Tantrism, and to complete the sacred story of Hinduism we must take note of this complicated form that arose in the medieval period. The goal of Tantra is moksha by means of elaborate ritual and yogic practices focusing on the power of the great goddess. Tantra is a vast collection of ideas and practices, but they center on the inseparability of Shiva and Shakti, of male and female, of divine and human, of the macrocosmos and the microcosmos. Since the body is a microcosmos, there is a sacred geography in the body, and through ritual practice it is possible to activate the sacred forces latent in the body, bring about the union of Shiva (passive, pure intelligence) and Shakti (active, creative energy), and achieve a sacred transformation.

The Tantrists distinguish between a right-handed and a left-handed path. The right-handed path is for all Tantrists and employs mantras (sacred sounds), mandalas (cosmic diagrams), and yogic-ritual techniques such as breath control to activate Shakti within to rise and be united with Shiva within. The left-handed path is considered appropriate only for advanced Tantrists, for it includes a special ritual called circle-worship (*cakra-puja*), using elements normally forbidden and associated with the lower bodily senses. These are called the "five M's" (each begins with the letter "M" in Sanskrit) and involve the use of wine, meat, fish, parched grain, and sexual intercourse. It is particularly the use of sexual impulses as ritual yoga to unite the powers of Shakti and Shiva that characterizes this form of Tantra. The orthodox tradition has strongly criticized left-handed Tantra for this seeming perversion of traditional morality. But Tantrists insist that the ritual practice must be done only by advanced adepts in the context of purity, self-discipline, and devotion to the goddess, under the guidance of a Tantric guru, not as gratification of desires but as the redirection of those desires into worship and transformation.

Muslim Presence and Impact in India

During the medieval period, the great expansion of Islam continued on into India. The first Muslim incursions came already in the eighth century, and the coming of the Mongols in the sixteenth century brought most of India under the rule of the Mogul dynasty. At first fiercely exclusive in religious practice, Muslim rulers, especially Akbar (r. 1556–1605), developed a toleration for Hinduism and even attempted a synthesis of these religions. Eventually tens of millions of Indians (Hindus and Buddhists) converted to Islam. Many clashes did, of course, occur between these very different religions, with Islam's radical

monotheism quite at odds with Hindu bhakti. But there was also mutual influence. For example, Hindu devotionalism and saints inspired the Muslim Sufis in India, and the Sufis in turn inspired many devout Hindus. One important development of this meeting of Islam and Hinduism was the emergence of the great religious leader Guru Nanak who attempted to combine features of both religions, creating the Sikh religion. By the eighteenth century Mogul power faded and the British entered to take control of India.

The Modern Era: Renaissance and Response to the West

Two Reform Movements: Brahmo Samaj and Arya Samaj

Western ideas brought to India by the British helped to raise questions among some Hindus about certain aspects of the tradition, especially the caste system and the sense that the world is the realm of samsara from which the goal is to escape. As Hindus learned Western thought, new ideas began to arise in Hinduism. One of the important early movements of reform was started by Ram Mohan Roy (1772–1833), who had worked for the East India Company. He spoke out against what he considered abuses in the Hindu system, such as polytheism, worship of images, neglect of women's education, and the practice of burning a widow alive at her husband's cremation (called sati or suttee). Influenced by Christianity but unwilling to accept the idea that Jesus was God, Ram Mohan studied the Vedas and Upanishads and found that they also taught a simple monotheism. In 1828 Ram Mohan founded the Brahmo Samaj (Society of Brahman) as a religious society advocating a rational, humanistic religion without all the Hindu rituals and customs. The members of the society would meet weekly to study the Upanishads, pray, and sing hymns.

Later, led by Debendranath Tagore (1817–1905), the Brahmo Samaj broke away from orthodoxy by asserting that reason and conscience, not the Vedas, are the final authority in religion; the truth of the scriptures is to be confirmed by the inner light, which all possess. The society revised the old rituals to excise references to the many gods, and they pressed for laws against child marriage and polygamy. Weakened by divided opinions toward the end of the nineteenth century, the Brahmo Samaj's religious ideas did not carry the day in modern Hinduism, but the society effected a significant change of attitude among Hindus with respect to the unquestioned rule of tradition.

In 1875 the Arya Samaj was founded by Swami Dayananda Sarasvati (1824–1883), representing another attempt to restore the original purity of Hinduism. Dayananda had been a Shaivite devotee, but under the influence of a fiery teacher who accepted only the oldest Vedic scriptures, he came to reject the puranas and all the popular gods of Hinduism, together with image worship and the caste system. In his book, *The Light of Truth,* he held that Hindus should rely on the early Vedas alone (the Samhitas) for all religious truth. Other religions, such as Islam, Christianity, and bhakti Hinduism, have corrupted this pure truth. The early Vedas are also the source of all scientific truth. Further, the caste system made up of numerous subcastes should be abandoned. Anyone can study the Vedas. Women should be educated, widows should be allowed to remarry, and child marriage should be abandoned.

Thus the Arya Samaj moved in somewhat the same direction as the Brahmo Samaj, but it differs in rejecting Western influences and in calling for a return to the early Vedas as supreme religious truth. Although the Arya Samaj did not come to dominate modern Hindu thinking, it together with the Brahmo Samaj helped to revitalize Hindu pride in the face of Western dominance and laid the groundwork for a Hindu spiritual revival by reasserting Hindu tradition as the source of value for modern society.

Ramakrishna and Vivekananda

As movements in India revived the sense of pride in India's spiritual heritage, many leading thinkers who had been influenced by the West began to turn to their own heritage for guidance in the modern world. Of the many who contributed to this task, we might single out Ramakrishna Paramahamsa (1836-1886) and his disciple, Swami Vivekananda (1863–1902).

Ramakrishna was a God-intoxicated Hindu who revitalized the Hindu tradition and channeled it into new directions. A temple priest of the goddess Kali who communed with her in trancelike meditation, he also worshiped other gods such as Krishna and practiced the Nondualist Vedanta type of meditation. He also followed disciplines of Christianity and Islam, experiencing visions of Christ and Muhammad; on that basis he came to believe that the ultimate reality may be approached by any tradition of worship. Thus Ramakrishna was able to develop an expansive Hinduism not by pruning it but by incorporating into it Western religious ideas and experiences, remaining all the while devoted to the Hindu tradition. Already in his lifetime he was widely regarded as a great Hindu saint.

One of the disciples of Ramakrishna was Swami Vivekananda who, after Ramakrishna's death, organized the Ramakrishna Order and the Ramakrishna Mission. He came to America to speak at the Parliament of Religions at the Chicago World's Fair in 1893 and excited many with his presentations on Hinduism. Thereafter he traveled about lecturing on Hinduism, founding the Vedanta Society to continue the work of teaching the Hindu tradition in America. In India, the Ramakrishna Mission was dedicated to a wide variety of charitable, missionary, and educational activities for the masses. By his example Vivekananda established a new sannyasin model, a holy man actively engaged in social concerns.

Independence Movement and New Visions: Gandhi and Aurobindo

As the Hindu renaissance represented by these movements brought Indians a new sense of pride and peoplehood, an independence movement arose that, under the leadership of people like Mohandas Gandhi (1869–1948), brought India independence from British rule. The motivation to work for independence came from many sources, of course, including many ultranationalists fighting for a "Mother India" purified from all Muslim and British influences. The man who became the leader, however, was a new kind of religious leader in Hinduism. Gandhi was born in the vaishya (mer-

Mahatma Gandhi at his spinning wheel, a symbol of national self-reliance.

chant) class and was not particularly learned in the Vedic texts and tradition, studying law in England and working for many years in South Africa before returning to India to lead the independence movement. His favorite Hindu scripture was the Bhagavad Gita, which he felt taught nonviolence and selfless action for the welfare of society, and he was also much influenced by the Sermon on the Mount in the New Testament. Drawing on these religious sources, he developed the philosophy and technique of *satyagraha* (holding to the truth), by which he meant a style of nonviolent resistance that awakens in the oppressors a sense of wrong-doing. It is wrong to seek personal victory over opponents, he taught; one must rather purify oneself of all selfish motivations and act without any violence and without any sense of anger. He was totally confident that this way of love and nonviolence (*ahimsa*) will always win out in any situation.

Gandhi became a kind of sannyasin, establishing a community that lived in simplicity and daily work—his spinning wheel become the symbol of his move-ment. Living in celibacy with his wife, wearing only the traditional loincloth of the sannyasin, exerting his energy to purify India of the sin of having made one class of people the "untouchables," and bringing the British to their knees in India by nonviolent resistance, Gandhi represented a spiritual moral force drawn from Hinduism that has had great impact not only on India but on the whole world.

Of the many other modern Hindu thinkers who have expressed a new and vital Hindu perspective, we might single out Sri Aurobindo (1872–1950), who lived through the same years as Gandhi but took a somewhat different course. Educated at Cambridge University in England, he got involved in the nationalist movement in India and was imprisoned in 1910. Discovering through visionary experiences that real human liberation went far beyond the political liberation of India, he chose thereafter to withdraw from the world and established an ashram (retreat) in the French enclave of Pondicherry for the practice of Tantric yoga. In his writings, *The Life Divine* and *Synthesis of Yoga*, he drew on India's ancient wisdom to develop the view that human life can be transformed into the highest forms of spiritual reality by the practice of an all-encompassing discipline of yoga. The divine forces are within us, though we are ignorant of them. If we search within and master these divine forces, making them pervade and transform all dimensions of our life, we will be able to live in the highest possible divine way. Society itself should be reshaped so that it is conducive to this human evolution into the divine life. Although Aurobindo draws on traditional Hindu ideas and techniques, what makes his vision a modern one is the way he integrates individual yogic means with the transformation of social conditions.

Hinduism in the West

Even though Hinduism has never been a missionary religion, the renaissance of Hinduism in India has spilled over to the West, and today many in Europe and America have had contact with the religion of the Eternal Dharma. We noted above the Ramakrishna Mission, which established Vedanta Society centers in various places in America and has for three-quarters of a century been providing Americans with solid knowledge of Hinduism. In recent years a variety of other Hindu movements have been transplanted to the West, including yoga, meditation, and bhakti of various sorts. The two movements most widely known are Transcendental Meditation and the International Society for Krishna Consciousness.

Maharishi Mahesh Yogi studied Shankara's Nondualist (Advaita) Vedanta meditation, but unlike the many other practitioners of this type of meditation he came to America and popularized this system for Westerners. Commonly known as Transcendental Meditation (TM), this practice emphasizes each person's inner divine essence and the creative powers that can be harnessed when this inner source is realized through meditation. TM is a natural process, the Maharishi emphasizes, employing the normal desire of the self to seek joy and happiness. Although some traditional Hindu forms are used, this type of meditation fits well with the American desire for personal success and well-being; by practicing meditation a person can find health and happiness in all areas of life.

A very different form of Hinduism is the Krishna bhakti group known as the International Society for Krishna Consciousness (ISKCON), a movement that has brought Chaitanya's Bengali Krishna worship into the streets of America's big cities. Swami A. C. Bhaktivedanta Prabhupada (1896–1977) became a sannyasin late in life in India and was sent by his master to bring Krishna Consciousness to the West. Arriving in New York City in 1965, he began to chant the names of Krishna in a park and in 1966 opened the first ISKCON center in New York. Soon the movement spread to all parts of the United States and to other countries as well. Prabhupada has also written many studies of the Bhagavad Gita, the puranas, and Chaitanya's writings, through his books making an impact on Western knowledge of Krishna Hinduism. Although there are many lay devotees and many Hindus from India who feel at home at the festivals held in the Krishna temples, the devotees who live in the temples and devote their whole lives to Krishna Consciousness form the heart of the movement. Their day begins about 3:45 a.m. and involves a full schedule of personal and corporate rituals, study sessions, chanting in the streets and elsewhere, worship of Krishna and the other deities, and so forth. The Hare Krishnas, with shaved heads and saffron robes, chanting in ecstasy and

Morning prayer and chanting at the Hare Krishna temple in Philadelphia.

inviting others to join in the delights of Krishna, have become a familiar touch of Hinduism in the West.

There are many other Hindu-related gurus and movements in the West today. Some of the more bizarre ones get much media attention, whereas others cultivate a traditional type of Hinduism in a Western context. It is clear, both from these new groups in the West and from the vital movements in India today, that Hinduism is alive and well and contributing to the future of humankind's religious experience. Already significant dialogue has been taking place between Hindus and people of other religions, especially Christians and Muslims. In the opinion of some scholars of such matters, Hinduism, because of its expansive conception of religious truth at many different levels, can be a resource for mutual understanding and cooperation between these very different paths we call the religions of the world.

DISCUSSION QUESTIONS

1. Who is a Hindu?
2. Discuss the relationship between the history of Hinduism in the modern Western sense of "history" and the traditional Hindu story as told especially in the Epics. Which is more important to Hindu identity?
3. What were some important features of the Indus Valley civilization, and what influences did this culture have on Hinduism?
4. List the main features of Aryan religion in the period of the Rig Veda.
5. What were the major concerns of the authors of the Upanishads?
6. What major aspects of Hinduism developed during the classical epic era?
7. Discuss the main interests of the religion of the Puranas.
8. Compare the Brahmo Samaj and the Arya Samaj as modern reform movements.
9. What were Gandhi's main ideas and activities? Why did he attract such attention worldwide?

CHAPTER 14

HINDU WORLDS OF MEANING

ULTIMATE REALITY IN HINDUISM: BRAHMAN, DHARMA, GOD/GODDESS

"What's it *all* about?" "What is really ultimate, the center of all?" Hindus have a long tradition of asking such questions, a tradition going back at least three thousand years. A hymn from Book 10 of the Rig Veda (ca. 1000 B.C.E.) puts it this way:

> Who really knows? Who will here proclaim it? Whence was it produced? Whence is this creation? The gods came afterwards, with the creation of this universe. Who then knows whence it has arisen? Whence this creation has arisen—perhaps it formed itself, or perhaps it did not—the one who looks down on it, in the highest heaven, only he knows—or perhaps he does not know.   (RG VEDA 10.129.6–7)[1]

Answering this question, the Hindu traditions have put forth many proposals and experimented with many conceptions of ultimate reality, from the gods of the early Aryans to the modern Hindu's God or gods, from the power of the fire sacrifice to the eternal cosmic order, from the Brahman of the Upanishads to the Shakti of Tantric ritual. In our brief look at these traditions several thousand years in the making, we focus on three prominent answers as to what the sacred ultimate is: Brahman, Dharma, and God or gods. These answers, as we by now have come to understand, are not exclusive, of course.

Brahman as the Sacred Ultimate

As noted earlier, the term *brahman* originally referred to the powerful words spoken by a priest in the ritual of fire-sacrifice. The priest who spoke the words was called brahmin, and the manuals about the ritual are the Brahmanas. Increasingly the term *Brahman* was used to refer to the sacred power that pervades and maintains all things. For a major portion of the Hindu tradition, Brahman is ultimate reality.

Brahman as the One Reality

According to the Upanishads, one of the first important ideas about Brahman is oneness, in contrast to multiplicity. A student once asked the sage Yajnavalkya how many gods there are, and Yajnavalkya answered that, as mentioned in a hymn, there are 3,306 gods. "But," the student presses on, "just how many gods are there?" "Thirty-three," is the answer. "Yes, but just how many gods are there?" "Six." "Yes, but just how many gods are there?" "Three." The student is still not satisfied: "Yes, but how many gods are there?" "Two." "Yes, but just how many gods are there?" "One and a half." "Yes, but just how many gods are there?" Finally Yajnavalkya answers, "One," and he explains that all the gods are but various differentiated powers of the One who is called Brahman (Brihad-aranyaka U-panishad 3.9.1–9).[2] Brahman is the one life of all the gods, the one soul of the universe, the one source of all. As the One, Brahman is primordial, prior to all forms and divisions. Brahman is without qualities and limiting attributes, transcending this universe.

What is soundless, touchless, formless, imperishable,
Likewise tasteless, constant, odorless,
Without beginning, without end, higher than the great, stable—
By discerning That, one is liberated from the mouth of death.   (KATHA UPANISHAD 3.15)[3]

Finally, the Brahman is indescribable, for it is the subject of all reality and thus is beyond speech and concepts. Yajnavalkya explains,

For where there is a duality, as it were, there one sees another; there one smells another; there one tastes an-other; there one speaks to another; there one hears another; there one understands another. But where everything has become just one's own self, then whereby and whom would one see? then whereby and whom would one smell? then whereby and whom would one taste? then whereby and to whom would one speak? then whereby and whom would one hear? then whereby and of whom would one think? then whereby and whom would one touch? then whereby and whom would one understand? whereby would one understand him by means of whom one understands this All? That Soul (Atman) is not this, it is not that (neti, neti).
(BRIHAD-ARANYAKA UPANISHAD 4.5.15)[4]

Yet it can be said that the Brahman is immanent, permeating all things, humans, gods, the physical universe, space, and time. "Verily, this whole world is Brahman" (Chandogya Upanishad 3.14.1). Most importantly, according to the Upanishads, one's own true self (atman) is none other than the Brahman:

This Soul of mine within the heart is greater than the earth, greater than the atmosphere, greater than the sky, greater than these worlds. Containing all works, con-taining all desires, containing all odors, containing all tastes, encompassing this whole world, the unspeaking, the unconcerned—this is the Soul of mine within the heart, this is Brahman. Into him I shall enter on de-parting hence.   (CHANDOGYA UPANISHED 3.14.3–4)[5]

Since the inner atman is really the Brahman, a central path toward liberation in Hinduism, as we see later, is to acquire knowledge of this inner atman, to fully realize, as the Upanishads say many times, that "This Atman is the Brahman" (Brihad-aranyaka Upanishad 2.5.19).

Two Levels of Knowing Brahman

To know Brahman as the ultimate is the goal—but that requires high spiritual understanding. Hindu thinkers have a long tradition of speaking of two levels of truth. One seer, for example, tells of two forms of Brahman, the formed and the formless. The formed Brahman is different from the wind and the atmosphere and thus is personal and worthy of worship. The formless Brahman *is* the wind and the atmosphere and thus is impersonal, described only by "Not this, not this" (*neti, neti*) (Brihad-aranyaka Upanishad 2.3.1–6).

The Hindu philosopher Shankara spelled out the two levels of knowing Brahman with characteristic thoroughness:

> Brahman is apprehended under two forms; in the first place as qualified by limiting conditions owing to the multiformity of the evolutions of name and form (i.e., the multiformity of the created world); in the second place as being the opposite of this, i.e., free from all limiting conditions whatsoever.[6]

The Brahman without qualities he called the *nirguna* Brahman; this is the very ground of existence, prior to any limiting characteristics, which can only be described negatively and known intuitively—the highest truth of Brahman, the ultimate. The Brahman with qualities, the *saguna* Brahman, is the creative power of the universe, the foundation of the phenomenal world—this lord of existence can be described and known and worshiped. This personal form of Brahman is a link between the idea of Brahman as ultimate reality and the worship of God or gods in theistic Hinduism.

The Eternal Dharma

Knowing the identity of the atman with the Brahman leads to moksha, ultimate liberation from the samsara cycle, so this is held forth by many Hindus as the highest goal. But alongside that basic idea of ultimate reality Hinduism puts forward another eternal ultimate reality, the cosmic order, the Eternal Dharma. "What's it *all* about?" In the context of living life the way we should, the answer turns out to be Dharma—not the underlying source and essence of reality, not a god to be worshiped, but the eternal order of things to be

followed. Dharma is something like the law of nature, eternal and unchanging. Following our dharma means living in accordance with reality. And it has as its correlate the law of karma, the law that there is an unfailing result that comes from every action. The whole world is supported and continues to exist on the foundation of Dharma and karma.

The eternal Dharma as ultimate stands in a certain tension with Brahman as ultimate. To realize Brahman means moksha, liberation from the world of samsara. But to live according to one's dharma means supporting and sustaining the world. This creative tension is built into the religious paths of Hinduism, and it provides much of the dramatic interest in the stories of the epics and the puranas, where the values of Dharma and moksha often conflict.

God as Supreme Sacred Reality

Down through the centuries, while philosophers were speaking of Brahman and other sages were working out their understanding of the eternal Dharma, people continued their worship of the gods. Spurred on by the stories of the gods in the great epics, theistic Hinduism came to be more widely accepted and practiced even by the scholars and philosophers, who developed new interpretations about God (gods) as the ultimate reality.

We noted the distinction between *nirguna* Brahman, Brahman without qualities, and *saguna* Brahman, Brahman that is rooted in the world as the creative power of existence. To Shankara, *saguna* Brahman is known at a lower level of truth, but to those Hindu thinkers who are devoted to their god, the argument is equally valid that God (*saguna* Brahman) is the highest level of truth. The philosopher who argued this most persuasively was Ramanuja (1017–1137), a leading thinker among the Vaishnavites of south India who worked out a theology of Vaishnavism that bridged Shankara's Nondualist philosophy of Brahman and his own devotion to the great god Vishnu. Ramanuja was mainly interested in promoting bhakti. With respect to the nature of Brahman, he held that whereas Brahman is one unified reality, there is *within* the one Brahman a qualitative distinction between the soul, the world, and the highest Lord. Using the analogy of soul and

Divine image, representing the great gods Brahma, Vishnu, and Shiva.

I see the gods
in your body, O God,
and hordes
of varied creatures:
Brahma, the cosmic creator,
on his lotus throne,
all the seers
and celestial serpents.
I see your boundless form
everywhere,
the countless arms,
bellies, mouths, and eyes;
Lord of All,
I see no end,
or middle or beginning
to your totality. . . .
only boundless strength
in your endless arms,
the moon and sun in your eyes,
your mouths of consuming flames,
your own brilliance
scorching this universe. . . .
You are the original god,
the primordial spirit of man,
the deepest treasure
of all that is,
knower and what is to be known,
the supreme abode;
you pervade the universe,
Lord of Boundless Form.
You are the gods of wind,
death, fire, and water;
the moon; the lord of life;
and the great ancestor.
Homage to you,
a thousand times homage!
I bow in homage to you
again and yet again (11:15–16, 19, 38–39).[7]

body, Ramanuja taught that, as body and soul are united and yet different, so the Lord is the soul of one's soul in a personal relationship that includes both identity and difference, so that one's soul can worship its lordsoul. Ramanuja put forth an intellectual system in which God (Vishnu) is the ultimate reality, and worshiping God, therefore, is the highest truth.

The Great God Vishnu

As we know, the Bhagavad Gita revealed Vishnu to be the highest Lord of all, transcending the cycles of samsara, evolving worlds forth from his own essence and absorbing them back again. The theophany (divine manifestation) revealed to Arjuna in Book XI of the Bhagavad Gita stands as one of the most impressive descriptions of God in religious literature. Arjuna prays to see Krishna's divine form, and the resulting vision of Krishna as the great god Vishnu is so awe-inspiring that Arjuna's hair stands on end.

All beings emerge from Vishnu, and he is the dissolution of all. His abode is far beyond the worlds of samsara. Vishnu as the universal lord concerns himself with cosmic stability. He is foremost the creator and preserver of the world, and his consort is Lakshmi, the goddess of wealth and abundance. When the world is periodically threatened by demons he embodies himself in an avatara (incarnation) to restore cosmic order, a factor that has become very important in Vaishnavite theology. The best-known incarnations of Vishnu are Rama, hero of the Ramayana epic, and Krishna, divine teacher of the Bhagavad Gita. The form of God as Krishna is amply filled out in the puranas, where delightful stories are told about his lovable nature and his exploits as a baby and as a young man among the cowherd people, as we saw earlier. Reflecting on the importance of these incarnations of God, Ramanuja says,

> [God's] divine form is the depository of all radiance, loveliness, fragrance, delicacy, beauty, and youth—desirable, congruous, one in form, unthinkable, divine, marvellous, eternal, indefectible, perfect. His essence and nature are not to be limited by word or thought. He is an ocean of boundless compassion, moral excellence, tenderness, generosity, and sovereignty, the refuge of the whole world without distinction of persons. . . . [By his incarnation] he can be seen by the eyes of all men, for without putting aside his [divine] nature, he came down to dwell in the house of Vasudeva, to give light to the whole world with his indefectible and perfect glory, and to fill out all things with his own loveliness.[8]

For Vaishnavites following Ramanuja's theology, Vishnu is the one supreme reality encompassing all gods.

The Great God Shiva

Many Shaivites have a theistic vision similar to the Vaishnavites, but consider Shiva to the great lord of all, the ultimate One. Yet the theology of Shaivism is quite different from that of Vaishnavism. When we think of what is really central to all existence, what holds everything together, we have to think of evil as well as good, pain and death as well as birth and growth. Divine creativity involves death and rebirth; life coming into this world means life leaving this world. Many in India, strongminded and dedicated to truth as it is really experienced, feel that ultimate reality is best experienced through Shiva and his Shakti (feminine side). Many, of course, worship Shiva and Shakti along with many other gods. For some single-minded visionaries, Shiva is the One, the ultimate form of the sacred.

The stories portray Shiva as the greatest, supremely powerful god. A story in the puranas relates how Brahma the creator god, before creation was complete, met Vishnu and the two argued over who was greater.

Suddenly a great pillar of flame shot up out of the darkness below and rose out of sight. Deciding to investigate this pillar, Brahma took the form of a swan and flew upward, and Vishnu took the form of a boar and pushed downward. A thousand years later the two gods returned, unable to find the top or the bottom of the pillar. The sound *Om* began to come from the pillar, and Shiva himself came forth from the pillar and received the worship of Brahma and Vishnu. The pillar was none other than Shiva's lingam, the infinite source of the whole universe.

Some Shiva devotees have moved toward a Shiva monotheism. For example, the Virashaivites, in their poems in praise of Shiva, often mock other practices and fiercely insist on Shiva as the one god:

> The pot is a god. The winnowing
> fan is a god. The stone in the
> street is a god. The comb is a
> god. The bowstring is also a
> god. The bushel is a god and the
> spouted cup is a god.
> Gods, gods, there are so many
> there's no place left
> for a foot.
> There is only
> one god. He is our Lord
> of the Meeting Rivers.[9]

Shiva is the power connected with the lingam and yoni, the power of yogic meditation, and the dancing divine energy. Central to the theology of Shiva is the encompassing of all dualities—male and female, good and evil, creation and destruction, eroticism and asceticism. As the cosmic generative power, Shiva is the very sap of existence, the vigorous creative power that permeates all life. As the divine model of yoga or the antisocial madman haunting cremation grounds (as in some myths), Shiva beckons people to search for the ultimate truth of liberation from the world. As the divine dancer Shiva expresses the ultimate truth that sacred power is continually creating and destroying the world. In Shiva these opposites are reconciled in a higher unity. Shiva's lingam is the axis of the universe and also extends infinitely beyond, showing that even the temporal and the eternal are united in him, as are manifested existence and unmanifested Brahman.

Shiva Nataraja, the great god dancing out the continual creation, preservation, and destruction of the world.

The Great Goddess: Mother and Destroyer

As we saw earlier, the great goddess has many forms in India, as Shakti, Durga, and Kali, for example, associated with Shiva but also worshiped as the one ultimate by single-minded devotees. She is the active female energy that complements Shiva's pure passive consciousness, the divine energy from which all creative processes derive. She is the creative power that constitutes the material world. So she is the divine mother, guarding and nurturing all the world. But creation also has its destructive side, and the divine mother kills and destroys her creation as well.

The nineteenth-century Hindu saint Ramakrishna, a lifelong devotee of the goddess Kali, expresses this vision of the divine mother as ultimate reality:

> Thus Brahman and Shakti are identical. If you accept the one, you must accept the other. It is like fire and its power to burn.... Thus one cannot think of the Brahman without Shakti, or of Shakti without Brahman. One cannot think of the Absolute without the Relative, or of the Relative without the Absolute. The Primordial Power is ever at play. She is creating, pre-serving, and destroying in play, as it were. This Power is called Kali. Kali is verily Brahman, and Brahman is verily Kali. It is one and the same Reality. When we think of It as inactive . . . then we call It Brahman. But when It engages in these activities, then we call it Kali or Shakti.[10]

Ramakrishna's words show that Hindus can encompass both nondualism and theism in thinking about ultimate reality. The truth of one ultimate Brahman does not prevent the experience of the ultimate in personal forms as god or goddess.

EXISTENCE IN THE WORLD: DHARMA AND SAMSARA

"What sense is there in life?" The Hindu vision of the nature of the world and of the situation of humans within it is complicated and varies from one period to another, from one group or community to another. One key idea found throughout most of the traditions is that somehow, behind all this multifaceted world of existence, there is a unitary source from which all evolved in a creative process. The nature of the world and of humans involves two levels or contexts: the phenomenal world and its ongoing process, and the underlying sacred source and its realization. Problems in human existence arise at both levels, because of our ignorance and selfishness. We fail to fulfill our place within the order of things, and we neglect the realization of the eternal source, with the result that existence becomes a wheel of suffering and repeated death.

The World and Human Nature in Hindu Thought

Throughout the three thousand years of Hindu sacred literature, many pictures have been presented of the creation of the universe, its nature and duration, and its dissolution and recreation. And the human role within this picture has been a prime concern of the sages. Finally, we already know, the role of humans is to seek moksha, liberation from the whole conditioned world of samsara. But we need to see that as the ultimate goal, not as the only thing to be said about the world and humans. Whatever the ultimate truth about the world, there is at least a penultimate truth: the world is here, it is real, it functions by the eternal Dharma, the gods work to keep it going, and humans have the duty to contribute to its welfare. There is more to be said, but we can at least begin with that.

Paradigms of the Creation of the World

Pictures of the creation of the world in the sacred texts vary from a mechanistic self-evolving process to a more theistic view of God or gods creating the universe. We have already mentioned the very influential Hymn to Purusha in the Rig Veda, which described the whole universe created from the sacrifice of the gigantic primordial reality, Purusha. From the one sacred, through the power of sacrifice, comes all the orders of the universe. We can mention two other well-known paradigms of creation, one from the Upanishads and the other from the Vishnu Purana.

The Upanishads elaborate on the creation of the world from the one sacred reality. One version runs like this:

> In the beginning this world was Soul (*Atman*) alone in the form of a Person. Looking around, he saw nothing else than himself. He said first: "I am." . . . Verily he had no delight. Therefore one alone has no delight. He desired a second. He was, indeed, as large as a woman and a man closely embraced. He caused that self to fall into two pieces. Therefrom arose a husband and a wife . . . He copulated with her. Therefrom human beings were produced. . . . She became a cow. He became a bull. With her he did indeed copulate. Then cattle were born. . . . She became a she-goat, he a he-goat; she a ewe, he a ram. With her he did verily copulate. Therefrom were born goats and sheep. Thus, indeed, he created all, whatever pairs there are, even down to the ants. He knew: "I, indeed, am this creation, for I emitted it all from myself."
>
> (BRIHAD-ARANYAKA UPANISHAD 1.4.1–5)[11]

Atman (Brahman) is the original solitary reality. This text and others tell how the primordial one desired to be many, and in the heat of that desire evolved itself into many, entering into and becoming this whole creation. The world is multiformed, but its sacred source is still the one dwelling in it all.

Let us, for one more paradigm, turn to a more theistic vision of creation from the Vishnu Purana. Here the great god Vishnu is the supreme lord, identical with Brahman, unified but containing the potential entire universe in his own nature. He unites within himself the primordial forms of spirit (purusha), matter, and time. Stirring himself, he engages in play to create the whole universe with these forms, evolving them into a vast egg resting on the cosmic waters. He enters the cosmic egg as Brahma (the creator) and creates the three worlds of sky, atmosphere, and earth, populating them with gods and all living beings. Then Vishnu becomes the preserver, supporting the world through its great time cycles (for millions of years) until it is exhausted. Now Vishnu becomes the destroyer and burns up the world in a great conflagration, bringing down rain until all is one vast ocean. Vishnu now sleeps on the coiled body of his great serpent (a setting often depicted in art), until he once again creates the world for another world cycle.

Here, in addition to the idea that the whole universe evolves from the one reality, we see that creation is really the "play" of the great god—suggesting both the exuberent divine energy and the temporary nature of the creation. We also learn that creation is a cyclical process of evolution and destruction over and over, a theme firmly set in the Hindu vision. Commonly, this picture of cosmic time cycles has smaller cycles (yugas) set within larger cycles (kalpas). It is said, for example, that the period from the beginning of creation to its destruction is one kalpa, but within each kalpa are 1,000 mahayugas ("great" yugas), each lasting 4,320,000 human years. Each mahayuga is made up of four lesser yugas, which progressively degenerate until a renewal takes place in the new mahayuga. The whole kalpa, made up of 1,000 mahayugas, is called one day of the Brahma, and it is followed by an equally long night of the Brahma in which Vishnu sleeps, until he again creates the universe for a second day of the Brahma. These kalpas continue for a lifetime of the Brahma, which is 100 years of 360 days and nights of the Brahma. Then at last the whole process is reversed until Vishnu alone remains in his primordial state of spirit, matter, and time—until he again decides to play and set the whole cosmic process in motion again.

Humans: Eternal Atman within the Dharma World

What am I, and what is my place within this whole world? The quest for understanding the self is as old as the human race, and Hindus have done their share of speculating on this question. It is important, Hindus believe, to make a distinction between the *real* self and the empirical self that appears to live in this phenomenal world. The empirical self is made up of the physical body comprised of the gross elements (earth, water, light, wind, and ether), and it also includes the subtle body made up of the vital breaths, the organs of action, and the organs of knowledge, mind, and intellect. This empirical self seems to be the "real me," for it has all my physical characteristics, and my distinct personality, my habits, my way of thinking also rest in this self. Isn't this the real self?

The wisdom of Hinduism says no. The real self is something other: the atman, eternal and formless, in essence is none other than the Brahman. A famous dialogue in the Upanishads between a father and son emphasizes this point. The wise father, Uddalaka, instructs his son Svetaketu, who is conceited about his knowledge of the Vedas, but doesn't know the secret, inner truth. Uddalaka tells his son:

> "Place this salt in the water. In the morning come unto me."
> Then he did so.
> Then he said to him: "That salt you placed in the water last evening—please bring it hither."
> Then he grasped for it, but did not find it, as it was completely dissolved.
> "Please take a sip of it from this end," said he. "How is it?"
> "Salt."
> "Take a sip from the middle," said he. "How is it?"
> "Salt."
> "Take a sip from that end," said he. "How is it?"
> "Salt."
> "Set it aside. Then come unto me."
> He did so, saying, "It is always the same."
> Then he said to him: "Verily, indeed, my dear, you do not perceive Being here. Verily, indeed, it is here. That which is the finest essence—this whole world has that as its soul. That is Reality. That is Atman (Soul). That art thou, Svetaketu." (CHANDOGYA UPANISHAD 6.13.1–3)[12]

"That thou art"—this is one of the most fundamental statements of identity. "That"—the Brahman that is the essence of all—is the same as your own true self, the atman. That self is eternal, formless, pure consciousness. That real self is the birthright of all living beings, and knowing it means attaining supreme bliss.

This is the highest self. Yet the lower realities of the self are not unimportant. This real self, atman, is attached to the empirical self made up of physical, mental, and psychological aspects, and it is in this condition that we live out our countless existences. Hinduism teaches that the eternal atman is embodied according to the working of the law of karma. The actions the atman performs in one lifetime, depending on their moral quality, create the conditions for the next embodiment of the atman. "According as one acts, according as one conducts himself, so does he become. The doer of good becomes good. The doer of evil becomes evil" (Brihad-aranyaka Upanishad 4.4.5).[13] The law of karma works neutrally and inexorably metes out the results of one's actions, rebirth after rebirth. There are countless living beings—each one embodying an atman—and countless levels of rebirth, from those in the hells to plants, animals, humans, and gods. One's evil karma may bring rebirth at lower levels, even as an animal or plant; one's good karma may bring rebirth at a higher human level or even as a god.

This whole process is samsara, the rebirth cycle, which is beginningless and endless. Since, as we saw, there is an eternal Dharma that prescribes the role of all things, every atman within samsara at any given time has its own dharma and thus its own role to fulfill. The dharma prescribes duties according to sex, caste, and so forth—all this is considered part of the nature of reality and is the basis for the operation of karma. If I am born as a servant, that is the karmic result of my previous lifetimes. In accordance with my dharma as a servant, my actions in this lifetime as a good servant or a bad servant will cause the level of my next rebirth.

The God of the Abraham religions created the world and said, "It is very good." In the Hindu vision, the world, evolved from the primordial One or created as play by the great god, is really neither good nor evil but neutral. On the highest level, the ultimate goal is to

Hindu woman feeding a sacred cow. In Hindu thought, all life forms embody eternal sacred reality.

this one might seem attractive, Hindus know that another lifetime—and countless more after that—means more of the same pain and death endlessly. Not that everything about life is unhappy—far from it. The dharma of Hindu householders, for example, includes the duties of pleasure and accumulating wealth. Hindus do not have an unduly pessimistic view of life in the world. But the Hindu tradition does stress the relative, transient quality of life clearly: it is not the lasting, most authentic state of the soul. Seen in the eternal perspective, one searcher discovered, it really is nothing to rejoice about:

> Sir, in this ill-smelling, unsubstantial body, which is a conglomerate of bone, skin, muscle, marrow, flesh, semen, blood, mucus, tears, rheum, feces, urine, wind, bile, and phlegm, what is the good of enjoyment of desires? In this body, which is afflicted with desire, anger, covetousness, delusion, fear, despondency, envy, separation from the desirable, union with the undesirable, hunger, thirst, senility, death, disease, sorrow, and the like, what is the good of enjoyment of desires? . . . In this sort of cycle of existence (samsara) what is the good of enjoyment of desires, when after a man has fed on them there is seen repeatedly his return here to earth? Be pleased to deliver me. In this cycle of existence I am like a frog in a waterless well.   (MAITRI UPANISHAD 1.3–4)[14]

The very heart of the human problem, according to Hindus, is ignorance. I don't know who I really am. My true self really is the atman, eternal and identical with Brahman—but I think this living, breathing, thinking, feeling, desiring, socializing body and personality is who I really am. The philosopher Shankara provided an astute analysis of our human problem. We commonly view the world as changing, full of different realities, persons, and things. But this arises from *maya* (illusion, a word used in the Vedas for divine creative magic). Although there is one absolute Brahman, we in the process of maya superimpose false notions on Brahman, notions of separate individual realities and selves. This maya then blinds us so that we react to that illusion as if it is real, and so we live our lives as if we are individual egos in relation to all the separate things of the world. In a cryptic statement, one teacher of the

seek moksha, liberation from samsara altogether. But on another level, our role is to live the good life according to the Dharma, the eternal law of the world, promoting the welfare of all beings in the interrelated cycle of life.

Samsara and the Problem of Existence

Why do things seem not right? Why is there so much pain and suffering? What's wrong with my life? Whereas to outsiders the idea of living another lifetime after

Upanishads said,

> By the mind alone is It to be perceived.
> There is on earth no diversity.
> He gets death after death,
> Who perceives here seeming diversity.
> (BRIHAD-ARANYAKA UPANISHAD 4.4.19)[15]

If I am ignorant of the unity of the Brahman, that is, if I think of myself as different and see this world as made up of various things, I get "death after death," trapped endlessly in the rebirth and redeath of samsara. Why? Because out of ignorance arises desire, and from desire comes the impulse to selfish action (karma). The law of karma is such that actions performed out of desire have evil repercussions in the next lifetime, bringing a state of suffering and pain for the embodied atman.

Ignorance, desire, karma, rebirth—that is why there is suffering in the world, that is why life isn't what it should be. It is a vicious circle: "He becomes as he desires. By whatever fruit of actions he is made, that kind of action he performs. Whatever actions he does, that [kind of fruit, good or evil] he obtains. . . . 'He who desires [pleasures] comes again to this world to perform actions'" (Brihad-aranyaka Upanishad 4.4.5–6).[16] What one does now, out of ignorance and desire, creates conditions for one's next lifetime under which one will continue to act in ignorance and desire—a vicious circle that is likely to spiral downward. That is why the sages of India have generally regarded samsara as a trap of existence, with the ultimate goal being moksha, liberation from samsara.

But that final goal of moksha requires great spiritual knowledge and perfection, and so at best it is many lifetimes away for most people. And so we ought at least strive to live the good life, doing good deeds instead of evil, so that our karma will create the conditions of a higher rebirth or at least not a lower one. But even knowing that, we find it difficult to get away from selfish actions time after time, desiring other things, experiencing feelings of anxiety and regret when we lose something. How can one keep from despairing over being trapped in samsara? How can one keep ignorance and selfish desires from bringing ever lower rebirths? The Hindu answer is to get on the path of transformation, at the level appropriate to one's spiritual status.

THREE PATHS TO TRANSFORMATION AND LIBERATION

"How can I start living *real* life?" "How can I reach liberation?" At first glance the answers to this question given within the Hindu tradition seem almost countless. We find almost every conceivable religious pursuit being practiced by someone or other. One devotes herself to a particular god or goddess; another studies the Vedas and performs sacrifices; another goes on pilgrimages. Then there is another who is deeply skeptical of these practices and prefers speculation and philosophy. One tries to fulfill moral duties and works for the good of the community. Yet another abandons his family and community and wanders about, seemingly uninterested in society and even in the gods. It's a bit confusing! What is the path of transformation for Hindus?

Fortunately, Hindus have traditionally grouped these various ideas and practices into three basic paths (*marga*) of transformation: the path of knowledge (*jna-na-marga*), the path of action (*karma-marga*), and the path of devotion (*bhakti-marga*). These three are broad paths and intersect at many points. Typically a Hindu may be following practices associated with all three paths, and the emphasis may change at different points in a lifetime. But each path does have a special focus and structure, and depending on a person's particular spiritual level and progress attention is given more to one or the other of these paths.

The Path of Liberating Knowledge

The theoretical basis of the path of knowledge was first worked out in the Upanishads, although no doubt the roots of this path go back to more ancient times, perhaps even to the Indus Valley civilization. The focus is on self-realization through meditation. Some Hindus consider the path of knowledge to be the highest path toward transformation, because it is the one

Moksha, the Realization of the Real Atman

"Whoever thus knows 'I am Brahman!' becomes this All" (Brihad-aranyaka Upanishad, 1.4.10).[17] So the final goal is to "know" that I am the Brahman. This is what brings moksha, the final and unconditioned release from the bondage of karma and samsara.

We should not be deceived by the simplicity of this answer. Knowledge here is not a merely intellectual knowing but rather a deep, experiential realization of the ultimate ground as one's true self. It far transcends the intellect and the mind, which are aspects of the subtle self involved in the rebirth cycle. The intellect can assist in reaching this knowledge, but eventually even the intellect is transcended in the pure consciousness of the true atman. This knowledge is to be felt, experienced, and lived, knowledge that transforms one's whole being.

How is it that knowledge can be transforming and liberating? We need to recall that ignorance is the root of the human problem. Because I am ignorant of my real atman, I take my empirical self to be my real concern and the focus of my desires. I look upon the other things in this world as separate objects, and I perform action (karma) out of desire to enhance my self, perpetuating the cosmic process that keeps me tied to the samsara cycle. But if I know that my true self is indeed the Brahman, and that the Brahman includes within itself the entire universe, then there is nothing for me to desire for my "self," for I already am all. "If a person knew the soul (*Atman*), with the thought, 'I am he!,' with what desire, for love of what would he cling unto the body?" (Brihad-aranyaka Upanishad, 4.4.12).[18] Since this knowledge destroys all desires and thus all karma, there will be no more rebirths once this knowledge is fully and completely realized. When the body dies, the subtle self of mind and the vital breaths do not draw together around the self to lead to a new rebirth; the true atman is liberated. "Being very Brahman, he goes to Brahman" (Brihad-aranyaka Upanishad, 4.4.6).[19]

Moksha is described in various ways in the Hindu tradition. Sometimes it is pictured as a dissolving of the atman into the one Brahman. Just as a lump of salt dissolves when thrown into water, leaving no salt to grasp but making the water salty wherever one may taste it, so the atman becomes one with the Brahman. The individuality characterized by the empirical self—the physical body and the traits of mind and personality—comes to an end in the pure oneness of the Brahman. Moksha, however, is not annihilation or extermination of the atman; it is rather expansion, becoming all by transcending the limited self of mortal existence. It is pure bliss, peace, freedom, and joy. It is endless and unlimited.

Meditation and Yoga

To follow the path of knowledge and reach moksha requires a high level of spiritual perfection. Therefore the path of knowledge is necessarily an elite path, although it is beneficial even for those at lower spiritual levels to devote some attention to it. A person who really wants to follow the path of knowledge should take the prior steps of self-discipline and preparation by becoming a sannyasin, a renouncer. By cutting off all ties to this world, by giving up possessions, family links, and all worldly concerns, one will have the freedom necessary to devote oneself to attaining the knowledge that will liberate from samsara.

A most characteristic method practiced on the path of knowledge is meditation, for it is by looking inward that one finds the true self, the atman. Many types of meditation have been developed in India, but in general the process is to withdraw one's consciousness from the outer sensual reality and turn it inward, by stages, until all dualities and conditions dissolve and one experiences the pure, unified consciousness of the Brahman. The Mandukya Upanishad suggests a four-stage process, based on the mantra OM (in Sanskrit, AUM). OM is often used in meditation, for it is considered the sacred sound that encompasses all sounds and therefore fittingly symbolizes the Brahman. The letter A of AUM corresponds to the waking state, with consciousness turned outward. U corresponds to the dreaming state, with consciousness turned inward but still not unified. M symbolizes the deep-sleep state, which is a blissful, unified, massive consciousness—

but still not the final goal. The fourth state, experiencing the real atman, corresponds to the silence that precedes and follows the saying of the mantra AUM. This state is neither cognitive nor noncognitive, it is indescribable and unthinkable. It is the unified, tranquil, blissful experience of the atman as the Brahman. "He who knows this, with his self enters the Self—yea, he who knows this!" (Mandukya Upanished 12).[20] This universal self is eternal and changeless, and in knowing it as one's real self one transcends death and rebirth completely.

Many forms of meditation are commonly spoken of as yoga. We can see the process of reaching knowledge of the Brahman by considering the classical eight-stage yoga practice developed by the ancient sage Patanjali and followed also in the Vedanta school, for these eight stages illustrate the movement from external control to inner knowledge. The first five stages have to do with eliminating external causes of mental distraction. First

A yogin in meditation.

comes restraint, getting one's life in moral order by abstaining from violence and greed. Second is observance, laying the moral foundation of purity and dedication. External control is perfected in the third, fourth, and fifth stages. Posture involves the proper sitting position to transcend the body. Breath control helps the meditator draw closer to the essence of reality. And withdrawal of senses detaches the mind from the sense-organs so that all powers of consciousness can be focused inward on the source of being.

The final three stages complete the inner rise of pure consciousness. Concentration focuses the mind on a particular object of thought, and meditation stabilizes the mind in an uninterrupted state of contemplation. The final state, trance (*samadhi*), is the culminating experience in which the object of meditation vanishes and the mind swells to encompass a limitless reality. Plural things and plural souls are no longer recognized; there is only an infinite sense of absolute knowledge, a consciousness of absolute freedom and liberation.

By becoming a sannyasin and following the path of knowledge to these spiritual heights, ultimate transformation can be attained, according to Hinduism. One reaches moksha, the fullest type of existence, and, if that moksha is complete and perfect, when this lifetime ends there will be no more rebirth. Being the Brahman, one attains the Brahman.

The Path of Action

While it might be recognized that the path of knowledge is the path that leads finally to complete moksha, most of us are a long way from that kind of spiritual perfection. Whereas practices like meditation are beneficial, there are other religious pursuits that provide us the most help along the way. Since the human problematic has to do with desire and the resultant action (karma) that binds us in the rebirth cycle at ever lower levels, it makes sense to work toward the lessening of desire and the cultivation of actions that will move us upward in the rebirth cycle. To a great many Hindus, following the path of action (karma-marga) is what Hinduism is all about as a way of transformation.

We learned that karma (action) was the cause of the samsara cycle. How can karma be the basis of a path of transformation? Hindus point out that there are different kinds of karma. Many—probably most—of the actions we do result from desire, from wanting something for ourselves. Action done out of desire or passion produces a "hot" kind of karma that has adverse effects in the future. We become as we desire, the Upanishads teach. This karma will bring fear and anxiety into our lives. And a whole lifetime filled with actions done out of passion and desire will inevitably result in rebirth at lower levels.

But there is another kind of karma, that is, action done without desire, "cool" karma. This kind of karma produces effects, of course, but these are good and beneficial effects. This kind of karma brings peace to life, and it will result in rebirths at higher levels in the samsara cycle. With enough good karma one can even be reborn as a god—though this, of course, is not yet moksha. Eventually, after many lifetimes, a person will reach the level of spiritual perfection in which she or he can follow the path of knowledge and reach ultimate liberation.

So the crucial question is, how can I eliminate action rooted in desire and cultivate action done without desire? The classical Hindu answer is simply to do what is expected of me according to my dharma, my place and role in the eternal order of things. If my karma has caused me to be born as a warrior, I should go about my duty of protecting people, not out of desire or hope for reward, but simply because it's my dharma. If I'm a woman, I should be a good woman; if a slave, I should simply serve others without desiring to be something else. The whole system worked out in the Law-code of Manu, which we discuss later, provides guidance for the path of action: caste, sex, and stage of life make up the essential elements of my dharma, and by performing that role properly, without desiring some reward, I move forward on the path of transformation.

In a sense the path of action is a universal path for Hindus, for everyone is born into it, and most Hindus keep practicing it until the end of their lives. Only some world-renouncers and devotees of certain gods claim to transcend the laws of the Eternal Dharma. The path of action is a way of transformation through discipline, ritual, and morality. Performing one's duty without desire leads to the higher spiritual levels. The Bhagavad Gita teaches:

> He incurs no guilt if he has no hope,
> restrains his thought and himself,
> abandons possessions,
> and performs actions with his body only. . . .
> Always perform with detachment
> any action you must do;
> performing action with detachment,
> one achieves supreme good.
>
> (BHAGAVAD GITA 4.21; 3.19)[21]

The Path of Devotion

There is yet another way. Only few can attain the liberating freedom of the path of knowledge. The path of action does not promise liberation and poses many problems itself, as we see in the great epics where examples of people caught between duty and love abound. Arjuna grieves for his slain relatives and wishes to avoid his duty as a warrior. King Yudhishthira mourns the countless lives sacrificed in the great battles and wishes he could renounce the world. We all know what our duty is; yet desires, longings, and even what appear to be higher values constantly keep us from performing our duty in a completely unattached way. Is there no hope, no other way? Yes, there is: the path of bhakti (devotion).

How Can God Save Us?

Generally in the Hindu system of thought, the gods, though powerful and blessed, are understood to be within the cycle of samsara and therefore not ultimate. From ancient time in India various gods were worshiped for all kinds of benefits. And still today Hindus perform rituals of worship for various reasons, such as worshiping Sarasvati to attain learning and art, Ganesha for success in business, Lakshmi for wealth, and the like. But how can such gods provide salvation? How can they liberate us from the effects of our karma?

We saw earlier how two great theistic movements developed in Hinduism, one centered on Vishnu, the other on Shiva and Shakti, in each case looking on the great god or goddess as the personal sacred power of the universe. Unlike the descriptions of Brahman in the Upanishads, these great gods are personal and present; they pervade all reality, they are present within the soul, and they can be worshiped and loved. Since, according to devotees, Vishnu and Shiva-Shakti are supreme and in fact none other than the Brahman, they can be sources of saving power, not only bringing limited benefits but transforming us and liberating us from bondage to samsara. It is not only knowledge of the inner Brahman, realized by the spiritually elite, that brings liberation; God, the lover of my soul, to whom I can abandon myself no matter what my spiritual status, can help me to liberation.

Bhakti means to love and devote oneself to one's god, fully and completely. By such self-abandonment, all desires and wants and needs are turned to God rather than to the self. United with the great God of the universe who is also the inner soul of one's heart, one rises above the bondage of karma and finds joy, peace, and ecstasy in the power of the Beloved One.

The Vaishnavite Path of Bhakti

The transforming power of Vishnu can be experienced in different ways by his bhaktas (devotees), whether through his presence in the universe as creator, preserver, and destroyer, or through his avataras Rama and Krishna. The important factor is the love and self-surrender on the part of the worshiper. In the Bhagavad Gita, for example, Krishna emphasizes this self-surrender:

> Keep me in your mind and devotion,
> sacrifice to me, bow to me,
> discipline your self toward me,
> and you will reach me!   (BHAGAVAD GITA 9.34)[22]

Our bondage to the conditions of karma—whether high caste or slave, woman or man, pure or sinful—is overcome in the power of God's love. Since Vishnu transcends even the samsara cycle, in loving union with him we too can rise to salvation:

> Even in Brahma's cosmic realm
> worlds evolve in incessant cycles,
> but a man who reaches me
> suffers no rebirth, Arjuna.   (BHAGAVAD GITA 8.16)[23]

God is lovable and invites us to love him. The puranas fill out the story of Krishna in the interest of the path of bhakti. A demon king by the name of Kamsa, the story goes, had seized rule of Mathura, and his power threatened even the gods. In answer to their appeal, Vishnu tells of his plan to be born into the world as the eighth son of King Vasudeva and his wife Devaki. King Kamsa, learning of this plan, kills the first six children of Devaki. Her seventh son is an incarnation of Vishnu, Balarama, who is transferred to the womb of Vasudeva's second wife and thus saved. When Krishna is born as Devaki's eighth child, he is exchanged for the newborn daughter of the cowherd woman Yashoda—and thus Krishna and his brother Balarama grow up among the cowherd people of Vrindavana.

Yashoda and the other cowherd people are filled with wonderful joy and love through the presence of the beautiful baby, dark as the lovely blue lotus petal. His playfulness and mischief endear him to everyone—untying village calves, mocking his elders, teasing babies, stealing butter and sweets, playing tricks on the villagers, dancing and sporting with his brother Balarama and the village boys—all of this brings the love of God to the people. How joyful to love God as a baby, as a free and playful child! God is present in spontaneous, tumultuous power, at the same time approachable and adorable. In the child Krishna, we can see that God's very nature is to sport and play, inviting us to share in the divine self-delight.

Child Krishna grows up and becomes young man Krishna—still adorable and beautiful and playful, now irresistible to the gopis, as the young women among the cowherd people are called. When he goes out to the forest and plays his flute, the divine sound is too enticing to resist, and the women leave their chores, husbands, and families and come out to be near Krishna. Krishna dances and plays with all of them, multiplying his form so that each can experience his love. It is a festival of love, full of intoxication, joy, and abandon. One purana describes this great romance:

> Some of the cow herdesses . . . out of fun forcibly took away the flute from the hands of Lord Krishna. Then they pulled his yellow dress. Some passionate girl denuded

him of his clothes, took away his yellow garment and then in jest returned it to him. . . . Some danced and sang with Krishna in the centre; others forcibly caused him to dance. Krishna also out of fun, dragged the clothes of some milk-maid, made her naked and then returned the clothes to her.

The scene grows more tumultuous, and Krishna, surrounded by this group of impassioned gopis, makes love to them all, a celebration that even the gods assembled to watch.[24] Among the gopis, Krishna's favorite is Radha, and the stories delight in telling of the many facets of the love affair between the divine lover and his beloved. They are drawn to each other passionately, they grow jealous and quarrel and make up, they consummate their love in ecstasy and abandon and bliss. Krishna plays and delights himself, and Radha and the gopis are drawn into this divine delight. Here all duty and obligation are forgotten, and the gopis and Krishna are drawn together out of sheer divine passion and delight. Here, some say, is the highest form of loving God. We can love God as a father or mother, as a brother or friend, as a beautiful baby—but to love God as a lover means totally forgetting self and surrendering to the ecstasy of divine joy and delight. And that experience helps the devotee toward transformation and liberation.

A seventeenth-century temple hanging showing the gopis (cowherd women) searching for Krishna in the night.

The Shaivite Path of Transformation Through Bhakti

Shiva appears to be a very different god from Vishnu, yet his devotees likewise experience transformation and liberation in worshiping him. In Shiva, the creative and the destructive powers of the sacred are held closely together. Shiva is often portrayed as bringing fierce destruction because of his quick temper and outrageous behavior. Sexually attracted to Parvati, daughter of the mountains, he marries her but then practices asceticism and refuses to impregnate her. Parvati has a son Ganesha, born from the dirt she removed from her body while bathing. Ganesha guards the bathhouse, but one day Shiva forces his way in and, enraged that Ganesha tried to stop him, cuts off Ganesha's head with a mighty blow. Parvati's anger now threatens to destroy the world, so Shiva agrees to restore Ganesha's life, taking the head of the first living thing that came by—an elephant—and placing this on Ganesha's body. This is the origin of the extremely popular elephant-headed god Ganesha, worshiped as the bringer of prosperity and good fortune.

Shiva also is described in the stories as the creator and nourisher of existence. He made it possible, for example, for the heavenly Ganges River to descend gently over the Himalayas to water the earth, cushioning the river's descent with his own divine head. Another well-known story tells how the gods and the demons were churning the great milk ocean to obtain the nectar of immortality. They used the great serpent Vasuki as the churning rope and a great mountain as the churning rod, but after a thousand years of furious churning, a terrible poisonous venom began to gush from the thousand mouths of the serpent. Now the lives even of the gods were threatened, so Shiva agreed to accept the poison as if it were the nectar of immortality, saving the gods and all existence from destruction. His supreme power kept him from harm, although the venom left his throat a dark blue color, still seen on artistic representations.

A central story in the puranas is the conflict between Shiva and Kama, the god of desire. As the great ascetic, Shiva is the epitome of chastity; yet he is constantly driven by desire for Parvati. His male powers are evident in that his semen is the seed from which the whole universe arises; yet he retains his seed and refuses to give in to Kama's enticements. A famous passage describes how Shiva destroyed Kama by burning:

> Kama assumed the form of a very subtle creature and entered Shiva's heart. Then Shiva was heated by a desire for sexual pleasure, and he thought of Devi, and his perfection vanished. . . . Then he saw Kama in his heart, and he thought, "I will burn Kama out of my body by means of withdrawal from worldly objects. . . ." [Kama] shot the arrow of Delusion into Shiva's heart, and in anger Shiva burnt Kama to ashes with the fire from his third eye.[25]

With Kama destroyed, of course, all life and fertility is threatened, and the gods beg Shiva to restore Kama; finally in his desire for Parvati he brings about a revival of Kama.

Based on stories and perceptions like these about Shiva, those devoting themselves to him often involve themselves in yogic austerities and meditation. Worshipers of Shiva may smear ashes on their bodies and haunt cemeteries. They express a deep sense of guilt and pain in separation from Shiva, and they revel in the overpowering holiness of the presence of Shiva. Looking to Shiva as a "madman with moon-crowned hair," devotees transcend themselves in divine ecstasy:

> But me he filled in every limb
> With love's mad longing, and that I might climb there whence is no return,
> He showed his beauty, made me his. Ah me, when shall I go to him? . . .
> Thinking it right, sin's path I trod;
>   But, so that I such paths might leave,
> And find his grace, the dancing God,
>   Who far beyond our thought doth live,
> O wonder passing great!—to me his dancing shewed.
> Ah who could win that which the Father hath bestowed?[26]

Transformation Through the Great Goddess

The Great Goddess (Devi) likewise brings transformation to her devotees. The goddess is worshiped in many forms and localities for a variety of benefits, but there are some who single-mindedly devote themselves to her as a way of salvation. The many faces of the goddess—grace, cruelty, creation, destruction, love, indifference—express the endless energy active at the heart of the world. So worshiping her, through meditation, Tantric rituals, and ecstatic devotion, can bring liberation through her gracious power. Even the form of the ferocious goddess Kali is worshiped by some strongminded ones as the source of salvation. The great Bengali poet Ramprasad Sen (1718–1775) sang the praises of the great goddess—Devi, Durga, Kali—who plays, tortures him, deludes him, brings misery and death, but in the end there is "Grace and mercy in Her wild hair":

> I'm sweating like the slave of an evil spirit,
> Flat broke, a coolie working for nothing,
> A ditch digger, and my body eats the profits.
> Five Elements, Six Passions, Ten Senses—
> Count them—all scream for attention.
> They won't listen. I'm done for.
> A blind man clutches the cane he's lost
> Like a fanatic. So I clutch You, Mother,
> But with my bungled karma, can't hold on.
> Prasad cries out: Mother, cut this black snarl
> Of acts, cut through it. Let life, when death
> Closes down, shoot rejoicing up
> Out of my head like a rocket.[27]

The modern Hindu saint Ramakrishna (1836–1886) often sang to Durga-Kali in ecstatic trance, as in this example:

> Thy name, I have heard, O Consort of Shiva, is the destroyer of our fear,
> And so on Thee I cast my burden: Save me! Save me, O kindly Mother!
> Out of Thy womb the world is born, and Thou it is that dost pervade it. . . .
> Thou art the Primal Power, O Mother! She whose senses are controlled;
> The yogis meditate on Thee as Uma, great Himalaya's daughter.

> Thou who art the Power of Shiva! Put to death my ceaseless cravings;
> Grant that I never fall again into the ocean of this world.[28]

For such devotees, Kali grants the ultimate boon of unconditioned freedom and release from concern over the samsara world; in worshiping Kali one confronts death head on, giving oneself over to her play, singing and dancing with the abandon and ecstasy of liberation.

Ramakrishna not only followed the path of devotion but he brought it together with the path of knowledge. He practiced meditation, and his deepest trances came as he focused on his beloved Kali. Once again we remind ourselves that these three paths of liberation in Hinduism are not exclusive, and it is more than likely that any given Hindu will be following at least two of them at the same time. Within these three paths are possibilities for all people, no matter how high or low spiritually or socially, to move toward transformation and liberation.

DISCUSSION QUESTIONS

1. Outline several prominent Hindu views of ultimate reality.
2. What is meant by different levels of knowing Brahman as proposed, for example, by Shankara?
3. Sketch out some of the main theistic visions, especially those associated with Vishnu, Shiva, and the Great Goddess.
4. Explain the Hindu notion of great world cycles.
5. What is samsara, and how does the Hindu tradition view this condition of existence? What is moksha?
6. Explain the main purpose and process of each of the three major paths of transformation in Hinduism.

CHAPTER 15

HINDU WORSHIP AND THE GOOD LIFE

SACRED RITUALS AND TIMES OF HINDUISM

"How can I find new power for life?" "How can I get in touch with what is *real*?" The Hindu answer, at least for the great majority, is to worship—to participate in the exciting, colorful rituals and festivals so close to the heartbeat of Hinduism.

Some spiritually advanced Hindus, withdrawn from the world and approaching the goal of moksha, feel little need for worship of the gods and festivals. Other Hindus would say that everything they do, following the traditional law-codes of Dharma, is worship and piety. But most Hindus acknowledge that worship of the gods,

rituals and pilgrimages, festivals, and life-cycle ceremonies are important and spiritually beneficial. Religion is not so much something to theorize about or
even to believe; rather, it is a thing to be *done*.

Vedic Sacrifice and Worship of the Gods

One important observation to begin with is the centrality of the notions of pollution and purity in the Hindu
way of life. Interaction with the sacred powers is essential for human welfare and spiritual transformation; yet
the limiting conditions of human life often make that
interaction difficult or even dangerous. The highest
gods must be worshiped by brahmins who are in a pure
state; polluted by contact with people of lower castes,
for example, a brahmin cannot offer the Vedic sacrifices, and the whole community suffers. A woman who
is menstruating should not prepare food to be offered to
the gods. The ordinary biological processes of the body
are polluting, so morning devotions should be preceded
by a purifying bath. Rituals, ceremonies, and festivals
always begin with the people purifying themselves.

Offering Vedic Sacrifices

The rituals and sacrifices prescribed in the Vedas
enjoy great prestige, just as the Vedas themselves do. In
earlier times powerful and wealthy individuals hired
brahmin priests to perform great public sacrifices (*yaj-
na*), offering food and drink to the gods to strengthen
them and harness their powers for the welfare of the
world and of the people. Equally ancient is the domestic Vedic fire ritual called *agnihotra*, still today performed by pious Hindus twice daily. The man of the
household arises at dawn and purifies himself with
water. The household fire is worshiped as the god Agni,
offerings are made, and ancient prayers are chanted.
Raising his arms to the sun god, the man chants this
Vedic mantra:

> OM. Earth, Atmosphere, Sky.
> We meditate upon the glorious splendour of the vivifier
> divine.
> May he himself illumine our minds   (RG VEDA 3.62.10).[1]

This important ritual destroys the effect of bad deeds,
drives away darkness, and harmonizes one's life with
the spiritual force of the universe.

Today brahmin priests perform Vedic sacrifices for a
variety of purposes. For example, one might see Vedic
rituals in drought-stricken villages in rural India in the
scorching days of summer, the dry season. The ground
is dried up, water is rationed, food is running low, and
famine threatens the community. Government agencies are busy sinking deep wells in the drought-afflicted
region and bringing water in from elsewhere to avert
calamity until, they hope, the refreshing rains of the
monsoon season will finally come. But the people of
the village are most interested in the group of brahmin
priests who go from village to village, spending the
whole day chanting Sanskrit mantras from the Vedas
and offering fire sacrifice. They are the real "experts" in
this crisis, and the people hope and believe that the
sacred vibrations set loose in their chanting and their
sacrifice will bring rain and benefit to the struggling
community. By participating in these Vedic rituals,
humans share in the ongoing processes of creation and
recreation of the world, nourishing the various gods
and spiritual powers so that they will continue to support and uphold the world.

Puja: Celebrating the Powerful Presence of God

Whereas Vedic rituals are restricted to the higher
classes (brahmin, kshatriya and vaishya), there are no
such restrictions on puja, the acts of worship paid to a
god or goddess, usually in the presence of the divine
image at a temple or domestic shrine.

The image of the sacred being plays a central role in
most puja. The image is made by craftspeople according to the special iconographic tradition for that particular god, and then a ritual calls down the vitalizing
presence of the god into the image. All worshipers, of
course, know that the image is not the whole manifestation of the god. The god, especially if it is a form
of Vishnu or Shiva, pervades the whole universe, and
the image is simply one local center for the operation of
the sacred power. There are a great variety of images of
the gods and goddesses. A most common symbol of
Shiva is the lingam (phallic symbol) placed on the yoni
(female generative symbol). Another favorite image is
the Dancing Shiva. Vaishnavites favor the *shalagrama*,
a black stone with fossil ammonite, or Vishnu reclining

An eighteenth-century illustration of
Shiva puja, worshiping the lingam-yoni
image of Shiva.

the goddess or god, a ritual accompanied with intense feeling and emotion in the large temples. It is particularly by the ritual "seeing" of the goddess or god that the worshiper feels united with the divine power and energy. Another important ritual is the taking of *prasad*, sacred food. The food that was prepared to be offered to the god or goddess is also given to the worshipers. By eating the food that the goddess has "eaten," we are doing great honor to the goddess and sharing in her power. Puja, especially as done in temples and at festivals, is a joyful, emotional, and exciting event, transforming both the individual and the community. For many Hindus, puja is the central religious activity of their lives.

Festivals and Pilgrimages

The rhythms of sacred time in India come in daily, weekly, monthly, and yearly cycles. Sacred times also have regional emphases, although certain great festivals are celebrated all over India. The same is true of the important practice of pilgrimage to holy places, sacred rivers and mountains, and the like. These are usually set during sacred periods and provide a dramatic experience of sacred time and renewal.

Rituals and Festivals

Depending on individual inclination, and also on caste and family custom, Hindus practice a rich daily series of ceremonies. A pious person rises before sunrise to meditate on the qualities of his god, bathe, and offer puja before eating his morning meal. If he or she is a brahmin, the daily Vedic rite is to be performed twice during the day, at sunrise and sunset, purifying oneself with water, making offerings and reciting mantras to the fire god (Agni) and to the sun god. Orthodox householders of the upper classes perform the five great sacrifices daily: studying the Vedas, offering food offerings to the gods, offering water to the ancestors, giving food to brahmins and students, and offering food to all beings. In modern times many Hindus do not find time for all these rituals. But almost all Hindus observe the ceremonies of purification, bathing in flowing water or pouring water on oneself (never bathing in a closed container, which retains the pollutions). And the rituals of cooking, serving, and eating daily food are

on his serpent Sesha, or images of Rama or Krishna. Shaktas might focus on the ferocious image of Mother Kali. The image is carefully and lovingly attended to. Large temples have rituals of putting the god to bed at night, waking the image in the morning, dressing, feeding, and entertaining her or him like a great queen or king, and taking the image out for joyous processions.

Puja at a temple generally begins with purification, invoking the presence of the god, and greeting the god with respect. The goddess (or god) is honored with *kirtana*, which includes offerings of items such as garlands of flowers and clothing, pouring water on the image, marking the forehead of the goddess with sandal paste, circling the goddess with incense, waving lights, singing devotional songs, and playing auspicious music. It is of great spiritual benefit to hold one's hands over the fire that has been offered before the goddess, then to touch the hands to the forehead. The devotees are particularly intent on taking *darshana* (seeing) of carefully observed; the kitchen is the citadel of the household, maintained with ritual purity against intrusions of pollution from the outside. In many families the serving of food is really an act of puja; the food is encircled with drops of sacred water while a mantra is recited. Thus the food is first offered to the god and the family meal becomes a form of prasad, eating food offered to the god.

Many families also have a household shrine, perhaps located near to the pure kitchen area. Images of the gods of special importance to the family are kept there, and worship rituals are performed daily, at least by the devout.

Certain days of the week and of the month, such as the new moon and the full moon, are times for special ceremonies and celebrations. Most characteristic of Hinduism is the annual festival cycle; a typical village in north India, for example, has over forty ceremonial occasions based on the lunar calendar of the year. Hindu religious life passes through seasons with various festivals and fairs, depending on the caste and sectarian affiliation of the community involved. Gods and goddesses all have their special festival times and seasons, far too many to attempt to describe. Here are three brief examples.

One great festival time throughout much of India, coming at the end of the rainy season (September-October), celebrates the triumph of good over evil, remembering especially the goddess Durga's victory over the buffalo demon, Mahisha. In the Belur Math temple in Calcutta (famous because of Ramakrishna's vision of Kali there), for example, a huge statue of Durga is consecrated and dressed, and prayers and songs ask Durga to drive away evil and bless the good. There are gala processions and dancing with lights and music. Another emphasis during this fall festival time is the Ram-lila, celebrating the victory of Rama over the demon Ravana, acted out in dramatic fashion by actors representing the divine heroes and demons, followed by communal celebrations.

Divali, meaning "cluster of lights," comes in October-November and is one of the most festive times of the year. The central ritual is the lighting of row upon row of lamps all over, outside the house and on the roof, as many as possible, for lights symbolize prosper-

Lighting the oil lamps at Divali, the festival of lights.

ity. Lakshmi, the goddess of prosperity, is a main patroness of this festival, and she is invited to come inside the house to a temporary altar containing symbols of wealth—coins, ornaments, and shells. The people perform puja with sweets and milk, and these are then passed around the family as sacred food. It is a time of housecleaning and refurbishing, a general renewal of life. This festival is especially important to merchants, beginning the new business year.

Probably the most popular festival in north India is Holi, celebrated on the full moon at the beginning of spring (February-March). For days the anticipation of the festival grows as people roam the streets seeking wood and combustibles for the Holi fire—with the accepted rule that everyone must contribute something for the fire. The fire is associated with the story of Prahlada, a virtuous young man who persisted in worshiping Vishnu even though his wicked aunt Holika tried to burn him in the fire. Holika had been given the divine boon of indestructibility by fire, so she held Prahlada on her lap in the flames—but Rama intervened and the lad emerged unscathed, whereas the demoness Holika was destroyed. With the rising of the full moon the great fire flames up, and people of all castes circle it, throwing cakes of cow dung into the flames, shouting obscene phrases of vituperation toward the blaze representing Holika.

The great fire signals the beginning of "Holi play," representing the play of Krishna and Radha, and a carnival atmosphere rapidly develops. Boys run about dousing people with mud and cow dung water; staid women dump buckets of buffalo urine on men's heads; colored water is thrown around on everyone; erotic dances portraying passion and copulation take place; many people drink *bhang* (marijuana) mixed with sweetened milk; and every street reverberates with hymn singing and shouts of Holi joy. Holi is a time of license and frenzy, negating the tight structure and rules of ordinary society, providing a catharsis for highborn and low-born alike. Marriott offers this interpretation:

> The dramatic balancing of Holi—the world destruction and world renewal, the world pollution followed by world purification—occurs not only on the abstract level of structural principles, but also in the person of each participant. Under the tutelage of Krishna, each person plays and for the moment may experience the role of his opposite: the servile wife acts the domineering husband, and vice versa; the ravisher acts the ravished; the menial acts the master; the enemy acts the friend; the strictured youths act the rulers of the republic . . . Each may thereby learn to play his own routine roles afresh, surely with renewed understanding, possibly with greater grace, perhaps with a reciprocating love.[2]

Pilgrimages: Experiencing the Sacred Geography of Mother India

To be a Hindu is to live in India and celebrate the presence of sacred power at the various holy places. Some holy places are naturally beautiful or awe-inspiring sites; others commemorate the exploits of gods and saints—and often the two types coincide. Like people of other religions, Hindus find it very spiritually rewarding to make pilgrimages to these holy places. A pilgrimage is a passage from the ordinary world of daily life to the world of the sacred. The pilgrimage begins with rituals of separation: shaving the head, putting on special clothes, and physically leaving the familiar neighborhood for a perilous journey. The journey itself represents a liminal, in-between state when the ordinary structures of social life are lifted. People walk in groups with little attention to social status and caste. Hymn-singing, popular religious recitations, and sleeping in makeshift tents all contribute to the sense of crossing the threshold from the profane to the sacred. At the pilgrimage center the pilgrims appropriate the sacred power through rituals and through the very fact of being there, taking *darshana* (seeing) of the sacred place with its temples and images.

All over India there are thousands of these sacred places, some visited regularly, some only at certain times—the famous Kumbha Mela festival in Allahabad, for example, is held only once every twelve years, when it attracts millions of pilgrims. Among the sacred places known as Dhamas (abodes of god) are Mt. Kailasa high in the Himalayas, the celestial abode of Shiva and Parvati; and Puri, on a beach on the Bay of Bengal, the abode of Krishna as Jagannath (Lord of the World). The great car festival at Puri commemorates Krishna's journey to Mathura to slay wicked Kamsa. To have *darshana* of the great image on the chariot (a chariot some forty-five feet high and supported by sixteen wheels each seven feet in diameter) provides great power for salvation.

There are also many sacred cities for pilgrims, the most sacred perhaps being Banaras (Kashi), the City of Light. Banaras is especially holy as the residence of Shiva and Parvati, but Vishnu and almost all the gods and goddesses are also present within the circle of this city. And the River Ganges flows through the city. Mother Ganga, the River of Heaven, agreed to flow on earth for the restoring of human life; Shiva caught the Ganges in his hair as she fell so the earth would not be shattered by her torrential force. Coming to Banaras, taking *darshana* of the sacred places of Shiva, Vishnu, and the other gods and goddesses, and bathing in the waters of Mother Ganga provide great blessing, the salvation of the dead, and the purification of the living. Another of the sacred cities is Mathura, loved by millions of Hindus as the birthplace of Krishna.

Rituals of the Passages of Life

The critical changes in life, such as birth, puberty, marriage, and death, are times when special rituals are needed to bring blessing and renewal. For this purpose Hindus have a series of *samskaras*, rituals of the rounds of life, focused on the individual's life changes but involving the community as well. For spiritual advancement there are also rituals of yoga, meditation, and even renouncing the world.

Samskaras: Rituals of the Life Cycle

Among the many prebirth rituals, some Hindus observe a "male-producing rite" and a rite for a healthy pregnancy called the "parting of the hair": the husband parts his wife's hair and applies a mark of red cosmetic powder as protection from malevolent spirits. About ten days after birth comes the important naming rite, and at about three years there is the first haircut, leaving only the sacred tuft, which some high-caste Hindus do not cut for the rest of their lives.

The great event for Hindu boyhood (for males of the upper "twice-born" classes) is the *upanayana* (initiation) ceremony. Usually performed when the boy is between eight and twelve, the initiation ceremony is the ritual introduction of the boy to his Vedic teacher (guru), who drapes the sacred thread over the boy's shoulder and chest, to be worn thereafter as the mark of a twice-born Hindu. The boy is now qualified to begin study of the Vedas, having died to the world of childhood and been reborn to the realm of responsibility. The initiation ritual is a joyous family and communal affair.

Another climactic family and communal celebration is marriage (*vivaha*), consisting of a series of rituals symbolizing this important passage of life. The wedding ceremony has the same kind of importance in a young girl's life as a young boy's initiation into the student stage. Parents arrange a suitable match and solemnize it with a betrothal. On the wedding day, chosen with the help of an astrologist, the bridegroom and relatives go to the bride's house, where brahmin priests conduct the special wedding rituals. Holding the bride's hand before the sacred fire, the groom says, "I seize thy hand for the sake of happiness, that thou mayest live to old age with me, thy husband.... The Heaven I, the Earth thou. Come let us marry." The bride places her foot on a stone to symbolize firmness, and the ends of their garments are knotted together. The most binding part of the ceremony is the seven steps, during which the husband says, "May you take

Elaborate rituals in the Hindu wedding ceremony.

one step for sap, second step for juice (or vigor), third step for the thriving of wealth, fourth step for comfort, fifth step for offspring, sixth step for seasons, may you be my friend with your seventh step!"[3] The husband touches his bride over the heart and paints the vermillion cosmetic mark on her forehead. In the evening they go out under the sky to look at the unchanging Pole Star, a symbol of faithfulness in their marriage.

After a person dies, he or she is washed and freshly clothed. Then quickly relatives and friends form a procession with the body to the cremation grounds, led by the eldest son of the deceased. The body is placed on a pyre of wood and the son sets it aflame with an ancient prayer to Agni to convey the soul to the place of the ancestors. The mourners recite verses urging the dead person to join the ancestral spirits, leaving sin behind and avoiding the dogs of Yama. After the cremation the mourners depart without turning around and take a purifying bath before entering their homes. Three days later is the bone-gathering ritual, and the eldest son will take them to the River Ganges or some other water symbolic of the Ganges. The final rituals are the shraddhas, the offering of balls of rice and water together with the recitation of sacred verses, nourishing the departed on the journey to the realm of ancestors. These rituals continue monthly for a year, and then are observed annually thereafter.

Rituals of Spiritual Transformation

For some few who have reached a high spiritual level of perfection, an important ritual of spiritual passage is the act of becoming a sannyasin, the fourth and final stage of life in the traditional system, the dramatic spiritual break that comes when a person decides it is time to renounce the world. He gives away all his possessions and performs his own funeral rituals, shaves his head, clips his nails, and takes a purifying bath. Performing his householder rites for the last time, he bids farewell to his family and walks away without looking back—never to mention or think of his family and village again. Now he lives as a wandering beggar, roving about freely. To help reach final perfection, the sannyasin may take a guru who gives him the final initiation, tearing off the sacred thread and cutting the tuft of hair—no longer is he bound by rules of caste or duties of social position. Now his one duty is to seek liberation.

The renouncer practices many rituals of meditation and yoga to work toward final liberation. But many Hindus who remain in society also practice these yogic rituals of self-transformation. These are generally individual rituals, often performed under the guidance of a guru, designed to master one's physiological system and tap into the deeper spiritual resources. The rituals are varied, including bodily posture and breath control, ritual chanting of mantras, sitting within a circle of fire, and much more.

Sacred Art in Hinduism

As in other traditional cultures, so also in Hinduism nearly all art is religious to some extent. The monistic vision of Hinduism means that the sacred is present in everything, so the function of art is to help us "see" the sacred. Hinduism is a strongly visual and sensuous religion. The sacred is present in this world and thus all the senses can be means of experiencing it. We see the sacred in the image, we touch the sacred by feeling the image, we hear the sacred sounds, we taste the sacred in the prasad and liquid offerings, and we smell the sacred by means of flowers and incense. Hindu religion is the cultivation of *aesthesis*, "perceiving" the sacred through sensuous forms.

The literary arts have been central in Hinduism since the ancient Sanskrit poems of the Vedas, and the art of chanting the sacred sounds is still important. The epics and mythic literature have been a vast artistic treasury from which Hindu artists have drawn their inspiration for many centuries. The literary art has continued especially in the poems and hymns of the God-intoxicated poets and saints who practiced bhakti.

Very characteristic of Hindu art is the sculpture or painting of the gods and goddesses. The creation of an image is an act of religious discipline or yoga on the part of the artist. The artist must see into the divine so that he or she can present the sacred in visual form, that others can take *darshana*—see and experience the sacred presence. A most popular artistic creation is the

Ten-armed Ganesha image, from the eighth century.

image of Vishnu as he lies sleeping on his cosmic serpent in the period prior to the creation of the world for the new world cycle. The artistic portrayal represents the endless cycle of the worlds, inhaled and exhaled as it were by Vishnu, who is represented as relaxed and serene, the eternal sacred reality. Another well-known image is the Dancing Shiva, portraying the great god simultaneously dancing out the destruction and the creation of the universe. Such artistic images, in countless forms throughout India, present the divine realities for us to "see," without words of explanation. Fiercely ascetic and terrifying images of Shiva and Kali, voluptuous and colorful paintings of Krishna's romances with Radha or of the great goddess in one of her many forms—there is no limitation on presenting the sacred through images in Hinduism.

Another important art form for Hindus is dance drama, in which the actors pattern their movements on the gestures and movements of the gods and goddesses. In the great religious festivals, they perform the lila (play) of the gods to the audience in tangible form, identifying with the divine models they portray. Through this artistic creation the audience is able to experience *rasa*, the flavor of sacred presence within our human world.

A very characteristic Hindu art form is the temple, the sacred architecture that fixes the sacred centers of the world, functioning as earthly dwellings of the gods and goddesses. Hindu temples are designed on the model of the square, reflecting the final perfection and order of divine space in contrast to the temporary, changing earthly spaces. A typical temple has a holy center or *garbha* (womb), which houses the image from which power radiates. The rest of the temple surrounds that center just as the human body surrounds the inner soul or atman. Many temples have great towers, representing a cosmic mountain to which one might ascend to the presence of the sacred. Other temples lead the worshiper into the depths, to the womb or navel of the cosmos from which the god sends out sacred power.

SOCIETY AND ETHICAL LIFE

"How should I live?" When one says she is Hindu, this means she belongs to Hindu society by birth, finding her place in that complicated, unchanging structure of society that all Hindus instinctively understand. So important is the Hindu societal system that it was long believed one could not really be a Hindu outside India—that is, outside traditional Hindu society. It is within this society that one finds one's place and knows how to live the good life.

The Structure of Hindu Society

Well known throughout the world is the unique Hindu social structure, the so-called caste system. It is certainly one of the distinguishing marks of Hinduism, rooted in the ancient scriptures and made prolific during the Middle Ages. Though caste discrimination is officially outlawed in modern times, for many Hindus this system still is a powerful and stable structure in their lives.

Origins and Development of the Class System

Whereas the caste system is well known throughout the world, it is often misunderstood. What is sometimes simply called the "caste system" is really made up of two social structures merged together: the *varna* (color) class divisions and the *jati* (birth) caste divisions. There are only four (or five) classes (varnas), but over two thousand castes (jatis) in Hindu society. Let us look first at the traditional class system.

As we noted earlier, one reason Hindu social structure is so highly respected and remains unchanged is that its origin is in the eternal Dharma, the order of the world. The four classes, into which all people enter according to their birth, are defined in terms of their religious and social duties.

The brahmins are the highest varna; their duty is primarily to study and teach Vedic learning and preside over the important rituals and sacrifices. The traditional duty of the kshatriya (warrior) varna is the protection of the people and the administration of a beneficial government. Today in India the Rajputs, for example, represent this class. The vaishya (producer) varna is to provide for the economic needs of the community. Today vaishyas are mainly businesspeople. These three upper classes are "twice-born" in that boys go through the initiation ceremony and receive the sacred thread. Thus all three classes are expected to study the Vedas.

The lowest class is the shudra varna, the menials, whose one profession is to serve the upper three. They are often domestic servants, doing work that is forbidden for the other classes. They cannot hear or study the Vedas, but they are permitted to participate in the path of bhakti. Hindu tradition places a fifth class below these four classes, called the untouchables or outcastes, people without varna. These people generally are to live outside the boundaries of cities and perform extremely polluting activities. Untouchables have to avoid contact with people of higher castes lest they pollute them; their occupations include fishermen, hunters, leatherworkers, sweepers, handlers of dead bodies, and the like.

The Structure of Castes (Jati)

Another social structure is superimposed on the class system to make up the characteristic subdivisions within Hindu society. This is the jati (birth) system of castes, subdivided into at least two thousands jatis, some very large, others little more than a group of families in a village. Each jati by tradition belongs to one of the four classes or the untouchable class. A jati is usually characterized by three restrictions on its members: endogamy, commensality, and occupational exclusivity. A jati is always endogamous, that is, one is permitted to marry only within one's own jati—a rule that still today is very widely observed throughout traditional Hindu society. Commensality means eating only with others of one's caste. And these castes are usually occupational groups, following a particular calling that has been handed down over the generations within the families that make up the caste.

One of the primary religious concerns in daily life is to maintain ritual purity, especially for the higher castes, otherwise they cannot perform their religious duties. There are complex rules about contacts between the castes, and settlement patterns are set up to minimize such contacts. When contact must be made, as at a village council meeting, seating is arranged so that the higher castes are elevated and distant from the lower castes.

All this seems very complicated. But Hindus know exactly where they belong in the caste system, and moreover they know how the castes are to be ranked and how people of each caste relate to the other castes. Each of the varna classes contains a large number of castes. There are perhaps hundreds of brahmin castes, for example, engaged in various occupations, and they rank each other, giving rise to the saying that where there are seven brahmins there will be seven cooking fires, each one believing himself or herself higher in the caste system and thus refusing to eat with someone lower.

For all its negative features, especially for the lower castes and the untouchables, the caste system provides a strong sense of security and identity. People know for sure where they belong. Their caste gives them a definite place in society, protects them, and makes it unnecessary for them to compete for higher places. It is accepted that they belong to their caste because of past karma, and therefore there is no reason to be bitter about their lot or to envy others.

Religious Leaders in Hinduism

Even though many brahmins pursue occupations other than being priests, the brahmin class is highly honored. Those brahmins who become priests have an important function for all in Hindu society, according to the Vedas. Even though some classes and castes cannot hear the Vedas or participate in Vedic rituals, the chanting of the Vedas and the performing of the rituals brings benefit across the board, maintaining the order of the world and society. Some brahmin priests are household priests, that is, they perform rituals and important ceremonies for various families. Other brahmins are temple priests, making their services available for the rituals and festivals centered in the temple for the benefit of the community. Another important function for learned brahmins is in teaching the Vedas.

Religious leaders in Hinduism include many other holy men and women who pursue the higher path of knowledge and who teach others in the many ashrams (retreats) scattered throughout India. The guru or learned person is one who has come to have deep insight into the truth and perhaps has attained a high level of spiritual realization, sometimes even recognized as God-realized or as an incarnation of one of the great gods. The widely revered saint Ramakrishna was one such spiritual master. Sri Aurobindo, a modern religious thinker, also founded an ashram for the study of yoga. In general there is high respect for those holy men and women who leave the world to advance their own spirituality and seek enlightenment. Even if they are simple wanderers seemingly doing nothing of benefit for the rest of society, they are supplying a continuous model and reminder of the high path toward moksha (liberation).

Living According to the Dharma

"How should I live?" Hinduism is suited for people with different temperaments and spiritual abilities; there is a place for everyone, with appropriate duties and ethical requirements. The ethical life is based on the major principles of Hindu society, namely, the class system (*varnas*), the four stages of life (*ashramas*), and the four aims of human life (*purusharthas*). The ethical life based on this pattern is spelled out in the classical writings and commentaries called *Dharma Sutras* and *Dharma Shastras*, the best known of which is the Law-code of Manu. Further, both the Mahabharata and the Ramayana Epics provide a broad and deep foundation for living out these Hindu ethical values.

The Centrality of Dharma for Hindu Ethics

The concept of Dharma, as discussed above, is central to the Hindu understanding of society. Dharma comprises comprehensive precepts having to do with the material sustenance and the spiritual welfare of human society and of the individual.

The Dharma includes universal ethical values that apply to everyone. For example, there are certain acts forbidden to everyone, such as disrespect for one's parents. And there are obligations that are common to all by reason of the human status, such as the obligation to act nonviolently. The Srimad Bhagavatam states, "Avoidance of injury to all beings, love of truthfulness and chastity, abhorrence of stealing, refraining from

anger and greed, striving to be of service to all beings—these are the universal duties of all castes."[4]

But for our human life the Dharma touches most concretely where we live and work in society, as it organizes our life through well-defined social classes and through stages of individual life. In its narrow sense, Hindu tradition has often equated the Dharma with *varna-ashrama-dharma*, that is, the ordained duties (*dharma*) of the four classes and the four stages of life. Our discussion of Hindu ethics can focus on this center field of the Hindu sense of the good life.

Ethical Life Based on the Classes and Castes

How should I live? The first answer is very direct: one should live in the way expected of one in the particular class and caste. The Law-code of Manu spells out in detail the duties of the four traditional classes. The duty of living according to one's class (varna) is commonly extended to include also the obligations, requirements, and prescriptions that belong to the particular occupational caste (jati) into which a person was born. The good life means abiding by the rules of one's caste about marriage, dining, occupation, and clothing. It means above all to avoid polluting the purity of one's caste and of the larger community by wrongful contact with those of other castes.

The ethical vision expressed in the caste system is widely misunderstood by non-Hindus. A chief ingredient in this system is the idea of maintaining caste purity, and it is true that this purity has a hierarchical order, for one brings pollution on his own caste by contact with someone of a lower caste. But it is important to understand that purity is a vital possession of the whole community, not just of one caste. Brahmins do have a special responsibility for maintaining the purity of the community because they study and teach the Vedas and perform the Vedic rituals—an activity of extreme importance for the whole society—and they cannot perform this service if they are polluted by contact with lower castes. But the purity of the community is also maintained by the people of lower jatis, such as the shudras and untouchables who wash clothes, cut hair, carry away garbage, and remove dead animals. The whole community is diminished by a breakdown of purity in its midst, but likewise the whole community is enriched by the purity, solidarity, cooperation, and contribution structured through the traditional caste system.

It is widely recognized by modern Hindu leaders that aspects of the caste system, such as the obligation to engage in the occupation of one's father or the practice of untouchability—seem to be in conflict with the basic Hindu ethical vision. Modern Indian law does not permit discrimination on the basis of caste, and untouchables are permitted to enter temples, sit in movie theatres, and eat in public restaurants. Gandhi took particular care for the untouchables in his movement to reform India, calling them Harijans (children of God) and himself engaging in unclean jobs reserved for the untouchables. Today efforts are being made to help those of the lower castes to improve their lot in modern society. But the Hindu ethical system remains based on the fundamental truth that one's birth is not an accident. It was determined by karmic causes from one's past existences in the samsara cycle. I am where I belong. Therefore the good and noble life consists of living according to my dharma, following the life prescribed for me by my caste.

This is not to say that life is completely free of ethical conflicts. The Mahabharata Epic contains the famous story of King Yudhishthira, who feels bitter inner conflict over his duty as a warrior-king and his higher vision of nonviolence and detachment. Yudhishthira wants to withdraw from life in the world and become a forest-dweller, for he knows that if he continues to live in the world as king he will have to inflict violence and pain on others. But King Yudhishthira did fulfill his duty, encouraged to do so by none other than Lord Krishna, waiting until he had grown old before he finally abandoned the world. So Hindus persist in the duties assigned by birth, knowing that the path of liberation ultimately leads beyond duties of class and caste.

The Four Stages of Life

Another key to living the good life is to be observant of the duties and opportunities incumbent in the different stages of life. Hinduism recognizes that the principles that bring a healthy and fulfilled human life change throughout the course of a lifetime, and thus the Dharma scriptures put forth the ideal of four stages of life, at least for males of the higher three classes. In the traditional system, the shudra and untouchable classes do not participate in the movement through different stages of life. Women also did not traditionally move through these stages in a direct way, at least not the student stage. But women certainly share in these stages insofar as they are related to the males in their families. The four stages of life are the stages of student, householder, forest-dweller, and renouncer (sannyasin).

The first stage of life is that of being a student, with the obligations of studying the Vedas, cultivating respect for one's teacher, developing self-control, and learning to be a contributing member of Hindu society. Brahmin boys of eight years of age, and kshatriya and vaishya boys of eleven or twelve, are to begin their student life with the ritual of initiation, after which traditionally they go to study with their teachers. In past times, girls were educated in the home to be wife, mother, and homemaker. The student stage is a rigorous way of life, learning rituals, values, duties, and patterns of behavior. The student is to remain celibate, ritually pure, begging for food, and acting as personal servant to the teacher.

Upon completing the period of being a student, the person moves on to the stage of householder, the keystone of Hindu life and society and an essential stage of personal spiritual development. Some few, it is true, seem spiritually prepared to omit this householder stage and pass immediately to the ascetic rigors of the renouncer stage of life, close to final liberation. But for almost all people, the householder stage is necessary and beneficial. During this major period of one's life, Hindu ethics require a happy, productive, ritually observant way of life. People should marry and raise children to continue the line. As householders they perform the proper sacrifices and rituals, maintain a ritually pure home, and engage in economic and political activity.

In the householder stage the woman's role, according to the Dharma scriptures, is significantly different from the man's role. The wife is subject to the husband

and should serve him, not presuming to eat, for example, until after he is finished. At the same time, the husband is required to honor his wife and protect her. The Law-code of Manu states,

> Women must be honored and adorned by their fathers, brothers, husbands, and brothers-in-law who desire great good fortune. . . .
>
> Her father protects her in childhood, her husband protects her in youth, her sons protect her in old age—a woman does not deserve independence.
>
> The father who does not give away his daughter in marriage at the proper time is censurable; censurable is the husband who does not approach his wife in due season; and after the husband is dead, the son, verily, is censurable, who does not protect his mother. . . .
>
> The husband should engage his wife in the collection and expenditure of his wealth, in cleanliness, in dharma [religious rituals], in cooking food for the family, and in looking after the necessities of the household. . . .
>
> Women destined to bear children, enjoying great good fortune, deserving of worship, the resplendent lights of homes on the one hand and divinities of good luck who reside in the houses on the other—between these there is no difference whatsoever.[5]

Deserving no independence and serving her family, on the one hand, and being honored as a goddess on the other—these are the two sides of the woman's role in traditional Hinduism. The pressure for offspring and for marrying daughters led to marriages involving child-brides. And the notion of self-sacrifice for one's husband sometimes led to the practice of young widows immolating themselves on the funeral pyres of their husbands—becoming thereby *sati* (sometimes called *suttee* in Western languages), a true woman who sacrifices bodily existence for the higher spiritual duty. Modern reforms have put a stop to these practices.

"When a householder sees his skin wrinkled and his hair gray and when he sees the son of his son, then he should resort to the forest."[6] Having reached the end of the productive householder stage, one should go into spiritual retirement and become a "forest-dweller." That is, a man together with his wife retire to a forest retreat (ashram), or at least to quiet quarters within the family residence, to devote themselves to self-discipline, study, and meditation. The responsibilities

of home management and business are turned over to the children, though the retirees may still be available for consultation. Abstaining from sex is recommended for this stage, as the withdrawal from householder life becomes more and more complete.

The final stage of life is that of the sannyasin, the "renouncer" who breaks all ties to enter the last part of the path toward liberation. "Having thus passed the third part of his life in the forest, he should renounce all attachments to worldly objects and become an ascetic during the fourth part of his life. . . . He should always wander alone, without any companion, in order to achieve spiritual perfection."[7] Those few who reach this stage of spiritual perfection have dissolved all sense of selfish needs and desires, and therefore, although not involved in society, they demonstrate the highest ethical values as a model for all others.

> He will patiently bear with hard words, despising none, nor out of attachment to the body will he bear enmity to anyone. To one who is angry with him he will not show anger in return, and him that curses him he will bless, nor will he utter any untrue word. . . . By curbing the senses, by destroying affection and hatred, by doing no harm to any living thing, he will conform himself to deathlessness.[8]

Most people will not reach the stage of sannyasin in this existence, but having that model before our eyes helps us to live out our own roles in the proper ethical perspective.

The Four Aims of Human Life

Hindus have traditionally summed up the vision of the good life by speaking of the four aims of human life (*purushartha*). These four good values of life that we should seek after are Dharma, material prosperity (*artha*), pleasure (*kama*), and liberation (*moksha*). This is a well-balanced ethical structure, verified by centuries of experience, designed to balance the concern for good life and happiness with the concern for spiritual development and liberation.

Of course, the balance of these four aims of life differ depending on one's particular stage of life. Fulfilling the Dharma is something that should always be central, for this is the key to how the individual's life in its different stages fits into the total order of reality. Seeking material prosperity is especially important at the householder stage, for involvement in business and politics is the foundation on which the whole society rests. Likewise, seeking pleasure and happiness is most directly appropriate at the householder stage, for without sexual pleasure and physical happiness the life of the family could not go on. Liberation (*moksha*) is understood to be the spiritual goal throughout one's life, but it becomes a more central concern in the forest-dweller stage of retirement, and one who reaches the *sannyasin* stage makes it his total and exclusive concern.

The Hindu Vision for Society and the World

It is sometimes said that Hinduism has no concern for the betterment of society, since it places so much stress on withdrawal from the world of senses and on individual meditation and pursuit of liberation. And it is true that Hinduism never developed the notion of having a mission to the whole world in the sense of spreading Hinduism to all. Yet the Hindu tradition does in its own way display deep concern for the welfare of the whole social order, and some modern Hindus have utilized those resources to improve the lot of all in society. The Hindu values of peace and nonviolence have made an impact on the whole world, and in modern times some Hindu thinkers have taken up the mission of transmitting the spiritual wisdom of India to the rest of humankind.

Toward the Betterment of Human Society

One perspective sees all life caught up in endless cycles of samsara, each lifetime determined by the karma of preceding ones, with the final goal being liberation from the whole cycle. This is the perspective of moksha. But another perspective complements this one, the perspective of Dharma. This present order has its own value and importance, and to maintain and promote the Dharma of this world is to enhance the welfare of all beings.

This is why the householder stage is so central, for the proper fulfilment of this role contributes significantly to the preservation and happiness of the whole

Worshipers strain to pull huge chariots with Lord Jagganath, Lord of the Universe, during a popular annual festival.

community. The fact that one of the four aims of life is material success (*artha*), involvement in the economic and political life of the society, shows that working toward the general welfare of all is a central Hindu concern. In fact, all the basic values and duties, such as respect for parents and maintenance of caste purity, prevent social breakdown and corruption and thus work toward the welfare of the whole society.

A major theme of the Hindu ethical tradition is compassion toward others, doing good for the benefit of others. The Mahabharata teaches,

> He succeeds in obtaining happiness who practises abstention from injuring (others), truthfulness of speech, honesty towards all creatures, and forgiveness, and who is never heedless. Hence one exercising one's intelligence should dispose one's mind after training it to peace towards all creatures. That man who regards the practice of the virtues enumerated above as the highest duty, as conducive to the happiness of all creatures, and as destructive of all kinds of sorrow, is possessed of the highest knowledge and succeeds in obtaining happiness.[9]

In modern times reform movements have drawn on the spirit of the Hindu tradition to better society by doing away with some evils that had developed within the tradition, such as child marriage, widows burning themselves, and the cruel lot of the untouchables. Mahatma Gandhi worked tirelessly against the evil of untouchability. He thought the class system, however, could still be the structure of society, for the classes are duties, not privileges, and those of the higher classes are more responsibile for the welfare of all. The hallmarks of Gandhi's ethical vision are simplicity, austerity, and nonviolence, and he felt these values could create the good life not only for Indian society but for other societies as well:

> There are two aspects of Hinduism. There is, on the one hand, the historical Hinduism with its Untouchability, superstitious worship of stocks and stones, animal sacrifices and so on. On the other, we have the Hinduism of the *Gita*, the *Upanishads*, and Patanjali's *Yoga Sutras*, which is the acme of *Ahimsa* [nonviolence] and oneness of all creation, pure worship of one immanent, formless, imperishable God. *Ahimsa*, which for me is the chief glory of Hinduism, has been sought to be explained away by our people as being meant for the *sannyasi* only. I do not think so. I hold that it is *the* way of life and India has to show it to the world.[10]

The possibility of reconciliation and peace through nonviolent means and through spiritual discipline and practice, as demonstrated by Gandhi and many others like him, has made a powerful impression on people of other cultures who are searching for a way to reverse the escalation of violence and materialism in the world.

Hinduism's Message for the World

Hinduism is not a missionary religion. It is fundamental to Hinduism to believe that there are many spiritual paths, appropriate to different peoples depending on their own past karma and spiritual perfection, and the idea of converting others to Hinduism does not fit with this. Yet Hindus do believe that the Vedas, as the Eternal Wisdom, present the truth in an ultimate way not found in any other religious path.

In modern times, under pressure from other religions like Islam and Christianity, some Hindu thinkers have attempted to reassert the primacy of Vedic Hinduism. For example, Dayananda Sarasvati, founder of the Arya Samaj, not only rejected many aspects of Hindu-

ism that he felt conflicted with the Vedas but also took an aggressive and militant approach to other religions. He argued that Christian belief was logically inconsistent and that the Quran presents a God unworthy of worship. Some members of this group engaged in attempts to gain Hindu converts from among Muslims.

On the other hand, other modern thinkers, like Sarvepalli Radhakrishnan, have responded to the challenge of Christianity and other religions by seeking out the universalist aspects of these religions that would be in keeping with the Vedantic teachings. Radhakrishnan argued that whereas Hinduism is the ultimate truth of religion, it is a truth that can be universally accepted by all. He brought his Hindu philosophy to the West through lectures and books, teaching that each religion is valid to the degree that it helps its followers achieve spiritual realization:

> If the Hindu chants the Vedas on the banks of the Ganges, if the Chinese meditates on the Analects, if the Japanese worships on the image of the Buddha, if the European is convinced of Christ's mediatorship, if the Arab reads the Quran in his mosque, and if the African bows down to a fetish, each one of them has exactly the same reason for his particular confidence. Each form of faith appeals in precisely the same way to the inner certitude and devotion of its followers. It is their deepest apprehension of God and God's fullest revelation to them. The claim of any religion to validity is the fact that only through it have its followers become what they are.[11]

Some Hindu groups today, such as the International Society for Krishna Consciousness, take the stance that Hinduism is the exclusive highest truth, and they bring it to the West as part of their commitment to this truth. Other modern Hindu thinkers follow the tradition that truth is found in many paths.. Convinced that Hinduism still is the highest of these many paths, many Hindus do feel a responsibility to help peoples in the rest of the world to become acquainted with the ancient wisdom, come to understand it, and incorporate its basic truths into their lives also. The world society will become enriched, they feel, more spiritual, and more peaceful if the perspective of Hinduism is better understood and appreciated.

DISCUSSION QUESTIONS

1. Why do the Vedic sacrificial rituals have such great prestige, even though people of the lower classes cannot perform them?
2. What is puja, and why is it so central to many Hindus?
3. What kind of religious experience is darshana? How is this important in activities like festivals, pilgrimage, and art?
4. Explain the class (varna) and cast (jati) systems and how they fit together in Hindu society.
5. Discuss how the story of King Yudhishthira (in the Mahabharata) illustrates the tension often expressed in Hinduism between doing one's duty (dharma) and seeking liberation (moksha).
6. Explain the four stages of life and the four aims of life, taking note also of the experiences of women.

CHAPTER 16

BUDDHISM:
SACRED STORY
AND HISTORICAL
CONTEXT

Buddhism, born in India but grown to become the light of much of Asia, shares many things with Hinduism. But the wisdom taught by Siddhartha Gautama turned Buddhism in a different direction, leading Buddhists to reject the idea of the eternal Brahman and atman (self), the authority of the Vedic scriptures, the caste system of society, and even for the most part the importance of worshiping the gods. Not unlike Christianity's turn away from the Jewish tradition and the Muslim turn from the Jewish and Christian traditions, Buddhism turned from the Vedic tradition to create a spiritual perspective very much like its sister Hinduism in so many ways—but so different in still more crucial ways. Buddhists and Hindus today can certainly recognize a family resemblance between themselves. But like relatives who have long gone in different directions, the things held to be most important are those things that are different.

THE STORY OF THE BUDDHA

"Who am I?" "I'm a Buddhist, on the Path of the Buddha." To be a Buddhist means to derive one's identity from the story of the Buddha, Siddhartha Gautama, who lived about 2,500 years ago in India.

Unlike Hinduism, Buddhism is a "founded" religion; a particular person and the things he did and said are the foundation of the religion. In that sense Buddhism is like Judaism, Christianity, and Islam, with the story of the founder at its heart. Whereas the Buddha was not divine or a prophet of God, he was like these founders in the sense of being the teacher and the model for the lives of his followers.

An important difference with those other founded religions is Buddhism's special sense of history in relation to ultimate reality. The fact that God is revealed in historical events and works through persons is important to Judaism, Christianity, and Islam, and thus the historical events and persons take on a special significance. Like Hinduism, Buddhism sees the historical events of this particular world age as fairly insignificant in the context of the great world cycles of samsara. Whereas Siddhartha Gautama's lifetime 2,500 years ago is indeed crucial as a model and guide, it is not necessarily the complete focus of revelation and truth. The Buddha existed many lifetimes before this, for example, and there have been other Buddhas. Historical events are part of the story; but equally important are mythological stories and revelations of eternal truth.

We must, of course, make use of scholarly historical research to provide orientation in the beginnings and development of Buddhism, but our primary interest is to understand how the sacred story is understood by Buddhists themselves to give meaning and identity. Even after the master story of Siddhartha Gautama, the Buddha, some important transformations took place in Buddhism, especially in the rise of Mahayana Buddhism. And we need to look briefly at the historical shaping of the Buddhist way beyond India, the land of its birth, as Buddhism developed in unique ways in response to different local cultures. The forms of the path that developed in Sri Lanka and Southeast Asia, and also in China, Japan, and Tibet are significant for understanding what it means to be a Buddhist today.

The Sacred Biography of the Buddha

The Buddha lived in northeast India in the sixth century B.C.E., at the time when fellow sages were composing the Upanishads and thus helping to create Hinduism. This was a most creative period, for at the same time the early Jain leaders were developing their religion, and there were other movements with new interpretations of the Vedas. Important religious figures in this northeastern part of India were wandering hermits who had withdrawn from society and lived in the forests. They often went about in groups, following a recognized teacher, practicing austerities, and discussing various theories about the truth of human existence. The ideas they were discussing were those found also in the Upanishads: karma, samsara, rebirth, the relation of the soul and the supreme reality, liberation, and the like. It was a time of searching, experimenting, and debating about the ultimate truths of human existence.

Among these wandering ascetics we find Siddhartha Gautama (and also Mahavira, leader of the Jains). Siddhartha searched for the truth for some years, experienced a great awakening, and became the Buddha, or "enlightened one"; then he taught a community of disciples for some forty-five years until he died. His life was in many respects not unlike that of other holy men of his time. But this teacher was different, as attested in the sacred biography. In his career, Buddhists believe, the ultimate truth for all human existence is found.

We do not know for sure when the first scriptures of Buddhism were composed or written down; Buddhist tradition says they were transmitted orally by disciples from the parinirvana (passing away) of the Buddha. The most important biographical accounts of the Buddha's life were not written until about five hundred years later, such as the very influential one by Ashvaghosha (ca. first century C.E.). Thus it is not possible to unravel the "historical" details from mythological elements. We cannot find the historical Buddha any more than the historical Jesus or the historical Moses. But the important thing is to see the sacred story as Buddhists understand it, and for that reason the legendary and mythological materials are as important as the historical facts. The story is more than just a history of certain people. It reveals the true path of life.

The Birth of the World Saviour, the Buddha

Siddhartha was born about 563 B.C.E in a tribe in northeast India called the Shakyas, who also used the traditional name of Gautama. So Siddhartha is often simply called Gautama or Shakyamuni (wise one of the Shakyas). His parents were royalty, King Shuddhodana and Queen Maya of Kapilavastu (in present-day Nepal). There he grew up, married, and had a child, until his spiritual experiences led him to go forth at about age twenty-nine to become a wandering ascetic, searching for the truth. A story not unlike many others of his time—but this one was different, as the tradition makes clear. The life of the Buddha, like other great religious founders, is larger than life. That one human lifetime is connected with transcendental power and meaning. The birth of Siddhartha comes as the result of aeons of preparation, and his lifetime and teachings have ramifications for people of all times and places.

Reaching beyond the boundaries of human finitude, many stories tell of the previous lifetimes of the Buddha in which he achieved merit and wisdom leading finally to Buddhahood. For example, the Buddha told his disciple Ananda about a wise and compassionate prince named Mahasattva who lived in the remote past. One day, strolling in a forest, he came upon a tigress surrounded by seven small cubs. The tigress was exhausted from giving birth to the seven cubs and was weakened by hunger and thirst. Mahasattva realized that if she found no fresh meat and warm blood, she would die, so he resolved to sacrifice his own body, which, he reasoned, was doomed to perish in the end anyway. Taking a vow to sacrifice himself to win enlightenment for the welfare of the world, he threw himself down in front of the tigress. But she was so weak that she could do nothing, so he cut his own throat with a sharp piece of bamboo. Finally, when she saw his body covered with blood, she ate up all his flesh and blood and was strengthened. Concluding this story, the Buddha told Ananda: "It was I, Ananda, who at that time and on that occasion was that prince Mahasattva."[1] So through many lifetimes the Buddha-to-be grew in compassion and perfected himself in wisdom.

But finally the decisive moment came. After a lifetime in the Tushita heaven, he decided to enter the womb of pure Queen Maya of Kapilavastu to be born one final time as a human and to reach Buddhahood. In a dream Queen Maya saw four guardian angels carry her away to the Himalayan Mountains and purify her. Lying on a couch, she saw a superb white elephant approach and seemingly enter her body so that she conceived. At the conception of the Buddha the world shook, the blind, deaf, and lame were healed, all fires in hell went out, flowers fell from heaven, and many other signs appeared showing an event of world significance had happened. When the time came for Maya to give birth, she went out to the beautiful Lumbini grove, accompanied by many waiting-girls. She gave birth standing up, and four angels placed the baby on a golden net. The young child stood, took seven steps, and said, "I am born to be enlightened for the well-being of the world; this is my last birth."[2] Learned Brahmins who were present saw the auspicious signs on his body and said that he was certain to become either the perfectly enlightened one, or else a universal monarch.

> Should he be a great, earthly sovereign, he will rule the entire world with courage and righteousness, leading all kings, as the light of the sun leads the lights of the world. If he seeks deliverance by living in a forest, he will acquire true wisdom and illumine the entire world.[3]

The Going Forth

Siddhartha's mother Maya died seven days after bearing him, and King Shuddhodana married Maya's sister Prajapati, who brought up the young prince as his foster mother. His father the king, of course, wanted him first to be a mighty king and then, perhaps, retire to the forest in his old age. From the sages he learned that if Siddhartha saw four special sights he would abandon his life in the royal warrior family and withdraw to the forest. What are the four sights? He was told that they are four realities of human existence: a decrepit old man, a diseased man, a dead man, and a hermit monk. Wanting Siddhartha to become a great world ruler, the king ordered that none of these sights should be allowed near him, surrounding him instead with luxury, pleasure, and martial training. He built three beautiful palaces for Siddhartha, and he arranged for him to marry the lovely maiden Yashodhara, who in time bore him a son, Rahula.

The gods knew that the time for Siddhartha's enlightenment was drawing near, so they intervened, according to the story. When Siddhartha was out on an excursion in his golden chariot, the gods created an old decrepit man, and Siddhartha exclaimed, "O charioteer! Who is this man with gray hair, supported by a staff in his hand, his eyes sunken under his eyebrows, his limbs feeble and bent?" And the charioteer had to explain old age to Siddhartha, who then asked, "Will this evil come upon me also?" And the answer: "Advanced age will certainly come upon you through the inescapable force of time, no matter how long you may live."[4] The young prince sat looking at the old man for a long time, disturbed that this human process of old age indiscriminately destroys beauty and strength, and yet people in the world are not changed from their selfish pursuits by such a sight. Again, on a second excursion, the gods created a diseased man, and then thirdly a dead man, with the same shattering effect on Siddhartha. Finally he saw a hermit monk, one who has withdrawn from the world and thus is in some way above all this. And Siddhartha moved toward his own decision to withdraw to the forest and devote himself fully to searching for the truth.

But, as we all know, such decisions are not made without a struggle between conflicting values and loyalties. Siddhartha was now twenty-nine, with a wife and a son, heir to the throne of the kingdom. His father, sensing Siddhartha's inner struggle, attempted to persuade him that his duty was to fulfil the role of a householder first before withdrawing from the world in his old age. But Siddhartha countered with a metaphor that has become famous in Buddhist literature: "It is not right to hold by force a man who is anxious to escape from a burning house."[5] The king made one

final attempt to keep Siddhartha from going forth to become a wandering hermit, providing the most pleasurable entertainments with dancing girls and lovely music. Siddhartha was unmoved, and as the night wore on all the women fell asleep in distorted postures and shocking poses—"some with their bodies wet with trickling phlegm and spittle; some grinding their teeth, and muttering and talking in their sleep; some with their mouths open; and some with their dress fallen apart so as plainly to disclose their loathsome nakedness."[6] Seeing all this the prince was filled with disgust and determined to go forth that very night. He bid a silent farewell to his sleeping wife Yashodhara and son Rahula. Mounting his faithful horse Kanthaka, with his servant Channa he rode to the edge of the forest, the gods having opened the palace gates that had been secured tightly by order of his father. He cut off his hair and beard and put on the robe of a monk in place of his princely robes, instructing Channa to bring his hair and jeweled sword back to his father. Thus took place the crucial turning point in the Buddhist story, the Great Renunciation.

Unlike Christianity's founder Jesus, who was born in poverty, Siddhartha was born and grew up in riches, luxury, and power. But it is precisely these things—which we all strive for—that keep us from seeing the real nature of human existence. When Siddhartha did finally see human existence as it really is, stripped of the veneer of luxury and pleasure, he realized that the princely life was an illusion and he cast it aside, going forth to search for the truth as a forest monk.

The Attainment of Enlightenment

For the next six years Siddhartha wandered about, begging for his food and searching for the truth. He followed two teachers who taught him yogic knowledge and techniques, but, although he quickly mastered these disciplines, after a time he came to feel that this was not the path to the ultimate truth he was seeking. Then for a time he practiced the path of extreme self-mortification, like that followed by Mahavira and the Jain monks, fasting and depriving himself of even the bare necessities of life in an attempt to attain victory and release. Five other ascetic monks were attracted to his struggle and they practiced fasting and other disciplines with him. However, near starvation, Siddhartha came to an important realization: "This is not the way to achieve passionlessness, enlightenment, liberation. . . . How can it be reached by a man who is not calm and at ease, who is so exhausted by hunger and thirst that his mind is unbalanced?"[7] Mind and body are united in this search; weakening the body means weakening the mind also. So Siddhartha resolved to follow the "middle path," avoiding the extremes of riches and luxury, on the one hand, and self-mortification, on the other.

At just that moment, inspired by the gods, a cowherd woman named Sujata brought milk-rice and offered it to the Buddha-to-be. He accepted it, bathed himself,

The Buddha pointing to the earth. From a twelfth-century stele with scenes from the life of the Buddha.

and ate it to nourish himself for his attainment of enlightenment. The five monks abandoned him because it appeared he had given up the search, but Siddhartha went alone to sit crosslegged in meditation under a wisdom (*bodhi*) tree at Bodh Gaya, making the mighty resolution, "Never from this seat will I stir, until I have attained the supreme and absolute wisdom!"[8] The struggle was on. Representing the forces of passion and death, the god Mara (Death) entered the picture to attempt to thwart the attainment of Buddhahood. Mara is the god of worldly desires; seeing that Siddhartha was passing beyond his control, Mara brought his battle legions to overwhelm the monk, frightening even the gods. But all his awesome powers were rendered harmless by the strength of Siddhartha's meditation. Now Siddhartha pointed to the earth, calling upon it to be witness to his merit and his right to achieve Buddhahood, and the earth responded with such a deafening roar of assent that all Mara's hosts were scattered and defeated.

The greatest event in human history was taking place, and the gods and all of nature were waiting in anticipation. Siddhartha continued in the power of his meditation, and on the night of the first full moon he attained Buddhahood. In the first watch of the night he reviewed all his former existences, and then he turned his compassionate mind toward the sufferings of all beings in the unending wheel of rebirth. In the second watch of the night he attained the divine eye by which he saw the entire world as in a spotless mirror, with all beings impelled by their deeds to undergo repeated death and rebirth; and he grew in compassion. Siddhartha turned his meditation in the third watch of the night to the real nature of this world, understanding the causes of all rebirth, suffering, and death, beginning with ignorance and yearning for existence, and thus he also perceived the path leading to the cessation of all this.

> He knew what was to be known : he became a Buddha
> awoke from his meditation and saw a self nowhere in the world
> > gained the highest peace by the eightfold noble path

I have attained this path : I have fulfilled this path
    which the great seers followed
    (who knew the true & the false)
    for the benefit of others
And in the fourth watch, when dawn appeared
    and the whole world was tranquil
He gained omniscience : the imperishable state
& the earth trembled like a drunken maiden when he
was enlightened
the heavens shone with his success
    and kettledrums sounded in the sky[9]

Turning the Wheel of the Dharma

For some time the Buddha stayed there at Bodh Gaya, looking into his own mind and knowing he had found freedom. But now the question arose as to whether this enlightenment should be shared with others. It seems the Buddha was thinking at first that humans would not be able to understand his teaching. But the god Brahma came and pleaded with him, persuading him that some beings would understand. The Buddha surveyed the whole world with his Buddha eye, and he had compassion for all living things, deciding to teach this way of liberation to the world. Making his way to Sarnath near Banares, he sought out the five ascetics who had earlier abandoned him and preached to them, turning the wheel of the Dharma (truth). He told them that the two extreme ways of life, living in luxury and practicing total self-mortification, were useless; it is the "middle path" that leads to enlightenment. Then he proclaimed the four noble truths:

> The Noble Truth of suffering (*Dukkha*) is this: Birth is suffering; aging is suffering; sickness is suffering; death is suffering; sorrow and lamentation, pain, grief and despair are suffering; association with the unpleasant is suffering; dissociation from the pleasant is suffering; not to get what one wants is suffering—in brief, the five aggregates of attachment are suffering.
>
> The Noble Truth of the origin of suffering is this: It is this thirst (craving) which produces re-existence and re-becoming, bound up with passionate greed. It finds fresh delight now here and now there, namely, thirst for sense-pleasures; thirst for existence and becoming; and thirst for non-existence (self-annihilation).
>
> The Noble Truth of the Cessation of suffering is this:

> It is the complete cessation of that very thirst, giving it up, renouncing it, emancipating oneself from it, detaching oneself from it.
>
> The Noble Truth of the Path leading to the Cessation of suffering is this: It is simply the Noble Eightfold Path, namely right view; right thought; right speech, right action; right livelihood; right effort; right mindfulness; right concentration.[10]

The vision of life and its goal of transformation expressed in these four truths is profound, and we look at it more closely later. The Buddha retained the Indian view of life as samsara, a series of deaths and rebirths caused by karma. He saw that this whole existence involves "suffering," that is, discontent, frustration, and the anxiety of being death-bound. He had seen that all this suffering arises from clinging, grasping, holding onto the self. But he had also experienced the liberation that comes when clinging is totally done away with and thus suffering ceases—this liberation he called nirvana, which means ending the samsara cycle and reaching complete freedom. And the way to reach this, he taught, was the noble eightfold path, a lifetime of disciplines focused on knowledge, ethics, and meditation, designed gradually to root out all clinging and bring about the transformation of existence, the attainment of nirvana, the imperishable and absolute state beyond all this.

The Buddha's teaching differed from the teaching of the Hindu Upanishads particularly in his doctrines of impermanence and no-self. There is nothing, he taught, that is permanent and absolute, not even Brahman, that which Hindus consider to be ultimate reality. Rather, everything is in a state of constant flux and change, birth and death, and therefore there is nothing to hold on to. Further, there is no permanent, eternal atman (self). I cling and crave because I mistakenly suppose that I have a permanent self; the goal of the path is to come finally to the full realization that there is no self to cling to, and with that realization comes the peace and freedom of nirvana. It is this new Dharma that the Buddha proclaimed.

Founding the Sangha

The five hermits accepted the Buddha's Dharma and were ordained as the first monks, and with that the

Buddha created the sangha, the community following the path to enlightenment. A tradition says the Buddha went to Kapilavastu and preached the Dharma to his father, who was overjoyed, and even went to the heaven where his mother dwelt and preached the Dharma for her and the gods there. He spent the rest of his long life, some forty-five years, traveling about northwest India, teaching the Dharma and gathering many disciples into the community of the sangha. When he had a community of sixty enlightened monks (Pali: bhikkhus), the Buddha sent them out as missionaries to travel about and bring the Dharma to all beings, and many converted to this path. The Buddha accepted all classes of people without regard to race or social status, thus breaking away from the Indian caste system. On urging from Ananda he also accepted women into the sangha in a separate order of nuns (Pali: bhikkhunis), with his foster mother Prajapati and

Statues of the Buddha and the monks that formed the sangha, with a prostrate worshiper in front, from Pagan, Burma.

her attendants as its first members. As he organized the sangha into a monastic community, he established the main guidelines for monastic life, including the basic precepts like chastity, having no possessions, begging for food, and nonviolence toward all living things. Whereas the early monks were basically wanderers, the Buddha did establish the custom of retreats during the summer monsoon season, often gathering in caves in northern India. Eventually the conversions got so numerous that the Buddha gave the monks permission to ordain new monks wherever they went, and thus the sangha spread as a kind of republican society of monastic communities in various places.

The Buddha also accepted lay adherents to the path—kings, princes, merchants, and others, teaching them to observe the basic moral precepts and attain merit by supporting the monastic community. He also insisted that the monks and nuns teach their lay supporters and help them live meritorious lives. So the sangha has four divisions: monks (bhikkhus), nuns (bhikkhunis), laymen, and laywomen.

With the founding of the sangha the Buddhist identity is complete. All Buddhists down to the present day have expressed this identity by saying the formula that is used for entry into the Buddhist community: "I take refuge in the Buddha, I take refuge in the Dharma, I take refuge in the Sangha."

The Death of the Buddha: Parinirvana

After a long, full lifetime of teaching, the Buddha knew the end of his human existence was near. He said to Ananda and the other monks,

> I am old now, Ananda, and full of years; my journey nears its end, and I have reached my sum of days, for I am nearly eighty years old. . . . So, Ananda, you must be your own lamps, be your own refuges. Take refuge in nothing outside yourselves. Hold firm to the truth as a lamp and a refuge, and do not look for refuge to anything besides yourselves.[11]

Ananda wept at the prospect of the teacher leaving him, but the Buddha told him not to grieve, reminding him that it is in the very nature of things that we must sever ourselves from all things near and dear to us. After ascertaining that none of the monks had any doubts or perplexities about the Buddha, the Dharma, the sangha, or the path, the Buddha spoke his last words: "All composite things must pass away. Strive onward vigilantly."[12] And in the midst of his final meditation he passed into parinirvana, complete liberation without any ties remaining to pull him back for another lifetime in samsara. At the passing of the Buddha, the earth shook, thunderbolts crashed, rivers boiled with water, and the trees over the Buddha's couch showered his golden body with flowers.

The grief-stricken laypeople of the area, the Mallas, honored the Buddha's remains for six days. Then they carried his body on a bier to a great funeral pyre, and fire consumed all but his bones. The bones and other relics of the Buddha were kept in golden jars and taken to the village hall, where they were venerated for seven days. Rulers of the neighboring regions also wanted relics of the great teacher so they could establish shrines, and after some resistance the Mallas allowed the relics to be divided into eight parts and taken by the kings of the region, who built stupas (memorial mounds) over them. The relics provide a sense of the ongoing presence of the Buddha who is beyond existence in the state of parinirvana.

The Tripitaka: Word of the Buddha
The Buddha had told the monks that the Dharma would be their leader, and so they looked especially to his sayings and teachings as the source for the Dharma. During the first rainy season retreat after the Buddha's parinirvana, the story says, five hundred arhants (monks who had achieved nirvana) assembled in the First Council at Rajagrha and collected the sayings and teachings of the Buddha so that the Dharma might abide. Since Ananda was the one who heard him speak most often, they asked Ananda to recite the Buddha's sayings. So Ananda recited the words that the Buddha spoke in his sermons and dialogues (the *sutras*). Another monk, Upali, recited the various rules that the Buddha had given to regulate the life of the monks and nuns (the *vinaya*). Thus arose two of the main parts or "baskets" (*pitaka*) of the scriptures, the Sutra (Pali: Sutta) Pitaka and the Vinaya Pitaka, containing the Dharma of the great teacher. Somewhat later, disciples produced a set of scholarly treatises on points of doctrine, the Abhidharma (Pali: Abhidhamma), also consid-

ered to derive from the word of the Buddha. These three sets of writings are the Tripitaka (Pali: Tipitaka), the "Three Baskets," the scriptures of Buddhism. Scholars of today think the formation of the scriptures was a longer and more complicated process than the tradition says. The sayings were passed on orally by different groups, interpreted and added to, and eventually written down in the Pali language centuries later. But what the Buddhist story emphasizes is that the Dharma of the scriptures derives directly from the word of the Buddha.

In the story of the Buddha, then, one finds the paradigm for what it means to be a Buddhist. The Buddha, the Dharma, and the Sangha are not just historical artifacts to be researched and reconstructed; they are living realities in which all Buddhists of all ages can participate. Further, the life story of the Buddha is in a real sense the life story of every Buddhist, showing how the path proceeds from ignorance and worldly attachment to knowledge, detachment, and complete liberation.

HISTORICAL TRANSFORMATIONS: SHAPING THE BUDDHIST WAY

The story of Buddhism, although it centers on the historical life of Siddhartha Gautama, is actually very open-ended. The ultimate truth can be expressed in many other persons and realities. For example, as we noted earlier, the Buddha himself had many previous lifetimes. And there have been other Buddhas in the great aeons of the past and there will be other Buddhas in the future. So the story could be expanded greatly as Buddhism developed in its various historical transformations. Because of its great influence on the identity of many Buddhists today, especially those of East Asia, we need to look particularly at the expanded version of the story that took place in that movement known as Mahayana.

Ashoka, the Second Founder of Buddhism
For two centuries Buddhism spread mainly in the Ganges Valley area of eastern India. But in the middle

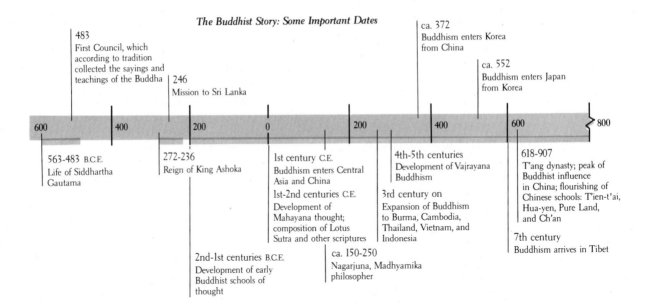

The Buddhist Story: Some Important Dates

483
First Council, which according to tradition collected the sayings and teachings of the Buddha

246
Mission to Sri Lanka

ca. 372
Buddhism enters Korea from China

ca. 552
Buddhism enters Japan from Korea

600 | 400 | 200 | 0 | 200 | 400 | 600 | 800

563-483 B.C.E.
Life of Siddhartha Gautama

272-236
Reign of King Ashoka

1st century C.E.
Buddhism enters Central Asia and China

1st-2nd centuries C.E.
Development of Mahayana thought; composition of Lotus Sutra and other scriptures

4th-5th centuries
Development of Vajrayana Buddhism

3rd century on
Expansion of Buddhism to Burma, Cambodia, Thailand, Vietnam, and Indonesia

618-907
T'ang dynasty; peak of Buddhist influence in China; flourishing of Chinese schools: T'ien-t'ai, Hua-yen, Pure Land, and Ch'an

7th century
Buddhism arrives in Tibet

2nd-1st centuries B.C.E.
Development of early Buddhist schools of thought

ca. 150-250
Nagarjuna, Madhyamika philosopher

of the third century B.C.E., it burst forth and spread throughout India and southward to Sri Lanka. One of the primary agents of this expansion was the great King Ashoka (r. ca. 272–236 B.C.E.), one of the most important rulers in Indian history and a zealous Buddhist. At the beginning of the third century B.C.E., the Maurya dynasty was engaged in extending control over much of India. The third Maurya king was Ashoka, who conquered Kalinga in northeast India, the last area to be subdued. But in the process the extensive bloodshed and destruction filled Ashoka with remorse, and he began to study the Dharma of Buddhism. He became a lay follower and even lived in a monastic community for a while, giving up the royal pastime of hunting because of the Buddhist precept not to harm living things.

Some five years after the bloody conquest of Kalinga, Ashoka proclaimed the new policy of the peaceful Dharma conquest. In a series of fourteen edicts engraved on rocks throughout his empire, he proclaimed that all people are his children and that they should live by basic Buddhist precepts: they should do no injury to any living things, they should be obedient to parents and elders, reverent to teachers, and the like. He abolished animal sacrifice and regulated the slaughter

of animals for food, provided for the welfare of the common people, built thousands of stupas, supported the monastic communities, and worked to have the developing sects of Buddhism recognize and tolerate each other. King Ashoka is fondly remembered by Buddhists as the "second founder" of Buddhism, establishing the model of the Buddhist layperson and the Buddhist state, complementary to the ideal of the sangha monastic community.

One of Ashoka's edicts says he sent Dharma-envoys to the Greek rulers of Syria, Egypt, Macedonia, Cyrene, and Epyrus, although these missionaries apparently did not have much success. Closer to home, however, in addition to spreading the rule of Dharma throughout India, Ashoka sent his son Mahinda and his daughter Sanghamitta as missionaries to Sri Lanka, and the two of them converted the king and the women of the court to Buddhism. Buddhism was on the way to becoming a world religion.

Theravada and Mahayana
In the course of its development, Buddhism came to be divided into two main branches: Theravada (Path of the Elders) and Mahayana (Greater Vehicle). Through

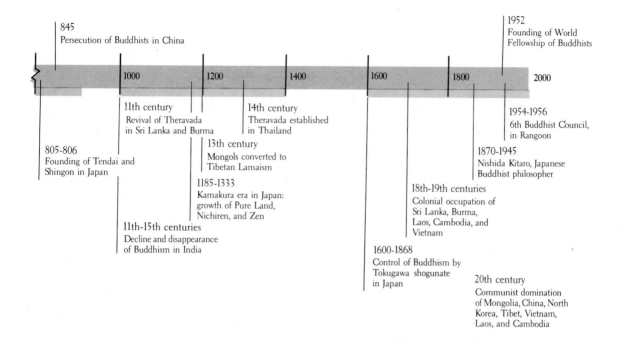

845
Persecution of Buddhists in China

1952
Founding of World
Fellowship of Buddhists

1000 1200 1400 1600 1800 2000

11th century
Revival of Theravada
in Sri Lanka and Burma

14th century
Theravada established
in Thailand

1954-1956
6th Buddhist Council,
in Rangoon

805-806
Founding of Tendai and
Shingon in Japan

13th century
Mongols converted to
Tibetan Lamaism

1870-1945
Nishida Kitaro, Japanese
Buddhist philosopher

1185-1333
Kamakura era in Japan:
growth of Pure Land,
Nichiren, and Zen

18th-19th centuries
Colonial occupation of
Sri Lanka, Burma,
Laos, Cambodia, and
Vietnam

11th-15th centuries
Decline and disappearance
of Buddhism in India

1600-1868
Control of Buddhism by
Tokugawa shogunate
in Japan

20th century
Communist domination
of Mongolia, China, North
Korea, Tibet, Vietnam,
Laos, and Cambodia

complex historical developments, Theravada came to be dominant in South Asia and Southeast Asia, whereas Mahayana spread through the lands of East Asia. A third branch, Vajrayana (Diamond Vehicle) or Tantric Buddhism, was accepted in Tibet.

In the first three or four centuries after the Buddha's death, there was much debate over basic questions of teaching and practice. By 200 B.C.E. reports indicate the existence of seventeen or eighteen "schools," each with a particular way of interpreting the path taught by the Buddha. One was the group that called itself Theravada, claiming to follow closely and to transmit the original teachings of the Buddha. Another early group was known as the Mahasanghikas (Great Sanghites), who admitted lay followers and nonarhant monks to their assemblies and taught that a transfigured Buddha exists with endless life beyond the world, appearing at different times and places. They also, of course, claimed that they carefully preserved the teaching of the Buddha.

All of these groups further splintered and eventually died out, with the exception of Theravada. The Theravadins established themselves in Sri Lanka, preserved the Buddhist scriptures in their Pali form, and have continued to exist to the present. Some of the teachings of the Mahasanghikas were taken over and continued in the Mahayana movement.

Contrasting them with Mahayana, all these early Buddhist schools were sometimes called Hinayana (Lesser Vehicle). Since this can be considered a derogatory term, it has become customary in modern times to replace it with Theravada, the one group among all these that continued to exist. In general, it may be said that Theravada did maintain the central teachings of early Buddhism, whereas Mahayana was more open to new ideas and practices.

Pressure for these changes came from several sources. In the sangha the arhants (enlightened monks) had formed an elite guild and insisted only they knew the true Dharma, alienating many other monks and laypeople, so in some communities there was a movement to include all, even laypeople, as equals on the path. The influence of Hindu bhakti (devotional) movements began to be felt, with many people desiring ways of expressing devotion and worship even as Buddhists. And the philosophical searching and speculation characteristic of thinkers in India led some Buddhists to explore the nature of reality in a more systematic, philosophical way, contributing new perspectives on the original Buddhist vision. These tendencies came to fruition in Mahayana Buddhism.

During the second and first centuries B.C.E. Mahayana ideas were being formed, and new scriptures, now in Sanskrit, were written expressing these ideas. The expanded story came to incorporate new conceptions of the sangha, the scriptures, the ideal saint, and the Buddha.

The Great Sangha and New Sutras

A major Mahayana innovation was to open the path to all people, monks and lay alike. The word Mahayana means "greater vehicle" or "greater course," and one implication of this new name is that the narrower concept of the arhant as the one reaching the goal was being broadened to include others, even laypeople. All can be equally on the path toward achieving Buddhahood. Of course, Mahayana communities continued to recognize monastic discipline as especially important in cultivating the higher virtues, but the path was thought to be within the reach of those who chose not to withdraw from the world and become monks or nuns. In contrast to the Greater Vehicle, the traditional form of Buddhism was designated as Hinayana, the Lesser Vehicle, since it offered salvation only to the few.

The Theravadins in turn criticized the Mahayanists for developing these new ideas rather than relying only on the Dharma of the Buddha. The new writings composed in Sanskrit by Mahayana were not just commentaries on the older Pali scriptures; they were claimed to be the secret teaching that the Buddha himself had given to his most advanced disciples. Mahayana thus taught a kind of progressive revelation of the truth; to those with lesser understanding the Buddha had revealed the preliminary truth embodied in the Tripitaka, the scriptures of Theravada, but to those with deep understanding he revealed the full truth, which was passed on orally and eventually written in the Mahayana sutras. All of these are still "word of the Buddha." Important early texts of Mahayana include writings like the *Sadharmapundarika* (Lotus), *Prajnaparamita* (Perfection of Wisdom), and the *Sukhavati* (Pure Land) sutras. In the following centuries a great number of additional sutras were added to the Mahayana corpus, filling out and refining the new understandings of the Buddha and the path.

The Course of the Bodhisattva

Mahayana is really the "great course" of the bodhisattva (Buddha in the making). It was one of the main innovations of Mahayana to teach that the Great Course leads directly to Buddhahood, whereas the Lesser Course (Theravada) leads only to arhant-ship. Theravada, it is true, had an idea of the bodhisattva path toward liberation, but they associated it with a few special beings like Gautama. But Mahayana began to teach that the course of the bodhisattva is the higher path that leads to Buddhahood and which, further, is for all to follow, open even to laypeople. Mahayana Buddhists cultivated devotion to bodhisattvas, great beings who are on the path to becoming Buddhas, and held this ideal up for all to strive after.

Inherent in Buddhism from the beginning was an emphasis on compassion, the sense of oneness with all living beings. But monastic religion seemed to some to place a great emphasis on striving for individual salvation. The arhant is one who perfects himself or herself through spiritual disciplines, roots out all clinging, and finally attains nirvana, liberation from the sufferings of the rebirth cycle in which all other beings are trapped. Whereas the arhant cultivates compassion as a virtue, the ultimate goal is release. But the bodhisattva, according to the Mahayana story, is a great being who aeons ago grasped the thought of enlightenment and took vows to work incessantly for the welfare and salvation of all living things, thus starting on the bodhisattva course. Through countless lifetimes the bodhisattva cultivates the ten perfections, eliminates all defilements, and reaches enlightenment and supreme Buddhahood. But having reached the goal, the bodhisattva delays entering into nirvana, continuing in the rebirth cycle in order to work for the salvation of all beings, in accordance with the bodhisattva vow.

An important factor in the idea of the bodhisattva is the Buddhist notion of merit, which is built up by moral, selfless deeds. The bodhisattva builds up a tremendous amount of merit in his long course, especially in voluntarily being reborn in samsara even after reaching enlightenment. And this merit can be transferred to others in need, delivering them out of physical distress and even helping them to rebirth in one of the paradises. One such bodhisattva vow says:

> I shall be the inexhaustible treasure of all the needy. I shall be in the vanguard with all kinds of means (for them). I shall give up all enjoyments in which by nature the ego is involved. I shall give up the merit that leads to all the three worlds and I shall do so for fulfilling the desires of all beings and without expecting any return. Nirvana is the renunciation of everything. My mind desires Nirvana. If everything is to be given up by me, it is better that I make a gift of everything to living things. I am the light for those who need light; the bed for those who need a bed; and the servant of those who need service. I am all these to all.[13]

The bodhisattva may be born in the world, appearing as an ordinary person, to help others. "Although the son of Jina [the conqueror] has penetrated to this immutable true nature of dharmas, yet he appears like one of those who are blinded by ignorance, subject as he is to birth, and so on. This is truly wonderful. It is through his compassionate skill in means for others that he is tied to the world."[14]

Some bodhisattvas are celestial beings, living in the heavens and working to help and save all beings. These bodhisattvas can be worshiped and prayed to for help, bringing the element of bhakti into Mahayana Buddhism. One such heavenly bodhisattva is Manjusri, who appears to humans in dreams. Hearing his name subtracts many aeons from one's time in samsara, and those who worship him are protected by his power. Another widely worshiped bodhisattva is Avalokiteshvara, who is described in the Lotus Sutra as an omnipresent saviour rich in love and compassion, taking many different forms to help living beings. Those who worship him and call on his name will be saved from all dangers, whether drowning in water, bound in prison, or burning in a fire. He grants women their desire for a daughter or son. In China and Japan the names Kuan-yin and Kannon are used for this bodhisattva, whose images are often represented as a compassionate woman, a "goddess of mercy."

The Mahayana Conception of Buddha

The Mahayana group also expanded the conception of who or what the Buddha is. They emphasized that the Buddha is really the eternal power of the Dharma, and that this "Dharma Body" of the Buddha is transcendent and universal, yet forever active in the world. The Dharma Body has lived for countless ages in the past and will continue forever in the future. This Dharma Body is the only real body of the Buddha; it is ultimate reality.

But the Dharma Body has various manifestations for the welfare of living beings, such as the human form, Siddhartha Gautama. And important manifestations are the heavenly Buddhas who preside over Buddhalands in which all the inhabitants are assured of attaining enlightenment. Moreover, some of these heavenly Buddhas can also be worshiped by people still living in this world, sharing merit with them so that they can be saved from a variety of sufferings and ultimately be reborn into one of the heavenly Buddhalands. One widely worshiped Buddha is Amitabha Buddha. He was a long-ago monk who made vows to become a Buddha and create a special Buddhaland (the Pure Land) in which there would be no evil destinies; everyone born there was sure to reach nirvana. Further, Amitabha vowed that those who meditate on him with faith will be reborn in his Buddhaland. Then he practiced the path of the bodhisattva for a trillion years and became the great compassionate Buddha, creating the Pure Land paradise in accordance with his vows.

Mahayana Schools: Madhyamika and Yogacara

As Mahayana thinkers speculated on the meaning of these new ideas about bodhisattvas and Buddhas, a new philosophical perspective emerged to become characteristic of the Mahayana approach, formulated especially by the Madhyamika school and its famous thinker,

Nagarjuna (ca. 150–250 c.e.). Early Buddhism taught that everything is a conglomeration of elements or "dharmas"; the chariot, for example, is only the sum of its parts and therefore not real, although its parts are real. The Madhyamika thinkers came up with the dramatic new idea that, since all these dharmas come into existence as a result of causes and conditions, they do not have an independent existence and thus are "empty" (*shunya*). This whole phenomenal world of samsara is empty. Taking this one step further, the Mahayana thinkers proposed that nirvana also is empty, since it is devoid of all definitions and discrimination. This means that the phenomenal world of samsara and the realm of nirvana are both empty, and thus they may be equated with each other. Nirvana is samsara. Rather than seeing nirvana as the opposite of samsara, nirvana is to be understood as the realization that all things are really empty and therefore there are no dualisms. One who understands this fully is enlightened and realizes the Buddha-nature within himself or herself.

Nagarjuna is famous for his logical reduction-to-absurdity method to show that every concept contains contradictions in itself and therefore is unreal, proving that the whole phenomenal world is empty or unreal because it is based on contradictory relations. The purpose of this method, he points out, is to free our minds of all theories and enable us to realize the unconditioned truth, beyond all words and concepts.

The other important Mahayana philosophical school, Yogacara, identified emptiness with what they called storehouse consciousness, the basis of all existence. The storehouse consciousness is the womb from which all Buddhas are born, and it is the embryo Buddha nature that is present in all things. This idea implies that all beings possess Buddhahood and that the goal is to realize that Buddhahood. If that is so, then many possible paths toward realizing that Buddhahood open up, from meditation and yogic practices to devotion and worship of the Buddhas. And in fact, especially in China, many Buddhist schools developed to cultivate the different paths toward realizing Buddhahood.

Buddhist Tantra: Vajrayana

Yet another form of Buddhism developed in India, influenced by Tantric aspects of Hinduism, which used many rituals, mantras (sacred words), mandalas (sacred diagrams), ritual sexual intercourse, and the like, to achieve realization of Buddhahood. Eventually the Tantric Buddhists produced new scriptures; these are manuals for rituals and meditations designed to lead directly to the realization of Buddhahood. These Tantras purported to come directly from the Buddha passed on secretly to his most advanced disciples, and they were written in a kind of code language so the uninitiated would not understand. Called Vajrayana (diamond vehicle), this form of Buddhism greatly extended the Buddha pantheon by adding many new Buddhas, bodhisattvas, feminine consorts, gods, and goddesses, representing the whole cosmos. Tantrists also believed that this sacred cosmos is replicated in the human body, that is, all these Buddhas and bodhisattvas reside within us, so with the proper rituals and meditation one can visualize or identify with these powers and realize Buddhahood. Vajrayana, later influential especially in Japan and Tibet, thus developed a path by which one could achieve Buddhahood even within this very lifetime.

Great Expansion of Buddhism in Asia

Unlike Hinduism, Buddhism from early times on considered the Dharma to be the truth for all living things, and therefore one of the important duties in following the path is to make it possible for others to share in the benefits of that Dharma. Buddhism spread to several major cultural areas and in transforming them was itself transformed, taking on a distinctive flavor in each region. First Buddhism spread throughout India and to Sri Lanka at the time of King Ashoka. Then with the Indianization of Southeast Asia it also became dominant in those lands. Since the Theravada form of Buddhism was strong in India during these expansions, those lands became Theravada countries, with indigenous cults and traditions still in place. When the expansion to Central and East Asia took place, Mahayana was in the ascendency, so East Asia emerged predominately Mahayana.

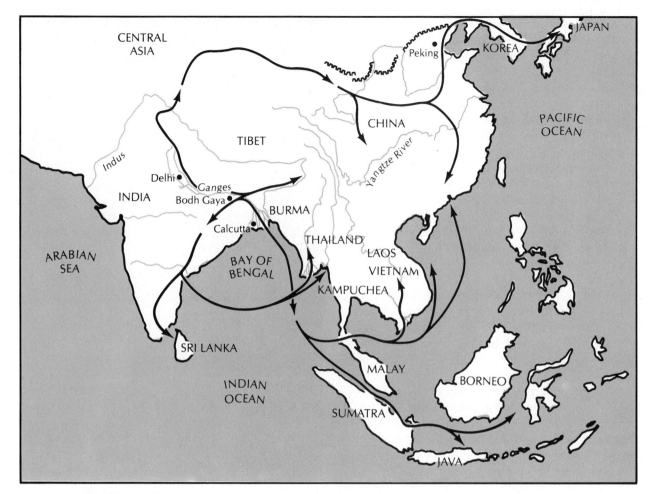

Expansion of Buddhism.

Within India itself, Buddhism remained fairly strong in most regions up to the seventh century, but over the next centuries a slow decline set in. By about the thirteenth century Buddhism had virtually disappeared from the land of its birth. One element in the demise of Indian Buddhism was perhaps the extent to which monastic Buddhism, with landed estates and royal grants, had grown unresponsive to the needs of the people. The general populace found their needs met more by theistic Hinduism and increasingly turned in that direction, incorporating some Buddhist worship and piety into popular Hinduism. Another factor in the weakening of Buddhism in India was the onslaught of outside invaders. Beginning with the White Hun invasions of the sixth century, the Buddhist monasteries of northwest India were devastated. Later Muslim invaders and Muslim rulers continued to demolish Buddhist temples and monasteries, along with Hindu temples. Hinduism, depending on village brahmins and devotional cults, survived, but Buddhism, focused on the monastic communities, weakened and eventually disappeared. But by this time Buddhism had already become the light of many other parts of Asia beyond its homeland.

Expansion to Sri Lanka and Southeast Asia

Beginning when King Ashoka's son and daughter converted the rulers of Sri Lanka, Buddhism has flourished there for over two thousand years, the longest continuity of Buddhism anywhere. At times there has been Mahayana influence in Sri Lanka, along with Hindu cults, but Theravada eventually became dominant. Sri Lanka boasts a tree said to have grown from a shoot of the tree at Bodh Gaya under which the Buddha reached enlightenment; the tree shoot was brought to Sri Lanka by King Ashoka's daughter. And a special temple in Kandy houses a tooth of the Buddha. From the beginning the sangha was strongly supported by the rulers of Sri Lanka. Buddhist kings were patrons of Buddhist art and learning, and they built many temples and monasteries, even helping to regulate the affairs of the sangha.

Since Burma provided a trade gateway for India to Southeast Asia, Indian merchants were bringing Buddhism with them into Burma already in the third century B.C.E., and some monks were also sent by Ashoka. Over the next centuries Buddhist influences continued, and gradually Burma became a flourishing center of Buddhist life. For a while Mahayana and Tantric influences were strong, but during the period of the Pagan kingdom, King Anawrahta (1040–1077) turned to Sri Lanka for inspiration, and thus Burma became a thriving center of Theravada Buddhism, retaining a pure form of Theravada ordination and tradition. Lay Buddhism in Burma took on a special character by adopting local cults of spirits (nats), so that side by side with the monastic community are found shamanistic practices involving women possessed by nats healing people and providing benefits for them.

A mixture of Mahayana Buddhism and Hinduism spread into Cambodia, Thailand, and Laos from about the fourth century C.E. onward. Theravada did not come to Cambodia until the twelfth century, when it

Ruins of the great Buddhist monument at Sukhothai, Thailand.

supplanted both Mahayana and Hinduism. The Thai states developed in the thirteenth century and accepted Theravada from Burma, although Thai kings used Hindu law and Brahmanical ceremonies. The first Laotian state developed in the fourteenth century and the Khmer missionaries from Cambodia introduced Theravada Buddhism, which became the official religion of Laos. Vietnam, though a part of Southeast Asia, received strong influence from China and has been predominantly Mahayana in orientation. Indonesia was Hinduized by the fifth century C.E., but Buddhism was also introduced and existed side by side with the cult of Shiva. At Borobudur on the island of Java was built the greatest and most glorious of all stupas, in the shape of a great mandala in stone representing the pilgrim's search for enlightenment.

Characteristic of the development of Buddhism in Sri Lanka and Southeast Asia is the interrelationship between the monastic community and the laypeople. The monks and nuns pursue the path toward nirvana, of course, and the laypeople carry on householder life in the cities and in rural areas. But each group lives in a certain dependence on the other. The monks need the support of the laypeople in terms of food, buildings, security, and the like. The laypeople need the services of the monks in terms of teaching, chanting scriptures, and providing spiritual power for the community. In some of these lands it has been customary for boys to spend at least some time as novices in a monastery before going on to adult secular life in society.

Development of East Asian Buddhism

As early as the first century C.E. Buddhist monks and laypeople made their way along the silk routes into central Asia. For a time both Theravada and Mahayana flourished in central Asia, until Buddhism was stamped out by Islam around the tenth century C.E. Scholars today are only beginning to recover the impressive achievements of Buddhists in central Asia, including temples, sculptures, and important translations of Indian Buddhist texts.

From central Asia monks and missionaries brought Buddhism to China, where in its Mahayana form it rose to become one of the three great religions of China, along with Confucianism and Taoism. Buddhism contributed to many transformations in Chinese society and religious thought, and in the process Buddhism itself took on characteristic Chinese forms, discussed in Part IV. Particularly important was the development of special lineages or "schools" of Chinese Buddhism, each with important writings and practices. The two schools that eventually became most important in China were Pure Land, centered on the worship of the compassionate Buddha Amitabha, and Ch'an (Meditation) Buddhism.

From China, Buddhism spread to Vietnam, Korea, and Japan, with the result that these cultures became predominantly Buddhist. Vietnam was influenced both from India and from China, but it was Chinese Mahayana especially in the Ch'an form that finally prevailed. Later Pure Land Buddhism came to dominate village-level Buddhism in Vietnam, whereas the monasteries remained predominantly Thien (Ch'an).

Buddhism was brought to the northern part of Korea in 372 C.E. by a Chinese monk, spreading throughout the rest of the land by the sixth century. Korean religion had been a form of shamanism, which still survives today as a cult of spirits. When Buddhism came in, the common people were much attracted to Pure Land Buddhism with its promise of salvation in the next world. During the eighth and ninth centuries, Ch'an (in Korean, Son) was introduced from China, and this became the most popular form of monastic Buddhism in Korea. The Buddhist scriptural canon was printed in Korea two times, as Korean Buddhism made a particularly important contribution to the spread of Buddhism. The wooden blocks from the thirteenth century printing are still preserved, and a new printing is being made from them.

From Korea Buddhism spread to Japan; around the year 550 Korean kings sent gifts of Buddhist sutras and Buddha images to the Japanese emperor. Buddhism in Japan was first adopted by the court and ruling families as a means of unifying the nation, but later it became an important part of popular Japanese life. Japanese Buddhism is discussed in more detail in Part IV.

The Special Shape of Tibetan Buddhism

In the seventh century C.E., Buddhist missionaries from India began to press northward to a new region in central Asia, the isolated Himalayan mountains of Tibet. The indigenous religious practice of Tibet was called Bon, and it focused on many spirits good and hostile. Shamans went into trances to communicate with these spirits, and the people offered animal sacrifices. Since during this period Tibet also had contact with central Asia and China, Ch'an Buddhism was successful in Tibet for a while, but at the same time the Tantric form of Buddhism, Vajrayana, was being imported from India. Toward the end of the eighth century the Tibetan king staged a remarkable international debate between Chinese Ch'an monks and monks from India. According to the Tibetan version of the story, the Chinese were defeated and expelled from the country, after which Tibet definitely turned toward India and Tantric Buddhism. The specific type of Buddhism created in Tibet in the interaction between Indian Tantrism and Tibetan culture is called Lamaism, from the term *lama*, which means a spiritual master.

Under support from the kings, Indian missionaries entered Tibet to teach, translate Sanskrit scriptures into Tibetan, and found monasteries. One missionary remembered in a host of legends was Padmasambhava, who arrived in Tibet in 747 and used his Tantric powers to subdue all the Bon demons who were hostile to Buddhism; after being subjugated, they were included in the Tibetan Buddhist pantheon as protectors of Buddhism. Under royal patronage Indian and Tibetan monks translated a vast number of scriptures into Tibetan, virtually creating the Tibetan literary language in the process. Many monasteries were established where scholar-monks practiced the disciplines of monastic life and mastered the classical Vajrayana doctrines. And countless wonder-working Tantric yogins wandered about, not concerned with monastic disciplines, often married and with families.

Tibetans, with their background in the popular shamanistic religion, accepted Tantric Buddhism from India but shaped it in their own way, enriching the pantheon with Lamaist saints, Tibetan gods and goddesses, demons, local heroes, and the like. The pantheon included many female figures, such as the bodhisattva Tara who became a kind of universal protectress worshiped by both monks and laity. Monks and nuns participated in popular Buddhism, but they also cultivated esoteric practices involving yogic meditation and Tantric rituals, with the goal of transforming the consciousness into the absolute Buddha reality. The religious specialists were the lamas, the highest spiritual authorities, often thought to be living gods, and under their direction the disciplines and rituals were practiced.

A significant event was the conversion of the Mongol leader Kublai Khan (1216–1294) to Lamaism, and several centuries later the peoples of Mongolia, northern China, and southern Russia also came to follow Lamaism. An important reform movement beginning in the fifth century was called the Gelukpa (partisan of virtue) sect, also known as the Yellow Hats, named after their hats in contrast to the red hats of the traditional Buddhist groups and the black hats of the Bon priests. Tsong-kha-pa (1357–1419), founder of the Gelukpa sect, advocated a return to the traditional Buddhist monastic life and also a modification of some of the Tantric magical practices. His third successor, his nephew Gendun Truppa, was recognized as an incarnation of the bodhisattva Avalokiteshvara and is counted as the first Dalai Lama, spiritual leader of Lamaism. Since lamas are recognized as incarnations in a continuing series, after the death of a Dalai Lama a search party goes out to find the new Dalai Lama, who will be an infant born forty-nine days later (the period of the intermediate stage). The searchers are guided by the dying lama's indications and other pertinent signs, and once the right child is found, he is brought to Lhasa to be educated for his role while regents rule

An esoteric paint-on-cotton rendering of the Buddha Ratnasambhava, from the Himalayan region.

temporarily. The present Dalai Lama is the fourteenth in this line.

Buddhism in the Modern Era

Developments in the modern era have often been disruptive to Buddhism as to other religions. Even before the modern era, as we saw, Buddhism disappeared in its motherland India. Then starting in the midsixteenth century, Western mercantilism, imperialism, and missionary work posed challenges to the other traditional Buddhist societies. In Sri Lanka, for example, the Portuguese attempted to convert the people to Catholicism, destroying Buddhist temples and relics and executing monks found wearing the yellow robe. And the challenges of rationalism, science, and secularism have affected Buddhist peoples as well as those of the Western religious traditions.

In the twentieth century, communism has proven to be a drastic challenge to Buddhism, as Communist governments now dominate the area that has for centuries been the heartland of Buddhism: China, Mongolia, North Korea, Tibet, and the Southeast Asian countries of Vietnam, Laos, and Cambodia. Mongolia, taken over by a Soviet-inspired Communist government in the early 1920s, replaced Buddhist teaching with Communist ideology and stripped the Lamaist leaders of their power. In China the Maoist procedure was to close the monasteries and force monks and nuns to return to secular life, gathering the remnants of Buddhism into a state-run Chinese Buddhist Association. The Chinese conquest of Tibet caused great disruption in this traditional Buddhist culture, which had not even experienced a period of modernization; the Dalai Lama and thousands of others fled the country, and apparently the Chinese took over administration of the monasteries with serious curtailment of Buddhist activities. It appears that the Communist governments in Southeast Asia are also seriously weakening the Buddhist institutions.

Revitalization of Buddhism Today

Yet there is a sense of revitalization of Buddhism today. Facing the challenge of Western influences and Christianity in the late nineteenth and twentieth centuries, Buddhists in various lands have responded with

Buddhist monk ringing the monastery bell at Eiheiji Temple in Japan.

a revival of Buddhist activity, especially in the area of scholarly work. To meet the challenge of modern secular values, Buddhist scholars have retrieved the sources of their own traditions and are reformulating Buddhist doctrines to meet modern questions. Some Buddhist thinkers, such as the Japanese philosopher Nishida Kitaro (1870–1945), have tried to relate Buddhist ideas with Western philosophical and scientific modes of thought. Other thinkers have stressed the relevance of Buddhist teachings for creating a just and peaceful society.

Within Buddhist lands there have been Buddhist reformers who have redirected the monastic life toward constructive religious and social roles. And much attention has been given to an increased activity of the laypeople in Buddhist affairs, through education, religious activities, and lay Buddhist associations. Interest in the revitalization of worldwide Buddhism is seen in the founding of the World Fellowship of Buddhists in Sri Lanka in 1952 to unite Buddhists of all nations. And in connection with the 2,500th anniversary of the Buddha's enlightenment, a two-year-long Sixth Great Council of Buddhism was held in Rangoon in the 1950s. There are even signs in the People's Republic of China that the newly issued policy of freedom of religion will assist a revival of Buddhist leadership.

In motherland India there are some first inklings of a revival of Buddhism. Small groups of Indian intellectuals have been attracted to Buddhism because it suits their ideas of social reform and rational spirituality. Refugees from Tibet live in communities in India, continuing some of the traditions of Tibetan Buddhism. And in 1956 the leader of Maharashtra's untouchables led 600,000 of his followers to a mass conversion to Buddhism, partly in protest against the caste system of Hindu tradition. Since then the number of Buddhist converts has doubled and constitutes a significant presence of Buddhists in India.

Another significant aspect of Buddhism today is its expansion in the West. Thriving communities of immigrant Buddhists have been established especially in such places as Hawaii and California, but increasingly in other areas as well. Many of these are organized into the Buddhist Churches of America and follow the Japanese True Pure Land school. But more recently immigrants from other parts of Asia—Korea, Thailand, Vietnam, and others—have strengthened the Buddhist presence in the West. There are also significant numbers of Westerners who have become Buddhist. This trend started especially with the writings of D. T. Suzuki, who interested many in Zen Buddhism, leading to the establishment of many Zen centers in the larger American cities. Then in the 1960s came a surge of interest in Tibetan Buddhism and the establishing of centers for studying and practicing this more esoteric form. Now there are a variety of other Buddhist traditions represented as well. The most significant development, perhaps, is the ordination of Western successors to Asian Buddhist masters, indicating a basis for the continuation of the fledgling Buddhist community in the West.

DISCUSSION QUESTIONS

1. According to the traditional Buddhist story, what was Siddhartha's early life like? Why did he decide to go forth to seek the truth?
2. Describe Siddhartha's attaining of enlightenment. What was the role of Mara and of the gods?
3. What was the content of the Buddha's first sermon given at Sarnath near Banares?
4. How, according to tradition, was the Tripitaka compiled?
5. Why is King Ashoka called the second founder of Buddhism?
6. What important new ideas came to expression in the Mahayana movement?
7. Outline the expansion of Buddhism in Asia and account for its virtual disappearance in India.
8. What are some special characteristics of Tibetan Buddhism?
9. What have been some major problems for Buddhism in the modern period? What are some indications of Buddhism's revitalization today?

CHAPTER 17

BUDDHIST WORLDS OF MEANING

THE ULTIMATE: DHARMA, NIRVANA, BUDDHA

"What's it *all* about?" "How can I make sense of everything that is?" "What is really ultimate in our existence?"

Buddhists, like Hindus, do not fall back on a simple single answer like God. God and gods, like everything else, are part of the samsara cycle and therefore cannot be ultimate. One of the central Buddhist teachings about reality is that everything is impermanent and conditioned; there is nothing, even God, that is eternal and absolute. Does this mean, then, that Buddhists have no ultimate reality at all? Some have suggested this, speaking of Buddhism as a philosophy rather than a religion.

But such a view would be misleading, for Buddhists for many centuries have found ultimate meaning and transformation in the path of the Buddha. What is really ultimate? The Buddhist Three Refuge formula gives us some help, for that to which a person goes for refuge must have something to do with the ultimate. According to the Three Refuge formula, a Buddhist goes for refuge to the Buddha, to the Dharma, and to the Sangha. The Dharma is the transcendental absolute truth, and the Sangha focuses toward the experience of nirvana, the unconditioned state of liberation. Whereas the Buddha as a human being is not ultimate, his example of reaching enlightenment and his role as teacher and guide is so central that we need to consider the Buddha within the concept of ultimate reality.

The Ultimate as Unconditioned Truth

It might appear to someone on the outside that Buddhists worship the Buddha as sacred reality. They build temples dedicated to the Buddha, perform rituals before statues of the Buddha, revere relics of the Buddha, and the like. Buddhist religious rituals and festivals can be as colorful and dramatic as any other. But, Buddhists insist, they are not worshiping the Buddha or any other object as ultimate reality, for the Buddha is beyond existence in the unconditioned state of nirvana, and all other objects of worship are conditioned and limited like everything else. Whereas it is beneficial to bow before a statue of the Buddha or invoke a guardian goddess, these objects of devotion are not ultimate and unconditioned. What then *is* ultimate and unconditioned? It is the Dharma as the truth of reality, and nirvana as the unconditioned state.

The Ocean of Dharma

Before the Buddha died, he counseled Ananda and the other disciples on what they should hold fast to: "So, Ananda, you must be your own lamps, be your own refuges. Take refuge in nothing outside yourselves. Hold firm to the truth [Dharma] as a lamp and a refuge, and do not look for refuge to anything besides yourselves."[1] The Dharma is to be found in the word of the Buddha transmitted in the scriptures. Of course, the scriptures themselves are conditioned, but the Dharma is not. It is the eternal truth that transcends even this world age, taught by all the Buddhas and known directly by those attaining enlightenment.

The word *dharma* was taken into Buddhism from the broader traditions of India, where it came to mean, as in Hinduism, the universal ordering principle that penetrates everywhere and is operative in everything. As such it is equated with things as they really are, and so the word *dharma* in Buddhism comes to mean ultimate truth, the knowledge of what really is. It is this truth that was realized by the Buddha when he reached enlightenment. Dharma is the truth about the way existence *really* is: the truth about the nature and function of the world, and the truth about liberation from the bondage of samsara. The story of the Buddha's enlightenment reveals the basic content of this Dharma. It tells how he saw the whole chain of his previous existences, and then he saw the whole universe as in a mirror, with the operation of the law of karma and rebirth. He perceived the Four Noble Truths about reality. Finally, according to Ashvaghosha's account of his enlightenment, he realized the principle of "dependent arising" (*pratitya samutpada*) as the last step to enlightenment and release from samsara.

A Sri Lankan sculpture of the Buddha in the meditation posture.

"Dependent arising" is essentially a doctrine of causality, showing the interconnectedness of everything. There is no god who causes everything; but it is also false to assert that everything happens randomly by chance. Rather, the truth is that everything and every event are caused by something prior in an interrelated process. Every condition contributes to the next, but it is itself conditioned by countless other determining conditions. This universal truth is often expressed in the abstract statement: "When that exists, this comes to be; on the arising of that, this arises. When that does not exist, this does not come to be; on the cessation of that, this ceases."[2]

Dependent arising is thus the most real knowledge about the world, and it is often simply equated with the Dharma—whoever sees one sees the other, and understanding it is tantamount to enlightenment. Since this Dharma was realized and taught by the Buddha, the Dharma is also often equated with the teaching of the Buddha. At the Deer Park in Sarnath, the Buddha first preached the truth and "turned the wheel of the Dharma."

The Dharma is not simply some mechanical law about reality. It is a transcendental principle immanent and operative in the world, real, valuable, and normative; at the same time it is infinite and eternal. The Dharma is alive in a sense; how well the sangha lives out its vocation in the world has an effect on the Dharma. When unhappiness and trouble come upon society, it is assumed that the ruler and the sangha have disrupted the Dharma by unfaithfulness. When the future Buddha Maitreya arises, Dharma will be stirred up again so that humankind will again know and live the truth. When monks chant scripture for the laypeople, they are unleashing the power of the Dharma for the benefit of the people.

The Dharma is a central aspect of ultimate reality to Buddhists. It is not a supernatural being or god. But, as unconditioned truth, the Dharma takes on a character of awesomeness, protection, and deliverance. It should not only be respected but worshiped and sought as a refuge. The hall of meditation in a monastery is often called the Dharma hall, the seat where the teacher sits is the Dharma seat, and the rule of King Ashoka is the reign of Dharma.

The Unconditioned State of Nirvana

Closely related with the Dharma is the unconditioned state of nirvana. The importance of the Dharma is that it leads to nirvana; fully realizing the Dharma means achieving nirvana. Nirvana is not a place like heaven or the realm of the gods, for all of these are part of samsara and thus conditioned and impermanent. Nirvana is freedom from samsara and therefore is a permanent, unconditioned state. The Buddha speaks:

> There is, monks, an unborn, not become, not made, uncompounded, and were it not, monks, for this unborn, not become, not made, uncompounded, no escape could be shown here for what is born, has become, is made, is compounded.[3]

As in this description, nirvana is often described negatively, for it is unlike anything else in our human experience. But how can such a negative idea be thought of as ultimate reality? The fact that nirvana is often described in negatives has led some outsiders to think of it as annihilation or as unreal. But this is a misunderstanding, for the Buddhist tradition applies many positive concepts to nirvana. Edward Conze draws from various texts some of the things that can be said in describing nirvana; in the texts we are told

> that Nirvana is permanent, stable, imperishable, immovable, ageless, deathless, unborn, unbecome; that it is power, bliss and happiness, the secure refuge, the shelter and the place of unassailable safety; real Truth and the supreme Reality; that it is the *Good*, the supreme goal and the one and only consummation of our life, the eternal, hidden and incomprehensible Peace.[4]

Such descriptions contain many attributes that Jews, Christians, or Muslims might apply to God, and they show that nirvana does function as ultimate for Buddhists. Yet nirvana is not in any sense like God, for it is not a sacred power outside oneself, operating in the world. Nirvana is a reality experienced within, as it were, a state of unconditioned freedom.

Still, nirvana is real. It is eternal, absolute, unconditioned, and ultimate. Therefore it is highly to be desired and looked to by every Buddhist as the supreme goal of human existence, even though it may be thousands of lifetimes away.

Emptiness and Suchness

Mahayana Buddhists go further in their view of the unconditioned real. Reflecting philosophically on the ultimate qualities of nirvana, they tend to emphasize positive terms like "emptiness" (*shunyata*) or "suchness" (*tathata*). Theravada makes a distinction between all conditioned things or dharmas and the one unconditioned dharma, the state of nirvana. But Mahayana teaches that emptiness (shunyata) is actually the common predicate of all dharmas, whether conditioned or unconditioned. Emptiness means the absence of "own-being," that is, something existing through its own power and having an immutable essence. So emptiness is really the same thing as the truth of dependent arising. But Mahayana points out that not only are all conditioned dharmas (that is, the phenomenal world of samsara) empty, but also the unconditioned reality of nirvana is empty. This leads to the conclusion that, since both nirvana and samsara are empty, there is no essential difference between them. Nirvana is samsara.

The fact that emptiness is a predicate both of nirvana and of samsara means a revaluation of living in the world. Nirvana is not a state found by fleeing from this world, but it is experienced precisely within this world. There is a nirvanic quality that can be experienced in life if we but awaken to it, because of the emptiness that characterizes all reality. Nirvana is precisely awakening to emptiness, seeing the world as it really is in its "suchness."

So among Mahayanists, especially in East Asia, emptiness is considered a positive and powerful basis of reality. Emptiness is actually the creative source of all that is. Emptiness is the womb that gives birth to all reality. In more direct terms, it is the silence that surrounds and supports every sound, the stillness that is the foundation of all movement, the pure consciousness that is the ground of all thought.

So, what's it *all* about? The Dharma. Nirvana. Emptiness. These terms together, all basically undefinable, point to the shape of the ultimate reality in Buddhism.

Going For Refuge to the Buddha

Along with the Dharma and nirvana, it seems that the Buddha has always had some place within the Buddhist idea of ultimate reality. It should be clear by now that the Buddha is not God, although he did live as a god in one of the heavens in a previous existence. He is not "supernatural" in the sense of a power that comes from beyond to save people. The Buddha was, in his final lifetime, a human being like the rest of us humans, and he remained a human being for forty-five years after becoming the Buddha, until he died and reached the state of parinirvana, beyond existence and nonexistence. His great achievement was done at the human level, and thus it is a goal that all living beings can reach, since all living beings have the possibility of being born at the human level.

The Perfections and Powers of the Buddha

Still, as a human being the Buddha was "supernormal," for he achieved all those supreme spiritual qualities that are far beyond the capabilities of most. Over countless lifetimes he reached the ten perfections, achieved miraculous powers, and attained complete omniscience, not to mention various other higher powers. Yet all these attainments and powers, which might appear to outsiders as possible for God alone, do

A statue of the Buddha Shakyamuni in the posture of turning the wheel of the Dharma.

not make the Buddha a god. Rather, they make him, still a human being, into the Tathagata, the "one who has arrived there," the victorious one, the very embodiment of the Dharma.

To put the Buddha in the proper perspective, we need to remind ourselves that there have been and will be other Buddhas in the infinite cycles of the rise and fall of the universe. And they will all reach the same perfections and powers and teach the same Dharma. The story of Siddhartha Gautama is the story of a being who, through a long series of lifetimes as a bodhisattva, made such spiritual progress that becoming a Buddha was inevitable, and he was born as a human at the time and place of his own choosing, to achieve the great breakthrough and become the Buddha, the world saviour to whom Buddhists in our world-age go for refuge.

So then, it is appropriate to chant in devotions every day, "Adoration to him the blessed one, the worthy one, the fully enlightened one." Whereas Buddhists know that the Buddha is not alive today as a god or saviour, the powers he achieved are real and present in our world, symbolized by his images and relics, present in his words and teachings, experienced in meditation, and actualized in those who follow his path.

The Mahayana Vision: Dharmakaya and Heavenly Buddha

Mahayana Buddhists go much further than Theravadins in their visions of the Buddha reality. The ultimate reality seen in the Dharma, in emptiness, and in the achievement of the Buddha are brought together in the Mahayana notion of "Buddhahood," expressed especially in the Three Body doctrine. The doctrine of the Three Bodies of the Buddha, as worked out by philosophers of the Yogacara school, is a way of formulating the dimensions of ultimate reality in terms of Buddha. There are three "bodies" (kaya) or dimensions of "Buddha": the Dharma Body (Dharma-kaya), the Bliss Body (Sambhoga-kaya), and the Transformation Body (Nirmana-kaya).

The idea of Buddha now moves far beyond the historical human Siddhartha Gautama, the teacher. The Buddha is really the eternal power of the Dharma. The Dharma Body of the Buddha encompasses all aspects of ultimate reality. Just as the Dharma is universal, eternal, and ultimate, so also is the Buddha. Just as nirvana is unconditioned and absolutely free, so is the Buddha. The Buddha is the same as suchness and emptiness. It is the Buddha-source identified as the Womb of the Tathagata, innate to all living beings, irradiated by the pervading power of Buddhahood. Mahayana, with its notion of a supermundane, universal Buddha essence, brings into Buddhism something like Brahman in Hinduism—an underlying ultimate reality. The Dharma Body is the fundamental Buddha-essence, which permeates and supports all things.

The human form of the Buddha (Transformation Body) now is seen as a kind of magical-appearance body by which the everlasting Dharma Body of the Buddha showed humans in our age the path to enlightenment. Siddhartha was really an apparition that took on the characteristics of human life and reached enlightenment as a model and guide to other living beings in this age. Likewise the Buddha reality has shown itself through Transformation Bodies in countless other ages and worlds.

Further, it makes sense that the Dharma Body, characterized by eternal, all-powerful compassion, should create bodies in all times and places in the universe, to respond to the needs of living beings everywhere. And so Mahayanists believe that the universe is filled with heavenly Buddhas (the Bliss Body of the Buddha) who use all kinds of means to lead all living beings to enlightenment and salvation, functioning almost like gods and saviours. There have been, according to the Lotus Sutra, an infinite number of Buddhas saving people, hundreds of trillions of kinds.

One of the most widely worshiped of the heavenly Buddhas is Amitabha (Unlimited Light). Countless aeons ago, Amitabha was a monk named Dharmakara who decided to become a Buddha. He was taught by the Buddha for ten million years and practiced meditation for five aeons, concentrating all the qualities of Buddhahood on the creation of one Buddhaland, the Pure Land. He vowed that his Buddhaland would contain no evil destinies, that all those reborn there would be destined for nirvana, and that all who meditate on him could share in his merit and thus attain rebirth in this paradise. After practicing as a bodhisattva for a trillion years, Dharmakara became the Buddha Amitabha, presiding over the Pure Land of the West, sending out unlimited compassion to all who call on him.

Another important heavenly expression of ultimate Buddhahood is Mahavairocana (great Shining Out), widely worshiped as the sun Buddha. One view is that Mahavairocana is actually the cosmic Dharma Body of the earthly Buddha. Important especially in Tantric Buddhism, Mahavairocana's body is really the whole cosmos, and his mind and power permeate the universe. In some schools of Mahayana, Buddha Mahavairocana, elevated to the status of the all-encompassing Buddha reality, approaches a monotheistic concept.

Of course, it is generally recognized that these countless Buddhas are not themselves the ultimate reality, but they are manifestations of the ultimate in various times and places to lead people to salvation. We need to understand that since truth is experienced at different levels, Buddhism can tolerate the worship of these heavenly Buddhas and much more, including bodhisattvas, gods, goddesses, and a variety of local spirits. And this is true both in Mahayana and in Theravada lands. For the common people these various divine forces are direct sources of help and salvation. For the spiritually advanced, these forces are but expressions of the universal Buddha nature or are simply divine beings operating within the samsara existence.

EXISTENCE IN THE WORLD

"What is this world all about anyway?" The origin of the world is not so important to Buddhists as the nature of the world and of ourselves. The Buddha said, "The first beginning of beings wandering and running round, enveloped in ignorance and bound down by the fetters of thirst is not to be perceived."[5] Questions about origin and purpose could imply a beginning and an end, and Buddhists think more in terms of a beginningless, endless process. Of more concern is the question: what is the nature of reality and what is one's own nature? Long wrestlings with these questions have produced both deep intellectual speculations and single-minded practices.

The Nature of the World

Origin of the World and of Humans

Buddhists like Hindus think of the universe as virtually endless both in time and in space. One illustration, for example, says that the amount of time this universe has existed is innumerable times greater than how long it would take to wear down to sea level a vast high mountain by touching it lightly with a piece of soft Banaras silk once every one hundred years. And texts talk of hundreds of trillions of worlds, so that our earth is but a small point in the vast canvas of the universe.

The Buddhist traditions agree with the Hindu view that there are periodic creations and destructions of the universe, like the rhythm of waves on the sea. As the various worlds are destroyed and evolve again, beings are born from one into another because of karma. The Buddha told a story about this process in which he skillfully rejected the idea of creation of the world through the god Brahma.

> There comes time, my friends, sooner or later, . . . when the world is dissolved and beings are mostly reborn in the World of Radiance [one of the heavens]. There they dwell, made of the stuff of mind, feeding on joy, shining in their own light, flying through middle space, firm in their bliss for a long, long time.
>
> Now there comes a time when this world begins to evolve, and then the World of Brahma [a lower heaven] appears, but it is empty. And some being, whether because his allotted span is past or because his merit is exhausted, quits his body in the World of Radiance and is born in the empty World of Brahma, where he dwells for a long, long time. Now because he has been so long alone he begins to feel dissatisfaction and longing, and wishes that other beings might come and live with him. And indeed soon other beings quit their bodies in the World of Radiance and come to keep him company in the World of Brahma.
>
> Then the being who was born first there thinks: "I am Brahma, the mighty Brahma, the Conqueror, the Unconquered, the All-seeing, the Lord, the Maker, the Creator, the Supreme Chief, the Disposer, the Controller, the Father of all that is or is to be. I have created all these beings, for I merely wished that they might be and they have come here!" And the other beings . . . think the same, because he was born first and they later.

And it might well be that some being would quit his body there and be reborn in this world. He might then give up his home for the homeless life; and . . . he might attain such a stage of meditation that with collected mind he might recall his former birth, but not what went before. Thus he might think: "We were created by Brahma, eternal, firm, everlasting, and unchanging, who will remain so for ever and ever, while we . . . are transient, unstable, short-lived, and destined to pass away."

"That," said the Buddha, "is how your traditional doctrine comes about that the beginning of things was the work of the god Brahma."[6] So the idea of creation of the universe by Brahma is an illusion. Really, the world and all living beings, including the gods, go on through successive stages of evolution and devolution, without beginning, without end.

According to the Buddhist tradition, the beings reborn on earth in this process begin to eat an earth essence and thus become dependent on subtle morsel food, their bodies becoming more substantial. Then they start eating a rice-pap sort of food, and male and female characteristics appear, and soon they indulge in sexual acts. Finally the earth-human society evolves to include the idea of private property with individual rice plots, stealing, and violence—and our human historical era begins.

The Real Nature of the World and of Humans

Like all the peoples from India, Buddhism accepts the basic idea of karma and samsara. There is a wheel of existence, both for the whole world and for the individual, and it is propelled by karma. But what is distinctive about the Buddhist view is the emphasis on impermanence, no-self, and dependent arising as doctrines about the nature of the world.

What is there to really hold on to in this world? Nothing. For there is nothing that is permanent, lasting, and absolute. Everything is impermanent, in a process of flux, coming into being and passing out of being endlessly. Even the gods, even the world itself, come and go. Even Brahman, central to Hindu belief as absolute reality, cannot be an eternal, unchanging reality. Whatever exists is a stream of becoming. A beautiful, fragile blossom is often used to exemplify this view. It blooms in beauty momentarily, but then it is driven to the ground by the rain or wilted by the sun. That is not particularly tragic or to be regretted; that is the nature of existence.

One aspect of the doctrine of impermanence regards one's own self. What is the real self? From Hinduism we learned that inward of the empirical self is the real atman, eternal and indestructible, which is embodied in existence after existence but itself does not change. The Buddha says there is no atman, no permanent reality we can call the self. Rather, that which we call the self or the person is really a changing process made up of a series of five aggregates combined together for a lifetime. This process of aggregates includes physical matter, sensations, perceptual activities, impulses to action, and bits of consciousness. These aggregates come together for a lifetime, constantly changing, and they dissipate when the lifetime ends. Where, beyond these aggregates, asks the Buddha, do you see a permanent self? There is none.

For understanding the nature of the world, it is important to remember the central Buddhist teaching about dependent arising, which shows the interconnectedness of everything. Everything is conditioned by other things, but it is false to assert that everything happens randomly by chance. Thus there is some continuity even in this world of change. For example, is an old man the same person as he was when he was a baby? On the one hand, he obviously is not, for everything about him has changed since babyhood. On the other hand, he still is the same because of the common stream of conditions that has made him what he is.

So it is the idea of dependent arising that makes it possible to understand how there can be rebirth cycles and yet no permanent self. Hinduism teaches that the eternal atman passes from one lifetime to the next. The question for Buddhism is: what is it that goes through the rebirth cycles if there is no atman? The answer is that *nothing* goes through the rebirth cycles. Rather each rebirth is caused by the previous existences in a chain of causation. It is like touching the flame of one candle to the wick of another and lighting it. Nothing is passed from the one candle to the next; there is no "candle-soul" or substance transmitted, yet the first burning candle is the cause of the burning of the second candle. It is the heat from the first flame that combusts the second candle, and likewise it is the karma from one lifetime that "combusts" the next lifetime.

Whereas the highest truth about the world consists in these doctrines of impermanence, no-self, and conditioned arising, there is still ample reason to carry on life in the world in a constructive, beneficial way. That I am no real self is the highest truth, to be realized by those reaching high spiritual perfection. Yet "my" life-process goes on, interrelated with all other living beings, and further teachings about reality provide guidance on the ideal way to live. One important idea is the interrelationship of all things: all beings are one in the ocean of life. What affects one affects all. Another important facet of reality is the nature of karma. As explained by the Buddha, the law of karma has a volitional aspect; it is not the working of a merely mechanical fate, but it involves will and desire. I am who I am now because of past existences, but every moment I have the freedom to perform moral rather than immoral actions, thus changing the flow of karma and my own future existence.

Mahayana Buddhists have additional things to say about the nature of the world and human existence. Since the essence of all reality is the Buddha nature, the very truths of impermanence and no-self point to this. That is, the samsara cycle of birth and death *is* Buddhahood; all things interpenetrate all else, and all are the Buddha nature. What is thought to be the self is illusory, but one's true nature is Buddhahood. So the goal in life is to realize the Buddhahood of the world and oneself. Whereas Mahayanists share the fundamental Buddhist outlook on the the world, these additional doctrines give a somewhat different color to their view of the goal and the problematic of human existence.

The Human Problem: Clinging

The evolutionary cycles of the world, the stream of karma and rebirth, the impermanence of all things—these are neutral facts of existence. That's the way things are. So what's the problem?

The Truths of Suffering and Clinging

The problem, the Buddha said in his first sermon, is *dukkha*, suffering (the first Noble Truth). All existence is permeated with suffering. The Buddha was not a grim-faced doomsayer or even overly pessimistic about human life. He allowed that people do experience moments of happiness and joy. But there always is that sense of anxiety and uneasiness, knowing that we are going to lose what we have, knowing that finally we will lose even our selves in death. So the problem is a matter of how we experience our existence, constantly fearful of losing what is important to us.

Why do we feel this kind of suffering and anxiety? It is because of clinging, answers the Buddha (the second Noble Truth). We try desperately to cling and hold on to things like happiness, to life itself, to ourselves. But the truth is that there is nothing to cling to, since everything is passing, so we lose what we try to hold on to, and in the process we experience suffering.

Buddhists have gone to great lengths to illustrate these truths of suffering and the cause of suffering. Once, according to a poem by Ashvaghosha, a relative of the Buddha named Nanda became a monk but was about to leave the order because of his longing for his wife. The Buddha took him to the paradise of King Indra, a heaven of indescribable beauty where beings who had built up much merit as humans now live happily as gods, perpetually young and free from suffering. Beautiful celestial nymphs reward all who come to this paradise by virtue of their previous austerities. Seeing the ravishing beauty of the nymphs, Nanda forgot his wife, and the world of humans seemed to him no better than a cemetery. So, having seen this paradise, Nanda resumed his austerities in order to reach this reward. But his fellow monk Ananda warned him that living in paradise is only temporary, and that one day the gods there also will fall to be reborn on earth—and just think of the tremendous suffering they will feel because of the great delights and pleasures they will finally be losing! "It is better, therefore," Ananda counselled, "to strive for final release. Even the dwellers in heaven, with all their might, come to an end. No intelligent man would set his heart on winning the right to a brief stay among them."[7]

Trapped in Ignorance

Why is it that we are trapped in an existence in which we are constantly desiring and therefore constantly suffering? To account for the arising of these conditions, Buddhists apply the principle of dependent arising to human existence. They picture a series of twelve causes of becoming, each cause conditioning the next cause. Frequently these twelve causes are pictured in the form of a twelve-spoked wheel, since there really is no beginning or end to the process. The hub of the wheel, the driving force, is made up of hatred, delusion, and greed. And the twelve groups of conditions are:

1. Ignorance, causing volitional actions
2. Volitional actions, causing consciousness
3. Consciousness, causing personal existence
4. Personal existence, causing the mind and the senses
5. Mind and senses, causing mental and sensorial contact
6. Mental and sensorial contact, causing sensations and feelings
7. Sensations and feelings, causing craving
8. Craving, causing grasping
9. Grasping, causing new becoming-forces
10. Becoming-forces, causing rebirth
11. Rebirth, causing aging and dying
12. Aging and dying—causing ignorance again

And the wheel rolls on and on. Buddhist art has developed a graphic form of this wheel, held in the claws and mouth of the demon Death.

The wheel of existence leads to the six realms or destinies of rebirth. The most degrading realms of rebirth are the hells (age-long but not eternal punishment), next the realm of the hungry ghosts, then the realm of animals. Fourth is the human realm, fifth that of the demigods, and the highest realm is that of the gods. Remember that even the gods, when their traces of karma run out, suffer death and lower rebirth, because they lack sufficient merit—and losing their heavenly joys causes indescribable suffering. Only in the human realm can virtue and wisdom be increased,

to proceed toward the goal, to transcend the wheel entirely.

So the whole wheel of life is really a trap, founded especially in ignorance, the delusion that I am a self and therefore I need things for myself. "I am—therefore I want." Our faint stirrings of morality, compassion, and goodness are quickly swallowed up by delusion, desire, and anger, and the wheel of selfish existence rolls on.

To stop this wheel of existence takes something more than struggle and selfish desire—it takes getting on the path of transformation.

THE PATH TO NIRVANA AND BUDDHAHOOD

"How can I start living *real* life?" "Where are meaning and peace to be found?"

Paradoxically, the Buddha taught that the only way to find real life is to withdraw from life, to work toward cessation of those attachments that keep existence going. Some therefore have thought of Buddhism as a negative, world-denying religious path designed to lead to extinction. But that is to misunderstand Buddhism. The path leads to cessation of attachments so that true life and meaning can be experienced—that which is called nirvana or Buddhahood.

The path of transformation is varied in Buddhism, as in Hinduism, although there is wide agreement on the basics of the path as taught by the Buddha, the noble Eightfold Path leading to nirvana. The Mahayana movement expanded the path, expressing the goal more in terms of Buddhahood or bodhisattvahood than in terms of nirvana.

Nirvana and the Noble Eightfold Path

The human problem, as we saw, is depicted in terms of suffering caused by craving or clinging in a universe that is characterized by impermanence. At the heart of the problem is human ignorance and the illusion of a permanent self. The Buddha described the human problematic only to show the way out, the means of conquering and reaching liberation.

Monks chanting Buddhist sutras, at Eiheiji Temple in Japan.

The Noble Truth of Nirvana

In his sermon at the Deer Park in Sarnath, after enunciating the first truth that human existence is suffering and the second truth that the cause of suffering is craving, the Buddha presented the third Noble Truth: "The Noble Truth of the Cessation of suffering is this: It is the complete cessation of that very thirst, giving it up, renouncing it, emancipating oneself from it, detaching oneself from it."[8] The suffering and frustration of our existence can be removed! It is removed by eliminating that which causes it, namely, craving. All craving can be eliminated by removing all the conditions on which it depends. The conditions on which craving depends are, we remember, depicted in the twelve-spoked wheel of existence: ignorance, wrong intentions, impure consciousness, the illusion of self, and so forth. Eliminating these conditions, and thus eliminating craving, will bring cessation of suffering. And this is the state of nirvana.

Nirvana is not the extinction of existence, nor is it a state to be experienced only after death. Nirvana (blowing out, cooling off) is the experience of full life and meaning achieved by eliminating all forms of grasping and attachment. It is complete freedom from conditions and limitations, permitting life to be lived in the full richness of the present moment, without fear or anxiety. Since the causes of bondage have been eliminated, one who attains nirvana will not experience further rebirths in the samsara cycle; the liberation is complete.

It sounds simple. But as we all experience over and over, eliminating craving is an awesome thing, and even the most painful results of our craving do not induce us to give up that craving. How can this state of nirvana be attained?

The Noble Eightfold Path

The Buddha was more concerned with practical spiritual results than with philosophical speculations about existence. He thought of himself as a physician or therapist. He showed people their symptoms (suffering), made a diagnosis of what causes the suffering (craving), made a prognosis that suffering can be stopped by stopping the cause (nirvana), and finally gave the prescription: the Path.

Not all the Buddha's disciples were satisfied with this practical approach. The monk Malunkyaputta felt the Buddha had left unanswered a whole set of important questions, like whether the world is eternal, whether it is infinite, whether the self and the body are identical, and whether one who reaches nirvana exists after death. So he challenged the Buddha, saying that he would leave the monastic life unless the Buddha would answer these questions. The Buddha reminded Malunkyaputta that he had never promised to answer such questions, and further he pointed out that the questions rested on so many assumptions and distinctions that they could not be answered in a lifetime. But, most important, these questions are simply beside the point.

> It is as if, Malunkyaputta, a man had been wounded by an arrow thickly smeared with poison, and his friends and companions, his relatives and kinsfolk, were to procure for him a physician or surgeon, and the sick man were to say: "I will not have this arrow taken out until I have learned whether the man who wounded me belonged to the brahmana, kshatriya, vaishya, or shudra class; the name of the person who wounded me and the clan to which be belongs; whether he was tall, short, or medium in height; whether he was black, yellow, or brown; what village, city, or town he was from; what kind of wood the bow was made from; what kind of

material the bow-string was made of; what kind of arrow it was, and with what it was feathered; what kind of sinews it was bound with; and what kind of point it had." That man would die, Malunkyaputta, without ever having learned this.[9]

This kind of speculation does not profit, nor does it have to do with the fundamentals of the religious path. Whether the world is eternal or not, there still remains birth, old age, death, and suffering. The important thing is to get on the Path.

The noble Eightfold Path sets forth a whole way of life leading progressively to higher levels of spiritual transformation. It consists in:

1. Right understanding ⎫ Wisdom
2. Right intention   ⎭
3. Right speech   ⎫
4. Right action   ⎬ Moral conduct
5. Right livelihood ⎭
6. Right effort   ⎫
7. Right mindfulness   ⎬ Contemplation
8. Right concentration ⎭

These eight norms are not separate steps, as if one followed the other in succession. Rather one should cultivate a way of life in which all eight norms are followed together, for each supports all the others. The eight are traditionally grouped in the three basic axioms of the path, namely Wisdom, Moral Conduct, and Contemplation.

First, Wisdom involves both some basic understanding of the nature of existence and also the intention to act in accord with this understanding. Right understanding would include knowing the four noble truths of existence, the doctrines of impermanence and no-self, the teaching of the conditionedness of all existence, and the like. Whereas understanding deepens as we follow the Path, some understanding is necessary to reverse our ignorance and motivate us to start on the path in the first place. This leads to the right intention of freeing ourselves from the conditions of craving by cultivating the virtues of selflessness, goodwill, compassion, and love for all beings.

Next, Moral Conduct results directly from Wisdom. Right speech is telling the truth, speaking in kindly and friendly ways, and saying only what is helpful. Right action means not killing or hurting living things, no stealing, and no wrong sexual activity; positively it fosters the welfare of all living beings. Right livelihood involves avoidance of occupations that bring harm to others, accepting only those occupations that promote peace and well-being.

Finally, Contemplation is made possible when all the other norms are in place, and it involves a steady discipline of mind that leads to awareness and insight. Right effort means achieving a strong will that prevents and gets rid of wrong states of mind and creates and develops wholesome states of mind. Right mindfulness means being carefully aware of what goes on in the body and in the mind, attentively mindful of all sensations, feelings, and thoughts. And finally right concentration is the attainment, through meditation, of higher stages of mental awareness by direct insight and enlightenment. Here all sense of self and selfishness drops away, and ignorant grasping is replaced by peace and total freedom. The "I am" conceit is rooted out, and nirvana is experienced.

So it is most characteristic of the Buddhist path of transformation to consider meditation to be the final means toward reaching nirvana. There are different types of meditation, of course, as Buddhists point out. One type, for example, involves concentrating and focusing the mind on an object or idea, leading to the calming of the mental processes and even to higher states of trance and supernormal psychic experiences. Whereas this type of meditation can be useful, the movement of meditation that leads toward nirvana involves developing insight and awareness, for finally it is "seeing" reality as it *really* is (the truth of dependent arising) that brings the nirvanic experience. So the Buddha taught *vipassana*, "insight" meditation, an analytic method based on mindfulness, observation, and total awareness of reality as it is.

The Buddha suggested that such meditation might profitably deal with four areas of life: the body, the feelings, the mind, and intellectual subjects. For example, the meditator might simply become totally aware of the bodily breathing process, watching and observing every minute aspect of breathing-in and breathing-out.

Or again, the meditator might observe and become mindful of sensations and feelings. A Buddhist scholar, Walpola Rahula, explains the process and the goal:

> First of all, you should learn not to be unhappy about your unhappy feeling, not to be worried about your worries. But try to see clearly why there is a sensation or a feeling of unhappiness, or worry, or sorrow. Try to examine how it arises, its cause, how it disappears, its cessation. Try to examine it as if you are observing it from outside, without any subjective reaction, as a scientist observes some object. Here, too, you should not look at it as "my feeling" or "my sensation" subjectively, but only look at it as "a feeling" or "a sensation" objectively. You should forget again the false idea of "I." When you see its nature, how it arises and disappears, your mind grows dispassionate towards that sensation, and becomes detached and free.[10]

So also through meditation one becomes totally aware of the operation of the mind, knowing the mind with lust as being with lust, the mind without lust as being without lust, the mind with hate as being with hate, the mind without hate as being without hate, and so forth, through all states of mind, cultivating total awareness and with it the cessation of attachment and clinging. Further, one may meditate on the truths about reality—the Four Noble Truths, the five aggregates, and so on. By becoming totally aware and thus seeing reality directly as it is, one facilitates the cessation of clinging and false sense of self, moving toward the experience of nirvana.

Arhants and Laypeople on the Path

Following the Path is a lifelong affair, indeed, a many-lifetimes affair for all but the most spiritually advanced. Because of the disciplines involved, to follow the Path fully one must leave society and become a nun or monk. Among the monastic community various levels of attainment are also recognized. At a high stage of spiritual perfection a monk or nun is recognized to be a "stream-winner," destined to have only a limited number of rebirths before reaching nirvana. Higher yet are the "once-returner," who will experience only one more rebirth, and the "nonreturner," who will achieve nirvana in this lifetime. The final stage is the arhant (worthy one), one who has already achieved nirvana and lives the completely enlightened, free life. Even for the monks and nuns at lower spiritual levels, the goal held out is victory over the world, the elimination of the illusion of self, the attainment of nirvana.

What about the laypeople in Buddhism? How can they follow such an elite religious path? Is there no hope for them? In Theravada Buddhism, it is true, the laity cannot expect to reach the goal of nirvana without eventually becoming a monk or nun. But laypeople can still get on the path and cultivate at least generosity and moral conduct. Besides deepening their understanding and intention, such disciplines also build up merit to counterbalance their store of bad karma. Merit can bring about more favorable rebirths; sufficient merit can even bring about rebirth as a god. The final goal of such merit, of course, is a lifetime in which the pursuit of nirvana will be possible. But that may be a long way off, and in the meantime it is better to be reborn in a happy state than in a despicable state. Some Theravadin laypeople do practice meditation, of course.

The Mahayana Enlargement of the Path of Transformation

Whereas Mahayana Buddhists accept the basics of the path as described above, their expanded vision of the sangha and the Buddha allows for additional possibilities on the path. Nirvana is understood as realizing one's Buddhahood, and this path is open to laypeople as well as monastics. The model to follow on the path is the bodhisattva rather than the arhant. And new possibilities of help from heavenly Buddhas and of realizing the inner Buddha-nature make this a much broader path of transformation. Yet it still is, we must remember, the same path of the Buddha.

Becoming the Buddha: The Broad Path

Since Mahayanists believe the Dharma Body of the Buddha is the source and essence of all reality, the goal of the path can be rephrased in terms of realizing one's Buddha-nature. Further, since the Buddha-nature (or nirvana) is not a state apart from this life but is in fact identical with the samsara world, the goal is to awaken to the Buddha-nature of this very life. The basic problem, for Mahayanists as well as Theravadins, is ignorance. We do not see the real Buddha-nature, and instead we cling to our illusory nature—and we suffer in this lifetime while creating an equally suffering future lifetime by our karma. How do we start living the real Buddha life?

The place to start is certainly the discipline of the Eightfold Path. But since the emphasis is on realizing the Buddhahood of all beings, the path stresses the awakening of the thought of enlightenment and the cultivation of compassion. Monastic disciplines are still important, but even laypeople can attain the realization of Buddhahood.

In a significant shift on the path of transformation, Mahayana Buddhists do not look to the arhant, reaching nirvana with great discipline and effort, as the supreme spiritual model. Rather, the Mahayana path is

Statue of a bodhisattva, probably Avalokiteshvara, from thirteenth century Nepal.

really the course of the bodhisattva, an enlightened being who reaches nirvana but voluntarily remains in the samsara existence for the purpose of helping others. The Mahayana scriptures record many bodhisattva vows, put forth as a model to guide all beings on the path of transformation. Here is one such vow:

> A Bodhisattva resolves: I take upon myself the burden of all suffering.... And why? At all cost I must bear the burdens of all beings, in that I do not follow my own inclinations. I have made the vow to save all beings. All beings I must set free. The whole world of living beings I must rescue, from the terrors of birth, of old age, of sickness, of death and rebirth, of all kinds of moral offense, of all states of woe, of the whole cycle of birth-and-death, of the jungle of false views.... I must not cheat all beings out of my store of merit. I am resolved to abide in each single state of woe for numberless aeons; and so I will help all beings to freedom, in all the states of woe that may be found in any world system whatsoever.[11]

The bodhisattva pursues a path of transformation based on the cultivation of compassion, of sharing merit with others, as the highest virtue that finally transforms one. The path of the bodhisattva is a model for all, showing the infinite transformations ahead on the path and the shape of the final goal.

Two Ways on the Path

Because of the idea of the universal Buddha-nature, in Mahayana there can be a number of approaches toward this path of transformation. It is possible, on the one hand, to practice meditation and see directly into one's Buddha-nature and the Buddha-nature of all reality. On the other hand, the compassionate nature of the Buddha reality makes it possible to receive help along the path from various bodhisattvas and Buddhas who are dedicated to the salvation of all beings. Frequently the path can be a combination of these two impulses.

Meditation plays an important role for many on the Mahayana path, as in Theravada. But a special emphasis is meditation on emptiness, that is, seeing the nirvanic quality of all reality. If one's real nature is the Buddha-nature, then transformation occurs by overcoming the illusion of separate selfhood and awakening to the Buddha-nature within. In this sense, one can "become Buddha" even within this very body and life—that is, awaken to one's innate Buddha-nature and thus live life in a transformed way. And this awakening is available for all people, not only for monks and nuns, for all people equally possess the Buddha-nature.

The meditation practices of Tantric Buddhism have often focused on the potential each person has for realizing the inner Buddha-nature through ritual practices. In Tibetan Buddhism, for example, one important ritual technique is visualization. Since the cosmos is filled with Buddha-nature, it is possible through ritual meditation using sounds, movements, and pictures to visualize and so mentally create that cosmic Buddha reality and to identify oneself with it.

The strong Mahayana ideas about the universal Buddha essence, the virtue of compassion, and the model of the bodhisattva mean that the path of transformation can include reliance on power from Buddhas as well as self-power for transformation and salvation. If one cannot follow the holy path of discipline and meditation to reach nirvana, and if one cannot even build up sufficient merit to hope for a better rebirth, there still is another way: one can rely on the power of the merciful Buddhas and bodhisattvas for help and salvation. This path has become very popular in East Asian Buddhism, both for laypeople and for monks and nuns.

How can I, sinner that I am and living in this degenerate age, have assurance of salvation from these lifetimes of suffering and evil? The Pure Land school would answer: have firm faith and recite the powerful name of Amitabha Buddha. If people practice this as a discipline and make it the center of life, they will receive spiritual assurances and growth in this life and salvation in paradise in the next life. Most Pure Land Buddhists acknowledge that rebirth in the Pure Land is not yet Buddhahood—but those reborn there will never again be born at lower states of woe, and they will achieve Buddhahood in just a few more lifetimes. Nichiren Buddhists in Japan believe that, since the Lotus Sutra is the supreme truth and contains all Buddha power, reciting the title of the Lotus Sutra enables one to receive the power of Buddhahood; it brings great blessings to the individual and to the whole community.

How can this "easy path" still be called Buddhism? Behind this path is the basic vision of Mahayana: all beings are one in the ocean of life, and merit achieved by one can be shared with others. Through faith the mind and heart lie open to the presence of the Buddha power. Reciting the sacred name actualizes that power and transforms us, breaking the bonds of past karma and bringing us to realization of the Buddha-nature. In these Mahayana Buddhist schools the path of salvation is not a matter of an individual struggling on her own merits to reach liberation; it is rather a path in which the individual can tap into the communal resource of saving power made available through the supreme Buddha Power.

We see, then, that the path of transformation in Buddhism is multicolored. There is the nirvanic path of Theravada monks, the karmic-merit path of laypeople, the Buddhahood-realization path of the Mahayana schools, and the salvation-through-saving power path of still other Mahayana Buddhists. Though they seem quite different, one can still recognize the basic Buddhist accents in all of them.

DISCUSSION QUESTIONS

1. Discuss the ultimate as unconditioned truth. What is signified by "dependent arising"?
2. What is nirvana? What is emptiness (shunyata)?
3. What is the Mahayana doctrine of the Three Bodies of the Buddha?
4. Explain the doctrines of impermanence and no-self. How can there be rebirth if there is no-self?
5. What, according to Buddhism, is the basic problem in human existence?
6. Explain the workings of the Noble Eightfold Path, showing how it leads toward nirvana.
7. In Mahayana, what are the two general ways toward realizing Buddhahood?
8. What is a bodhisattva?

CHAPTER 18

Buddhist Worship and the Good Life

WORSHIP AND RITUAL

"How can I find new power for life?" "How can I get in touch with what is real?" Buddhists feel these needs as do people of other religions, and the answer lies in ritual practices and observance of sacred times.

Buddhism has a strong sense of individual mindful effort as the means of transformation, and with that has always gone a relativizing attitude toward worship and ritual. The goal of ultimate transformation, that is, nirvana, can be reached only by individual discipline and mindful meditation, not by acts of worship or ritual directed toward sacred beings. Certainly worship cannot provide forgiveness or expiation for sins. Bad karma can be diminished only by discipline and meritorious action.

335

Yet there still are many reasons and goals for worship and ritual in Buddhism, even for the spiritually advanced monks and nuns. Many rituals are commemorative, remembering and respecting the Buddha and the great saints of the past. Rituals can also be expressive, a way of showing emotions of thankfulness, respect, and devotion to the Buddha, the Dharma, and the sangha. Performing such rituals can remind and guide people in their practice of the path, and they can help to create the refreshed and peaceful mental attitude necessary for mindful meditation and meritorious action.

Many Buddhists believe that worship and ritual are also instrumental in bringing about blessings in life and even inner spiritual transformation. Worship can be beneficial in concerns like health, wealth, rainfall, coping with crises, passing through stages in life, and the like. And worship can contribute toward happy rebirths, because of the merit involved in making offerings to the Buddha and also because worship creates a favorable mental state—and it is the mental state at death that largely determines the nature of one's next existence. Sacred rituals like ordination as a monk, chanting the scriptures, and making pilgrimages can help to bring about important inner spiritual transformation.

Central Rites and Ceremonies of Buddhism

The Structure of Buddhist Ritual

For all the variety of ceremonial in different places of the Buddhist world, there are several basic rites that Buddhists perform no matter where they are. They always include some form of giving or offering in worship. Making offerings with the proper attitude and motivation serves to bring merit, and it is especially appropriate to show homage to the Buddha, the monks, and the spirits by making offerings of lighted candles, flowers, water, and food. Of course, the Buddha does not need or receive these offerings, for the state of parinirvana is beyond all this. But making the offerings brings merit for the future and blessings for this life; it reminds one of the Buddha and his teaching so as to

better contemplate his attributes; and it helps on the way toward selflessness and compassion.

Another rite that all Buddhists perform is bowing before the Buddha image, the pagoda in which Buddhist relics are kept, or other symbols of the Buddha or bodhisattvas. A person may bow to the rosary and to the cushion used for meditating. And parents may bow to their ten-year-old son who has just been initiated as a temporary novice monk. This ritual of bowing is not that of a humble sinner petitioning a holy God for pardon and blessing. Rather, it shows respect for the Buddha, the Dharma, the sangha, parents, teachers, and all beings on the path. By bowing a person experiences the truth of no-self, symbolically turning away from self-centeredness to the real Buddha-nature of compassion and love.

Buddhists also use words of prayer, devotion, commemoration, and petition. A widely used Buddhist common prayer runs like this:

> I beg leave! I beg leave! I beg leave! By act, by word, and by thought, I raise my hands in reverence to the forehead and worship, honor, look at, and humbly pay homage to the Three Gems—the Buddha, the Law, and the Order—one time, two times, three times, O Lord [Buddha]! . . . By this act of worship may I be free from the four States of Woe [in hell, as an animal, a ghost, a demon], the Three Scourges [war, epidemic, and famine], . . . the Four Deficiencies [tyrannical kings, wrong views about life after death, physically deformed, dull-witted], and the Five Misfortunes [loss of relatives, wealth, health, proper belief, morality], and may I quickly attain Nirvana, O Lord![1]

Buddhists often recite the Three Refuges and other important formulas, and monks and priests spend much time chanting words of scripture. In words of worship they share merit with all others, especially wishing love for all beings:

> May all creatures, all living things, all beings, all persons, all individuals, all males, all females, all Aryans, all non-Aryans, all gods, all mankind, all spirits be free from enmity, from care, and from oppression. May they all live happily. May they all be free from trouble and adversity. May they all enjoy prosperity. May they all help themselves through the law of karma.[2]

Meditation, of course, is one of the central practices of Buddhism, especially for monks and nuns but also for spiritually advanced laypeople. Whereas meditation is not necessarily a part of all Buddhist worship and ritual, typically it is done in a context of worship. Before Buddhists sit to meditate, they bow to the image of the Buddha and perhaps to images of bodhisattvas and other masters, and they chant scriptures together. After meditating they offer incense and bow again. Whereas meditation takes one beyond outward ritual to the higher truths, the ritual context is beneficial for calming the mind and developing the proper will and intent.

Universally used objects of worship include images of the Buddha and bodhisattvas. For some centuries after the Buddha's death no images of him were used. Instead people paid homage to symbols of the Buddha such as an empty throne, a pair of footprints, a wheel, or a lotus plant—symbols still used in Buddhist art. Later Buddhists began using images of the Buddha, and today people will almost always turn to such an image

as they worship. Other widely used objects of worship include relics of the Buddha, such as the famous Buddha tooth at the temple of Kandy in Sri Lanka, and also the stupas and pagodas in which the relics have been kept. Homage is paid also to monks and nuns and to the yellow robe they wear.

Daily Rituals and Worship

Traditional, pious Buddhists usually have a small shrine in their home, perhaps a simple shelf with a small Buddha image and a vase for offering flowers. The first act in the morning and the last act in the evening is worship, offering fresh flowers and/or food offerings, lighting a candle, bowing, reciting prayers, and sometimes saying the rosary of 108 beads.

Monks and nuns, on the path toward victory, of course, have a much more demanding ritual schedule throughout the day. Many of the common daily activities are accompanied with rituals of devotion and homage to the Buddha and the other sacred realities. From 3:00 a.m. in the morning until 10:00 p.m. at night there is typically a busy scheduule of chanting scripture, meditating, making offerings to the Buddha and to other monks, saying prayers, reciting the Three Refuges and the monastic rules, listening to talks on the Dharma, participating in the communal tea ceremony, and much more. Even daily work like gardening and cleaning can be ritual opportunity for spiritual transformation, as practiced especially in the Ch'an (Zen) monasteries of China and Japan.

Holy Days and Festivals

The rhythm of renewal follows a regular pattern on certain days of the month and the year, with variances, of course, in different Buddhist lands.

The Uposatha Holy Day

Although Buddhists do not have a weekly holy day like Saturday or Sunday for communal worship, some do observe a similar type of regular holy day (*uposatha*). This rhythm is based on the lunar calendar, with the days of the full moon and the new moon, together with the eighth day after each. On these days the monks have special observances, and these are appropriate

The great stupa at Sanchi. The gateway has important early Buddhist artistic depictions.

times for laypeople to visit the monastery or the temple for worship. This is not something required as a religious duty, and there is no demerit in not observing this worship—many good Buddhists only keep this day occasionally. But there is merit and benefit in going to the monastery or temple to show respect to the monks and the priests, hear them chant scripture, give offerings, receive the precepts, and listen to instruction. Even if one does not understand the words the monks are chanting, there is spiritual blessing just by being in their presence and honoring them. This is an opportunity for laypeople and monastics to meet together and share spiritual benefit.

These holy day observances provide an opportunity for some devout laypeople to live temporarily according to the rules of monastic life. A person who has a job and a family normally takes only the five precepts for laypeople (to refrain from taking life, from stealing, from wrong sexual relations, from wrong speech, and from drugs and liquor), but on this holy day the person can take some of the additional precepts followed by monks and nuns and stay overnight in the monastery, practicing the discipline of a novice monk, before returning to normal householder life the next day.

The Great Annual Festivals

Perhaps not a lot of Buddhists participate in the uposatha holy day, but the great annual holy days and festivals are central to the rhythm of religious life, providing occasions for all the people to gather at the temples and holy places. These annual festivals often commemorate events in the life of the Buddha or the great bodhisattvas and celebrating them provides an opportunity to get in on the sacred story and make it real once more. Other festivals have to do with the seasonal changes in monastic life and with the veneration that is due for the ancestors. Among the most important and most widely celebrated festivals are the New Year's festival, the Buddha's birthday, the beginning of the Rainy Season Retreat, the presentation of robes to the monks, and the Ullambana festival celebrated in China and Japan.

In Theravada countries, the New Year comes at the end of the dry season and the beginning of new life in nature, falling in the month of April. It is a time of cleaning up, washing away the demerits of the past, and starting afresh. The first two days are celebrated in a carnivallike atmosphere as a water festival—for water cleans away the old and the dirty. Besides the spiritual cleansing, it is great fun to douse each other with water! The third day of the festival is a time for rededication to the Buddhist path, worship at the temples, taking the precepts, and giving offerings. It is especially meritorious on this festival, as on other festivals, to set animals and fish free into enclosures or ponds where they will be safe from harm for the rest of their lives. Since the release of the animals is accompanied by a monk or priest reciting the Three Refuges and the Precepts, the animals become "children of the Buddha" and have increased advantage of better rebirths.

The birthday of the Buddha is a joyful celebration, observed on the last full moon in May in Southeast Asia and on the eighth of April in China and Japan. Besides the usual worship activities, this festival is marked by the ritual of washing the Buddha image—a ceremony based on the tradition that the Buddha was bathed with scented water poured down by the gods after he was born. Another important ceremony is the procession of Buddha images, amidst the cheering and shouting of the people setting off firecrackers, burning incense, scattering flowers, and the like. Children love this festival—on this day they can dress up in their finest clothes, themselves little Buddhas.

In Theravada communities the beginning of the Rain Retreat is an especially important sacred time. The practice of the Rain Retreat goes back to the Buddha's time in India, when monks gathered in caves during the rainy season for intensified spiritual practice. When the Rain Retreat begins, the monks and nuns dedicate themselves to study and meditation, and the laity present specially prepared candles to the monastery to burn throughout the retreat. Other special offerings of food, money, and items of personal use are also made to the monks, and the senior monk leads the laypeople in the recitation of the precepts and the prayers. During the month at the end of the Rain Retreat (October-November), the laypeople perform the ritual of presenting newly made yellow robes to the monks, together with other elaborate gifts. High government officials also participate in these ceremonies, showing that the continued presence of the monastery is essential for the welfare of society. Pagodas and houses are decorated with lamps during this time, and crowds of people throng the streets at night during this festival of lights.

A most popular festival in China and Japan is the Ullambana festival (All Souls' festival), which will be discussed in Part IV. There are many special festivals held in sacred places in addition to these widely observed festivals. For example, the Temple of the Tooth in Kandy, Sri Lanka, has a big ten-day celebration in August, featuring a procession of great elephants carrying the precious relic of the Buddha's tooth. Temples celebrate the birthdays of special Buddhas and bodhisattvas. Pilgrimage to the sacred places often takes place in the context of festivals.

Rituals of the Changes of Life

Buddhists, like other humans, have special rituals for the critical passages in life. Less concerned with birth and growth than with spiritual transformation and death, emphasis in Buddhism is especially on the rites of initiation and funeral rites.

The Rites of Passage

All over the Buddhist world, families and communities observe many prebirth and birth rituals. Some rituals ensure safety during pregnancy, and others are directed to the health and welfare of the baby: the first head-washing, placing into the new cradle, naming, and so forth. These rituals are observed according to local tradition with little Buddhist context, although monks may bring blessing to the family by their presence. Likewise, the variety of wedding rituals has little reference to Buddhist concerns, and Buddhist monks and priests do not usually attend the actual wedding ceremony. They, of course, may be invited to chant sutras for the safety of the new home and to be fed by offerings from the family. Buddhists recognize that birth, growth, sexuality, and happiness in life are important, and it is all right to perform rituals dedicated to those gods and spirits who provide these blessings. But the world is transitory, and the deeper Buddhist truth teaches one to keep all this in perspective by cultivating detachment and preparing for a holy death.

Much more important, as far as Buddhism is concerned, are the rites of passage that focus on the higher truths. In many Theravada communities the ritual of initiation for a young boy is one of the most important events of community life. The initiation corresponds to a puberty rite of passage, but its meaning is a spiritual transformation: the young boy becomes a novice monk for a temporary period. Typically this ceremony is carried out amid great festivities, the family inviting many relatives and friends for a joyful celebration complete with food, songs, dancing, and the like, in honor of the young prince decked out in his finest. In some communities an ear-boring ceremony is performed for young girls at the same time so that they share the attention, although this ceremony does not indicate a spiritual passage in the Buddhist sense. It is after all these festivities, when most of the guests have left, that the real ceremony takes place. Some monks assemble, the boy's head is shaved, and he takes the vows of the monastic life. Now he spends the night in the monastery and, when he goes out begging the next day, even his parents bow to him to honor his elevated spiritual state. After a few days or weeks the boy may return to normal life, but now he is spiritually an adult and may reenter the monastery again sometime in the future.

All things are impermanent. So Buddhists believe they should keep death in mind always, and funerals are times to remember most directly the transitory nature of existence. Buddhists also believe that a person's rebirth is determined at least in part by her state of mind immediately before death, so preparation for death is vitally important. And if the departed person is reborn in one of the states of woe, as a hungry ghost or in one of the hells, it becomes important for the descendants to offer prayer and merit to ease the sufferings and make deliverance possible.

To help the dying person to a peaceful, unattached, calm state of mind, Buddhist devotions are recited at the death bed, and monks may come to recite sutras. Pure Land Buddhists recite the name of Amida Buddha over and over, on the basis of Amida's vow to save all beings who recite his name. After death the body is washed and the head shaved. Many friends and relatives come to call, and on the day of the funeral a Buddhist service is held in which the priests chant scriptures and burn incense. Then the body is taken in a procession to the crematorium or to the burial ground, and the memorial tablet may be taken back to the house and placed in the household shrine. A variety of rituals during the funeral may offer food to hungry ghosts, keep the soul of the deceased from returning to the house, and transfer the merit of the monks to the departed one. After the funeral, regular rites are held on the seventh day and at regular intervals thereafter, including annual anniversaries of the death. Although rites for the dead differ widely among areas such as Burma, Tibet, and China, they all symbolize that this most critical passage of life is taken seriously and affects everyone, the living as well as the dead. Hope for a favorable rebirth is a central concern. Yet at the same time, Buddhists believe we should think of the higher truth that our own life with its karma causes rebirth and that ultimate liberation from the rebirth and redeath cycle is the final goal.

The Great Spiritual Passage of Life

These natural passages of life have spiritual importance. But the highest and most beneficial passage is that critical step of leaving normal life with all its cares and clingings, passing through the narrow passage to become a mendicant to follow the higher path of the Buddha. Ordination into monkhood is therefore a very important community affair, and those who bear its expense build up a considerable amount of merit. Some Buddhist communities, especially in China, traditionally had a tonsure ceremony that preceded ordination. The candidate was accepted by a spiritual master, who performed the head-shaving ceremony and thus established the candidate as a trainee, learning the discipline to be a monk. In Theravada lands, it is customary for ordination as a novice to come before full ordination. The novice takes the Three Refuges and the Ten Precepts in the "going forth" ceremony.

Full ordination (*upasampada*) as a monk or nun is a drastic step and not to be taken lightly. The candidate must be at least twenty years of age, and much training and preparation are involved. For the ordination ceremony there must be an assembly of at least ten monks. The candidate is presented by his tutors, and he petitions the assembly for admission to the sangha. His tutors examine him to make sure he has his begging bowl and proper monk's robes, and then he is questioned to ascertain that he is free from certain diseases, and that he is a freeman, debtless, exempt from military service, at least twenty years old, and furnished with his parents' permission. The candidate then kneels and asks the assembly for ordination. Silence indicates assent, and the interrogation is repeated a second time. The proclamation is made: "If any approves, let him be silent. If any objects, let him speak." If silence follows three repetitions of the proclamation, the tutors announce that the candidate has received ordination, noting down the date and the hour of the ordination into the sangha, since seniority is determined not by age but by time of ordination. Then the new monk is given an exhortation to the effect that from now on his four reliances are to be alms for food, old rags for clothing, the shade of a tree for shelter, and cow's urine for medicine. The ordination of a nun is much the same as that of a monk.

Art in Buddhism

With its focus on escaping the world and reaching nirvana, it might seem that Buddhism would hardly be conducive to art's sensous, earthy aspects. For example, monks and nuns vow to wear no ornamentation and to go to no shows or music. But Buddhism, like most other religions, does harness the various human creative activities to produce art expressive of the Buddhist vision of life. Though the emphasis is on enlightenment and nirvana, the path proceeds through human life with its many activities and arts. And the aesthetic expressions that most deeply and compellingly express the real meaning of human life are those that arise from the creative power of one who has awakened to the Truth by following the path.

Since the Dharma rests on the word of the Buddha, it is fitting that Buddhists have always cultivated the literary arts. From the very beginning up to the present the sacred words have been memorized, recited, reiterated, elaborated, written, chanted, and sung with an enormous inlay of artistic power and creativity. The narrative art has been especially important: the creation of stories about the previous lives of the Buddha, elaborations on the events in the Buddha's life, stories about many other Buddhas and bodhisattvas, and stories about saints to provide inspiration and a model to follow. Poetry is another characteristic Buddhist literary art, for the sense of oneness with nature and the immediacy of insight into the truth can be especially well expressed in a poem. From the earliest disciples of the Buddha come poems like this:

I am thin
I am sick & weak
but leaning on my stick I go
climbing the mountain
I lay aside my robe
turn my bowl upside down
lean against a rock
& smash the mass of darkness
today I went to beg for alms
shaven & dressed in robes
I sat at the foot of a tree
& attained to nonthinking
all bonds are loosed
human & heavenly
I have destroyed all drunkenness
I have become cool : quenched[3]

Probably the most characteristic Buddhist art form is the Buddha sculpture, omnipresent wherever there is a temple, shrine, or altar. In the early centuries Buddhists refrained from creating images of the Buddha, possibly reflecting the transcendence of the Buddha, plus the practical consideration of educating the people not to worship him as they were accustomed to worship Hindu gods. Beginning around the first century B.C.E. or C.E., artists began creating statues of the Buddha standing, seated, or reclining, illustrating different qualities of Buddhahood. Of particular importance are the hand gestures (*mudras*) on the statue. Of the many gestures, these might be mentioned: the mudra of the fulfilling of the vow, with the palm lowered and turned outward in a gesture of offering; the mudra that grants the absence of fear, with the hand raised, palm facing outward; the mudra of appeasement or teaching the Dharma, hand raised, palm outward, with thumb touching the end of the index finger; the mudra of touching the ground, with right hand pointing downward; and the mudra of concentration, with the hands in the lap. Representational art, of course, also includes paintings and drawings; one important type is

The Sri Mahatat Temple in Bankok, Thailand.

the mandala, a depiction of the whole universe emanating from the cosmic Buddhas.

Architectural expressions of Buddhism include the early stupas, gravemounds that housed the relics of the Buddha and many other artistic symbols. Outside of India a most impressive stupa is that at Borobudur in Java, a giant mandala in stone, with the pilgrim path representing the search for enlightenment adorned with more than two thousand reliefs. The Buddhist temple takes many forms, influenced by the different indigenous cultures, from the pagoda form in southeast Asia to the massive temples of China and Japan, complete with statutes of the Buddhas, bodhisattvas, and arhants.

BUDDHIST SOCIETY AND THE GOOD LIFE

"How should I live?" To be Buddhist is to take the Buddha's story as one's own, to find one's place in the community of those on the path of the Buddha, that is, the sangha, following the ethical precepts given by the Buddha.

The Structure of Buddhist Society

The Sangha as Monastic Community

In one sense the sangha is restrictive, focused in the community of monks and nuns. But in another sense it is wide open, open, that is, to all who genuinely search for the truth. Buddhism rejected the caste system of Hinduism and accepted people of all classes and castes and of both sexes into the sangha. The major requirement is that people enter voluntarily and in good faith, willing to dedicate themselves totally to seeking enlightenment.

The main purpose of the monastic community is to strive for nirvana. This means that the social ideal for monks and nuns is radical world renunciation, for nirvana can be achieved only by the extinction of all attachments to the world and its vanities. It might seem that the sangha monastic community, the ideal social order for Buddhists, is antisocial in its very essence. The monk or nun rejects many normal social values, begs instead of works, does not marry or have a family, and cannot participate in politics or defense of the community. If all people joined the sangha, there could be no society!

But the sangha does have a constructive role in society. First of all, its very presence is a constant reminder to all Buddhists of the ultimate goal of the Buddhist path—to transcend attachment to the world and reach nirvana. Only a small percentage of the people in society join the monastic community, of course. It is estimated that in the 1950s somewhat under one percent of Thailand's population were in the monasteries. There may be about five percent of Burma's population who are monastics.[4] But for all of the laypeople the monastic life represents the final goal of the path. Further, the monks and nuns perform valuable spiritual services for the laypeople, even though all recognize this is not their primary function. The temple-monastery complex also contains halls where the laity can participate in the ceremonies and school buildings where the local boys and girls can be instructed. Monks and nuns regularly chant scriptures and perform rituals at the temple and at people's homes. The basic idea is that some of the purity and merit built up in the monastic life can be channeled into the community for the benefit of all.

The Role of the Laypeople in Buddhist Society

Buddhist laypeople are not following the nirvanic goal; rather, they pursue the karmic goal of a good life and better rebirths. Along with living according to Buddhist moral precepts, one of the most important roles of the laity is to support and maintain the sangha, making it possible for the monks and nuns to strive for nirvana. Supporting those who are on the monastic path brings a good deal of spiritual merit. It might be said that, whereas in some other religions the clergy serve the people and help them reach transformation and salvation, in Buddhism the people serve the monk to help him attain nirvana. In the process, the people build up merit for their own benefit and better rebirths.

We might use the simile of a sports team and its followers to explain the relationship of the sangha and the laypeople. The real team is the sangha, struggling for victory on the field of the Dharma. The laypeople are the supporters of the team, cheering them on, supporting them so that they can devote themselves fully to the struggle, and reaping the benefits of having a victorious team in the community.

Religious Leadership

Religious leadership in Buddhism is again bound up with the monastic community, although there are popular religious specialists and lay leaders outside the monasteries that are also important to laypeople.

Like Hinduism, Buddhist society focuses on the religious adept, the virtuoso who, like the Buddha, has experienced the truth at a high level and can thus be a model and illumination for others. It is, of course, within the monastic community that these religious leaders are found. The social structure of the monastery is hierarchical, from the young novice at the bottom to the abbot of the monastery at the top. Seniority is determined by how many years the person has worn the monk's robes. The abbot and the senior monks provide leadership for the monastery. For the laypeople, the monks and nuns provide spiritual leadership by instructing, performing ceremonies, and chanting scripture. Especially in Mahayana communities the ordained monks are often thought of as "priests" as they serve the local people in various ways.

Of particular importance, especially in the Mahayana tradition, is the "master" who founded the lineage and who passed on his authority to designated Dharma successors. The head of a monastery will be recognized as a Dharma successor of the founder, and he in turn may choose one or more monks to be his successors. The relationship between master and disciple is like that between father and son, forming an important social structure within Buddhism.

Outside the realm of "official" Buddhism, there are in some Buddhist lands additional religious specialists who perform a variety of rituals and exorcisms, dealing with the spirits and gods who affect the immediate welfare of the people. This has nothing to do with the goal of nirvana, so generally monks and nuns pay little attention to such things. But for the people involved with concerns of birth and sickness, marriage and wealth, such religious specialists can offer immediate help and benefit.

Buddhist monks at Myoshinji Temple in Kyoto, Japan.

The Buddhist Vision of the Good Life

So how should I live? Since the doctrine of no-self is fundamental to the Buddhist conception of existence, the ideal way of life would be one that demonstrates as little sense of self as possible. This may sound like a negative approach to life, but really it aims to bring out the fullest potential. This task is not easy, of course, and Buddhism offers many guidelines and practices to help one move more toward that kind of good life. It is recognized that not everyone is at the same grade of spiritual development, however, and so the ethical life needs to be expressed at different levels. Whereas it is the same ethical life, the forms it takes differ somewhat for the monastic life and for the life of lay householders.

The Life of Love and Compassion

Among the many traditional subjects for meditation in Buddhism is one that has to do specifically with relationship to others, that is, with ethics. This meditation is on the four "sublime states," which are (1) boundless love, (2) boundless compassion, (3) sympathetic joy, and (4) limitless equanimity. These four states give expression to the way Buddhists cultivate their own inner life with respect to others, and so they reflect the Buddhist ethical vision. They all spring from the enlightened wisdom that knows there is no separate self and that all beings exist in interdependence.

Boundless love (*metta*) is related to friendliness. But many of our experiences of friendly love are intertwined with feelings of need, dependency, lovability of our friend, and so forth. Buddhists cultivate love that is unconditioned and unlimited, based on the knowledge that all are one in the ocean of life. The well-known sutra on boundless love states that one should direct her thoughts by reflecting in this way:

> May all beings be happy and secure; may their minds be contented.
>
> Whatever living beings there may be—feeble or strong, long, stout, or medium, short, small, or large, seen or unseen, those dwelling far or near, those who are born and those who are yet to be born—may all beings, without exception, be happy-minded!
>
> Let not one deceive another nor despise any person whatever in any place. In anger or illwill let not one wish any harm to another.
>
> Just as a mother would protect her only child even at the risk of her own life, even so let one cultivate a boundless heart towards all beings.
>
> Let one's thoughts of boundless love pervade the whole world—above, below and across—without any obstruction, without any hatred, without any enmity.
>
> Whether one stands, walks, sits or lies down, as long as one is awake, one should maintain this mindfulness. This, they say, is the Sublime State in this life.[5]

If one has anger in his heart, he takes it out on all, regardless of who or what they are. So also, when one's mind is filled with thoughts of boundless love, that love radiates out to all, regardless of who they are or whether or not they are deserving of love.

The second sublime state, boundless compassion (*karuna*), is the intense fellow-feeling one should have for all living beings who suffer pain, anxiety, ignorance, and illusion. It was Siddhartha Gautama's compassion that led him, after achieving enlightenment, to devote the rest of his life to teaching the way to liberation for the benefit of all beings suffering in the ocean of life. Compassion is knowing that when one living being suffers, we also suffer, for we are not separate from any being but are one with all. Mahayana Buddhists have raised this sublime state of compassion to a supreme virtue as displayed by the bodhisattva who takes a vow to devote him- or herself unceasingly to bearing the sufferings of others and sharing merits for the salvation of all others. Out of compassion the bodhisattva vows:

> All creatures are in pain, all suffer from bad and hindering karma . . . so that they cannot see the Buddhas or hear the Law of Righteousness or know the Order. . . . All that mass of pain and evil karma I take in my own body. . . . I take upon myself the burden of sorrow; I resolve to do so; I endure it all. I do not turn back or run away, I do not tremble. . . . I must set them all free, must save the whole world from the forest of birth, old age, disease, and rebirth, from misfortune and sin.[6]

Of course, this is the vow of the highly perfected bodhisattva! But then all Buddhists are "Buddhas-in-the-making" (bodhisattvas), and so these sentiments of compassion can be cultivated by all.

Whereas compassion is sometimes thought to dwell on the negative aspects of human existence, sharing the suffering and pain of all, the third sublime state of sympathetic joy moves one to seek out the prosperity and happiness of others and rejoice with them. Strangely, this is difficult to do, for in selfish inclination people seem more ready to gloat over the misfortunes of others. However, when the sense of our needy, grasping self is extinguished, we no longer need to feel superior and therefore can genuinely not only promote the welfare of others but join in sympathetic joy in their material and spiritual happiness.

The final sublime state, limitless equanimity, is in the mind of some Buddhists the culmination of these four states. It expresses that sense of nonattachment to self and to world that the arhant achieves by following the path of transformation and rooting out all desire and clinging. In terms of the ethical life, equanimity is that fundamental sense of impartiality that makes it possible to treat all others equally with love, compassion, and joy, with no aversion to them and no desire to win their approval. Unthreatened by the evil vibrations of others, not seduced by the bribes or temptations offered by others, one can radiate love, compassion, and joy to all beings equally.

Ethical Steps on the Path

These four sublime states portray a high-minded ethical vision of selflessness and giving. But is it practical? Who can live according to such principles in the real world? Buddhism is above all a practical religion, and the emphasis is on the actual practice of these ideals. There are many scriptures that spell out practical guidance and concrete disciplines for the good life. The Dhammapada, for example, offers over four hundred statements to give direction in how to live. Here are there samples:

> "He abused me, he beat me, he defeated me, he robbed me"; the hatred of those who harbour such thoughts is not appeased.
> One should not pry into the faults of others, into things done and left undone by others. One should rather consider what by oneself is done and left undone.
> Conquer anger by love, evil by good; conquer the miser with liberality, and the liar with truth.[7]

To get a feeling for the practical dimension of Buddhist ethics, we can concentrate on the Five Precepts, recited often and respected as a model for life by all Buddhists. They are: to refrain from taking life, from taking what is not given, from wrong sexual relations, from wrongful speech, and from drugs and liquor. Through these precepts Buddhist ethical ideals are put into everyday practice.

The principle to refrain from destroying life is especially central to the Buddhist vision; this is the principle of nonviolence (ahimsa), shared in common with Hinduism and Jainism. The concept of not taking life and not harming life does not apply only to human life but also to animal life, and so it has always been the Buddhist principle to refrain also from killing animals,

even for food, thus making vegetarianism the ideal way of sustenance. It is true that, given the reality of the natural world order with its continual struggle for existence, some provision has been made in Buddhism for laypeople to eat meat and even for monks and nuns to eat meat if it is received as a gift—provided that they did not see the killing of the animal and that the animal was not killed for their sake. But the positive side of the principle is important: one should do all possible to promote and support the well-being of fellow humans and of all living beings, assisting them, whether near or far, to live with honor, dignity, and security. It is particularly meritorious to save animals from harm and death by setting them free in a safe place.

To refrain from taking what is not given, that is, stealing, of course, means also to avoid all forms of cheating or dishonest dealings to gain an advantage over others. Rather, putting away selfish motivations, one should share with them and promote ways in which they can lead a peaceful and secure material life.

When Buddhism teaches to refrain from wrongful sexual behavior, it does not mean that everyone should totally avoid sex. That is true, of course, for monks and nuns on the higher path of perfection. But the Buddha had many lay followers also. It is expected that lay householders should indeed marry and have sexual intercourse in a rightful way. But the sexual impulse is one of the most powerful human drives, and therefore it can easily upset one's self-control. It can lead one to take advantage of others, harming both them and oneself.

To refrain from wrongful speech goes far beyond just avoiding lies and only telling the truth. It does, of course, mean to avoid all falsehoods, because they are always harmful to others and to oneself as well. The Buddha said that there is no evil that will not be done by one who is not ashamed to lie. But right speech means also to refrain from all slander and recriminations that would bring about hatred, enmity, and disharmony among people. It means to avoid all abusive, harsh, rude, and impolite language, for this is offensive to others. And it means to stay away from all gossip, all disparaging of others, and all idle and useless babble. Avoiding these kinds of wrong and harmful uses of words, one's conversation with others will deal with the truth, with that which is friendly, pleasant, meaningful, and beneficial to others.

To refrain from drugs or liquor is important, for these tend to cloud the mind and make insight and awareness difficult, thus hindering one's progress on the path. Further, intoxication can lead to reckless behavior and violence of various kinds to others, thus leading to the breaking of the other precepts.

These Five Precepts form an ethical guide to the kind of profession and social involvement that would be consistent with the virtues of love and compassion. Obviously one should avoid any activity that, directly or indirectly, brings harm to others. This would obviously include professions that have to do with harming and killing people, such as making or trading in arms and lethal weapons, serving in military forces, or even supporting the making of weapons and military actions by our taxes. Occupations having to do with killing animals are also to be avoided—slaughtering animals, hunting, working in leather, and the like. Since intoxicating drinks and drugs are harmful to the minds and lives of people, one should avoid activities that promote or use such harmful materials. It is not justified to claim only to be a middleman or to argue that what others do with what one has produced is not one's responsibility. To earn wages by engaging in activities that contribute to causing harm to living beings is inconsistent with the Five Precepts. Rather, one's personal livelihood should at the same time be service for the welfare of the community of living beings.

These Five Precepts are practical, down-to-earth principles for leading the good life of compassion, love, and fulfilment. In the wisdom of the Buddha, however, they are at the same time steps along the way to transformation. The more we practice these disciplines, the more we root out clinging and become self-giving and loving.

The Ethical Life for Monks and Nuns

The Buddhist path of transformation is such that one becomes a nun or monk to pursue the higher stages—and thus there is a higher ethical life also, that of the mendicant. The basic principles of boundless love, boundless compassion, sympathetic joy, and limitless equanimity are the same, simply intensified in practice. The main difference is that the monk or nun has gone beyond society and practices a high level of detachment from those material, economic, and social attachments that characterize life for laypeople. Yet the presence of these mendicants within society helps to set the ethical tone for the community: they are the conquerors, near to the goal, and their lifestyle is the model to approximate whenever possible.

The ethical life of monks and nuns is characterized first of all by the Ten Precepts, which they take at their ordination as novices. The first Five Precepts are taken by laypeople also, but they are intensified by monks and nuns. The Ten Precepts are to refrain from (1) taking life, (2) taking what is not given, (3) sexual misconduct, (4) lying, (5) drinking liquor, (6) eating after noon, (7) watching shows, singing, and dancing, (8) using adornments of garlands, perfumes, and ointments, (9) sleeping in a high bed, and (10) handling gold and silver. These basic principles are elaborated in the Vinaya scripture as the rules of discipline for monks and nuns. Over two hundred rules define categories of offenses, prescribe punishments, and regulate the conduct of the monks and nuns. The two dominant ethical concerns are not harming life and sexual continence, but many other matters are dealt with as the code defines the proper mendicant lifestyle.

The code defines four most serious offenses that warrant expulsion from the order: sexual intercourse, theft, intentionally killing a human being, and falsely claiming spiritual attainments. Many rules deal with improper sexual conduct; for example, a monk is put on probation if he intentionally ejaculates, touches a woman, speaks suggestively to a woman, urges a woman to gain merit by yielding to a monk, or serves as a go-between in arranging a meeting between a man and a woman. Other serious offenses meriting probation include false accusations against another monk, causing divisions in the monastic community, and refusing admonishment from other monks. Some offenses require forfeiture and expiation, such as accumulating more than one begging bowl or buying articles with gold or silver. There are quite a few offenses that require expiation, such as lying, stealing another monk's sleeping place, digging in the ground, destroying any vegetable, taking animal life, drinking liquor, or going near an army drawn up for battle. Whereas many of the rules seem trivial and quaint, taken together they shape a life-style designed to facilitate the rooting out of clinging and desire and to promote love and compassion for all living beings.

The Dharma Model for Society and the World

With the highest ideal being withdrawal from society and the world, how does Buddhism have anything to offer for the betterment of human society? The Buddha likened life in the world to a burning house from which one should escape as soon as possible. Isn't it the position of Buddhism just to let the house burn itself down?

Of course, Buddhism, like all religions, has a vision for the betterment of society. It is true that much attention in the scriptures is given to the role of the monks and nuns, and little is said about laypeople and their lives in society. But from the beginning the Buddha did have lay disciples and he did give them guidance on life in society.

The Buddhist Model for Society

The earliest Buddhist societal reform was the sangha itself. Whereas Indian society was stratified into the different classes, the Buddha accepted people from all classes to be in the sangha. He argued that biologically all humans are of one species, and therefore the different classes were simply convenient designations for different occupations. When some brahmins tried to maintain the superiority of their class, he asked, "Do the brahmans really maintain this, when they're born of women just like anyone else, of brahman women who have their periods and conceive, give birth, and nurse their children, just like any other women?" And he went on to assert that people from all classes can equally live the high spiritual life. He asked his questioner,

And if [a person] avoids grave sin, will he go to heaven if he's a brahman, but not if he's a man of the lower classes?

No, Gautama. In such a case the same reward awaits all men, whatever their class.

And is a brahman capable of developing a mind of love without hate or ill-will, but not a man of the other classes?

No, Gautama. All four classes are capable of doing so.[8]

The Buddhist view of ranks in society is summed up in this passage:

No brahman is such by birth.
No outcaste is such by birth.
An outcaste is such by his deeds.
A brahman is such by his deeds.[9]

Essential to the Buddhist vision for society is the fundamental principle that all types of people are equal and that honor depends not on circumstances of birth but on moral and spiritual achievement.

But what about life in family, in community, in society? Doesn't Buddhism downgrade the importance of this, so that it really has nothing to offer except the advice to escape the burning house? In one important discourse the Buddha set forth great respect for family and social life, saying that one should "worship" parents, teachers, wife and children, friends and counselors, slaves and servants, and ascetics and brahmins.

Sunday services at Chua Giac Minh, a Vietnamese Buddhist temple in Palo Alto, California.

There should in fact be mutual honor and care and help from children and from parents, from students and from teachers, and so on. With respect to the relation between husband and wife, the Buddha taught:

> A husband should serve his wife . . . in five ways: by honoring her; by respecting her; by remaining faithful to her; by giving her charge of the home; and by duly giving her adornments. And thus served by her husband . . . a wife should care for him in five ways: she should be efficient in her household tasks; she should manage her servants well; she should be chaste; she should take care of the goods which he brings home; and she should be skillful and untiring in all her duties.[10]

The Buddha occasionally spoke about the needs of material, economic life. He clearly stated that poverty is the cause of immorality and crime; this cannot be suppressed by punishment, but rather the economic condition of the people needs to be improved. When a layperson asked him how laypeople can improve their welfare, the Buddha told him that there are four things conducive to welfare. First, a person should be skilled in his profession. Second, he should protect the income that he has earned righteously. Third, he should have good and helpful friends. And, fourth, he should spend reasonably, in proportion to his income, not hoarding and not being extravagent. But along with this, of course, the person should cultivate spiritual values, keep the precepts, be generous, and develop wisdom.[11] Wealth is not bad, according to Buddhism; in fact, proper care for economic security can be conducive to a peaceful and spiritually minded society.

What about political power and the necessary force to keep order in society? The Buddhist scriptures do not say a lot about states and government, but one text does put forth these ten duties of the king: he should be generous, of high moral character, sacrificing everything for the good of the people, honest, gentle, austere, free from hatred, nonviolent, patient, and not opposing the will of the people.[12] A government based on these principles would surely create a happy, peaceful nation! Actually, the great Buddhist King Ashoka (r. 273–232 B.C.E.) put many of these principles into practice as he ruled according to the Buddhist Dharma, treating people with forgiveness, extending his kindness

also to animals. One of Ashoka's edicts states: "For this is my rule—to govern by Righteousness, to administer by Righteousness, to please my subjects by Righteousness, and to protect them by Righteousness."[13] Describing how painful his earlier bloody conquests were to him now, Ashoka publicly declared that he would never draw his sword again for any conquest; from now on the only conquest would by that by righteousness. At the zenith of power, Ashoka renounced war and violence and turned instead to nonviolence and peace.

Following Ashoka's model, Buddhists generally are pacifists, not abandoning the world to its self-destruction but seeking to conquer violence and terror by kindness and righteousness. Today Buddhists are at the forefront of movements for peace in the world. The fact that it was a predominantly Buddhist country, Japan, that experienced the only military unleashing of nuclear terror so far has further motivated Buddhists to promote world peace by nonviolent means. The Buddhist aim would be to create a society in which the ruinous struggle for power and supremacy is renounced and where hatred is conquered by kindness.

Spreading the Dharma to the World

The missionary nature of Buddhism derives from the Buddha himself, from the compassion he felt after his enlightenment as he surveyed the whole world and saw suffering, ignorant beings everywhere. He preached the first sermon and began the turning of the wheel of Dharma. And when there were sixty enlightened monks, he sent them out to proclaim the Dharma for the benefit of all, out of compassion for the world, for the welfare of humans and of gods. The human condition analyzed in the Dharma is universal, and the path put forth in the Dharma is universal—so the motivation to bring the Dharma to others naturally arises out of the Buddhist sense of compassion.

This does not mean that Buddhists are intolerant of other peoples' beliefs and religious practices. They acknowledge that many of the world religions recognize something of the fundamental problem of human ignorance and clinging, and the religions also incorporate many elements of the path of transformation in their own various ways. On one of his rock edicts King Ashoka engraved this message, referring to various sects within India:

> The Beloved of the Gods [King Ashoka]...honors members of all sects....But he does not consider gifts and honors as important as the furtherance of the essential message of all sects. This essential message varies from sect to sect, but it has one common basis.... Whoever honors his own sect and disparages another man's, whether from blind loyalty or with the intention of showing his own sect in a favorable light, does his own sect the greatest possible harm. Concord is best, with each hearing and respecting the other's teaching.[14]

Not all Buddhists, of course, demonstrate this religious tolerance toward others as stated by King Ashoka, especially when threatened by aggressive members of another religion. But with its emphasis on love and compassion, and with its insight that it is finally the mind, not faith, that brings one to liberation, Buddhists have generally chosen the style of spreading the Dharma by rational explanation, practical advice, and personal example.

One important consideration for the spread of the Buddhist Dharma is the flexibility Buddhism allows in matters that religions traditionally focus on. There is plenty of room in the Buddhist cosmology for gods and goddesses, demons and devils, ancestors, nats, shen, kuei, kami, and whatever other spiritual beings people believe they have to deal with to live a happy life. As Buddhism spread from people to people, it left many of the traditional religious practices intact—for finally they have little importance, positively or negatively, for the Buddhist path of liberation. Let the nat wives, the shamanesses, the exorcists, and the ritualists ply their trade and deal with the supernatural world for the material welfare of the people. The path of liberation is a different matter, and when one advances far enough in the Dharma she will find herself beyond these gods and spiritual beings. Different concerns arise, of course, when religious claims for ultimate liberation and salvation are made on the basis of worshiping God, as in world religions like Judaism, Christianity, and Islam. And so some Buddhists of today have entered into dialogue with members of other religions, showing respect and tolerance, yet affirming the ultimacy of the Dharma.

DISCUSSION QUESTIONS

1. With the Buddhist idea of only the unconditioned truth as absolute, what is the meaning of worship, ritual practices, and images of the Buddha?
2. Describe several great annual festivals of Buddhism.
3. Describe the ordination ritual (upasampada). Why is this so important in Buddhism?
4. Explain what the sangha is, and how there can be both nirvanic and karmic goals on the path.
5. What are the Five Precepts?
6. What basic principles of Buddhism do you think would be helpful for the betterment of human society?

CHAPTER 19

THE PATH OF THE JAINS

SACRED STORY AND HISTORICAL CONTEXT

"Who am I?" To call oneself a Jain means to follow the teaching and model of the Jinas, the "conquerors." The Jinas, also called "Ford Builders" (*Tirthankara*), are those who have conquered by reaching liberation from the wheel of existence and who show the way across the ocean of suffering. The most recent Jina in our world cycle is Mahavira, whose story, though 2,500 years in the past, provides in a very direct way the model of life for Jains.

350

At the beginning of his study of the Jaina path, Padmanabh Jaini presents this story of a modern follower of Mahavira:

> It is August, 1955. On the holy mount of Kunthalagiri, in the state of Maharashtra in India, an old man called Santisagara (Ocean of Peace) is ritually fasting to death. He is the *acarya* (spiritual leader) of the Digambara Jaina community; now, after thirty-five years as a mendicant, he is attaining his mortal end in the holy manner prescribed by the great saint Mahavira almost 2,500 years earlier. Santisagara has owned nothing, not even a loincloth, since 1920. He has wandered on foot over the length and breadth of India, receiving food offerings but once a day, and then with only his bare hands for a bowl; he has spoken little during daylight hours and not at all after sunset. From August 14 until September 7 he takes only water; then, unable to drink without help, he ceases even that. At last, fully conscious and chanting the Jaina litany, he dies in the early morning of September 18. The holiness and propriety of his life and the manner of his death are widely known and admired by Jainas throughout India.[1]

Shocking perhaps to many outside India, this ascetic manner of life and death is greatly admired in India, and not only among the Jains. To understand this path, we need to look to the Jaina sacred story.

Mahavira Becomes the Jina for Our Age

Jains conceive of the universe as a vast structure subject to endless cycles of time, each cycle consisting of a progressive half-cycle and a regressive half-cycle. Twenty-four Jinas (Tirthankaras) will arise in each half-cycle as teachers, leading others to attain liberation. The first Tirthankara of our present half-cycle was Rsabha, who established civilization, taught the path, and lived approximately 600,000 years. The twenty-third Tirthankara was Parshva who lived in the middle of the ninth century B.C.E. and established an order of mendicants. Mahavira was born as the twenty-fourth and last Jina of our cycle, no more to come for many thousands of years. Whereas Jains pay worship to all twenty-four Tirthankaras, it is Mahavira who is the most recent Jina and thus the most important model for following the path.

The Sacred Life Story of Mahavira

The stories about Mahavira differ slightly between the two main sects of Jainism, the Svetambaras (white-clad, that is, clothed), and the Digambara (sky-clad, that is, unclothed). But the general outline of his life is accepted by all, centering around the five auspicious moments that Jains still celebrate: his conception, birth, renunciation, enlightenment, and final death (nirvana). Mahavira (Great Hero) is said to have been born in 599 B.C.E. at Kundagrama near modern Patna. Stories about his birth make it clear that this child was intended for a high destiny. For example, his mother had a series of dreams involving things like a white elephant, the rising sun, and an enormous heap of jewels, dreams that are still celebrated in ritual and art. Within the womb, the Jina-to-be showed the virtue of *ahimsa* (nonviolence), lying still lest his kicks should cause his mother pain. Like the Buddha, he was born to royal parents of the kshatriya (warrior) caste and lived in wealth and luxury. The second of two sons, he married and had a daughter (the Digambara sect says he remained a bachelor) and, even though he wanted to renounce the world, he fulfilled the duties of a householder until both his parents died. When he was thirty, certain gods appeared and urged him to make the great renunciation: "Awake, reverend lord of the world! Establish the *dharma-tirtha* (teaching of the holy path) for the sake of every living being in the entire universe; it will bring supreme benefit to all."[2]

The Great Renunciation is celebrated as a glorious occasion, as it is for all renunciants in Jaina communities even today. The story says Mahavira was adorned with garlands by the gods and carried on a palanquin to a large park. There he fasted, renounced all possessions, removed all his clothing, pulled out his hair by hand, and set forth on the mendicant path. The Svetambara sect says he wore a loincloth for thirteen months until it accidently caught on a thorn bush and was pulled off, after which Mahavira went about unclad.

He joined a group of hermits for a while, but then he came to believe one must practice a more severe form of asceticism to win release, and he went wandering about and practicing extreme austerities for the next twelve years. He begged only for the most minimal food, and often he practiced complete fasting, that is, abstaining from both food and water for long periods of time, sometimes as long as a week. Further, he was convinced that a most essential practice was ahimsa, nonviolence toward every living thing. The scriptures report, for example:

> Ceasing to inflict injury on living beings, abandoning concern for the body, and having perceived the true nature of the self, the Venerable One, houseless, endured the thorns of the villages [that is, the abusive language of the peasants]. . . . Once when he [sat in meditation], his body unmoving, they cut his flesh, tore his hair, and covered him with dirt. They picked him up and then dropped him, disturbing his meditational postures. Abandoning concern for his body, free from desire, the Venerable One humbled himself and bore the pain. Just as a hero at the head of a battle is surrounded on all sides, so was Mahavira there. Undisturbed, bearing all hardships, the Venerable One proceeded [on the path of salvation].[3]

He walked carefully to avoid stepping on living things, moving not at all during the four-month rainy season when the paths teemed with living things. Insects and other things gathered on his body and caused pain, but he did not wash or scratch so as to avoid hurting them. In the cold he sought out cold places to meditate, and in the heat he sat in the sun.

After twelve years of the harshest self-deprivation, Mahavira reached the highest enlightenment (*kevela*), the infinite, supreme, omniscient state, and thus he became the twenty-fourth and final Jina of the present world cycle.

Jina Mahavira and the Jaina Community

Digambara stories say that after his enlightenment Mahavira was completely free from all defects of human existence—hunger, thirst, disease, and so forth. He engaged in no mundane activities but sat in omniscient meditation in a special hall created by the gods. Disciples were attracted to his victorious nature and the Jaina community was thus established. Other stories from the Svetambara sect say he preached to the gods, then converted three brahmin priests who were offering a Vedic sacrifice. These were Indrabhuti Gautama and his two brothers, who with their 1,500 followers were

Colossal statue of Bahubali, with crowds gathered around at a huge festival.

taken into the new order. Soon eight other brahmins were converted, completing the inner circle of eleven chief disciples (*ganadharas*), who with their followers swelled the Jaina order to over 4,000.

Whereas Mahavira primarily demonstrated for his followers a way of life to reach liberation, some basic teachings about the nature of reality and human existence guided his followers. Although the soul has knowledge, bliss, and energy, because of past actions the soul becomes enmeshed in karmic matter, which leads to embodiment at the level appropriate on account of the past actions. Fettered with karma of passion and desire, the soul commits more such actions, leading to more and more rebirths. Every soul passes through tens of thousands of incarnations, ranging from fire, mineral, air, and vegetable bodies to animal, human, and god bodies. In most of these existences the soul experiences great suffering, and so the goal of liberation from the whole cycle is the most important thing, according to Mahavira's teaching. The path toward liberation involves an awakening of knowledge, faith in liberation, and conduct that will lead finally to that liberation.

Death of Mahavira and Life of the Community

When he was seventy-two years old, Mahavira passed into nirvana as the result of voluntary self-starvation, thus becoming fully liberated, forever free of rebirth and embodiment. He "cut asunder the ties of birth, old age, and death, became a siddha, finally liberated."[4] And thus he became the model for all Jains ever since, including Santisagara in 1955.

All eleven of Mahavira's chief disciples attained enlightenment either during the master's lifetime or shortly thereafter. His closest disciple, Indrabhuti Gautama, was so deeply attached to his master that he could not attain this goal. On the last day of his life Mahavira exhorted Indrabhuti not to linger on the path:

> As a dewdrop clinging to the top of a blade
> of Kusa-grass lasts but a short time,
> even so the life of men;
> Gautama, be careful all the while!
> You have crossed the great ocean; why do
> you halt so near the shore? Make haste
> to attain the other side;
> Gautama, be careful all the while![5]

Mahavira died that day soon after giving this exhortation, and Indrabhuti attained enlightenment also that very day.

The Jain story says that when Mahavira preached, his words took on a divine sound, and this divine sound was translated into the scriptures by the chief disciples, especially Indrabhuti, who passed them on through oral transmission. The main scriptures are called the Angas (limbs), giving Mahavira's teaching on conduct for monks and nuns, false doctrines to avoid, basic teachings, and exhortations for the laity. Many secondary scriptures arose after the time of the chief disciples, and Jains also composed numerous commentaries and philosophical writings interpreting the teachings of the enlightened Jina.

Historical Transformations in Jainism

The Jain teachings and practices have remained remarkably constant over the 2,500-year history of this religion. The community was disrupted by one major schism, which still exists. They incorporated many Hindu rituals and practices and have built great temples and statues. Even in the modern world they retain their commitment to nonviolence and honesty.

The Great Division: Digambaras and Svetambaras

Shortly after the time of Mahavira, a difference of opinion arose over a number of points, leading to a schism into two major sects. One group insisted that being real monks meant going totally unclad as Mahavira had done, for clinging even to a loin cloth is a form of attachment. This group, called the Digambaras (sky-clad), also insisted that women could not be allowed into the monastic life; they can become monks and reach enlightenment only after rebirth as men. The other group is called the Svetambaras (white-clad), holding that it is not important whether one is clad or unclad, as it was not important to Mahavira. The Svetambaras allowed women into the monastic community and felt they also could reach enlightenment. In fact, according to the Svetambaras, the nineteenth Tirthankara, Malli, was a woman.

The split between these two groups happened when one part of the community fled southward in the face of a great famine about 360 B.C.E. After twelve years they returned, but they found that the other group had prepared an official recension of the sacred texts containing many things that were unacceptable. Furthermore, the "northern" monks had taken up lax habits like the wearing of clothes. So the southern group, the later Digambaras, considered themselves the "true"

Jains and eventually wrote their own stories about Mahavira.

Other points have accumulated to divide the two groups. Digambaras think a Jina, who has omniscient cognition, cannot engage in worldly activity and bodily functions, whereas the Svetambaras hold that he can. Svetambara monks carry small begging bowls and beg for food door to door, not entering the houses to eat. But Digambara monks receive food offerings only in their upturned palms, and they may enter a house and eat if they have gone there only to beg. Eventually the two communities also became separated geographically, the Digambaras moving to the south and the Svetambaras to the west. The schism between the two groups has not lessened through the centuries, although there have been attempts at cooperation in modern times.

Jains and the Culture of India

Jain monks and nuns have tried to strike a balance between perpetuating orthodox faith and practice, on the one hand, and fruitful intercourse with Hindu society, on the other. Adopting elements of Hindu ritual and worship, Jains incorporated worship of Hindu gods like Rama and Krishna, with appropriate adjustments to Jain values, in addition to the twenty-four Jinas whom they worship. They took over the use of ritual offerings, mantras, and holy fire. Also, rituals of the passages of life were adapted from Hindu models. Over the course of centuries they erected over forty thousand temples, many renowned for their architectural beauty.

To be a Jain means above all not harming any living thing—thus there are some occupations that Jains must avoid, occupations that involve taking life or making profit from the slaughter of living things. So Jains have generally been restricted from being soldiers, butchers, exterminators, leatherworkers, or even farmers. Because of this, Jains have tended to enter commercial professions, where their reputation for honesty and morality have made them quite successful and generally wealthy. They have also made significant contributions to the public welfare by founding institutions such as public lodgings, public dispensaries, and

schools. They have established libraries and contributed to Indian literature and philosophy.

The basic principle of nonviolence has become firmly embedded in Indian tradition, also in Hinduism and Buddhism, partly because of the persistent Jain adherence to this principle of ahimsa. Mahatma Gandhi, who successfully put this principle into practice in modern times in the movement leading to India's independence and brought it into the moral recognition of the whole world, acknowledged that he had been strongly influenced by Jains, especially the saintly layman Raychandbhai Mehta.

WORLDS OF MEANING

Ultimate Reality: Eternal Universe, Liberation

"What's it *all* about?" "What is really the center that holds everything together?" Jainism is decisively atheistic, somewhat like the Upanishads and early Buddhism. Yet—as we have learned in India—there is not just one way. Jains also worship the Jinas and a number of gods.

Jains do not believe in a creator god or supreme being. Rather, the world process operates according to its own innate laws, in world cycles of evolution and degeneration without beginning and without end. In a sense we could say that ultimate reality is this eternal universe, with its laws of operation and its constituents of space and time, matter and infinite individual souls. What is really central and permanent on the Jaina path is the pure state of blissful omniscience achieved by the soul that reaches complete liberation from the embodied condition of samsara. But even this liberation process is controlled by the laws that are inherent in the universe.

In a sense, then, ultimate reality is the truth taught by those Jinas who attained this state of omniscience and liberation. According to the laws of the eternal universe, in each world half-cycle there will arise twenty-four Jinas, conquerors, who attain complete omniscience and thus can teach the truth for others to follow. Our world age has already seen its twenty-four

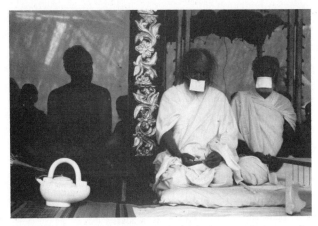

Jain Saddhus (holy men), two with cloths over their mouths to keep from doing injury to organisms with air bodies.

Jinas, the last one being Mahavira, and, with increasing degeneracy until the end of our age, no one will even be able to attain enlightenment (the last one who did so was a saint who lived shortly after Mahavira). So it is proper to worship and venerate the Jinas, not as "gods" who hear our prayers and save us, but as conquerors whose souls now enjoy the bliss of eternal liberation and omniscience. The other gods worshiped for various benefits are souls who have attained rebirth in the god-realm but who still must in some future rebirth become humans in order to achieve liberation.

Karmic Matter and Eternal Souls

"What is this world all about?" The Jain view of the world resolutely rejects any creator or any beginning or end to the process of the universe. Jain writers through the ages have raised deep questions about a theistic idea of creation:

> If God created the world, where was he before creation? If you say he was transcendent then, and needed no support, where is he now?... If he is ever perfect and complete, how could the will to create have arisen in him? If, on the other hand, he is not perfect, he could no more create the universe than a potter could.... If out of love for living things and need of them he made the world, why did he not make creation wholly blissful, free from misfortune?... Know that the world is uncre-

ated, as time itself is, without beginning and end, and is based on the principles, life and the rest. Uncreated and indestructible, it endures under the compulsion of its own nature.[6]

The Jaina Universe and Human Existence

The Jain view of the world and human nature is very complex. Jains envision the universe, eternal and uncreated, as a vast three-dimensional structure, often pictured as a man or woman with arms and legs apart, with three levels. The lower level contains 8,400,000 hells, the middle level houses worlds in which humans and animals live, and in the upper level live the gods, who are always young and beautiful. Crowning the whole structure, beyond the celestial realms, is the crescent-shaped abode of the liberated souls. Surrounding the cosmic structure is absolute nothingness. The complex physical structure of the universe is further complicated by the idea that the middle regions are subject to endless time cycles. Each cycle contains a progressive half-cycle followed by a regressive half-cycle. The progressive half-cycle moves through six stages from an extremely unhappy to an extremely happy stage, and the regressive half-cycle moves through six stages from extremely happy to extremely unhappy. Only in the middle portions of each half-cycle—when conditions are neither extremely happy nor extremely unhappy—can beings be moved to seek enlightenment. As mentioned above, twenty-four Jinas are said to arise in each half-cycle.

All existing things, besides time and space, can be divided into matter and souls. Space contains an infinite number of immaterial, eternal souls whose essential nature is pure consciousness, bliss and energy. But all these souls—except those who have attained liberation and dwell in the pure state in the highest realm—are embodied in matter and always have been so. Existence in an embodied state is accompanied by desire, which causes more karma to accumulate, leading to further defilement and endless embodiments in the cycles of rebirth (samsara). The possibilities of rebirth are enormous, from the crudest life forms to the most exalted gods. And these are not mere possibilities. Jains hold that in the vast world cycles every soul already *has* been born in all these states and will continue in virtual endless repetition of these rebirths. The four main categories of birth destinies are as gods, humans, hell beings, and animals and plants. These four categories have from earliest times been illustrated in Jain art by the swastika-shaped wheel of life. The animal-plant category is almost infinite, including even microscopic creatures with only the sense of touch and single-sense organisms whose body is air, water, fire, or earth. It boggles the mind: I have already existed as all these beings.

The Bound Soul: Karma

Why is my soul bound like this? The Jain view of karma and how it affects the soul is distinctive among the religions, for Jains see karma as a subtle form of matter. The universe is filled with tiny imperceptible particles of material karma, floating about freely until attracted to an embodied soul. Because of its defilement, the soul's inherent energy creates vibrations that attract the karmic particles. Because of the passions of desire and hatred the soul is "moistened" and the karmic particles stick to it, clouding its pure consciousness, giving rise to more desire and hatred, which attracts more karma, and on and on.

The influx of karma leads to an actual change in the soul, like drinking wine involves an actual alteration in one's internal chemistry. Some forms of karma cause the soul to become confused and desirous, other karma obstructs the qualities of the soul, and still other types of karma bring about embodiment and determine the precise type of embodiment (whether the soul will be born human or plant, male or female, etc.) and also the duration of that embodiment. The effect of the karma depends on the type of act that attracted it. For example, if greed leads to robbery, the attracted karma will eventually cause loss of one's own possessions; and if I slander someone else, the karma I attract will cause me to be slandered sometime in the future.

The rebirths caused by the accumulated karmic matter adhering to the soul include not only the relatively pleasant life of humans and the blessed life of the gods, but also the untold lifetimes spent as hell-beings and as incarnations in animal, plant, even air and water

bodies. The intense sufferings experienced by the soul in these unimaginably vast numbers of lifetimes is portrayed with deep feeling by the young prince Mrgaputra as he begs his parents to allow him to take up the life of a mendicant to cut the bonds of suffering once and for all:

> From clubs and knives, stakes and maces, breaking my limbs,
> An infinite number of times I have suffered without hope.
> By keen-edged razors, by knives and shears,
> Many times I have been drawn and quartered, torn apart and skinned.
> Helpless in snares and traps, a deer,
> I have been caught and bound and fastened, and often I have been killed.
> A helpless fish, I have been caught with hooks and nets;
> An infinite number of times I have been killed and scraped, split and gutted.
> A bird, I have been caught by hawks or trapped in nets,
> Or held fast by birdlime, and I have been killed an infinite number of times.
> A tree, with axes and adzes by the carpenters
> An infinite number of times I have been felled, stripped of my bark, cut up, and sawn into planks.
> As iron, with hammer and tongs by blacksmiths
> An infinite number of times I have been struck and beaten, split and filed. . . .
> Ever afraid, trembling, in pain and suffering,
> I have felt the utmost sorrow and agony. . . .
> In every kind of existence I have suffered
> Pains which have scarcely known reprieve for a moment.[7]

When we remember that one can only seek liberation when born on the human level, we realize that, passing up the chance in this lifetime, it may be millions of lifetimes before we again are born as humans. That's why Jains—laypeople as well as monks and nuns—are intent on following the path of transformation.

The Path of Liberation

"How can I reach liberation?"

The Jain view of the human problematic, as we saw, is quite bleak: eternal souls trapped for millions of lifetimes because of karmic matter, born in material bodies mostly at lower levels full of suffering. The path of transformation, then, consists of a process of purifying the soul, eliminating the karmic matter so that the soul can move upward toward ultimate liberation. There is no possibility that this can be accomplished in this lifetime, for according to Jain doctrine we are now in the degenerate part of this half-world-cycle when no one can any longer reach enlightenment. Still, the consequences of passing up this human lifetime with no strenuous efforts at purifying the soul would be drastic, trapped ever again at lower rebirth levels. So there is strong motivation to follow the path, not only for monks and nuns, but also for laypeople.

Jains reject the idea that a divine power from outside can help the soul, and they also reject the idea that the soul is hopelessly trapped with no possibility of changing its fate. Rather, the soul, even in its defiled state, retains certain capacities that can change the effect of the karmas, especially the central capability to start, under certain conditions, in the direction of knowledge and liberation. The soul has an innate tendency toward self-improvement, and time and again it progresses to higher states only to fall back again because of onrushing karmas. But, Jains believe, a moment can come when two factors coincide: the soul both is in a relatively pure state, and it encounters a set of outside conditions that activate the energies of the soul toward liberation—the outside conditions could be, for example, an encounter with a Jina or his image, or hearing the Jain teachings. That transforming event completely redirects the soul toward moksha so that, no matter how many lifetimes it may take, it never falls back; the bonds of samsara begin to unravel, and ultimate liberation is assured.

Once started on the ladder upward, the soul progresses fourteen rungs (stages of purification) until it reaches ultimate liberation and pure consciousness at the top of the universe: Every embodied soul dwells at the first stage (ignorance) until the great shift occurs, the first awakening when the soul, blind until now, has its first glimpse into its true nature. The soul achieves certain attainments of knowledge and energy that eliminate masses of accumulated karmas, melting away like ice before a flame, and the soul, with growing insight and energy, eventually reaches the fourth stage

on the ladder, the state of true insight. The significance of this stage is that the soul now is irreversibly on the path to moksha. It will fall back to lower stages, for the deluding karmas have been suppressed but not entirely eliminated yet. But even in falling back the soul retains true insight and will eventually make its way upward again. It is said that the soul that has reached true insight will remain in bondage no longer than the time it requires to take in and use up one-half of the available karmas in the universe—which may seem a tremendous time but really is tiny compared with what the soul has already gone through! Before reaching this stage of true insight, following the religious path is not possible. But to progress beyond the fourth stage requires voluntary restriction of activities tying one to the material world, and for this purpose the Jains have two paths, that for laypeople, and that for mendicants.

The path for Jain laypeople is ascetic, actually a modified and simplified version of the mendicant path. Central to the path are the "restraints" that govern behavior, including the great restraints of nonviolence, not lying, not stealing, refraining from illicit sex, and nonpossession or nonattachment. In addition to their ascetic disciplines, laypeople participate in rituals such as worshiping the Jinas, keeping holy days, and going on pilgrimages. Laity are also expected to visit and venerate the mendicant teachers, fast, give alms, and, ideally, die a holy death in fasting meditation. Laypeople can progress spiritually until their religious disciplines are almost as rigorous as the monks' and nuns'.

To be a Jain monk or nun means basically to observe all the restraints and other disciplines on a path of total renunciation, in contrast to the "partial" renunciation of the laity. In the case of nonviolence, for example, nuns and monks extend this principle to *all* living things, even one-sense beings. They thus cannot dig in the earth, bathe or walk in the rain, light or extinguish fires, fan themselves, or touch a living plant—for all of these activities harm delicate one-sense beings who have earth, water, fire, air, or vegetation as their bodies. A monk or nun possesses only things like a begging bowl, a whiskbroom, scriptures, and a loincloth (Digambara monks renounce even those). By observing all the restraints in a radical way, they reduce

Two unclothed Jain monks with lay Jain devotees.

WORSHIP AND LIFE

Ritual and Worship Among the Jains

"How can I find new power for life in my everyday existence?" Jains have always taken a skeptical attitude toward ritualism and worship of the gods. Still, the Jain tradition recommends that people worship the five worshipful ones, perform the rites of the life cycle and the festivals, and above all engage themselves in prayer and meditation. There is, of course, considerable difference between the worship life of mendicants and that of laypeople, but it is a difference of degree, not of substance.

Jains are sometimes called atheistic, and to some extent that is true, as they do not accept an ultimate creator god to whom they should direct their worship. How then can one worship, and who does one worship? It is beneficial to practice the ritual of worship directed to the "five worshipful ones." These are not gods, of course, for Jains believe that final perfection can happen only at the human level. These worshipful ones are humans who have reached perfection or are well on the way toward perfection. The first category is that of the Arhantas, that is, the Jinas or Tirthankaras who have conquered and who are no longer to be seen in their embodied state; statues of these Jinas are installed in temples to remind Jains of the spiritual attainments for which they are adored. The second category is that of the Siddhas, the perfect liberated souls who live in eternal bliss but who, therefore, cannot easily be imaged or even imagined. The other three types of worshipful ones are the true ascetic aspirants: the masters, the teachers, and the spiritual guides who are worthy of veneration. These great ones can be worshiped—not that they hear prayers and grant favors, but because it elevates one's soul to dwell on their ideal perfection.

It is not wrong for the common people also to worship gods and goddesses who control and protect various aspects of human existence. This kind of worship can be distracting, of course, since these gods are not ultimate. Yet many Jains do find it helpful to worship, for example, the guardian gods of the regions, Sarasvati the goddess of learning, and the spiritual guardians who are attendants of the Jinas.

activities in the world that would generate the influx of karmas and the rise of fresh passions. Rigorous meditation techniques are used to attain deeper insight, and finally, after a lifetime of such severe disciplines, the monk or nun may attain the highest spiritual state of enlightenment. But even then the last step remains to be taken: elimination of those activities that accrue to embodiment. Just before death the enlightened one ideally enters a trance in which he or she stops all activities of mind and body, including even heartbeat and breathing, so that the soul, now freed from all embodied activity, may at the moment of death dart upward to liberation at the top of the universe.

We who are still a long way from such perfection and bliss can take comfort in remembering that even those most exalted souls at the top of the universe were once trapped in bondage just as we are.

Daily worship (puja) for Jains involves bathing in the morning and repairing to the temple, standing respectfully in front of the statue of the Jina, reciting sacred formulas, and making some offerings of food or flowers. They may also say the rosary of 108 beads and devote a few minutes to the study of the scriptures. If more time is available, such as on festival days, devotees may bathe the image of the Jina with pure water and make more elaborate offerings, symbolizing the desire to attain eventually to the status of the Jina. Jains might conclude the daily worship with this prayer for peace:

> May Lord Jinendra bestow peace on the land, the nation, the city and the state, and welfare on all the citizens, may the rulers and administrators be strong, law-abiding and righteous, the rains be timely and adequate, all the diseases and ailments disappear, no one in the world be afflicted with famine or scarcity, with theft, loot, plunder and devastation, nor with epidemics, even for a moment: Peace to all!!![8]

Jains observe many fasts and festivals along with visits to temples and pilgrimages to holy places. Since the practice of austerities is important, there are various fasts, such as the important fast of Paryushana, which lasts for eight to ten days in the month of Bhadra. On these days all the people assemble at the temple in the mornings, perform worship and study, and fast to their abilities—some taking no food at all for these days, others eating only once a day. It is especially important during these fast days to prevent any animal life from being taken. Other festivals include events like the nine-day saint-wheel worship done twice a year by Svetambara Jainas, the birthday of Lord Mahavira (the only festival commonly celebrated by all sections of the Jain community), the day of worshiping the sacred books, and great Indian festivals such as Divali observed by Jains along with Hindus.

Holy places for the Jains are the beautiful temples built for the worship of the Jinas. In these temples laypeople can come near to the statue of the Jina, just as some in ancient times encountered a living Jina sitting in omniscient glory. The image can be a tangible aid to visualization of this sacred being, stirring up the soul for awakening. The most renowned temples are the lovely marble temples of Vimalasaha and Vastupala.

Jain saddhus worshiping at the foot of the huge statue of Bahubali at Shravanabelogola, India.

Rituals of the passages of life observed by traditional Jains are many—one listing for Digambaras adds up to fifty-three ceremonies from cradle to nirvana, beginning with the conception ceremony between husband and wife, and ending with the ceremony of achieving final deliverance.[9] Many ceremonies surround birth, naming, and tonsure of the child. The initiation ceremony comes at about eight, when the child adopts the cardinal virtues and becomes a student. The marriage ceremony, of central importance in the life of a householder, is generally similar to the Hindu rite. A person on her deathbed offers final prayers, does repentance, abstains from food, and dies in meditation. The body is cremated and the ashes thrown into a river, while the family meditates on the transitory nature of life. No days in honor of the dead person are observed. In cases when the dying person has taken the vow of *sallekhana* (fasting to death), the end is considered especially laudable and a model for the survivors.

For sacred times and rituals, Jains have created art and architecture that ranks in the foremost of the cultural heritage of India. The most distinctive contribution is in the area of icon-making. Innumerable images of Jinas have been created of all kinds of materials, to be consecrated in temples and worshiped by the faithful. These sculptures—sometimes colossal in size, radiant in selfless contemplation, often unclad, epitomizing the perfection of the saint who has conquered—provide the main focus for Jain worship and pilgrimage. Jain temples with their richly carved and sculptured pillared chambers have contributed significantly to Indian architecture and art. The way of Jainism, leading far beyond the world, still is grounded in the basic stuff of this world through ritual, art, and architecture.

Society and Ethics

The Jain Sacred Community: Mendicants and Laity

"How should I live?" The good life means to live as one of those on the Path of the Jina, the Conqueror.

The Jain community, which Jains believe to be the oldest continuous religious community in the world, has never grown large by standards of the other religions—there are perhaps two million adherents in India today. Yet Jainism did survive in India, whereas the other non-Vedic movements (like Buddhism) did not.

One reason for the vitality of the Jain community has been the close association of the monks and nuns with the laypeople. Monks and nuns do not withdraw to monastic centers of learning far removed from the laypeople. Rather they stay in close contact and in effect simply practice a more radical and austere form of the same path that the laypeople are following. The role of the laity is to support the monastic community.

It is interesting that the number of women in monastic life has always been very high, more than men. Buddhism also, of course, allowed women into the mendicant life, but orders of Buddhist nuns have been very small in number, and today only the Chinese order of nuns still exists. According to a 1977 census, there are approximately 1,590 monks and 3,972 nuns among the Jains.[10] Many of the nuns are widows, but the numbers still show a striking participation of women in the highest levels of the path to liberation.

Whereas the role of women in Jainism thus differs from Hinduism, the Jains have adopted some aspects of the Hindu social caste system, especially the caste of Jain-brahmins. However, Jains interpret the origin of the castes not as stemming from the eternal order of things, as in the Hindu understanding, but as simply necessitated by events. Rshabha, the first king and the first Jina of our world half-cycle, originated the organization of human society. All humans belonged to a single *jati* (birth), but Rshabha, while still a layperson, took up arms and became a king to curb the excessive lawlessness, thus establishing the kshatriya caste. As he invented new means of livelihood and various arts and crafts, the vaishya and shudra castes also arose. Finally, Rshabha's son Bharata arranged a kind of "ahimsa test" for the people. He scattered the courtyard of his palace with fresh flowers and sprouting grain, and then he invited the people to a festival. Those who were careless in their vows of nonviolence walked on the flowers and grains, whereas the most virtuous refused to enter the place lest they harm the living things. Those then were honored by Bharata, given the sacred thread, and called divine brahmins. Those of the shudra class generally have been excluded from the full mendicant life, but they can perform nearly all the lay ceremonies and can attain to a quasi-mendicant status.

How does one become a Jain monk or nun? The distinction between advanced laypeople and the mendicants comes about with the formal assumption of the great vows in the *diksa* (initiation) ceremony. The new monk or nun casts off all lay possessions and abandons his or her former name. The relationship between the laity and the mendicants is demonstrated in the initiation ceremony, which is supported financially by laypeople. Besides renouncing everything (even a loincloth in the case of a Digambara) and receiving a whisk-broom for gently removing insects, Jains enter the mendicant status by slowly pulling hair from the head in five handfuls. On the day following the initiation there is great excitement as the new monk goes begging for the first time. The householder who provides these alms is considered to earn great merit.

The Jain View of the Good Life: Nonviolence

The Jain vision of the good, ethical life is strongly shaped by the underlying idea of karma, which attaches to the soul through certain types of deeds. The Jinas are the conquerors who by strenuous self-discipline, asceticism, and meditation, mastered the flesh, annihilated all karmic forces, and attained the highest spiritual perfection. The path they taught is for everyone to follow, and it involves the same kinds of self-discipline and asceticism practiced by the Jinas. Perhaps the best way to approach an understanding of Jain ethics is to consider the five vows or restraints taken both by laypeople and by mendicants—the laypeople observing them less strictly, the mendicants observing them with stringent completeness. The five vows are nonviolence, abstaining from falsehood, nonstealing, celibacy, and nonpossession.

Of these vows, the one that stands in the forefront of Jain ethics is nonviolence (*ahimsa*). In fact, nonviolence is the driving principle in almost every aspect of Jain conduct. It is intentional violence toward living organisms that causes karmic matter to adhere to the soul, so the most important ethical principle would be to abstain from such violence in any form. Violence is understood to be doing any kind of harm or injury to any living organism—including the billions of microscopic organisms of one or two senses. A distinction is made between violence done with intention and non-intentional violence; intention here means through selfish motivation but also through pleasure, wantonness, or avoidable negligence. It is permitted for laypeople to harm one-sense organisms (such as vegetable life), for the obvious reasons of providing food for society, but they are strictly enjoined from harming animals and thus practice vegetarianism. Monks and nuns avoid doing harm to all organisms, even to one-sense organisms. For example, they carry a whiskbroom to clear the path so they do not inadvertently step on microscopic creatures, and they strain their water before they drink it. Some orders of monks and nuns even wear a cloth over their mouths so they do not harm air bodies (one-sense organisms that have the air as their body) by sudden rushes of air while breathing.

Nonviolence is not just something negative. One Jain saint, Samantabhara, said that nonviolence is the highest bliss known to beings in the world. Violence not only causes pain to other beings but it results in calamity for oneself in this world and in future existences. But nonviolence brings blessings and bliss. It means showing benevolence toward other beings, feeling joy at the sight of virtuous beings, showing compassion toward the suffering, and displaying tolerance toward the ill-behaved. The Jain path is really the path of total nonviolence.

The second vow, speaking truthfulness, is related to nonviolence, since all lying is motivated by the passions and damages the soul. Further, particular care should be taken not to use any speech acts, even if true, that cause harm or damage to living beings. This requirement, of course, may lead to complicated situations. For example, when asked by a hunter where a deer is, a layperson should probably mislead the hunter rather than cause destruction to the deer by her speech. Nuns and monks, of course, must observe this vow perfectly and thus could only keep silence in the face of the hunter's question.

The third vow is not to steal, that is, not to take

anything not given, since doing so always arises out of greed and causes violence. Necessarily, then, a person should not engage in any activities involving gain at the expense of others, such as substituting inferior goods for the original, using underhanded measures, accepting stolen goods, and the like. Even finding and keeping something that has been lost by another person is wrong.

The fourth vow, celibacy, means for the layperson to refrain from all illicit sexual activities, practicing moderation in sexual behavior strictly within marriage, and avoiding all types of sexual thoughts or contacts with persons besides one's spouse. As laypeople progress toward higher spiritual development, they may late in life take the more stringent vow of complete celibacy. Monks and nuns, of course, avoid all sexual feeling, since that is always accompanied by the passions, and all sexual contact, since that always causes violence and slaughter for the microscopic organisms dwelling in the generative organs.

The fifth vow is nonpossession or nonattachment, and for monks and nuns that means giving up all possessions entirely, even clothing, as we noted, for monks of the Digambara sect. Merely thinking about possessions is damaging to the soul. For laypeople, some possessions are necessary for the welfare of society in general, but one should not be attached overly to one's possessions. Rather, people should impose restrictions on themselves so as to check their greediness; once they have the amount of possessions they need for a decent life, they should voluntarily refrain from further acquisitions.

Jainism thus envisions a human society based on the central principle of nonviolence with its related corollaries. Whereas ethical practice is primarily directed toward the end of perfecting the soul and finally reaching liberation, Jains have always been concerned about the welfare of the whole society and of the entire ecological sphere with its countless billions of living organisms. Some modern Jain thinkers have pointed out that the basic Jain principles of nonviolence can make a great contribution to world society. The Jain ethical vision has an answer to the modern problems of racism, economic inequality, the inadequacies of both capitalism and communism, the disastrous destruction of our ecology, modern sexual exploitation, overpopulation, intolerance, and above all warfare.

Jains are not missionaries out to convert the world. But leading thinkers clearly articulate for all thinking people the universal benefit of following the Jain principles, as in these words of Jyotiprasad Jain:

> And, it is today, more than ever, when suspicion and distrust are vitiating the atmosphere of international peace and brotherhood, when the world is filled with fear and hate, that we require a living philosophy which will help us to discard them and recover ourselves. Such a living wholesome philosophy, bearing the message of love and goodwill, ahimsa and peace, internal as well as external, personal as well as universal, is the Jaina philosophy of life. It is this system of Jaina religion, thought and culture that stands for the highest and noblest human values, moral elevation and spiritual uplift, eternal and universal peace and happiness.[11]

DISCUSSION QUESTIONS

1. What is a Jina or Tirthankara?
2. Describe how Mahavira became a Jina. Why is his story, of all the Jinas, of particular importance to the Jains?
3. Describe the two major groups within Jainism.
4. What is the Jain conception of the universe?
5. Describe the particular Jain notion of the working of karma.
6. What insights into the Jain perspective do you find in the poem by young prince Mrgaputra?
7. How does the soul move upward on the path of transformation?
8. Describe the practice of nonviolence (ahimsa) as observed by a Jain monk or nun.

CHAPTER 20

THE WAY OF THE DISCIPLES: THE SIKHS

Sikhism, beginning in the sixteenth century C.E., is the youngest of the major religions to arise in India, and it was influenced by the interaction of Hinduism with Islam, that strongly monotheistic religion from the outside of India that seems so opposed to the Hindu vision of life but that became such an important factor in Indian culture and religion. In a remarkably fertile religious and intellectual climate, spiritual forces from these sharply contrasting religions were drawn together in Sikhism, the path of the disciples of the Gurus. Sikhism provides an Indian way, still within the worldview of samsara and rebirth, to find salvation by union with the one God, through love experiencing the person of God dwelling within and responding with the heart to the voice of the Divine Guru.

SACRED STORY AND HISTORICAL CONTEXT

"Who am I?" To be a Sikh means to be a "disciple," a disciple of the Guru. And who is the Guru? Of course, it is Guru Nanak and the other gurus, ten in all. But then the Guru is also the Holy Book, the Adi Granth. In the final analysis, God is the Guru. The identity of Sikhs is tied up with the sacred story about the Gurus, the Holy Book, and God.

Nanak and the Other Gurus

The time for the founding of this new religion of India came when Islamic spiritual influence became strong in India and, in Hinduism, the great Vaishnavite bhakti movement was popular. This movement had begun in the Tamil country in the south, but in the fourteenth and fifteenth centuries it spread all across north India and had much contact with Islam. These devotees maintained that Vishnu is the one and only divine reality, though known by many other names, and that the best way to salvation is by singing God's name and approaching God in love. The Muslim Sufis in India were cultivating a similar path of mystical love and devotion to God, with emphasis on the master who guides the devotional meditation.

Among the Vaishnavites an important predecessor of Nanak, the founder of Sikhism, was the poet Kabir (1440–1518), who rejected the authority of the Vedas and combined Hindu and Muslim ideas in his syncretistic approach. He taught that all should worship the one God, that images and rituals such as pilgrimages provide no help, and that the simple love of God that captures the heart is sufficient to free one from the wheel of rebirth. The path of Kabir is still followed by groups in India called the Kabirpanthis. And Sikhs look to Kabir for spiritual inspiration—many of his hymns and verses appear in the Adi Granth.

Nanak Becomes the Guru

Nanak was born in 1469 in the village of Talwandi near Lahore (in present-day Pakistan) to a Hindu kshatriya (warrior) family. His father was a revenue officer for the Muslim overseer of the village, and Nanak received a Hindu upbringing along with considerable exposure to Islam. Whereas Sikhs consider Nanak's writings in the Adi Granth to be the only completely authentic information about him, they have many other popular stories about his life. He was a precocious youth, a poet by nature, more given to meditation and searching for religious truth than to the business affairs his father tried to interest him in. In this heavily Muslim area he explored Islam as an alternative to Hinduism, and he took every opportunity to talk with holy persons of any sect. Eventually he was married and had two sons, and he worked for a while for a Muslim official in the nearby town of Sultanapur. He became close friends with a Muslim family servant, Mardana, who played the rebec, a stringed instrument, and together they sang the hymns that Nanak composed, gradually attracting a small community of seekers.

When Nanak was thirty came a crucial, intense religious experience that transformed his life. One morning after bathing in the river he disappeared in a forest and experienced being carried up to God's presence, where he was given a cup of nectar and a divine call:

> This is the cup of the adoration of God's name. Drink it. I am with you. I bless you and raise you up. Whoever remembers you will enjoy my favor. Go, rejoice in my name and teach others to do so. I have bestowed the gift of my name upon you. Let this be your calling.[1]

Emerging from the forest three days after he disappeared and had been thought drowned, Nanak was silent for one day, and then he said, "There is neither Hindu nor Mussulman [Muslim], so whose path shall I follow? I shall follow God's path. God is neither Hindu nor Mussulman and the path which I follow is God's."[2]

Now Nanak was a guru, one who drives away darkness and teaches enlightenment, giving voice to the word of God who is the true Guru. The story says he pursued his divine calling by spending many years traveling about India, often accompanied by Mardana, teaching and singing evangelistic hymns in market-places, street corners, and open squares. One tradition says he and Mardana even traveled to Mecca, Medina, and Baghdad. To emphasize his pronouncement that there is neither Hindu nor Muslim, on one occasion he wore a Hindu dhoti (lower garment) and a mango-colored jacket with a white sheet over both, a Muslim hat, and a necklace of bones, and on his forehead he had a Hindu saffron mark. Later in his life he adopted the common garb of a householder, to show, perhaps, that his religious path did not mean abandoning the world.

After many years of traveling, in about 1521 Nanak decided to settle down with his family, establishing a religious center in Kartarpur, a village whose residents were Sikhs. Then he devoted the rest of his life to teaching and serving this community. His teachings revolved around God as the sole reality who is formless and beyond all conceptions, whose self-manifestation is the whole creation so that in a sense everything is in God. Yet the transcendent, unknowable God is experienced as personal through love and devotion. One of the most important passages in the Adi Granth, the first part of the Japji (recited by Sikhs in every morning devotion), was composed by Nanak immediately after his enlightenment experience. It well expresses his experience of God:

> There is one God,
> Eternal Truth is His Name;
> Maker of all things,
> Fearing nothing and at enmity with nothing,
> Timeless in His Image;
> Not begotten, being of His own Being:
> By the grace of the Guru, made known to men.[3]

The primary problem in human existence, Guru Nanak taught, is separation from God through ignorance and self-centeredness. The soul is capable of pure union with God, but in self-centeredness it turns to the world as something separate from God and allows itself to be dominated with passions and pride. The soul that is trapped in evil will have to endure countless rebirths, sufferings, and deaths. But the way to union with God is revealed by the guru, through whom God's word reverberates. By meditating on this word and on God's name, disciples are given God's grace and favor and enabled to hear his voice and open their hearts to salvation.

Since the true path is an inward preparation of the heart to receive and experience God, Nanak rejected the traditional Hindu and Muslim rituals and scriptures. And since all beings are God's creation, he rejected discriminations on the basis of sex or caste. The path Guru Nanak taught includes techniques and disciplines for preparing the heart, particularly singing God's praises (*kirtan*) and meditating on God's name, repeating it so that the divine sound fills one's whole being: "Repeating [the Name] of the True God means engrafting [Him] in the *man* [soul]."[4]

The Ten Gurus and the Sikh Community

Before his death in 1539, Guru Nanak named Lehna, a former devotee of the goddess Durga, to be his successor as head of the Sikh community, renaming him Guru Angad (part of me), implying that Angad did indeed possess Nanak's own spirit. Henceforth God's word would continue to come through the gurus, leading the community to union wtih God. For a succession of ten gurus, the position of guru continued to be central to the Sikhs, because the gurus were vehicles through whom God's message was expressed. When the third guru, Amar Das, began collecting the Sikh scriptures, he included not only hymns of Guru Nanak but also hymns composed by Guru Angad, himself, and a number of non-Sikhs such as Kabir, for they all were regarded as transmitting the voice of God. This holy book became known as the Adi Granth (Original Collection) and is also often called Granth Sahib (Sacred Collection), itself called Guru.

The third guru also created a system of Sikh parishes and established rituals and festivals for Sikh observance in place of Hindu celebrations. Ram Das, the fourth guru, enjoyed the favor of the tolerant ruler Akbar, and set up the village Amritsar near a pool of water that had been especially beloved by Nanak. Amritsar became the religious center for Sikhs and their most holy city.

A Sikh reading at the Golden Temple at Amritsar.

later in martyrdom by the ninth guru, Tegh Bahadur (1675). These martyrs have also become an important part of the Sikh sacred story and are remembered in festivals.

Yet another important component of the story comes under the tenth guru, Gobind Singh. Part of a male Sikh's identity is his long hair, dress, and his name Singh; and when Sikhs worship together they glorify the *Khalsa*. What is this all about? Already in the time of Guru Arjan, the Sikh community began to realize that it needed to develop military preparedness to defend itself, and the gurus were trained as military leaders. The tenth guru, Gobind Singh, in preparation for a momentous struggle for Sikh survival, founded the khalsa military society in 1699. According to the traditional story, Guru Gobind addressed an assembly of Sikhs on New Year's Day and stressed the seriousness of the times and the need for strength, unity, and loyalty to the guru. With his sword uplifted, he called for five volunteers to come forward to die for the Sikh cause to show their loyalty and conviction. After a fearful silence, one Sikh came forward and was led into the guru's tent. Guru Gobind emerged with his sword dripping with fresh blood and asked for more volunteers. One by one four more brave Sikhs came forward and were escorted into the tent. In a dramatic climax, Guru Gobind emerged from the tent with all five Sikhs still alive; he had substituted a goat for the sacrifice of the five men.

Now Guru Gobind performed a ceremony of initiation of the Five Beloved Ones, as they are called. Mixing nectar in water with a two-edged sword, he gave them to drink of it and sprinkled it over them, initiating them into the khalsa (pure) Order. Then he himself received initiation from them. As the physical sign of the khalsa all vowed to wear the five K's: uncut hair (*kais*), a comb (*kangha*), a sword or dagger (*kirpan*), a wrist guard (*kara*), and short pants (*kachha*). The uncut hair was to be kept in a topknot under a turban.

After these first members, the guru threw open membership in the khalsa to everyone of all castes, including women. Men entering the khalsa adopted the common surname Singh (lion), and the women took the name Kaur (princess). And the guru set up a special code of discipline, prohibiting tobacco, eating meat of

Now the guruship became hereditary. Under the next guru, Arjan, the Sikhs began to build the Golden Temple at Amritsar. The hymns of the first four gurus and other inspired hymns and poems were gathered into the final, authoritative edition of the Adi Granth and this was enshrined in the Golden Temple, to be from that time the central focus of Sikh faith and worship.

But now political adversity comes into the story. The Muslim successors to Akbar were less tolerant and began persecuting non-Muslims, and Arjan had to choose between accepting Islam or death. Choosing death, he became the first Sikh martyr (1606), followed animals slaughtered in the Muslim way, and sexual contact with Muslims, but enjoining regular singing of the guru's hymns and congregational worship with men and women participating on a equal basis. Thousands of men and women were initiated on that founding day, and afterward people of all castes eagerly entered the khalsa. Although, of course, not all Sikhs became members of the khalsa, it did sustain the Sikh community through times of grave crisis, and still today the ritual of initiation, accepting the prohibitions, and wearing the five K's are important aspects of Sikh identity.

Guru Gobind's four sons died in the struggle with the Muslim forces, and Gobind fled to south India where he was assassinated by a fanatic. But before he died he declared that the line of gurus ended with himself, the tenth guru. From now on, he decreed, the Adi Granth would be their Guru. From that time onward, except for a couple of small Sikh sects who retained human gurus, Sikhs have looked to Guru Granth Sahib, the Holy Book, for God's word.

Developments, Struggles, Transformations

Religious Developments in Sikh History

As time went on and the Sikh community spread, more congregations were established, and in every locality they erected *gurdwaras*, buildings for worship and meeting together. Often these included a kitchen area (*langar*) where a free common meal would be served for all. This, together with the worship gatherings in which men and women participated together without priests and without class distinctions, served to maintain the sense of unity and equality in the Sikh community.

Although maintaining Guru Nanak's emphasis on a religion of the heart rather than ritual and pilgrimage, Sikhs did adopt many of the festivals of Hinduism in northern India, together with traditions and lore from the Hindu epics. Guru Gobind Singh produced a supplement to the Adi Granth, called the Granth of the Tenth Guru, not considered as sacred as the Adi Granth but still used widely for edification. Along with his own hymns, Gobind included much material from

the Hindu epics, especially about the gods Rama and Krishna and their renowned exploits. He also included stories about the great goddess Durga and her victories over evil. Such heroic material could be used especially to instill bravery in the khalsa to stand firm in their faith and fight against the enemies of the Sikhs.

After the death of the tenth guru, the hostility between the Sikhs and the Mogul rulers continued to increase, and members of the khalsa took to the hills to carry on guerrilla warfare for the survival of the Sikh community. The Sikhs emerged victorious in the area of Lahore, and a Sikh kingdom was set up under Ranjit Singh (1780–1839) that controlled most of the Punjab area. But the British had taken the place of the Mogul Empire, and a period of running battles between the Sikhs and the British led ultimately to the complete surrender of the Sikhs to British control. Because the British treated them with fairness and justice, the Sikhs turned out to be loyal subjects, serving with bravery and distinction in the armies through which the British maintained their control of India.

But the longstanding desire for freedom and an independent Sikh state could not be entirely suppressed, and the Sikhs tended to join the movement for India's independence from the British. However, they were devastated by the decision to partition their homeland, the Punjab, between the newly created Muslim state of Pakistan and India. With immense suffering, two and a half million Sikhs had to leave their homes and move across the new border to India, leaving behind rich farms and sacred places such as the birthplace of Guru Nanak.

The Sikh Community Today

Today Sikhs still make up the majority in the Punjab in India. Whereas the Sikh community has maintained a strong sense of unity, several divisions did develop in the course of history. Today the Singh group (the khalsa) makes up the great majority of Sikhs. A small order called Udasi is inclined toward asceticism and celibacy, going about in yellow robes with begging bowls, often with shaved head and no beards. The Sahaj-dhari group, also clean-shaven, is a nonkhalsa group that refused to go along with the militant stance of the tenth guru. Within the large Singh group there are some differences as well. One faction takes a rather militant stance and carries martial implements. Another faction leans toward contemplation and scholarship.

The vision of a Sikh state has always been a part of Sikh belief. Many Sikhs have been working toward and demanding a Sikh-dominated state in the Punjab, a demand that in recent years has caused considerable violence and bloodshed, even at the Golden Temple. The Sikh community has not been able, to date, to unify itself on the question of what course to take within the extremely complicated politics of India. A Sikh has been president of India; but others advocate violent uprising against the Hindu-dominated government.

Another problem Sikhism faces today, like all the major religions, is the lure of secularism and the loss of tradition. Many young people abandon the khalsa emblem of unshorn hair, and there is some tendency, especially among Sikhs living outside of strong Sikh settlements, to lapse back into Hindu society. To combat these tendencies, Sikh leaders promote a revival of Sikh tradition, stressing those features that are unique to the Sikh heritage.

Sikhism is a world religion today, with perhaps fourteen million adherents in various parts of the world. Some twelve million live in India, but there are about one million living in thriving Sikh communities in the United States and Canada, and around half a million Sikhs live in England.

WORLDS OF MEANING

The Sacred Ultimate: God

"What's it *all* about?" "What is really the center that holds everything together?"

For Sikhs, as for Jews, Christians, and Muslims, the answer is God. Guru Nanak and the other gurus certainly were influenced by the radical monotheism of Islam. But the "monotheism" of Sikhism is born of

Sikh leaders at the Golden Temple of Amritsar. Recent conflicts have brought much bloodshed and violence to this holy shrine.

India, counting also Vaishnavite theologians and poets among its sources, signaled by Guru Nanak's important teaching that God is neither Hindu nor Muslim.

At the heart of the world's existence is the one God, who is immortal, unborn, self-existent, omniscient, formless, and totally beyond human conceptions and categories. God is the creator of the universe and transcendent far beyond it. At the same time, the universe is an emanation from God's being, a manifestation of God's own essence, so in a sense we can say that God is in everything and everything is in God. The world exists within the unity of God, and even the Hindu gods can be seen as manifestations of the supreme one name: "He, the One, is Himself Brahma, Vishnu and Shiva; and He Himself performs all."[5] God rules over the world in the samsara cycles of existence and even over the law of karma.

But God is not simply like the Hindu Brahman, impersonal and beyond conception. God is personal, being revealed to the human heart through the word in all creation and especially through God's name, the dimension of God that can be known and loved by humans. "The Name is the total expression of all that God is and this is Truth. *Sati Nam*—His name is Truth."[6] Thus God is the true Guru, granting self-revelation through the creation, and through grace enabling humans to hear the divine voice. Persons who thus open their hearts to God's presence and follow the path will ultimately attain nirvana, absorption into God's being like water blending with water. In this way the Sikh experience of God as ultimate reality blends monistic and monotheistic, impersonal and personal dimensions.

Divine Creation and Human Nature

In thinking about the creation of the world and human nature, often we encounter two opposite views: belief in one creator God who creates humans for a single lifetime, or belief in world cycles with karma and rebirth as the human lot. The first is characteristic of the Abrahamic religions, and the second is typical of the religions arising from India. We have already been chastened in holding this assumption too strictly, for we found within Hinduism groups believing in one creator God. Now in Sikhism we have a religious perspective that specifically combines elements of both these views.

The Divine Creation: World and Humans

"What is this world all about?" Just as Sikhs combine the ideas of a transcendent, impersonal God and an immanent, personal God, so also they combine views of the world as God's creation and the world as an emanation of God's being. God, formless and eternal, created all existence, and God sustains all forms of existence by dwelling in them. Originally there was darkness everywhere with only the Omnipotent One existing in abstract meditation. Then God willed, and from the word expressing the divine will the universe came into existence as a hot nebula spinning out the planets.

> Through uncountable ages,
> Complete darkness brooded
> Over utter vacancy;
> There were no worlds, no firmaments.
> The Will of the Lord was alone pervasive;
> There was neither night nor day, nor sun nor moon
> But only God in ceaseless trance. . . .
> When He so willed, He shaped the Universe;
> The firmament He spread without a prop to support it.
> He created the high gods, Brahma, Vishnu and Shiva.
> And Maya the goddess, the veil of illusion,
> Who maketh Truth dark and increaseth worldly attachment.
> To some, to a chosen few, the Guru revealeth the Lord's Word.
> The Lord creates and He watcheth His Creation;
> He made the heavenly bodies,
> Our Universe in the endless space,
> Above, below and around it.
> And out of the Unmanifested, Unmovable ground of His Being,
> To us and in us, He made Himself manifest.[7]

God creates the universe and dissolves it time and again in divine play. The universe is real, but it is not eternal and has no independent existence. God creates both good and evil, but the overall existence of the world is good and beneficial, and accordingly Sikhism does not advocate asceticism or withdrawal from the world. God also preserves the world according to the divine will or norm expressed in the orderly functioning of existence. In accordance with the divine norm, the Adi Granth says, we are born and we die, and everything, ahead and behind, is pervaded by this norm.

What is one's real self? Human souls are part of the creation emanating from God, like sparks arising from the fire. God is infinite, but the soul is finite and has its own individuality; yet it is deathless. It takes bodily form according to the will of the creator, and it gives consciousness to the body. Mind and intellect are the outer coverings of the soul; it is through the mind and intellect that the soul controls the working of the bodily senses. It is the soul that is conscious of truth or falsehood, that determines virtue or sinfulness. The soul is the basic link with God, as the receptacle of God's love. When the body dies the soul leaves and continues forever, transmigrating to other bodies in the rebirth cycle in accordance with karma. There are heaven and hell into which one can be reborn, although these are not eternal or ultimate, and we can be reborn as animals or plants. At death the soul leaves the body and appears before the God of justice. Depending on its karma, it may be sent to be reborn as an animal, a bird, or an insect. It may be sent to heaven or hell. Or it may be sent to be born again as a human being for its further development. The goal of the Sikh religious life is to attain final nirvana, that is, total union of the soul with God, thus transcending heaven and hell and the rebirth cycle.

The Human Predicament
Although the world and humans were created by God and thus are not essentially evil, our self-centeredness and pride lead to attachment to the pleasures and concerns of the world. The result of this is separation from God and all the manifold human sufferings, including the endless cycle of rebirths.

The main human problem is the ego, that is, self-centeredness, which arises because we are enveloped in *maya*, delusion, which also is part of God's creation. It is not inevitable that humans give in to self-centeredness. Sikhs do not believe in a predestined course of the soul nor do they hold to the belief that the soul is basically evil. The soul and the world are both good and pure. If the world is seen as God's creation, it

is like a beautiful gem; and if the soul is pure, it reflects God's purity and love. But most of us give in to self-centered tendencies and turn our attentions to the pleasures of the world rather than to God. We fill our souls with self-love rather than love for God, and such a soul is trapped by the passions into a life of sin and evil.

> Those who do not cherish the Lord's Name
> Wander, deceived and bewildered;
> Without such cherishing of the Lord's Name,
> Without the love of His Eternal Being,
> Man can have no destiny except remorse and anguish.[8]

The curse of the self-centered person is separation from God. Such a person suffers deprivation of God's love and grace, sinking ever deeper into a life of fear and anxiety. Yama, the lord of death, uses the evil tendencies to snare those who are separated from God and lost in the world; their lot is the endless cycle of rebirths.

> O Self-love, Self-will, thou root of births and deaths,
> Thou soul of sin, thou makest a man to
> Estrange friends and increase the enmity of enemies:
> He thinketh ever of heaping up more wealth,
> And his soul exhausts itself in deaths and rebirths
> And suffers uncountable delights and agonies.
> Thou makest man to lose himself in error's dark wood,
> And thou strikest him mortally sick with covetousness.[9]

Such wanderings can only stop when we meet a true perceptor, a guru, who will guide us onto the path of transformation.

The Path of Transformation
"How can I start living *real* life?"

The human problem is selfishness, which makes one love the world rather than God, causing one to be separated from God. The answer? In Guru Nanak's words,

> What keepeth me in my detachment
> Is meditating on the Ungraspable One,
> Through the One Divine Word
> God is made real to us,
> And the saints destroy the flames,
> Of attachment to the little self.[10]

Nanak repeatedly rejected the need for various religious practices like sacrifices, pilgrimages, fasting, and the rest. Rather the path is essentially an inner discipline aimed at opening the heart to God's presence. The heart needs to be purified so it can resonate to God's name.

Sikhs believe that God's word reverberates throughout creation as the revelation of God's own being. It is the means through which God can be known, and it reveals the path leading to union with God. It comes first of all through God's grace, awakening our minds and hearts. Guru Nanak said, "*Karma* determines the nature of our birth, but it is through grace that the door of salvation is found."[11] Every person has the capability to hear and respond to this word. As God's word is divine revelation in creation, so God's name is the revelation of God's personal being whom we can know and love. By focusing on the divine name we enter into a personal relationship with God. But how can we, selfish and forgetful, hear and respond to God's name?

Sikhs believe that to get on the path of transformation it is necessary to hear the word of the guru, for it is through the gurus that God channels grace to humankind. A modern Sikh scholar explains:

> To be communicable, the Supreme Being chooses one of his created men to be his vehicle and speak to humanity through that chosen vehicle in a language that man can understand. "He places himself in the Guru," the specially chosen form, says Guru Nanak. . . . They [the gurus] only proclaimed what was inspired in their holy beings by the Master as a command or communication. The voice thus received was recorded in human language and it, so preserved, became the eternal Guru. The voice "vibrates in the pages of the Guru Granth."[12]

The ten gurus were illuminated by the inner truth of God's word, and by their perfection they were able to be illuminators of that truth to bring others to salvation. After the death of the tenth guru, the truth that the gurus illuminated was understood to be merged into the Adi Granth. The path of transformation is above all to focus on the word of the guru, for that word inspires and transforms human life:

> And as music has a strange fascination for the mind, the Guru's Word is to be sung to fire one's mind with an experience that sinks in the soul, and turning the usual, habitual tide of the mind, makes the soul experience the nature of God within one's emotional self. Yea, and then this God-nature will outflow into secular activity as well, deflect man's mind from his immediate environs and personal pulls and passions, and yoke it to the service of the others in order that the Name, the all-pervading Spirit, is seen through all creation.[13]

Thus the path involves honoring, reading, singing, and meditating on the words of the gurus as they are written in the Adi Granth.

Achieving this realization naturally affects the way people live their lives. They control their desires and their sense of ego, not withdrawing from the world but seeing it as God's creation and God's revelation. As people advance in spiritual perfection, they deepen their piety, knowledge, effort, and fulfillment, until finally they attain to God-realization, entering into union with God's own true, formless being. The realm of birth and death, even the realm of heaven and hell, are left behind in this eternal bliss.

> They who think on Thee, they who meditate on Thee,
> In this dark age have their peace.
> They who think on Thee: they are saved, they are liberated;
> For them death's noose is broken.
> Those who meditate on the Fearless One
> Will lose all their fear;
> Those who have worshipped the Lord,
> In the Lord they are now mingled.[14]

WORSHIP AND LIFE

Ritual and Worship Among the Sikhs

"How can I find new power for life?" The Sikh answer is love, God's love, experienced and expressed in service, ritual, and worship. The active love and worship of God, focused on the divine revelation in the Adi Granth, God's presence in the gurdwara, and God's word brought through the gurus, characterize the Sikh religion. The proper way to relate to God is in prayer, submission, study of God's word, thankful praise, and a lifestyle that reflects this love.

Worship starts with the word of God, which is experienced concretely in the Adi Granth. Daily worship at home means reading and meditating on the sacred word, the Adi Granth, which is kept in a special room of the house. Devout Sikhs rise before sunrise and bathe, followed by saying prayers, reciting scriptures, and concentrating on the name of the Lord. When the day is done, they again recite prayers and scriptures before retiring for the night.

Worship also means visiting the gurdwara, daily, perhaps, and participating in worship there—this is the heart of the Sikh religion. Since there are no priests or ordained worship leaders in Sikhism, each person is free and empowered to perform the rituals of worship. The central object of worship is the Granth Sahib, the Holy Book, which is placed on a low cot and draped in embroidered silks with a royal awning above. People remove their shoes and cover their heads when entering the gurdwara. Often they bring some flowers and copper or silver coins to deposit before the Holy Book. They walk solemnly to the Holy Book, bow and perhaps touch their foreheads to the edge of the sheet covering the Book. Then they move back to sit on the carpeted floor with the rest of the congregation.

The pattern of worship in the gurdwara consists of two main activities: reading and explaining the scriptures, and singing the hymns (*kirtan*). Both men and women read from the Holy Book. Often there are trained musicians who lead the faithful in the devotional music, which is a valuable means of lifting the soul to communion with God. After the prayers, Sikhs receive *karah parshad*, a sacred food made of flour, sugar, and ghee.

Generally Sikhs observe the usual festivals of northern India, such as Holi and Divali. There are also specifically Sikh festivals commemorating the birthday of Guru Nanak, the martyrdom of the fifth Guru Arjun, and the like. In celebrating a festival, the Holy Book is placed in a decorated palanquin carried on a flower-bedecked lorry. The joyful procession is led by men marching with drawn swords, and many enthusiastic and gaily dressed devotees participate, some in singing parties, others as sword-stick performers, and the like. Often the festival includes a common meal for the worshipers at the kitchen (*langar*) of the gurdwara.

Sikhism does not approve of excessive ritualism.

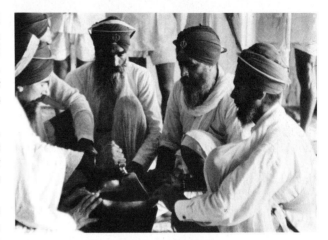

Sikhs preparing holy water for ritual use.

Still, there are commonly observed ceremonies relating to the main passages of life. Some Sikhs follow the tradition of reciting the first five verses of the morning prayer in the ears of a newborn child. In the naming ceremony, the Holy Book is opened and the child is given a name starting with the first letter of the first word on the top of the page. Religious instruction is provided privately or at the gurdwara, and the first day when the child learns to read the Granth Sahib is a day of great festivity. When Sikh boys and girls come of age they are formally initiated into the order of the khalsa. Five Sikhs perform this ritual before the congregation, stirring sugared water (*amrit*) with a steel double-edged dagger accompanied by the recitation of sacred verses. The holy water is poured into the cupped hands of the initiates and they drink of it, and it is then sprinkled all over their bodies.

A Sikh marriage takes place in the gurdwara before the Adi Granth. The main ceremony is circling the Adi Granth four times accompanied by the singing of special verses. After each round the couple bow down before the Holy Book. After the fourth round the marriage is complete.

When a Sikh dies, the body is bathed and dressed in the emblems of the faith and taken in solemn procession to the crematorium. No wailing is permitted, only recitation of the holy word and the distribution of food to the family and mourners. A short period of mourning is observed, and on the last day family and friends assemble in the house for singing hymns and reciting the Adi Granth.

The worship life of Sikhs gives expression to the love of God in a variety of art forms. Shunning sculpture because of the worship of images in India, Sikhs celebrate the artistic beauty of nature in its manifold forms. Since the word of God is central, the literary arts have been highly cultivated, especially that of religious poetry, with the powerful poems of the gurus taken as models. Another art beloved by the Sikhs is music, used in singing the sacred songs to uplift the soul. Guru Nanak spoke:

> In the house in which men sing the Lord's praises
> And meditate upon Him,
> In that house sing the songs of praise
> And remember the Creator;
> Sing the song of praise of thy fearless Lord,
> Let me be a sacrifice unto that song,
> By which we attain everlasting solace.[15]

A Sikh writer explains the importance of the art of music in this way: "Music carries an individual above the mundane and helps in merging the not-Self with the Self. By music the soul is lifted into an almost mystic union with God."[16]

Society and the Good Life

Sikh Society: Khalsa and Gurdwara

"How should I live?" A Sikh should live as befits one who belongs to the Panth (path), the Sikh community of believers, disciples of the gurus.

Many Sikhs think of themselves as part of the khalsa, the special form of the Panth founded by Guru Gobind. Their salutation to one another is, "The khalsa belongs to God; victory to Him!" Historically, the khalsa is the community founded by the tenth guru to keep the Sikhs in military readiness and bravery, but it has become a symbol of belonging to the Sikhs, an identity expressed concretely by the uncut hair and turban worn by men. Although there are birth rituals for Sikhs, the real entrance into the Sikh community is through the initiation into the order of the khalsa held when the individual comes of age.

The Sikh community differs from the other religions arising from India in having no priests, mendicants, or other holy persons as worship leaders. It is an egalitarian community, and any person with reasonable proficiency in the Punjabi language, including women, can conduct congregational services and act as readers of the Adi Granth.

Leadership in the Sikh community is found in the committees formed to manage the gurdwaras (temples). These are local autonomous bodies, elected democratically. These groups not only manage the temples but run many educational institutions and publish religious literature, playing a leading role in political developments as well. But there is also a central authority that decides on the major issues that affect the larger Sikh community. This group is made up of the leaders of four major gurdwaras in India, including especially the one at Amritsar. The decisions of this central authority are binding upon the Sikh community.

The Sikh Vision of the Good Ethical Life: Self-realization

In answer to the question, "How should I live?," Sikhs could answer in the words of Guru Nanak,

> Men of contentment serve their Lord and dwell upon the True One.
> They do not put their feet in sin; they do good deeds and practise Dharma.
> They loosen their sensual bonds and eat but sparingly.
> And the Grace of God is heaped upon them.[17]

Love of God and the guru is the basis of the good ethical life, leading to happiness, grace, and self-realization. And that good life is the natural life, following the highest law that is in the human heart. "Act according to the Universal Will that is written within one's Self," said Guru Nanak.[18]

The primary human problem that stands in the way of the good life is the ego, that is, attachment to self apart from God. Sikhs believe that one's present life has been shaped by karma in past existences, and futher that the Will of God controls all existence. However, even though much of our existence is beyond our ability to control, we do have a realm of free will in which we can cultivate the love of God and follow the guidance of the guru in order to break our attachment to selfishness. The good life is seen as the way to move away from ego to the union of the self with God and thus complete self-realization. This means cultivating concrete virtues and avoiding attachments to sins and vices, thus becoming a true Sikh.

There are, of course, springs of action that hinder the moral life; these are concupiscence, anger, covetousness, attachment, and pride, the "evil ones and thieves" that continuously steal away our virtues. Against these vices Sikhism does not advocate extreme asceticism or withdrawal from social relations. Rather, recognizing one's place in God's Will, one should cultivate the central virtues. Guru Nanak said that "as many are the vices, so many are the chains round one's neck. One removes vice with virtue, for virtue is our only friend."[19]

Heading the list of virtues would be wisdom, as the foundation for the good life, and truthfulness, as a fundamental quality growing from the love of God and one's fellow humans. Another central human virtue is justice, regarding all others as equal to oneself, respecting their rights, and not exploiting them. Sikhs further emphasize the virtue of self-control, living one's life in moderation and governing the lower impulses by the higher, not through extreme asceticism but through moderation: eating less, sleeping less, and talking less, as Guru Nanak suggested. A related virtue would be contentment, that is, accepting both success and failure calmly.

Still one more characteristic virtue in the Sikh view of the good life is courage. Sikhs are enjoined to be fearless and unflinching in standing in their faith, no matter what the suffering. Beginning with Guru Gobind Singh, the tenth guru, the virtue of courage was extended to taking arms and struggling on the battlefield in the cause of righteousness: "When the situation is past all remedies, it is righteousness to take to sword."[20] Such militant courage is to be used only when all other avenues are closed and together with the other virtues of justice and love. The virtue of courage is embodied especially in the khalsa with its code of discipline and the symbolic wearing of the sword.

But how does one apply these virtues concretely to life in family and in society? Sikhism teaches that all should perform the duties associated with their particular station in life. Further, all should observe the duties of right livelihood, not depending on the charity of others and not being dishonest in trade. They should help the needy, regarding such help as an act of service to the guru. Extramarital sexual relations are immoral, and intoxicants and narcotics are forbidden.

As part of their vision of the good life in human society, Sikhs reject the Hindu caste system in favor of the principle of universal equality. One concrete symbol of this social equality is the characteristic Sikh institution of the community kitchen (langar), where people of all sorts sit together and partake of the same food without any distinction between the high and the low. Further, women are to be accorded equal status and respect with men, conducting worship services, leading Sikh armies, voting in elections, and the like. Guru Nanak said,

> Of a woman are we conceived,
> Of a woman we are born,
> To a woman are we betrothed and married,
> It is a woman who is friend and partner of life,
> It is woman who keeps the race going. . . .
> Why should we consider woman cursed and condemned
> When from woman are born leaders and rulers.
> From woman alone is born a woman,
> Without woman there can be no human birth.
> Without woman, O Nanak, only the True One exists.[21]

To realize human brotherhood, Sikhs are taught to do away with slander of others and all enmity toward them. In a positive sense they are to practice altruism toward all, involving themselves in social service for the poor and needy—for in serving humanity one is serving the guru and serving God. In the Sikh vision of the good life for the world today, peoples of all nationalities and religions are considered equal. The tenth guru proclaimed:

> Let it be known that mankind is one, that all men belong to a single humanity. So too with God, whom Hindu and Muslim distinguish with differing names . . . There is no difference between a temple and a mosque, nor between the prayers of a Hindu or a Muslim. Though differences seem to mark and distinguish, all men are in reality the same.[22]

All religions originated with good intentions and are like different roads leading to the same destination. Sikhs feel they should not enter into arguments about the truth of other religions. Rather the gurus encourage the cultivation of a rational attitude, finding out for oneself what is right and what is wrong. In doing so, Sikhs believe one will find that the path taught by the ten gurus is the highest path of self-realization.

A modern Sikh thinker, Taran Singh, has interpreted the khalsa in such a way as to transcend a narrow sectarian view. There is one universal Spirit, he holds, who belongs to all people, whatever their color, country, caste, or religion; there are no privileged people or superior faiths. He writes,

> The doctrine of the Khalsa or the Universal Brotherhood of the Pure, proceeds from the doctrine of the all-pervasive and indivisible ultimate Reality. The Wonderful Lord manifests himself in a wonderful drama . . . of the cosmos and creation. In fact all the actors in this cosmic play are Khalsa or Pure; they are all saints and no sinners. . . . So the brotherhood of the Pure is the brotherhood of the entire humanity.

And those initiated Sikhs who make up the actual khalsa are to be seen as an ideal society of humankind who have a mission to perform: "It is a society of humanity so that they might transform the world into the Kingdom of Heaven."[23]

DISCUSSION QUESTIONS

1. Relate the beginnings of Sikhism to developments in India in the fourteenth and fifteenth centuries C.E.
2. What was the experience that transformed Nanak and made him a guru?
3. What is the role of the ten gurus in Sikhism? Why is the Adi Granth also called Guru?
4. Describe the special Sikh form of monotheism. How is this similar to, or different from, the monotheism of the Abrahamic religions?
5. How do the Sikhs maintain both the idea of God's creation of the world and belief in samsara and rebirth?
6. According to the Sikhs, what is the major human problem? What is the main movement on the path of transformation, and what is the spiritual goal?
7. Describe worship at a gurdwara.
8. What is the khalsa?

PART IV

RELIGIONS OF CHINA AND JAPAN

INTRODUCTION

East Asia is a tremendously diversified cultural area, with many different ethnic and linguistic groups. Moreover, it has a mind-boggling number of people—perhaps one-fourth of the world's five billion people live in the area of East Asia! The peoples of East Asia have the same human experiences as others on this planet, and they ask similar questions about human existence, finding the answers in their long experience. Their answers fall in many ranges, for they have seriously experimented with many world visions, philosophies, and ways of life. These traditions are called by different names—Confucianism, philosophical Taoism, religious Taoism, Mahayana Buddhism, Shinto, and many new religions. But there is some commonality of vision underlying all this, even in the divergent practices and teachings.

A complete study of the religions of East Asia would include

377

many peoples, such as those of Korea, Mongolia, Tibet, the Philippines, even Vietnam. We concentrate our investigation here on the dominant traditions of China and Japan, for these are representative of East Asia and have been most influential throughout the whole area.

The family of religions that we find in China and Japan is perhaps not as closely knit historically as the Abraham religions or those arising in India. Even within China the vast land and the variety of ethnic groups promoted a diversity of religious traditions, and Japan developed in isolation until Chinese influence began to infiltrate in the sixth century C.E. East Asia embraces religious traditions of three totally different origins: Confucianism and Taoism arising in China, Shinto arising in Japan, and Buddhism imported from India.

Yet it is still possible in a certain sense to speak of the religions of China and Japan as a family of religions, for they do share important historical developments and religious ideas. Historically, China had developed a great civilization by the second millennium B.C.E., and its Confucian and Taoist religious traditions were passed on later to Japan and the rest of East Asia to become the heart of the common East Asian vision. And Mahayana Buddhism, though originally foreign to China, was accepted and transformed into a Chinese religion, and this also was shared with Japan and the rest of East Asia to form another major component. So the common history is largely a matter of Chinese civilization, developing stage by stage, moving outward to permeate the rest of East Asia with its culture, written language, and a common religious outlook, tempered, of course, by the indigenous traditions such as Shinto in Japan.

But what are some main elements of that common East Asian religious vision? A good word to start with is *harmony*—the functioning harmony of a cosmos filled with sacred forces. There is a close interrelationship of the human and natural orders, and the sacred forces—gods, kami, spirits, yin-yang forces—stand at the heart of the sacred ecology. This is one unified world—no transcendent God or eternal world outside this unified sacred cosmos. We are a part of this one world together with all the sacred forces and all of nature, and our highest good comes in maintaining harmony and balance within it.

The natural social links to family, community, and nation are key arenas of religious involvement for the peoples of China and Japan. The family in particular is the realm of sacred power most directly and concretely affecting one's existence. And the family is founded on the ancestors, so worship of ancestors is a most characteristic form of religious expression. Many gods and spirits are associated with the home and most religious rituals are based in the family.

The pattern of family relationships is also the basis for one's relationship to the community and to the nation as a large sacred family.

The religions of China and Japan are typically "this worldly," in the sense that some transcendent world or a future life after death is not the center concern. It is true that Mahayana Buddhism did bring into East Asia a concern about the fate of the souls of the dead. But the strongest emphasis is on the good, balanced life here and now. The world is good and beautiful, human nature derives from positive sacred forces like Heaven and the kami, and the religious path means to achieve and enhance the potential life of sacred harmony in the world and in human society. There is no sharp division, then, between sacred and secular parts of life, between spiritual and humanistic concerns, for all are joined together in balance.

We should note that one strong common factor throughout East Asia is the worldview of Mahayana Buddhism. Though originally a foreign religion from India, Mahayana Buddhism was thoroughly transformed into an East Asian religion, itself transforming East Asia at the same time. The key concepts of shunyata (emptiness) and the universal Dharma Body of the Buddha have permeated the culture and the arts of China and Japan in very fundamental ways, in a creative union with the Chinese notion of the Tao as the source and support of all reality.

Founded on these common ideas, the cultures of China and Japan demonstrate a profound appreciation for ritual and for the aesthetic quality of life. Important aspects of life tend to be highly ritualized, for ritual helps to create and sustain harmony. Art is united with religion, for it is in the good and beautiful material of human life that the fullest expressions of the religious vision can be created. And it is not only the product of art but the process of artistic creation—the "way" of art—that is considered important in East Asian religions.

As with the other families of religions, it is tempting to put great emphasis on the common elements, for this provides a basic arena in which to compare and understand these particular religions. But this can be misleading if it covers up the fact that each tradition has its own special shape and integrity. Among the religions of China and Japan the interplay between common elements and distinctive traditions is somewhat complicated. First of all, the Chinese religious traditions form their own unity, and the Japanese religious traditions also make up a unified culture. But within China it is important to recognize the distinctiveness of the separate traditions: Confucianism, philosophical Taoism, religious Taoism, and Mahayana Buddhism. And yet actual Chinese religion as practiced by the people consists of a synthesis of these traditions and includes common popular religious practices as well. The situation is similar in Japan. Shinto is the indigenous tradition, still alive and well today, but Mahayana Buddhism also receives the allegiance of most Japanese; and Confucian values and popular religious practices are also part of Japanese religion as it is lived in local communities.

Because Buddhism is detailed in Part III, we devote more of our attention here to the Confucian, Taoist, and Shinto traditions of China and Japan.

CHAPTER 21

CHINA: SACRED STORY AND HISTORICAL CONTEXT

"Who am I?" To be Chinese is to be from one of the most ancient societies on earth, to respect the ancestors and the land. Called the Middle Kingdom, this ancient great people and vast land were felt to be the reflection on earth of the mandate of Heaven, the society of the cultivation of the perfect human.

For many Chinese, the three paths—Confucianism, Taoism, and Buddhism—are one story. Traditional Chinese honor the teachings of Confucius and strive to attain that ideal; they respect the practice of harmony with nature shown by Lao Tzu, legendary founder of Taoism; and they take inspiration from the deep insights into human existence and liberation taught by the Buddha. This is the Chinese way—the way of harmony. Still, each of these three traditions has its own story and its devotees in China, each tradition putting forth a total vision of sacred reality and human existence.

The Chinese story begins in very ancient times with great kingdoms and ideal rulers. Important classical writings were produced that have guided Chinese thinking ever since. The story includes the diversification of the tradition in the forms of Confucianism and Taoism, and the coming of Mahayana Buddhism fills out the religious universe of the Chinese people.

Each of the three great traditions underwent centuries of growth and decline and revitalization, interacting with each other and contributing to the common popular religion of most of the Chinese people. But in this diversity of traditions and schools there remains a striking unity, based on a common written language, an overriding sense of the centrality of the family, an abiding concern for the harmony of the Tao, common classical writings, and an overall sense of this vast group of peoples as one national family.

Because the Chinese religious traditions are so intertwined, we treat their beginnings together in this chapter, looking at the later historical developments and transformations in Chapter 22.

THE BEGINNINGS OF THE CHINESE STORY

The beginnings of the Chinese story go back to far ancient China, long before Confucius and Lao Tzu. China is one of the oldest continuous civilizations in the world, and thus this story is the accumulation of wisdom over many, many centuries. Confucius and Lao Tzu did not start totally new traditions—they simply reshaped and revitalized what had long been present in China.

The Ancient Rulers and Their Ancestors

Humans have lived in China for hundreds of thousands of years. Near Peking (Beijing) important discoveries of so-called Peking Man have been made in caves, the human culture of Homo Erectus dating from about 500,000 years ago. Humans here had learned the use of fire, used tools and hunted big game animals, and had developed speech and social structures. After the last glacial period, abundant evidence of Neolithic culture is found in China, agricultural peoples who lived in villages, made coarse pottery, used the stone-bladed hoe for agriculture, and kept domestic animals like pigs, horses, and cattle.

Chinese traditions tell the story of important sages who lived during the third millenium B.C.E., namely, the Three Sovereigns and the Five Emperors. The Three Sovereigns domesticated animals, instituted family life, and invented agriculture. Heading the list of the Five Emperors, Huang Ti, the Yellow Emperor, is traditionally seen as the symbolic ancestor of all Chinese people. Appropriately, he and his court are credited with inventing many of the cultural boons so important to later Chinese: writing, music, medical arts, wooden houses, carriages, bronze mirrors, silk cloth, weapons, and the like. The last of the Five Emperors is said to have founded the first Chinese dynasty, the Hsia (ca. 2200–1750 B.C.E.). Although archaeological work has not substantiated the existence of the Hsia dynasty, it is clear that there was a fountainhead of culture in this period, whose people knew the art of casting bronze, the cultivation of the silkworm, the use of the wheel, and perhaps the value of written symbols. Surely they venerated their ancestors, and they paid great concern to the fertility of the earth and the presence of many sacred powers of nature.

The History of the Shang Rulers

History—that is, ancient life known from written materials and supported by archaeological evidence—begins in the Shang period (ca. 1751–1111 B.C.E.). Shang kings mastered neighboring tribes in northeast China and marched to northwest China to incorporate the Hsia alliance. Under the Shang rulers, important features of Chinese culture developed: ceramics, carving, bronze casting, the chariot, architecture, the feudal system, the calendar, and the art of writing. Most important to the story are the religious forms that found expression during the Shang era.

The Shang rulers established a kind of theocracy with themselves as divine rulers who worked for the welfare of their people by worshiping the gods, the ancestors, and especially the high god, Shang Ti. All the forces of the world—sun, wind, rain, rivers, and earth—are gods to be worshiped and served. But they are all part of the pantheon presided over by Shang Ti, the "Lord Above," who can be worshiped only by the Shang ruler—perhaps being the ruler's primordial ancestor. The hierarchy of the ruler and his people is reflected in the hierarchy of the supreme god and the lower gods and goddesses, and that establishes a central dimension of Chinese religious tradition: the pattern of social ranks and divine ranks making up the total order of nature and society.

Besides structuring the hierarchy of the gods and of society, the story of the Shang kings establishes the model for two additional basic tendencies in Chinese religion. The Shang kings worshiped their ancestors, and they performed divination rituals to understand the will of their ancestors and of the forces of nature.

Worshiping the ancestors was a very elaborate affair, and for the Shang rulers it involved establishing a royal genealogy and a well-organized ritual cycle. Further, it was important for each king to become an ancestor when he died, and so elaborate burials were performed, including burial of carriages, utensils, ritual vessels, jewelry, weapons, food, and the like. Even wives and slaves, with their chariots and horses, were buried alive with their master, to continue the total royal life into the next world when the ruler would be an ancestor. The practice of burying wives and servants with the

Bronze ritual vessel from the late Shang period, decorated with designs of birds, dragons, serpents, and fish.

dead ruler was stopped later, of course, with clay representations sometimes substituted; but the important truth that the ancestor continues to live and rule in an effective way is a long-time heritage of Chinese religion.

In order to determine the will of the ancestors and the operation of the various forces of nature, the Shang rulers consulted divination experts, just as some Chinese have continued to do up to the present time. Their favored form of divination was to use bones and shells heated in a fire and plunged in water, the cracks being read by experts and the answer inscribed on the bones. These oracle inscriptions—nearly 100,000 examples from the Shang capital city—represent the first clear use of Chinese writing in pictographs and ideographs, appropriately designed as an operational method of achieving harmony with the forces of nature.

The Everlasting Ideal: Chou Society

A rebellion by the Chou tribal alliance brought down the Shang kingdom in the eleventh century B.C.E. and inaugurated the Chou dynasty (ca. 1123–221 B.C.E.), whose early ruler created a realm remembered ever after as a model for the ideal Chinese society. It was the evils of the Shang nobility that brought about the rebellion of the Chou family, we are told by the early Chou writings, *The Book of History, The Book of Poetry*, and inscriptions on bronze vessels. A new religious consciousness had evolved, which held that the supreme God cannot merely be a patron deity of a ruling tribe. Rather, the supreme God, which now is called Heaven (*T'ien*), is a universal righteous God for all. Heaven will give its mandate to rule only to a righteous king governing a righteous state, taking the mandate away from unrighteous rulers and peoples. Morality is of the essence before Heaven, and the welfare of all humans and all nature equally before Heaven becomes a prominent theme in the tradition.

> Without pity *T'ien* has brought destruction on Yin [Shang], since Yin has lost its mandate to rule, which we of the house of Chou have received. I do not dare to affirm that what we have established will continue forever in prosperity. Yet, if *T'ien* assists those who are sincere, I would not dare to affirm that it will end in misfortune.[1]

The Duke of Chou developed the notion of the moral mandate and righteous rule into a complete feudal political system, with the king as "Son of Heaven," and the whole Chou society was stratified hierarchically according to the relationship with the royal family. Here is the pattern that later generations looked to as the ideal human society.

The Chou rulers developed ceremonialism to a degree perhaps unknown in many other cultures. Why do Chinese put so much emphasis on ceremonies, rituals, bowings, and the like? Performing the proper reverential ceremonies (li), according to the ancient sages, is an expression of cosmic order. The ceremonies make connections with the larger forces of existence, especially with the ancestors, so that the people continue in their blessing. From the ancient Classic of Songs we read this description of a ceremonial sacrifice for the ancestors in the early Chou era:

> We proceed to make fermented liquor and to prepare viands for the offerings and for sacrifice. We seat the representatives of the dead and urge them to eat. Thus we seek to increase our bright happiness. We with grave looks and reverent attitude choose our sacrificial victims without blemish, oxen and sheep, to serve in the autumn and winter sacrifices. Some slay the animals; others attend to the cooking; some put the meat on stands; some arrange it for sacrifice. The master of ceremonies stands at the temple gate to await the arrival of the ancestor spirits. The sacrifice is all ready in brilliant array. The ancestor spirits arrive and accept our offerings. Their filial descendant receives their blessing. The spirits reward him with happiness and long life. Some reverently tend the fires, whilst others place in position the great stands [for the meat]. The queen reverently sets out a large number of smaller dishes. The guests and visitors draw near and a toast is drunk. All the ceremonies are meticulously observed; each smile, each word in perfect decorum. The personators of the ancestor spirits arrive and promise every blessing and ten thousand years of happiness. We have done all within our power and performed the rites without error. [2]

Ancient Religious Ideas: Yin-Yang and the Five Elements

The personal wills of the ancestors and the gods of nature are important, of course. But there are also impersonal forces that shape everything humans are and do, as discovered by the Chou sages. These are forces that are powerfully helpful and productive when they are in harmony, but they cause destruction and death when they are out of harmony. One of the most significant discoveries in the Chinese story is the bipolar activity of the yin and yang forces. All reality is made up of the interaction of two polar forces: yin forces of darkness, femininity, coldness, wetness, and passivity; and yang forces of brightness, masculinity, heat, dryness, and activity. Keeping these forces in harmony brings benefits and happiness, but disharmony causes disaster and suffering.

The Chinese also discovered by the early Chou period that all reality operates through the five elements, which are qualities that act and transform things. These are water, fire, wood, metal, and earth, all operational qualities that cause things to be the way they are.

To deal with these forces of the gods, the ancestors, yin and yang, and the five elements, people in the early Chou period continued the practices of divination they inherited from the Shang peoples. The system of divination that now came to be widely used is the system of trigrams made up of broken and unbroken lines (e.g., ☲ and ☷), the unbroken lines representing yang and the broken lines representing yin. Each trigram has its own referent in cosmic forces operating in this particular context. By placing one trigram on top of another, a system of sixty-four hexagrams is developed, each with a special operational meaning. Commentaries on these hexagrams are written in the I Ching, the Classic of Changes, begun during the early Chou period and certainly one of the most influential books in all of Chinese history. Still today people consult the I Ching for guidance on all sorts of matters.

FOUNDINGS: THE STORIES OF CONFUCIUS AND LAO TZU

Some of the most important religious developments come when bad times overtake the stable institution that seems to be the religious ideal. In ancient Israel, for example, when King David, King Solomon, and

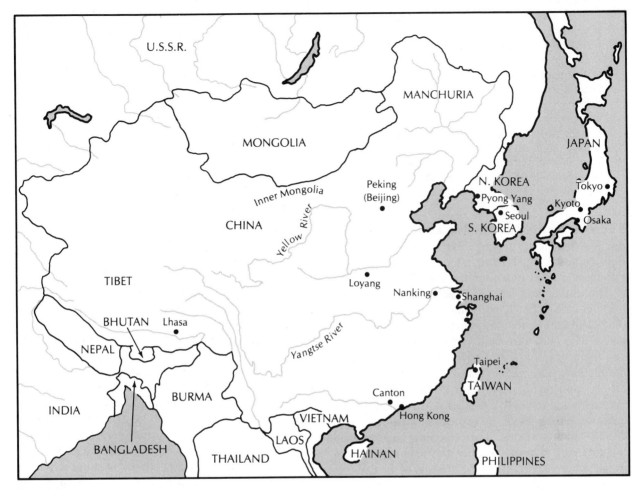

East Asia.

their successors reached the highest power, adversity set in and prophets arose to bring about a far-reaching religious transformation in Israel. So, too, in China, the ideal Chou kingdom fell onto bad times, and in the ensuing questioning and searching, there was a great period of religious transformation in which the most important Chinese religious traditions were founded.

Anarchy and Search in the Middle Chou Period

Troubles for the Chou rulers started around 800 B.C.E. when their power dwindled with the emergence of a number of independent states headed by powerful princes. The struggle for supremacy among these states continued for five centuries until the rulers of the Ch'in state emerged victorious and unified China under a dictatorship in 221 B.C.E.

A striking picture of the situation in the eighth and seventh centuries is given in some of the poems in the *Book of Songs*, reflecting the suffering and disruption felt during these times. If the rulers are really ruling according to the Mandate of Heaven, why are all these misfortunes and wars occurring? Is Heaven (T'ien) really the moral force that oversees all rulers and all nations?

I raise my eyes to August *T'ien*, but it does not pity us. It sends down great afflictions without respite. There is no stability in the land. Officers and people alike suffer.

Oh, great far-spreading *T'ien*, whom we call father and mother! Though guiltless, on me these troubles fall. Great *T'ien*, you are too stern. I have examined myself and am without fault. Great *T'ien*, you send down afflictions, but I am blameless.

Vast, far-spreading *T'ien* does not extend its virtue but sends down death and famine to destroy the land. Pitiful *T'ien* now strikes terror without rhyme or reason. It is right that sinners should be punished for their crimes, but why should innocent people be overwhelmed with ruin?[3]

The poets lamented the fact that people look to Heaven but find no clear guidance. With the questioning of the traditional beliefs came a tendency toward a more rationalistic and humanistic interpretation of life.

The middle and late Chou periods, in spite of the troubles of society, are remembered as the classical age of ancient China, for many creative developments took place. The laws were written down for the first time, and there were important advances in agriculture and production. The earlier classical writings of poetry, history, and divination were read and memorized by statesmen and scholars. Teachers set up schools to train boys for public office or instructed small groups of disciples in their homes. Their teachings had to do with the ancient traditions, but they also took up the burning religious, political, and social issues of the day. The words of some of these teachers were remembered and written down by their disciples. Among the teachers were Confucius and Lao Tzu, along with Mo Tzu, Mencius, and Chuang Tzu. The most important religious traditions—Confucianism and Taoism—developed from these foundations.

The Story of Confucius

The man whose teachings transformed Chinese society and guided the Chinese state and educational system for the past two thousand years was of fairly obscure birth and was not widely recognized in his own lifetime. His disciples carried on his teachings after him, transforming it in the process, and eventually in the Han period his philosophy of life was enshrined as the official way of Chinese thought and the Confucian cultus became the state religion of China. The heart of the story is the vision of life articulated in the Confucian tradition. But the life story of Confucius is also important.

The Life of Confucius

Although there is a biography of Confucius from several centuries after his lifetime, supplying a detailed ancestry that makes him a direct descendant of the Shang royal house, contemporary records say little about his background. The collection of his sayings, the Analects, does not give much biographical information about his life. We know nothing for sure about his parents, for they are never mentioned in the materials from Confucius' time, leading to the supposition that he was orphaned at an early age. We do know of a daughter and a son, but from the early sources we know nothing about his wife.

He was born in the small state of Lu in the northeast part of China in the year 551 B.C.E. Confucius said of himself that he was of humble status and he owned little personal property. Yet all the traditions suppose that he came from an aristocratic ancestry, and he certainly was well educated and had leisure time to pursue such arts as music and archery. In his day there were many members of formerly wealthy aristocratic families who were not able to maintain their high social status, for there were not enough government positions available for all of them. According to Mencius, Confucius was once a keeper of stores and once he was in charge of pastures. One of his disciples said that Confucius did not have a regular teacher, so perhaps he was largely self-taught. It is clear, however, that he excelled in learning the classical writings of the past.

Like most educated people of his day, Confucius aspired to political office, and there are persistent traditions that he was a minister in the state government of Lu for a time. His special goal was to restore the culture and religion of China as under the ideal reign of the Duke of Chou. His service in public office, however, was not recognized, and he was repeatedly rebuffed in his attempts to attain responsible public positions for which he felt he was suited. He turned to teaching to make his great contribution to Chinese culture. Confucius, perhaps because of his own background, had developed a sympathy for the common people, and when he set up his own school he resolved never to turn away an aspiring student no matter how poor he was.

Confucius had a full life teaching in his state of Lu and seeing his disciples attain government positions so as to shape culture and society. But in his fifties he was frustrated and disillusioned with the lack of moral leadership in the state, and he decided to leave and journey to other states to instruct rulers and attempt to find a way of putting his principles into practice. Although he was respected and well received by many rulers, and even offered a position here and there, he did not find the kind of moral commitment and understanding necessary to revitalize the ideal Chou rule and society.

Finally Confucius was invited back to the Lu state, after a decade of wandering, when he was nearly seventy. Outwardly it perhaps seemed that he had failed, for no ruler had heeded him and put his ideals into practice. But these journeys and challenges contained the sparks of the future, when other Confucianists would journey and teach and create a society that would use this fundamental vision as the standard of culture and religion.

After several years with his disciples back in Lu, Confucius fell sick and died. We do not know the details of his death, but the Analects tell about an earlier sickness when his disciples feared he was dying. His disciple Lu Yu was agitated that the master was dying and suggested that sacrifice and prayer be offered. Confucius dryly commented, "Is there such a thing?" When his disciple quoted the ancient classics to support such prayer, Confucius said simply, "My prayer has been for a long time" (Analects 7.34). His life was his death prayer.

Death in Chinese society is a very important communal affair, and the mourning rituals—up to three years of mourning—are a high priority for the family. Although they were not his family, Confucius' closest disciples observed the three years of mourning after his death. He is like the sun and the moon, one disciple said (Analects 19.24); he was the uncrowned king, in the eyes of later generations.

The Way of Life According to Confucius

Perhaps we do not know a great deal of certain facts about the life of Confucius. But then the most important dimension of the Confucian story is not the life of Confucius but the way of life that he taught as recorded in the Analects. Many Chinese have found identity in following the Way of Confucius.

The way of life that Confucius walked and taught to his students was not a new, revolutionary change from the traditional Chinese way. He felt that the main problem was a breakdown in morality and values resulting from turning away from the standards of the early Chou society. Now rulers usurped power and oppressed their subjects, ruling by laws and punishments, and the people responded with violence and hatred. So Confucius taught that the people needed to return to the basic principles of virtue as these were enacted by the Duke of Chou and the other virtuous rulers of the early Chou period, who followed the Mandate of Heaven and presided over realms of peace and harmony.

What does it take for people to transform themselves

A Manchu period portrait of the great sage Confucius; relief from a stele.

into people who live in peace and harmony? Confucius articulated an important goal, that of *jen*, humane goodness. Like so many ideographs among the written Chinese characters, *jen* is most expressive: the sign for a person plus the sign for two—that is, two persons in harmonious interaction, representing society in harmony. Confucius felt that all humans have the capability for this basic goodness. The reason people act selfishly and harmfully toward others is the influence of social anarchy and immorality of the rulers. How can this be turned around so that the people can become people of jen?

People need a discipline, Confucius taught, and the best discipline is the deliberate cultivation of the tradition of the ancient sages. That is the key to harmony and peace and prosperity. By studying their words and modeling one's actions after their actions, a person can become humane like they were. So Confucius led his disciples in studying the classics, writings traditionally held to stem from the sage-kings of earlier times. Some traditions say Confucius even had a hand in writing or at least editing these classics, which form such an important part of the Chinese tradition. The heart of the Confucian scriptures has always been the Five Classics. As they took their final form in later times, these include the Classic of History (*Shu Ching*), recording words and deeds of the ancient sage-rulers from the prehistoric Yao period to the early Chou period. The Classic of Poetry (*Shih Ching*) is a collection of some three hundred poems dating mostly from early Chou times, examplifying the quintessence of moral virtue and poetic beauty. The Classic of Changes (*I Ching*) is a book of divination that includes interpretations and commentaries explaining the patterns of the universe. A sacred text on ritual is the Classic of Rites (*Li Ching*), giving detailed accounts and interpretations of the rituals of the ancient sage-kings, plus additional philosophical teachings. And the fifth classic is the Spring and Autumn Annals (*Ch'un-Ch'iu*), a record of events in Confucius' native state of Lu between 722 and 481 B.C.E., together with several commentaries. There apparently was a sixth classic, the Classic of Music, which is no longer extant.

In transmitting and perhaps editing these classics, and in leading his disciples into a path of self-transformation based on their study, Confucius established the model of a life of study that has been so influential in providing the shape of the Chinese way.

The key principle in the sages' way of life, Confucius taught, is *li*, a word that means "propriety" or "respectful ritual." This word originally referred to the sacrifices and rituals directed toward the ancestors, actions filled with respect and performed with great care and thoroughness: The heart of propriety is filial piety directed toward parents and ancestors. But Confucius showed how this attitude of respect can permeate all actions; we can practice propriety as we live our daily lives, performing the proper rituals and ceremonies as an outer discipline so that we transform ourselves inwardly into people of *jen*. Confucius saw a close relationship between ritual and human goodness, as illustrated in this dialogue:

> Yen Yuan asked about humanity. Confucius said, "To master oneself and return to propriety is humanity. If a man (the ruler) can for one day master himself and return to propriety, all under heaven will return to humanity. . . . Do not look at what is contrary to propriety, do not speak what is contrary to propriety, and do not make any movement which is contrary to propriety."
> (ANALECTS 12.14)[4]

The purpose of practicing propriety, Confucius taught, is to establish the proper relationships in family and in society. As these outer relationships are in order, so the inner nature is also in order.

In teaching the discipline of study and the practice of rituals to transform people toward humaneness, Confucius knew he was putting forth a way of life that had its foundation in sacred power. He spoke of his practice as the Tao (way), a term used from earlier times to designate the way of the universe. To follow the Tao means to be in harmony with the ancestors and spirits, with the forces of yin and yang and the five elements. Yet Confucius was not overly interested in what we might think to be the "religious" aspects of the Tao, that is, the gods, spirits, and natural forces. His concern was human life in family and society, not invocation of gods and spirits. Once a student asked him about worshiping gods and spirits, and his answer was: "If we are not yet able to serve man, how can we serve spiritual beings?" And when the student asked about death, Confucius replied: "If we do not yet know about life, how can we know about death?" (Analects 11.11).[5] The gods and spirits should not be the focus of attention; much more important is the transformation of human society into a society characterized by humaneness.

But this is not to say that Confucius had no vision of the sacred in relation to human life. He was deeply religious in his conviction that Heaven as the supreme moral authority ruled over all through its decree or mandate. And he believed that his own way was in harmony with the mandate of Heaven, although he preferred to leave the demonstration of that to the real evidence of his life. Once, when he was in danger, he said: "If (my) Way is to prevail, it is (Heaven's) Mandate. If it is to be stopped, it is (Heaven's) Mandate. What can Kung-po Liao do about (Heaven's) Mandate?" (Analects 14.38).[6]

So it is that through Confucius' teaching and life the Way of Heaven became a central part of Chinese identity. Even Chinese who do not call themselves Confucianists still follow his model in studying the classics, practicing the traditional rituals, cultivating the proper family relationships, and striving to live together in peace and harmony according to his teachings.

Disciples of the Confucian Way

Many of Confucius' disciples went on to become important government officials, for Confucius was particularly concerned with educating the superior person who could lead the people with virtue and propriety and thus help them develop their humanity. As these disciples passed on the teachings of Confucius, they also developed and shaped them. Two new writings in the Confucian tradition were produced that had a great effect and became part of the story, helping to shape Chinese identity ever since. These are the Doctrine of the Mean and the writings of Mencius.

The Doctrine of the Mean (*Chung Yung*), attributed to Tzu Ssu, a grandson of Confucius, teaches that the Way of Heaven that prevails throughout the universe also underlies the moral nature of humans. Our nature has been imparted to us by Heaven. Therefore we can develop this Heaven-given nature, assisting in developing the nature of others, even reaching the point of assisting in the transformation process carried on by Heaven and Earth. The Doctrine of the Mean set forth the very influential image that humans can become a unity with Heaven and Earth in the nourishing and transforming process of the Way.

Mencius (ca. 372–289 B.C.E.) is said to have studied under disciples of Tzu Ssu, and he has been accepted by many as the chief interpreter of the Confucian tradition. His writings rank second only to Confucius in their importance for shaping the Confucian way of life. Mencius established the philosophy that humans in their original nature are "good," and from this he drew the principle that all political and social institutions exist for the benefit of the people. We are to serve Heaven, Mencius taught, by fulfilling human nature and living the good moral life. "He who knows his nature knows Heaven. To preserve one's mind and to nourish one's nature is the way to serve Heaven."[7] Mencius followed the lead of Confucius in teaching a humanism rooted in the Way of Heaven—a humanism that for many centuries has been a foundation of the Chinese way of life.

Lao Tzu and the Beginnings of Taoism

The Tao has long been a central concern of Chinese. In the experience of Confucius, the Way is realized especially in social relations, in the family structures, the ruler-subject relationships, and the like. But there were others in this fertile middle Chou period who took a sharply different approach to harmony with the Tao. These Taoists (as they later came to be called) felt the Way of Confucius was too artificial and structured. Real harmony with the Tao is to withdraw from the structures of society and experience the natural rhythms of the universe itself. Taoism later developed institutions of priesthoods and rituals that identify it as a particular religion of China. But as a philosophy of life, complementing Confucianism as its polar contrast, the vision of Taoism has greatly influenced many Chinese people.

The Story of Lao Tzu and the Tao Te Ching

Who was Lao Tzu, the founder of Taoism? There are legends about his life, although some suspect these legends are collective representations of many sages who protested against the tight structuring of society by withdrawing to the mountains as recluses, to practice methods of harmonizing with nature. Details of his life are rather scanty. Even the great historian Ssu-ma Ch'ien, writing in the midsecond century B.C.E., despaired of writing an accurate biography of Lao Tzu. And that is properly so. For one who attunes himself so completely with the flow of the Tao as did Lao Tzu passes beyond the limitations of human history.

But the legend has its importance. Lao Tzu was born in about 604 B.C.E., it is said, making him an older contemporary of Confucius. He was conceived sixty-two years before this at the time when his mother had admired a falling star. When time came for his birth, his mother gave birth while leaning against a plum tree, and he was able to speak when he was born. Since his hair was already white, he was called Lao Tzu, "Old Master."

Later Lao Tzu became palace secretary and keeper of archives for the court of Chou at Loyand. Many knew of his wisdom and the spiritual depth of his meditative practices and came to be his disciples. The story reports that even Confucius came to visit Lao Tzu in 517 and was overwhelmed by his deep insight and spirituality.

But by the time he was 160 years old, Lao Tzu had become disgusted with the way people lived in the world, and he decided to withdraw from society to pursue the higher virtues in the mountains of the west. As he departed through the Han-ku Pass, riding a chariot drawn by a black ox, the keeper of the pass recognized him as a sage and prevailed upon him to write his wisdom in a book. Lao Tzu responded by writing down the 5,000 characters of the book called the Tao Te Ching (also called simply the Lao Tzu), and then he departed for immortal sagehood.

These legendary stories of Lao Tzu's life do not connect with historical events very well. He appears to be representative of the approach developed by a group of recluse thinkers, especially in the fourth and third centuries B.C.E., who resisted the Confucian structures of society and advocated instead a simple nature mysticism. Whereas Lao Tzu is an important character, it is not so much the legend of his life as the sacred writing associated with him, the Tao Te Ching, that has profoundly shaped Chinese life and thought.

This short text with its vision of living in harmony with the flow of the Tao has been a most influential book in Chinese history. People of almost all religious schools in China have gone to it for inspiration. And its influence has not been limited to China—no book except the Bible has been translated into Western languages as often as this text! It is, of course, a special

Lao Tzu, the legendary founder of the Taoist philosophy. Stone rubbing from the Ming Dynasty.

book of those who call themselves Taoists, the ones who follow the Tao.

The title, *Tao Te Ching*, means "Classic of the Tao and its Power." It puts forth a vision of the Way that stands in sharp contrast to the Confucian notion of the Way of Heaven. The Tao is the sacred principle immanent in nature, that which is the source of all and that to which all returns. In a typically cryptic statement the Tao Te Ching describes the Tao:

> There was something undifferentiated and yet complete,
> Which existed before heaven and earth.
> Soundless and formless, it depends on nothing and does not change.
> It operates everywhere and is free from danger.
> It may be considered the mother of the universe.
> I do not know its name; I call it Tao. (CH. 25)[8]

Everything in the world is produced by this universal Tao, so all of nature has an inherent harmony and balance in its natural process.

Since the Tao is the source of all, the greatest human good is to be in harmony with the Tao. And people get in harmony with the Tao not by following rules of propriety or structuring their activities in society, but by *wu-wei* (no action). That is after all how nature itself operates: passively, quietly, in a natural rhythm. The tree grows, water flows, winter changes into spring—all without effort or striving. And so the Taoist sage will follow that pattern of no-action and nonstriving, withdrawing from the activities of society, harmonizing the inner self with the flow of the Tao.

In weakness and passivity there is strength, the Tao Te Ching teaches. The softest things in the world overcome the hardest things. Water washes away mighty mountain cliffs. The sage who attunes with nature, who does not use aggression and violence, who seeks not reward and position, who lives spontaneously without rules and plans, who accepts weal and woe with equanimity—such a one is kingly and free. "Being one with Nature, he is in accord with Tao. Being in accord with Tao, he is everlasting and is free from danger throughout his lifetime" (ch. 16).[9]

Taoist Freedom and Creativity: Chuang Tzu

Nearly as important as Lao Tzu in the formation of the Taoist story is Chuang Tzu (ca. 369–286 B.C.E.)—

and his life is almost as legendary and obscure. It appears that he was a government official at one time, but probably he lived most of his life as a recluse doing, apparently, some very unconventional things. The traditional story counts him as the main successor and interpreter of Lao Tzu and, most importantly, the author of the very influential book called the *Chuang Tzu*. It is from Chuang Tzu's stories and parables more than anything else that we have derived our image of the free, unimpeded, nonconventional, roaming Taoist saint. Chuang Tzu thus plays a significant role as a model for the Taoist way of life.

Chuang Tzu was not concerned with good government or society; he proposed no plan to remake the world to improve the human situation. Rather, he used his great literary skills to advocate emancipation from the shackles of conventional values and thought and a total identification with the very process of nature, namely, the Tao. Our conventional way of thinking tells us that some things are good and others evil, that pleasure is different from pain, that life is desirable and death is undesirable. But the Tao encompasses all forms of existence without such distinctions and dualities. To be in tune with the Tao is to transcend ordinary judgments and emotions and attain absolute happiness by understanding the real nature of things. The Tao, embracing all things, is in a constant process of change and transformation. Rather than reacting to these changes with pain or pleasure, the wise one accepts them as the natural process and goes along with them.

Chuang Tzu delighted in shocking conventional wisdom by extolling creatures that (by ordinary values) were ugly, misshapen, or useless; to Chuang Tzu, they display the freedom and naturalness of the Tao. He told a story about a horribly deformed man, Tzu-yu, who had a hunched back, internal organs on top of his body, and his shoulders higher than his head. But when asked whether he disliked this condition, Tzu-yu replied,

> No, why should I dislike it? Suppose my left arm is transformed into a cock. With it I should herald the dawn. Suppose my right arm is transformed into a sling. With it I should look for a dove to roast. Suppose my buttocks were transformed into wheels and my spirit into a horse. I should mount them. What need do I have for a chariot? When we come, it is because it was the

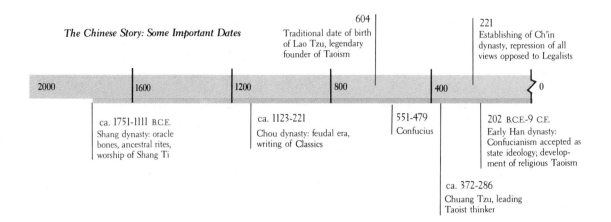

The Chinese Story: Some Important Dates

604
Traditional date of birth
of Lao Tzu, legendary
founder of Taoism

221
Establishing of Ch'in
dynasty, repression of all
views opposed to Legalists

2000 | 1600 | 1200 | 800 | 400 | 0

ca. 1751-1111 B.C.E.
Shang dynasty: oracle
bones, ancestral rites,
worship of Shang Ti

ca. 1123-221
Chou dynasty: feudal era,
writing of Classics

551-479
Confucius

202 B.C.E.-9 C.E.
Early Han dynasty:
Confucianism accepted as
state ideology; develop-
ment of religious Taoism

ca. 372-286
Chuang Tzu, leading
Taoist thinker

occasion to be born. When we go, it is to follow the natural course of things. Those who are contented and at ease when the occasion comes and live in accord with the course of Nature cannot be affected by sorrow or joy. This is what the ancients called release from bondage.   (CH. 6)[10]

Living with the Tao frees one from the limitations imposed by normal, conventional life. In fact, Chuang Tzu told stories about the ability of Taoist sages to fly through the air above the clouds, avoiding all harm, achieving miraculous longevity, and otherwise transcending normal human limitations. So one is freed from the conventions imposed by social life, laws and rules, ceremonies and etiquette, and all other forms of artificiality. Providing an alternative to the dominant Confucian philosophy of life, Chuang Tzu has embedded in Chinese tradition a vision of spontaneity and naturalness that has given a special shape to culture, art, and religion.

Development of Religious Confucianism and Taoism

The teachings of Confucius and Mencius, on the Confucian side, and of Lao Tzu and Chuang Tzu, on the Taoist side, are very important to the Chinese religious perspective; but they do not yet represent completely what average Chinese think of as Confucianism and

Taoism. There is something more to these religious ways, something more involving temples, altars and shrines, gods and spirits, rituals and festivals. Moreover, the story is the story of the three Ways, and we have not yet mentioned the founding of the third Chinese Way, Buddhism. It was during the Han dynasty (202 B.C.E.–220 C.E.) that beginnings were made in the direction of a more specifically religious orientation of these Ways, and we include some of these key developments to conclude our look at the story of the founding of Chinese religion.

Confucian Triumph and the Cult of Confucius

For some centuries after the time of Confucius, the Confucian approach to the humanization of society existed as one philosophy among others. There was the Taoist alternative, of course. Another important alternative to Confucianism was the movement founded by Mo Tzu (ca. 471–391 B.C.E.), who lived soon after Confucius and taught an approach to life that rejected certain Confucianist principles. Mo Tzu held a strong belief in a righteous God (Heaven) who loves all people impartially. The evils of the day, Mo Tzu taught, are directly caused by the fact that people do not love one another altruistically but only selectively and partially—as exemplified by the Confucian notion

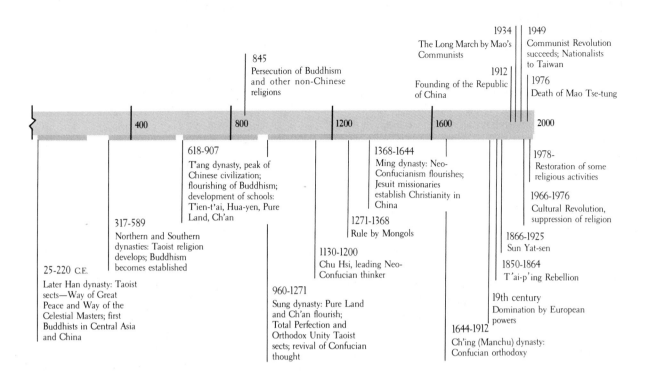

845
Persecution of Buddhism and other non-Chinese religions

1934
The Long March by Mao's Communists

1912
Founding of the Republic of China

1949
Communist Revolution succeeds; Nationalists to Taiwan

1976
Death of Mao Tse-tung

618-907
T'ang dynasty, peak of Chinese civilization; flourishing of Buddhism; development of schools: T'ien-t'ai, Hua-yen, Pure Land, Ch'an

1368-1644
Ming dynasty: Neo-Confucianism flourishes; Jesuit missionaries establish Christianity in China

1978-
Restoration of some religious activities

317-589
Northern and Southern dynasties: Taoist religion develops; Buddhism becomes established

1271-1368
Rule by Mongols

1966-1976
Cultural Revolution, suppression of religion

1130-1200
Chu Hsi, leading Neo-Confucian thinker

1866-1925
Sun Yat-sen

1850-1864
T'ai-p'ing Rebellion

25-220 C.E.
Later Han dynasty: Taoist sects—Way of Great Peace and Way of the Celestial Masters; first Buddhists in Central Asia and China

960-1271
Sung dynasty: Pure Land and Ch'an flourish; Total Perfection and Orthodox Unity Taoist sects; revival of Confucian thought

19th century
Domination by European powers

1644-1912
Ch'ing (Manchu) dynasty: Confucian orthodoxy

of filial piety with its concern directed mainly to one's own family and clan. This kind of unequal treatment of others must be replaced by "universal love," loving all others as oneself, equally and impartially, showing the same respect for their lives and possessions as for one's own. Mo Tzu was strongly against war and violence, and he taught that the highest good is that which benefits people, gaining for his movement the name Utilitarianism. Mohism had many devout followers for several centuries and provided strong competition to the Confucian vision of human life.

Another significant alternative to mainline Confucianism grew up within the Confucian tradition itself, stemming from Hsun-Tzu (ca. 300–238 B.C.E.). Hsun Tzu turned away from the Mencius perception of the fundamental goodness of humans to take the more realist position that humans by nature are basically inclined toward evil. Consequently, he advocated a strict system of discipline so that people's natural evil

inclinations might be overcome and peace and order might exist. He also rejected all superstitious beliefs about supernatural powers and taught a naturalistic understanding of the world and of the value of rituals and ceremonies. Some of Hsun Tzu's ideas found expression in the school of the Legalists, who advocated a system of authoritarian government with strict laws and punishment to enforce order. These Legalists managed to gain control of the state of Ch'in, and eventually it was the Ch'in rulers who conquered the other Chinese states and established a unified empire in 221 B.C.E. The Ch'in Empire lasted only a few years, but it enforced a uniform order by the repression and wholesale slaughter of all opponents. It was, in fact, made a capital crime to discuss Confucian writings and principles, and books representing all views opposed to the Legalists were burned.

Here was a profound crisis for the Confucian tradition, as well as for the other non-Legalist schools of thought. But the story tells how some scholars, at risk to their lives, managed to save some of the classic writings so that the ancient wisdom was not lost in this book-burning frenzy. The Ch'in dynasty fell rapidly, to be replaced by the Han dynasty (202 B.C.E.–200 C.E.). The first Han rulers continued to be of the Legalist persuasion, although without the violent excesses of the Ch'in rulers. But now Confucian scholars managed to revive their teachings and work out a complete cosmological basis for a unified state under an emperor who served as the representative of Heaven, channeling the cosmic forces and providing harmony in society. The turning point for Confucianism came when Emperor Wu-ti (r. 140–87 B.C.E.) ascended the throne and, realizing the need for well-educated officials, ordered scholars to appear for interviews. Among some one-hundred scholars to be interviewed was Tung Chung-shu (176–104 B.C.E.), who convinced the emperor to practice the teachings of Confucius only and dismiss all other theories and scholars. Emperor Wu appointed Tung to be the chief minister of the state, and soon he established doctoral chairs for the classics, thus making Confucianism the state ideology. Later Tung convinced the emperor to found a national university for which fifty of the most talented students in the classics were selected. Now all state officials had to pass civil service examinations in the Confucian classics, ensuring that Confucianism would remain as the official state ideology and thus as the leading component in the Chinese identity—a position it held until the beginning of the twentieth century.

Together with this intellectual triumph of Confucianism went a new emphasis on the rituals and ceremonies associated with Confucianism and the state. State-supported temples for Confucian ceremonies were established all over China, Confucius' home became a national shrine, spirit-tablets of Confucius and his disciples were venerated in elaborate rituals, and the so-called state cult of Confucius was born. Soon new versions of the texts began to assert the semidivine status of Confucius, and eventually Confucius even came to be considered a god in the popular religion of China.

Through all of this, the very broad range of teachings, rituals, education, and social structures that bears the name Confucianism had become the central focus of the Chinese cultural tradition.

The Beginnings of Religious Taoism

The philosophical Taoism of Lao Tzu and Chuang Tzu is not the complete story of Taoism. There were other streams of practice that merged with those basic Taoist insights to produce that broad, complex religious tradition that we can call religious Taoism. All of these streams were in existence in pre-Han times, although the full development of religious Taoism complete with its writings, priests, and sects took many centuries.

The common denominator of these Taoist streams is the concern about long life and immortality. Lao Tzu and Chuang Tzu already made some statements about the freedom from human limitations that can be experienced by getting into complete harmony with the eternal Tao. Around this central notion there began to draw together many popular practices and beliefs cultivated from ancient times by shamams, mediums, and diviners, all rooted in the fundamental idea that humans can get in tune with the larger spiritual forces of our universe. The so-called hygiene school emphasized breathing exercises and various methods of controlling the bodily processes of decay as a way of prolonging life. A search was on to use the five elements in such a way as to produce an elixir of life, a movement that later became known as alchemy. And expeditions were organized to sail across the seas and find the Isle of the Blest, where it was believed there grew a plant that could renew a person's life and vitality. The emperor of the Ch'in dynasty already sent out such expeditions, and they continued in the Han period.

This search for immortality began to extend also to the common people, and it combined with the ancient interest in gods and spiritual beings. For example, around the year 3 B.C.E. a popular religious movement erupted centered on a mother goddess named Hsi Wang-mu (Queen Mother of the West). All over China people turned to her with singing and dancing, believing that by worshiping her and wearing charms with her name written on them they would be able to avoid death. As these movements spread, other gods, goddesses, spirits, and Taoist immortals (sages who were thought to have become immortal) came to be included in the powers who could grant long life and immortality. One Taoist group called itself the Way of Great Peace (T'ai P'ing Tao). Their leaders functioned as both priests and military officers, and their chief god was Lord Lao, that is, Lao Tzu, author of the Tao Te Ching, now worshiped as a god and as the creator of the world. They had a sacred book, the *Scripture of Great Peace*, which revealed how to restore good government, encourage peace, and bring good health and long life to the people. Another group in western China during the later Han period was the Way of the Celestial Masters (T'ien Shi Tao), which set up its own state ruled by a Master of Heaven with priest-officials as assistants. They also worshiped Lao Tzu as a god.

These communities, worshiping Lao Tzu and other gods and immortals and centering on rituals performed by priests on the basis of sacred texts, were the forerunners of religious Taoism. Here the philosophy of Lao Tzu and Chuang Tzu was taken over and put in concrete form through rituals, priests, techniques for attaining immortality, and community forms. Religious Taoism developed many more scriptures, organizations, rituals, and techniques over the next centuries, but its basic role in the Chinese story was already established: the philosophy of Taoism combined with rituals, gods, priests, and a search for long life and immortality.

The Beginnings of Chinese Buddhism

So we have the Way of Confucius and the Way of Taoism. But when traditional Chinese think of who they really are, the Way of the Buddha also plays a part, and so we should include the beginnings of Chinese Buddhism in the foundational history. The acceptance of Buddhism came gradually, over a number of centuries, and it was the Mahayana form of Buddhism that most connected with the Chinese story.

A tradition says that Han emperor Ming (58–75 C.E.) had a dream in which he saw a golden man, taken by his wise men to be the Buddha; so he dispatched envoys to northwest India to bring back scriptures and teachers. We know that already in the first century C.E. Buddhist monks and laypeople made their way along the silk routes into Central Asia

Buddhism became one of the major religions of China; here is a modern Chinese monk at the Big Wild Goose Pagoda in Xian.

(through present day Afghanistan) and on into China. For a time Buddhism flourished in central Asia until stamped out by Islam around the tenth century C.E. But from central Asia monks and missionaries went to China, and Buddhism came to be firmly planted in China and rose to become one of the three great religions of China, along with Confucianism and Taoism. This remarkable development—a religion from India being adopted by the Chinese and from the Chinese also by the Koreans and the Japanese—led to rich new transformations of Buddhism.

How did it come about that such a foreign way of thinking came to be so important in China? It is not easy to answer that, for there were things about Indian Buddhism that the Chinese people could not understand or accept. What was most problematic about Buddhism as it arrived in China was the monastic system: monks and nuns leaving their families, not working but begging for their food, taking the vow of celibacy and thus cutting off the family line. Traditional Chinese society strongly advocated the centrality of the family and the individual's duty to respect and care for parents and to continue the family by marrying and having children. Chinese values affirmed living in society, seeking happiness, and working productively for the good of all. Buddhist monks were accused of being lazy and idle because they went about begging and did nothing for the welfare of society. The notion that life is suffering and that worldly pleasure should be renounced also seemed strange to the Chinese, as did the "no-self" teaching of Buddhism. And Chinese scholars pointed out that Buddhism was a foreign, barbarian philosophy, not mentioned in the Chinese classical writings.

And so Buddhism was not widely accepted at first in China. But the incursion of Buddhism continued. Mahayana scriptures were brought in and translated into Chinese, and gradually the Chinese came to understand what Buddhism was about, transforming it in the process to fit better into the Chinese worldview. The upheaval that came with the end of the Han dynasty (220 C.E.) led many Chinese to turn away from Taoism and Confucianism and embrace Buddhism. From the fourth to the sixth centuries C.E., Buddhism consolidated its place and then became, for a time, the most powerful and vital religious force in the country.

The appeal of Buddhism was manifold and soon outweighed the initial negative reactions on the part of the Chinese. The disunity and warfare surrounding the end of the Han dynasty induced many to turn to the relative security and peace of the Buddhist monasteries, escaping among other things serving in the armies. And Buddhism in China showed itself not to be opposed to the importance of family life. By becoming a monk or nun, a child could actually fulfill a great amount of filial piety, praying for the family, accumulating merit for the welfare of the ancestors of the family, erecting pagodas to perpetuate the memory of the parents, chanting scriptures for their welfare, and performing the funeral rituals and the rituals for the release of the ancestral souls from purgatory. The monasteries in China tended to be like settled communities, supported by landholdings, serving as art centers, hostels, retreats, and centers of life. Although joining a monastery meant leaving one's family, it was like becoming part of a new family, especially in the son-father relationship with one's Buddhist master.

When Buddhism came to China, it brought important new ideas about human existence that were enlightening to the people of China. The Chinese traditions had virtually nothing to say about life after death or the causes of one's present existence, and here Buddhism was influential. The law of karma, for example, helped to explain why people were born in particular circumstances, whether slave or king. And the Buddhist doctrine of samsara helped people to understand that there are rebirths for all in future existences, on many different planes. In addition, Buddhism supplied a great variety of conceptions about Buddhas and bodhisattvas, heavens, and hells. The cult of Buddhas and bodhisattvas could be added to other popular Chinese cults, and the idea of rebirth in the heavens was not unattractive. The Mahayana notion that each person possesses the Buddha-nature and is capable of salvation appealed to the common people. Buddhism from India contributed great scriptures and works of art to enrich Chinese culture and religion.

One way in which Buddhism was transformed in China was through the translation of Buddhist scriptures into Chinese. At first Theravada scriptures were translated, but as time went on the great Mahayana texts of India were translated into Chinese or—scholars think some of them may actually have been composed in China—attributed to a translator. The high regard the Chinese have for the ancient classics led them to respect these translations and seek more. At the same time, putting Indian texts into Chinese inevitably meant coloring those ideas by Chinese vocabulary and concepts. Perhaps the greatest translator was Kumarajiva (344–413), who translated or revised translations of most of the popular Mahayana sutras and treatises from

Nagarjuna's school, thus introducing the very important philosophy of emptiness into Chinese thought. Kumarajiva's translations are still in use today.

DISCUSSION QUESTIONS

1. What were the main religious activities of the Shang rulers (in the Shang dynasty)? What was the origin of writing?
2. How did the beginnings of Confucianism and Taoism reflect the social situation in the middle Chou period?
3. Explain the basic Confucian ideas of jen, li, and study of the tradition.
4. It is sometimes said that Confucius's ideas were humanistic, not religious. How would you define the matter?
5. What does the Tao Te Ching put forth as its basic perspective on the world?
6. What were some of Chuang Tzu's major contributions to the Taoist tradition?
7. How did Confucianism triumph and become the leading ideology of the Chinese state? What is the "state cult of Confucius"?
8. What were the streams that went into the making of "religious Taoism"? How were these related to the ideas of the Tao Te Ching and Chuang Tzu?
9. Discuss factors that worked for and against the Chinese accceptance of Buddhism.

CHAPTER 22

TRANSFORMATIONS IN CHINESE RELIGIOUS HISTORY

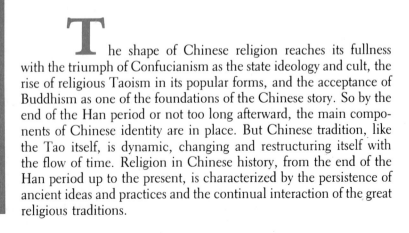

T he shape of Chinese religion reaches its fullness with the triumph of Confucianism as the state ideology and cult, the rise of religious Taoism in its popular forms, and the acceptance of Buddhism as one of the foundations of the Chinese story. So by the end of the Han period or not too long afterward, the main components of Chinese identity are in place. But Chinese tradition, like the Tao itself, is dynamic, changing and restructuring itself with the flow of time. Religion in Chinese history, from the end of the Han period up to the present, is characterized by the persistence of ancient ideas and practices and the continual interaction of the great religious traditions.

After the disintegration of Han rule around 220 C.E., China entered into a period of political disunity until the end of the sixth century. During this time Buddhism gathered in acceptance and vigor, and Taoism was also in ascendancy, whereas Confucianism was gradually eclipsed. A high point of Chinese culture came in the T'ang (618–907) and Sung (960–1280) eras, when there was a brilliant flowering of literature, art, and philosophy that signaled China as perhaps the greatest world civilization of the time. Winds of change came with the Mongols ruling all of China in the Yuan era (1280–1368). Chinese rule was temporarily reestablished with the Ming dynasty (1368–1644), and Neo-Confucian orthodoxy won the day. But now European influences started to penetrate China with the first Jesuit missionaries and all that followed, opening up contact with the West that was to continue unbroken. The Revolution of 1911 destroyed imperial China and disrupted its traditions, although the traditional religions continued in some form in the Republic of China (since 1949 confined to Taiwan). The disruption of all the religious traditions has been much more drastic in the People's Republic of China, controlling the mainland since 1949.

FLOURISHING OF THE RELIGIONS IN POST-HAN CHINA

Buddhism Expansion and Crystalization

During the centuries of disunity following the downfall of the Han dynasty, Buddhism gradually became more and more accepted by the Chinese people, working its way into Chinese society and integrating Chinese ideas into its own religious vision.

The Golden Era of Buddhism in China

Part of the reason for Buddhism's great success in China was its acceptance by various emperors, such as Emperor Wu of the Liang dynasty (r. 502–549), who abolished Taoist temples and built Buddhist ones and who himself entered a monastery as a lay servitor. The Sui emperors (581–618) and the T'ang emperors (beginning in 618) continued imperial support of Buddhism. The emperors were particularly attracted to the intellectual systems of the Buddhist schools, which could serve as a unifying ideology.

The whole Chinese cultural landscape was being made over under Buddhist influence. Thousands of monasteries and shrines were built, tens of thousands of people became monks and nuns, and often the monasteries had huge land holdings. Elaborate Buddhist rituals came to supplement the Confucianist and Taoist ones, and Buddhist festivals such as the Lantern festival, the Buddha's birthday, and Ullambana (All Souls' Day) came to be universally observed. Monasteries became social centers for money lending, medical care, serving also as hostels and retreats. Buddhist influence fostered literature and art, with particularly significant contributions in Buddhist sculpture.

Schools of Chinese Buddhism

Very important and characteristic of Chinese Buddhism was the development of a number of different schools or "lineages" that took place during the seventh century. Mahayana teachings had opened the way for a variety of different practices to reach the goal of liberation, whether by help from Buddhas and bodhisattvas or by one's own discipline and meditation—and many combinations in between these two paths. And it had produced many scriptures, purporting to be the Buddha's own word, explaining these paths. Why there are so many scriptures and paths was easily explained: the Buddha uses skillful means and thus teaches different doctrines and practices to suit the condition of the audience. So monks could devote their attention to one or several of the great scriptures and develop a school that would specialize in certain teachings and practices. Whereas some ten such Chinese Buddhist schools are recognized, a number were of relatively minor importance, and only two continued past the persecutions at the end of the T'ang period, that is, Pure Land and Ch'an. Two others did contribute a great deal to Chinese thought, however, and also to Buddhist developments in Japan: T'ien-t'ai and Hua-yen.

The T'ien-t'ai school, founded by Chih-i (538–597) at the monastery on Mount T'ien-t'ai, can be seen as a synthesis and harmonization of all Buddhist teachings and practices. According to this school, the great mass of scriptures taught by the Buddha can be classified into five periods in which the Buddha taught the different scriptures. In the earlier periods he taught the Theravada scriptures and then, when the people were more enlightened, the elementary Mahayana scriptures; finally in the last period he taught that all paths leading to salvation are united in the one path as taught in the Lotus Sutra, which is the full and perfect teaching.

The Hua-yen school devoted its attention mainly to the Garland Sutra, teaching that the absolute reality and the temporary phenomenon are completely interfused with each other and that all phenomena interpenetrate each other. Thus every thing or event in this passing world is a manifestation of the absolute, which means that everyone possesses the Buddha-nature and thus each is related to all other beings. Both T'ien-t'ai and Hua-yen, harmonizing many basic strands of tradition, deepened the Mahayana sense of the Buddha-nature as a universal reality present in all beings.

The cultural climate of China lent itself to the creation of more simple and direct versions of Buddhism, which had greater appeal to the masses than the complex philosophical teachings of T'ien-t'ai and Hua-yen. The inspiration for both these new forms, Pure Land and Ch'an, came from India, of course, but as they developed in China they took on special Chinese characteristics and greatly increased the popular appeal of Buddhism in China. They surfaced strongly in the T'ang era partly as reformist reactions against the increasing worldliness of the powerful monastic establishment.

Amitabha Buddha, the compassionate heavenly Buddha who created the beautiful and peaceful Pure Land paradise and assisted living beings to be reborn there, had been known in China from earlier texts, and meditation on Amitabha was practiced in monasteries. In the T'ang era, Tao-ch'o (562–645) and his disciple Shan-tao (613–681) began to preach salvation in the Pure Land solely through the power of Amitabha, open to all who recite his name orally with a concentrated and devout mind. They interpreted the practice of concentrating on Amitabha to mean vocal recitation of Amitabha's name through which all the merit of Amitabha would be available and one would be assured of rebirth in the Pure Land. By saying Amitabha's name over and over with faith in his vows to save all beings, even sinful people could hope for rebirth in the Pure Land paradise. It is easy to understand that the Pure Land school appealed directly to the common people with its simple but effective teachings and practices, and its influence also permeated the other schools. Here was a form of Buddhism that could spread through the populace and be practiced in independent communities and societies outside the monasteries. Pure Land Buddhism soon became the most popular form of Buddhism in China and was taken also to Japan, where some centuries later it likewise became immensely popular. As it developed, Pure Land Buddhism became a characteristic form of East Asian culture.

The other distinctively Chinese school of Buddhism is Ch'an (meditation) Buddhism, likewise simple and direct and popularly supported. Ch'an is a unique creation of Chinese Buddhism, yet it draws on the early Indian practices and texts that emphasize meditation. Meditation was, of course, practiced in all the schools but as only one aspect of many disciplines of study and ritual. Ch'an's achievement was to make meditation the one practice to be almost exclusively pursued to reach enlightenment. In this sense it was a reform and simplification, somewhat parallel to the Pure Land movement.

According to Ch'an tradition, the founder of this school was Bodhidharma, an Indian meditation master who came to China around 470 C.E. When Emperor Wu of Liang asked him what merit he had earned by his donations and temple building, Bodhidharma answered, "No merit at all." Banished by the emperor, Bodhidharma went to north China and settled in a mountain temple, where he spent nine years sitting in meditation gazing at a wall, it is said, until his legs fell off. He also, the story says, cut off his eyelids so that his gaze would not falter. Among the successors of Bodhidharma the most famous was Hui-neng (638–713), known as the sixth patriarch, who supposedly was illiterate but demonstrated a flair for the direct, sudden awakening taught in Ch'an. His legendary career provided a model for Ch'an life, and all later masters claim to be descended from him. Two schools of Ch'an

Bodhidharma, the legendary founder of Ch'an Buddhism in China, crossing the Yangtze River on a reed.

Ch'an is characteristically Chinese in the way it brings Buddhism into contact with Chinese ideas and practices, especially those of Taoism. The emphasis on meditation carries with it a certain anti-intellectual tendency, for, according to Ch'an, thoughts and concepts cloud the mind and therefore the mind must be emptied so that we can see directly into our Buddha-nature. In order to empty out the mind and see the truth directly, relationship with a master is crucial, for there is a special transmission of the truth outside the scriptures that goes from mind to mind, without words. Sayings and dialogues of the masters were collected and came to be used as themes for meditation. These "public documents" (*kung-an*; Jap. *koan*) were used to show that ordinary logic must be transcended in order to see directly into one's real nature.

This school of Buddhism first became influential in the T'ang era, advocating group meditation in the context of disciplined communal life in a monastery. Monasteries were established in remote areas, and frugality and shared work characterized the communal life. Whereas Ch'an did not become a "popular" movement in the sense of great numbers of people joining the monasteries, it did achieve widespread support among the people of China. The Ch'an form of Buddhism is distinctively a creation of China, and in the stories about the masters, the iconoclastic attitude toward rituals and doctrines, the practice of meditation to realize Buddhahood, and the poems and paintings by Ch'an artists, we find some basic shadings of Chinese identity.

The golden age of Buddhism was glorious—but brief. Although it enjoyed wide support from all levels of society, there remained opponents among the Confucianists and Taoists, some of whom thought of Buddhism as a "foreign" religion. And the relative independence and growing wealth of the monasteries were often seen by the rulers of the state as a distinct threat. Finally in 845 an ardent Taoist emperor, Wu-tsung (r. 840–846), ordered the suppression of Buddhism, leading to the destruction of some 4,600 monasteries and 40,000 temples and shrines, and forcing some 260,500 monks and nuns to return to lay life. Wu-tsung died the next year and the order was rescinded, but Buddhism never regained its former pres-

eventually became particularly influential, Lin-chi and Ts'ao-tung, differing on whether enlightenment should come suddenly or as a gradual process.

tige and position. The only schools that survived the persecution were the popularly supported Pure Land and Ch'an schools, and they did continue to exercise considerable influence on Chinese culture.

A new development in the Sung era (960–1279) was the emphasis on the compatability of the two Buddhist schools. In the monasteries both meditation and recitation of Amitabha's name came to be employed together as two techniques toward achieving the same end of emptying the mind and reaching awakening. Another important development was the growth of lay Buddhist societies, including both men and women, both gentry and commoners, who devoted themselves to good works and recitation of the Buddha's name.

The Maturing of Religious Taoism

The search for long life and immortality continued to dominate the Taoist movement throughout the period of disunity following the Han era and also during the T'ang and Sung periods. Sometimes patronized by the rulers, Taoist masters perfected a great variety of ritual techniques for the controlling of the forces of the cosmos, reversing the forces of decay and establishing the forces of renewal. Great scriptures were revealed, written down, and memorized for use in the rituals. Many sects developed, founded by recognized masters based on a particular scripture, and each sect developed its own ritual experts or priests.

Neo-Taoism in Philosophy and Life

Before following the growth of religious Taoism, we might note that interest in the more philosophical aspects of Taoism was revived in the period after the fall of the Han dynasty. Taoist philosophers like Wang Pi (226–249 C.E.) and Ku Hsiang (d. 312) wrote commentaries on the Tao Te Ching and the Chuang Tzu, talking about the Tao as nonbeing or vacuity, the primal source of all the myriad things of the world. Interestingly, they thought of Confucius as the greatest sage because he, unlike the Taoist writers, did not talk about the mysterious operations of the Tao and thus exemplified vacuity.

Other Neo-Taoists were more romantic and practical in their approach, mainly poets and painters who tried to practice the Tao in a life of freedom and ease without conforming to conventions. Since they wanted all their talk to be pure, aesthetic, and in harmony with nature, this group is sometimes called the Pure Conversations movement. Well known are the Seven Sages of the Bamboo Grove, who refused office, sought enjoyment of life and freedom from cares, glorified drinking wine, and lived in complete harmony with nature.

These Neo-Taoist attitudes and styles had a profound effect especially in the shaping of Ch'an Buddhism, as is clear in the well-known Ch'an saying: "Here is a miracle of Tao! I draw water, I chop wood."[1] And this philosophical Taoism continued to influence thinkers, artists, and poets in China. Theories of aesthetics came to be based in the notion of the resonance of the Tao, which gives rise to artistic inspiration and expression. The artist meditates, gets his spirit in tune with the Tao, and spontaneously lets the artistic form create itself.

Religious Taoist Experts: Interior Gods and Alchemy

The rise of religious Taoism has many facets, but a central focus is on the *yuan ch'i*, the primordial breath or substance from which humans like all nature evolve. The *ch'i* comes ultimately from the Tao, and it is present especially in the cosmic gods, the astral bodies of the universe, and in the other manifestations of nature. The problem is that under the conditions of our existence our vital breath becomes stale and exhausted, and thus our life becomes weak and short. Religious Taoism consists of the various techniques for renewing and restoring that vital *ch'i*, so that long life and even immortality may be achieved.

The human body is a microcosm of the great cosmos of nature, and so within each organ of the body there reside gods, and furthermore the great Tao forces of the cosmos can be called down and actualized within the human body. Taoist specialists developed ritual techniques by which they could visualize these interior gods of the body and the cosmic bodies and planets as they descend into the body, purifying and preserving the vital organs.

Carrying over the interest from ancient China in the five elements and how these can be used to promote long life, Taoist experts cultivated various techniques for creating substances to be ingested into the body to renew the vital breath. The science of alchemy developed, based on the idea that the ingestion of gold and other chemicals can renew the vital breath and prolong life.

But there were also the "inner elixir" techniques for renewing and prolonging life. Ritual techniques were developed by Taoist priests involving breathing techniques and gymnastics. By special breathing and bodily exercises the breath could be circulated through the various zones of the body to nourish the vital powers. At the same time, it was felt that much care should be given to diet, especially avoiding grain foods that, coming from the yin earth, nourish the three "worms" or principles of death in the body. Some advanced adepts practiced ritual techniques of sexual intercourse, the idea being that the forces of yin and yang nourish each other and thus restore the vital forces.

Development of Taoist Sects

Something new happened in the rise of religious Taoism—there developed communities or congregations of Taoists led by priestly authorities, something unheard of in the Chinese tradition up to this point. The Yellow Turbans who followed the sacred text called Classic of Great Peace, whose rebellion brought on the end of the Han dynasty, was one of the first such group religious movements.

The most important Taoist religious group movement was the Way of the Heavenly Masters (T'ien-shih Tao), which established a state in northern Szechuan that was organized like a church, having a Celestial Master at its head and local parishes under the authority of "libationers" or priests. The first Heavenly Master was Chang Tao-ling (died between 157–178 C.E.) who received revelations from Lao Tzu, now thought of as a god, and instituted various communal rituals. Since almost all sects of religious Taoism trace themselves in some manner back to Chang Tao-ling, he is often considered the "founder" of religious Taoism. Faith-healing was practiced in this sect, based on the idea that sickness was caused by sin, and therefore repentance, confession, and good deeds were part of the healing process. Documents inscribed with the sins and the penances were transmitted to the rulers of Heaven, earth, and the waters, to ensure healing and blessing. This communal Taoist movement had a strong emphasis on moral, virtuous living as part of the requirement for healthy, long life. Following this, one of the characteristics of religious Taoism in general has been the emphasis on the practice of moral virtues in addition to the rituals and ceremonies.

During the T'ang era (618–907) Taoism received considerable support from some of the emperors, enabling it to flourish and develop. Emperor Kao-tsung (r. 649–683) conferred on Lao Tzu the title of emperor, thus confirming Lao Tzu's divine status and claiming him as a royal ancestor. The political power of Taoism reached its zenith with the suppression of Buddhism and other non-Chinese religions in the 840s.

The most important Taoist order during the T'ang era was the Mao-shan sect, based on Mao-Shan Mountain where many temples were built, scriptures edited, and disciples trained to be priests. There, under the direction of a hierarchal priesthood headed by "masters of doctrine," they carried on ritual activities of purgation and cosmic renewal, calling down the gods of the stars and practicing ritual meditation. Their outstanding leader was Ssu-ma Ch'eng-cheng (647–735), who authored many works and was well known for his calligraphy. He emphasized ritual meditation focused on "emptiness," for, he wrote, "only the heart which has been emptied can be the dwelling place for the Tao."[2]

Among the many new sects of Taoism that developed in the Sung era (960–1280), two were lasting and are still influential in the twentieth century. A scholar named Wang Che (1113–1170) became the founder of the Ch'uan-chen (Total Perfection) sect in northern China. Wang experienced two mysterious encounters with Taoist immortals that led him to dig a grave and live in it for three years, after which he lived in a thatched hut for four years before burning it down and setting out to start the new Taoist order. He selected seven disciples who lived as eccentric ascetics, but they attracted lay followers from all classes, including women. Influenced by Ch'an Buddhism, this sect spiritualized some of the ritual practices. Wang taught celibacy and sitting in meditation to control the mind and the will and to nourish one's nature and life force. As the first Taoist sect to base itself in monasteries, the Total Perfection sect aimed for a rigorous life of simple monastic discipline, including celibacy and abstinence from wine and meat. Founder Wang stressed practices of inner alchemy and self-perfection as well as Confucian and Buddhist doctrines, teaching the unity of the three religions.

One of Wang's disciples made a three-year trek to visit Chinggis Khan at his central Asian court in 1222, ensuring the continuation of imperial support for this Taoist sect even into the time of the Mongol rule. For a while the Total Perfection sect was favored over Buddhism by the Mongol rulers, but a conflict developed when the Taoists started to teach that the Buddha was one of the eighty-one transformations of Lao Tzu. After a series of debates Khubilai Khan ordered the Taoist Canon burned and the Taoist priests returned to lay life, and the sect went into a long eclipse. But as late as the 1940s, the seat of the sect, the White Cloud Monastery of Peking, retained influence over the monastic Taoist priests of China.

The other major Taoist sect that came to influential status during the Sung era was the Cheng-i (Orthodox Unity) sect, which was a continuation of the Way of the Heavenly Masters of earlier times. Its patriarchs were believed to be descendants of Chang Tao-ling, and they based their headquarters at Dragon-Tiger Mountain (Lung-hu Shan) in Kiangsi Province. The thirty-sixth generation Heavenly Master, Chang Tsung-yen, was invited to the capital by the emperor in 1277 to perform a "Grand Offering of the Entire Heaven," and shortly after that the emperor appointed him head of all Taoists in southern China. Then in 1295 the emperor decreed that Heavenly Master liturgical texts be used throughout the empire, and since then this sect has generally had the highest influence in ritual and liturgical matters. Under the first Ming emperor, toward the end of the fourteenth century, the Heavenly Masters were put in charge of all Taoist affairs.

In contrast to the celibate monks of the Total Perfection sect, the priests of the Orthodox Unity sect do not live in monasteries nor do they restrict themselves to a vegetable diet. They hand down their esoteric ritual arts in their families. Since they marry and live with their families, they are sometimes called Fire Dwellers, that is, living by the family hearth. This sect of the Heavenly Masters continues to the present day, although the Heavenly Master in 1949 had to leave the Dragon-Tiger Mountain and flee to Taiwan, where he set up the organization of religious Taoism.

Other Taoist sects arose in the Sung era and afterward, and many of the sects contributed new works to the burgeoning Taoist Canon. The present Taoist Canon was commissioned and completed by 1447, under the Ming emperors. The emperors brought the growing sectarianism under control by decree of the court, limiting to three the monastic centers authorized to grant licences of ordination, without which the local Taoists masters were forbidden to practice. But popular, unauthorized Taoist movements continued to rise and spread throughout the Ming (1368–1644), Ch'ing (1644–1911), and even modern periods. This created a polarization between the traditional classical orders and the popular Taoist priests of local origin. The traditional orders were given the title "orthodox," whereas the popular groups were called "heterodox." On Taiwan the orthodox priests are known as "Blackhead" and the heterodox as "Redhead," based on a slight difference in their usual ritual attire.

The Resurgence of the Way of Confucius: Neo-Confucianism

Confucianism, of course, remained a strong component of Chinese government and family life, the main foundation for morality, social custom, and status even after the fall of the Han dynasty. But as a vital religious force it was eclipsed by Buddhism and religious Taoism for many centuries, as the best philosophical and religious thinkers of China devoted themselves to Buddhism, and Taoism attracted government support because of its expertise in rituals of health and long life. To be sure, there were a few Confucian philosophers in this period, such as Han Yu (768–824), who reasserted the central Confucian theme of the goodness of human nature and sharply attacked both Taoists and Buddhists for belittling humanity and human relations. But in general there was not much fresh thinking in Confucianism from the fourth to the tenth centuries.

However, suddenly in the eleventh century, during the Northern Sung dynasty, a series of important think-

Confucius, the Buddha, and Lao Tzu. Despite the occasional conflict between leaders of these three religions, there is a long-standing Chinese vision of their unity.

ers appeared who attempted to revive Confucianism as a philosophical vision of life. They were influenced by Buddhism and Taoism, but they turned back to Confucian sources to articulate a new philosophy of life, focused on positive human nature, family life, and social reform. Neo-Confucianism arose vigorously in the Sung era, became dominant in the Ming era, and controlled Chinese thought throughout the Ch'ing era down to the twentieth-century revolutions.

The Northern Sung Masters and Chu Hsi

The beginnings of a Confucian revival can be seen in the T'ang era, centered in the class of people known as "literati" (*ju*). The T'ang government kept a huge bureaucracy to administer its vast empire, and the examination system required that higher status in the government was won by those who mastered the study of the Confucian classics. In the following Sung era these literati established themselves as dominant in the political and intellectual spheres. Many of the literati, of course, got caught up in the expediency of government politics, but there was a minority who devoted themselves to study and teaching in an attempt to recover the ancient Confucian ideal of the "noble man," the one who perfects his moral qualities.

Actually the Neo-Confucians went further than the noble man ideal, cultivating themselves to become "sages" like the ancient sages who had revealed the truth of the Way in the classics. The true sage, they believed, reaches the ultimate of true humanity by complete identification with the nature of all things. This is possible, they believed, because the heavenly principle is universal, possessed both by the self and by all things. One who meditates on that universal principle becomes more wise, mature, and in control, so that he can help to bring order and harmony to family, society, and government.

In the eleventh century there was a group of outstanding Confucian thinkers who worked out a Neo-Confucian cosmology and metaphysics based on redefining concepts from the Confucian classics. For example, Chou Tun-i (1017–1073), sometimes considered the real founder of Neo-Confucian philosophy, taught that the Great Ultimate (*t'ai chi*) generates yin and yang, which, through their alternation, give rise to the five elements, which in turn produce the myriad of things, of which humans are the most intelligent. But the many are actually the one reality, and the one is differentiated in the many. Chang Tsai (1020–1077) identified material force with the Great Ultimate, functioning through yang and yin; he also redefined the gods (*shen*) and evil spirits (*kuei*) as positive and negative spiritual forces involved in the expansion and contraction of material force. Chang is famous for his short essay *The Western Inscription*, which he inscribed on a panel in the western window of his study, reflecting on the ethical implications of the doctrine that all creation is united by the universal underlying principle. He wrote in part:

> Heaven is my father and earth is my mother, and even such a small creature as I finds an intimate place in their midst. Therefore that which extends throughout the universe I regard as my body and that which directs the universe I consider as my nature. All people are my brothers and sisters, and all things are my companions.[3]

A key idea of these early Neo-Confucianists is that of "principle" (*li*). The Ch'eng brothers (Ch'eng Hao, 1032–1085, and Ch'eng I, 1033–1107) based their teaching entirely on principle, which they conceived of as self-sufficient, extending everywhere, and governing everything. It is that by which all things exist, and it is possessed by everyone and all things, binding all together into a unity. The principle is one, but its manifestations are many. Since the one principle is identical with all things and with one's mind and nature, moral and spiritual development comes through the investigation of things and through the cultivating of one's nature and mind.

These basic Neo-Confucian ideas of the Northern Sung masters were synthesized and organized by Chu Hsi (1130–1200). He taught that the whole universe is but one principle, the Great Ultimate, which is prior to form and which contains all principles and is the source of all principles. At the same time each phenomenon has its own defining principle. Chu Hsi explained this by using the metaphor of the single moon that is reflected in many lakes and rivers; everything has the Great Ultimate, yet the Great Ultimate remains one. But, according to Chu Hsi, principle never exists in isolation but always is attached to material force (*ch'i*), that which exists within form.

Now humans have principle as their original nature, good and humane. But principle needs to be attached to material force to be actualized, and this aspect of human nature is often characterized by selfish desires, clouding principle and leading to evil results. Therefore it is important, Chu Hsi taught, for humans to cultivate themselves to rectify the mind and penetrate to the underlying principle. The way to self-cultivation is through intellectual learning, meditation, and the investigation of things, both in the external world and within oneself.

Other Neo-Confucian thinkers put more emphasis on the mind as morally self-sufficient, innately endowed with knowledge of the good and ability to do the good. This Mind School of Neo-Confucianism, represented especially by Wang Yang-ming (1472–1529), has as its central thesis the view that principle and mind are one. Since the mind, which innately contains all principles, is the master of the body, to cultivate oneself one need only follow the impulses of the mind's innate knowledge. Thus, Wang argued, the way to self-cultivation is not through the investigation of external things, as Chu Hsi taught, but through the cultivation and extension of the innate knowledge of the mind, through inner moral and spiritual cultivation.

The idealistic concern for awakening the moral consciousness of the mind, as put forth by Wang Yang-ming, continued to have influence in later generations of Neo-Confucianists, but Chu Hsi's more rationalistic concern for the ordering principle tended to remain dominant. The Manchu rulers, who conquered China in 1644 and inaugurated the Ch'ing dynasty, affirmed Chu Hsi's Neo-Confucianism as the orrthodox ideology of their reign, and so it remained until the onslaught of Western imperialism and the revolutionary forces of the twentieth century both brought down imperial rule in China and put the whole Confucianist tradition in jeopardy.

Persistence and Transformation of Popular Religion

The Chinese story revolves around the three religions as they developed to their full space by about the end of the Sung era—Buddhism, religious Taoism, and Confucianism (both in the state cult and in Neo-Confucianism)—continuing more or less in that form down to the modern era. But we should not neglect a vast area that overlaps with these three religions but includes much more—Popular Religion. The popular religious tradition goes back as far as the records go, and it includes a great variety of religious activities practiced by the whole population except those who specifically opted out, that is, the strict Confucian scholars, Buddhist monks, orthodox Taoist priests, and state officials in their public roles.

In ancient times most Chinese shared in religious

activities like ancestor worship, exorcism, use of spirit mediums, divination, sacrifices to spirits, and belief in ghosts and demons. These activities were based in family, clan, and village, and they continued effectively even as the great religions developed. By the end of the Sung era, the various strands of popular religion came together and incorporated Buddhist and Taoist ideas about karma and rebirth, Buddhas and bodhisattvas, and gods and spirits, forming the more-or-less coherent popular religious system that has continued to the present day, at least in Taiwan and Hong Kong.

Although popular religion does also promise salvation from hell and favorable rebirth, generally it has focused on practical, immediate human concerns like protection of property, health and long life, expulsion of evil spirits, obtaining favor from the gods, peace and harmony in the home, good livelihood, repose of ancestors, and the like. For these benefits, the most important sacred powers are the ancestral spirits and the popular gods. These powers bring benefits and protection in life and in death.

Most of the gods of popular religion were originally human beings who were gradually deified over time as more and more people recognized their power and efficacy. The gods have a reciprocal relationship with the humans: they understand the needs of the worshipers, and they need the offerings and recognition of the worshipers if they are to keep their position as gods. New gods are recognized as their power and fame is effective; but gods can also be demoted and forgotten if their benefits no longer are felt. Under Taoist influence, the gods of popular religion were organized into a bureaucratic system with each one having a particular function, like protecting fishermen, bringing children, causing rain, protecting the village, and so on. The Jade Emperor presides over the gods, parallel to the emperor in the human realm, and the Jade Emperor appoints the various gods to their offices, promoting them for effective help but also demoting them when their effectiveness fails.

The popular gods maintain order over and against the vast array of demons and ghosts that can bring sickness and death. These demons (*kuei*) usually are spirits of the restless dead who died unjustly or who were not cared for by their descendants, and they need to be expelled by a spirit-medium or a Taoist priest in

Chinese pilgrims pray at a Buddhist shrine on Heng Mountain in Hunan Province.

the name of a powerful god. Harm can also come from ancestors who have been aggrieved, and harmony can be restored by a medium communicating with the ancestor to learn what the family should do to make amends.

Popular religion has always been carried on in the midst of the family, village, and city neighborhood, and so there are usually no full-time specialists. The temples are run by local people who have other jobs. Some people have special talents as spirit-mediums, spirit-writers, healers, and the like, and Taoist priests and Buddhist monks can also be employed to perform special rituals. Popular religion is associated with a rich cycle of annual festivals, funeral rituals, and rituals of geomancy (*feng-shui*), the process of locating the proper place for a house or a grave.

These activities of popular religion have given a special character to most Chinese families and communities, even as the people also pursued Confucianist, Taoist, and Buddhist practices. In modern times popular religion has been questioned in some areas and is ranked as superstition in the People's Republic, but it still is a significant factor in Taiwan, Hong Kong, and some overseas Chinese communities.

WESTERN INCURSION AND REVOLUTIONARY CLIMATE

One major foreign influence that transformed traditional China was, of course, Buddhism; but Buddhism was indigenized and contributed much to the shape of Chinese religion. More disruptive were the incursions of religions and ideas from the West, followed in the nineteenth century by foreign imperialism in China. The upheaval in traditional Chinese society culminated in the Revolution of 1911, ending two millennia of imperial rule and inaugurating the Republic of China. More disruption followed the Communist takeover of the mainland, with the result that Chinese religion today is somewhat minimal in the People's Republic, although it is still alive in other Chinese communities.

Foreign Religions and Western Domination

We should note that other foreign religions besides Buddhism did play a part in China's religious history. During the T'ang period, for example, Zoroastrianism and Manichaism (teaching a cosmic dualism) came into China as a result of contact with Persia, and they dealt some influence on Taoism and Buddhism. A large Muslim minority and a small Jewish presence added to the religious landscape of China; and Christian missions combined with Western influence to have a significant impact on Chinese religious history.

During the T'ang and Sung periods, increased Muslim dominance of the western edges of China led to the presence of a significant Muslim community in northwestern China. When the Mongols established the Yuan dynasty in China (1260–1368), Muslim merchants, soldiers, and religious leaders settled throughout China, and numerous Chinese converted to Islam during this period. But Muslims maintained the purity of their faith, refusing to blend it with other Chinese religions, and adherents of Islam tended to be from minority non-Han tribal groups, lumped together as the Hui peoples. Generally they retained their own language and culture, thus maintaining a separate religious and ethnic identity. Today Muslims total some twenty-five million people in China. In general they have been given a good bit of autonomy under the Communist government. Whereas they like other religious groups suffered during the Cultural Revolution, they have revived quickly and today practice their religion actively. Yet, because they have stood aloof from the syncretistic tendencies of the traditional Chinese religions, the overall impact of Islam on Chinese religion has been limited.

There is also an interesting though brief story of Jewish presence in traditional China. During the Sung dynasty a Jewish community was established in Ka'i-feng, and an impressive synagogue was built there in the style of a Chinese temple. But cut off from contact with other Jews, the small Jewish communities in China eventually lost their identity and were totally assimilated.

Traces of Christian presence in China go back as far

as the T'ang period, when Nestorian Christians came to China. And in the thirteenth century the pope at Rome dispatched Franciscan monks overland to China, during the time when the Mongols ruled all of central Asia and Marco Polo had made Europe aware of China. But with the fall of the Mongol dynasty the Ming rulers closed the door to foreigners, and the fledgling Christian communities died out.

The real beginning of Western Christian impact on Chinese culture came with the Jesuit mission in the sixteenth and seventeenth centuries. Around 1500 Portuguese traders came to southern China, and Christians started entering China especially from the Spanish Philippines. The newly founded Jesuit order devoted itself to a missionary-scholar approach, both in Japan and in China. The first Jesuit missionary in China was Matteo Ricci (1552–1610), who went to China in 1582 and set out to learn the ancient Chinese writings, accommodating Christianity to the best of classic Chinese culture. The Jesuits took on the role of Chinese literati, wrote works in Chinese, and proved helpful to the Chinese rulers by providing maps and Western learning in science and astronomy.

The Jesuits found acceptance in the scholarly, governmental circles partly because they tried to integrate Christianity into what they considered the best of Chinese culture. They made Christianity acceptable to many Chinese by, for example, using the Chinese words *Shang Ti* and *T'ien* for God in the Christian sense, adopting the ceremonies of respect for Confucius, teaching that Confucian ethics were consonant with Christian faith, and interpreting the ancestral rituals as acceptable within the Christian understanding. But before long rival religious orders attacked the Jesuit methods of accommodation, accusing them of not imposing fasting and not teaching that Confucius was in hell. After much discussion of this so-called rites controversy, the pope at Rome finally decided against the Jesuit position, leading to the breakdown of the Jesuit relationship with the Chinese emperor and the suppression and expulsion of Christian priests.

Around the beginning of the nineteenth century came English and Dutch traders to China, and with them the first Protestant Christian missionaries arrived.

These missionaries tended to work with the working classes, not the literati. The Western presence was fortified by military power, which forced the Chinese to open up ports and allow foreigners to travel in the interior and teach Christianity. By the end of the nineteenth century, there were some 2,000 Christian missionaries in China. Some mission groups, like the China Inland Mission in particular, began to adapt more to Chinese customs and carried on much educational and medical work, which had a considerable impact on Chinese society. But the close association with Western imperialism and the general failure to recognize the drastic changes in modern China kept Christianity from gaining wide favor, and the revolutionary movements of the twentieth century turned against the Christian movement.

Revolutionary Movements and Communist Society

Responding to the West and to Christianity, China was gripped by new religious movements, rebellions, and revolt against its own traditional imperial system. An early response to Christian influence was the T'ai-p'ing Rebellion in the middle of the nineteenth century. A farmer boy named Hung Hsiu-ch'uan, influenced by Christian pamphlets, had visions of ascending to heaven where he learned that Confucius had confused the people and that he himself was the Father's son next younger to Jesus. Hung organized a religious movement based on some Christian ideas, baptizing, throwing out the ancestral tablets, and destroying shrines and temples. The movement drew on the centuries-old peasant frustration with the old hierarchical system; they advocated an egalitarian social structure, equality of the sexes, and the redistribution of land. In 1851 Hung proclaimed himself the Heavenly King of the Heavenly Kingdom of Great Peace (T'ai-p'ing T'ien-kuo). The movement grew rapidly and started to attack armies in Peking and elsewhere, but in 1864 the whole group, now 100,000 strong, was defeated and massacred. But the rebellion had devastated China and almost toppled the Ch'ing dynasty.

The winds of change blew strongly as the twentieth

century began. The abortive Boxer Rebellion in 1899–1900, a vast antiforeign movement that tried to drive out Western influences and attacked Christian missions in the name of Chinese gods, was symptomatic of the growing conflict between traditional values and the impact of the West. The imperial government, humiliated by defeat at the hands of the Japanese in 1894–1895, was not able to stem the growing tide of dissatisfaction. Reforms were attempted, such as abolishing, in 1905, the long-standing Confucian examinations for government service. But it was too little too late, and the Ch'ing government fell in the 1911 revolution, the final end of many centuries of imperial rule.

Whereas the majority of Chinese continued their traditional religious practices, many intellectuals turned to Western ideas and philosophies, including Marxism. The leader of the revolution and of the republican government that followed, Sun Yat-sen (1866–1925), had received a Western, Christian education, as did his successor as leader of the Nationalist party, Chiang K'ai-shek. Sun and Chiang followed a kind of modern, liberal Protestantism; Chiang even promoted the revival of ancient Confucian virtues during his leadership of the Nationalist government. Other leading intellectuals were influenced by the antireligious attitudes of Western liberal thinkers like John Dewey and Bertrand Russell and took a strong stand against all traditional religion. The famous May 4, 1919, student protest, for example, demanded a New China based on humanistic liberal principles, free of all old literature, education, and religion.

But Western liberalism could not control the spirit of anarchy that had developed, and in 1920 a group of Marxists secretly formed the Communist party. The Communists cooperated for a number of years with the Nationalist party, but by 1928 an irrevocable split had occurred. Chiang K'ai-shek led the Nationalist government, relying on rural landlords and the urban business class, whereas the Communist party built support among the peasantry. The Nationalists began a notorious "bandit extermination" campaign against the Communists, but under the leadership of Mao Tse-tung (1893–1976) the Communists escaped to the north in the famous Long March of 1934, creating a

mythology that supported Mao's domination of the Chinese Communist party. In the chaos following World War II, Mao and his followers successfully carried through a revolution and established the People's Republic of China in October 1949, sweeping Chiang's forces out of the mainland and into an exiled Nationalist government on the island of Taiwan.

The religions of China have been subjected to disruption under Maoist rule unlike any previous period in Chinese history. The constitution of the People's Republic does establish the freedom both to support and to oppose religion. In practice, however, sharing the Marxist attitude that religion is an instrument that oppressive overlords use to pacify and exploit the ener-

A scene from the Cultural Revolution—Red Guards chatting at the entrance to Sun Yat-sen's mausoleum near Nanking.

gies of the people, the Chinese government mounted a series of campaigns to turn people's loyalty away from the traditional religions to support the new Chinese order. People were encouraged to "struggle against Confucius," for that system of thought supported the old hierarchical state. Popular Taoist practices were denounced as superstitions, not to be tolerated in the modern society. For a time state-controlled Buddhist and Christian associations were tolerated. But during the so-called Cultural Revolution, which began in 1966, all religious institutions were subjected to intense persecution by fanatical Red Guards in the struggle to rid China of the "four olds": old habits, old ideas, old customs, old culture. The Red Guards invaded homes to expose people practicing religion and to destroy religious art, scriptures, and literature. Temples and churches were closed, images destroyed, leaders returned to lay life, and books burned. All over China there was an attempt to get rid of everything that looked like a remnant of the "bad old days" before the 1949 revolution. It seemed that the thousands of years of religious tradition in China had come to an abrupt end.

Coinciding with the attack on the traditional religions, there grew up a new "religion" in China: the cult of Maoism. The philosophy of Marxism, as has often been pointed out, has some of the characteristics of a religious philosophy, with its call for repentence, conversion, and unconditional commitment, and also with its view of history moving toward the consummation of a classless society. In China, communism took over some of the traditional religious forms: Mao has been revered almost like a state deity, and national holidays are celebrated complete with popular music, art, drama, parades, and banners to create the atmosphere of a sacred state. During the Cultural Revolution, Maoism went further in taking on many of the characteristics of a religious cult. Some people looked to Mao almost as a god, and young people carried the "bible" of his sayings around, studying, memorizing, and reciting his teachings. It was in the intolerant furor of this cult of Mao that the excesses against everything having to do with the "old" religions and institutions were carried out.

The Cultural Revolution came to an end with the death of Chairman Mao in 1976 and with the downfall of his wife and three other leaders (the Gang of Four) who tried to continue these policies. Though traditional religious ideas had been drastically shaken and reduced in influence, they were not dead. Under more moderate leadership, China entered into a new phase in which more relaxed and practical programs have been emphasized in order to attain the "Four Modernizations": science, agriculture, industry, and defense. Along with all this has gone a liberalization of government policies toward religion. Hundreds of churches, temples, and mosques have reopened, and the government is even paying back rent for the religious buildings that were confiscated during the Cultural Revolution. A few seminaries, monasteries, and religious training centers have been opened, and priests and ministers are again available, though in comparatively low numbers, to serve Buddhist and Christian needs. Sacred scriptures are being published, and religious scholars again publish writings about religious subjects.

Reports from China today indicate a general flourishing of Christianity, free from control of foreign churches and dedicated to the socialist ideals of the new China. In addition to overflowing churches in some of the cities, there are countless "house church" groups throughout China guided by lay leaders. The revival of Buddhism has not been as dramatic but nonetheless is apparent as some temples are again busy, priests chant sutras and perform rituals, and some monasteries and training centers again have accepted young people for training. Islam, as a recognized ethnic group in China, did not suffer as drastically during the Cultural Revolution and has managed to continue its religious practices somewhat outside the mainstream of Chinese social and political life.

Religious Taoism has not shared very much in the general revival of religion, partly because many of its practices are still looked upon as superstitions harmful to the new society. Likewise, Confucianism, that is, the whole religious, ethical, and literary tradition based on the Confucian Canon, has been deeply damaged by the persistent Maoist attack on this backbone of Chinese "feudal" civilization. Whereas scholars again can study and write about the classics, there seems little likelihood that the Confucian philosophy will again become the guiding vision of thinkers in modern China. There is some evidence on the popular level of a renewed interest in religious practices like ancestor worship and funeral rituals. And certainly attitudes of respect for the family and for elders, loyalty to the community and the nation, and the acceptance of reciprocity as the basis of human relations continue in present-day China, evidence that deeply based religious attitudes persist even in drastically changed conditions.

It must still be said that religious activities take place only on a small scale in the People's Republic of China today, and that the vast majority of the people simply no longer seem interested in religion. Their concern is for good jobs, education for their children, modern appliances, and working to better Chinese society. Whether the basic human religious questions and concerns will again play a part in their lives appears to be an open question.

The religious situation in Taiwan, Hong Kong, and among the overseas Chinese is quite different, of course. The religious practices differ greatly from place to place, and modernization affects religious ideas and practices as elsewhere in the world. But in general traditional religion still flourishes, based in a strong family system and community support of temples, monasteries, festivals, and various popular religious rituals.

DISCUSSION QUESTIONS

1. Describe the major Buddhist schools or lineages in China during the T'ang period. Why were Pure Land and Ch'an able to survive the persecutions of 845?
2. What were the most important Taoist sects or orders during the T'ang and Sung periods? Which have survived to modern times?
3. Explain the development of Neo-Confucianism.
4. Why must we include a category such as "Popular Religion" in addition to Confucianism, Taoism, and Buddhism in China?
5. Sketch the history of Islam and Judaism in China.
6. How did Christianity rise to become influential in the sixteenth and seventeenth centuries? What caused its subsequent decline?
7. What was the T'ai-p'ing Rebellion?
8. What were the roles of Sun Yat-sen, Chiang K'ai-shek, and Mao Tse-tung in twentieth-century events?.
9. Discuss the status of traditional religion during the four decades of the People's Republic of China.

CHAPTER 23

CHINESE WORLDS OF MEANING

THE SACRED ULTIMATE IN THE CHINESE VISION

"What's it *all* about?" "What holds it all together?" "Where do we look for the absolute center, the real?" Chinese people know about these questions, having learned them from the sages of ancient times. "Is Ti [Lord] going to order the rain within the fourth month?," asks an oracle inscription in one of the earliest written texts in China. Ancient skeptics raised questions: "Now the people in their peril look to T'ien [Heaven], but find no clear guidance." Others affirmed that there is a sacred center of all: "T'ien loves the whole world universally. Everything is provided for the good of

413

mankind."[1] These ancient ideas were refined in the Confucian teachings and in philosophical Taoism. Religious Taoism and popular religion have continued the emphasis on a multiplicity of sacred beings all working together in cosmic harmony.

The Supreme Sacred Power: Heaven

The early Chinese worldview was naturalistic. The whole universe was felt to follow the basic laws of cyclical processes, growth and decline, and the bipolar operation of the forces of yin and yang. In a sense, the world itself was ultimate reality, operating in harmony and following the natural laws without any supreme creator or law-giver. This "universism" has remained central to Chinese experience and has colored all thinking about sacred beings and powers. But, as we saw earlier, there was belief in a supreme being from early times on, called Shang Ti (Ruler Above) or T'ien (Heaven), and these terms have figured centrally in the Chinese conception of ultimate reality ever since.

Shang Ti, as worshiped by the rulers of the Shang dynasty, was not the ultimate or unlimited god over all, of course, but did function as the power of conspicuous importance that controlled nature and brought both good and evil on the Shang rulers. Although Shang Ti may have been the special god of the Shang rulers, perhaps even thought of as the high ancestor of the ruling house, this was not just a tribal god. Shang Ti had control over all the natural forces and over human welfare, bringing the benefits of rain, military victory, and building cities, but also the punishment of drought, defeat, and ruin of cities. The texts show that Shang Ti was felt to have divine personality and intelligence, could issue orders to the wind and rain and other natural forces, and could bring things and events into being.

Beneath Shang Ti there was a full pantheon of gods of nature—Sun, Moon, Wind, Rain, Earth, Mountain, River, and gods of the Four Directions—functioning as divine subordinates of the supreme god. In addition, all the ancestral gods of the house of the Shang rulers were members of Shang Ti's pantheon. The deceased kings of the Shang dynasty were worshiped especially as mediators to approach and obtain Shang Ti's approval. It seems that deceased queens were also worshiped as accompanying Shang Ti, and perhaps even the ancestral dukes, ministers, and diviners found their place among the ancestral gods. The sacred powers of nature and of human ancestry were linked in harmony around the center provided by the supreme god.

Heaven as Universal Moral Authority: T'ien

T'ien (Heaven), as worshiped by the rulers of the Chou dynasty, was assimilated to Shang Ti and was conceived as the all-powerful, all-knowing, purposeful god who sent down blessings or disasters in accordance with divine pleasure or displeasure with the people. When kings prospered, it was believed that they had received the mandate of Heaven; in the case of corrupt or unworthy rulers, Heaven would withdraw the mandate and the ruler would fall.

Texts from the Classic of Poetry and the Classic of History describe T'ien:

> Be reverent! Be reverent! T'ien has revealed its will. Its mandate is not easy to preserve. Do not say that T'ien is far distant above. It ascends and descends, concerning itself with our affairs, and daily examines all our doings.
>
> T'ien inspects the people below, keeping account of their righteousness, and regulating according to their span of life. It is not T'ien who destroys men. They, by their evil doing, cut short their own lives.[2]

Here there is a strong emphasis on the universal moral authority of Heaven along with the notion of Heaven as an impersonal governing authority. When we live in accord with Heaven's will, we prosper, but when we go against that will, our lives are short and bitter.

Chinese ideas and feelings about Heaven are colored by the sayings of Confucius, who emphasized this universal moral power. Confucius had a strong belief in the mandate of Heaven, and he was convinced that he had a sacred mission that had been conferred on him by this purposeful supreme power. To Confucius, Heaven was the guardian of humanistic culture. Once, mistreated by the people of K'uang, he said,

> Since the death of King Wen [founder of the Chou dynasty], is not the course of culture in my keeping? If it had been the will of Heaven to destroy this culture, it would not have been given to a mortal [like me]. But if it is the will of Heaven that this culture should not perish, what can the people of K'uang do to me?
>
> (ANALECTS, 9.5)[3]

Some leading thinkers continued to emphasize the personal character of Heaven as a supreme being to be loved and worshiped. Mo Tzu (late fifth-century B.C.E.) described Heaven as the father who loves all people equally, who accepts sacrifices from all and is concerned about the moral conduct of the people. Others emphasized more the impersonal qualities of T'ien. Hsun Tzu (ca. 300–238 B.C.E.), for example, denied that Heaven acts in response to human actions or pleas. Rather, T'ien is simply the operation of the physical universe according to its inherent laws.

Since these ancient thinkers, many have continued to ask the question whether Heaven is personal and interactive with humans or whether Heaven operates impersonally and naturally. For example, the Neo-Confucianist Liu Yu-shi (772–842 C.E.) summed up both positions and proposed his own theory about the mutual interaction of Heaven and humans:

> There are two theories about Heaven today. Those who are bound by what is obvious say that Heaven and man really influence each other. Calamities will surely descend on us because of our sins, and blessings will surely come when induced by good deeds. If we are in distress and cry out, we will be heard, and if we keep our suffering to ourselves and pray, we will be answered. There seems to be definitely someone who rules them. Hence the theory of silent recompense wins.
>
> On the other hand, those who are bigoted about what is hidden say that Heaven and man are really different. Lightning hits animals and trees without anyone committing any sin, and the spring nourishes flowering bushes without selecting any good deeds to reward. . . . It seems there is no one who rules us. Hence naturalism wins.
>
> Therefore I have written "A Treatise on Heaven" to bring the argument to its final conclusion. For every-

thing that is included in the realm of physical forms and concrete objects, there are things it can do and things it cannot do. Heaven is the largest of things with physical form and man is the best among living things. What Heaven can do, man cannot, and what man can do, there is some that Heaven cannot do. Therefore I say that Heaven and man mutually overcome each other. The explanation is this: The way of Heaven lies in producing and reproducing, and its function is expressed in strength and weakness, whereas the way of man lies in laws and regulations and his function is expressed in right and wrong.[4]

Temple of Heaven in Peking (Beijing).

As suggested by this example, the Neo-Confucianists did a lot of speculating on the nature of Heaven, the powerful reality that somehow is involved in controlling human existence.

The importance of Heaven can be seen in the emperor's practice, continued down to the twentieth century, of making special sacrifices to Heaven and to the ancestors and other gods. One part of the prayer offered to Heaven by the emperor on the festival of the winter solstice reads:

> Thou madest heaven; Thou madest earth; Thou madest man. All things with their re-producing power, got their being. O Te [Heaven], when Thou hadst separated the *Yin* and the *Yang*, Thy creating work proceeded. Thou didst produce, O Spirit, the sun and the moon and the five planets. . . . I, Thy servant, venture reverently to thank Thee, and, while I worship, present the notice to Thee, O Te, calling Thee Sovereign. Thou hast vouchsafed, O Te, to hear us, for Thou regardest us as a Father.[5]

Heaven, whether personal god or naturalistic power, has an important role in holding everything together for human benefit. And according to the traditional Chinese conception, the emperor as the representative of humans shares in the responsibility of nourishing the process of life with sacred power.

The Chinese Vision of the Way of Nature: Tao

The ancient conception of the Tao, or the way of nature, has also played an important part in Chinese views of ultimate reality. Tao has many meanings, but as ultimate reality Chinese think of Tao as the source and origin of everything and also as that power that maintains harmony and balance in the world. This eternal Way of the universe can be thought of at many different levels, as evidenced by the fact that all the religious traditions of China have focused in one way or another on this reality. But it is the texts of philosophical Taoism that have most deeply explored this dimension of ultimate reality. In religious Taoism, the Tao is associated with the various gods and sacred powers of the universe.

Tao as the Undifferentiated Source of All

Chinese thinkers and searchers from early times have talked of a primordial source of all reality, itself undivided and prior to all the multiplicity of things that make up our existence. The famous passage in chapter 25 of the Tao Te Ching, in its mysterious, cryptic language, sets forth this understanding:

> There is Something undifferentiated and yet complete in Itself,
> It existed before the birth of heaven and earth.
> Soundless and formless,
> Independent and unchanging,
> Pervasive and invincible.
> It can be regarded as the Mother of the Universe.
> I do not know Its name.
> I name It "Tao," only when I was forced to give It a name.
> I regard It simply "Great,"
> For in greatness, It produces.
> In producing, It expands;
> In expanding, It regenerates. . . .
> The way of man follows after the law of Earth.
> The law of Earth follows after the law of Heaven.
> The law of Heaven follows after the law of Tao.
> The law of Tao follows after Its own naturalness.[6]

So Tao is one, prior to all differences. Nothing produced Tao, nor is it limited or affected by anything. Whereas everything else is dependent on Tao, Tao only follows its own nature. It is that eternal, primordial reality that contains within itself the inexhaustible source and creativity of the whole universe. It is the "mother" of all and operates within everything, pervasive and invincible, producing all and regenerating all.

This rich description of Tao in the Tao Te Ching uses many terms and qualities that might be ascribed to God in the monotheistic Abraham religions, although it is said that Tao contains all within itself and is immanent in all—far different from the monotheistic concept that the creator is transcendent beyond the creation. But Taoists hold that such terms and qualities are only pointers to a deep, mysterious reality that cannot be grasped by word or concept. It is important that Lao Tzu's 5,000-character description of Tao in the Tao Te Ching begins with the assertion that such a description is impossible:

> The Tao that can be told of is not the eternal Tao;
> The name that can be named is not the eternal name.
> The Nameless is the origin of Heaven and Earth;
> The Named is the mother of all things.[7]

Once Tao is named and described, it is limited and thus no longer the primordial Tao. Chung Tzu once said:

> The fish trap exists because of the fish; once you've gotten the fish, you can forget the trap. The rabbit snare exists because of the rabbit; once you've gotten the rabbit, you can forget the snare. Words exist because of meaning; once you've gotten the meaning, you can forget the words. Where can I find a man who has forgotten words so I can have a word with him?[8]

Tao is immanent in heaven and earth and all things as the undifferentiated stuff out of which all namable things are articulated—but Tao in itself can only be known intuitively by getting one's mind and whole being in harmony with the movement of Tao.

Tao operates as the inner law of all things, even the most common and insignificant, as we see in this dialogue in the Chuang Tzu:

> Tung-kuo Tzu asked Chuang Tzu, "What is called Tao—where is it?"
> "It is everywhere," replied Chuang Tzu.
> Tung-kuo Tzu said, "It will not do unless you are more specific."
> "It is in the ant," said Chuang Tzu.
> "Why go so low down?"
> "It is in the weeds."
> "Why even lower?"
> "It is in a potsherd."
> "Why still lower?"
> "It is in the excrement and urine," said Chuang Tzu. Tung-kuo gave no response.[9]

So Tao, prior to everything, operates in even the most insignificant realities. How does it operate? Not through power and coercion, not through commands or absolute structures, but simply as the innermost universal way of nature. "Tao invariably does nothing, And yet there is nothing that is not done" (ch. 37).[10]

The Tao is really the operation of the way of the universe in its totality.

> The Great Tao flows everywhere.
> It may go left or right.
> All things depend on it for life, and it does not turn away from them.
> It accomplishes its task, but does not claim credit for it.
> It clothes and feeds all things but does not claim to be master over them   (CH. 34).[11]

Chuang Tzu describes the Tao as the final harmony and unity of all realities, all forms, even all gods:

> Tao has reality and evidence but no action or physical form. It may be transmitted but cannot be received. It may be obtained but cannot be seen. It is based in itself, rooted in itself. Before heaven and earth, Tao existed by itself from all time. It gave spirits and rulers their spiritual powers. It created heaven and earth. It is above the zenith but it is not high. It is beneath the nadir but it is not low. It is prior to heaven and earth, but it is not old. . . . The Great Dipper obtained it and has therefore never erred from its course. The sun and moon obtained it and so they have never ceased to revolve. The deity K'an-pi obtained it and was therefore able to enter the high K'un-lun mountains.[12]

Not only those who call themselves Taoists but most Chinese have been deeply impressed by this vision of Tao as the source of existence. Even as many adhere to other views of ultimate reality, these views somehow cohere with the world view represented by Tao.

The Taoist Gods of the Prior Heavens

To the thinkers and experts of religious Taoism, the abode of the transcendent, eternal Tao is most associated with the stellar constellations, the Prior Heavens, and in these Prior Heavens there are great gods who are exempt from the changes that take place in the visible world (the Posterior Heavens). The great gods are one with the eternal Tao and thus are the source of life, primordial breath, and blessing for our visible world.

At the summit of the gods are the Three Ones, headed by T'ai I, the original one divine reality. These are the "three primordial breaths," whose origin is described in an early religious Taoist text:

> The *Tao* gives forth a subtle breath
> The colors of which are three:
> *Hsuan* [dark], *Yuan* [primordial], *Shih* [origin].
> The *Hsuan* is blue-green, and formed the heavens.
> The *Yuan* is yellow and made the earth.
> The *Shih* is white, and is the *Tao* [of man].
> From the center, the three breaths rule heaven and earth.[13]

In present-day Taoist rituals, these Three Pure Ones or Three Heavenly Worthies are Yuan Shih, the Primordial Lord of Heaven, Ling Pao, the Lord of Earth, and Lord Lao, the Lord of Humans. The Three Heavenly Worthies head a pantheon of gods that includes the Five Primordial Spirits, the Five Great Mountains of China, and many more deputies and helpers.

In the Taoist conception of reality, these great gods are not only resident in the Prior Heavens. Since our world and our human body make up a microcosm (small cosmos) corresponding to the macrocosm (great cosmos), these gods are also present within our world and within our body. For example, the Lord of Heaven is also Lord of the head and the primordial breath; the Lord of Earth is also Lord of the chest and the spirit; the Lord of Humans is also Lord of the belly and the seminal essence. The power that originates in the primordial Tao is very present and active in the several spheres of our existence. Since favorable activity of these gods is essential for human happiness and success, people look to the Taoist experts to summon and revitalize these powers within the community.

The Gods of Popular Religion

Some Taoist texts identify one of the Three Heavenly Ones as the Jade Emperor; other texts seem to think of the Jade Emperor as another sacred being. In any case, popular religion in China has looked to the Jade Emperor as the supreme arbitrator over life in this changing, human world—perhaps as the deputy of the Lord of Heaven in administering the heavenly bureaucracy and in governing the world of humans. It is widely believed among traditional Chinese that the Jade Emperor is the head of the heavenly court, and that he has many helpers and deputies to govern our

Worshipers at the temple of Wong Tai Sin in Kowloon; Wong Tai Sin, a shepherd boy, became a god who provides good health and success in business.

world. There is, for example, the god of T'ai Shan, the great mountain of the East, who is the Jade Emperor's regent on earth. Then there are the city gods (the Gods of Moats and Walls) who have been given the administration of particular villages and cities. Another important local god is T'u Ti, the earth god, guardian of the local community in all its fortunes and misfortunes. Then there are important household gods, including especially Tsao Chun, God of the Cooking Stove, who keeps the ledger of good and bad deeds committed by the members of the family and, in general, looks after the welfare of the home.

All these deputy gods, it is believed, come to the Jade Emperor's court once a year to report and hand in accounts of their administration over the past year. And then they are promoted or punished accordingly, for their beneficial administration must harmonize with the work of the human emperor and the local administrators. If the larger good of human society is not served, the fault must lie somewhere within these human and divine bureaucracies.

Where did all these gods come from? Well, many (probably most) were originally humans who died and as ancestral spirits displayed such power and benefit that they were promoted to the ranks of the higher gods. The simple test of divine status is efficacy—does this god really come through with beneficial power or not? This approach is very practical-minded. When sacred power from a particular deceased human is experienced by many in the community and beyond, clearly an important god is in the making, for the gods are channels of sacred power as it is dispersed for the welfare and growth of the human community.

As important among the divine powers, we should mention two outstanding gods who are worshiped all over the Chinese communities, Ma Tsu and Kuan Yin. Ma Tsu is a favorite goddess, "Old Granny." Her story is especially important, for it illustrates how a human soul becomes a most universal, beneficial channel of sacred power. The story originates on an island in south China, where a teenaged girl showed special powers in communicating with and helping fishermen at sea. She knew when her father and brothers were experiencing a horrible shipwreck, and she flew to them in spirit to save them. She carried her brothers to safety in her arms but lost her father, for she was carrying him in her mouth and had to open her mouth in reply to a question from her mother. She died as a young woman, but soon other fishermen experienced her assistance, and then still others, until before long all across southern China, Ma Tsu was revered as a most efficacious sacred power. Eventually even the emperor recognized her powers and she was raised to the status of Imperial Consort of Heaven—certainly a high position in this whole realm of sacred beings. Ma Tsu provides much help in the practical circumstances of life—childbirth, healthy children, happy marriages, and much more.

Gods can make their appearance from many different directions, and Kuan Yin is one who came in from Buddhism. As the great Bodhisattva Avalokiteshvara in India, this sacred being was widely known for saving and helping people, and in China the power continued and increased. Now known as Kuan Yin, the Lord Who Looks Down (a translation of the Sanskrit name), this bodhisattva has become one of the most widely worshiped gods in China. The compassion and mercy of this bodhisattva have come to be expressed in feminine symbols and images, and many think of Kuan Yin as the great goddess of mercy who grants help in the most critical areas of life.

Ma Tsu, Kuan Yin, and many more—Chinese people know that these gods, goddesses, and spirits are not ultimate and universal in their power, but they represent the ways, the avenues in which the ultimate Tao shows effective presence within daily human existence. These sacred powers are tangible and real elements of the operating everyday universe, and to stay in harmony with them is a most important practice of life.

The Inner Principle of All: Neo-Confucian Metaphysics

"What really holds everything together?" The Confucian tradition made important intellectual advances in China during the Sung era, and this Neo-Confucian philosophical attitude became central to the vision of ultimate reality held by many Chinese. What we call Neo-Confucianism was really known as the school of "Principle," that is, the underlying Principle that holds everything together, and thus it is precisely what we are looking for in this investigation, ultimate reality as Chinese understand it. The theory of principle (li) attaches itself to the earlier views, incorporating the concepts of Heaven and Tao. These terms flow together in the Neo-Confucianism notion that all is principle and that the mind itself reflects and resonates with this principle.

We can take Chu Hsi's (1130–1200) synthesis of Neo-Confucian thought about ultimate reality as representative, though, of course, there were alternate ideas and emphases in some of the other thinkers. As the very source of all Chu Hsi posits the Great Ultimate (t'ai chi), another term used from ancient times. The Great Ultimate transcends time and space. It is both the sum total of the principles of all things and also the highest principle within each. As the repository for all actual and potential principles, the Great Ultimate is present in the universe as a whole and in each thing individually. Chu Hsi explained this relationship in this way:

> The Great Ultimate is merely the principle of heaven and earth and the myriad things. With respect to heaven and earth, there is the Great Ultimate in them. With respect to the myriad things, there is the Great Ultimate in each and every one of them. Before heaven and earth existed, there was assuredly this principle. . . . Fundamentally there is only one Great Ultimate, yet each of

the myriad things has been endowed with it and each in itself possesses the Great Ultimate in its entirety. This is similar to the fact that there is only one moon in the sky but when its light is scattered upon rivers and lakes, it can be seen everywhere. It cannot be said that the moon has been split.[14]

So the real center of all, that which holds all together, is ultimate principle, both transcendent and completely within all things.

But how can we understand principle within each individual thing? Chu Hsi made a distinction between principle and "material force" (ch'i). Principle is eternal, unchanging, indestructible, and incorporeal. On the other hand, material force is transitory, changing, destructible, and corporeal. Yet these two do not exist separately. Principle needs material force to adhere to, and material force needs principle as its essence. Understandably, someone asked Chu Hsi which came first, principle or material force. Principle has never been separated from material force, Chu answered, even though if we talk about origins we would have to say that principle is prior.

But what about the Lord Above and Heaven? What about gods and spirits? In answer to questions like these, Chu Hsi consistently interpreted all such ideas as simply the operation of principle. One questioner referred to passages in the classics about Heaven's creative activity and said: "I ask whether these and similar passages mean that there exists above the blue sky a real master and governor; or whether, Heaven having no mind, it is Li that is responsible." Chu Hsi's answer was direct: "These passages have all the same meaning—it is Li [principle] alone which acts thus."[15] Thus in its view of ultimate reality Neo-Confucianism has effectively excluded the idea of a personal creator God who rules over all. Finally it is principle that holds things together and keeps the world running.

The Chinese Buddhist Vision of the Ultimate

If the Chinese perspective on the ultimate is not too complicated already, we should add that many Chinese also have accepted the Mahayana Buddhist view of ultimate reality as emptiness and as the Dharma Body of the Buddha (discussed in Part III). Many distinctive Chinese ideas associated with the sense of cosmic harmony and the Tao have colored Buddhist views of the ultimate in China. The Hua-yen school, for example, articulated a complicated teaching about the interpenetration of the transcendental Dharma (suchness) and the dharmas of the conditioned world of rebirth, so that all phenomena enter into and are identical with each other. To illustrate this, one great Hua-yen master placed a Buddha image illuminated with a lamp in the middle of a hall, setting up mirrors in all the ten directions (the four cardinal directions, the four intermediate directions, and up and down). Each mirror thus reflects the Buddha image—and each also reflects the Buddha image as reflected in all the other mirrors, showing the interpenetration of all reality infused with the Buddha nature.

Ch'an Buddhism perpetuated the basic Mahayana conceptions of the ultimate and presented them in direct, forceful form in China: nirvana as nondifferent from samsara, the Buddha essence of all reality, and the Dharma Body (equated with the Tao) as universal. The second patriarch of Ch'an in China, Hui-ko, is reported to have taught:

> The deep principle of the True is "utter nondifferent." From of old, one is confused about the Gem and thinks it is a piece of tile. When suddenly "oneself" wakes up, there is the real jewel. Ignorance and wisdom are the same and without difference. Know that the myriad things are all identical with suchness. When you regard the body and do not distinguish it from the Buddha, why go on to seek [nirvana] without the remainder?[16]

In characteristic Ch'an language, the message is that ultimate reality is no different from the suchness of life in every moment as we live it.

So the Chinese tradition puts forth a number of important answers to the question about what is ultimate, what really holds everything together. One may believe in the Lord Above, Heaven, as the power that runs the world. Or one may look to the Tao of nature as the center of all. Again, one may find that the great gods of the Prior Heavens, together with their deputies on earth, provide the real center and support for existence. Or, one may take the view that all these forces are really the natural, impersonal functioning of Principle. Finally, there is the Buddhist view of ultimate reality as the Dharma Body of the Buddha and as emptiness. The truth of the matter is that many Chinese have held to all these views in varying degrees. Chinese religious thought has produced many creative visions of ultimate reality on the basis of these fundamental patterns.

COSMOS AND HUMANITY

"So what sense or meaning is there in life?" "What is this world all about anyway?" Ancient Chinese thinkers spent a great deal of time speculating and arguing on precisely questions like these, and their positions have influenced Chinese religion ever since. There are ancient myths of the creation of the universe and of humans within it. And there are philosophical theories about the origin of all and about how the sacred forces operate together in this world. Much concern has been given to the nature and place of humans in the world, especially with regard to the question of whether humans are good or evil by nature.

Origin of the Cosmos and Human Nature

One ancient myth about the creation of the cosmos has special standing in the Chinese tradition: the P'an Ku myth. But additional theories about the Tao, the yin-yang forces, and the five elements have also given shape to the Chinese cosmology. All these stories and theories point to a cosmology in which humans are closely interwoven with the various aspects of the world in the harmony of the sacred power that is within, not outside, nature.

The P'an Ku Myth of the Origin of the Cosmos

Stories about P'an Ku are well known in Chinese popular tradition. The ancient myth, from a third century C.E. text, goes like this:

Heaven and Earth were in the chaos condition [hun-tun] like a chicken's egg, within which was born P'an-ku [perhaps "coiled-up Antiquity"]. After 18,000 years, when Heaven and Earth were separated, the pure yang formed the Heaven and the murky yin formed the Earth. P'an-ku stood between them. His body transformed nine times daily while his head supported the Heaven and his feet stabilized the Earth. Each day Heaven increased ten feet in height and Earth daily increased ten feet in thickness. P'an-ku who was between them daily increased ten feet in size. After another 18,000 years this is how Heaven and Earth came to be separated by their present distance of 90,000 li [roughly 50,000 kilometers].[17]

Another version of the myth about this cosmic person, from a sixth-century C.E. text, tells that after P'an Ku died he was transformed into the universe. His breath became the wind and the clouds, his voice the thunder, and his eyes the sun and moon. His blood became the rivers, his flesh the soil, his hair and beard the constellations, his skin and body hair the plants and trees, and his teeth and bones the metals and stones. And the parasites on his body, impregnated by the wind, became human beings.[18]

The origin of all things in a condition of chaos, called Hun-tun, is an ancient and widespread Chinese idea. It is, of course, found in other religious traditions also, such as the ancient Babylonian and Hebrew stories of the creation of the cosmos from a condition of chaos. Hun-tun is the great void, the undifferentiated, formless, watery source that through a process of differentiation engendered our universe. A recently discovered text from ancient China gives this striking description of primordial chaos:

In the beginning of the ancient past,
All things were fused and were identical with the great vacuity.
Vacuous, and blended as one,
Resting in the [condition of] one eternally.
Moist and chaotic,
There is no distinction of dark and light. . . .
From ancient times it [Tao] had no form,
It penetrated greatly but was nameless.[19]

This chaos is beyond all categories, characterized by flexibility, simplicity, and spontaneity, with inexhaustible potency to create the cosmos. As an eternal reality, it underlies the cosmos as the perpetual source of regeneration.

The P'an Ku myth describes chaos as a chicken's egg, a notion that is widespread in ancient China and also in many other cultures. Early Chinese writers likened the universe to an egg, with the heaven enclosing the earth from without as a shell does the yolk of the egg, the earth being the yolk suspended in the midst of heaven. The symbolism is appropriate, for the egg contains creative potentiality, with all the aspects of life already present, ready to evolve and burst out. All the multiplicity of things, all opposites, even yin and yang, are united in this source of creativity.

The cosmic person, P'an Ku, is engendered and nurtured within chaos to become the universe itself. There is no creator god here, working from the outside, as in the Hebrew creation story. Rather creation grows organically from within as that which is born in the chaos-womb grows to become the universe. There is a complete unity between the producer and that which is produced; the chaos-source evolves itself into the universe, still of the same essence. There is a continuing process of transformation, as P'an Ku grows and Heaven and Earth become established. The transformation continues with the death of this cosmic Person. P'an Ku, the macrocosm (great universe), becomes all the various aspects of the world, so that each part of the world is organically linked to the whole.

Here is a self-evolved world. The original chaos is completely unified with the resultant world in a continuous process of creation and regeneration.

The World Process: Tao, Yin-Yang, and Five Elements

Lao Tzu and later Taoist thinkers identified the primordial chaos as none other than Tao. They held that Tao is not only the origin of all but the inner source of the continual transformation of the whole universe. That process involves generation and evolving forth; it

Working in the rice paddies; the sense of the rhythms of nature is prominent in Chinese religious thought.

also involves devolving and returning to the source, the "uncarved block," the Tao.

How does the Tao operate? The Tao Te Ching says,

Tao produced the One.
The One produced the two.
The two produced the three.
And the three produced the ten thousand things.
The ten thousand things carry the yin and embrace the yang, and through the blending of the material force they achieve harmony.   (CH. 42)[20]

Chinese cosmological views have always given an important place to the forces of yin and yang in understanding the nature and operation of the world. A widespread view of how the world originated is that Tao, in the great primordial chaos, engendered a separation between the finer and brighter elements, which became Heaven (yang), and the coarser and darker elements, which became earth (yin). From yang come fire and the sun, from yin water and the moon—and so on in the total operation of the world, the Tao functioning in the interaction of yin and yang. All of this is closely related to human welfare and happiness:

Therefore the Yin and the Yang are the great principles of Heaven and Earth. The four seasons are the great path of Yin and Yang. Likewise, punishment and reward in government are to be in harmony with the four seasons. When punishment and reward are in harmony with the seasons, happiness will be produced; when they disregard them, they will produce calamity.[21]

As we see from the four seasons, the Tao operates in yang-yin cyclical processes of rise and decline. We can also understand the Tao as the operation of the five elements or forces. The five elements are wood, fire, earth, metal, and water, but these are identified with many other sets of five: planets, weather, seasons, cardinal directions, sense organs, tastes, viscera, moods, and so forth. These are dynamic operational agents that are continually moving in cyclical changes from one to the other. Each element has its time to rise, flourish, decline, and be taken over by the next. The relationships are complicated processes of mutually produc-ing, conquering, and transforming. Thus, for example, wood conquers earth, metal conquers wood, fire conquers metal, water conquers fire, earth conquers water. In this whole cyclical process an ecological balance is maintained. For example, over-forestation would be stopped by forest fires, which would be stopped by rain. On the other hand, water can produce forests faster than metal cuts the trees down. This ecological balance is extended into all facets of personal, social, and political life.

The Human Position in the World

"Where do we come from and why are we here?" The P'an Ku myth, describing how everything in the world came from different parts of the cosmic P'an Ku, tells how the parasites on P'an Ku's body were impregnated by the wind and became human beings. This may seem to be a rather modest view of human origins and of the human function in the world, unlike the view in the three Abraham religions that humans were made specially as the crown of creation to be God's representative over all. Actually, the point of the P'an Ku story of human origins does not seem to be that humans are parasites on the world. Rather, humans are from the same one source as the whole universe, organically related to the rest of nature. Humans are not masters of the universe, but they are evolved from the same source and share the common process of life with all.

The P'an Ku myth is important, but it is especially the classics and the writings of the Confucian and Taoist philosophers that define the nature of humans and their position in the world. There is general agreement that human nature is intricately related to all the sacred forces inherent in the universe. One of the clearest statements of human nature is in the Book of Rites: "Humanness is consistent of benevolent virtue of Heaven and Earth, the co-operative union of Yin and Yang, the joint assembly of ghost [kuei] and spirit [shen], and the finest breath contained in the Five Elements."[22] Human nature is the finest cooperative product of the universe itself, containing the basic substance and elements of the universe.

This passage from the Book of Rites refers to "the joint assembly of *kuei* and *shen*" within human nature. Chinese traditionally conceive of two souls within humans, appropriately, since humans are the "cooperative union of yin and yang." One soul is the yang soul (*hun*), which comes from Heaven, the realm of pure yang. The other soul is the yin soul (*p'o*), from the pure yin source, Earth. The yang dimension is also thought of as the spiritual aspect, and the yin as the physical aspect, of a person. During life yin and yang are united, but at death they again separate. The yang soul, stemming from Heaven, becomes *shen*, a spiritual being or god. The yin soul is *kuei*, an earthy spiritual force to be returned to its original source, the earth, in burial. If the *kuei* is not properly buried and cared for by descendants, it may become an unhappy wandering spirit, or "ghost."

Thus we see that human nature is a microcosm of the great universe itself. Human nature reflects all those powers writ large on the cosmic scale, now active and focused on the human scale. Many philosophical texts delight in spelling out the correspondences between the human body and the forces of Heaven and Earth, yin and yang, and the five elements. One text says,

> The roundness of the head imitates Heaven, and the squareness of the foot imitates Earth. Like Heaven has four seasons, Five Elements, nine divisions and 360 days, human beings also have four limbs, five viscera, nine orifices and 360 joints. Like Heaven has wind, rain, cold, and heat, human beings also have the qualities of accepting, giving, joy and anger. Therefore gall corresponds to clouds, the lung to vapor, the spleen to wind, the kidneys to rain, and the liver to thunder. Thus human beings form a trinity with Heaven and Earth, and the human mind is the master.[23]

The suggestion here that humans form a triad with Heaven and earth is an important idea in the Chinese view of human nature and makes it clear that humans have an important role to fill. Philosophical discussions of human nature inevitably come to that question of what special role humans have in the universe.

According to Lao Tzu and Chuang Tzu, human beings have received the special quality of "virtue" (*te*) from the Tao, the life principle inherent in each individual. Therefore, humans simply need to discover that virtue within and live according to it.

For Confucius and his followers, the ideal human position in the world could best be characterized by the concept of *jen*, "humaneness," a notion that puts strong emphasis on interrelationship between people, in kindness and morality. It is this morality that makes humans different from animals; humans have the Heaven-given qualities of love or commiseration, righteousness, propriety, and wisdom; and they have the potential of fulfilling these qualities. Tung Chung-shu (178–104 B.C.E.), a great Confucianist who synthesized the ideas of yin-yang, five elements, and Tao within Confucianism, had a bit to say about the high position of humans in the universe.

> Of the creatures born from the refined essence of Heaven and Earth, none is more noble than man. Man receives the mandate from Heaven and is therefore superior to other creatures. Other creatures suffer troubles and defects and cannot practice humanity and righteousness; man alone can practice them. . . .
>
> The highest humanity (*jen*) rests with Heaven, for Heaven is humaneness itself. It shelters and sustains all creatures. It transforms them and brings them to birth. It nourishes and completes them. Its works never cease; they end and then begin again, and the fruits of all its labors it gives to the service of mankind.[24]

In this Confucianist interpretation is summed up the high Chinese view of the role of humans in the world, to be in union with Heaven and earth not only physically but also spiritually and thus help to maintain harmony in the universe through moral life.

The Realities of Human Existence in the World

"Why do things seem so uncertain and confused?" "Why is there so much evil and suffering in the world?" "What keeps us from living the way we should?" Since ancient times Chinese philosophers have debated questions about why humans seemingly do not reach their full potential in their own nature and in society. Sometimes, usually among Confucian thinkers, the discussion focuses on the question of whether humans are good or evil by nature, seen within the social context. Those inclined toward the Taoist vision see the problem more in terms of humans trapped in artificiality and conventional strictures instead of living in full harmony with the Tao. Buddhists emphasize the problems of ignorance, desire, and karma. Those concerned about our relation to the gods and spirits feel that problems arise because humans forget them or fail to make use of their power of renewal. Whichever view is chosen, there is consensus on one thing: we humans do not live the full life of happiness, because we are out of harmony with the sacred power at the heart of our existence.

Life in Community: Are Humans Good or Evil by Nature?

It is not hard to see that things are not right in the world. True, there have been eras of relative peace and harmony—Chinese thinkers often took a nostalgic look back to the early Chou period (starting ca. 1100 B.C.E.) as a time when sage-kings ruled according to the mandate of Heaven in an era of peace and prosperity. But even that peaceful era was short-lived. Both Confucius and Lao Tzu lived in a time of upheaval and anarchy. At no time could it be said that humans reached their full potential in peace and prosperity.

Chinese thinkers of all persuasions have offered theories as to why humans fail to live up to their possibilities. There are many possible theories, but it is characteristic of Chinese thinking that good and evil behavior is seen as a human problem, not something that is determined by divine forces, whether god or evil power. Of course, humans do interact with many spiritual forces, and hungry wandering spirits can cause suffering and misfortune. But in the final analysis the human problem of failure lies within humanity itself, in the individual, in society, or in both.

It is a time-honored view in China to consider human nature as essentially good and positive, in spite of the reality of evil and suffering in human society. This was the view suggested by Confucius and articulated clearly by Mencius. Confucius based his whole approach on the educability of human beings, including the common people whom he accepted in his school. He held that it was lack of moral leadership and the attempt to rule by laws and penalties that prevented the people from developing a sense of honor. It is not that people by nature are hurtful and cruel; it is the anarchy of society and especially the greed and brutal power of rulers that turn human behavior to negative and harmful directions.

Mencius articulated clearly the basic notion that humans are essentially good by nature but turn to evil because society and its leaders fail to cultivate and nourish that goodness of nature. All people have four intrinsic virtues: the feeling of commiseration, the feeling of shame, the feeling of courtesy, and the sense of right and wrong. Famous in this discussion is Mencius' parable of a child falling into a well:

> Why I say all men have a sense of commiseration is this: Here is a man who suddenly notices a child about to fall into a well. Invariably he will feel a sense of alarm and compassion. And this is not for the purpose of gaining the favor of the child's parents, or seeking the approbation of his neighbors and friends, or for fear of blame should he fail to rescue it. Thus we see that no man is without a sense of compassion, or a sense of shame, or a sense of courtesy, or a sense of right and wrong. The sense of compassion is the beginning of humanity [jen]; the sense of shame is the beginning of righteousness; the sense of courtesy is the beginning of decorum [li]; the sense of right and wrong is the beginning of wisdom. Every man has within himself these four beginnings, just as he has four limbs. Since everyone has these four beginnings within him, the man who considers himself incapable of exercising them is destroying himself. [25]

These four beginnings are motivations and possibilities that are inherent in everyone. Starting with commiseration, these originating impulses in human nature motivate us to become humane, righteous, proper, and wise.

But, Mencius holds, these beginnings of goodness need to be nurtured and developed—and for many people that fails to happen. It seems that what we call evil in human nature is really due to lack of completion and development of the innate goodness. Mencius explains:

> Can it be that any man's mind naturally lacks Humanity and Justice? If he loses his sense of the good, then he loses it as the mountain lost its trees. It has been hacked away at—day after day—what of its beauty then? However, as the days pass he grows, and, as with all men, in the still air of the early hours his sense of right and wrong is at work. . . . Indeed, if nurtured aright, anything will grow, but if not nurtured aright anything will wither away.[26]

So evil does not arise within human nature but comes, in a sense, from without, from lack of nourishing by society. The tendency of human nature is to do good, Mencius said, like water flowing downhill. Of course, you can interfere and splash water uphill, but this is due not to the nature of water but to the force of circumstances. Similarly, humans may be brought to do evil, but that is because something has been forced onto human nature. Lack of nourishment of our good nature, corrupting influences from outside—from these arise the human problematic of evil and suffering.

But there is an alternate way of looking at the problem, and this was best articulated by another disciple in the Confucian tradition, Hsun Tzu (ca. 313–238 B.C.E.). Hsun Tzu, taking a "realist" position, held that human nature is essentially selfish and hateful, and any kind of goodness can only be acquired by training or enforced through laws and punishment. Heaven—which to Hsun Tzu is a mechanistic force without moral qualities—produces a human nature that loves profit, envies and hates, and strives and plunders selfishly. Hsun Tzu wrote,

> The nature of man is evil; his goodness is acquired. His nature being what it is, man is born, first, with a desire for gain. Second, man is born with envy and hate. If these tendencies are followed, injury and cruelty will abound and loyalty and faithfulness will disappear. . . . Hence to give rein to man's original nature and to yield to man's emotions will assuredly lead to strife and disorderliness, and he will revert to a state of barbarism (CH. 23).[27]

If left to itself, our evil human nature would destroy any goodness in our civilization. Yet, for all his pessimistic view of human nature, Hsun Tzu was optimistic that humans could be reshaped through the laws and training produced by the sages.

Since Mencius and Hsun Tzu seem to hold opposite positions, it is inevitable that there might be a view of human nature somewhere between the two. Some later Confucianists argued that both Mencius and Hsun Tzu were right; human nature is partly good and partly evil. If the good aspect is cultivated and nourished, the goodness increases; but if the evil aspect is cultivated, the badness increases. One thinker put it this way: "Man's nature is a mixture of good and evil. He who cultivates the good in it will become a good man and he who cultivates the evil in it will become an evil man."[28] This view suggests that Mencius and Hsun Tzu were perhaps not as far apart as might appear at first glance. The basic problem is still a genuinely human one: evil tendencies (whether from society or from human nature) often grow and spread, whereas good tendencies (whether from human nature or from society) often wither and diminish. And the struggle goes on not in the cosmos but on the stage of human life in society. The Confucian path of transformation is designed to reverse that human situation so that humaneness and righteousness prevail.

Life in Nature: The Problem of Artificiality and Coercion

There is still another position on the question of whether humans are good or evil by nature. One thinker challenged Mencius by claiming that there is no distinction between good or bad in human nature: "The nature of man may be likened to a swift current of water: you lead it eastward and it will flow to the east; you lead it westward and it will flow to the west. Human nature is neither disposed to good nor to evil, just as water is neither disposed to east nor west."[29] Perhaps asking whether human nature is good or evil is the wrong approach, for that very judgment is artificial and may in fact contribute to the problem. Perhaps our basic problem is that we pass such judgments about good and evil!

This is the general approach to the human problem taken by philosophical Taoism. It is artificiality and coercion that lie at the root of our problems in the world. The Tao by nature grows and wanes, operating in everything in harmony, and the good life is always to be in complete harmony with the Tao. But our human tendency is to try and take charge of our lives, change things in accordance with our own strategies, and force structures onto nature and ourselves. We judge wealth and power to be good, and we judge poverty and weakness to be evil—and we spend our lives struggling for one and trying to escape from the other. But in doing so we are alienated from the harmony of Tao.

Chuang Tzu stated the problem with his characteristic flair for imagery:

> The duck's legs are short, but to stretch them out would worry him; the crane's legs are long, but to cut them down would make him sad. What is long by nature needs no cutting off; what is short by nature needs no stretching. That would be no way to get rid of worry.[30]

It is in going against the givenness and spontaneous fitness of nature that we experience suffering, frustration, and defeat. All of our problems come from trying to force things in artificial, unnatural ways.

Where does this human tendency come from? Lao Tzu and Chuang Tzu do not really say whether it is inherent in human nature or whether it stems from institutions of society. Probably even these distinctions are false and misleading. Nature itself is the operation of Tao, and evil embodies all that resists pristine nature through coercion, artificiality, and intellectual skill. However they originate, these tendencies at least are promoted by social institutions such as laws, education, ceremonies, rules of morality and etiquette, and the like. This means that the people who do the most to worsen our human problems are the law-enforcers, the teachers, and the ritualists—all of them imposing restraints on what should be natural and free.

Of course, this perspective of philosophical Taoism pertains most directly to those following the path put forth by Lao Tzu and Chuang Tzu. But the same basic notion flows over into the more widespread religious Taoist view of the human problem: we are out of balance with the cosmic forces that support and sustain us. These forces are the great gods of the stellar constellations, managing the operation of yin-yang and the five elements. Through neglect and ignorance we often live out of harmony and bring deprivation and evil upon ourselves. In popular religious understanding, these forces are the gods and goddesses that make up the pantheon of the state and the local community; they are the ancestral spirits that oversee the family and dispense weal or woe in accordance with our harmony with them. One need only look at one's failures and frustrations, conflicts and tragedies to recognize that the general disharmony with Tao and yin-yang is reflected in daily life in family and community.

Chinese Buddhist Views of Human Existence

In bringing to China ideas of karma arising out of ignorance and desire, the wheel of existence, rebirth, and so forth, Buddhism contributed much to the Chinese conception of human nature and the human problem. We can briefly note two tendencies in Chinese Buddhist thought regarding the human problem, one that emphasizes ignorance of the Buddha quality of human nature, and the other that finds life in this degenerate world-age to be well-nigh hopeless.

The Hua-yen, T'ien-t'ai , and Ch'an schools emphasized the classical Mahayana doctrine of the universal Buddha-nature that all people possess, holding that it is human ignorance that keeps us from seeing this Buddha-nature and thus remaining trapped in suffering. A clear statement about human nature and the human problem comes from the fifth patriarch of the Hua-yen school, Tsung-mi (780–841):

> The Doctrine of the Manifestation of the Dharmanature . . . preaches that all sentient beings possess the true mind of natural enlightenment, which from time immemorial has always been there, clear and pure, shining and not obscured, understanding and always knowing. It is also called Buddha-nature and Tathagatagarbha (Store of the Thus-come). From the beginning of time, it has been obscured by erroneous ideas without knowing its own (Buddha-nature), but only recognizing its ordinary nature, loving it and being attached to it, accumulating action-influence, and suffering from the pain of life and death.[31]

Chinese popular imagination was fascinated by Buddhist ideas about bad karma accumulated during one's existence and rebirth in purgatories and hells, and lurid descriptions of the horrors of those purgatories abound in popular literature. Buddhist notions of purgatory were expanded by Chinese notions of trial and punishment for the guilty. One popular tract first issues a plea for the sinner to repent, and then presents a portrait of what is in store for him if he does not. Here is the general policy:

> The Judges of the Ten Courts of Purgatory then agreed that all who led virtuous lives from their youth upwards shall be escorted at their death to the land of the Immortals; that all whose balance of good and evil is exact shall escape the bitterness of the [worst three of the Six Paths], and be born again among men; that those who have repaid their debts of gratitude and friendship, and fulfilled their destiny, yet have a balance of evil against them, shall pass through the various Courts of Purgatory and then be born again amongst men, rich, poor, old, young, diseased or crippled, to be put a second time upon trial. Then, if they behave well they may enter into some happy state; but if badly, they will be dragged by horrid devils through all the Courts, suffering bitterly as they go, and will again be born, to endure in life the uttermost of poverty and wretchedness, in death the everlasting tortures of hell. Those who are disloyal, unfilial, who commit suicide, take life, or disbelieve the doctrine of Cause and Effect (i.e., karma) . . . are handed over to the everlasting tortures of hell.

After a long description of the most horrid punishments imaginable, the tract reflects on the foolishness of human nature, illustrated by those shades who, having passed through the purgatories and through the Terrace of Oblivion (where they are caused to forget all that has happened to them), now rejoice at the prospect of being born again as humans:

> Yet they all rush on to birth like an infatuated or drunken crowd; and again, in their early childhood, hanker after the forbidden flavours. Then, regardless of consequences, they begin to destroy life, and thus forfeit all claims to the mercy and compassion of God [the Jade Emperor]. They take no thought as to the end that must overtake them; and finally, they bring themselves once more to the same horrid plight. [32]

THE PATH OF TRANSFORMATION

"How can I start living the life that is real?" "How can I find power for renewal and transformation?"

The portrayals of the human problematic in the Chinese traditions, against the background of the human potential for goodness and happiness, help to set the stage for the Path of Transformation, the kind of praxis that leads to renewal of harmony with Tao, the gods, the spirits, and the innermost sources of life.

Confucianism: Transformation Through Study and Ritual

The Confucian tradition, disdaining as it does some of the usual religious practices like calling on the gods for

Decorated steles in a Confucian temple in Peking.

help, has sometimes not been considered a religious path at all but rather a kind of philosophy for improvement of self and society. Are these questions, having to do with the search for real life and renewal, even applicable to the concerns of Confucianists?

Of course they are, for these are basic, universal human concerns. Confucianists are just as concerned as anyone else about real, authentic life and self-transformation. The emphasis is not on life after death or salvation through help from the gods, it is true. But perhaps for that very reason there is a very strong emphasis on achieving the life that is truly human and fulfills our full potential for peace, harmony, and happiness—according to the design of Heaven. Confucianism is clearly a path of spiritual transformation, stressing both the intellectual pursuit of education and study and also the practical and social pursuits of ritual behavior and propriety. We look more closely at the Confucian rituals and ethical actions later; here we want to understand the theoretical basis of the path: how can study, ritual, and moral behavior be the basis of self-transformation, the path to real life?

Transformation Through Study and Moral Cultivation

Confucius was above all an educator, and those following in his tradition have always stressed the path of study and education as the means toward transformation. The human problem, as we have seen, is that our fundamentally good nature gets stunted for lack of nourishment and even misdirected by the anarchy that tends to rule in society because of selfish rulers, repressive laws, and wrongful social relationships. But we have the potential to realize our humanness and become noble people, if we have noble teachers and rulers, if we allow ourselves to be educated, if we study our own nature and the nature of things as determined according to the will of Heaven. This means using the intellect for education, study, and moral self-cultivation.

Confucius taught that the sage-kings of old had deep insight into the will of Heaven and perfected their own humanity in harmony with Heaven. Therefore the classics that tell about their sayings and their lives can mediate that wisdom and perfection to those who read

and study these sacred writings. Study of the classics accordingly has been the primary mode of education in China down into modern times—not always used, of course, for the noble goal of self-transformation. But the ideal has remained that through study and education one's human goodness can be nourished and perfected.

In a famous passage in the Analects, Confucius points to the way of learning as a lifelong process of self-cultivation:

> At fifteen, I set my heart on learning. At thirty, I was firmly established. At forty, I had no more doubts. At fifty, I knew the will of Heaven. At sixty, I was ready to listen to it. At seventy, I could follow my heart's desire without transgressing what was right (2.4).[33]

There is no quick fix here, no sudden conversion and transformation. The path is a long, gradual movement of study and learning, awakening the inner knowledge of the will of Heaven and growing into that will so that the very springs of motivation are in complete harmony with it. So study is not just for knowledge's sake, but for inner cultivation and growth in realizing the will of Heaven—thus becoming a true Noble Person.

The study of the classics actually involves all the major liberal arts, providing a thorough humanistic education. The six disciplines are based on the Six Classics, and they include study of poetry for refinement of thought and expression; study of history for understanding the tradition and refining moral judgment; study of ritual for understanding propriety; study of music for inner transformation; study of politics for social transformation; and study of cosmology to harmonize with the sacred forces. By such study and practice it is possible to cultivate the innate human capabilities to become good and noble and superior; and such noble persons can then lead and guide others to become humane and good.

The Neo-Confucianists developed the path of study into a total system of moral and spiritual self-cultivation, and to many Chinese this Neo-Confucian model of the path has been their highest aspiration. Learning and knowledge cross over into transforming the will and mind and personal life, and this strength of personal character influences the whole social setting of the family, the community, and even the world. One of the most important descriptions of this path of self-cultivation is in the Book of Great Learning:

> The Way of learning to be great consists in manifesting the clear character, loving the people, and abiding in the highest good. . . . The ancients who wished to manifest their clear character to the world would first bring order to their states. Those who wished to bring order to their states would first regulate their families. Those who wished to regulate their families would first cultivate their personal lives. Those who wished to cultivate their personal lives would first rectify their minds. Those who wished to rectify their minds would first make their wills sincere. Those who wished to make their wills sincere would first extend their knowledge.

So all the good expressions of character depend on steps of self-cultivation that finally rest on extending one's knowledge, as the very first movement. The text continues:

> The extension of knowledge consists in the investigation of things. When things are investigated, knowledge is extended; when knowledge is extended, the will becomes sincere; when the will is sincere, the mind is rectified; when the mind is rectified, the personal life is cultivated; when the personal life is cultivated, the family will be regulated; when the family is regulated, the state will be in order; and when the state is in order, there will be peace throughout the world.[34]

Here are eight steps toward the transformation of human society in the world! The last three have to do with family and society—reflecting the importance of parents, teachers, rulers, and others on the path of transformation. But the focal point still is the cultivation of personal life. The text goes on to say, "From the Son of Heaven [the emperor] down to the common people, all must regard cultivation of the personal life as the root or foundation. There is never a case when the root is in disorder and yet the branches are in order."[35]

So the important question is, how can one cultivate personal life so as to become a noble person? The text lays out some basic steps, namely, investigation of things, extension of knowledge, the will becoming sincere, and the rectification of the mind. These form the heart of the path of transformation, leading to the moral, and spiritual cultivation of personal life. The investigation of things means to study the nature of the world and of oneself, arriving at true understanding of the underlying moral principles of the universe. In this process the will becomes sincere, resolving on the goal with calmness and unflagging determination. The path of transformation specifically involves rectification of the mind, becoming one with the whole universe by understanding its principles and looking upon the whole cosmos as one's own self. All of this adds up to cultivation of personal life, that is, self-discipline and practice with diligence and zeal, in study, meditation, and cultivation of moral virtue.

Transformation Through Ritual

In addition to the mental disciplines of study and extension of knowledge, the Confucian path places great emphasis on the practical disciplines of self-transformation. We have seen how ritual and ethical behavior according to God's law play a major part in the Jewish and in the Islamic paths of transformation. Confucianism does not think in terms of God's law, but it finds ritual and ethical behavior (propriety) in society to be powerful instruments of self-transformation. Both ritual and the rules of propriety, in fact, correspond to the patterns immanent in the whole of reality.

It is important to understand that what we are calling ritual and ethical behavior both are the same one word in Chinese: *li* (not the same word as *li* meaning principle). As the inherent ritual pattern of the universe, *li* is followed and practiced both in the various traditional rituals and in one's proper roles in family and society.

In traditional China there were rituals for almost every purpose—sacrifice to the ancestors, political occasions, family events, great public occasions, receiving a guest, and so on. And many great thinkers have written about the meaning of ritual, following the lead of the Classic of Rites, the ancient text that describes many rituals and also provides important ideas about the meaning of the rituals. Chinese have always thought of ritual as closely connected with the underlying principles of the whole universe. In ancient China, for example, rituals of divination were used to connect with the sacred powers of the world and even to direct and control them. Thus, by performing ritual correctly, we are harmonizing ourselves with the forces of Heaven and earth.

One Confucian thinker who wrote a lot about ritual, Hsun Tzu (ca. 313–238 B.C.E.), has this to say about the origin of ritual:

> Rites (Li) rest on three bases: Heaven and earth, which are the source of all life; the ancestors, who are the source of the human race; sovereigns and teachers, who are the source of government.... Hence rites are to serve Heaven on high and earth below, and to honor the ancestors and elevate the sovereigns and teachers.

So ritual has both a cosmological origin and a social origin. It issued forth from Heaven and earth as part of the very principle of the universe. And it also was transmitted by ancestors and shaped by teachers and rulers.

Indeed, it is ritual that upholds and unifies the whole realm of the world, as Hsun Tzu writes:

> It is through rites that Heaven and earth are harmonious and sun and moon are bright, that the four seasons are ordered and the stars are on their courses, that rivers flow and that things prosper, that love and hatred are tempered and joy and anger are in keeping. They cause the lowly to be obedient and those as high to be illustrious.... Rites—are they not the culmination of culture?[36]

Therefore ritual can effect the great transformation of harmonizing us with the world, so that we humankind do become, as the classics state, a trinity with Heaven and earth. Through rituals our innate goodness is nourished and we conform ourselves more and more into the pattern of Heaven and earth, becoming people of humanity.

Moral Cultivation Through Propriety in Society

Confucius taught that we can become people of humanity (jen) especially by practicing the rules of li, "propriety" (the same word as ritual). Here the focus is on relationships in society, in accordance with the will of Heaven, transforming ourselves by practicing and fulfilling our proper roles.

The Confucian tradition talks about the "rectification of names," that is, transforming oneself so as to practice one's proper roles in family and society. Confucius said, "Let the prince be the prince, the minister be minister, the father father and the son son" (Analects 12.11).[37] Each person is related to all the others in society, so each needs to fulfill the particular role and duty that she has. Much of the breakdown in society today results from people not fulfilling their proper roles, usurping the roles of others, rulers looking after their self-interest, teachers misleading students, and all the rest. Many people do not live according to their proper role in family and society—they usurp the authority of their elders, they fail to respect and obey the rulers, they consider themselves above their teachers. To transform ourselves into our potential human goodness, we need the discipline and practice of rectifying our social roles, Confucius taught. We need to discipline ourselves to live as a father, a son, a sister, a ruler, a subject. Only in this way will we be able to inject humaneness (jen) into our lives and into our relation with others. "Without knowledge of the rules of propriety," Confucius said, "it is impossible for one's character to be established" (20:3).[38]

What makes this pursuit of ritual and propriety a religious path is the deep sense that the elaborate systems of ritual and the rules of propriety are based in the pattern originating in the cosmic principle of the universe, according to the mandate of Heaven. "Without knowing the Mandate [of Heaven], it is impossible to be a superior man," Confucius said (20:3).[39]

The Taoist Path of Transformation

"How can I start living *real* life?" "Where do I find power for life and immortality, beyond failure and death?" The Taoist tradition is very much concerned with these questions, and it proposes one fundamental answer: get into harmony with the Tao!

The basic human problematic from the Taoist perspective, as we recall, is forcing our lives against the flow of Tao, engaging in the human tendency of artificiality, judging others, planning strategies, forcing people into roles, and generally struggling selfishly against the stream. This is what causes evil and misery, war and violence, sickness and early death.

So what can one do to transform all this? The path offered by those of the Toaist persuasion consists of ideas, disciplines, and practices to lead to harmony with Tao and with all the spiritual forces that operate within our universe. In the words of Lao Tzu,

> Being one with Nature, he is in accord with Tao.
> Being in accord with Tao, he is everlasting,
> And is free from danger throughout his lifetime.
>
> (CH. 16)[40]

According to philosophical Taoism, the way to ultimate transformation involves the practice of inaction, meditation, and withdrawal from society. Religious Taoism offers many more rituals and practices that restore the powers within our bodies, call down the great cosmic gods, all together balancing yin and yang forces to bring blessed life and immortality. Some scholars have held that philosophical Taoism and religious Taoism are very different modes of religious practice. The understanding we will follow, on the contrary, will see these two movements as basically related paths. One emphasizes harmony with Tao through personal meditation and experience; the other looks to gods and other sacred forces to establish the balance needed for blessed life and immortality.

The Path of Transformation According to Philosophical Taoism

The kind of existence that can be attained, according to Lao Tzu, Chuang Tzu, and other Taoist thinkers, is one beyond all limitations, hindrances, and finite borders. We can become transcendental, realizing our body as part of the universe. That means we need have no worries or anxieties, for the real truth transcends normal knowledge and moral principles. Invincible and immortal, we can live fully in tune with Tao.

The most important movement on the path of transformation, according to the Tao Te Ching, is to practice "no action" (*wu wei*). This seems like a contradiction in terms—how can you practice no action? Of course, what the path prescribes is a way of life in which nothing is done against the course of nature, no actions are forced, no mental concepts are imposed on the Tao, and judgments about good and bad or desirable and nondesirable are completely avoided. The Tao in itself is neither good or bad, neither right or wrong, so there is no need for actions on our part to

Workers crossing the Yellow River near Loyang. Taoist philosophy cultivates harmony with the flow of nature.

resist or change the natural transformations. The course of the Tao is simply the natural, universal course of the Tao—and our highest good is to be in harmony with that Tao just as it is. That calls for a life in which we dedicate ourselves to disciplines and practices that open us up toward the Tao—disciplines of nonstriving, noncontrol, nonstructure, and nondirection. Never do anything that is against the natural flow of Tao—that is the basic meaning of wu-wei, no-action. Stated positively, it means to do everything in accord with the flow of Tao.

This kind of life requires practice. And the Taoist texts put forth a program designed to cultivate the no-action type of life: withdrawing from society, living simply, cultivating one's inner nature. Early Taoists were hermits and recluses, following the Tao in the mountains and valleys, through winter and summer, alone and in groups, practicing the discipline of no-action. Central to this is meditation, emptying out the plans, structures, and strategies of the mind so that the natural flow of Tao might fill the whole being. An important text in the Tao Te Ching says:

> Attain complete vacuity,
> Maintain complete quietude,
> All things come into being,
> And I see thereby their return.
> All things flourish,

But each one returns to its root.
This return to its root means tranquility.
It is called returning to its destiny.
To return to destiny is called the eternal (Tao).   (CH. 16)[41]

What is proposed here is a type of meditation that empties the mind of all ideas and concepts that limit and restrain, so that the mind can directly experience the flow of Tao, the rise and return of all things to the root and source of all. Through such meditation we can harmonize ourselves with the Tao so that we are not affected by change, by feelings of good and bad, even by death. By being one with the Tao we can live totally freely and spontaneously, letting everything happen as it will.

This path of transformation does not involve study and learning, for such activities only serve further to cloud over our minds so that we cannot open ourselves to the flow of Tao. Nor does this path mean learning our proper roles in society, for such structures only increase artificiality and coercion. Rather the ideal path would be that of a mountain hermit, roaming about freely and carelessly, fully atuned to the rhythms of nature, acting only in full harmony with the flow of Tao. It is possible to follow this path without becoming a mountain hermit, of course, but the method of withdrawing from societal structures and meditating in harmony with nature is still important even for those who remain in society.

Since words and concepts do not help on the path of Tao, it is misleading to offer too many rationalized explanations. Fortunately, Chuang Tzu was a great storyteller, and through these stories we can develop some sensitivity for what it means to practice no-action and follow the Tao. Once, Chuang Tzu said, Prince Wen-hui's cook was cutting up a bullock. "Every touch of his hand, every shift of his shoulder, every tread of his foot, every thrust of his knee, every sound of the rending flesh, and every note of the movement of the chopper was in perfect harmony." Prince Wen-hui was impressed and praised him for his perfect skill, but the cook replied:

What your servant loves is the Tao, which I have applied to the skill of carving. When I first began to cut up bullocks, what I saw was simply whole bullocks. After three years' practice, I saw no more bullocks as wholes. Now, I work with my mind, and not with my eyes. The functions of my senses stop; my spirit dominates. Following the natural markings, my chopper slips through the great cavities, slides through the great cleavages, taking advantage of the structure that is already there. . . . A good cook changes his chopper once a year, because he cuts. An ordinary cook changes his chopper once a month, because he hacks. Now my chopper has been in use for nineteen years; it has cut up several thousand bullocks; yet its edge is as sharp as if it just came from the whetstone.

Now the prince understood and said, "Excellent. I have heard the words of this cook, and learned the way of cultivating life" (ch. 3).[42] This way of cultivating life is the way of no-action, that is, not scheming and forcing things but working spontaneously with one's spirit in harmony with the Tao. That approach brings success and happiness in life; in fact, one completely in tune with the Tao overcomes the normal human limitations, as Chuang Tzu says somewhat playfully:

Let me try speaking to you in a somewhat irresponsible manner, and may I ask you to listen to me in the same spirit. Leaning against the sun and the moon and carrying the universe under his arm, the sage blends everything into a harmonious whole. He is unmindful of the confusion and the gloom, and equalizes the humble and the honorable. The multitude strive and toil; the sage is primitive and without knowledge. He comprehends ten thousand years as one unity, whole and simple. All things are what they are, and are thus brought together.   (CH. 2)[43]

The Path of Religious Taoism

There is no sharp division between the path of transformation as understood in philosophical Taoism and that in religious Taoism. Religious Taoism starts from the basic perspective of Lao Tzu and Chuang Tzu and offers a path that relates more concretely to the human concerns of health, material happiness, well-being of family and community, and even immortality. Whereas the path of philosophical Taoism is mostly a private pursuit of individuals, the path of religious Taoism is a community concern and focuses on experts and priesthoods, temples and festivals, for the welfare and transformation of the community. Still, the priests and experts follow the path for their own personal transformation, for only in that way can they share the transforming power with others. The path of religious Taoism really operates at two levels, then: the level of the expert or priest and the level of ordinary people in the community.

The Taoist view of the human situation holds that our problems arise because we are out of balance with the cosmic forces that support and sustain us. Religious Taoism sees these forces as the great gods of the stellar constellations who manage the operation of yin-yang and the five elements, related also to the ancestral spirits and the gods and goddesses of everyday life. So how can one start living *real* life? The basic answer is to follow the path that restores one's balance with these cosmic forces.

An important theory in understanding the path of religious Taoism is the microcosm-macrocosm relationship. The macrocosm or "great cosmos" is the Tao operating through the gods of the stellar constellations, yin-yang, and the five elements. The microcosm or "small cosmos" is our limited world, our local temple, and even our human body, a small-scale replica of the great cosmos. This means that the regions of the temple and of the human body correspond to the regions of the cosmos. And the forces of the cosmos are also present within the temple and the human body, or they can be called down to inhabit them.

The path of the priest is first of all a path of study and discipline, for it is necessary to memorize the spirit registers and the appropriate rituals for summoning the gods. Typically a priest would pass this knowledge and expertise on to one of his sons—the rule being one priest in each generation of the family. So through a long discipline of study and practice the Taoist priest becomes adept at the rituals, able to summon the great powers into this realm and into his own body to bring about renewal and transformation.

In ancient times the path included the practice of alchemy, creating a kind of gold-dust fluid to drink for the purpose of nourishing the inner forces and prolonging life. More important for Taoists today, the path includes various practices of bodily exercises and meditation designed to nourish the life-forces. It is believed that the most important elements in the body

are the breath, the spermatic essence, and the spirit. These are present throughout the body but are especially concentrated in the three Cinnabar fields, namely, the head, the heart, and just below the navel. These three fields are also the special realms of the Three Pure Ones, the great stellar gods that inhabit the body. The processes of yin and yang are also at work in the body, for the yang soul came from Heaven and the yin soul from earth. As life goes on, yang gradually is used up and yin increases, leading to an imbalance. And finally breath, seminal essence, and spirit are dissipated in death.

The path followed by the Taoist adept is designed to reverse this process, to renew the heavenly yang forces and thus restore vitality to breath, seminal essence, and spirit. There are methods of inner contemplation in which the One Tao is meditated upon; and through a visualization technique the Three Pure Ones are summoned into the three fields of the body to bring renewal. There is also visualization of the gods who dwell in each point and each organ of the body, and visualization of the heavenly bodies and planets that also descend into the body. Further, there are breathing techniques, gymnastics, and dietetics to free the body of impurities, clear the channels of circulation throughout the body, and nourish the primordial breaths. One important practice is guiding the breath through the different fields of the body to nourish the vital forces.

Since it is only the Taoist priests who know the names and characteristics of each of these spiritual forces, together with the elaborate techniques for summoning them to provide renewal, this is a path of transformation that is followed by the priests and adepts, not by the common people, even through they also reap benefits from it.

But what about the average person? Does she have no path of transformation, no way to find the life that is whole and blessed with harmony? Of course, an important part of the religious path for the common people is relying on the priests and experts for their services, in the great festivals, critical life events such as marriages and funerals, and times of sickness and other need. The priests and experts can restore the balance of sacred forces by exorcising the evil spirits and calling down the great gods to renew life force and restore harmony. In this respect religious Taoism resembles other religions, such as some forms of Christianity or Hinduism, in which there is reliance on the authority of ritual experts to effect the desired transformations. For example, only those with proper training and authority can say the Christian mass or chant the Hindu Vedas for the desired transformation. So, too, in religious Taoism, one part of the path for laypeople is to respect and rely on these ritualists and experts in the Tao.

But laypeople themselves have appropriate involvement on the path, for the sake of maintaining a balance of sacred forces in their personal lives, in family, and in community. These practices go beyond religious Taoism strictly speaking, including Buddhist and Confucian elements together with long-held local folk traditions. The popular religious path has many variables, but it centers around the cult of popular gods and goddesses, the ancestral cult, and personal spiritual cultivation.

Whereas the priests summon the great cosmic gods of the Prior Heavens that bring renewal and harmony to the universe, there are other powers in our world that have a lot to do with health and happiness in our lives, and when we are out of balance with these powers we suffer in various ways. So people can go to the local temple and worship the gods who have demonstrated their power and importance. For example, Kuan Yin, a Buddhist bodhisattva of great mercy, is to many people a compassionate mother, the giver of children, and a source of help in time of need. The Jade Emperor, a Taoist cosmic god, is also the supreme god to whom all the local gods report. The path of the laypeople means invoking and worshiping these gods and many more, so that the sacred balance may be maintained in their personal lives.

The theory of the ancestor cult is rooted in the conviction that the souls of the dead ancestors continue existence after death, and that the original family relationship remains in full force, with the ancestors possessing even more spiritual power than they had in life. The dead and the living are mutually dependent on each other, the living providing sacrifices and care for the graves, the ancestors providing blessings. To maintain harmony in this reciprocal relationship, people need carefully to fulfill the requirements for proper funerals and graves, offer continuing sacrifices to the ancestors, and observe the seasonal visits to clean and repair the graves. In all of these activities, the family and clan maintain a continuing sense of wholeness and cohesion, bound together in the love and remembrance of the ancestors.

Of course, laypeople involve themselves in varying degrees of religious discipline for personal transformation. Some, usually among the older, retire from normal life and spend much time in devotion, praying, and reading sacred texts. Some practice meritorious deeds, such as being vegetarian to avoid killing animal life. And it is not uncommon for laypeople to practice some kind of meditation, for spiritual advancement or for promoting health and longevity.

Buddhist Paths of Transformation in China

The path followed by average Chinese people has been significantly influenced by Buddhism as by the other Chinese religions. We discussed (in Part III) the basic Buddhist path, but we need to take note of the important Chinese contributions to the shaping of the Mahayana path of transformation. We can focus on the two major schools, Pure Land and Ch'an.

Worship of Buddha Amitabha (Amita) was known from early times in India, but the main emphasis had been on the discipline of meditation. Two major new ideas were introduced by the Chinese Pure Land masters to make this path more appealing and more usable by the common people. Amita's original vows were interpreted to mean that simply reciting the name of Amita with faith in one's heart is sufficient to attain rebirth in the Pure Land through Amita's power. And, based on the Mahayana emphasis that all living beings possess the Buddha-nature, the Chinese Pure Land masters taught that even those who have committed evil deeds and atrocities can be reborn in the Pure Land if they sincerely desire it. Here is a Chinese path of salvation open to everyone, and as a result Amita became very widely worshiped in China.

The path of transformation offered by the Ch'an school focuses almost exclusively on meditation, with many similarities to Theravada and early Buddhism in

Buddhist monks at a temple in Peking in 1966.

this regard. Becoming totally aware of the true nature of reality is what brings transformation. But meditation in the Ch'an school is based on Mahayana principles— that all reality is the universal Buddha-nature, that nirvana is not different from samsara, and that one's original nature is the Buddha-nature. Through meditation it is possible for anyone, learned or unlearned, to awaken to this true Buddha-nature. Scriptures and orthodox doctrines are not necessary, for the Ch'an masters held there was a special transmission of the truth outside doctrines, a direct transmission from mind to mind. The basic path was simply to strive constantly to have no notions but to see directly into one's nature.

Therefore the master-disciple relationship was crucial in the Ch'an path; in private interviews the master would teach and provoke the disciple, until finally, at a critical moment, the disciple would experience a spontaneous awakening to the Buddha-nature. Stories about these master-disciple encounters were later collected and became a characteristic part of Ch'an literature. A typical example is the story told about Lin-chi I-hsuan (d. 867). Lin-chi went to talk with Master Huang-po, asking him the real meaning of Bodhidharma coming from the West (a standard question in Ch'an interviews). Immediately Huang-po struck him. Lin-chi came back to visit the master three times, but each time he received blows. Finally, on Huang-po's advice, Lin-chi went to visit another master, Ta-yu, who asked him what Huang-po had taught him. Lin-chi answered, "When I asked him for the real meaning of Buddhism, he immediately struck me. Three times I put this question to him, and three times I received blows. I don't know where I was at fault." But Master Ta-yu cried out, "Your master treated you entirely with motherly kindness, and yet you say you do not know your fault." Upon hearing this, Lin-chi was suddenly awakened and stated, "After all, there isn't much in Huang-po's Buddhism!"[44]

It appears that Ch'an was influenced considerably by the Taoist path of meditation and cultivating freedom of living in the world. Ch'an emphasized that one need not try to escape from the change and flux of the world. The path itself is enlightenment and freedom. The Buddha-nature is universal and can be realized without any special searching, in the commonness of daily existence. Often-quoted words of Master Lin-chi I-hsuan make this point in a dramatic way:

> Seekers of the Way. In Buddhism no effort is necessary. All one has to do is to do nothing, except to move his bowels, urinate, put on his clothing, eat his meals, and lie down if he is tired. The stupid will laugh at him, but the wise one will understand. . . .
>
> Seekers of the Way, if you want to achieve the understanding according to the Law, don't be deceived by others and turn to [your thoughts] internally or [objects] externally. Kill anything that you happen on. Kill the Buddha if you happen to meet him. Kill a patriarch or an arhat if you happen to meet him. Kill your parents or relatives if you happen to meet them. Only then can you be free, not bound by material things, and absolutely free and at ease. . . . My views are few. I merely put on clothing and eat meals as usual, and pass my time without doing anything. You people coming from the various directions have all made up your minds to seek the Buddha, seek the Law, seek emancipation, and seek to leave the Three Worlds. Crazy people! If you want to leave the Three Worlds, where can you go? "Buddha" and "patriarchs" are terms of praise and also bondage. Do you want to know where the Three Worlds are? They are right in your mind which is now listening to the Law.[45]

The path in the Ch'an tradition is not a matter of striving to escape the samsara world and achieve nirvana. The path itself is enlightenment.

DISCUSSION QUESTIONS

1. Reflect on the nature of the Tao as the source of all existence.
2. What is the difference between the Taoist gods of the "Prior Heavens" and the gods of popular religion?
3. What are some basic implications about the world to be drawn from the P'an Ku myth?
4. How do yin and yang and the five elements operate as part of the world process?
5. What does it mean to say the human body is a "microcosm" of the great universe itself?
6. Review the discussion in the Confucian tradition about whether humans are basically inclined to good or evil. Which view becomes dominant?
7. What view does Taoism (the Tao Te Ching and Chuang Tzu) put forth as to the nature and problem of human existence?
8. How can study be transformative? How can ritual and the practice of social propriety be transformative?
9. Explain the Taoist principle of nonaction (wu-wei). How can this be transformative?
10. Describe the path of transformation as taught in Pure Land and Ch'an Buddhism.

CHAPTER 24

WORSHIP AND THE GOOD LIFE IN CHINA

RITUAL RENEWAL AND WORSHIP

"How can I find new power for life, new meaning in my everyday existence?" Ritual has always been very important in Chinese society—after all, one of the ancient texts is the Classic of Rites. Confucian thinkers have taught and written a lot about the proper practice of ritual and what it means. From time immemorial Chinese have ritualized all facets of family life and life within the state's political community, and there are frequent colorful and spectacular Taoist rituals and folk festivals. Since the religious traditions of China are so interwoven, it is not possible to draw sharp distinctions between the rituals of the different traditions in all cases.

We look first at what are generally recognized as Confucian and as Taoist rituals, and then we consider the more general festivals and rituals of the life cycle. Although we speak of Chinese ritual and worship in the present tense, it should be remembered that this applies to pre-Maoist China and to Chinese communities in Taiwan, Hong Kong, and overseas.

Worship and Ritual in the Confucian Tradition

Confucianists traditionally placed a strong emphasis on ceremony and ritual. The term "ritual" or "propriety" (*li*) as used by Confucius goes back to the ritual sacrifices offered to the ancestors. Confucian scholars thoroughly investigated the function of ritual to show how it serves to transform and renew life. In fact, ritual is a cosmological principle upholding the whole universe, according to Hsun Tzu (ca. 298–238 B.C.E.):

> It is through rites that Heaven and earth are harmonious and sun and moon are bright, that the four seasons are ordered and the stars are on their courses, that rivers flow and that things prosper, that love and hatred are tempered and joy and anger are in keeping.[1]

Performance of ritual helps to uphold the universe, to stay in communion with the ancestors, and to harmonize human society.

Ritual in the Family and the Cult of the Ancestors

The Confucian emphasis on ritual is most apparent in aspects of family and community life that have to do with the principles of hierarchy and reciprocity. It is through ritual that the relationship is maintained between parent and child, between ancestor and descendent, between friend and friend. Perhaps the most important rituals are those that hold the family together in proper order, that is, the rituals expressing and cultivating filial piety. The idea of reciprocity, of mutual dependence of younger and elder, of living and dead, is basic to these ritual actions.

Each traditional home will have an altar on which the ancestral tablets are kept and also where images of the gods important to the family are worshiped. Incense is offered on the table before the altar daily, usually by a woman of the house. On important occasions, the central ritual actions in worshiping the ancestors and the gods include offerings of food, offering of spirit money, acts of reverence such as kowtowing (prostrating oneself), and prayers. Since the ancestors are kinspeople, they are offered food in much the same form as the family's guests. The table in front of the altar is set with rice bowls, chopsticks, spices and condiments, and fully prepared dishes hot from the stove, including cooked rice. Food offerings are also made to the gods in the home, and on certain occasions meals are offered to the homeless spirits—but these are always placed outside the house. Paper spirit money is also sometimes offered at the altar, usually silver for ancestors and gold for the gods. Kowtowing before the ancestors and the gods is an essential act of reverence, and the number of kowtows depends on the status of the spirit being worshiped—a person may kowtow four times before ancestors, for example, only twice before the Stove God, and a hundred times before Lord Shang Ti. Further, kowtowing is done in the proper order in the family hierarchy.

Here are some excerpts from a description of family worship during the ancestor festival of the seventh month, in a town in southwestern China in the early 1940s.

> The dishes offered on this occasion are all elaborately prepared and contain chicken, pork, fish, and vegetables. Each dish is topped with flower designs. If the household worships as one unit, all dishes, together with at least six bowls of rice, six cups of wine, and six pairs of chopsticks are laid on the offering table in advance. Members of the household then kowtow one after the other before the altar....
>
> They kowtow before the altar, the elder before the younger, and men before women. The usual number of kowtows appears to be four, but often individual members perform this obeisance five, nine, or even more times....
>
> When the offerings and homage at the family altar terminates, the same dishes are taken by a male member of the household (or branch of the household) to the clan temple. There the food is briefly offered at the main altar, and the male who delivers it kowtows a number of times. After this, the offering food is taken back to the

house, and all members of the household come together to feast on it. . . .

After the meal the *shu pao* (burning the bags) ceremony begins. Each bag contains a quantity of [paper] silver ingots and bears the names of a male ancestor and his wife, of the descendants who are providing the bag for them, and the date on which this is burned, together with a brief plea entreating the ancestors to accept it. . . .

A big container with some ashes and a bit of fire is placed in the middle of the courtyard just outside the west wing of the house. A young member of the household then kneels on a straw cushion beside the container, facing the west wing. The rest of the household may be sitting or standing around him. All the bags are heaped beside the kneeler. He first picks up the bag for the most ancient lineal ancestor, reads slowly everything that is written on it, and then puts it on the fire. . . . After all bags are burned, the ashes are poured into a stream which finally carries them into the lake.[2]

Worship in the Community and the State

Beyond the family, the Confucian principle of ritual permeates community and government life. At the local level, officials, magistrates, and governors perform rituals for the harmony and happiness of the community. And at the highest levels, up until the twentieth century, the emperor and the supreme officials performed rituals directed to Heaven and earth and the royal ancestors, for the harmony and welfare of the whole people.

An example of worship in the state cult would be the emperor's sacrifice to Heaven at the winter solstice, during the longest night of the year. The emperor and his officials arose before dawn and climbed to the top of a great stone altar south of the city (the direction of yang). The ancestors and other gods were represented by inscribed tablets on the altar, and food was placed before them. A young red bull (a symbol of yang) was offered to Heaven, and wine, incense, and silk were presented together with music from bells and drums. It was important that all the ritual be done well on the emperor's part, so that Heaven and the ancestors would do their part and assist in the rebirth of yang and the coming of spring once again, for the benefit of all nature and society.

The Altar of Heaven in Peking.

In traditional China, officials were assigned by the imperial government to have charge over a particular locality, and it was each official's job to worship the spiritual powers for the welfare of his territory. Important in the local capital was the Confucian temple, whose main hall contained the spirit-tablets of Confucius and other sages. Sacrifices were held here twice yearly, in midspring and midautumn, with the city magistrate as the chief celebrant and the senior officials in attendance. At dawn sacrifices were placed before the tablet of Confucius, including a roll of silk, chalices of wine, bowls of soup, other food dishes, an ox, a pig, and a sheep. The officials lined the sides of the courtyard below the hall, and six ranks of young students in traditional costume postured with long wands tipped with pheasant feathers. Drums and an orchestra playing an ancient melody accompanied the ceremonies, as the celebrant made each offering, together with kowtows and hymns of praise. An observer marked that

> . . . it is in reality one of the most impressive rituals that
> has ever been devised. The silence of the dark hour, the
> magnificent sweep of the temple lines, with eaves curv-
> ing up toward the stars, the aged trees standing in the
> courtyard, and the deep note of the bell, make the scene
> unforgettable to one who has seen it even in its decay. In
> the days of Kubilai the magnificence and solemnity of
> the sacrifice would have required the pen of a Coleridge
> to do it justice. The great drum boomed upon the night,
> the twisted torches of the attendants threw uncertain
> shadows across the lattice scrolls, and the silk embroi-
> deries on the robes of the officials gleamed from the
> darkness.
> The flutes sounded, and the chant rose and fell in
> strange, longdrawn quavers.
> "*Pai*," and the officials fell to their knees, bending
> forward till their heads touched the ground.
> "*Hsin*," and they were erect again.
> Within the hall, the ox lay with his head toward the
> image of Confucius. The altar was ablaze with dancing
> lights, which were reflected from the gilded carving
> of the enormous canopy above. Figures moved slowly
> through the hall, the celebrant entered, and the vessels
> were presented toward the silent statue of the sage, the
> "Teacher of Ten Thousand Generations." The music
> was grave and dignified, and the sound of the harsh
> Mongolian violin was absent. The dancers struck their
> attitudes, moving their wands tipped with pheasant
> feathers in unison as the chant rose and fell.
> It would be hard to imagine a more solemn and
> beautiful ritual, or one set in more impressive sur-
> roundings. . . .[3]

At the local level, town officials go out on every new
and full moon to worship and burn incense to T'u Ti,
the local earth god, and to pray for the welfare of the
people, so that the reciprocal relationship will be maintained and harmony and prosperity will continue. One
simple but typical prayer to the earth god reads:

> *Wei!* The efficacy of *shen* [the earth god] extends so far as
> to transform and sustain, to preserve and protect all
> [within these] city walls. *Shen* defends the nation and
> shelters the people, and all we officials rely upon him
> completely. Now, during the mid-spring (or, mid-
> autumn), we respectfully offer animals and sweet wine
> in this ordinary sacrifice. Deign to accept them.[4]

Worship in Religious Taoism and Popular Religion

Just as some aspects of worship and ritual are linked
with Confucian ideas and principles, we can identify
other kinds of rituals more specifically with religious
Taoism. Of course, the line between religious Taoism
and the more general popular relious rituals and festivals is indistinct and there is no particular need to
separate them rigorously. Some of the rituals are performed specifically by priests or experts for their own
transformation, but most of them are to help and benefit the people whom the priests serve. Reciprocity is
also a principle of Taoist religious ritual, the mutual
exchange of gifts and benefits between people and
gods, the setting up of a reciprocating contract or
relationship.

Summoning the Gods: Cosmic Renewal

Taoist priests are recognized primarily by the level of
their command of the sacred powers. The people are
also served by exorcists, those who are familiar with the
local gods and can use rituals to bring their power to
bear on evil spirits that cause sickness and ill fortune.
Taoist priests (*tao shih*), in addition, are familiar with
the great gods of the universe, knowing their names
and their characteristics, able to summon them when
needed. Taoist priests chant scriptures and use written
formulas, ritual implements, and ritual dances to accomplish what is necessary for repulsing evil spirits
and obtaining boons from the higher gods. In addition,
the priest makes use of internal rituals such as meditation, visualization, and ritual breath control.

The rituals used by Taoist priests have a long history,
going back to the methods for attaining immortality
practiced by the Heavenly Master sect and other sects
from the later Han era on. The rituals are based on the
belief that the Taoist's body is a microcosm of the great
cosmos, and that therefore the great gods of the stellar
constellations can be summoned into the body to supply power of renewal. Today the main ritual that still
contains the purely Taoist rituals is the Chiao, the Rite
of Cosmic Renewal, performed in Taiwan by Taoist
priests to renew a particular community's covenant

with the highest gods. Chiao are held at different intervals depending on the community, and they may last from one to as many as seven days, although three days is the most likely duration.

What makes the Chiao different from the many other popular rituals and festivals is that the powers addressed are not the gods of local popular religion but the Three Pure Ones, the threefold primal expression of the Tao. The Three Pure Ones receive only "pure" offerings (wine, tea, cakes, and fruit), in contrast to the meat sacrifices offered to the popular gods. And they are worshiped by the Taoist priests inside the temple, unseen by the people who carry on their own popular religious rituals outside in the community during this festival. Occasionally the two celebrations come together when the Taoist entourage emerges to perform some rituals for the people, but essentially what goes on inside the purified temple is something that can be done only by qualified Taoist priests: summoning the great gods and renewing the whole community through the primordial power of the Tao. The people's participation is in the form of contributions and support for the Taoist experts.

To prepare for the Chiao the temple is sealed except for one door, and the gods of the people are removed from their places of honor along the north wall and placed on the south, to prepare for the coming of the Three Pure Ones and the other Heavenly Worthies from the realm of pure yang. The temple area is set up as a model of the Prior Heavens, with scrolls representing the Three Pure Ones on the north wall and other important gods represented on the east and west wall. In the center is an altar at which the priests stand, with a brass bowl on the east side giving forth yang sounds when struck and a hollow wooden sphere on the west side to give forth yin sounds when struck. The chief priest stands in the center, while acolytes to the east and west chant the liturgy alternately, representing the alternation of yin and yang in the universe. The vestments worn by the priests are symbolic of the powers of the universe, including the flame-shaped golden pin on top of the chief priest's crown, showing that he is lighted from within by the eternal Tao.

The rituals performed by the priests are very elaborate and complicated. They include summoning all the spirits to attend and then the very dramatic ritual of purifying the sacred area, sealing it off so no forces of yin can enter. Perhaps some sense of the intense religious drama can be felt in Michael Saso's description of a Chiao in which he participated (as a Taoist priest):

The chief Taoist and all present are then purified by the reciting of prayers that penetrate deeply into every part of the body. . . . Through the purificatory cleansing of the ritual, all three of the microcosmic sections of the body, with eight orders of spirits in each, corresponding to the three times eight or twenty-four cosmic realms, are filled with the *Tao*. . . .

The Taoist then calls upon the orthodox spirits of the seven Pole Stars to come and fill the body; he asks specifically that the three Pole Stars of the Dipper's handle, which control man's destiny, come and fill the three realms of the body, upper, middle and lower, in order to give birth to, nourish, and protect the "*Tao*-life" conceived within. It is specifically into the Taoist's body that the spirits are called; and with the Taoist as mediator, they are infused into the bodies of all those present.

Next the Taoist performs a sacred dance called the "Steps of *Yu*," based upon the nine positions of the magic square called *Lo Shu*, dragging one foot behind the other, imitating the lame pace of *Yu* when he stopped the floods, . . . with the same efficacy that *Yu* the Great had when he paced around the nine provinces of the ancient empire, ordering nature and stopping natural calamity. . . .

Now the climax has been reached, as the Taoist begins to trace another heavenly dance step, that of the seven stars of the Great Dipper, in the center of the area. He summons the exorcising spirits of the north to close all entrance to the sacred area from spirits of malevolence, *Yin*, or death. Next, he summons all the heavenly spirits [and a long list of all the great sacred powers] to assemble now at once in the sacred area, right at the devil's door, and seal it forever.

Taking the great sword in his right hand, the Taoist then draws a circle on the floor, three revolutions from left to right, that is, clockwise, going toward the center. Then over this he draws another circle, this time from right to left, counter-clockwise. Over these two concentric circles he then draws seven horizontal lines, representing heaven, and seven vertical lines, representing earth. By thus sealing the Gate of Hell, that is, the northeast position, the primordial breath of earth and the seminal essence of wood can no longer flow away, but they with the *Tao* (spirit) can now be kept within, that is, in the Yellow Court of the center. Finally, he draws the character for demon, *"Kuei,"* in the center of the figure, and runs it through with the sword, spraying the purifying water on it from his mouth. The Gate of Demons is now sealed, with primordial breath, semen, and spirit kept within, and the evil influences of *Yin* locked without. The sacred *T'an* area having been purified, the members of the entourage are filled with the orthodox *Yang* spirits of the heavens, the five elements are now in their life-giving order bearing *"Yang,"* and the liturgy of the encounter with the spirits of the Prior Heavens may begin.[5]

The liturgy goes on with continuous reading of scriptures, offerings to the heavenly guests, and lighting of the new fire of yang. As physical rituals are performed by the assistants, the chief priest performs internal meditation, summoning the great gods of the universe, visualizing within himself the process of restoring the universe to the pristine vigor of yang. The high priest has special audiences with the Three Pure Ones to make them present, and finally he brings the Three together in the center to offer them a great banquet accompanied by a heavenly ritual dance. Then the petitions of the whole community are sent off to the assembled gods by burning the paper slips on which they were written. Finally, the priests go outside the front of the temple and present the petitions of the community to the Jade Emperor and the other gods who rule this changing world. The whole community has now been renewed through the powers of the heavenly world of pure yang.

In addition to these essential Taoist rituals, the Chiao contains many rituals promoting the welfare of the people. The presence of the ancestors is especially felt, for they have been invited to attend by the Taoist priests, and there is a great procession to float paper lanterns in the rivers, to summon the souls from the underworld. After the presentation of the petitions to the Jade Emperor outside the temple, a twenty-four-course banquet is laid out for the ancestors and the orphan spirits, and the Taoist priests come out to perform the ritual to release all souls from hell. The great

celebration that follows is a fitting conclusion to the Rite of Cosmic Renewal; meantime, the Taoist priests alone in the temple send off the gods to the realms from which they came.

Rituals of Exorcism and Divination

Whereas the Chiao, held only occasionally, is the special time for the advanced Taoist priests to perform their highest role, much more common are the other rituals that the priests and exorcists perform for the service of the people in their everyday needs. The most important needs are illness, bad luck, and death, already experienced or anticipated. The Taoist priest, for example, will perform a brief ceremony for one in need, presenting a written memorial calling on the gods in charge, in exchange for offerings, to cause good fortune to come to the one named in the memorial. The memorial is read and then transmitted to the gods by burning. Mediums offer the service of communicating with the dead for various purposes, and both exorcists and priests perform rituals to deliver souls imprisoned in hell.

A most important occasion for Taoist ritual, of course, is a time of sickness. A Red-head Taoist priest on Taiwan, for example, in curing a child's sickness, first computes from the daily almanac the relative yin and yang influences for the child, depending on the date of birth, and then he determines the cause of illness (both natural and supernatural). The Taoist then summons the various gods at his command. On a piece of yellow paper he draws a talisman and signs it with a special seal. Lighting a candle, he recites an exorcistic mantra such as this:

> I command the source of all pains in the body—
> Muscle pains, headaches, eye sores, mouth sores
> Aching hands and aching feet
> [insert the particular ailment of the child]—
> With the use of this magic of mine,
> Here before this Taoist altar,
> May all demons be bound and captured,
> May they be chased back into Hell's depths.
> "Ch'iu-ch'iu Chieh-chieh"
> You are sent back to your source!
> Quickly, quickly, obey my command![6]

The priest casts the divination blocks, and once he receives a positive answer from the blocks the talisman is burned. Water with some of the ashes mixed in it is given to the child to drink, along with a prescription for medicines the priest thinks will cure the natural causes of the illness.

Some forms of exorcism pit the priest or exorcist against the power of the evil spirits causing the trouble. A major source of trouble is the soul of a person who has died violently or tragically and thus becomes a wandering spirit, and in such cases dramatic rituals of exorcism are needed. For example, a child drowned in a village pond in Taiwan and, since it happened while the image of the chief god of the village was away for a different village's festival, people thought an angry ghost had pulled the child in. But now the child's spirit would also become very harmful, having died so tragically. So the village leaders prepared an exorcism using divination chairs. These are small chairs each held by two bearers. Gods descend on these chairs and cause them to move about, sometimes violently, providing instructions on how to perform the exorcism by tracing out characters on a tabletop with one of the protruding arms. In this ritual, a local god became present on one chair and instructed the people to avoid speaking bad words to each other, since the death had caused disharmony in the village; furthermore, they should keep their children away from the fish pond. Then a second chair was possessed by the chief village god, who gave them instructions for the exorcism. The two gods would go into the pond to drive out the "bad thing" (avoiding the word "water ghost," which should not be spoken), and the people should stay away so that it would not lodge in their bodies. The wielders of the chair were instructed to carry spirit money signed by one of the gods—who proceeded to cause the arm of the chair to dip in ink and make a blot on sheets of spirit money that had been laid out on the table. The anthropologist's report becomes vivid:

> The men stuffed these into their pockets and left in a great hurry for the fish-pond, following the two wildly swinging divination chairs, which fairly dragged their wielders along the road. Upon arrival at the pond the chairs ran madly about the perimeter of the pond, then

hurled themselves and their bearers into the water, where they circled the pond several times more swinging up and down into and out of the water to drive out the bad thing. At the same time the onlookers shouted high-pitched shouts, hurled burning firecrackers over the pond, and threw handfuls of sesame seeds into the water. The shouting, the rain of sesame seeds, and the continual and ubiquitous explosions of firecrackers were all calculated to terrify the ghost, and added to this were the chairs of the gods ploughing through the water, hot on the trail of the startled ducks. When the gods climbed out at one bank, they would leap in wildly elsewhere and beat the water with renewed vigor.[7]

The key force for the exorcism is the command from the village god to the ghost—in this case conveyed rather dramatically to that ghost.

As seen in this example, rituals of divination are important in many Chinese ceremonies, for it is through divination that communication is established with the spirits, gods, and sacred forces. They can make their will known through a divination chair held by two bearers writing on a table, as we have just seen. Again, they can speak through a Y-shaped stick suspended above a shallow tray of sand, handled by a stick-wielder possessed by a particular god, scratching out characters that are "read" by a trained expert. Much of the revelation received from the gods comes through such spirit-writers.

There are other forms of divination based on reading the forces of yin and yang. The system contained in the I Ching (Classic of Changes) has been used continuously in China since ancient times. This system began as eight trigrams, consisting of all the possible combinations of three broken lines (yin) or unbroken lines (yang). This developed into sixty-four hexagrams by placing one trigram on another, working out all the possible combinations of six broken or unbroken lines. These patterns can be divined in various ways, such as by throwing coins to determine the yin or yang character of each line. The I Ching then is consulted, for it contains judgments and commentaries on each of the hexagrams, helping people understand how the universal forces are operating and how to stay in harmony with them.

Another example of rituals of divination is the practice of *feng-shui* (wind and water), which is the science of reading the interaction of the yin-yang forces at a particular place, to determine the best location and shape of a house or an ancestral grave. The geomancer (feng-shui expert) ritually determines where the yin and yang "breaths" are pulsating, finding the outlines of the azure dragon (yang) and the white tiger (yin) in the landscape and devising the best way to retain the breaths in maximum harmony and vitality. To accomplish this, trees are often planted behind the house to counteract evil exhalations and a freshwater pond placed in front.

But much worship and divination need not involve Taoist priests or experts. Anyone can go to the temples to visit the local gods, give offerings to them, and seek their help. After all, they are in their position as gods because they have shown that they can provide benefits to the people as they worship them. The whole community—people and gods—are bound up in a reciprocal relationship. The gods are housed in temples, their official residences, lesser gods first and then the principal god in the center. The temple doors are open at all times, and people can go in at any time to bring personal problems to the gods. The worshiper lights several sticks of incense and places them in the brazier on the altar. She bows before the altar to show respect, sometimes burning paper spirit money or offering different kinds of food. Then she consults the god about her personal problem or question, and for this she can use rituals of divination to see what the divine answer is so that she knows what course of action to take. One simple ritual is to throw two divination blocks on the floor before the altar. The blocks are rounded on one side and flat on the other (like the halves of a banana that has been split lengthwise). A flat side down signifies yin in the ascendancy, and a rounded side down signifies yang in the ascendancy. So it is when one rounded side and one flat side are up together that yin and yang are in harmony—and that is an affirmative answer from the god. Another method of divination is

Worshipers at the Wong Tai Sin Temple in Kowloon lighting joss sticks; some are shaking bamboo containers to obtain a numbered stick by which their fortune can be told.

to shake numbered sticks out of a vase, taking the first stick to fall out to the attendant, who matches the number with a slip of paper and interprets one's destiny for the occasion from what is written on the paper.

Buddhist Influences in Chinese Worship and Ritual

Buddhist rituals and worship in the home and at temples or monasteries, as described in Part III, have been a part of Chinese worship life for many, even those who also participate in Confucian and Taoist rituals. In popular religious practices, Buddhist rituals and prayers, for example, those dedicated to the great bodhisattva Kuan-yin, mingle together with other non-Buddhist rituals. Some temples have room for Buddhas and bodhisattvas along with Confucian and Taoist deities, so rituals can be directed to whichever one or ones are appropriate for the current need. Among people more specifically committed to the Buddhist path, many have altars in their homes, near the shrine that holds the ancestral tablets, and they offer incense to the Buddha image and recite sutras. In addition to worship in families and in temples, some join lay societies that meet together regularly for worship, reciting favorite Buddhist scriptures or chanting Buddha Amita's name, sometimes six or seven hours a day.

Ritual and worship at Buddhist monasteries in traditional China developed some characteristic Chinese forms. The ritual of tonsure symbolizes the beginning of life as a novice monk. In the presence of other monks and novices, the master and the candidate prostrate themselves before the Buddha image and offer incense. Then the candidate hands a razor to the master, saying, "I, your disciple, today beg Your Reverence to be the Teacher who shaves my hair. . . . I wish to renounce lay life as your dependent." After admonishing him about the meaning of shaving his head, the master cuts off his hair and the novice changes into a monk's gown.[8]

Full ordination in Chinese Buddhism involves elaborate rituals. According to the traditional pattern, after a training period of several weeks at the ordaining monastery, a first ordination is held in which the ordainees recite the Three Refuges and the Ten Precepts. After a night of penance, followed by ritual bathing, they process to a secluded ordination platform and accept the monastic vows collectively, then go up to the platform in groups of three to be examined and accepted as monks or nuns by the three ordination masters. A week later they recite the "Bodhisattva Vows," which impose a commitment to lead all sentient beings into nirvana before attaining it themselves. A special feature of Chinese Buddhist ordination is the ritual of burning "incense scars" into the scalp at the end of the ordination ceremonies. Cones of moxa are placed on wax on the novice's head and then lighted by a head monk. As the cones burn down into the scalp other monks hold the novice to help control the pain, and all chant prayers until the ordeal is over—and the new monk or nun is branded for life.

Buddhist rituals are most fully practiced in the monastic setting, and Homes Welch has provided a detailed description of the daily ritual routine in a Ch'an monastery.[9] The monks are awakened at 3:00 a.m. to wash and march to the great shrine hall to recite morning devotion to the accompaniment of a liturgical orchestra of monks sounding a handchime, wooden fish, bell-and-drum, cymbals, and hand-gong. The liturgy consists of scriptures, poems of praise to the Buddha, the Three Refuges, and reciting the Buddha's name. Then the monks recite Buddha Amitabha's name while processing in a serpentine course around the shrine hall and in the courtyard. At breakfast an acolyte takes seven grains of rice from a bowl in front of a Buddha image and places them out for the hungry ghosts, after which the monks eat in silence, meditating on the debt they owe to those who provided the food. After visiting the latrines, the monks join in circumambulation, a rapid walking or "running" while swinging their arms, meditating all the while.

At 7:00 a.m. they go to the meditation hall, sitting in exact order of rank. They sit erect in silence with crossed legs, while a meditation patrol observes carefully. If someone dozes, the patrol goes before him and strikes him with the incense board on the upper part of the back as a reminder. At 8:00 there begins another cycle of "running" and then sitting in meditation. At 9:00 they go to the refectory for some rice and then, back at their seats, are served tea, the first of three teas served to them during the day. There is a "noon meditation" period, followed by yet another meditation period, lasting until 2:00. Then comes another meal, after which the monks may go to the apartment of the abbot or an instructor for discussion about their progress. Around 3:00 comes the afternoon worship in the great shrine hall, the liturgy including the reading of the Pure Land sutra. For about two hours the monks have a rest period in the meditation hall, but then comes the longest and most important meditation period of the day, lasting an hour and a half. At 8:00 a meal is served to them in their seats, followed by "running," an exhortation by the abbot, and still another period of sitting in meditation, ending at 10:00 with lights out.

During special intensive training for seven weeks starting on the fifteenth of the tenth month, the daily regimen is much stricter, with monks leaving the meditation hall only for meals and once a week to bathe. Their running and sitting cycles add up to fifteen hours a day.

In addition to their monastic rituals, the monks are often called on to perform rituals of chanting scripture on various occasions for laypeople, especially for funerals and for anniversaries of deaths.

Sacred Times in the Chinese Traditions

Although much of the worship and ritual in China depends on the specific needs of the people, one major need is to have regular times for renewal of life—that is, seasonal festivals, special holy days, sacred times that occur periodically to revitalize life and the bonds with family, ancestors, and community.

Birthday Festivals of the Gods

One of the favorite days of communal celebration is the birthday festival of the god, whether this is one of the great gods traditionally worshiped throughout China or one of the local gods worshiped especially by the people of the local community. Widely celebrated with great excitement, for example, are the birthday festivals of the Jade Emperor (ninth day of the first lunar month); Lao Tzu (fifteenth of the second month); Bodhisattva Kuan-yin (nineteenth of the second month); Ma Tzu, the goddess of seafarers and Consort of Heaven (twenty-third of the third month); the Buddha Shakyamuni (eighth day of the fourth month); Kuan Kung, the warrior-protector (twenty-fourth of the sixth month); and Confucius (twenty-seventh of the eighth month). But each community also celebrates the birthday of its own local T'u Ti, the earth god, and the other important gods of the village or community.

These divine birthday festivals have colorful processions in the city streets, packed with sightseers and worshipers. There are offerings of food, lighting of candles and incense, and burning of spirit money. The honored god is carried in a large sedan chair, with firecrackers to announce his or her coming and a band playing traditional music. Multitudes join in the parade, dressed in court clothes and carrying placards. People hail the god as she or he passes by, holding infants in arms to be blessed and protected. All such festivals include standard theatricals or operas to entertain the gods as well as their human audiences.

The festival of the Buddha's birthday, unlike the other birthday festivals, is completely Buddhist in orientation. A small image of the Buddha is placed in a basin of fragrant water with flower petals. Worshipers ladle dippers of water over the image in honor of the gods bathing the Buddha immediately after his birth.

New Year's Festival and Other Annual Festivals

The New Year, of course, has important symbolic meaning for all peoples as the renewing of time and of life that has run down in the course of the past year. In China the New Year's Festival has long been the most important and elaborate of all the festivals. The Chinese New Year, fixed according to the lunar calendar, comes in late January or early February, a time of renewal and celebration before the start of spring planting. Events begin ten days earlier with housecleaning and closing of business offices. About a week before New Year's eve, the God of the Cooking Stove is sent off to heaven to report to the Jade Emperor on the behavior of the family members for the past year. It is traditional to take his printed image from the wall and smear his mouth with syrup before sending him off by burning, so that he will only tell sweet things. He returns home on New Year's eve, when a new picture is pasted up over the stove, to be present for the main event of the New Year festival: the family feast on New Year's eve, when important rituals of family bonding are held.

On New Year's eve, the family members worship Heaven and earth, the tutelary gods of the home, and the family ancestors. At the conclusion of these rites, all family members who can possibly be there—but no outsiders—join in the family feast. Then, to show respect for the living elders, each family member comes forward in order of precedence to kowtow to the family head and his wife. Firecrackers are set off, and on New Year's day and several days afterward courtesy visits are made to relatives and friends. The season ends at the full moon (fifteenth day of the first month) with a celebration of light called the Lantern Festival.

Two other major annual festivals are the Dragon Boat and the Mid-Autumn Festivals. The Dragon Boat Festival ("double fifth," i.e., fifth day of the fifth lunar month), popular in south China, features dragon boat racing and making triangular-shaped rice dumplings wrapped in bamboo leaves. The festival has to do with the summer solstice that occurs about this time, the high point of yang and the beginning of its displacement by yin. The Mid-Autumn Festival (fifteenth of the eighth lunar month), celebrating the autumn harvest as in many cultures, features enjoyment of the beauty of the harvest moon and round sweet pastries called "moon cakes."

Two other main festivals have to do primarily with honoring the ancestors: the Ch'ing Ming (pure and bright) Festival on the third of the third lunar month (early April), and the Feast of Souls on the fifteenth of the seventh lunar month (late August). For the Ch'ing Ming Festival, the people bathe in flowing streams to wash away the dirt and harmful forces that have accumulated during the winter, and they put out all old fires for three days before starting new fires by rubbing two sticks together—the rebirth of spring yang power. Most importantly, family members process out to spend the day at the ancestral graves, cleaning the tombs, offering food to the ancestors, and renewing family ties with a joyful, hearty picnic feast.

The Feast of Souls (Ullambana) was influenced by Buddhist ideas of souls in purgatory. The souls of the

Worshipers and onlookers at a Buddhist temple in Hangchow.

ancestors are worshiped on the fifteenth day, when family members give offerings and sometimes burn spirit money and other paper equipment for the comfort of the dead souls. But during the whole month it is believed the gates of purgatory stand open and the souls from purgatory—the hungry ghosts—wander about before being sent back to purgatory on the last day of the month. Out of compassion for their plight and in recognition that one's own ancestors might be suffering in purgatory, families set out offerings of food for them. During this festival many rituals are performed by Buddhist monks (and Taoist priests, to a lesser extent). In the great services in the middle of this month, the monks recite the Chinese Buddhist scripture which tells how the monk Mu-lien descended to the deepest hell to rescue his mother from her miseries there, and how this festival was instituted to save the ancestors, at least temporarily, from the tortures of purgatory. The ritual is called "ferrying across [to salvation] all [souls]," and the general population joins in the extensive ceremonies associated with this ritual of universal salvation.

Rituals of the Life Cycle in China

Since the family is the locale of meaning in an individual's life, the rituals connected with the important passages in a person's life—birth, puberty, marriage, and death—are, as in most cultures, closely connected with the family. And since the family is focused on the ancestors, these rituals are performed with close attention to the ancestors.

Not much attention is paid to individual birthdays in China—the real birthday for everyone is New Year's day when everyone is counted a year older—and so there are no particularly important religious rituals associated with birth. There are, of course, customs having to do with propitiating hungry ghosts that could cause harm during pregnancy and birth. And, naturally, offerings are made to the ancestors, the God of the Cooking Stove, all the gods in the family shrine, and the local patron god.

After years of education involving training both for livelihood and for carrying on the family traditions socially and ritually, young people enter into adulthood. Years ago there were special ceremonies of initiation, giving a new adult name and cap to a man in a "capping" ceremony, and providing a special hair-do and new clothes for a woman. In recent times the special coming-of-age ceremonies tend to be celebrated just before marriage.

As befits the strong emphasis on family and ancestors, the two most important celebrations in a lifetime are at marriage and death. A traditional Chinese marriage consists essentially in the ritual transfer of the bride from her own patrilineal group to that of her husband-to-be, accompanied by exchange of gifts and agreements between the two families. They will consult a diviner to make sure the horoscopes of the couple are compatible and to set an auspicious date for the wedding ceremony. Then they formalize the engagement with exchange of gifts and visits of the young man and woman to their future parents-in-law. Gifts from the bridegroom's family go toward the woman's dowry, especially to buy furniture and other items for the new household. On the day of the wedding the woman's dowry is sent to the man's home in a procession through the streets. The groom's family hires a special red sedan chair to be sent to the bride's house to receive the bride, the groom himself riding in a blue sedan chair. This ritual leave-taking is full of the symbolism of separation, as shown in this description from

Taiwan:

> The arrival of the groom and his party to claim the bride quickens the pace of activity.... The go-between then calls the couple to the family altar to bow first to the gods and then to the girl's father's ancestors. At this point the sedan chair... is carried into the living room, and parents and daughter begin to exchange the ritual formulas of farewell, wishing each other long life, wealth, happiness, and for the bride, many sons. By this time mother and daughter are weeping uncontrollably.... The chair is closed, and the bearers carry it out of the house. The house doors are quickly slammed behind the bride's chair to prevent the wealth of the family from following the bride. Her brother spits or throws water on the departing chair to indicate that just as spilt water cannot be returned to the container, so the bride cannot return to her natal home.[10]

When the sedan chair procession arrives at the groom's home, the couple bows before the gods of Heaven and earth, the God of the Cooking Stove, and the ancestors, indicating that the bride is now part of her husband's lineage. Then the couple pays respects by kowtowing before the groom's parents, uncles, aunts, older brothers and sisters-in-law, and any other senior relatives. A great many guests have been invited, and the feasting may go on for several days.

Death rituals represent the culmination of life—the safe passage to ancestral status, with the soul secure in the family grave (the yin soul) and in the tablet kept on the ancestral altar (the yang soul). These funeral rituals are the most serious and protracted of all traditional Chinese rituals, and they are described only in brief outline here. Chinese are well aware of death and begin to prepare a proper coffin and a grave long before, though the actual duty of making funeral arrangements falls on their sons. When a person is near death, he or she is moved into the main hall of the home, where the ancestral tablets are kept. When the person dies, the body is covered with a coverlet red on top and white (the color of death) on the bottom, and food offerings are placed at the feet. The family don mourning garments and wash the body; and they send out cards announcing the death to relatives and friends, who come to wail and mourn. A soul-tablet is made with the name of the deceased and set up by Taoist or Buddhist priests to receive the prayers of the mourners. The grave jacket (longevity jacket) is put on the body, the corpse's mouth may be filled with rice, and the deceased is placed in a coffin together with paper spirit money. The family is in no hurry to remove the body from the home; they may wait weeks or even months for the auspicious day chosen for taking the coffin out for the final funeral rites.

After the coffin is taken outside, sacrifice is offered to the deceased and the coffin is sealed. Then the funeral procession is organized with a banner, musicians, and many symbolic palanquins. Most important is the sedan chair for the soul-tablet, followed by Taoist or Buddhist priests and then the coffin itself, carried by four or more pallbearers. The oldest son walks behind the coffin, followed by the other sons and all the rest of the mourners. The mourning clothes typically are of sackcloth, with different colors and types showing different relationships to the deceased. At the grave the soul-tablet is placed on an altar and the coffin is lowered into the pit. The filial son kneels with the soul-tablet, and it is dotted with a brush dipped in vermilion ink, signifying that it is now the actual residence of the soul of the deceased. This soul-tablet is carried home by the eldest grandson, seated in the sedan chair; finally the tablet is placed in the main hall to join the other ancestors.

Mourning continues for quite some time, showing proper respect and ensuring that the deceased person's soul will be in a beneficial relationship to the family as an important ancestor. The intensity of mourning and the length are determined by how closely one is related to the deceased; traditionally there were five degrees of mourning. First-degree mourning is for the sons, daughters, and spouse of the dead person, lasting from two to three years, in which they eat simple food and wear coarse clothing. Others are to observe mourning in a lighter tone; for example, the great grandsons wear clothes of joyous colors showing that the lineage of the dead ancestor will continue on.

Ritual and Art in Chinese Religions

As in all cultures and religions, art forms have always been intricately bound up with religious expression in China. Since the goal of religion in China is the fullest harmony with the natural forces, art enters in to express and perhaps even to create that harmony. The Taoist sense of letting the innermost truth of nature express itself is a key principle of art, and this was reinforced also by Ch'an Buddhism. And the Confucian notion of self-transformation through ritual also lends an importance to artistic pursuits.

The ancient Chinese emphasis on ritual led to the full cultivation of the aesthetics of movement, dance, drama, chanting, clothing, and especially music. The ancient texts particularly extol the art of music—meaning music and dance together—as expressive of full human emotions. Hsun Tzu had this to say about the art of music:

> This is the symbolism of music: the drum represents a vast pervasiveness; the bells represent fullness; the sounding stones represent restrained order; the mouth organs represent austere harmony; the flutes represent a spirited outburst; the ocarina and bamboo whistle represent breadth of tone; the zither represents gentleness; the lute represents grace; the songs represent purity and fulfillment; and the spirit of the dance joins with the Way of Heaven.[11]

Many art forms developed in typical Chinese ways under the influence of the religious vision, like poetry, novels, architecture, sculpture, painting, and more. We might single out architecture as particularly influenced by ideas about the yin-yang forces. A temple, for example, is typically surrounded by an outer wall with a high, decorated main gate opening to the south (yang influences) and has its back to the north (where baleful yin influences come from). There may be another inner gate, and then the central main hall with the god's throne and altar, with lesser halls to the sides and back, balancing each other to reflect cosmic order and thus to create sacred space.

A striking Chinese art form is monochrome ink landscape painting (plain black ink against a plain white background). Early Taoist painters strove to capture the authentic, spontaneous forms of nature, and later Ch'an Buddhist painters brought the ink landscape painting to a peak of naturalness and simple harmony. One of the main principles of Chinese painting was called "Spirit Resonance and Life Movement," and painters interpreted this to mean being filled with the creative power of nature (Tao) so that it could be expressed in spontaneous brushstrokes that were not so much skills of the painter but movements of the Tao itself. A few comments Su Shih (1036–1101) made about Yu-k'o (d. 1079) help us see the attitude:

> When Yu-k'o painted bamboos he was conscious only of the bamboos and not of himself as a man. Not only was he unconscious of his human form, but sick at heart he left his own body, and this was transformed into bamboos of inexhaustible freshness and purity. . . .
>
> In his earlier years Yu-k'o painted his bamboos

Seven Pines, by Tang-Tse-Hua from the Yuan period (1280–1367).

whenever he found some pure white silk or good paper. He grasped the brush quickly, brushing and splashing with it freely. He simply could not help (doing) it. . . .

> Painters of to-day draw joint after joint and pile up leaf on leaf. How can that become a bamboo? When you are going to paint a bamboo, you must first realize the thing completely in your mind. Then grasp the brush, fix your attention, so that you see clearly what you wish to paint; start quickly, move the brush, follow straight what you see before you, as the buzzard swoops when the hare jumps out. If you hesitate one moment, it is gone. Yu-k'o taught me thus.[12]

To paint bamboo, one should first sit down and meditate, harmonize one's spirit with Tao, become a bamboo—then pick up the brush and let the bamboo paint itself!

This Taoist approach to painting was further shaped by Confucianists into a way of self-cultivation and by Ch'an Buddhists into a way of enlightenment. Ch'an painters in particular influenced the Chinese theory of painting with Ch'an ideas of spontaneity and emptiness. The effortlessness and sudden insight of Ch'an meditation are reflected in the quick, spontaneous creation of a painting. And Ch'an painters sometimes made use of empty space more so than brushstrokes, reflecting their experience of the "emptiness" of reality. Reality is formless, and thus the function of what has form in the painting is to help one experience formlessness.

SOCIETY AND THE GOOD LIFE

"How should I live?" One who is Chinese belongs to a huge, multiethnic grouping of peoples speaking a variety of dialects, yet unified around Confucian traditions of the family and the nation. The good life consists in fitting into this society at appropriate places and observing the moral principles taught in the religious traditions.

The Structure of Chinese Society
Sometimes it is said that in the Asian religions, in contrast to the Abraham religions, the individual is not important, for only the group has value. That is, of course, not true. The individual is very important in China, so much so that rituals of individual life passages such as marriage and funerals are the focus of

much attention. And personal, individual self-transformation is the goal of the path as set forth in Taoism, Neo-Confucianism, and the different schools of Chinese Buddhism. The value and the religious needs of the individual are surely not forgotten in China!

Yet the individual is seen in balance with the larger community in Chinese society. Individual worth and meaning are closely tied to roles within the social nexus of family, local community, and nation. What meaning would a person have if he cut himself off from these reservoirs of meaning to move out as an "individual" into some new world? The key to Chinese social tradition is that full personal worth and belonging comes with the cultivation of fellow-humanness—in family, in community, in nation.

Family-ism, the Heart of Chinese Society

In China, religious affiliation is not primarily a matter of belonging to a particular religion or a denomination (although there are such things in China, too), but it centers on the family or clan. We have already seen how the cult of the ancestors has formed the basis of Chinese society both historically and theoretically. In practical terms, the ongoing life of the ancestors and their continued influence comes in the arena of the family, as each family elder who dies becomes a *shen* and is enshrined in the spirit-tablet on the family altar. Within the family, the virtue of filial piety is all important, and it is this virtue that underlies all the different roles of the various individuals within the family structure—the head of the family and his wife, the oldest son and his younger brothers, the daughters, the sons-in-law and daughters-in-law, the oldest grandson, the other grandchildren, the various uncles and aunts, and the rest. All have their proper roles in the family structure, and by fulfilling this role each individual realizes personal fulfillment.

The family structure is based on the patrilineal clan or lineage, those who share a common surname and a shared descent from common ancestors, usually supported in written proof in geneological records. Within this larger clan, the individual households revolve around a male of the older generation who was a part of the original household, one who "shared the stove" of the house. The family is multigenerational. And those who have died are present as ancestors, and those yet unborn are present in potential in the lives of the young people who cultivate their bodies and grow up to marry and produce offspring who will carry on the family and its life. The sons will keep the family surname and continue the family into the next generation. The daughters are brought up in order to be transferred into other lineages through marriage contracts.

The family thus is the primary focus of meaning and identity for all members. The worst imaginable tragedy is to be cut off from the family with its network of obligations and support; this would be to lose all meaning and purpose while living and to become a "hungry ghost" after death.

The National Family

The Confucian tradition built on the family structure with its central virtue of filial piety and, in fact, extended the basic structure to the larger community groupings, to the village or town, and especially to the nation. The family is the prototype of all these concentric circles of human relationships. A filial son will certainly also be a good citizen, and a ruler or superior who lives as a good parent will also be an ideal ruler. During the long successions of dynasties in China (from the third century B.C.E. up to the twentieth century), the state was conceived as a "national family," with the emperor fulfilling the role of "father" and the guiding principles being filial piety and paternal love. As the head of the national family, the emperor was concerned both with the welfare of the people and with the spiritual welfare of the national ancestors.

Along with this ideology of the national family, the Confucian state also developed a centralized bureaucracy based on the principles of ceremonials (*li*) and penalties. Under the emperor there was a large bureaucracy made up of Confucian scholars from the gentry, chosen on the basis of an examination in the Confucian classics.

Even though the national family was considered sacred, this is not completely a "chosen people" ideology. The emperor, called the "Son of Heaven," was thought to be given a mandate from Heaven to rule as long as he kept order and prosperity for his people. He therefore was held responsible both for mismanagement in government and also for natural disasters that befell the nation. If disasters occurred, it was believed that the mandate of Heaven was being taken away from the emperor.

There are other religious communities besides the family and the state, certainly. The village or town is an important social unit, with respected local leaders performing the important rituals on occasions of community festivals. The people of the community unite in support of the local temples, and often there are special gods whose duty it is to guard the community and bring prosperity to its people. Further, there are special voluntary religious groups, such as Buddhist monasteries or nunneries, lay Buddhist associations, and the various orders of Taoist priests.

Religious Leaders in China

Religious leaders correspond to the major social groupings in China. Perhaps most important of all is the head of the family, the one responsible for continuing close communion with the ancestors, governing the activities of the family, presiding over the important family rituals, and so forth. It is imperative that the head of the family have a wife to perform many of the important household rituals. And many duties fall to the oldest son, who in a special way is the representative of his grandfather and thus is very important for carrying on the worship of the ancestors and the family well-being.

In the traditional feudal hierarchy in China, those responsible for governing at the different levels also had corresponding roles of religious leadership. The village elders, the city administrators, and the province governors all had specific roles to play in the local and state cults. They were ranked in a hierarchy just as the gods are accorded different ranks. At the top, corresponding to Heaven and earth, is the emperor, the father of the nation and the only one empowered to perform the essential rituals that bring renewal and harmony to the whole land.

Among the other important religious leaders are the Confucian scholars, the literati, who attained their leadership by virtue of mastering the classics and passing state examinations, who also presided at important Confucian rituals, often connected with the state cult.

Then there are the various types of ritual specialists, especially the Taoist priests, who go through long training in the secretive scriptures and rituals and receive an ordination rank depending on how extensive their command of the spirit world is. Today there is generally recognized a distinction between the monastic Taoist priest who pursues the Taoist disciplines for his own transformation, and the "fire-dwelling" priest, that is, one who has a family and serves as a ritualist for the community. In Taiwan today, those fire-dwelling priests who can perform the great festivals in the "orthodox" way are sometimes called Black-head priests (from their black headdresses), whereas the priests performing the more popular rituals and exorcisms are called Red-head priests. Finally, there are also Buddhist monks and nuns who pursue their own spiritual growth but who also have special spiritual powers that they can share for the benefit of the laypeople in chanting scriptures, saying prayers, and the like.

A type of religious leader that cuts across religious traditions in China is the "master," one who has reached a high level of spiritual achievement and who takes a small number of disciples. Unlike a teacher who simply passes information to students, the master imparts something of himself, his secret insights, and his special disciplines to the disciples. And he remains in that master-disciple relationship with them as long as they live. Great masters established "lineages" that continued for many generations as the conduit for transmitting advanced spiritual insights and practices. In modern times abbots of Buddhist monasteries, Ch'an masters, and Taoist chief priests still fulfill this important religious role of master.

The Confucian Vision of the Good Moral Life

"How should I live?" We saw earlier how Confucianism sees Heaven (T'ien) as the ultimate moral authority by whose mandate all human decisions and actions are measured—not as an external law-giver and judge but as the cosmic law that is also inherent in our human nature. We also saw that Confucianists have generally considered human nature as basically good and positive, so that living according to our moral nature is possible. The famous opening passage of the Doctrine of the Mean sums it up succinctly:

> That which is bestowed by Heaven is called man's nature; the fulfillment of this nature is called the Way; the cultivation of the Way is called culture. The Way is something that may not be departed from even for one instant. If it could be departed from, it would not be the Way.[13]

What does it mean to cultivate the Way in day-by-day situations? The place to start is by molding all one's actions to the principle of filial piety. Moving out from there, the same basic attitude of respect and reciprocity is extended to all others through acts of propriety (*li*) as the humanizing force in social relationships.

In spite of the practical bent of Confucian principles, they are not based simply on utilitarian motivations. It is true that the influential thinker Mo Tzu (ca. 470–391 B.C.E.), or at least his disciples, advocated a form of utilitarianism: "Any word or action that is beneficial to Heaven, spiritual beings, and the people is to be undertaken. Any word or action that is harmful to Heaven, spiritual beings, and the people is to be rejected."[14] And that kind of practical test of moral actions—whether they bring good and happiness to the people—is often used to evaluate a ruler's actions. But Confucius spoke strongly against doing a moral action simply because of the reward that would be received: "The gentleman understands what is right; the inferior man understands what is profitable" (Analects 4.16).[15]

The Good Life of Filial Piety

Confucius often described the ideal moral life as the life of humaneness (*jen*), that is, fully displaying one's innate human goodness in relationship to others. The very root of that humaneness, he taught, is in filial piety (Analects 1.2). The Chinese character used for filial piety (*hsiao*) is very illuminating, made up of the graph for old person, supported by the graph for son placed underneath it. And that means, according to the Classic of Filiality,

> In serving his parents the filial son is as reverent as possible to them while they are living. In taking care of them he does so with all possible joy; when they are sick he is extremely anxious about them; when he buries

them he is stricken with grief; when he sacrifices to them he does so with the utmost solemnity. These five [duties] being discharged in full measure, then he has been able [truly] to serve his parents.[16]

Out of all crimes and wrongs, there is none worse than being unfilial—in traditional China such a crime, in fact, could be punished by death. To get some feeling of the kind of total devotion that filial piety calls for, here are some examples from a long list of instructions in the Classic of Rites. First of all, sons and sons' wives, on the first crowing of the cock, should proceed to where their parents are.

> On getting to where they are, with bated breath and gentle voice, they should ask if their clothes are (too) warm or (too) cold, whether they are ill or pained, or uncomfortable in any part; and if so, they should proceed reverently to stroke and scratch the place. They should in the same way, going before or following after, help and support their parents in quitting or entering (the apartment). In bringing in the basin for them to wash, the younger will carry the stand and the elder the water; they will beg to be allowed to pour out the water, and when the washing is concluded, they will hand the towel. They will ask whether they want anything, and then respectfully bring it. All this they will do with an appearance of pleasure to make their parents feel at ease.[17]

Among the primary obligations of filial piety is the duty to marry and have offspring, so that the ancestral sacrifices can be continued and the family line will not die out. But beyond the duty to honor and support parents, perform the sacrificial rites for the ancestors, and produce offspring to continue the family, filial piety is a moral virtue that permeates how one lives all of life. Mencius lists some of the things that are unfilial:

> There are five things which in common practice are considered unfilial. The first is laziness in the use of one's body without attending to the support and care of one's parents. The second is chess-playing and fondness for wine, without attending to the support and care of one's parents. The third is love of things and money and being exclusively attached to one's wife and children,

without attending to the support and care of one's parents. The fourth is following the desires of one's ears and eyes, thus bringing his parents to disgrace. And the fifth is being fond of bravery, fighting, and quarreling, thus endangering one's parents.[18]

The last point is interesting: in what way do bravery and fighting endanger one's parents? Getting oneself killed or maimed is, in effect, to cut off filial service to one's parents. A dead son will not get married to produce offspring. Even to be maimed in some part of the body is to do dishonor to the parents who gave one's body in a state of wholeness. Therefore a pious son "avoids climbing to great heights, he avoids going near precipices, he avoids cursing or laughing incautiously; he avoids moving in the darkness; he avoids climbing up steep slopes: he fears to dishonour his parents!"[19] What a person does with his personal life is no private matter; reckless sports, brawling, even careless accidents are slaps at one's parents.

Filial piety thus forms the heart of practicing the good ethical life. And it extends beyond considerations of parents and family to the other areas of life. "Filiality begins with the serving of our parents, continues with the serving of our prince, and is completed with the establishing of our own character."[20]

The Good Life of Propriety

But what about the rest of life besides considerations of parents and family? What are the basic ethical principles having to do with community, business, politics, and the rest? In a sense these principles are derived by extending the respectful, serving attitude of filial piety to embrace all other relationships. At the heart of his ethical system Confucius put the practice of rites (*li*), usually translated as "propriety" when it refers to social relationships. As we have seen, this word originally was used for the sacrificial rites offered to the ancestors. The Confucian tradition held that even Heaven and earth are upheld by Li as a cosmological principle, and so it makes sense to pattern social relationships after this: one should always treat others with respectful reverence.

To get a feeling for what the traditional Chinese mean by respectful reverence, here is a description of how one should receive a guest.

> Whenever (a host has received and) is entering with a guest, at every door he should give place to him. When the guest arrives at the innermost door (or that leading to the feast-room) the host will ask to be allowed to enter first and arrange the mats. Having done this, he will come out to receive the guest, who will refuse firmly (to enter first). The host having made a low bow to him, they will enter (together). When they have entered the door, the host moves to the right, and the guest to the left, the former going to the steps on the east, and the latter to those on the west. If the guest be of the lower rank, he goes to the steps of the host (as if to follow him up them). The host firmly declines this, and he returns to the other steps on the west. They then offer to each other the precedence in going up, but the host commences first, followed (immediately) by the other. They bring their feet together on every step, thus ascending by successive paces. He who ascends by the steps on the east should move his right foot first, and the other at the western steps his left foot.[21]

Such attention to ritual detail may seem extreme, also to modern Chinese, but the idea is that social relationships are nourished in proper balance and harmony through these rituals.

When asked exactly what were the essential ingredients of the principle of propriety or respectful reverence, Confucius stated that it all was based on reciprocity (*shu*) and loyalty (*chung*) (Analects 4:15). In explaining these basic principles, the Analects give two versions of a golden rule:

> What I do not want others to do to me, I do not want to do to them. . . . A man of humanity, wishing to establish his own character, also establishes the character of others, and wishing to be prominent himself, also helps others to be prominent   (5:11; 6:28).[22]

The first statement is expressed negatively and the second positively, but both together show that propriety is really the expressing of mutual, reciprocal relationships of trust, loyalty, and respect, in which one is actively concerned for the well-being of the other.

Confucian thinkers have generally defined these reciprocal relationships in a hierarchical scheme, for there needs to be an orderly structure so that trust, loyalty, and respect can prevail, avoiding confusion and anarchy. And where there is structure, there is superior and inferior, older and younger. Such hierarchy does not mean arbitrary power, for the superior in each case must show the appropriate moral virtues. Of course, there are many types of human relationships, but Confucian thinkers since Mencius have talked about the five basic human relationships, that is, five fundamental patterns into which all social relationships fit so that the proper forms of propriety can be practiced. These five paradigmatic relationships are father-son, husband-wife, elder brother-younger brother, ruler-subject, and older friend-younger friend. In each of these relationships there is a particular quality of propriety that is to be shown. The son is to show filial piety to the father, for example, and the wife should show obedience to the husband. The younger brother shows respect to the older brother, the subject shows loyalty to the ruler, and the younger friend should show deference to the older friend. But these are reciprocal relationships, so the appropriate virtues should also be shown from the superior party: the father should show kindness, the husband caringness, the older brother nobility, the ruler benevolence, and the older friend humaneness.

Within this structure the moral principles can be brought into daily life, for these reciprocal relationships provide the basic patterns for all social involvement. For example, the father-son relationship is the pattern for parents and children and also for ancestors and descendents. And the ruler-subject relationship is the pattern for all cases where one is in authority and the other is under that authority. And all of this, Confucius teaches, corresponds with the will of Heaven for living the good life in human society.

Live the Best Life at Your Place

Confucianism has a positive, life-affirming outlook. One should not withdraw from society in favor of some higher, purer spiritual pursuits. Political and economic involvement is necessary and good, and wealth and success do not corrupt the morally superior person. Physical needs and desires are not evil and should be fulfilled through the proper social means for food and provisions, clothing, and sexual relations with one's

Jade carving depicting sages of ancient China; they each taught their vision of the good life.

spouse. Always the guiding principle is the welfare of the family and the community.

The ethical philosophy expressed in the Doctrine of the Mean might be summed up as doing one's best according to one's place in life.

> The superior man does what is proper to his position and does not want to go beyond this. If he is in a noble station, he does what is proper to a position of wealth and honorable station. If he is in a humble station, he does what is proper to a position of poverty and humble station. If he is in the midst of barbarian tribes, he does what is proper in the midst of barbarian tribes. In a position of difficulty and danger, he does what is proper to a position of difficulty and danger. He can find himself in no situation in which he is not at ease with himself.[23]

The Confucian ethical vision has a strong interest in the leaders and rulers of society, for these people set the tone for all the rest. An evil ruler will fail to promote the goodness of the people and will create anarchy and disaster, but a good ruler will educate and nourish the moral nature of the people. One of Confucius' sayings hits this point directly:

> Lead the people with governmental measures and regulate them by law and punishment, and they will avoid wrongdoing but will have no sense of honor or shame. Lead them with virtue and regulate them by the rules of propriety [Li], and they will have a sense of shame and, moreover, set themselves right (ANALECTS 2.3).[24]

There were Legalists in ancient China who tried to rule the people with strict laws and punishment, based on the theory that people are evil by nature. But the Confucian tradition advocates the power of moral action as the key principle for social and political ethics.

The Taoist Perspective on the Good Life

The good life seen from a Taoist perspective has quite a different hue from that of Confucianists, though it is not as fully articulated. The thrust toward withdrawal, no-action, and meditation tends toward a more quietistic and carefree type of life, at least for those looking to philosophical Taoism. A fundamental principle of religious Taoism would be the need to maintain a balance in all activity; giving in unduly to the senses can lead to an exhausting of life powers and an unhealthy imbalance.

No-Action as a Basis for Living

Whereas the Confucian approach has definite principles of right and wrong, good and evil in human behavior, it is characteristic of the Taoist view to take a relative position on such issues, as we saw. To a duck, short legs are good, but to a crane, long legs are good. Making judgments about right or wrong is forcing something artificial on the natural process. Thus the fundamental Taoist approach to the good life would be to do everything in the natural way, freely and spontaneously, without artificiality or coercion. That is, no-action should be one's basic principle. This does not necessarily mean withdrawal to a life of reclusion

and quietism, although some Taoists have done that. In family and in community, in work and in play, it means to always act spontaneously and naturally, not according to plans or schemes or strategies.

This approach to the good life works best, it is true, at the personal level, although even then it may strike others as bizzare or even immoral. The Seven Sages of the Bamboo Grove (ca. 210–263 C.E.) were notorious because they flaunted customary mores to live their lives freely and spontaneously. They dropped out of politics, lived impulsively, and had drinking parties in which they drank wine from a common bowl on the floor, sharing it even with pigs. One of them, Liu Ling, liked to go around naked in his house, scandalizing others when they came to visit. But to them he replied, "The whole universe is my house and this room is my trousers. What are you doing here inside my trousers?"[25]

Of course, Taoism does not advocate simply giving in to every whim, but cultivating a style in which the natural events of life are not stifled through emotional judgments about good and bad but are simply accepted and lived for what they are. A good example of this approach to life is Chuang Tzu's behavior when his wife died. A friend came to offer condolences, but he found Chuang Tzu squatting on the ground and singing, beating on an earthen bowl instead of performing the mourning rites. The friend was scandalized and rebuked him: "To live with your wife, and see your eldest son grow up to be a man, and then not to shed a tear over her corpse—this would be bad enough. But to drum on a bowl and sing; surely this is going too far!" "Not at all," replied Chuang Tzu.

> When she died I could not help being affected by her death. Soon, however, I remembered that she had already existed in a previous state before birth, without form or even substance; that while in that unconditioned condition, substance was added to spirit; that this substance then assumed form; and that the next stage was birth. And now, by virtue of a further change, she is dead, passing from one phase to another like the sequence of spring, summer, autumn and winter. And while she is thus lying asleep in eternity, for me to go about weeping and wailing would be to proclaim myself ignorant of these natural laws. Therefore I refrain. (ch. 18)[26]

One should not let emotional judgments about good and bad stand in the way of living the natural life.

Of course, Taoism does provide certain guidance about ideals and virtues in life. Here is a description of the kinds of virtues the ancient Taoists held:

> Not to be encumbered with popular fashions, not to be dazzled by the display of things, not to be unfeeling toward other men, and not to be antagonistic to the multitude; to desire peace in the world for the preservation of the life of the people; to seek no more than is sufficient for nourishing oneself and others, thus setting one's heart at peace—these were some of the aspects of the system of the Tao among the ancients. . . . To be impartial and nonpartisan; to be compliant and selfless; to be free from insistence and prejudice; to take things as they come; to be without worry or care; not to rely on one's wits; to accept all and mingle with all—these were some of the aspects of the system of the Tao among the ancients. (CHUANG TZU, CH. 33)[27]

Many of the virtues and ideals listed here have to do with relationships with others, even though the emphasis is on the individual's style of life. Like Confucianism, Taoism is also concerned with how leaders and rulers should live their lives for the benefit of their people. But, in contrast to the Confucian ideal of a ruler who leads with the rules of propriety, the Taoist notion of a good ruler is one who lets the people develop naturally. Already in the Tao Te Ching is this statement about the good ruler:

> Govern the state with correctness.
> Operate the army with surprise tactics.
> Administer the empire by engaging in no activity.
> How do I know that this should be so?
> Through this:
>   The more taboos and prohibitions there are in the world,
>   The poorer the people will be.
>   The more sharp weapons the people have,
>   The more troubled the state will be.
>   The more cunning and skill man possesses,
>   The more vicious things will appear.
>   The more laws and orders are made prominent,
>   The more thieves and robbers there will be.
> Therefore the sage says,
>   I take no action and the people of themselves are transformed.

> I love tranquillity and the people of themselves become correct.
> I engage in no activity and the people of themselves become prosperous.
> I have no desires and the people of themselves become simple. (CH. 57)[28]

A leader who uses laws and punishments, weapons and force, even cunning and strategy will inevitably rule by force and coercion, thus doing injury to the natural flow of life. A leader who follows the Taoist vision will rule through no-action, that is, practicing the virtues of Taoism and thus allowing the people also to live freely and spontaneously.

It is true, of course, that most rulers in Chinese history have been Confucianists!

Religious Taoism: A Life of Balance

In that large realm of Chinese life that we have associated loosely with religious Taoism, the people, of course, follow moral principles derived both from Confucianism, especially with regard to the family, and from the philosophical Taoist texts. The scriptures of religious Taoism do put forth some principles for the good and wholesome life, arising from the Taoist view of the balance of sacred forces in the universe and in the body. Some of these principles have to do with the ancient notion that certain types of food nourish the yin processes of the body and should be avoided, and others come from the idea that certain types of actions use up the the vital forces of the body and should be avoided. One Taoist text states, for example:

> When the five organs are ruled by the heart [mind] and are not perverse, then a regulated will overcomes, and does that which is not evil. When a regulated will overcomes and does not do evil, then seminal breath and spirit flourish, and life breath is not dissipated. When seminal breath and spirit flourish and life breath is not dissipated, then there is order. . . . When ear and eye are seduced by sensual pleasure of sound and color, then the five organs are shaken and unstable. When the five organs are shaken and unstable, then breath and blood [will] overflow and are wasted, never resting; when breath and blood overflow and are wasted, never resting, then seminal breath and spirit gallop forth unbridled and are not kept within.[29]

There is an ancient tradition in one form of religious Taoism that the inner gods will be beneficial for renewal only if the adept practices virtues and good works. So some Taoists did good deeds like repairing bridges, endowing orphanages, and caring for the poor and sick. Still today, in preparation for a Taoist festival, the people of the community will give attention to alleviating their wrongdoings and to doing good deeds, such as giving money to repair temples, giving alms to the poor and the crippled, and presenting offerings of food to the hungry ghosts who flock about on the last day of the festival. The underlying motivation is that of maintaining harmony and balance among the forces that affect the lives of all. When someone suffers, whether through poverty or as a hungry ghost, all the people are responsible in some way, and the baleful effects of that suffering are felt also in their lives. When people help those unfortunate ones, the benefits of that are also shared because of the enhanced harmony and peace that results.

Patterns and Paradigms for World Society

The religions of China, except for Buddhism, have traditionally been seen simply as Chinese religions, of benefit specifically for those varied peoples who came to call China their sacred land. In theory both Confucianism and Taoism are universal religions, that is, the basic principles apply to the whole world and even the whole universe, although the Chinese have not attempted to draw other peoples of the world into the Chinese religions. In modern times attempts to reform and better Chinese society have often included breaking the hold of the traditional religious system, especially of Confucianism. But there are modern thinkers who believe the traditional wisdom of China has some important things to contribute to the peace and welfare of the whole world.

Throughout the centuries, the Chinese religious traditions have held up the ideal of harmony and balance in the universe and in society. And the model

The Great Wall of China, symbol of the unification of China during the Ch'in dynasty (ca. 210 B.C.E.).

CHAPTER 24: *Worship and the Good Life in China* / **459**

structure for living that harmony is the family. The lineage, the community, even the state have been structured after the paradigm of the family. Within the paradigm of the family, the notion of reciprocal relationships is central; when conflict arises, when injustices become apparent, when needs change, the whole structure works toward reconciliation so that the harmony can be restored.

This model was extended to all of society in China, operating slowly to bring reforms and changes, all the while maintaining harmony and balance. The big question is whether it can continue to work today. The heavy blows against this Confucian-based ideal have been modernization and the Communist movement in China, both purporting to liberate the people from the shackles of tradition. The future of the traditional models of society is indeed clouded in China, although in Taiwan, Hong Kong, and overseas communities the pattern has remained more intact. But, at least according to some observers, the basic paradigm of family, reciprocity, and reconciliation to maintain harmony still plays a central role even in the People's Republic of China. Maoism has been described as a quasi-religion, patterned very much after the Confucian tradition, with Mao taking the part of the sage-father, and the state (or the party) as the family. However the new China develops, it appears that the ideals of reconciliation and harmony will always play a key role.

With nearly a quarter of the world's population, China is a not-so-small world in itself, and with its own problems there has been little time to think of responsibility for the rest of the world. But since ancient times the theme of a "grand unity," not just of humanity but of the whole universe, has fascinated Chinese thinkers, and these visions can still excite imagination today and suggest an enduring world message of China's wisdom. Here are three passages based on the Confucian vision, one from the time of Confucius, one from the Sung era, and one the twentieth century, representing the Chinese vision of the great unity.

In this passage from the Classic of Rites, these words were purportedly spoken by Confucius:

The practice of the Great Way [Tao], the illustrious men of the Three Dynasties—these I shall never know in person. And yet they inspire my ambition! When the Great Way was practiced, the world was shared by all alike. The worthy and the able were promoted to office and men practiced good faith and lived in affection. Therefore they did not regard as parents only their own parents, or as sons only their own sons. The aged found a fitting close to their lives, the robust their proper employment; the young were provided with an upbringing and the widow and widower, the orphaned and the sick, with proper care. Men had their tasks and women their hearths. They hated to see goods lying about in waste, yet they did not hoard them for themselves; they disliked the thought that their energies were not fully used, yet they used them not for private ends. Therefore all evil plotting was prevented and thieves and rebels did not arise, so that people could leave their outer gates unbolted. This was the age of Grand Unity.[30]

Another passage famous in Chinese tradition is the Western Inscription by Chang Tsai (1020–1077), which he inscribed on a panel of his west window:

Heaven is my father and Earth is my mother, and even such a small creature as I finds an intimate place in their midst. Therefore that which fills the universe I regard as my body and that which directs the universe I consider as my nature. All people are my brothers and sisters, and all things are my companions. The great ruler [the emperor] is the eldest son of my parents, and the great ministers are his stewards. Respect the aged. . . . Show deep love toward the orphaned and the weak. . . . Even those who are tired, infirm, crippled, or sick; those who have no brothers or children, wives or husbands, are all my brothers who are in distress and have no one to turn to. . . . He who disobeys [the Principle of Nature] violates virtue. He who destroys humanity is a robber. . . . But he who puts his moral nature into practice and brings his physical existence into complete fulfillment can match [Heaven and Earth]. . . . In life I follow and serve [Heaven and Earth]. In death I will be at peace.[31]

K'ang Yu-wei (1858–1927), making the following radical proposals based on Confucianism, was actually considered a Confucian reactionary because he advocated restoring Confucianism as the state religion.

Having been born in an age of disorder, and seeing with my own eyes the path of suffering in the world, I wish to find a way to save it. I have thought deeply and believe the only way is to practice the way of Great Unity and Great Peace.... The Way of Great Unity is perfect equality, perfect impartiality, perfect humanity, and good government in the highest degree.... My way of saving people from these sufferings consists in abolishing [the] nine spheres of distinction. First, do away with the distinction between states in order to unify the whole world. Second, do away with class distinctions so as to bring about equality of all people. Third, do away with racial distinction so there will be one universal race. Fourth, do away with the distinction between physical forms so as to guarantee the independence of both sexes. [So also he advocates doing away with all other distinctions, and with restrictive social institutions including marriage, nations, private property, and taxes!].... In the Age of Great Peace, there are no emperors, kings, rulers, elders, official titles, or ranks. All people are equal, and do not consider position or rank as an honor either. Only wisdom and humanity are promoted and encouraged.[32]

In spite of its idea of a Great Unity, the Confucian vision has fallen on hard times in the modern secular, liberated, Marxist-oriented world of China. Taoism is also in deep trouble, because many religious Taoist practices are considered superstitious and thus antimodern. But the message of Taoist philosophy has also been heard by many in the world today—through the many translations of the Tao Te Ching, through overseas Chinese who still consult the Almanac and the I Ching, through people who are interested in arts like t'ai ch'i. This is hardly the kind of missionary outreach that is done in Christianity and Islam. It is rather people in the Western world discovering a vision of the world and a practice of harmony that fascinates and compels them—not to become Chinese, but to accept something of lasting value from that ancient wisdom.

DISCUSSION QUESTIONS

1. Describe the various rituals by which the family maintains relations with the ancestors.
2. What goes on in the Taoist Chiao festival? Describe both the actions of the Taoist priests and the community celebration outside the temple.
3. In an exorcism ritual, who are the main antagonists?
4. Outline the daily rituals in a Ch'an monastery.
5. Show how Chinese monochrome ink landscape painting was especially expressive of Taoist and Ch'an ideas.
6. What are the main aspects of filial piety?
7. What are the five basic patterns of reciprocal social relations, according to the Confucian tradition?
8. How does Chuang Tzu's behavior when his wife died illustrate Taoist perspectives?
9. What advice do Confucianism and Taoism have toward bettering government?

CHAPTER 25

JAPAN: SACRED STORY AND HISTORICAL CONTEXT

"**W**ho am I?" To be Japanese is to find one's real identity in the story of Japan, that is, the religious and cultural heritage of the land and the people of Japan.

Japanese religious identity is complicated, made up of perhaps half a dozen important religious traditions from earlier times. Some of these traditions have developed institutional forms, but Japanese characteristically find no problem in sharing in a number of religious traditions simultaneously. The life story of a typical person can illustrate this. When the person was born, his parents took him to the family Shinto shrine to dedicate him to the kami (gods, sacred beings) traditionally worshiped by the family. He goes to the shrine on New Year's Day and other holidays, and he was married in a Shinto wedding ceremony. But the wedding date was determined in accordance with lucky and unlucky days according to the Taoist calendar. In his family relationships he strives to uphold the Confucian virtue of filial piety toward parents and relatives, and his associations in school and business build on the Confucian attitude of loyalty. He has studied Christian teachings and especially respects Christian morality, finding the Christian idea of love even for the poor and downtrodden a most commendable attitude for modern society. He likes the local festivals, legends, and other activities of his hometown, folk religious practices unique to his region and dating from who knows when. He turns to Buddhism as he remembers his parents and ancestors who have died. His intellectual commitment is to the Buddhist vision of life and the final goal of liberation and the peace of nirvana.

Shinto, Taoism, Confucianism, Christianity, folk religion, Buddhism—a Japanese person often is involved in the sacred stories of all of these. Since we discussed the major traditions like Confucianism and Buddhism in previous chapters, here we pay particular attention to the Shinto tradition of Japan. It should be kept in mind that "Shinto" (shen-tao) is a word taken over from China to designate the indigenous religious practices of Japan. It was not an organized religion but included both the traditions of the ruling family and the various practices throughout the different localities of Japan. Today the Association of Shinto Shrines is an organization that includes the main part of those who consider themselves Shinto, but generally various local folk practices and new religious movements are also included in this designation.

THE STORY OF THE JAPANESE PEOPLE

Although the early Japanese did not have any system of writing to record their sacred stories, they did pass them on orally generation by generation in the different clans and communities. In early Japan there was no orga-

nized religion, so the stories about the kami and the origins of the people varied from place to place. Many of these stories were never written down, whereas others were collected and shaped into larger narratives that focused on the imperial clan and the important families and localities. These stories, some recorded in the eighth century in the first writings in Japan (the Kojiki and the Nihon Shoki), have provided the origins of a general national story for many generations of Japanese. The sacred stories about the kami go back to the Time of the Beginnings and tell of the creation of the world, moving without a break into the origins of the land of Japan and the sacred people.

The Prehistoric Heritage of Japan

To provide some orientation, it is helpful to set the stories of the kami and the people into historical context. The very late development of writing in Japan means that essentially everything before the eighth century C.E. is in the prehistoric period. The first Japanese writings—the Kojiki (712) and the Nihon Shoki (720)—were written in Chinese characters under considerable influence from Chinese civilization and the political developments of the imperial rule in Japan.

Origins of the Japanese: Hunters and Rice Planters

The Japanese story goes far back into prehistoric times in Japan, to the Jomon period (ca. 4500–250 B.C.E.) when the early humans in this land lived by hunting and fishing. Since the Japanese islands are bounded on all sides by seas, a somewhat unified cultural sphere developed. Some people in the ancient period perhaps had matriarchal societies. They lived in pit dwellings and made pottery with a rope pattern. They placed flexed bodies decorated with red ocre in burials, indicating some hope of a passage to the afterlife. They had a special sense for the power of the sun, building many stone circles used apparently for rituals related to the sun. The kami associated with the sun, we know from the myths, is a dominant kami in the Japanese story. Other religious ideas are indicated by ritual objects similar to ones found in China, especially curved beads, swords, and mirrors—symbols of the emperor later on. They also made ritual use of phallic

A *figurine from the late Jomon period.*

stones, clay masks, and fertility figurines. Whereas we do not know a lot about the religious vision of these stone-age ancestors of the Japanese, we can recognize some later Japanese ideas and practices having their origins in this dim past.

But new migrations of people came into Japan during the Yayoi period (ca. 250 B.C.E.–250 C.E.), and now an important new development becomes central: wet-rice cultivation. Later it is taken for granted that growing rice is the heart of the Japanese way of life, and many festivals and rituals have to do with planting and harvesting rice. Traditional Japanese religion, associated with the cultivation of rice, is concerned with fertility, growth, birth, and renewal. In the communal religion of the Yayoi peoples, we can discern the origins of the Japanese way of life. Probably the Japanese language was developing in this period, and the artistic

expressions of the people show many of the aesthetic characteristics of later Japanese art. These people are Japanese.

Some of the descriptions in the records of Chinese dynasties are illuminating about the people in this formative period. We are told that men tattooed their faces and decorated their bodies with designs, and women wore their hair in loops. They enjoyed liquor and practiced a form of divination to tell whether fortune will be good or bad. Whenever they would go on a sea voyage, they would select a man who did not comb his hair, rid himself of fleas, or wash his clothes, also abstaining from meat and lying with women. This man behaved as a "mourner," and he would be rewarded if the voyage met good fortune or killed if ill fortune occurred. Earlier these people of "Yamatai" had been ruled by a man, but after much warfare they accepted as their ruler a woman, Pimiko, who remained unmarried and practiced magic. When she died a great mound was raised in her honor, and over a hundred attendants followed her to the grave, according to the Chinese account.

Such glimpses into ancient Japanese society show that communication with the kami through divination and reliance on shamans and shamanesses were part of Japanese religion from very ancient times.

Clans, Shamans, and the Imperial Rule

The formation of Japanese society and religion was completed in the Kofun (tomb mount) period (ca. 250–600 C.E.), characterized by the large mounds that served as tombs for rulers and their attendants. Possibly there were new migrations of peoples from the continent and from the southern islands of the Pacific Ocean during this era, and the people constituted many large families and clans. Before long one clan attained dominance over the others, and this became the imperial clan. The head of this clan was the ruler, the emperor—and gradually traditional Japanese society made up of emperor and people took shape. The head of each clan served as priest of the kami of the clan, and the emperor, as head of the whole people, was recognized as high priest of the kami for the sake of all the people.

As the imperial clan established its rule, a new cultural impetus developed. The emperors built huge mound-tombs for their burials, and the art produced for these tombs is strikingly Japanese in character. Of particular significance are the *dogu*, clay representations of animals and people, which were placed in the tombs to accompany the deceased ruler. Archaeological evidence makes it clear that by the end of the prehistoric period the imperial family was firmly in place in this area of Japan, ruling over a people whose religion and culture is the fountainhead of Japan as we know it from the historical period. The mythology recorded in the Kojiki and the Nihon Shoki seems to reflect the religious ideas and practices of this formative period, at least from the point of view of the imperial clan.

Sacred Nation: The Story of the Kami

The Japanese sense of identity as a people in this sacred land was influenced by traditions of interaction with the kami of the land—the kami of the mountains, the rivers, the rice fields and the rest of nature, together with the kami of ancestors and families. The story has many local variants, but an important part is told in the Kojiki and Nihon Shoki in the mythologies about the kami who created the world and the land. The story includes the origin of the imperial family and of all Japanese from the kami. It tells how sacred government spread over the land and how many festivals and rituals originated. The myths establish the basic Japanese way of looking at nature, the land, the kami, and the people.

Izanagi and Izanami: Creating the Land and Culture

Among the kami generated on the Plain of High Heaven in the beginning time, Izanagi and Izanami are most important because they are the ones whose creative power brings forth the land and Japanese civilization. The myths tell how Izanagi and Izanami, descending to the Floating Bridge of Heaven, stir up the brine below and thus create an island to which they then descend to give birth to the various kami of the world. The whole world is interpenetrated with kami power—the myths talk of eight hundred myriads of kami on the Plain of High Heaven, to say nothing of the kami of earth.

Why do Japanese have so much concern for purity?

Why do they venerate the sun kami as special among all the kami? Why do they celebrate festivals at shrines with prayers, music, dancing, and the like? These are age-old traditions that provide a special identity, and they have models in the sacred story.

When Izanami died (after giving birth to the kami of fire) she went to the underworld. Izanagi descended there to try and bring her back, in his impetuousity breaking in to see her in her state polluted by death, which made her rather angry so that she pursued him. Escaping from her, now Izanagi needed to purify himself from the pollutions of the underworld, so he washed in a river, purifying and exorcising the evil from himself. Thus was established the model for purification rituals.

Finally when Izanagi washed his left eye, Amaterasu (Heaven Illuminating Kami, that is, Sun Kami) was born, and from washing his right eye and his nose, Tsukiyomi (Moon Kami) and Susanoo (Valiant Raging Male Kami) were born. Izanagi rejoiced at these kami of the sun, moon, and storm, and he gave his necklace to Amaterasu and entrusted her with this mission: "You shall rule the Plain of High Heaven." To Tsukiyomi he gave the mission of ruling the night, and to Susanoo the rule of the seas. Thus it is that Amaterasu, the sun kami, born in this sacred land, became the ruler of all the heavenly kami.

The narrative goes on to tell of the conflict that developed between Amaterasu and Susanoo, her boisterous storm kami brother. Amaterasu withdrew to the rock cave of heaven, so that now constant night began to reign on the Plain of High Heaven and in the Central Land of Reed Plains, with cries rising everywhere and all kinds of calamities occurring. So the eight hundred myriads of heavenly kami held a great festival. They set up a sasaki tree and hung strings of curved beads, a large mirror, and white and blue cloth in its branches. They presented offerings and intoned prayers. And Kami of Heavenly Headgear performed a shamanistic dance on a bucket, exposing her breasts and genitals and entertaining the kami so that the Plain of High Heaven shook with kami laughter. Intrigued by the raucous festival, Amaterasu was enticed out of the cave, and the Plain of High Heaven and the Central Land of Reed Plains were illuminated once more. Following this model, Japanese perform festivals of entertaining the kami at the shrines, so that the blessing of kami power will continue.

The Divine Descent of the Imperial Family

In the beginning times, the story says, the kami of the earth were unruly, so from time to time heavenly kami were sent down to pacify and subdue them. Finally the Central Land of Reed Plains was subdued, and Amaterasu decided to send down her descendants to rule the land. To her grandson Ninigi she gave the commission: "The Land of the Plentiful Reed Plains and the Fresh Rice-Ears has been entrusted to you to rule. In accordance with the command, descend from the heavens." Then Amaterasu gave Ninigi the three symbols of divine rule: the myriad curved beads, the mirror, and the sacred sword, saying, "You have this mirror as my spirit; worship it just as you would worship in my very presence" (Kojiki chs. 38–39). Then came the great descent: Ninigi pushed through the myriad layers of the trailing clouds of heaven until he stood on an island by the Heavenly Floating Bridge. Then he descended from the heavens to the peak of Mount Takachiho to inaugurate kami rule on earth. Emperor Jimmu, the legendary first emperor, was the great-grandson of Ninigi.

According of the traditional way of thinking, all emperors of Japan are direct descendants from this line, descendants of the great kami Amaterasu, and thus they are fit to rule the land and people. Other myths say the Japanese people are also descended from the kami. Many people today, of course, do not understand these myths in a literal, factual way. But the myths do say something important about land, people, and emperor: all are bound together in the sacredness of Japan.

People and Kami in Communion

In early times, as the story tells it, life centered on family, clan, hunting, planting and harvesting rice, the people responding to the goodness of the kami in the rhythm of the seasons, the beauty of mountains and forests, and the fertility of the land. The head of the family or clan acted as a priest for the kami of the clan, worshiping and honoring the kami at a shrine on a hill or in a forest. The shrine probably had no building, at

least in early times, but a rope boundary was stretched around the sacred space and the kami was called down to be present there to receive gifts of prayer and food and to give blessings to the people. The chieftain of a large clan would sometimes set up a special pure house near the shrine and appoint a female relative to be priestess for the kami, communicating with the kami through shamanistic trances and providing information for the chieftain.

The story tells how the emperor, chieftain of the ruling clan, at first worshiped Amaterasu, his kami ancestor, right in the imperial palace. But Sujin, the tenth legendary emperor, was not at ease living with such awesome power in the palace, so he established a special shrine for Amaterasu to reside in and appointed Princess Toyosukiiri to act as high priestess. Later, at the time of the next emperor, the sun kami revealed this wish: "The province of Ise, whose divine winds

Worshipers ascending to the ancient Inner Shrine at Ise, where Amaterasu is enshrined.

blow, is washed by successive waves from the Eternal Land. It is a secluded and beautiful place, and I wish to dwell here."[1] So the shrine for Amaterasu was built at Ise, the most important shrine in all of Japan for the worship of the sun kami, the divine ancestress of the emperor.

All of Japan was dotted with shrines for worshiping the kami, both the kami of the various clans and also many other kami of various localities, of mountains, trees, waterfalls, rice fields, and the like. Each community had seasonal festivals at these shrines, during which the kami came to provide their powerful presence for the people and grant blessings so the rice crops would grow and the people would be healthy and prosperous. When calamities struck, great purification ceremonies would be conducted to rid the community of the pollution and restore purity for the continued blessing that comes through the kami.

The Coming of Buddhism and Chinese Culture

In the sixth century C.E. this early Shinto world was penetrated by a very different religion and culture, a way of looking at existence that seems nearly contrary to the early Shinto vision. Buddhism, with its view of the passing nature of this world and the goal of nirvana, made its appearance in Japan, together with Chinese culture such as Confucianism, Taoism, scriptures, art, and writing. Now the story of Japan was transformed and drastically redirected—yet that story goes on, as the Japanese absorbed Buddhism and the other aspects of Chinese culture while continuing the main lines of their traditional society.

Sacred Buddha Image and Scriptures

In 552 C.E., according to the Nihon Shoki, a provincial king in Korea sent gifts to Emperor Kimmei, and among these gifts were a Buddha image and Buddhist scriptures. Of course, something was known about Buddhism before this, since Korean immigrants had recently come to Japan. But now for the first time the Japanese emperor, father of the people and high priest of the kami, was confronted directly with the claims for the superior power of this new teaching of the foreign Buddha. Along with the gifts the Korean king sent this message:

> This [Buddhist] Law is superior to all other teachings. It is difficult to understand and to comprehend, and even the wise Duke of Chou and Confucius had no knowledge of it. However, this Law will bring about boundless rewards and blessings, and enable men to attain supreme enlightenment. To have this wonderful Law is like having a treasure which would bring about everything one asks for according to his wish, because everything one asks the Buddha in prayer will be fulfilled without fail. Therefore, from India in the distant west to Korea in the east everyone upon receiving the Law pays utmost respect to it.[2]

Now the Japanese leaders were in a dilemma—they who had always looked to Amaterasu and the kami as the divine forces who bring all good and blessing in the world. They had never seen this mysterious kami in seated position with eyes closed, so contrary to the Japanese tradition of not making images or statues of the kami. And they had never used any form of writing, so they could not understand these mysterious scriptures.

Emperor Kimmei was overjoyed at this gift, but he was undecided about what he should do, so he consulted his three trusted ministers, saying, "We have never seen such a dignified face as that of the Buddha which has been presented to us. Should we worship [the Buddha]?" Soga no Iname felt the superiority of the Chinese culture should determine the answer: "How can [Japan] refuse to worship the Buddha, since all the nations in the west without exception are devoted to Him?"[3] But the other two ministers were from the Mononobe and the Nakatomi families, both hereditary priesthood families, and they saw a potential risk. Since it has always been the custom of the emperors to worship the Japanese kami, they argued, should a foreign kami be worshiped instead, it might incur the wrath of the kami of our nation. In this dilemma, Emperor Kimmei compromised, giving the Buddha image to Minister Soga to worship privately as an experiment. Soga was overjoyed; he enshrined the Buddha image in his house and began to follow Buddhist disciplines and practices in worshiping the Buddha.

This was a momentous step—a court minister worshiping the foreign kami, the Buddha. Shortly after this a pestilence prevailed in the land, and the Mononobe and Nakatomi ministers petitioned the emperor, saying that this pestilence broke out because their advice had not been followed; now happiness could only be secured by throwing the Buddha image away. So the emperor ordered the Buddha image to be thrown into a canal—whereupon a sudden fire swept away the great hall of the imperial palace! Thus the dilemma of how to respond to the power of the Buddha continued to rage in the land of the kami.

But the attraction of the new religion was not to be denied, even as the question of its relation to the traditional way of Japan was unresolved. The next year people reported hearing Buddhist chants coming like thunder from the sea, together with a great light from the west. Investigating this, they found a piece of shining camphor wood floating on the water, and the emperor ordered an artist to make images of the Buddha from this wood. In the following years more Buddhist images and scriptures came from Korea, and also Buddhist monks and nuns who could teach the Buddhist disciplines, meditation, making of images, and building of Buddhist temples. The Soga family continued its dedication to Buddhism. Soga no Umako, son of Soga no Iname, worked tirelessly for the acceptance of Buddhism and for Japanese to study the Buddhist scriptures and disciplines. Gradually the teaching of this "foreign kami" attained a foothold among the leading families of Japan.

Transformation of Japan Through Buddhism and Chinese Culture

One of the most brilliant rulers in Japanese history, Prince Shotoku (573–621), who administered the nation as prince regent, was a key figure in the Buddhist transformation of Japan. Shotoku continued the traditional worship of the kami, issuing an edict saying that all ministers should pay homage to the kami of heaven and earth from the bottom of their hearts. But Shotoku also studied Buddhism and Confucianism and attained deep understanding of both. In 604 he issued the famous Seventeen Article Constitution, in which he advocated the Confucian virtues of harmony, propriety,

and loyalty to the emperor. But most importantly, he stated in this constitution: "You should sincerely venerate the Three Treasures, namely, the Buddha, Buddha's Law, and the Buddhist Order, which are the final refuge of [all creatures] and have indeed been venerated by everyone at every age."[4] Prince Shotoku was strongly committed to the Buddhist teachings and even gave lectures on the Buddhist sutras. For this he has won veneration in the sacred story as the founder of Buddhism in Japan. Through Prince Shotoku the transformation was realized that set Japanese culture firmly on three foundations: the kami way, Buddhism, and Confucianism. The relationship among these foundations has been debated through the centuries and still today. But Japanese life and culture are shaped by these traditions.

As Japan moved into the Nara period (710–784), with the capital no longer shifting about with each new emperor but now set permanently at Nara, Buddhism and Chinese culture became ever more an integral part of the Japanese story. The city of Nara was laid out in the style of the current Chinese capital city, for example. And the structure of government with bureaucracies and systems of ranks was modeled after the Chinese pattern.

The Confucian influence from China was perhaps not as direct as that of Buddhism but still it was pervasive, in its emphasis on social harmony through a system of hierarchical relationships in which the subordinate one is loyal and obedient, and the superior one is protecting and benevolent. The Japanese sense of family was reinforced with the Confucian notion of filial piety. And Confucianism supported the traditional respect for the emperor as the head of the leading family by its notion of loyalty of subjects to rulers. One difference retained in Japan was that the emperor, equated with Heaven in the Chinese Confucian view, ruled not only according to mandate of Heaven but according to his descent from Amaterasu. Whereas Chinese emperors could be deposed if they lost the mandate of Heaven, the traditional Japanese story makes the imperial line permanent and eternal.

The influence of Taoism from China was subtle but extensive. Following the Chinese bureaucratic model, the Japanese government set up a Bureau of Divination, officially incorporating Taoistic practices of divination for determining auspicious dates for government activities and interpreting good and bad omens. Gradually ideas and practices from religious Taoism merged with traditional Japanese ideas of kami and nature and filtered into all the Japanese religious traditions.

The importation of Buddhism by means of monks and nuns, images and scriptures, masters and searchers, continued strongly in the Nara period, when the first important Buddhist philosophical schools developed in Japan. Important for the story is the increasing acceptance of Buddhism first by the nobility and the imperial court, followed by a general turn to Buddhism also by the common people of the land. Wandering shamans and charismatic leaders adopted the new Buddhist vision and became evangelists for the new teaching. One shamanistic Buddhist priest, Gyogi, had no education or ordination but because of his zeal and ability to unify the people around Buddhism was

The great statue of the Sun Buddha at Todaiji Temple in Nara.

made archbishop of Buddhist priests in Japan. In 752 Emperor Shomu decided to build a great Buddhist temple in Nara as the central temple for all Japan, and he enlisted Gyogi and others to raise money from the common people for erecting a colossal statute of Lochana, the Sun Buddha (Vairocana) there.

But what about the sun kami, Amaterasu? What did the imperial Ancestress feel about this foreign sun deity? The story says that the emperor sent Gyogi to inquire of Amaterasu at the Grand Shrine of Ise, and the august Ancestress communicated that the Sun Buddha Lochana was really a manifestation of the kami and could be worshiped as identical with the sun kami, Amaterasu. Since the protection provided by the Buddha was now considered important, the emperor also set up temples in all the provinces where monks and nuns could live and pray for the welfare of the nation.

Thus the sacred history was transformed to include both Confucianist virtues and Buddhist worship. The Japanese story is based on relationship to the kami. But it is also the story of Confucius, and it is especially the story of the Buddha who came to the Japanese land.

HISTORICAL TRANSFORMATIONS OF THE JAPANESE WAY

After the formative periods in the prehistoric and Nara eras, the Japanese tradition has seen many historical transformations. These have resulted both from internal developments and from political and social changes, especially pressures on Japan from the outside.

Transformations Along the Way

The Japanese path, now accepting Buddhism and Chinese cultures as part of the story, widened and deepened during the Heian (974–1185), Kamakura (1185–1333), and Muromachi (1333–1600) periods. One of the chief characteristics of Japanese history is the periodic influence that came from the Chinese mainland. Japanese people responded—usually scores of years later—to religious and cultural developments in China, and the shaping of the Japanese way was closely related to these influences. Some powerful religious personalities came forth during these times to provide dynamic leadership and founded Buddhist movements that transformed religious life in Japan.

Firming Up the Foundations: The Heian Period

When the capital city was moved to Heian (Kyoto) in 794, a classical period of refinement and deepened religious understanding commenced, under imperial courtly rule. The emperor was the nominal ruler, but real power was held by the Fujiwara family, which cultivated a courtly style of elegance and taste well illustrated, for example, in Lady Murasaki's *Tale of Genji*, a masterpiece of early Japanese literature. Much of the stimulus for culture came from two new Buddhist schools imported from China, Shingon and Tendai. Each established an important monastic center in Japan and acted as a wellspring for Buddhist education and the transmission of culture.

A young monk named Saicho (767–822) studied at the T'ien-t'ai (Jap. Tendai) monastery in China and upon his return to Japan established a Tendai monastery at Mt. Hiei near Kyoto. Tendai in Japan actually included practices from some of the other schools, like Ch'an, Pure Land, and Tantric Buddhism. The Tendai monastery on Mt. Hiei flourished for a number of centuries and became a center for many of the later developments in Japanese Buddhism.

The founder of the Shingon school, Kukai (773–835), is considered to be one of the most gifted and brilliant religious leaders in Japanese history. Trained first for government service, Kukai spent years in austere Buddhist practices. He studied the Tantric (esoteric) form of Buddhism in China and advocated these practices for the Japanese people, greatly influencing the emperor and others of the court from his monastery at Mt. Koya. The Shingon practices included the use of mantras (sacred formulas), ritual gestures (mudras), mandalas, and other forms of meditation and ritual. Kukai excelled in the arts and literature, and he established a special school that gave instruction in both religious and secular education. His writings describe the development of all religions through ten stages, with Shingon as the highest level;

and he taught the doctrine of becoming a Buddha in this very body through the Tantric practices. Shingon became a kind of national religion for Japan, and literature and the arts were widely promoted under Kukai's influence.

Now that Buddhism was firmly established as a central factor in the Japanese way, Shinto also went through some new transformations. In earlier times Shinto was simply a variety of folk beliefs and practices loosely held together by the leading clans and their mythologies. Now there was an attempt to create a more self-conscious Shinto tradition based on the ancient way of the kami. Imperial edicts called for the people to be pure, bright, and upright, in accordance with the kami way, and a work on history as transmitted in a Shinto priestly family was compiled, the *Kogoshui* (Gleanings from Ancient Accounts). Rules were put forth regulating the shrines and priests and designating a number of important shrines as "specially privileged," receiving support from the court. Now Shinto, at least as represented by the larger shrines and their priesthoods, was becoming an institutionalized religion.

But important internal transformations of Shinto were also occurring. Shinto priests were not oblivious to the powers of the Buddha and of Chinese culture. The feeling eventually developed that the kami themselves could benefit by the help of the Buddha, and in some shrines Buddhist chapels were set up and Buddhist scriptures recited before the presence of the kami. These popular attitudes were reinforced by ideas that the kami were "protectors of the Buddha's Law." Therefore kami were enshrined in Buddhist temples. Before long the idea developed that Buddhahood was the "original essence" of the kami, and so the kami could be worshiped as manifestations of the Buddha, some of them even given the title *bosatsu*, bodhisattva.

As Shinto was transformed by Buddhist influence, Buddhism was also being influenced by the Japanese traditions, especially the this-worldly attitude of the Shinto way. Many people took to a path that combined ideas and practices from both Shinto and Buddhism. For example, there were many shamanistic holy men who underwent spiritual disciplines in the mountains and practiced healing and exorcism. Typically they based their practice in esoteric Buddhism, using the fire

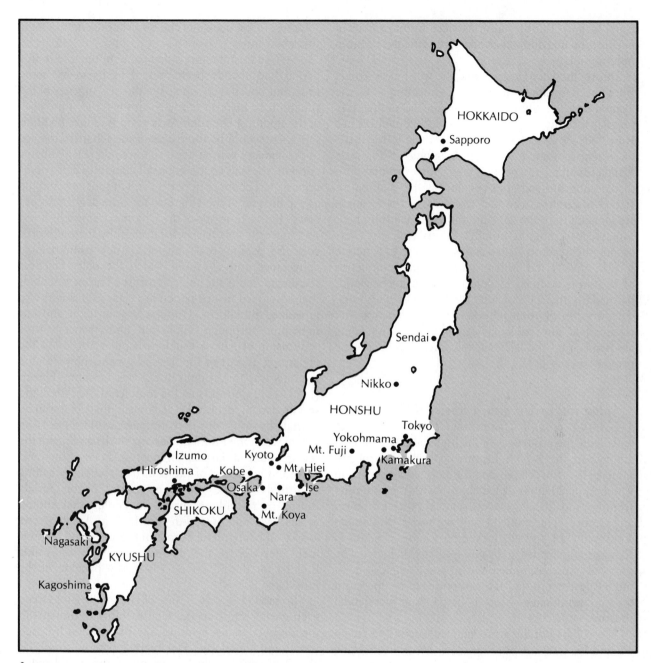

Japan.

ritual (*goma*). But they also practiced Shinto rituals of purification and abstinence and made retreats to Shinto holy mountains.

During the later Heian period the worship of Amida Buddha grew rapidly in Japan, permeating both the Tendai and the Shingon schools and becoming very popular with the aristocrats. Shamanistic Buddhists like Kuya (903–972) took the gospel of Amida to the masses, teaching them to sing the Nembutsu, "Praise to Amida Buddha," to a popular tune. Also extremely popular among the common people was the Bodhisattva Jizo (Ksitigarbha), who had taken a vow not to attain Buddhahood until the last soul was redeemed from hell. Since fear of suffering in hell was very real, especially among the peasants, Jizo was a good figure to which to turn in anxiety and distress, for he mediates on behalf of the souls destined to descend to the lower world, particularly the souls of infants and children who die. The worship of Amida Buddha and of Jizo was not confined to any particular school or locality, being absorbed into the general religious system of the people.

Salvation in Uncertain times: the Kamakura and Muromachi Eras

Rule by the aristocracy of the imperial court came to an end in the twelfth century with the rise of the *samurai* (warrior) classes and the new feudal system in which landed barons called *daimyo* with their samurai retainers and vassals vied with one another for power and control. The strongest military leader, Minamoto Yorimoto (1147–1199), moved the center of power to Kamakura and ruled as *shogun* (military dictator). The imperial house continued to exist and to exercise ceremonial leadership, but the real power from now until the nineteenth cnetury was in the hands of such feudal shoguns.

The collapse of the aristocratic culture of the Heian era and the outbreak of more or less continual fighting between the various daimyo brought a new sense of uncertainty and despair among the people. How can we find order and meaning in life? How can we be delivered from this passing world and attain assurance of salvation in the next world? Such questions were foremost to the people of the Kamakura period in these uncertain times.

The Buddhist traditions that came to the fore in this period had already been present in Japan for some time, but now they resonated to the new urgency of the situation. In the eyes of many, this was the "third age" of the Buddhist Dharma. An ancient Buddhist tradition said there would be three ages of the Dharma: the age of the perfect Dharma when many could reach enlightenment; the age of the copied Dharma, when conditions would be more imperfect and degenerate; and the age of the end of the Dharma, the time of great degeneracy. In this third age of the Dharma, many felt, it was no longer possible to reach salvation by the traditional path. So people were looking for new assurances of deliverance and salvation, which the older practices seemingly could no longer provide. The new schools that developed in this period are clear expressions of a Japanized Buddhism, emphasizing salvation and enlightenment through simple faith and practice.

Worship of Amida Buddha, popular already in the Heian era as part of the Tendai system, now became the only way to salvation in the eyes of many. Honen (1133–1212), considered the founder of the Pure Land sect in Japan, declared, "It is clear that for ordinary mortals living in this contaminated world there is no way to reach the Pure Land except by depending on the saving power of Amida."[5] Honen was one of the most persistent advocates of the path of salvation by calling on Amida's name with the words, "Namu Amida Butsu," a formula of praise to Amida that should be said over and over with firm faith in Amida's vows to save all beings. The Pure Land sect became a movement devoted to the exclusive worship of Amida Buddha for the gift of rebirth in the paradise of the Pure Land.

Shinran (1173–1262), one of Honen's disciples, laid even greater stress on the total inability of humans in this degenerate age to move toward salvation by one's own merit or efforts. The highest path is simply to accept the gift of salvation promised through Amida's vow to save all beings and, out of thankfulness, to chant Amida's name and rely completely on his grace. To emphasize that humans can have no merit in this degenerate age, Shinran gave up monastic life, married, and raised a family—starting the tradition of married Buddhist priests in Japan. The sect founded by Shinran, the True Pure Land, became very popular in medieval Japan and has continued to be the religious practice of a large segment of the Japanese people down to the present day.

A similar answer to the question of salvation was provided by Nichiren (1222–1282), a humble fisherman's son who became, in the eyes of many, "the pillar of Japan, the eye of the nation, and the vessel of the country." Nichiren was convinced that the woes Japan was experiencing resulted from the abandonment of the true Buddhist path. The true path is the teaching of the Lotus Sutra; this is the supreme teaching of the Buddha Shakyamuni, revealing the one and only way to salvation both for individuals and for the whole nation. Now, Nichiren felt, the different Buddhist schools had abandoned this pure and simple truth, and because of that Japan was suffering various misfortunes. To return to the true path people need only to take on their lips the name of the Lotus Sutra through the formula, "Namu myoho rengekyo" (Praise to the wondrous truth of the Lotus Sutra). Nichiren himself was identified as an incarnation of a bodhisattva, and he made it his mission to save Japan from the political and social evils that he felt came from wrong Buddhist teachings. He condemned the other Buddhist schools, caused great difficulty for the government, was twice exiled, and narrowly escaped execution. But he received considerable recognition when the Mongol invasion that he predicted actually occurred, and many were attracted to his simple religion and his vision of Japan as an earthly Buddha-land. Nichiren's zeal and his straightforward path appealed to many in this broken age, and the Nichiren sect grew to a large movement. Through the centuries Nichiren Buddhism has been a special Japanese form of Buddhism, and today many people in Japan belong to Nichiren groups.

Not all people were looking for salvation through sacred power that comes to us from outside, whether from Amida Buddha or from the Lotus Sutra. Some in this turbulent period were looking to Buddhist roots for something that would transcend the disorder and anxiety and restore calmness in the heart. And they found this in the practice of Zen (Chinese Ch'an)

Buddhism. The Zen meditation type of Buddhism was known in Japan in the Nara and Heian periods along with the other forms of Chinese Buddhism, but the impetus for developing Zen as a separate school in Japan came from fresh importations from China. Eisai (1141–1215) is credited with bringing Zen anew to Japan; he found favor with the military rulers and emphasized the nationalistic value of Zen, as in his tract, "Propagate Zen, Protect the Country." It was Dogen (1200–1253) who provided the intellectual foundation for Zen in Japan. As a Tendai monk, he was bothered at an early age with the question that if all living beings have the Buddha-nature, then why does one have to engage in religious practices to gain enlightenment? His search took him to China, and when he returned he established a monastery where he taught the single practice of *zazen* (sitting in meditation). It is not by "other power" that one is saved, Dogen taught; rather it is through self-power, simply sitting in meditation, that one reaches enlightenment. Since one already possesses the Buddha-nature, all one has to do is awaken to that nature.

Dogen founded the Soto (Chin. Ts'ao-tung) Zen sect in Japan, which advocates "gradual enlightenment," that is, an unhurried, purposeless, nonstriving practice of zazen, which gradually deepens one's experience of enlightenment. The other main school that developed is Rinzai (Chin. Lin-chi), the "sudden enlightenment" school. Rinzai masters typically gave their disciples koans, Zen questions and riddles from the sayings of the Chinese masters. The disciple would concentrate on this koan, eventually experiencing a sudden breakthrough, an awakening.

Zen monasteries in Japan practiced an austere mode of life with heavy emphasis on meditation as the path to enlightenment. Critical of the "easy paths" of Pure Land and Nichiren Buddhism, Zen adherents cultivated a strong-minded approach to the spiritual life that brought calm and control in the midst of the troubles of the age. There is no need to rely on the Buddha from far off or to long to be reborn in the Pure land of the West. The Pure Land is right here; the Buddha is within oneself! Anyone, taught Dogen, even women and common people, can sit in meditation and realize Buddhahood.

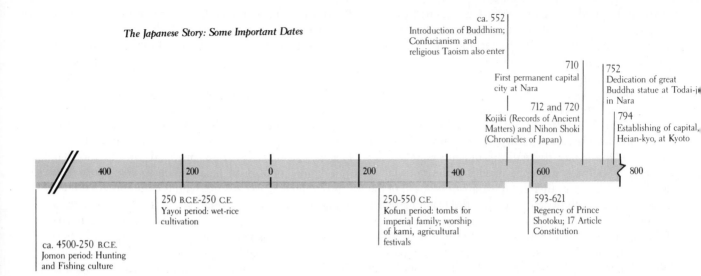

ca. 552
Introduction of Buddhism;
Confucianism and
religious Taoism also enter

710
First permanent capital
city at Nara

712 and 720
Kojiki (Records of Ancient
Matters) and Nihon Shoki
(Chronicles of Japan)

752
Dedication of great
Buddha statue at Todai-ji
in Nara

794
Establishing of capital,
Heian-kyo, at Kyoto

400   200   0   200   400   600   800

250 B.C.E.-250 C.E.
Yayoi period: wet-rice
cultivation

250-550 C.E.
Kofun period: tombs for
imperial family; worship
of kami, agricultural
festivals

593-621
Regency of Prince
Shotoku; 17 Article
Constitution

ca. 4500-250 B.C.E.
Jomon period: Hunting
and Fishing culture

Of course, the common people were not drawn to Zen as they were to Pure Land and Nichiren, but one important class did find the Zen approach most attractive—the samurai. This newly rising class of warriors and military lords found meaning in the discipline, self-reliance, strong commitment, and mental control involved in Zen practice. Zen's strong sense of enlightenment directly within the pursuits of the ordinary world gave strong impetus to martial arts like swordfighting and archery, and it likewise contributed greatly to other traditional arts like poetry, classical Noh drama, and the tea ceremony. Great artistic masters like Zeami (Noh drama), Rikyu (tea ceremony), and Basho (haiku poetry) drew inspiration from Zen. Although the total number of Zen adherents during these times was perhaps never large, through the important Zen monasteries and the dedication of the warrior class and artists Zen had a transforming effect on all Japanese society and culture.

Zen provided a new avenue for Confucianism to permeate Japanese society—now the Neo-Confucianism of the late Sung period in China. With emphasis on loyalty to superiors and self-transformation through discipline and study, Neo-Confucianism com-

bined with Zen to provide a foundation for the "Way of the Warrior," or *bushido*. Samurai became retainers of a particular daimyo master and dedicated themselves with total loyalty to that master, practicing military discipline as a kind of spiritual training. Bushido placed a heavy emphasis on bravery, duty, and being fearless to meet death in the service of one's lord.

Shinto continued to be an important influence during the medieval era, existing both in its local popular forms and in the amalgamation with Buddhism. For the first time in Japan, leading thinkers tried to articulate the Shinto basis of the Japanese way, acknowledging the contributions made also by Confucianism and Buddhism but beginning the intellectual process that eventually attempted to separate Shinto from Buddhism.

This cultural synthesis involving Shinto, Buddhist, and Confucian religious traditions formed the basis for the aesthetic pursuits that blossomed in the Muromachi era (1333–1600). So much of what we consider to be typically Japanese cultural forms in architecture, literature, and the other arts grew out of this synthesis. Main elements were contributed by the different religious traditions: the sense of the purity, beauty, and

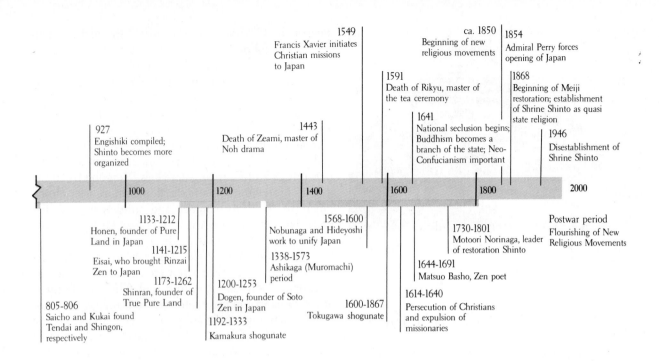

927
Engishiki compiled;
Shinto becomes more
organized

1443
Death of Zeami, master of
Noh drama

1549
Francis Xavier initiates
Christian missions
to Japan

1591
Death of Rikyu, master of
the tea ceremony

ca. 1850
Beginning of new
religious movements

1854
Admiral Perry forces
opening of Japan

1641
National seclusion begins;
Buddhism becomes a
branch of the state; Neo-
Confucianism important

1868
Beginning of Meiji
restoration; establishment
of Shrine Shinto as quasi
state religion

1946
Disestablishment of
Shrine Shinto

1000   1200   1400   1600   1800   2000

1133-1212
Honen, founder of Pure
Land in Japan

1141-1215
Eisai, who brought Rinzai
Zen to Japan

1173-1262
Shinran, founder of
True Pure Land

805-806
Saicho and Kukai found
Tendai and Shingon,
respectively

1200-1253
Dogen, founder of Soto
Zen in Japan

1192-1333
Kamakura shogunate

1568-1600
Nobunaga and Hideyoshi
work to unify Japan

1338-1573
Ashikaga (Muromachi)
period

1600-1867
Tokugawa shogunate

1614-1640
Persecution of Christians
and expulsion of
missionaries

1644-1691
Matsuo Basho, Zen poet

1730-1801
Motoori Norinaga, leader
of restoration Shinto

Postwar period
Flourishing of New
Religious Movements

goodness of nature; the realization of spiritual realities through art forms; and the experience of self-cultivation and transformation through the artistic practice. Such elements as these combine in the Japanese *geijutsu-do*, the "way of art." Among the arts widely practiced as spiritual aesthetic paths were poetry, painting, Noh drama, calligraphy, the tea ceremony, flower arranging, gardening, and even martial arts like sword-fighting and archery. The heritage from the medieval religio-aesthetic synthesis has been a strong factor in shaping Japanese identity.

The Coming of the West and the Modern Period

The first real encounter with the West and with Christianity came in the middle of the sixteenth century, near the close of the Muromachi period. The unification of Japan under the Tokugawa shogunate together with the reaction against Christianity and foreign influence had its effect on the Japanese religious traditions.

Unification, Christian Impact, and Reaction

The close of the Muromachi period was signaled in the gathering strength of three military dictators who finally unified Japan during the last thirty years of the sixteenth century: Nobunaga, Hideyoshi, and Tokugawa Ieyasu. The long medieval period of wars and conflicts ended when Tokugawa Ieyasu (1542–1616) established the Tokugawa Shogunate, instituting a peaceful period for Japan from 1600–1867.

By the time Oda Nobunaga (1534–1582) came to power, the various Buddhist groups had attained considerable land and even military power in Japanese society, and there was also much fighting between the Pure Land and the Nichiren groups, each with its own army of solider-monks. With power, of course, came a tendency toward political involvement, and a power struggle ensued between Nobunaga and the Buddhists, especially the Pure Land group. In several attacks Nobunaga massacred tens of thousands from this sect. The violence of these events considerably weakened

Himeji Castle, typical of castles in Japan dating from the medieval period.

the influence of the Buddhist groups, at least for a while.

But the religious situation during the unification of Japan was complicated by the intrusion of a new foreign religion: Christianity. European explorers and traders began to arrive in the 1540s, and the Jesuit missionary Francis Xavier arrived in 1549, followed by other Jesuit missionaries and priests of the Franciscan and Dominican orders. Christian and European influence rose sharply for half a century and then just as sharply declined and virtually disappeared in the Japanese reaction that led to the closing of Japan. But the Christian story, so foreign to Japan, touched and contributed to the Japanese story.

The Society of Jesus, formed by Ignatius Loyola in 1540, sent forth an army of Christian monk-soldiers into the Asian world. Pursuing a policy of accommodation to the best of the local cultures, Frances Xavier and other Jesuits attempted to convert the Japanese feudal leaders to Christianity, with some success for a time. Following the lead of certain feudal lords, tens of thousands of people took over the Christian vision. The spread of Christianity was aided perhaps by Nobunaga's hostility toward the organized Buddhist groups.

But suspicions about the connections of Christians with the foreign European powers soon surfaced, and Nobunaga's successor Hideyoshi (1537–1598) turned against the Christians and instigated the first persecutions, to be followed by the more systematic attempts by the early Tokugawa rulers to control and wipe out the European-Christian intrusion. There were heroic martyrdoms and even a peasant-based revolt of some 37,000 people, mostly Christian, in Shimabara in 1637–1638, who stood against government forces for several months before being massacred. Finally the Tokugawa authorities enforced their ban on all Christian priests and Christian activities. Responding to the threat of foreign intrusion and domination, they closed Japan to Western contact and influence, and the Christian century was over. The ban on Christianity was enforced by requiring all people to register with their local Buddist temples, and reports of continuing involvement in Christianity were investigated and the offenders punished. A number of Christian families and groups in more remote areas did manage to continue practicing Christianity in secret; some groups of these "Hidden Christians" still existed two hundred years later when Westerners again were permitted into Japan.

Neo-Confucianism and Resurgence of Shinto

Whereas the Tokugawa government made Buddhist temples into the guardians of the state against Christianity, the ideological leanings of the regime were toward Neo-Confucianism. A strict separation of the classes of society was developed, with duties assigned to each: the samurai, the farmers, the artisans, and the town merchants. But changes were coming, and before long the samurai class became relatively nonproductive, the farmer-peasant class became impoverished, and the merchant class rose to create a flourishing urban culture with new religious and artistic dimensions. In the urban centers, the "Floating World" of painters, writers, and geisha girls put its stamp on Japanese culture.

Neo-Confucianism inspired Japanese scholars to go back to the original classics of China. But before long scholars were also going back to the Japanese classics, and the Shinto Restoration movement was born. Earlier medieval scholars had begun to resist the dominant theory that kami were reflections of the original Buddha reality; they suggested that the kami represented the sacred essence, and the Buddhas were but reflections of this original reality. Now a School of National Learning developed to promote the study of original Shinto writings and to attempt to restore an authentic Shinto way purified of foreign (Buddhist) influence. Scholars like Motoori Norinaga (1730–1801) argued that the Kojiki provided the best and universal principle for Japan and for the human race. The Shinto Restoration movement exerted much influence on the political scene and helped to create the climate that led to the restoration of imperial rule.

The Meiji Restoration and Nationalistic Shinto

Internal pressure from Restoration Shinto and from peasant uprisings combined with pressure from the West to bring great changes: Japan was opened to the West, the Tokugawa regime fell, and imperial rule was restored in 1867 under Emperor Meiji. The Meiji Restoration combined two quite different tendencies. On the one hand, Japan became a modern nation and adopted many Western forms of government and education, including freedom of religion. On the other hand, the government attempted to restore a kind of "pure" Japanese society on the basis of the classic Shinto texts. The emperor was thought of as the father of the nation. And Shinto was separated from Buddhism and taken over under the administration of the state. So that there could be freedom of religion and still universal participation in Shinto, the government declared that state Shinto was not a religion but rather the cultural heritage of all Japanese. Even Buddhists and Christians were expected to participate in Shinto rituals to show their loyalty to the emperor and the nation.

In the rising tide of Japanese nationalism, the government used the educational system to teach the Shinto mythology as the basis of its claim to the divine origin of Japan and its manifest destiny to rule Greater Asia. There were dissenting voices to this misuse of the Shinto tradition, but they were considered unpatriotic and dealt with harshly. After the defeat of Japan in World War II, the Occupation Forces insisted on the complete disestablishment of Shinto, removing government support of the shrines and making Shinto simply one religion alongside Buddhism and Christianity in Japan. The emperor remained as the symbolic head of the nation, but he renounced the nationalistic use of the Shinto traditions.

Religion in the Post-War Period

Today Japan is a very modern, technologically advanced nation. The people are highly educated and outwardly very Westernized. Secularization has played a big role in Japan in recent years, and many people find it unimportant to participate in the traditional religious activities. Modern urban life does not lend itself to the family and clan-centered focus that was the heart of so much of the religious activity in the past.

This does not mean that religion is dead in Japan today—far from it. After the great disruption caused by its disestablishment after the war, Shinto has stabilized and continues to find support in the local communities. The Association of Shinto Shrines sees to it that priests are educated in the Shinto traditions and rituals, assigning them to shrines as needed. Although many smaller shrines do not have resident priests, they still

Priests and worshipers observing the Mifune Boat Festival in Kyoto. Such Shinto festivals attract large crowds of worshipers and sightseers in modern Japan.

can be administered by local people and served by priests from time to time. Even though many people no longer keep a *kamidana* (household shrine) in their homes, they visit the shrines on festival days and participate in Shinto community activities.

Buddhism still holds the intellectual allegiance of most Japanese, even though they may not actively take part in Buddhist activities. Many who are quite secular still turn to Buddhism in times of crisis or when a family member dies. Japanese Buddhism has outstanding scholars who have contributed much to the revival of Buddhist scholarship in the world. Buddhist scholars and leaders are also much engaged in dialogue with leaders of other religions and with movements seeking peace throughout the world.

One of the most striking developments in Japanese religion in the modern period has been the emergence of many "New Religions," which have captured the imagination of a good portion of the Japanese people. Some of these started in the nineteenth century, but most are more recent movements, and the real spurt of growth has come in the post-war period. In a sense, these are not really "new" religions, for they generally adopt elements from the traditional religions and combine them in new ways. Some draw mainly on Shinto traditions, others stem from Buddhism, and still others draw from a variety of traditions, including Christianity.

A common characteristic of the New Religions is a strong, charismatic founder or leader who has new revelatory experiences. Another characteristic is their emphasis on concrete, this-worldly benefits and goals, especially healing from sickness and success in life. They have simple teachings and practices, and above all they offer a caring community in which people, lost in the frustrations of modern life, can find identity and meaning.

These New Religions run the whole range of traditional religious emphases in Japan. One movement that has many Shinto and shamanistic elements is Tenrikyo, founded by a farmwoman, Nakayama Miki (1798–1887), through whom a monotheistic God spoke, providing a narrative of the creation of the world and establishing rituals to bring humankind back to God. Many groups have arisen from Nichiren Buddhism, among them Soka Gakkai, a lay movement that emphasizes chanting the name of the Lotus Sutra for immediate health, happiness, and success in life. Yet another type is represented by P. L. Kyodan (Perfect Liberty Order), which advocates a balanced life and graceful rituals in keeping with its slogan, "life is art."

So the Japanese sacred story still goes on today, with many changes and transformations. It is difficult to predict the future in the Japanese context. Certainly the story of the traditional religions, Shinto and Buddhism, will continue, and perhaps renewal and revitalization will take place. And just as certainly the widespread secular attitudes of many people will continue and perhaps grow. Less certain is the future story of the New Religions, whose growth has stabilized after the great surge in the early post-war period. Perhaps these religions will mature, enter into associations with others, and become a continuing part of the Japanese religious story.

DISCUSSION QUESTIONS

1. What are the half-dozen religious traditions that share in making up the identity of many Japanese?
2. In what ways has the mythic tradition about the creation of the world and the rule of Amaterasu provided identity for the Japanese people?
3. What does the story about the first introduction of a Buddha image into Japan reveal about the early Japanese reaction to Buddhism?
4. What was Prince Shotoku's importance for Buddhism in Japan?
5. Outline the teachings of three Buddhist sects that developed in the Kamakura period. What concerns did they have in common?
6. What might account for the success of Christianity in the sixteenth century in Japan? And why was it soon banned?
7. What were the concerns of the leaders of the Shinto Restoration movement in the Tokugawa period?
8. What are some main characteristics of the so-called New Religions of Japan?

CHAPTER 26

JAPANESE WORLDS OF MEANING

ULTIMATE REALITY: KAMI AND BUDDHA-NATURE

"What's it *all* about?" "What is really the central meaning of life?" "Where do we look for the power that is ultimate?" The Japanese answer, of course, includes many of the Chinese and Buddhist ideas that have been incorporated in Japanese religion. The basic Shinto answer to these questions centers around the kami.

Reality as Myriads and Myriads of Kami

The word *Shinto*, modeled after Chinese terms, means in native Japanese terms the "Way of the Kami" (*kami no michi*). This refers primarily to Japanese religion as a way of life according to the will of

479

the native kami. But the Japanese people have never given much concern to working out theoretical doctrines about kami nature. It was not until the Shinto Restoration movement in the Tokugawa era that Shinto theoreticians articulated basic teachings about the nature of the kami. More important to Japanese understanding are the ancient myths about the kami preserved in classical texts like the Kojiki and Nihon Shoki, and the numerous other stories and beliefs passed on in the various shrines in Japan.

Myths About the Kami: Generation of Sacred Life

Are the kami eternal, or where did they come from? The myths are not really interested in whether the kami are related to some eternal transcendent being or principle. Rather, the emphasis is on the generation of kami as a continuous rhapsody of sacred life, from an indescribable and inexhaustible source.

The myths telling the origin of the kami begin quite simply with the primordial chaos and a spontaneous generation of a series of kami:

> In the time of the beginning of heaven and earth, on the Plain of High Heaven there came into existence first Lord of the Heavenly Center Kami, then High Generative Force Kami, and then Divine Generative Force Kami. These three kami came into existence as single kami, and their forms were invisible. When the world was young, resembling floating oil and drifting like jellyfish, something like reed-shoots sprouted forth, and from this Excellent Reed Shoots Male Kami and Heavenly Eternal Standing Kami emerged. These two kami also came into existence as single kami, and their forms were invisible. These are the Separate Heavenly Kami. Then there came into existence Earth Eternal Standing Kami and Abundant Clouds Field Kami. These two kami came into existence as single kami, and their forms were invisible. Next there came into existence the Clay Male and Female Kami, Post Male and Female Kami, Great Door Male and Female Kami, Complete Surface Kami and his spouse, Awesomeness Kami; and Izanagi and his spouse, Izanami. These are the Seven Generations of the Kami Age.

> (FROM THE KOJIKI, CHS. 1–2)

The kami sprang forth without progenitors, independently, in some mysterious generation out of the fertile, primordial, divine chaos. The last pair, Izanagi and Izanami, became the bearers of sacred life as they created the first land and descended to it to begin the creation of everything.

For understanding the kami nature, it is important to realize that everything that Izanagi and Izanami gave birth to is called kami—rivers, sea, wind, trees, mountains, plains, and fire. They overflowed so much with kami power that they spontaneously generated many more kami from their tears, blood, purification water, and so forth, in complete continuity with the originating kami.

Japanese generally make a distinction between the Kami of Heaven—such as those in the myths discussed so far—and the Kami of Earth. The Kami of Heaven are the powerful kami of the Plain of High Heaven, headed by Amaterasu, connected with the greater forces of nature such as the sun, moon, wind, and the like. The Kami of the Earth are those myriads of kami who are resident in all facets of nature throughout the earth, usually associated with certain localities.

The myths provide a large canvas of kami activity on earth, with stories about various kami of the different regions and their interaction with the people. Already in the Age of the Kami, Susanoo, too unruly for the Plain of High Heaven, was forced to descend to the region of Izumo, and Susanoo's descendant O-Kuninushi (Great Land Master Kami) held sway in the Izumo region and finally agreed to accept the rule of the descendant of Amaterasu. But the divisions between the Kami of Heaven and the Kami of Earth are not rigid. Even the sun kami herself, though she rules the Plain of High Heaven, is in close relation to the people; the stories tell how the emperor enshrined his august Ancestress in the shrine at Ise. Ever since that time the emperor has performed special ceremonies of worship to Amaterasu at Ise for the welfare of the whole people.

Nature and Role of the Kami

These myths in the Kojiki and Nihon Shoki, and many stories and rituals associated with the kami at the thousands of shrines throughout Japan, provide a general view of the kami. Japanese have a personal, intuitive sense of the kami as the center of existence, without trying to define fully who or what they are. Still, there are some basic ideas that can be expressed about the nature of the kami and especially about their role in our world.

Scholars have often attempted to find the etymological meaning of the ancient word *kami*, but there are no theories that have gained widespread consensus. The only way to understand the word is to pay attention to how the people feel and act toward the kami. Perhaps the best definition was given by the famous Shinto scholar Motoori Norinaga (1730–1801), who wrote,

> The word *kami* refers, in the most general sense, to all divine beings of heaven and earth that appear in the classics. More particularly, the *kami* are the spirits that abide in and are worshiped at the shrines. In principle human beings, birds, animals, trees, plants, mountains, oceans—all may be *kami*. According to ancient usage, whatever seemed strikingly impressive, possessed the quality of excellence, or inspired a feeling of awe was called *kami*.[1]

So kami are defined principally by the awesomeness and striking impressiveness that they demonstrate, calling forth feelings of respect, fear, and appreciation of beauty and goodness.

Thus anything that seems imbued with kami quality is thought of as kami. This can include the qualities of growth, fertility, and productivity; various natural phenomena and objects, such as wind and thunder, sun, mountains, rivers, trees, and waterfalls; animals such as the fox and the dog; and ancestors, especially the ancestors of the imperial family. Further, kami can include the guardian spirits of the land and of occupations; the

The so-called "Married Rocks" at Futamigaura in Mie Prefecture. Beautiful spots of nature often are considered sacred to the kami, as indicated by the torii gateway.

spirits of national heroes; and even spirits that are piti-able and weak, such as those who have died tragic deaths.

Unlike conceptions of the creator God in the Abrahamic religions, and unlike Indian and Chinese conceptions of transcendent gods or eternal principles, Shintoists believe the kami, even the Kami of Heaven, to be entirely immanent within the forces and qualities of the world. They are not preexistent beings who create the world and then stand above it. Rather the kami are the inner power of all nature, constituted from the sacred nuclei of the world itself. As such, they are the forces that bestow and promote all life, growth, and creativity.

Some distinction in rank among the various kami can be made, but only in terms of how they contribute to life and growth. There is some tendency to think of the Kami of Heaven as superior, with Amaterasu having the leading position of all the kami. Yet even Amaterasu is not absolute in her power and authority. She pays her respects to other kami and consults them; and even though Japanese revere her, they also worship other kami and go to them for concerns that fall under their functions. And certainly there are kami that are inferior, such as kami of flora and fauna, who also need to be respected and appeased with religious rites when their domain is impinged upon. The kami who are negative and destructive are also respected, those who bring vengeance and calamity on humans. For these kami, too, are manifestations of life-power, turned to the destructive side, and they also are worthy of reverence and worship.

The kami sometimes communicate important knowledge to those who worship them. It was taken for granted in ancient Japan, for example, that the kami communicated their will to the clan leader and to the people through oracular means, usually through a shamanistic priestess. This revelation was kept and passed on as important truth for the family and community. For example, when a special spate of calamities struck, Emperor Sujin inquired of the kami through divination. A powerful kami spoke through the "kami-possession" of Princess Yamatototohimomoso: "Why is the emperor worried over the disorder of the nation? Doesn't he know that the order of the nation would be restored if he properly venerated me?" This kami identified himself as Omononushi-no-Kami, the kami who resides in Yamato, and further designated a particular man to be his chief priest.[2]

Under Buddhist influence there was some tendency in medieval Shinto to look for some kind of kami essence or principle that could be compared to the Buddhist notion of the universal Buddha-essence. Some, for example, thought of the kami as local reflections or forms of the Buddhas, all of whom really go back to the one Buddha-reality. Later some Shinto scholars held that the Japanese kami are really the "original essence" and the various Buddhas are the reflections of this. And there was a tendency to regard one particular kami, such as Heavenly Center Lord Kami, the first kami to be generated in the mythological account, as the supreme original kami who existed before the creation of the world. But today Shinto leaders reject any notion of a supreme creator kami, affirming instead the independent dignity of each kami in the Shinto pantheon, still giving the central position, of course, to Amaterasu.

"What holds it all together?" Monotheistic religions have one absolute God, and monistic or nondualistic religions have some one principle that holds everything together in a unified whole. It is sometimes said that a polytheistic religion necessarily understands the world in a fragmented way, with the different aspects of the world under the domain of different gods. But Shintoists believe that the myriads of kami function together in complete harmony so there is no division of the cosmos against itself. The kami generate all life, growth, happiness, creativity, also all suffering and destruction. The way of the kami is a cosmic harmony.

Perspectives on Ultimate Reality in Japanese Buddhism

The perspective of Buddhism, as discussed in Part III, plays an important role in Japanese thinking about ultimate reality. The ideas of the Dharma Body and emptiness (shunyata) are central in Japanese Buddhist thought. Japanese Zen thinkers reinforced the Mahayana nondualistic interpretation of reality: samsara is nirvana. In a series of writings Dogen, for example, argued forcefully that there is a universal Buddha-nature. Whereas Mahayana scriptures had said that all beings have Buddha-nature, Dogen wrote that all beings *are* Buddha-nature. Thus Buddha-nature is not some unchanging entity beyond the world but it is precisely inseparable from the transiency common to all beings. In fact, Dogen wrote, impermanence and even birth-and-death—the conditioned character common to all beings—are Buddha-nature. In this way Dogen pushed the Mahayana teaching that samsara is nirvana to a radical level of understanding.

One tendency in Mahayana Buddhism, to elevate a particular Buddha toward ultimate status, may be seen in some of the Japanese sects. For Pure Land Buddhists of Shinran's school, Amida is the supreme Buddha for this age, the only saving power available; and his Pure Land paradise is almost identified with nirvana itself. For Shinran, Amida is not just one Buddha among others, limited to his period of enlightenment ten kal-

pas ago. Rather, he is the eternal Buddha, the formless Dharma Body that took form to manifest his essential nature, making his eternal compassion and wisdom available for the salvation of living beings.

Tantric Buddhism in Japan, that is, Kukai's Shingon school, elevated Mahavairocana, the Sun Buddha (Dai Nichi, Great Sun) to the status of the all-encompassing Buddha reality whose body is the whole universe. Shingon thinks of Mahavairocana as the eternal Dharma Body of the Buddha. But whereas the Dharma Body was traditionally thought of as formless and totally beyond conceptualization, Mahavairocana's attributes are represented in the Buddhas and gods of the universe. Mahavairocana transcends the universe, yet this material universe is his body. Kukai wrote, "The Buddha Dharma is nowhere remote. It is in our mind; it is close to us. Suchness is nowhere external. If not within our body, where can it be found?"[3] So the Dharma Body is the ultimate pantheistic-monotheistic reality with personality, wisdom, and compassion, who is found in the world and in our mind.

For the Nichiren Buddhists of Japan, it is the Lotus Sutra that embodies all the power and perfection of Buddhahood. Shakyamuni Buddha is the eternal reality, of whom all other Buddhas are emanations. But the absolute truth of Shakyamuni Buddha and the whole universe is embodied in the Daimoku, the sacred title of the Lotus Sutra that is chanted in the formula "Namu myoho rengekyo" (Praise to the wondrous truth of the Lotus Sutra).

THE WORLD AND HUMAN EXISTENCE

"How can we make sense out of this world and our lives?" "Why are things so filled with confusion and violence?" Questions about the meaning of life and the cause of evil have been felt by the Japanese long before atomic bombs exploded over Japanese cities. Since Buddhism has been a leading factor in Japanese thinking since the eighth century C.E., Buddhist views of the nature of the world and human existence are widely accepted by the Japanese people. The Shinto tradition also exhibits a particular vision of the world and of

At Sanjusangendo Temple in Kyoto, a thousand and one statues of the thousand-armed Bodhisattva Kannon (Avalokiteshvara) provide an overwhelming sense of sacred reality.

human existence, a vision that influenced Japanese Buddhism and that still today forms part of the Japanese way of looking at human existence.

The Shinto Perspective on the World and on Humans

The world in its essence is good, pure, and beautiful, as we learn from the myths and from the unsystematized traditions. This is because the kami are good, pure, and beautiful, and the world originated from them.

A World Replete With Kami

The Shinto myths of the creation of the world really do not tell how the world was created; rather they tell how the kami of everything in the world came into existence, and that is equivalent to the origination of the things themselves. We are told how the kami of the mountains were born, how the kami of forests came into existence, how the kami of sun, moon, and storm were engendered. In this vision there is no such thing as neutral matter that makes up the world; all operates in the will and activity of the various kami.

The main cosmology assumed in the early myths is a vertical, three-layered one, consisting of the Plain of High Heaven, the Manifest World, and the World of Darkness. The Plain of High Heaven is the locale of the spontaneous generation of the first series of kami, but how the Plain of High Heaven itself originated is not told. The unformed world is described as "resembling floating oil and drifting like jelly-fish," and some of the kami were born from reedlike shoots that sprouted from the floating chaos.

The beginnings of the Manifest World came when Izanagi and Izanami, from the Floating Bridge of Heaven, stirred the brine below with their Heavenly Jeweled Spear and, when they lifted the spear, the brine dripping from it heaped up and formed an island. Descending to the island, they had sexual intercourse and bore as kami-children the Great Eight-Island Land (Japan) and then the other lands and the kami of other things. But when Izanagi gave birth to the kami of fire, she was badly burned and died, now descending to the World of Darkness, the abode of the dead. Even in her death more kami came into existence from her vomit,

feces, and urine—all these things are highly charged with kami power.

The overall sense we get from the myths of creation is that the whole world is replete with kami essence, symbolized by the phrase, "800 myriads of kami." This is a kami-saturated cosmos, for all the kami are immanent within the world. There is no such thing as nature in distinction from the sacred power, as is the case in the monotheistic religions. Furthermore, the world gradually progresses from chaos to order, from confusion and conflict to harmony and unity, as the kami engender the whole world and then bring it all into peaceful functioning under kami rule. All things, organic and inorganic, fit together in this divine harmony—humans, animals, mountains, rivers, forests, and so forth. An early poem from the *Manyoshu* expresses this feeling:

> Between the provinces of Kai and Suruga
> > Stands the lofty peak of Fuji.
> Heavenly clouds would not dare cross it;
> > Even birds dare not fly above it.
> The fire of volcano is extinguished by snow,
> > and yet snow is consumed by fire.
> It is hard to describe;
> > It is impossible to name it.
> One only senses
> > the presence of a mysterious kami.[4]

The whole universe is essentially a sacred community of living beings, all together contributing to the development of inexhaustible kami power. This-worldly values are not negated in Shinto, for there is no need to transcend the Manifest World for a different kind of world. This world—the only world for humans—is inherently good, pure, and beautiful.

Humans as Children of the Kami

Unlike the creation stories of the Abrahamic religions, the creation of humans does not receive special attention in the Japanese myths. Humans are "children of the kami," just like the mountains, rivers, animals, and all the rest. There really is no sharp line separating humans from kami, for in a sense all humans have the kami nature. After death humans can be thought of as kami, though this term is usually reserved for great and important ancestors. Since humans received life from the kami, they have that kami essence within themselves. They are originally pure and clean.

The meaning and purpose of life is implied in the truth that humans are children of the kami. Owing life to the kami, humans should show gratitude by contributing to the continuing evolution of the kami-based world.

The Reality of Human Existence: Pollution and Failure

"Why do we fail to live in harmony and happiness?" For all its optimism, Shinto does know of human failure and inadequacy. Whereas this does not stem from the essence of human nature, it still is real and often felt in our lives. Where does it come from?

The Shinto tradition is realistic about life in this good and beautiful world. The myths of origins describe how the world evolved slowly from chaos, as even the originating kami experienced failure and suffering in the process of generating this world and humans within it. Izanagi and Izanami failed in their first attempt at producing kami-land offspring, giving birth to a leech-child because of a ritual failure when Izanami spoke before Izanagi. And the dark scepter of death and the World of Darkness rose up when Izanami gave birth to the kami of fire; she died amid vomit and feces and descended to the underworld, where she was seen by Izanagi with maggots squirming around her body amid great pollution. Failure and death, it appears, are bound up with the generation of life.

As the world evolves through kami-generation, a persistent theme in the myths is the unruliness of many aspects of the world. This is symbolized already by Susanoo, the storm-kami brother of Amaterasu. Whereas Amaterasu represents the purity and sovereignty of the sun, Susanoo rages against her, plays dirty tricks, and instigates Amaterasu's withdrawal into a cave, which brings about a disasterous darkness over the whole world. The kami of the Plain of High Heaven depose Susanoo—to, of all places, the Central Land of the Reed Plains (the human world, specifically Japan), where he and his descendants continue their unruly ways and are only gradually pacified so that finally Amaterasu's grandson Ninigi can descend to inaugurate kami-rule on earth. The world evolves toward peace and harmony—but unruliness, failure, suffering, and death are always present in the process.

To get a picture of the realistic Shinto view of human existence, we can turn to the ancient ritual prayers (*Norito*), to the prayer for the great exorcism to be celebrated on the last day of the sixth month, to purify the whole nation from defilements. Included in the prayer is this statement illustrating human existence in a realistic way:

> With the increase of the descendants of the heavenly kami, various offences were committed by them. Among them, the offences of destroying the divisions of the rice fields, covering up the irrigation ditches, opening the irrigation sluices, sowing the seeds over the seeds planted by others, planting pointed rods in the rice fields, flaying living animals or flaying them backwards, emptying excrements in improper areas, and the like, are called the "offenses to heaven," whereas the offences of cutting the living or the dead skin, suffering from white leprosy or skin excrescences, violating one's own mother or daughter, step-daughter or mother-in-law, cohabiting with animals, allowing the defilements by creeping insects, the thunder or the birds, killing the animals of others, invoking evils on others by means of witchcraft, and the like, are called the "offences to earth."[5]

This interesting listing of the various offenses among the descendants of the heavenly kami (that is, the nobles and officials of the land) seems to indicate that people have always been the same, greedy, selfish, unruly, and thoughtless of others. That's just the way humans are—and that's why, of course, the Great Purification was necessary every year.

But the Shinto view does not find evil and offense as something inborn in human nature. This listing of offenses is realistic, but there is no idea here of some original, innate sinfulness. Shinto texts do talk of offense or sin, but the word for this, *tsumi*, might better be understood as defilement or pollution. These offenses are harmful because they bring pollution, and pollution stands in the way of life, harmony, and happiness. Since the kami are pure, they dislike impure deeds, and thus our pollution hinders the flow of blessing and life from the kami.

There are some suggestions in Shinto tradition that

even evil happenings stem from the kami, that is, the evil and violent kami. When Izanagi fled from the World of Darkness, he brought pollutions with him, and from these pollutions were born the Kami of Great Evils. To counteract this evil, the Kami of Great Good were also born at the same time. Some Shinto thinkers have interpreted these kami as the origin of all evil and all good events in the world. The great Shintoist Motoori Norinaga (1730–1801) explained it like this:

> It goes without saying that every event in this world is willed by the kami. There are various kinds of kami, noble and humble, good and evil, and just and unjust. Among the events there are some which may be regarded as unreasonable or unjust; these are operated by evil kami, such as the events which cause troubles to the nation and harm to the people. The evil kami is one who came out of the nether world with the great kami Izanagi when he [returned from there and] purified himself. Although the heavenly kami attempt to overcome the power of evil kami, they cannot always restrain him. There are certain reasons, established already during the divine age, why evil is mingled with good.[6]

Norinaga's reason for emphasizing this is to advocate the Shinto attitude of accepting evil and death as part of life without resorting to foreign teachings (as in Buddhism and Christianity) that deny death by hoping for some kind of life after death. There is nothing sadder than death, Norinaga noted; but the authentic human emotion, knowing death is caused by evil kami, is to weep and mourn, respecting and pacifying the malevolent kami. Other Shinto thinkers like Hirata Atsutane (1776–1843) have held that the Kami of Great Evils are those who hate pollution and therefore become violent and rough when there are pollutions and wrongdoing. In other words, kami do not originate evil, but they do become rough and violent when humans commit defilements and pollution.

The Shinto tradition sees human nature as originally pure but also imperfect and limited. Humans are not at war with kami, there is no fall into sin, and evil is not a cosmic force overpowering us. But evil and pollution are accumulated in the ordinary course of living, like dirt and dust. Since humans are finite and imperfect, they do sometimes act with a black heart rather than with a bright pure heart; they make errors and mistakes, bringing pollution and shame upon themselves, hindering the flow of life and happiness from the kami. These pollutions affect not only the individual but also the whole community, for relation to the kami is always a social affair, and almost all offenses are social offenses.

Consequently, what humans need to move toward better and fuller life is the path of purification.

The Japanese Buddhist Perspective on Human Existence

Though Japanese culture is permeated with the Shinto sense for the world and human nature, Japanese people have also been deeply influenced by the perspective of Buddhism, discussed in Part III, on topics of the universal Buddha-nature, impermanence, no-self, conditioned arising, and karma. This perspective operates for many people in a complementarity (or in a certain tension) with the Shinto perspective.

Whereas Shinto teaches that nature and humans are originally bright and pure, Japanese Buddhists stressed, for example, the notion of "original enlightenment" (*hongaku*), the innate enlightenment or Buddha-nature that all people, and even plants and animals, possess. This means that there is a Buddha quality about life and nature—a quality that was aesthetically explored in poetry, painting, and other arts. But, as Shinto holds that pollution and impurity obscures the original nature, Japanese Buddhists teach that original enlightenment is obscured by ignorance and desire. As Kukai said, "All sentient beings are innate bodhisattvas; but they have been bound by defilements of greed, hatred, and delusion."[7]

Some schools of Japanese Buddhism have taken over the notion of the "three ages of the Dharma" from China, the idea that we are now living in the third, totally degenerate age of this world cycle. Consequently, life in the world is depicted as corrupt and degenerate, and the purgatories and hells awaiting after death are described or painted in pictures with gory details. Other schools resist such a gloomy picture of human existence. But all agree on the basic Buddhist perspective that it is ignorance and clinging that cause suffering and continued samsaric existence.

Japanese writers have provided striking portrayals in literature of this human problem. For example, building on a traditional theme, a short story by a modern author, Akutagawa Ryunosuke,[8] tells how one day the celestial Buddha, sauntering by the lotus pond of paradise, happened to look down through the crystal water and saw hell far below. Among the sinners squirming on the bottom of hell he spotted Kandata, a great murderer and robber. The Buddha remembered that, among his innumerable crimes, Kandata had one good deed to his credit: one day he had spared a spider's life rather than step on it. Thinking he might deliver him from hell, the Buddha took some silvery thread from a spider of paradise and let it down to the bottom of hell. Below, Kandata chanced to see the thread and, wearied though he was from all the torments, began to climb with all his might to get out of hell. He was having a fair amount of success and began to think he might even climb to paradise, even though hell is myriads of miles removed. Finally he stopped to rest, but now he noticed to his horror that countless other sinners were climbing eagerly after him, like a procession of ants. How could this slender spider thread support these hundreds and thousands of sinners without breaking? He cried to them that this thread was his and they should get off. At that moment the thread, which had shown no signs of breaking, snapped above Kandata and he fell headlong back into the Pool of Blood at the bottom of hell.

Selfish struggle and desire are common human tendencies, but they do not lead to liberation.

THE PATH OF PURIFICATION AND RENEWAL

"How can I start living the life that is *real?*" "Where do I find sacred power to give meaning and goodness to life?" These concerns are felt by Japanese as by everyone else, and the answers found in Shinto are shaped by the special history and experience of the Japanese people. Japanese are also much influenced, of course, by the Chinese perspective, especially the Mahayana Buddhist path of transformation.

The Shinto Path of Purification

Whereas Shinto sees the world as originally good and beautiful and human nature as pure, it recognizes that humans do not fulfill their potential in life, that they often fail and suffer. The reason for this, as we saw, is that humans become polluted through wrongdoing or through contact with evil and death. Because the kami are pure, pollution cuts one off from this source of life and goodness, so that people suffer personally and communally. So the most important need is for a path of purification so as to become bright and clear once again.

The Pure and Bright Heart

The Shinto tradition has not worked out theories of how people become transformed and in harmony with the kami. Rather it is in myths, rituals, and poems that we understand the path of purification. The primordial model for purification is Izanagi, who was polluted when he visited Izanami in the world of darkness. He bathed in a stream, washing his body with water and thus cleansing the pollution from himself. In a certain sense all pollution originates in the world of darkness, and people repeat Izanagi's act of purification every time they purify themselves with water or by other means.

Hundreds of thousands of people visit Meiji Shrine in Tokyo on New Year's Day, purifying themselves for the new year.

Something of a theory of how pollution is done away with is found in the Great Purification Ritual of the sixth month. According to the Norito (ancient prayers), this is a national, communal purification to cleanse all Japan from pollution. In this ritual the defilements of the nobles and officials are transferred to narrow pieces of wood and sedge reeds, which are then thrown into the river and carried out to the sea. When this exorcism is performed, the liturgy says, the kami of the various river shoals and the kami of the ocean depths cooperate in carrying the pollution from the river to the sea and to the distant ocean depth. Then the kami of the ocean depths swallow the pollution and blow it away to the world of darkness from which it originally came. "And when the offences are thus lost, it is announced that from this day onward there is no offence remaining among the officials of the sovereign's court and in the four quarters of the land under heaven."[9] Pollution comes from the world of darkness, and the kami assist in cleansing the world by returning pollution to the world of darkness.

But Shinto teaches that outward purification of the body and community should be accompanied by inner purification, a cleansing of the heart that restores it to its original uprightness. Very frequently in imperial edicts, poems, and other Shinto literature, terms like "the bright and pure heart" or "the honest and sincere heart" are used. The Shinto scholar Kitabatake Chikafusa (1293–1354) quotes a revelation from the kami that says, "Fast and prepare yourself purely and fairly with a bright, red heart and not a dirty, black heart."[10] Chikafusa explains that the true way of purity consists in discarding one's own desires and keeping oneself lucid and clear in any situation, just as a mirror reflects objects—alluding to the bright mirror of Amaterasu the sun kami that she transmitted to her grandson Ninigi when she commissioned him to descend and establish kami rule on earth.

The Path of Dedication to the Kami

Purification of the body and a bright and pure heart are required before coming into the presence of the kami. Further transformation comes from worshiping the kami through rituals of dedication, as people offer sprigs of the sacred sasaki tree and other offerings, present music and dance, and read the solemn prayers. The prayers are permeated with praise of the kami, petitions for protection and blessing, dedication to the will of the kami, and vows to live an upright pure life.

Shinto believers do not try to formulate a theory of what happens when one comes into contact with the kami. But as one approaches the kami, the inner heart changes with a sense of awe and reverence and a strong feeling of appreciation and gratitude. This feeling was well expressed by a fourteenth-century Buddhist priest by the name of Saka who made a pilgrimage to worship the kami at the shrines of Ise and found the experience so transforming that he shed tears of gratitude:

> When on the way to these shrines one does not feel like an ordinary person any longer but as though reborn in another world. How solemn is the unearthly shadow of the huge groves of ancient pines and chamaecyparis, and there is a delicate pathos in the few rare flowers that have withstood the winter frosts so gaily. The crossbeams of the Torii or Shinto gate way is without any curve, symbolizing by its straightness the sincerity of the direct beam of the Divine promise. . . . And particularly is it the deeply-rooted custom of this Shrine that we should bring no Buddhist rosary or offering, or any special petition in our hearts and this is called "Inner Purity." Washing in sea water and keeping the body free from all defilement is called "Outer Purity." And when both these Purities are attained there is then no barrier between our mind and that of the Deity. And if we feel to become thus one with the Divine, what more do we need and what is there to pray for? When I heard that this was the true way of worshiping at the Shrine, I could not refrain from shedding tears of gratitude.[11]

Becoming one with the kami, what more does one need? In and through these forms of worship of the kami, people are helped to regain their original purity and brightness and to live life in reverence for the kami. Fellowship with the kami helps one discover the inexhaustible sacred life that has its source in them, for renewal and transformation, enabling one to contribute to the continuing evolution of the kami-based world.

The need for transformation extends to the family and the community as well, and so the path provides family rituals as well as communal festivals. The family rituals serve especially to bond the family together with the ancestors, as people renew their sense of gratitude to the ancestors for giving life, protection, and blessing; and they resolve to realize their hopes and ideals by passing love and care to their descendents. Many of the rituals of worshiping the ancestors are Buddhist rituals, but reverence and gratitude to the ancestors and the continued transformation of the family through their blessings is certainly also a central Shinto concern. Festivals also have a transformative effect on the community, for these are sacred times when the whole community purifies itself and renews its life and harmony by joyful communion with the kami.

So the path of transformation begins with purification of the physical world and of the inner heart, and it leads to renewal of life in communion with the kami, the source of all goodness and blessing.

Buddhist Paths of Transformation in Japan

Many, if not most, Japanese follow in some degree the Mahayana Buddhist paths of transformation, either exclusively or together with the Shinto path. Buddhists in Japan have taken over the full path from India and China, and they have given it characteristic Japanese accents. We find these accents in the path as taught, for example, in Shingon, Pure Land, Nichiren, and Zen, and carried over into some New Religions of today.

Resonating to the concrete, this-worldly emphasis of Japanese culture, one strand of the Buddhist path in Japan has long focused on the possibility of achieving Buddhahood in this very body, this very existence. Kukai, founder of Shingon, provided particular emphasis on this goal, as he taught the esoteric (Tantric) form of Buddhism, but these basic perspectives came to permeate other schools of Japanese Buddhism as well. The whole universe is really the body of the great cosmic Buddha, Mahavairocana or Dainichi (Great Sun), Kukai taught. Since our real nature in the great Buddha, it is possible by meditation and ritual action to realize one's Buddhahood. The body, speech, and mind of Mahavairocana—the Three Mysteries—permeate the whole cosmos. But these three mysteries are innate to all living beings, and therefore it is possible through meditation and ritual to integrate the micro-

cosmic activities of our body, speech, and mind into the Body, Speech, and Mind of Mahavairocana. This is done in meditation by symbolic ritual acts of body, such as sitting in meditation and use of hand gestures (mudras); by recitation of mantras, symbols of Mahavairocana's cosmic speech; and by rituals of the mind involving thinking, imagining, and visualizing, focusing especially on symbolic paintings of the sacred cosmos (mandalas). Kukai wrote:

> If there is a Shingon student who reflects well upon the meaning of the Three Mysteries, makes mudras, recites mantras, and allows his mind to abide in the state of samadhi [meditative trance], then, through grace, his three mysteries will be united with the Three Mysteries [of Mahavairocana]; thus, the great perfection of his religious discipline will be realized. . . . If there is a man who whole-heartedly disciplines himself day and night according to the prescribed methods of discipline, he will obtain in his corporeal existence the Five Supernatural Powers. And if he keeps training himself, he will, without abandoning his body, advance to the stage of the Buddha. The details are as explained in the sutras. For this reason it is said, "When the grace of the Three Mysteries is retained, [our inborn three mysteries will] quickly be manifested." The expression "the grace . . . is retained" indicates great compassion on the part of the Tathagata and faith on the part of sentient beings. The compassion of the Buddha pouring forth on the heart of sentient beings, like the rays of the sun on water, is called ka [adding], and the heart of sentient beings which keeps hold of the compassion of the Buddha, as water retains the rays of the sun, is called ji [retaining]. If the devotee understands this principle thoroughly and devotes himself to the practice of samadhi [meditation], his three mysteries will be united with the Three Mysteries, and therefore in his present existence, he will quickly manifest his inherent three mysteries.[12]

Kukai's words reflect the characteristic Japanese Buddhist double emphasis on the grace or power of the Buddha and on meditation and discipline on the part of the meditator. These two emphases are reflected, in somewhat different configurations, in the Pure Land and Zen paths of transformation.

The one strand of the path takes over the Chinese Pure Land tradition of depending on the power of Amida Buddha. Honen, considered the real founder of the Pure Land movement in Japan, felt deeply that humankind had entered into the third stage of the Dharma, the "latter end of the Dharma," the period of hopeless degeneracy. In this situation it is no longer possible to follow the path of meditation and discipline and reach enlightenment, so the only hope is to rely on the power of Amida Buddha, on the basis of Amida's original vows to save all those who have faith in him and call on his name. The power of Amida is made available through his name, so it is by repeating the Nembutsu, that is, the phrase "Namu Amida Butsu" (Praise to Amida Buddha), that the mind becomes fixed on Amida and, at death, one is reborn in the Pure Land paradise. Honen taught:

> The method of final salvation that I have propounded is neither a sort of meditation, such as has been practiced by many scholars in China and Japan, nor is it a repetition of the Buddha's name by those who have studied and understood the deep meaning of it. It is nothing but the mere repetition of the "Namu Amida Butsu," without a doubt of His mercy, whereby one may be born into the Land of Perfect Bliss.[13]

Shinran, a disciple of Honen, articulated this emphasis on help from Amida into a full theology of salvation by grace and faith. If we have feelings of merit, Shinran felt, these can stand in the way of total dependence on Amida's saving grace. Likewise, if we feel we first need strong faith and goodness before Amida helps us, we will despair. Rather, Shinran taught, even before we are moved to recite Amida's name, we are already embraced by Amida's saving light from which we will not be forsaken. Faith is really a gift from Amida, transforming our minds and giving hope and confidence of salvation. It matters not whether one is saint or sinner—Amida's original vow saves all. Honen had taught that since Amida can save even an evil person, surely he can easily save a good person. To make his point effectively, Shinran turned this saying around: "If even a good man can be reborn in the Pure Land, how much more so a wicked man!"[14] Self-confidence and reliance on "self-power" (jiriki) are grand illusions, for in this degenerate age good deeds are impossible for mortal beings. In place of such pride and illusion, Shinran urged complete reliance on the "other power" (tariki) of Amida, for it is through the Buddha's act of compassion and his gift that faith arises in our hearts, and that is none other than attaining the Buddha-nature:

> One who lives in faith is equal
> To Tathagata, the Buddha.
> Great Faith is the Buddha Nature.
> This at once is Tathagata.[15]

At the moment that faith arises in the mind, according to Shinran, one has total assurance of salvation, for she has entered into the company of the assured, to remain in this state of nonretrogression until she is born into the Pure Land paradise. So the moment of faith brings salvation now, determining once and for all the destiny of the individual and thus assuring salvation. Thus the life of faith is marked by joy, gratitude, and thankfulness.

In contrast to the "other power" emphasis of Pure Land, Zen (Ch'an) Buddhism in Japan has self-consciously cultivated an approach to transformation that relies on one's own powers and abilities to see the Buddha-nature within. The Japanese Zen master Dogen said, "Any person at any time can attain enlightenment by following the path of the Buddha. . . . In following the Law of the Buddha, there is no difference in the kinds of people. Every being in the realm of man is endowed with the capacity to follow the Law of the Buddha."[16] There is no need to rely on "other power," or to look to future rebirth in the faraway Pure Land paradise. The Buddha is our own mind; the Pure Land is here this very instant.

Like Ch'an in China, Japanese Zen teaches a path of transformation that is without goal or purpose. There is no goal to be attained, no purpose to strive for. Goal, purpose, future reward, striving for—all such concepts suggest that the Buddha-nature is something other than the immediate here-and-now existence. All such concepts of the mind need to be discarded, for they only stand in the way of direct seeing. Just sit quietly and do nothing, Dogen counseled, emptying the mind and seeing directly into your own nature. This is to realize the pure mind of Buddhahood and to experience awakening—satori. There is no difference between the

Work is considered a part of the path of meditation for Zen Buddhist monks, here at Eiheiji Temple in Fukui Prefecture.

practice of meditation and enlightenment itself; doing zazen is itself experiencing enlightenment.

Dogen's school of Zen, the Soto school, teaches the path toward a "gradual enlightenment," a deepening experience of awakening arising from daily zazen. The Rinzai school has traditionally practiced the path with a view toward "sudden enlightenment," an intense experience of awakening that comes suddenly after much practice and floods the consciousness. To help disciples toward that experience, Rinzai masters make use of the koan (Chinese kung-an), a question or riddle often taken from the sayings of the early Chinese Ch'an masters, as we saw in our discussion of Chinese Ch'an Buddhism. A favorite koan tells how Chao-chou, when asked about the Buddha-nature of a dog, replied simply: "Wu" (nothingness). One koan often used in Japan stems from Japanese master Hakuin: "Listen to Sound of the Single Hand." Hakuin explained: "What is the

Sound of the Single Hand? When you clap together both hands a sharp sound is heard; when you raise the one hand there is neither sound nor smell."[17] The disciple meditates on the koan, striving to understand it and explain it in daily interviews with the master. Since the koan cannot be answered by ordinary rational, logical thinking, gradually the conceptual operation of the mind breaks down, and the disciple may experience the "great doubt" and the "great death," which culminates in the "great enlightenment," in Master Hakuin's words.

If you take up one koan and investigate it unceasingly your mind will die and your will will be destroyed. It is as though a vast, empty abyss lay before you, with no place to set your hands and feet. You face death and your bosom feels as though it were afire. Then suddenly you are one with the koan, and both body and mind are cast off. This is known as the time when the hands are released over the abyss. Then when suddenly you return to life, there is the great joy of one who drinks the water and knows for himself whether it is hot or cold. This is known as rebirth in the Pure Land. This is known as seeing into one's own nature.[18]

Whether through gradual enlightenment or sudden enlightenment, the Zen path leads to the transformation of life that results from seeing the "suchness" of reality, the Buddha quality that is inherent in every moment of existence.

So we see that, with the Mahayana emphasis on realizing Buddhahood, Japanese Buddhists shaped paths that emphasize either "other power" or one's own discipline and meditation—with many different shadings of these possibilities. We should remember that many Japanese have retained a sense of the basic identity of kami and Buddhas and that the Confucian path of transformation has also remained influential for many Japanese. So it is typical in Japan not to remain strictly within the confines of the Shinto path or the Buddhist path but to integrate elements of Shinto, Buddhism, and Confucianism in a "way" (*michi*) of self-cultivation. Examples of such syntheses abound, such as the way of the warrior (bushido) or the way of the mountain priests. Even though most of the "New Religions" tend to fall into either the Shinto or the Buddhist tradition, the way as practiced in many of them combines elements from Shinto, Buddhism, Confucianism, and folk traditions. Finally, we might mention that for some Japanese even the practice of the traditional arts, such as poetry, Noh drama, the tea ceremony, and flower arranging, is filled with disciplines and rituals and considered a way of self-transformation.

DISCUSSION QUESTIONS

1. What is the nature of the kami? What does it mean to say this is a "kami-saturated" cosmos?
2. What does the Buddhist idea of the Three Ages of the Dharma imply about the nature of human existence?
3. What is the importance of "purification" in the Shinto path of transformation? What is meant by a "pure and bright heart"?
4. Explain Kukai's view of the use of the Three Mysteries in the path of transformation.
5. What is the double emphasis in the Japanese Buddhist path of transformation, as exemplified in Pure Land and Zen?
6. What is meant by "gradual enlightenment" and "sudden enlightenment"? What is a koan and how is it used?

CHAPTER 27

WORSHIP AND THE GOOD LIFE IN JAPAN

WORSHIP AND RITUAL

"How can I find new power for life?" "How can I find meaning in the humdrum of daily existence?" Answers to questions like these are given through worship and sacred times in Japan as elsewhere. Japanese religion is practical more than theoretical. Colorful ceremonies, exuberant sacred dances, quiet meditation sessions, pilgrimages to sacred mountains—more than articulating doctrines and beliefs, Japanese traditionally have performed their religion.

The worship and ritual of Confucianism and Taoism are intertwined in varying degrees in Japanese religious life. But most characteristic of Japan are the specifically Shinto practices of worshiping the kami and the Buddhist worship of Buddhas and rituals of meditation. For many Japanese these are not exclusive practices. For example, traditional families often have both a kamidana (altar for the kami) and a butsudan (altar for the Buddha) in their home, with appropriate daily rituals performed at both.

Rituals of Worshiping In Daily Life

Worshiping the Kami

Since all life, growth, and goodness come from communion with the kami, the Japanese have from ancient times cultivated the art of worshiping the kami, based on the patterns given in the mythology. When, for example, Amaterasu the sun kami withdrew into a cave, all the myriads of kami celebrated a matsuri (festival) to please her and entice her to come out of the cave. Shinto worship and festivals today are patterned after that event. The main ingredients of worshiping the kami are purification, an attitude of respect and gratitude, presenting offerings, and saying prayers—accompanied, of course, with a dedication of one's life in harmony with the will of the kami.

Where does one worship? Wherever the presence of kami is felt it is appropriate to worship them. Primarily this will be at home, at the shrines, on neighborhood streets during community festivals, and, of course, in beautiful places of nature.

Actually, since all life is lived in communion with the kami, even ordinary daily life is thought of as matsuri, service to the kami. But it is important to maintain harmony and unity with the kami by specific rituals of worship growing out of a sincere heart, in a sacred time and a setting of purity.

Devout Japanese often begin the day by worshiping the kami at the kamidana (kami-altar) in the central room of the home, a high shelf with a miniature shrine containing talismans of the kami, with a rope stretched over the shrine. The ritual of worship is very simple. The worshiper washes the hands and rinses the mouth and then places fresh offerings before the kami, consisting of clean rice, water, and salt. On special occasions, rice cakes, sea fish, fowl, seaweed, vegetables, or fruit might also be offered. Facing the shrine, a slight bow is made, followed by two deep bows. A brief prayer may

be offered audibly or silently. Then the worship is ended with two deep bows, clapping the hands together twice, another deep bow and a slight bow. Later the special food offerings may be served at mealtime when a special act of reverence would again be made.

On many special occasions individuals or families go to a shrine to worship the kami, and the general attitude of worship is the same as at home. Proceeding on foot, the worshipers pass through the first *torii* (shrine gate) with a sense of entering sacred space. At the ablution pavilion they purify their mouth and hands with water from a wooden dipper. Standing in front of the worship hall, they jangle a bell, toss a coin into the offering box, and then perform the bows, hand claps, and prayers. On occasions of special significance, such as starting a new business venture or entering college, they may go inside the worship hall with a priest for a more formal ritual before the kami, with offerings and a prayer. Before leaving the shrine they may obtain a printed oracle that tells what fortune or misfortune lies ahead, and after reading these they usually twist them around a twig of a tree or some other convenient object, as a petition to the kami for fulfillment (or warding off, if a misfortune is predicted). They leave the shrine with an inexpressible feeling of peace and renewal.

Some of the most joyous and renewing times come when the whole community shares in a Shinto festival. It is said that many people in Japan today are secular, and perhaps not a large percentage would call themselves Shinto believers. But when a community festival comes along, many of these people join in. Communal worship at a shrine typically includes four major movements: purification, presentation of offerings, intoning of prayers, and communal participation.

In preparation for a festival the priests do many acts of purification, cleaning the shrine and abstaining from forbidden acts. The people also purify themselves with water upon entering the shrine. The festival typically begins with the priests appearing in their special garments, and one of them performs a formal purification, waving a purification wand with sweeping arm movements and sprinkling salt.

As all bow deeply, the chief priest opens the doors of the inner sanctuary (where the symbol of the kami is kept) to the accompaniment of music and a special "oo-ing" sound. Then the special food offerings, having been ceremonially prepared and purified and arranged on trays with exquisite aesthetic taste, are passed from one priest to another until they are placed before the kami. The food items typically consist of rice, rice wine, salt, vegetables, seafood, and fruit. There may also be other special offerings of silk, money, or other items from the Association of Shinto Shrines or, in the case of some shrines, from the Imperial Household.

With the offerings in place, the priest recites the ancient prayers (Norito) in a dignified, high, chanting voice. The prayers thank the kami for benefits over the past year, asking for continued health and prosperity. After the prayers, the offerings are removed, later to be consumed by the priests and their families, and the chief priest closes the doors to the inner sanctuary, accompanied by the "oo-ing" sound.

At this point the fourth movement of the matsuri begins, the communal participation. Laypeople may come forward to make offerings and receive a sip of the wine offered previously to the kami. Often there will be a dance (kagura) performed by the young shrine maidens, both solemn and colorful, according to the tradition of the local shrine. Another special dance is the ancient Chinese court dance called bugaku. In addition, there will usually be a variety of other entertainment presented at the festival, such as horse races, archery, folk dancing, Japanese wrestling (sumo), pageants, and processions—all designed to entertain the kami and the human participants as well. A special part of local shrine festivals is the procession of the palanquin with the kami-symbol through the streets of the community. These processions can be solemn, but nowadays one may see sturdy young men carry the palanquin on their shoulders, zigzagging down the street shouting "washo, washo," under the watchful eyes of the shrine priests. Usually the people go to visit the kami; during the procession the kami comes to visit the people and bless the community with divine presence.

Buddhist Elements of Worship in Japan

Traditional homes also have a *butsudan* in the central room, a lacquered cabinet containing images of Buddhas and small containers for offerings. Offerings

The Gion Festival held during July in Kyoto is one of the most famous festivals in Japan.

are made to the Buddhas and prayers and sutras recited in daily devotions. The butsudan also typically contains the wooden tablets representing the spirits of the family ancestors, so worshiping at the butsudan is at the same time venerating the ancestors, praying to them to ensure their continued blessing for the family.

Worship at Buddhist temples has a somewhat different character from that at Shinto shrines. Whereas shrines are usually simple and natural, without statues, in Buddhist temples there are usually elaborate altars and statues of Buddhas and bodhisattvas, the inner darkness of the ornate temple rooms illuminated with candles that reflect light off the gilded statues and decorations. Many villages and neighborhoods have parish Buddhist temples, where not only Buddhas but also the ashes of ancestors of parish families are enshrined. Often these parish temples have cemeteries where families erect memorial stones dedicated to the ancestors. As at the butsudan in the home, so also at the temple people make offerings and speak prayers and sutras before the altars. Priests associated with these temples perform worship services, commemorative rituals, memorial rites, and the like, for their own needs and for the welfare of the laypeople. The temple cultic life is especially active, of course, during the major annual and seasonal festivals.

The ultimate purpose of Buddhist worship is to attain enlightenment and Buddhahood, but, as we have seen, the path toward the ultimate transformation is broad and can find expression in many types of ritual and worship. One prays before the Buddhas and ancestors to achieve ends such as the protection of the nation, success in life, healing of the sick, or repose for the dead. Several of the Buddhas and bodhisattvas are widely worshiped for such benefits. Very popular is Kannon (the bodhisattva Avalokiteshvara), the "goddess of mercy," who provides help in almost any kind of need, such as conceiving a child, easy childbirth, safe travel, and much more. In times of sickness people pray and recite scripture before a statue of Yakushi, the healing Buddha; and to request response and merit for the dead, people pray before statues of Jizo, patron saint of the spirit of the dead, especially of dead children. Whereas such acts of worship are directed toward immediate needs, we should remember that the power for these benefits comes from the wisdom and compassion of those beings who have achieved Buddhahood and who are believed, through various means, to lead their devotees toward that goal.

Many of these activities of worship can be carried out by laypeople with little or no priestly help. Sometimes a group of laypeople will form their own association for the purpose of worshiping a particular Buddha, holding regular meetings in their homes during which they have simple services and social gatherings.

Japanese following the popular Pure Land and Nichiren traditions exemplify typical patterns of group worship, whether at home or temple, with or without priests participating. The Pure Land worship service includes the usual elements of Buddhist worship, but a special focus is on reciting the Nembutsu, "Namu Amida Butsu," over and over again, for this is the formula by which the worshipers receive the merit and compassion of Amida Buddha. Worship might include chanting verses from Shinran's writings, reading Shinran's biography, listening to sermons, and discussing the teachings.

Buddhists following the Nichiren tradition, one of the most lively and populous of the various traditions in modern Japan, follow Nichiren's special design for worship, focusing on the gohonzon as the object of worship and using the daimoku chant. The gohonzon, as designed by Nichiren, is a kind of mandala without pictorial images; it is a scroll inscribed with names of leading Buddhas and bodhisattvas of the Lotus Sutra, with the sacred words of the daimoku chant at the center. This is the chief object of worship both in homes and in temples. The daimoku is the formula, "Namu myoho rengekyo" (Praise to the wonderful truth of the Lotus Sutra), which Nichiren considered to contain the universal Buddha nature. Nichiren worship thus consists of reciting the daimoku before a gohonzon, to the accompaniment of drums, with worshipers often fingering the particular Nichiren rosary of 108 beads. The worship is dramatic and intense and is felt to produce many spiritual benefits as well as benefits for everyday life. Modern Nichiren groups in Japan often include informal small group discussion sessions that provide opportunity for individuals to share their personal problems and receive Buddhist insight in dealing with them.

In contrast to the Pure Land and Nichiren forms, the characteristic Zen Buddhist rituals are carried on primarily by Zen monks and nuns, although certain laypeople may also participate on occasion. Whereas priests of Zen temples may perform the usual types of Buddhist worship, also for the benefit of the laypeople, the distinctive Zen ritual discipline is meditation. The typical daily ritual in a Ch'an (Zen) monastery is discussed earlier concerning traditional China. Here let us look more closely at the actual practice of zazen, sitting in meditation. The simplicity of the meditation hall and rituals of sutra-chanting, bowing, and offering incense before a statue of the Buddha help set the atmos-

Zen monks sitting in meditation at Eiheiji Temple, with one monk receiving "encouragement" from a fellow monk.

phere for the period of quiet sitting. Practitioners in the Soto tradition sit facing the wall; in the Rinzai tradition, the meditators face into the room, looking down to the floor in front. The basic ritual discipline is the art of sitting itself. Here is Master Dogen's famous description of how to sit:

> At the site of your regular sitting, spread out thick matting and place a cushion above it. Sit either in the full-lotus or half-lotus position. In the full-lotus position, you first place your right foot on your left thigh and your left foot on your right thigh. In the half-lotus, you simply press your left foot against your right thigh. You should have your robes and belt loosely bound and arranged in order. Then place your right hand on your left leg and your left palm [facing upwards] on your right palm, thumb-tips touching. Thus sit upright in correct bodily posture, neither inclining to the left nor to the right, neither leaning forward or backward. Be sure your eyes are on a plane with your shoulders and your nose in line with your navel. Place your tongue against the front roof of your mouth, with teeth and lips both shut. Your eyes should always remain open, and you should breath gently through your nose. Once you have adjusted your posture, take a deep breath, inhale and exhale, rock your body right and left and settle into a steady immobile sitting position. Think of not-thinking. How do you think of not-thinking? Non-thinking. This in itself is the essential art of zazen. [1]

During the meditation session, which may last thirty to forty minutes, one monk may walk slowly among the seated meditators carrying the long flat *keishaku* stick; when someone feels drowsy or unalert, she may bow toward the monk who will then strike her sharply on her shoulders, an act of compassion to assist in meditation. In the Soto tradition, the meditator simply empties the mind, without effort, without purpose. In the Rinzai tradition, the meditator may work on such koans as "The sound of one hand clapping," "What was your face before you were born?" or simply "Mu!" (nothingness), allowing that koan to break through ordinary dualistic notions of self and object. Regular interviews with the master for testing and growing insight also form part of the meditation discipline and ritual.

Sacred Times in Japan

There are a great number of festivals in Japan, depending on the region and specific community, and these festivals may be predominantly Shinto or Buddhist, often containing elements from both traditions together with many local popular traditions. Probably the most highly ranked festivals are those at the Grand Shrines of Ise where Amaterasu is enshrined: the Spring Festival, the Autumn Festival, and especially the Niiname-sai (November 23–24) at which the emperor offers the first fruits of the grain harvest. The Niiname-sai is modeled on the ancient ceremony in which a newly enthroned emperor first offers the new food to Amaterasu and the other kami. Other important local Shinto festivals are widely attended by tourists, such as the Aoi Matsuri in Kyoto on May 15, involving a procession through the streets with ox-drawn carts, horses with golden saddles, and everything decorated with wisteria.

Among the universally celebrated festivals are some that no longer have specific religious significance such as the Doll Festival (for girls) on March 3, Boys' Day on May 5 (now Children's Day, a national holiday), and the Star Festival on July 7. Of important religious significance are the Great Purification celebrated at local shrines on June 30 and also the spring and fall festivals for the tutelary kami. There is also the festival of the Buddha's birthday, celebrated in Japan on April 8, when temples perform a special ritual of pouring sweet tea over a statue of the infant Buddha, in memory of the story of Shakyamuni's birth when flower petals and sweet tea rained from the sky. More solemn than this festive springtime celebration is the observance marking the Buddha's attainment of enlightenment, generally held on December 8. At this time Zen monasteries hold specially intensive training sessions over a seven-day period, culminating in all-night sitting until the dawn of December 8.

The Obon Festival (Ullambana), celebrated in the middle of the seventh lunar month (today most Japanese observe it in the middle of July), is Buddhist-inspired and related completely to the ancestors, like the similar festival in China discussed earlier. The spirits of the ancestors are welcomed in the home at the butsudan with special offerings, and the families visit the ancestral graves and clean the area and place new flowers. Although the festival has to do with the dead, it tends to be joyful, with the spirits warmly welcomed on the night of the thirteenth day of the month, entertained with colorful dances and singing, and then, after two days, sent off by fires to the graveyards. In some places lanterns are floated on a nearby river. Obon festivals often conclude with people dancing around a temporary tower holding singers and drummers. During the festival Buddhist priests hold memorial services in temples and homes. Services remembering the dead and visits to the family graves also take place during the spring and autumn equinoxes (Higan-e); rituals include repenting of past sins and praying for enlightenment in the next life.

The New Year Festival, now almost universally observed at the beginning of January (the old lunar calendar has it in February), is the most vigorously celebrated festival of the year and the most important family event. Toward the end of December there is much bustle as workers leave the cities to journey back to the country to be with their families. Business and industry shut down for a number of days, and the perpetual smog over industrial cities even lifts a bit. Shrines perform a great purification to purify people of defilements from the previous year. Each family cleans and symbolically purifies the house, putting a pine branch on the outside gate and hanging a straw rope over the entrance. Special New Year foods are prepared, especially dried fish and o-mochi, a sticky rice cake. Offerings are made to the ancestors, the family eats, drinks, and relaxes together, and with midnight the cry goes up, "Akemashite omedeto gozaimasu!" (Happy New Year!). At Buddhist temples at midnight the temple gongs are struck 108 times, signifying the 108 kinds of blind passions that should be purged out in the coming year.

On New Year's Day people make their first visit of the New Year to the local shrine, wearing traditional kimono, to begin the New Year with luck and happiness. Buddhist temples are also visited, but the bulk of the seventy million people who make the New Year visit go to Shinto shrines. Many buy new shrine symbols and paper to place in their household shrines, since the old ones have been used up in absorbing all the bad luck and illness in the past year. For the next few days there is general relaxing and visiting of family and friends. Gradually the festivities end, people journey back to the cities, and around January 15 in a bonfire celebration the New Year decorations are burned. So the people have purified the home and the community, renewed family bonds and contacts with the ancestors, visited the kami and Buddhas anew, and now they start off the new year with fresh vitality.

Besides these rituals and festivals there are still other opportunities for personal spiritual growth. People can go individually to the shrine and apologize to the kami for wrongdoing, or, for stronger penance, perform the ritual of the "hundredfold repentance"—walking between two stone markers one hundred times reciting repentance. Going on pilgrimages to special temples, shrines, sacred mountains, and the like, is another well-used ritual of spiritual transformation. Since the Heian era (794–1185) there have been people who engaged in special training and practices on sacred mountains, combining Buddhist practices with local Shinto traditions, and these mountain priests (yamabushi) would serve as guides to pilgrims going on retreats to these mountains. Today there still are some Shinto organizations that continue the traditions of these earlier mountain ascetics, and there are in addition many formal and informal mountain pilgrimage groups. A popular Buddhist pilgrimage takes the devotee to eighty-eight special temples on the island of

Shikoku, worshiping the main Buddhas enshrined in these temples. The main emphasis on the Shikoku pilgrimage is "walking with St. Kukai," the holy man born in Shikoku who founded Shingon Buddhism in Japan and is widely believed to be alive yet today, walking with the pilgrims and helping those who need assistance. The pilgrimage is made by individuals, family groups, groups of friends, and even more formally organized pilgrimage groups.

Rituals of the Passages of Life

At the great moments of life passages or crises, many Japanese look especially to the assistance of guardian kami, whose protective arms enfold all their children. Unlike Western ideas of change and decay, the Shinto view is of life as a clear and pure river with endless change, freshness, and renewal. As so the main passages of life are dedicated to the kami for purification and renewal.

The kami are frequently invoked to assist couples who want to have a baby. In earlier times there were many avoidances associated with childbirth, an impure situation especially because of the blood involved. After a month the child is considered free from impurities and is taken to the shrine of the tutelary kami, to be dedicated to the kami who is affirmed as the source of life and protection. There are special events the family celebrates with the young child, on the first birthday, for example, or the first participation in the Doll Festival or Boys' Day. A special festival on November 15 is "Seven-Five-Three Festival"—for girls of seven and three and boys of five—when the children dress up in their best and visit the shrine.

The passage from childhood to adulthood is marked in a number of ways, for example, when a young man first participates in the local festival by helping to carry the portable shrine. For many Japanese youth, the "examination hell," which finally leads to entrance to a good university, is a critical passage in life, and there are visits to the kami for help in learning. Today Japan has a national holiday on January 15 called "Adult Day," on which all twenty-year-olds are formally recognized as adults and show their gratitude by visiting a local shrine. This very modern tradition is a good ex-

The bride and groom worshiping the kami at a modern Shinto wedding ceremony.

ample of how Shinto has adapted its institutions to modern-day life.

Marriage is an important affair, joining not only two lives but also two families. Even in modern Westernized Japan, many families prefer to arrange marriages for their children, using a family friend as a "go-between," with, of course, considerable input from the young people about the prospective mate. Weddings traditionally occurred in the home, and the crucial ceremony was the ritual exchange of *o-sake* (rice wine) between the bride and groom. In modern times it has become customary to have the wedding ceremony at a shrine with very formal Japanese (or Western) dress. The couple sit before a priest in the presence of family and close friends. The priest waves the purification wand and offers prayers that they may be free of ill fortune and blessed by good things. And all present receive some o-sake as a sharing with the protective kami who have been invoked. If and when the new couple is able to build their own house, they will have a Shinto priest perform a purification ritual at the site, and there will also be a framework-raising ceremony to thank the kami and invoke their continued protection.

Whereas Japanese turn to the kami during the changes in the flow of life, when death approaches their thoughts turn to Buddhist teachings, and most observe Buddhist funeral practices. In a sense, Shinto has to do with life, fertility, and growth; Buddhism in Japan has to do especially with death and the ancestral existence after death. So the funeral service is conducted by Buddhist priests, reciting Buddhist scriptures at the wake, in the funeral service, and at the cremation. A Buddhist posthumous name is given to the deceased and written on a memorial tablet, which is set up in front of the butsudan in the home. The family is in mourning for forty-nine days, after which the dead person is considered to be transformed into an ancestral spirit. After this memorial masses are held on the anniversary days of the death, often ending with the thirty-third anniversary, when the deceased joins the more general generations of ancestors.

Art in Japanese Religion

A deep aesthetic sense permeates Japanese culture, and this sense has roots both in Shinto and in Buddhist-Confucianist traditions from China. Many of the arts are closely related to Buddhism, especially Zen, but the indigenous Japanese outlook on life first established the integration of art and religion that is so characteristic of Japanese culture.

The Shinto attitude is that the elements of nature are the pure and beautiful children of the kami, and humans are to cooperate with the kami to promote this goodness and beauty. The land itself is pure, sacred, and beautiful as created by the kami, and therefore the presence of the kami is revealed not only by words but especially an aesthetic awareness of the beauty of nature. Leaders of craft guilds in ancient times acted as priests, invoking the kami of the tree and the metal before cutting wood or forging metal to create cultural objects. Still today carpenters may intone prayers to the kami when raising the head beam of a building. Further, the idea that human cultural creations are made in service to the kami inspires artists to create the most aesthetically pleasing houses, shrines, clothing, food, and the rest. The Shinto perspective has contributed an emphasis on the natural and the simple in art forms, a reflection of the true pure heart.

The Shinto tradition has not done much with iconography—rarely have there been statues or images to represent the kami, for example. Rather, the arts to which Shinto has contributed are those related to ritual, such as dance, music, drama, poetry, clothing, food, and so forth. The shrine dance, kagura, with its musical accompaniment, has many forms throughout Japan and is carefully cultivated. Poetry, as in the ancient prayers (Norito) and the early collection of poems in the Manyoshu, shows how the Japanese language grew up together with religion.

Buddhist art in Japan is influenced both by developments in China and by the pre-Buddhist Japanese sensitivity for the natural and the simple as appropriate for sacred power. Much use is made of art in Buddhist practice in Japan, serving to enhance rituals, create a sense of sacred time and space, make present the Buddha power, or assist in realizing the Buddha-nature. Chinese Buddhist art was carried over into Japan—iconography, including sculptures and paintings of Buddhas and bodhisattvas, paintings of mandalas, temple architecture, literature, music, drama, and the like. But in appropriating this art the Japanese also transformed it in keeping with the Japanese aesthetic tradition, as is evident in the simple, natural, and open architecture of some monastery halls, slender and graceful sculptures of Buddhas and bodhisattvas, simple gardens of rocks and sand, and Buddhist poetry inspired by nature.

Kukai, the founder of Shingon Buddhism in Japan and himself an excellent calligrapher, laid a strong foundation for the use of art in Japanese Buddhism by emphasizing the universal Buddha-nature in all of nature. Using the art of poetry, Kukai wrote:

> The three Mysteries [body, speech and mind of Maha-vairocana] pervade the entire unvierse,
> Adorning gloriously the mandala of infinite space.
> Being painted by brushes of mountains, by ink of oceans,
> Heaven and earth are the bindings of a sutra revealing the Truth.
> Reflected in a dot are all things in the universe;
> Contained in the data of senses and mind is the sacred book.[2]

Kukai influenced the arts especially by promoting the Tantric idea that through ritual and art forms one experiences the universal Buddha-nature. Since, as he taught, all the world is the Dharma Body, identical with the cosmic Sun Buddha Mahavairocana, through aesthetic forms like hand gestures, chanted formulas, paintings, and the like, it is possible to experience that Buddha-nature. One must take care, Kukai cautioned, not to take the finger pointing to the moon for the moon itself. The highest truths cannot be expressed in words or forms. Yet through ritual use of speech and

A rock garden at a sub-temple in Daitokuji Temple in Kyoto.

forms, especially paintings of mandalas, in meditative practice, one can act out the cosmic drama of Mahavairocana's self-activity, "entering self into Self [Mahavairocana] so that the Self enters into the self."[3] The aesthetic forms thus aid in awakening to the Buddha nature.

Zen Buddhist art in Japan, deeply influenced by Chinese aesthetic developments in the Sung era, uses restraint, empty space, and natural materials to heighten the Mahayana awareness that "form is emptiness, emptiness is form." A painting such as Sesshu's (1420–1506) misty landscapes often leaves much empty space and merely suggests the lines of the form. Zen temples may have rock gardens, such as the one at Ryoanji Temple in Kyoto, created from scattered rocks on a base of raked sand; here emptiness and form seem to interact with each other, creating an atmosphere of stillness and tranquility resonating with the "suchness" that underlies all reality.

Buddhist art in Japan, like Shinto art, has always reflected a concern for the natural and the simple, bringing to fruition the notion that life is art lived beautifully and purely. Under Buddhist influence, many of the traditional Japanese arts are thought of as "ways," complete with spiritual training and discipline—for example, the way of the sword, the way of poetry, the way of painting, the way of Noh drama, the way of flowers, and the way of tea. Basic to these arts is the Mahayana Buddhist sense of the nonduality of samsara and nirvana—that is, the experience of the Buddha-nature can be expressed aesthetically in the commonness of daily life, whether that is the sparse brushstrokes of a landscape painting, a few common words put together in a short poem, or a social gathering for a cup of tea.

For example, the poems of Japanese Buddhist poets attain a deep sense of the immediacy of the nirvanic experience in the midst of natural life. A waka poem from Saigyo (1118–1190) expresses the sense of impermanence:

> In deep reverie
> On how time buffets all,
>   I hear blows fall
> On a temple bell . . . drawing out more
> Of its sounds and my sadness.[4]

In even terser form, haiku (seventeen-syllable) poems present a snapshot of reality that can only be understood intuitively by the mind, as in Basho's (1644–1694) celebrated haiku:

furu ike ya	An ancient pond, ah!
kawazu tobikomu	A frog leaps in—
mizu no oto	Water's sound.

Such a poem presents the suchness of reality in its undivided immediacy, devoid of our mental and emotional interpretations; it returns one, for a moment at least, to the "original mind" of enlightenment.

The way of tea (chanoyu or chado) is perhaps the epitome of a "secular" Japanese art that was interpreted by some great masters of the art as a way of enlightenment. The way of tea is a way of life focused on the tea ceremony, encompassing many of the traditional arts like gardening, architecture, flower arranging, and calligraphy. In involves stringent training and discipline, and it moves toward self-transformation and awakening. But the materials of the art are precisely common everyday experiences: rustic utensils (highly valued, of course, for their rustic beauty) for preparing tea, a simple hut, a tranquil garden, a sprig of flowers, some food and a cup of tea shared between friends. But this ritual art slows down this common everyday experience, as it were, savoring the aesthetic quality of each movement, sound, sight, and taste. Every action, every sense, every aesthetic form is attuned to the real. The tea ceremony is "a one-time meeting once in a lifetime"—that is, it focuses all of life's experience in the timelessness of the present moment, touching that depth of reality that, to Buddhists, is none other than the Buddha-nature. A great tea-master, Sen Rikyu (1521–1591), is said to have expressed the spiritual meaning of the tea ceremony art in this way:

> The essential meaning of *wabi* ["poverty," applied to Rikyu's style of tea ceremony] is to manifest the Buddha-world of complete purity free from defilements. In this garden path and in this thatched hut every speck of dust is cleared out. When host and guest together commune direct from the heart, no ordinary measures of proportion or ceremonial rules are followed. A fire is made, water is boiled, and tea is drunk—nothing more! For here we experience the disclosure of the Buddha-mind.[5]

SOCIETY AND THE GOOD LIFE

"How should I live?" To be Japanese means to live as part of the Japanese people. The sense of community in Japan has been strong from ancient times, and the good life means living in accordance with the role one has within the family, the community, and the nation.

Structure of Japanese Society: Sacred Community

An outstanding feature of Japanese society is the strong group solidarity, as in China. The sense of individualism is minimized; it is the social nexus that provides identity and meaning. Perhaps because of insular isolation, Japanese society is more homogeneous than Chinese society. Emigrants from outside were assimilated already in the prehistorical period, and since that time there have been only a few divisions in Japanese society along ethnic or cultural lines. So the concentric circles of group solidarity move out without disruption from family to clan to village/town to the whole people as one large family.

The importance of the family in Japan is much like that in China, and indeed the influence of Confucianism imported from China played a big part in structuring the family values of Japan. But even before Confucian influence, ancient Japanese society was already based in clans (*uji*) that bound familial groups together around tutelary kami, clan shrines, and a clan leader. The clans in ancient Japan each had their own family kami (*uji-gami*), which they worshiped through the head of the clan acting as the priest of the kami. This tradition of tutelary kami has continued in a modified form up to the present, at least in areas where families have maintained connections with their family shrines or with local tutelary shrines. Children, for example, are taken to the family shrine a month after birth to be dedicated to the tutelary kami. The family is certainly the keystone of Japanese society and religion; in fact, most participation in society and in religious practices is based in the family.

The traditional family often includes at least three generations, the oldest son of a family continuing the primary line and the other sons setting up branch families. The importance of the family for one's personal identity is illustrated by the common practice of referring to family members by their particular position or roles in the family. A sociological study of a village in Japan provides this typical conversation of a mother speaking to her small daughter:

> "Ma-chan, has West-Grandmother gone across to the store yet?"
> "No, she went out to see Eldest-Sister-Uphill first."
> "Well, go tell her that Grandfather-Within wants her to bring him something from the store."[6]

Whereas everyone has a personal name, in this short conversation only the little girl's name (in diminutive form) is used, the others being designated by their place within the extended family.

The cohesion of the family is closely linked to the ancestors. A traditional family will place ancestral tablets on a butsudan (Buddhist altar) in the home and make offerings and prayers to the ancestors in household rituals. They believe that the ancestors make special visits to the family homes during the New Year celebrations and during the festival of the dead in late summer. In this way the ancestors provide blessing and protection within the ongoing family unit.

The family naturally broadens out through participation in the local community, which traditionally was the village but in modern Japan is often a city or an urban district. In the rural areas a number of farming families form a village community for economic and religious cooperation, making practical decisions for the welfare of the community and sponsoring the village shrines and festivals. Neighborhood groups in the cities sponsor local shrines and festivals in which many of the people participate.

The notion of the Japanese people as a sacred nation (*kokutai*) has been a long and powerful tradition, reaching back to the ancient mythology of the descent of people from the kami and continuing in varying forms up to the disestablishment of Shinto after World War II. Throughout much of Japanese history religion has been closely bound up with the nation, focusing on the emperor as the head of the people, descended from Amaterasu, the sun kami. Often this was expressed in terms of a "father-child" relation between emperor and people, with the people expected to dedicate themselves wholeheartedly to the welfare of the emperor and the whole nation. It is true that this ideology of loyalty to the emperor and the nation was abused as a tool of totalitarianism in the hands of military expansionists in the World War II tragedy. But at the end of the war Emperor Hirohito issued an Imperial Rescript to renounce the emperor's "divinity" and reinterpret the relationship:

> The ties between us and our people have always stood upon mutual trust and affection. They do not depend upon mere legends and myths. They are not predicated on the false assumption that the Emperor is divine and that the Japanese people are superior to other races and fated to rule the world.[7]

And under the Allied occupation, the disestablishment of Shinto and the separation of government and religion in Japan were carried out.

But still today the nation has a semireligious character for many Japanese. Many have deep respect and reverence for the emperor as the symbol of the unity of the whole people. They recognize that the state no longer supports religious activities but feel it is important nevertheless, for example, that the special shrine of Amaterasu at Ise is maintained, that the emperor performs the special thanksgiving rites at harvest time for the welfare of the whole nation, and that those who died for the nation be remembered through special rituals at Yasukuni Shrine (the national shrine for war

Children dressed in their finest, visiting a shrine for the Seven-Five-Three children's festival.

dead). National observances like these are somewhat controversial today, given the official separation of state and religion. But the important point is that the Japanese people are more than just a people who happen to live in a certain place; the people still in some sense make up a sacred community that gives its people a special sense of belonging.

There are, of course, other kinds of community identity in Japan. In the early Tokugawa period, following Neo-Confucian ideas, the samurai (warriors) cultivated loyalty to superiors into a path of self-transformation called bushido (way of the warrior). That same kind of group loyalty focused on a master or leader can be seen in schools of the traditional arts, where the head of the lineage (the *iemoto*) is the focus of intense group tradition and loyalty. Some sociologists have pointed out that a similar type of group loyalty operates in many modern Japanese corporations.

Other groups are more specifically religious. There are Buddhist lay societies, for example. Community identity is especially important for members of the New Religions, which are recently formed religious movements that have incorporated many of the traditional religious forms but offer to the believers a more personal and intimate sense of belonging to a large family of like-minded believers. These New Religions usually have a powerfully charismatic founder or leader, and the new believers can enter into a "parent-child" relationship with that leader. Typically there are many group activities, including regular meetings, pilgrimages, and even sports events, to recreate the sense of belonging that perhaps has been lost with the decline of the traditional communities in Japan. These New Religions have grown tremendously in Japan since World War II and for many Japanese appear to provide a most important sense of community identity and belonging.

Religious Leadership in Japan

From ancient times there has not been a sharp line separating kami and humans, and Japanese have always looked on great ancestors and powerful leaders as personifications of kami. In certain periods the emperor was considered "manifest kami" as direct descendent of Amaterasu and as father of the Japanese national family. Through the centuries the role of the emperor waxed and waned, but in general he (or she, in some early cases) always had the double role of being the chief of state and the chief priest of Shinto, since politics and religion were closely bound together. Even though Shinto is disestablished from state support today, the emperor still performs certain rituals such as the harvest thanksgiving ceremony, acting in his capacity as the spiritual head of the traditional Japanese religion.

In early times the head of each clan had special responsibilities to act as priest in worshiping the kami, sometimes communicating with the kami through a priestess or shamaness. Gradually special families of Shinto priests developed, regulated by the government, and today the priests of most of the shrines are educated and certified under the auspices of the Association of Shinto Shrines. There is no longer a hereditary priesthood. During the wartime shortage of priests, wives of some priests performed the priestly duties in place of their husbands, and today some 1,300 of the nearly 20,000 Shinto priests are women.

Of course, as in other Buddhist lands, Buddhist monks and nuns are also holy persons who provide important religious leadership for the Japanese people. A special characteristic of Japanese Buddhism is the tradition, starting with Shinran of the Pure Land school, of married Buddhist priests. Shinran broke with the Buddhist tradition of celibacy for monks because of his conviction that in this degenerate age such practices bring no merit and are not helpful. Following Shinran's example, the tradition of a "household Buddhism" developed in all Japanese Buddhist schools, with married Buddhist priests in charge of local temples.

Among the holy persons in Japan is also the shaman or medium who lives among the people and serves as healer and exorcist apart from the organized religions. One important tradition in northern Japan was the blind shamaness who received special training and was able to communicate with the dead. Founders of some of the New Religions have also shown shamanistic traits, believed to be possessed by sacred power and thus qualified to give revelation and guidance. It is not unusual that the leader of one of these religions is considered to be a "living kami" (*ikigami*).

The Good Life in the Japanese View

"How should I live?" "What is the good life for me and my community?" Like people of all cultures, Japanese also are interested in these questions. It is typical of the Japanese to be directed more toward actually living the good life rather than discussing what it is. It goes without saying that the Buddhist and the Confucian ethical views, discussed earlier, are very important for most Japanese. But the Japanese understanding of Buddhist and Confucian ethics has been tempered and shaped by the traditional Shinto outlook on life.

Unlike many religions, Shinto has never had any standardized written law code to guide behavior, nor are ideas of morality and ethics discussed in the sacred texts. Once, in Tokugawa times, a Confucian scholar argued that the lack of such codes showed the ancient Japanese were morally deficient: "As proof of this there is the fact that no native Japanese words exist for the concepts of humanity, righteousness, decorum, music, filial piety, and fraternal affection." A leading scholar of the Shinto restoration movement, Hirata Atsutane (1776–1843), responded indignantly:

> Humanity, righteousness, filial piety, and the rest are all principles governing the proper conduct of man. If they are always automatically observed and never violated, it is unnecessary to teach them. . . . The ancient Japanese all constantly and correctly practiced what the Chinese called humanity, righteousness, the five cardinal virtues and the rest, without having any need to name them or to teach them.[8]

It is Shinto belief that a moral sense is a natural property of human beings. In proper harmony with the kami, people will naturally do what is good and right in their personal lives and in family and community.

Not only does Shinto not have any written moral code, but it also does not have a strict sense of what is right and what is wrong or what is good and what is evil. Nothing is unconditionally evil, even illicit sexual relations or killing. Good and evil are relative notions, to be understood in the context of family, clan, community, nature, and the rest. The meaning and value of a particular action depend on the motivations, purpose, circumstances, time, and place. In the myths and legends about the kami and the early ruling families, there is much killing, sex, stealing, and the like. But "evil" arises when a kami becomes angry and rough and obstructs the processes of life, and "good" occurs when the kami is quieted down and brings benefits. Similarly, something is good when fortunate things happen and bad when unlucky things happen, apart from considerations based on some standard of morality.

This is not to say that Shinto is immoral or amoral. Traditions of proper behavior have been passed on in families and communities, and there is wide consensus on the general outlines of the good life. It is recognized, according to Shinto scholar Sokyo Ono, that "that which disturbs the social order, causes misfortune, and obstructs worship of the kami and the peaceful development of this world of kami is evil." There is also consensus on what is good: "Generally speaking, however, man's heart must be sincere; his conduct must be courteous and proper; an evil heart, selfish desire, strife, and hatred must be removed; conciliation must be practiced; and feelings of goodwill, cooperation and affection must be realized."[9]

The emphasis here is on the inner motivation, the need for a sincere and pure heart. Thus the important moral quality of an act depends on intentionality, on the sincerity or honesty (*makoto*) of the heart. That sincerity is common to kami and to humans, and if one is in harmony with the kami and acts in sincerity, she will be doing the best, being "true" to the whole situation.

From this perspective we can see that the Shinto view of right behavior is not only situational and intentional; it is also naturalistic. Since our nature, and the nature of all the world, is pure and good as given from the kami, the good life is also the most fully natural life. There is no fundamental breech between humans and the natural world. This means that all natural needs, instincts, desires, and passions are also good and can be indulged in with a sincere and honest heart—sexuality, acquiring wealth, drinking and eating, playing, and the rest. It further means that the good life brings people into close harmony with nature itself, for together the world and humans are siblings, children of the kami. So the good life means an ecological balance, with respect and love for nature as well as human society. One aspect of this ethical harmony with nature is the value Japanese have always placed on art; part of human responsibility is to assist the kami in making human life and nature as beautiful as possible.

Buddhist Ethical Contributions in Japan

The Buddhist ethical system has also been very influential in Japan, of course. The most characteristically Japanese developments in Buddhism—Pure Land, Nichiren, and Zen—have each contributed to the shaping of the Japanese view of the good life. Shinran's writings place much stress on the gratitude that should permeate the life of one who knows she is saved by Amida's power. "When I consider well the Vow upon which Amida Buddha thought for five aeons, (I reflect) it was for me Shinran alone. O how grateful I am for the Original Vow which aspired to save one who possesses such evil karma."[10] The sense of deep obligation to the compassion of the Buddha is to find expression not only in reciting the Nembutsu but also in showing sympathy for others and in refraining from speaking ill of others. Later interpreters of Pure Land ethics tended somewhat toward a passive quietism, based on the view that human life is inevitably under the sway of passion even for those who have faith in Amida. Rennyo (1414–1499), for example, constructed a theory of two levels of moral truth: the believer should obey the conventional morality, at the same time knowing that he is free from such obligations because his destiny is determined solely through faith in Amida.

Nichiren Buddhism, at least in some of its sects, has tended to emphasize the affirmative value of the world and ordinary human activities, arising from the Mahayana equation of nirvana and samsara. Some of the new Nichiren movements of today, such as Soka Gakkai, explicitly direct concern toward human fulfillment and worldly benefits that accrue to the person following the Nichiren path.

Zen Buddhism, in a somewhat different way, also affirms a this-worldly ethical outlook, building on the Mahayana idea that the ultimate truth transcends all dualities, including those of right and wrong or good and evil. Of course, Zen masters do not promote immorality, but they remind Buddhists that all moral values are relative. Right conduct does not result from following rules but from the spontaneous expression of inner awakening. A popular figure in the Japanese Zen tradition is Ikkyu Sojun (1394–1481), an eccentric Zen master who gained a reputation for tavern and brothel hopping, claiming they were far better places for attaining enlightenment than the corrupt establishment temples. But despite his flaunting of accepted standards of morality, Ikkyu pursued the rigors of the meditative life in preference to the pomp and rewards that could have been his through the established Zen institutions. The ideal Zen life transcends standards of right and wrong—but it results in a life of selflessness and compassion.

Principles of the Good Life: Filial Piety and Loyalty

We have emphasized the personal, subjective aspect of the good life. But we cannot forget that the main context for this life is the community—the community that includes the kami and the Buddhas, the family together with the ancestors, and the larger community and nation. In traditional Japan, questions about how one should live are inseparable from the welfare of family and nation. This does not mean that the individual is sacrificed to the group—although that mentality did have some backing during the nationalistic World War II period. The central paradigm, as in China, is the family, writ large as the national family, and the twin ethical principles are filial piety and loyalty. These principles the Japanese learned from China and Confucianism, but they are simply ways of expressing deeply held ancient Japanese values. Hirata Atsutane, a Shinto thinker deeply influenced by Neo-Confucian values, summed up this context in these words:

> Inasmuch as we originally came out of the creative spirit of the kami, [we] are endowed with the way of the kami. It implies therefore that we have the innate capacity to venerate the kami, the sovereign, and our parents, to show benevolence to our wives and children, and to carry out other obligations.... To live according to these [kami-gives virtues] without distorting them is nothing but to follow the way of the kami.[11]

Hirata uses the same word, *venerate*, to speak of proper actions over against kami, parents, and emperor—and this is appropriate, since in the traditional Japanese view humans are children of the kami, children of their parents and ancestors, and children of the emperor. Here we see the concentric circles of the good life, with duties over against family and nation simply extensions of worship of the kami. The good life is really a way of showing gratitude to the kami by contributing to the continuing evolution and welfare of the kami-based family and nation.

Duties within the family have tended to be defined in Confucian terms, with the virtue of filial piety as the core. This is broadened to put emphasis on each person's responsibility upward toward seniors or superiors. There is, of course, a family hierarchy, and the specific grade of privilege and responsibility of each member is clearly understood—whether that be where to sit for meals, in what order to bathe, what subtleties of speech formality to use, or the degree of authority over the family budget. A major obligation, as a member of the family, is to live up to the standards of the family and do nothing to discredit it. Such "loss of face" for the family would be a serious affront to one's parents and ancestors.

The traditional Japanese idea of the good life maintains the centrality of the family, at the same time incorporating the nation itself as the larger context. Here the Confucian key term is loyalty. Since early times the political rule of Japan has been closely united with religion, and loyalty to the rulers, especially the emperor, has been highly valued. This sense of loyalty to one's superior was highly cultivated in bushido, the way of the samurai.

One of the reasons Japanese society has never needed strong law enforcement is the deep sense of reciprocal social obligation and duty that forms the heart of the social system. A key term is *giri*, the social obligation to help those who have helped one and to promote the welfare of the group of which one is part. Each person has obligations to live up to the standards of his or her family, rank, class, or group and to do nothing to discredit them. To fulfil these obligations, no matter what the cost, is the highest moral worth. To fail in this is *giri-shirazu*, "not knowing *giri*"—one of the worst insults imaginable. This system of reciprocal obligations works in many contexts. One important arena is

the workplace, where a person is a part of a large family, the business company. Here loyalty to the company and to superiors in the company takes on important moral force. As in the family and in the nation, there are reciprocating relationships in the company structure, with duties going both ways among superiors and employees.

Concern for the Betterment of Human Society

The strong Japanese sense of group loyalty translates into a feeling of responsibility for the welfare of society. The most dramatic evidence of that is the way the person in charge assumes complete responsibility when misfortune or disaster befalls the people—whether the person is a government official or a company head. In present-day Japan the ethic of productive work for the welfare of the group (the company) and the whole nation is likewise strong. Each company employee has responsibility for the good of the whole.

According to Shinto thinkers, there is in the Shinto outlook a vision that lends itself to social change and progress. As children of the kami, people show their gratitude to the kami by working toward the fuller goodness of this evolving kami-world. As one modern Shinto author says,

> It is further believed that the *kami* who created this land are those who bless and sustain life in this world and that human participation in and advancement of this life constitute at once a realization of the will of these deities and the fulfillment of the meaning and purpose of individual existence. . . .
>
> Some people, not yet understanding Shinto, criticize it as a religion that has a primary interest in this-worldly benefits. From a Shinto perspective, however, an interest in tangible benefits that will promote life in this world is regarded as a perfectly natural consequence of its esteem for the *kami* that bestow and enhance life.[12]

From this Shinto point of view, Japanese people can participate wholeheartedly in promoting the betterment and further evolving of life in the world, realizing it as the unfolding of kami-life that is infinite and inexhaustible.

In a land that has had its share of bloody violence down through the centuries, many Japanese today draw on the harmony promoted in Shinto and the pacifism of Buddhism to present to the world a voice for peace and reconciliation. Like all religions, the Japanese religions also have in the past been used to lend support to violence and war. But many religious leaders today, freed from political ideology, continue to support the unique heritage of Japan while seeking the betterment and harmony of the whole world. The Association of Shinto Shrines has stated these three principles:

1. To express gratitude for divine favor and the benefits of ancestors, and with a bright, pure, sincere mind to devote ourselves to the shrine rites and festivals.
2. To serve society and others and, in the realization of ourselves as divine messengers, to endeavor to improve and consolidate the world.
3. To identify our minds with the Emperor's mind and, in loving and being friendly with one another, to pray for the country's prosperity and for peaceful co-existence and co-prosperity for the people of the world.[13]

Some Buddhist groups in Japan have been engaged actively in promoting interreligious cooperation and in efforts to end the risk of nuclear war in the world. Interestingly, one of the groups leading the peace movement is Rissho Koseikai, a new religious movement in the Nichiren tradition. Nichiren groups have traditionally been known for their nationalism and exclusive claims to truth, but Rissho Koseikai has launched an international movement for attaining world peace through interreligious cooperation. With Japan's unique status as the only country to have suffered from nuclear bombing, these Japanese voices for peace carry a compelling message to the rest of humankind.

DISCUSSION QUESTIONS

1. What are the four main movements of matsuri (Shinto shrine festivals)?
2. What is the main worship for Pure Land Buddhists? For Nichiren Buddhists?
3. Describe zazen.
4. Outline the interaction of Shinto and Buddhism in the rituals of life and death in Japan.
5. What is the religious significance of the artistic ways in Japan, such as poetry, Noh drama, the tea ceremony (chanoyu), and others?
6. In what senses is the Shinto vision of the good life situational, intentional, and naturalistic?
7. Discuss the importance of group loyalty in Japan, as well as the sense of *giri*, in terms of Shinto and Confucianist ideals.

EPILOGUE: CROSSINGS AND GUIDEPOSTS ON THE PATHS

As we reach the end of our study of the sacred paths of the world's religions, we need to remember that our journey has been only a beginning and that a vast store on these paths remains to be explored. We have seen that the paths are really a multifaceted human pilgrimage made up of family groups of religions, each one with its own path that provides full and compelling meaning for life. We have seen that these individual religions are dynamic, changing homes for communities of peoples, sources of identity and meaning, reservoirs of values, and storehouses of motivation and action. Throughout the many millennia of human life, these various paths have guided, shaped, and inspired our human adventure.

The Religions and the Future of Humankind

It is perhaps important to pause for a moment to reflect on the significance these religious paths might have in the world today. Things have changed; it is a new day in our common human history. Each of us can make our own list of what is new today, different from the past, in the areas of life that are of central concern to religion. Here are some starters.

As never before, the religions of the world are being bombarded with rapid change, unimagined secularity, rampant materialism, and competitive ideologies.

As never before, peoples who practice the religions are educated in a modern secular way and taught knowledge and value judgments that are often in basic conflict with their traditional worldview.

As never before, people come into daily contact with many people of the other religions and cultures of the world.

As never before, at least in recent human history, women are becoming aware of their own religious experience and religious heritage; and both women and men are recognizing how patriarchal religions have oppressed women and how religions today need to revive the feminine aspects of religious experience.

As never before, the peoples of the world are bound together into a global village, through interconnections of communications, economy, politics, and concerns of common survival.

As never before, there are forces in the world that have the very real potential of devastating all or most of the human community: overpopulation and starvation; dwindling natural resources and greater competition for their use; and nuclear weapons of awesome and incomprehensible destructive power. Never before (since the early stages of human evolution) has the human race faced such imminent threat of total devastation. Never before has the power to control and drastically affect human destiny been so completely in the control of secular forces far removed from religious visions and values.

Enough—let the reader go on with her or his own list. Given all of this, perhaps the religions of humankind can only be relics of the past! In the view of some, the sacred paths, which in their almost endless variants have nourished the families of humankind ever since the beginning, are in the process of withering and dying. We face, they say, a religionless future. Perhaps, some think, that future will be humankind coming of age, throwing off the shackles of religion and superstition; perhaps, others warn, it will be the Brave New World of totalitarian thought control. Or—more likely—it will be a continuing slide into a one-dimensional, secular, materialistic world culture.

The point of view adopted here, which of course cannot be proved, is that religion will continue to play an important role in the future. To have religious experience appears from our study to be a central dimension of being human, and thus we might suppose that religion will continue in changing and adapting forms as long as there are humans. Religious traditions, as we have seen, possess great adaptability to new needs and pressures. Every religious tradition, in fact, is an organic composite of developments over many years in changing circumstances, always managing to maintain a continuity of identity in the midst of transformations.

So the real question is not whether there will be religion in the future. It is whether the sacred paths can help shape the future of humankind in a creative, beneficial, hopeful way. Each religion and each family of religions have done this within their own sacred peoples and sacred lands. But what of the future of this interconnected global community?

The position taken here is that the religions of humankind provide important resources and guideposts for shaping the future of our human adventure. Most of the religions we have studied are "universal," that is, they claim some kind of universality for the whole human race. Of course, each religion is bound to its own past, its own claims, and its own mission, and one possible scenario is a bloody eruption of holy wars as people are pressed closer and closer together but revert all the more to fundamentalistic exclusive religious claims. Such a pessimistic outlook, however, is not warranted by our study of the families of religions. For all the intolerance, conflict, and violence that each of the major religions bears in its history, there is peace and reconciliation at the heart of each. Each one has a vision for the welfare and happiness of the whole world, with important blueprints for achieving that. How can these great religious resources be tapped in the common human search for hope and welfare?

There are many ways, and there are dedicated people in each of the religions today who are utilizing these resources in their efforts toward justice, peace, and reconciliation in the world. This book is dedicated to the view that studying, learning, and understanding the different religions will make some contribution toward world peace and reconciliation. The crossings and the guideposts on the paths represent interconnections and high points in the common human religious experience, and the better people come to know and understand these the more consciously they can join others in using these resources to work toward peace and well-being for all. Here are four suggestions as to how the resources of the religions could contribute to the common human welfare.

One important area in which the religions are involved is the pressing need in our world today for mutual understanding and respect among the different peoples of the world. Whereas this seems obvious, it still is true that much of the conflict in the world today stems from, or is worsened by, lack of understanding between the peoples involved. Every culture has been influenced by religious traditions, so to understand another culture means understanding the religious vision that the culture is bound up with. Some tragic mistakes have been made—and are still being made—simply by the failure of one people or government to understand and respect the values and religious commitments of another people. One need only mention the treatment of the Native Americans, the conflict in Vietnam, the Arab-Israeli conflict, the partitioning of

India into India and Pakistan, and the civil war in Northern Ireland. Sometimes it is said that religions cause conflict, but that is not the case. Most of these conflicts developed over nonreligious issues. It is not religion but rather ignorance and lack of understanding about religion that lends its support to the conflict. Conversely, better understanding and mutual respect among the peoples of different religions would contribute greatly to world peace.

A second point of importance is that each major religion has a compelling vision of the good world, of the ideal goal of peace and happiness for all humankind. No religion wishes evil and destruction on the other peoples of the world—such perversions have indeed occurred at infamous points in the history of each religion, but that does not negate the honest, peaceful, compassionate motivation at the heart of each. There are many and various approaches, to be sure, to the question of how to create a better world. We might say that the religions from India tend toward pacifism and self-sacrifice; the Abrahamic religions advocate justice, love, and equality; the religions of China and Japan emphasize harmony and reconciliation. By now we have learned, of course, that such terms are oversimplifications, and within each religion there are many variant tendencies. But each approach is valid and helpful, and through better understanding of each other these resources can become more effective in our interconnected global village.

A third point is the transnational character of religious commitment. Whereas religious values and commitments, even of people of the world religions, are always located in specific communities and even nations, religious commitment has the quality of transcending national or group loyalties and ideologies. "Is it better to serve God or man?" (asked by followers of Jesus Christ in a situation of conflict between religious and national commitment) is a question found in some form in all religions, especially the world religions that transcend national boundaries. Whereas religions can be, and often have been, used by the state or other groups for selfish, propaganda, even violent purposes, religious commitment can also be the motivation for people to say no, to pursue values and goals different from those of the ruling authorities. Most governments, in fact, have recognized that religion can be a subversive force! In our world, there are many cases, for example, in which people with the same religious commitment are split into political camps that are hostile to each other. There are Christians on both sides of the Berlin Wall, supposedly loyal to conflicting political ideologies but united in higher Christian commitments. There are Muslims both in Pakistan and in India, bound together in religious belief even though citizens of hostile states.

A fourth, related point is the potential for people of the religions to cooperate together, across religious, ethnic, national, and ideological lines, to deal with our

Pope John Paul II making a historic visit to the Jewish synagogue in Rome with Rome's chief rabbi, Elio Toaff.

common human concerns, which seem so overwhelming today. The secularization of all values, the great god of materialism, the devaluing of human life, the oppression and exploitation of minorities and women, the rape of our natural resources, and above all the great threat to humanity posed by the militarizing and nuclearizing of our global village—the religions do have important things to speak in common about all such concerns. A paradigm of such interreligious cooperation might be the worldwide peace movement, in which people from all the different religious traditions work together to achieve reconciliation, peace, and disarmament throughout the world. It is urgent that those who are steeped in the religious ideal of a peaceful world rather than those who trade in weapons and conflict be the visionaries who shape the future of humankind.

Dialogue: Crossings on the Paths

These suggestions about the contribution the religions can make to the future of humankind are based on the presupposition that people will get to know and understand their own religious traditions and the traditions of others better. What is needed is not a turn back to the dark ages of irrational religious dogmatism but a clear and accurate understanding both of the religions and of the modern world. Once the other religions (and also one's own, in many cases) were shrouded in mystery and lack of knowledge, and therefore misguided religious prejudices abounded. Today there is no longer any excuse for that, for accurate information and opportunities for contact with peoples of the different religions abound.

In fact, one the striking developments in recent religious history, at least within some of the traditions, is the increase of dialogue between people of different religions. Since this has the potential of creating new levels of intercultural understanding, let us look more closely at the attitudes and movements that are involved in understanding through dialogue between people of different religions.

Dialogue can take place on different levels. Important dialogue takes place today between leading scholars and experts in the different religions, each representing her or his own religion and entering into conversation with those of different religions on a deep religious-theological level. But dialogue also can take place as ordinary people of the different religions meet each day as neighbors, fellow employees, students, or tourists. In particular, dialogue occurs between people of different religions as they face the common concerns and problems of daily life together, working toward understanding and dealing with the social, political, and economic issues that affect all of us.

Expectations about the results of religious dialogue depend on how one views the relationship between the common human religious experiences, on the one hand, and the concrete, specific forms taken in the different religions, on the other. Is there one perennial religious essence shared by all peoples, or is there only a multitude of special forms everywhere different and incompatible? Or is there some view in-between?

One approach to dialogue with people of different religions holds that all religions are essentially the same. Whereas outer forms and trappings differ from culture to culture, the real inner essence is all the same. A similar attitude says that, whereas religions are taking different paths, the goal for each is the same. In practical terms, the result of these attitudes is to look for the emergence of a superreligion, an all-inclusive religion made up of the best of the present religions, that will eventually supercede all the religions today. A related attitude, widespread today, is that we can pick and choose among the religions, adopting elements that suit us and discarding all the other uninteresting or nonappealing elements. In this way new religious movements are begun—or at least we develop our own brand of religion.

One problem with these attitudes is that they neglect the wholeness and integrity of each religion. Our point of view here, as studied in the introduction to this book, is that each religion is a whole meaning system with its own central and primary symbols. Often it is the unique and different points—rather than the points in common with other religions—that are most important to a particular religion. That means that to attempt to create some kind of superreligion or arbitrarily to select one symbol or another without regard to the rest is to do injustice to the religion's full integrity.

Another kind of attitude would hold that dialogue is not really possible between people of different religious commitments. This attitude is often associated with religious fundamentalism, the attitude that one's own religion is the exclusive truth and therefore truth claims of another religion can only be argued against and shown to be false. From another perspective, certain cultural-linguistic theories of religion also suggest that people from different religions have differing linguistic systems and therefore cannot really understand the vocabulary and semantics of another religion. A Hindu, a Christian, and a Taoist may all use the English term *God*, but the term carries quite different meaning for each. If we cannot understand each other's words, real dialogue would seem rather impossible.

Both of these approaches remind us of important characteristics of religion. It is well to remember that claiming to be the *real* truth is essential to any particular religion. And it is also important to realize that each religion is a unique cultural-linguistic system, whose terms and concepts cannot simply be interchanged with those of another religion.

But it is not necessary to press these ideas to the conclusion that real dialogue between people of different religions is impossible. One can claim to possess the real truth and still listen to, and even understand, the truth claims of others. Our religions are differing cultural-linguistic systems, yet there is a common quality of human experience that does allow cross-cultural communication and understanding. All humans have lived on the same mother earth, under the same sky and sun, experiencing birth, sex, food production, fellow-human relationships, and death in common. It is not necessary to suppose there is a common essence of religion in order to believe that it is possible for humans to communicate their religious ideas to each other.

Furthermore, there have been and continue to be many crossings on the paths—for millennia peoples of different religions have interacted, learned from others, and adopted elements from other religions into their own. Today, of course, the interaction is more intense and widespread, but there is plenty of evidence from the past that people can communicate across the cultures, and that they can learn and grow through such communication.

The Attitude and Process of Dialogue

The process of dialogue between people of different religions has been tried and tested in many settings. Dialogue is going on between Christians and Jews, Jews and Muslims, Muslims and Hindus, Hindus and Buddhists, Buddhists and Christians, and many more. Dialogue often involves more than just two partners, with representatives of three or more religions involved, such as Jews, Christians, and Muslims, or Hindus, Buddhists, and Christians. It is generally agreed that a number of basic attitudes are important, so that the process of dialogue can take place. Among the most important attitudes are the following.

1. Real dialogue presupposes a firm standing in one's own religion. It is interesting to float above all religions, coming down only where something useful is found. But dialogue means to share that which is most essential and innermost to oneself, and that comes from deeply held religious convictions. This does not mean there are no doubts, questions, or dissatisfactions with one's own tradition—we have seen that such doubt and questioning are essential to change and development within each tradition. But dialogue means "talking through to another," presupposing one sharing her or his religious commitment with one of another faith—not people with no commitments looking around for what suits them best.
2. The goal is to grow in understanding, of the other religions and of one's self. The goal is not to convert the partner in dialogue, nor is it to convince oneself to convert to the other religion.
3. Dialogue presupposes a respect for the people of the other religion and a willingness to see how that religion really makes sense to the people who live by it.
4. Dialogue presupposes a willingness to learn from

the other, taking the risk of growing and changing in one's own understanding.

5. Dialogue includes the readiness to share one's own religious commitments and convictions about truth, yet without arrogance or defensiveness, without belittling the beliefs of others or attempting to convert them. To open out in sharing one's beliefs and values means becoming vulnerable, letting others in on one's inner convictions.

It may seem difficult to bring these attitudes into an area as personal and subject to strong feelings as religion. It is in the nature of religious belief to make claims to truth. If I were not convinced that my religion is the truth about existence, it would no longer be my *religion*. Each person has experienced sacred reality by means of a particular religious tradition, and based on that there are certain absolute and irreducible convictions by which he or she lives. The whole issue then of competing truth claims cannot be avoided when two people of different religions talk together: is one religion true and the other not? are they both true? do they both possess partial truth? These are important questions to think about and to discuss.

The experience of people engaged in dialogue today is that it is possible to remain firmly convinced of the truth of one's own religion and still respect the truth claims of others. One can acknowledge the fact that each religion claims to be the real truth about human existence—and leave open the question whether such claims have to be exclusive. The attitude of dialogue is based on the realization that in religion we enter into the sacred mystery of life (remember our definition of religion in Part I), and that the sacred can never be fully grasped or limited by our own understanding or experience. However much we are convinced of the truth of our own religious understanding, we can acknowledge that the sacred mystery is still greater and deeper, and that others may have valid religious experiences, which, if we but listen to them, may be illuminating also to us.

Of course, it is not necessary to give up critical thinking in order to dialogue with people of different religions. Dialogue involves a give-and-take that includes questions and challenges as well as respect and acceptance. Comparing religious ideas and practices calls for accurate information and good critical thinking. But experience has shown that this can be done in an atmosphere of respect and willingness to learn and grow.

The process of dialogue between people of different religious beliefs involves four main movements:

1. It is important, first, to become aware of one's own religious values and commitments. It is possible, then, to "bracket" them so as to enter into the other person's religious world, as much as possible, without preconceived notions and prejudices.
2. Next comes a movement of passing over to enter into the universe of symbols that makes up the other person's religion, seeing it from the inside as the other person does.
3. The next movement is returning to one's own world view, but bringing new ideas and comparisons from the other person's religion.
4. Now integration and growth can take place, seeing one's own religious ideas more clearly and deeply.

These movements, of course, are essential for learning and growth in all areas of life—moving outside ourselves to experience something new, then returning and integrating that with what we already are, as the process of growth goes on. The four movements listed above take place over and over again, sometimes occurring simultaneously, as the dialogue with people of other religions goes on.

The increase of interreligious dialogue today coincides with revival and renewed vitality in most of the world religions. As the dialogue between the peoples of the different religions continues and deepens, on all levels, the potential contribution of the sacred paths to the common life and well-being of humankind will become stronger. What this will bring cannot be fully predicted, of course, but it appears as one hopeful sign in the outlook for the future of humanity.

DISCUSSION QUESTIONS

1. In what ways is the present age a new critical time for the religions—and for humanity?
2. Sometimes it seems that religions cause divisions and conflict. What are some resources of the world religions that could contribute to the common human welfare?
3. Does what is common and universal to the religions seem more important to you, or what is unique and particular to each tradition? Do you see ways in which both these tendencies might be promoted?
4. What kinds of attitudes are presupposed for dialogue between people of different religions? What are the four main movements of such a dialogue process?

NOTES

PART ONE
UNDERSTANDING THE SACRED PATHS

Chapter 1
Basic Dimensions of Religion

[1] Ruldolph Otto, *The Idea of The Holy*, trans. John Harvey (London: Oxford University Press, 1958).

[2] Joachim Wach, *Sociology of Religion* (Chicago: University of Chicago Press, 1944), pp. 17–34.

[3] Mircea Eliade, *The Sacred and the Profane: The Nature of Religion*, trans. Willard R. Trask (New York: Harcourt, Brace & World, 1959).

[4] The terms *kenosis* and *plerosis* are used by Theodor H. Gaster, *Thespis: Ritual, Myth, and Drama in the Ancient Near East* (New York: Doubleday, 1961), pp. 23–49.

[5] The structure of the rites of passage was first analyzed by Arnold van Gennep, *The Rites of Passage*, trans. Monika Vizedom and Gabrielle Caffee (Chicago: University of Chicago Press, 1960).

[6] Eliade, *The Sacred and the Profane*, pp. 20–65.

Chapter 2
Religions of Ancient Peoples

[1] *Ancient Near Eastern Texts Relating to the Old Testament*, ed. James B. Pritchard (Princeton, NJ: Princeton University Press, 1950), p. 407.

[2] Ibid., p. 164.

[3] Ibid., pp. 434–437.

[4] *Ajax*, lines 126–133, trans. John Moore in *Sophocles*, vol. II of *The Complete Greek Tragedies*, eds. David Grene and Richmond Lattimore (Chicago: University of Chicago press, 1959), p. 219.

Chapter 3
Religions of Nonliterate Peoples

[1] Mircea Eliade, *The Sacred and the Profane: The Nature of Religion*, trans. Willard R. Trask (New York: Harcourt, Brace & World, 1959) p. 95; *Myth and Reality* (New York: Harper & Row, 1963), pp. 6–7.

[2] Sam Gill, "Nonliterate Traditions and Holy Books: Toward a New Model," in *The Holy Book in Comparative Perspective*, eds. Frederick Denny and Rodney Taylor (Columbia: University of South Carolina Press, 1985), p. 226.

[3] Frank Waters, *Book of the Hopi* (New York: Viking Press, 1963), pp. 114–115.

[4] See Sam Gill, *Native American Religions: An Introduction* (Belmont, CA: Wadsworth Publishing, 1982), p. 24.

[5] See John Middleton, *Lugbara Religion: Ritual and Authority Among an East African People* (London: Oxford University Press, 1960), especially pp. 230–238.

[6] Adolf Jensen, *Das religiöse Weltbild einer frühen Kultur* (Stuttgart: August Schoeder Verlag, 1949), pp. 33–40.

[7] Jonathan Z. Smith, "A Pearl of Great Price and a Cargo

of Yams: A Study in Situational Incongruity," *History of Religions*, 16 (1976), 1–19.

8 James Mooney, *The Ghost Dance Religion and the Sioux Outbreak of 1890*, abridged (Chicago: University of Chicago Press, 1965), p. 181.

9 See J. Omosade Awolalu, *Yoruba Beliefs and Sacrificial Rites* (London: Longman, 1979); and E. Bolaji Idowu, *Olodumare: God in Yoruba Belief* (New York: Frederick A. Praeger, 1963).

10 Sam Gill, *Sacred Words: A Study of Navajo Religion and Prayer* (Westport, CT: Greenwood Press, 1981), pp. 50–55; *The Portable North American Indian Reader*, ed. Frederick W. Turner III (New York: Viking Press, 1973), pp. 175–205.

11 Gill, *Native American Religions*, pp. 20–22; *North American Indian Reader*, pp. 36–39.

12 Ronald M. Berndt, *Djanggawul: An Aboriginal Religious Cult of North Eastern Arnhem Land* (New York: Philosophical Library, 1953), pp. 24–28.

13 Marcel Griaule and Germaine Dieterlen, *Le renard pale* (Paris, 1965); see the briefer account in Griaule and Dieterlen, "The Dogon," in *African Worlds: Studies in the Cosmological Ideas and Social Values of African Peoples*, ed. Daryll Forde (London: Oxford University Press, 1954), pp. 83–89.

14 John S. Mbiti, *Concepts of God in Africa* (London: SPCK, 1970), pp. 171–177.

15 Gill, *Sacred Words*, pp. 61–84.

16 Ibid., p. 66.

17 *The Sacred Pipe: Black Elk's Account of the Seven Rites of the Oglala Sioux*, ed. Joseph Epes Brown (Baltimore: Penguin Books, 1971), p. 50.

18 Arthur Amiotte, "Eagles Fly Over," *Parabola*, I, no. 3 (1976), 34.

19 Mircea Eliade, *Shamanism: Archaic Techniques of Ecstasy*, trans. Willard Trask (Princeton, NJ: Princeton University Press, 1964).

20 Vilmos Dioszegi, *Tracing Shamans in Siberia* (New York: Humanities Press, 1968), p. 62; quoted in John A. Grim, *The Shaman: Patterns of Siberian and Ojibway Healing* (Norman: University of Oklahoma Press, 1983), p. 46.

21 Eliade, *Shamanism*, pp. 115–120.

22 Amiotte, "Eagles," p. 29.

23 Eliade, *The Sacred and the Profane*, pp. 68–72.

24 Ruth M. Underhill, *Papago Indian Religion* (New York: AMS Press, 1969), pp. 77–79.

25 Hans Schärer, *Ngaju Religion: The Conception of God Among a South Borneo People* (The Hague: Martinus Nijhoff, 1963), especially pp. 27–38, 94–97, 131–141.

These rituals are interpreted by Sam D. Gill, *Beyond "the Primitive": The Religions of Nonliterate Peoples* (Englewood Cliffs, NJ: Prentice-Hall, Inc., 1982), pp. 81–85.

26 See John Batchelor, *The Ainu and Their Folklore* (London, 1901); Kyosuke Kindaichi, *Ainu Life and Legend* (Tokyo, 1941); and Joseph M. Kitagawa, "Ainu Bear Festival (Iyomante)," *History of Religions*, I (1961), 95–151.

27 John Batchelor, "The Ainu Bear Festival," *Transactions of the Asiatic Society of Japan*, 2nd Series, IX (1932), 42.

28 John Witthost, *Green Corn Ceremonialism in the Eastern Woodlands* (Ann Arbor: University of Michigan Press, 1949), pp. 52–70.

29 K. H. Basso, *The Cibecue Apache* (New York: Holt, Rinehart and Winston, 1970), pp. 53–72. The quotations here are from pp. 65, 66.

30 Victor Turner, *The Forest of Symbols: Aspects of Ndembu Ritual* (Ithaca, NY: Cornell University Press, 1967), pp. 151–279.

31 John S. Mbiti, *African Religions and Philosophies* (New York: Doubleday, 1970), p. 141.

32 Awolalu, *Yoruba Beliefs*, pp. 69–91, 108–126.

33 Baldwin Spencer and F. J. Gillen, *The Arunta*, vol. I (London: Macmillan, 1927), p. 388.

34 *The Sacred Pipe*, pp. 31–43.

35 Ibid., pp. 41–42.

36 From J. W. MacMurray, "The 'Dreamers' of the Columbia River Valley in Washington Territory," *Transactions of the Albany Institute XI* (Albany, 1887), pp. 241–248; quoted in Sam D. Gill, *Native American Traditions: Sources and Interpretations* (Belmont, CA: Wadsworth Publishing, 1983), pp. 156–157.

37 John (Fire) Lame Deer and Richard Erdoes, *Lame Deer: Seeker of Visions* (New York: Washington Square Press, 1972), pp. 254–255.

PART TWO
FAMILIES OF ABRAHAM

Chapter 4
Judaism: Sacred Story and Historical Context

1 Translated in Judah Goldin, *The Fathers According to Rabbi Nathan* (New Haven: Yale University Press, 1955), p. 34.

Chapter 5
Jewish Worlds of Meaning

1 Louis Jacobs, *A Jewish Theology* (New York: Behrman House), p. 62.

[2] C. G. Montefiore and H. Loewe, comps., *A Rabbinic Anthology* (New York: Schocken Books, 1974), p. 217.

[3] Jacobs, *Jewish Theology*, p. 93.

[4] Jacob Neusner, *The Life of Torah: Readings in the Jewish Religious Experience* (Belmont, CA: Dickenson Publishing, 1974), p. 19.

[5] Milton Steinberg, *Basic Judaism* (New York: Harcourt, Brace & World, 1947), p. 86.

[6] Montcfiore and Locwe, *Rabbinic Anthology*, p. 305.

[7] Neusner, *Between Time and Eternity: The Essentials of Judaism* (Belmont, CA: Dickenson Publishing, 1975), pp. 79–80.

[8] Steinberg, *Basic Judaism*, p. 58.

[9] Neusner, *Between Time and Eternity*, pp. 77–78.

[10] Steinberg, *Basic Judaism*, p. 61.

[11] Abraham J. Heschel, *Between God and Man: An Interpretation of Judaism*, edited by Fritz A. Rothschild (New York: The Free Press, 1959), p. 72.

[12] Howard R. Greenstein, *Judaism—An Eternal Covenant* (Philadelphia: Fortress Press, 1983), pp. 31–32.

[13] Jacobs, *Jewish Theology*, p. 256.

[14] Neusner, *Between Time and Eternity*, pp. 91–94.

[15] Heschel, *Between God and Man*, p. 164.

[16] Montefiore and Loewe, *Rabbinic Anthology*, p. 140.

[17] Ibid., pp. 607–608.

Chapter 6
Jewish Worship and the Good Life

[1] Jacob Neusner, *The Way of Torah: An Introduction to Judaism*, 2nd ed. (Belmont, CA: Dickenson Publishing, 1974), p. 41.

[2] Isadore Twersky, "The Shulhan Aruk: Enduring Code of Jewish Law," in *Understanding Jewish Technology: Classical Issues and Modern Perspectives*, edited by Jacob Neusner (New York: KTAV Publishing House, 1973), p. 146.

[3] Abraham J. Heschel, *Between God and Man: An Interpretation of Judaism*, edited by Fritz A. Rothschild (New York: The Free Press, 1959), p. 183.

[4] Ibid., p. 164.

[5] C. G. Montefiore and H. Loewe, comps., *A Rabbinic Anthology* (New York: Schocken Books, 1974), p. 433.

[6] Ibid., p. 535.

[7] Ibid., p. 200.

[8] Ibid., p. 108.

[9] Ibid., p. 536.

[10] Ibid., p. 226.

[11] Louis Jacobs, *A Jewish Theology* (New York: Behrman House, 1973), pp. 292, 300.

Chapter 7
Christianity: Sacred Story and Historical Context

[1] Henry Bettenson, ed., *Documents of the Christian Church* (New York: Oxford University Press, 1947), pp. 72–73.

Chapter 9
Christian Worship and Ethical Life

[1] John Burnaby, *Augustine: Later Works*, vol. 8, in *The Library of Christian Classics* (Philadelphia: Westminster Press, 1955), p. 316.

Chapter 10
Islam: Sacred Story and Historical Context

[1] A. Guillaume, trans., *The Life of Muhammad: A Translation of Ishaq's Sirat Rasul Allah* (London: Oxford University Press, 1955).

[2] Passages from the Quran in the chapters on Islam, unless otherwise indicated, are from Arthur J. Arberry, trans., *The Koran Interpreted* (New York: Macmillan, 1955).

[3] Guillaume, *Life of Muhammad*, pp. 69–81.

[4] Ibid., p. 106.

[5] Ibid., pp. 106–107.

[6] Ibid., p. 552.

[7] Ibid., pp. 651–652.

[8] Ibid., p. 682.

[9] Ibid., pp. 682–683.

[10] A. J. Arberry, *Muslim Saints and Mystics* (Chicago: University of Chicago Press, 1966), p. 51.

[11] Frederick Mathewson Denny, *An Introduction to Islam* (New York: Macmillan, 1985), p. 250.

[12] Ibid., p. 262.

[13] W. Montgomery Watt, *The Faith and Practice of al-Ghazali* (London: Allen and Unwin, 1953), pp. 56–57.

[14] Mohamad Jawad Chirri, *The Brother of the Prophet Mohammad (the Imam Ali)*, Vol. I (Detroit: Islamic Center of Detroit, 1979), pp. 128–133.

Chapter 11
Muslim Worlds of Meaning

[1] Seyyed Hossein Nasr, *Ideals and Realities of Islam* (Boston: Beacon Press, 1975), pp. 18–21.

[2] Wing-tsit Chan et al., comps., *The Great Asian Religions: An Anthology* (New York: Macmillan, 1969), p. 352.

[3] Abul A'la Mawdudi, *Towards Understanding Islam*, translated by Khurshid Ahmad (Plainfield, IN: Muslim Students' Association of the U.S. and Canada, 1980/1400 A. H.), p. 19.

Chapter 12
Muslim Worship and the Good Life

1 Kenneth Cragg and R. Marston Speight, eds., *Islam from Within: Anthology of a Religion.* (Belmont, CA: Wadsworth Publishing, 1980), p. 50.
2 W. Montgomery Watt, *The Faith and Practice of al-Ghazali* (London: Allen and Unwin, 1953), p. 115.
3 Frederick Mathewson Denny, *An Introduction to Islam* (New York: Macmillan, 1985), p. 317.
4 Cragg and Marston, *Islam from Within*, p. 202.
5 Wing-tsit Chan et al., comps., *The Great Asian Religions: An Anthology* (New York: Macmillan, 1969), p. 377.
6 Abul A'la Mawdudi, *Towards Understanding Islam*, translated by Khurshid Ahmad (Plainfield, IN: Muslim Students' Association of the U. S. and Canada, 1980/1400 A. H.), p. 101.
7 Ibid., p. 26.

PART THREE
RELIGIONS ARISING FROM INDIA

Chapter 13
Hinduism: Sacred Story and Historical Context

1 Wendy Doniger O'Flaherty, trans., *The Rig Veda: An Anthology* (New York: Penguin Books, 1981), pp. 211–212.
2 Ibid., p. 149.
3 Wing-tsit Chan et al., comps., *The Great Asian Religions: An Anthology* (New York: Macmillan, 1969), p. 13.
4 O'Flaherty, *Rig Veda*, p. 134.
5 Ibid., p. 25.
6 Chan et al., *Great Asian Religions*, p. 24.
7 Robert Ernest Hume, trans., *The Thirteen Principal Upanishads Translated from the Sanskrit*, 2nd ed. (New York: Oxford University Press, 1931), p. 76.
8 Barbara Stoler Miller, trans., *The Bhagavad-Gita: Krishna's Counsel in Time of War* (New York: Columbia University Press, 1986), p. 39.
9 Ibid., p. 87.
10 John M. Koller, *The Indian Way* (New York: Macmillan, 1982), p. 257.

Chapter 14
Hindu Worlds of Meaning

1 Wendy Doniger O'Flaherty, trans., *The Rig Veda: An Anthology* (New York: Penguin Books, 1981), pp. 25–26.
2 Robert Ernest Hume, trans., *The Thirteen Principal Upanishads Translated from the Sanskrit*, 2nd ed. (New York: Oxford University Press, 1931), pp. 119–120.
3 Ibid., p. 353.
4 Ibid., p. 147.
5 Ibid., p. 210.
6 Troy Wilson Organ, *Hinduism: Its Historical Development* (Woodbury, NY: Barron's Educational Series, 1974), p. 256.
7 Barbara Stoler Miller, trans., *The Bhagavad-Gita: Krishna's Counsel in Time of War* (New York: Columbia University Press, 1986), pp. 99–105.
8 Ramanuja on Bhagavad Gita 6.47, in R. C. Zaehner, *Hinduism* (London: Oxford University Press, 1962), p. 99.
9 A. K. Ramanjuan, trans., *Speaking of Shiva* (Baltimore: Penguin Books, Inc., 1973), p. 84.
10 Swami Nikhilananda, trans., *The Gospel of Sri Ramakrishna* (New York: Ramakrishna-Vivekananda Center, 1952), pp. 134–135.
11 Hume, *Thirteen Principal Upanishads*, p. 81.
12 Ibid., p. 248.
13 Ibid., p. 140.
14 Ibid., pp. 413–414.
15 Ibid., p. 143.
16 Wing-tsit Chan et al., comps., *The Great Asian Religions: An Anthology* (New York: Macmillan, 1969), p. 45.
17 Hume, *Thirteen Principal Upanishads*, pp. 83–84.
18 Ibid., p. 142.
19 Ibid., p. 141.
20 Ibid., p. 393.
21 Miller, *Bhagavad-Gita*, pp. 52, 43.
22 Ibid., p. 87.
23 Ibid., p. 79.
24 David R. Kinsley, *The Sword and the Flute* (Berkeley: University of California Press, 1977), pp. 52–53.
25 O'Flaherty, *Shiva: The Erotic Ascetic* (Oxford: Oxford University Press, 1981), p. 149.
26 Manikka Vasager, quoted in R. C. Zaehner, *Hinduism*, pp. 133–134.
27 Translated in Leonard Nathan and Clinton Seely, *Grace and Mercy in Her Wild Hair: Selected Poems to the Mother Goddess* (Boulder: Great Eastern, 1982), pp. 62, 25.
28 Nikhilananda, *The Gospel of Sri Ramakrishna*, pp. 261–262.

Chapter 15
Hindu Worship and the Good Life

1 Robert C. Lester, "Hinduism: Veda and Sacred Texts," in *The Holy Book in Comparative Perspective*, edited by

Frederick M. Denny and Rodney L. Taylor (Columbia; University of South Carolina Press, 1985), p. 128.

2 McKim Marriot, "The Feast of Love," in *Krishna: Myths, Rites, and Attitudes*, edited by Milton Singer (Chicago: University of Chicago Press, 1968), p. 212.

3 Mariasusai Dhavamony, *Classical Hinduism* (Roma: Universita Gregoriana Editrice, 1982), pp. 181–183.

4 Patrima Bowes, *The Hindu Religious Tradition: A Philosophical Approach* (London: Routledge and Kegan Paul, 1977), p. 296.

5 Law-code of Manu, 3:55; 9:3-4, 11, 26, in Wm. Theodore de Bary et al., comps., *Sources of Indian Tradition* (New York: Columbia University Press, 1959), p. 233.

6 Law-code of Manu, 6:2, in de Bary et al., *Sources*, p. 234.

7 Law-code of Manu, 6:33, 42, in de Bary et al., *Sources*, p. 234.

8 Law-code of Manu, 6:45–81, in R. C. Zaehner, *Hinduism* (London: Oxford University Press, 1966), p. 113.

9 Pratap Chandra Roy, trans., *The Mahabharata*, vol. IX (Calcutta: Oriental Publishing, 1927–1932), p. 110.

10 Written in *The Harijan* for December 8, 1946; in Troy Wilson Organ, *Hinduism: Its Historical Development* (Woodbury, NY: Barron's Educational Series, 1974), p. 368.

11 S. Radhakrishnan, *Eastern Religions and Western Thought* (Oxford: Clarendon Press, 1939), p. 327.

Chapter 16
Buddhism: Sacred Story and Historical Context

1 From the Suvarnaprabhasa, a Mahayana text, in Edward Conze, trans., *Buddhist Scriptures* (Baltimore: Penguin Books, 1959), pp. 24–26.

2 From the Buddhacarita, a Sanskrit poem said to have been composed by Ashvaghosha between the first and second centuries C.E., Wm. Theoodore de Bary, ed., *The Buddhist Tradition in India, China and Japan* (New York: Vintage Books, 1972), p. 58. We follow the main outlines of the Buddhacarita in telling the Buddha's story.

3 Ibid., p. 59.

4 Ibid., pp. 61–62.

5 Ibid., p. 66.

6 Henry Clarke Warren, *Buddhism in Translation: Passages Selected from the Buddhist Sacred Books* (Cambridge: Harvard University Press, 1947), pp. 60–61.

7 de Bary, *Buddhist Tradition*, p. 68.

8 Warren, *Buddhism*, p. 76.

9 Stephan Beyer, *The Buddhist Experience: Sources and*

Interpretations (Belmont, CA: Dickenson Publishing, 1974), p. 197.

10 From the Samyutta Nikaya; in Walpola Rahula, trans., *What the Buddha Taught*, rev. ed. (New York: Grove Press, 1974), p. 93.

11 From the Mahaparinibbana Sutta, in de Bary, *Buddhist Tradition*, p. 29.

12 From Digha Nikaya, in ibid.

13 From Bodhicaryvatarapanjika, in Wing-tsit Chan et al. comps., *The Great Asian Religions: An Anthology* (New York: Macmillan, 1969), p. 74.

14 Edward Conze, ed., *Buddhist Texts Through the Ages* (New York: Harper and Row, 1964), p. 130.

Chapter 17
Buddhist Worlds of Meaning

1 Wm. Theodore de Bary, ed., *The Buddhist Tradition in India, China and Japan* (New York: Vintage Books, 1972), p. 29.

2 Majjhima Nikaya, in David J. Kalupahana, "Pratityasamutpada," *Encyclopedia of Religion*, vol. 11, edited by Mircea Eliade (New York: Macmillan, 1987), p. 486.

3 Edward Conze et al., eds., *Buddhist Texts Through the Ages* (New York: Harper and Row, 1964), p. 95.

4 Conze, *Buddhism: Its Essence and Development* (New York: Harper and Row, 1959), p. 40.

5 From the Samyutta Nikaya, in Wapola Rahula, *What the Buddha Taught* (New York: Grove Press, 1974), p. 27.

6 Digha Nikaya, *Sources of Indian Tradition*, compiled by Wm. Theordore de Bary et al. (New York: Columbia University Press, 1958), pp. 130–131.

7 Conze, trans., *Buddhist Scriptures* (Baltimore: Penguin Books, 1959), pp. 222–224.

8 From Samyutta Nikaya, in Rahula, *What the Buddha Taught*, p. 93.

9 From Majjhima Nikaya, in John M. Koller, *The Indian Way* (New York: Macmillan, 1982), p. 158.

10 Rahula, *What the Buddha Taught*, p. 73.

11 Siksasamuccaya Vajradhvaja Sutra, in Conze, *Buddhist Texts*, p. 131.

Chapter 18
Buddhist Worship and the Good Life

1 In Melford E. Spiro, *Buddhism and Society: A Great Tradition and Its Burmese Vicissitudes* (New York: Harper and Row, 1972), p. 210.

2 Ibid., p. 212.

3 Stephen Beyer, *The Buddhist Experience: Sources and In-*

terpretations (Belmont, CA: Dickenson Publishing, 1974), p. 241.

4 Spiro, *Buddhism*, pp. 283–284.

5 Suttanipata, I, 8; in Walpola Rahula, *What the Buddha Taught* (New York: Grove Press, 1959), pp. 97–98.

6 Siksasamuccaya, pp. 278–283, in Wm. Theodore de Bary et al., *Sources of Indian Tradition* (New York: Columbia University Press, 1958), pp. 163–165.

7 Dhammapada, vss. 3, 50, 223, in Rahula, *What the Buddha Taught*, pp. 125–132.

8 Majjhima Nikaya, 2:147ff., in de Bary et al., *Sources of Indian Tradition*, pp. 144–145.

9 Sutta Nipata, v. 136, in ibid., p. 143.

10 Digha Nikaya, 3:180ff, in ibid., pp. 125–127.

11 Rahula, *What the Buddha Taught*, pp. 81–84.

12 Ibid., pp. 84–85.

13 First Pillar Edict, in de Bary et al., *Sources of Indian Tradition*, p. 148.

14 Twelfth Rock Edict, in ibid., p. 151.

Chapter 19
The Path of the Jains

1 Padmanabh S. Jaini, *The Jaina Path of Purification* (Berkeley: University of California Press, 1979), p. 1.

2 Ibid., pp. 11–12.

3 Ibid., p. 26.

4 Ibid., p. 38.

5 Ibid., pp. 45–46.

6 Wm. Theodore de Bary et al., comp., *Sources of Indian Tradition* (New York: Columbia University Press, 1958), pp. 79–81.

7 Ibid., pp. 59–60.

8 Jyotiprasad Jain, *Religion and Culture of the Jains* (New Delhi: Bharatiya Jnanpith Publication, 1975), p. 114.

9 Vilas Adinath Sangave, *Jaina Community: A Social Survey*, rev. ed. (Bombay: Popular Prakashan Private, Ltd., 1980), pp. 245–247.

10 Jaini, *Jaina Path*, p. 247, n. 8.

11 Jain, *Religion*, p. 176.

Chapter 20
The Way of the Disciples: The Sikhs

1 W. Owen Cole, *The Guru in Sikhism* (London: Darton, Longman and Todd, 1982), pp. 15–16.

2 Ibid., p. 15.

3 Trilochan Singh et al., trans., *Selections From the Sacred Writings of the Sikhs* (London: George Allen and Unwin, 1960), p. 28.

4 W. H. McLeod, *Guru Nanak and the Sikh Religion* (New York: Oxford University Press, 1968), p. 216.

5 Ibid., p. 165.

6 Ibid., p. 196.

7 Trilochan Singh et al., *Selections from the Sacred Writings of the Sikhs*, pp. 103–105.

8 Ibid., p. 91.

9 Ibid., p. 203.

10 Ibid., p. 102.

11 McLeod, *Guru Nanak*, p. 205.

12 Taran Singh, quoted in Cole, *The Guru*, p. 89.

13 Gopal Singh, *The Sikhs: Their History, Religion, Culture, Ceremonies, and Literature* (Madras: M. Seshachalam, 1970), p. 64.

14 Trilochan Singh, *Selections*, p. 56.

15 Ibid., p. 60.

16 Pritam Singh Gill, *Heritage of Sikh Culture: Society, Morality, Art* (Jullundur: New Academic Publishing Co., 1975), p. 229.

17 Ibid., p. 159.

18 Avtar Singh, *Ethics of the Sikhs* (Patiala: Punjabi University, 1970), p. 29.

19 Ibid., p. 85.

20 Ibid., p. 112.

21 Trilochan Singh, *Selections*, p. 93.

22 McLeod, *Textual Sources for the Study of Sikhism* (Totowa, NJ: Barnes and Noble Books, 1984), p. 57.

23 Quoted in Cole, *The Guru*, pp. 93–94.

PART IV
RELIGIONS OF CHINA AND JAPAN

Chapter 21
China: Sacred Story and Historical Context

1 Howard Smith, *Chinese Religions: From 1000 B.C. to the Present Day* (New York: Holt, Rinehart and Winston, 1971), p. 16.

2 Ibid., pp. 22–23.

3 Ibid., pp. 27–28.

4 Wing-tsit Chan, *A Source Book in Chinese Philosophy* (Princeton, NJ: Princeton University Press, 1969), p. 38.

5 Ibid., p. 36.

6 Chan et al., comps., *The Great Asian Religions: An Anthology* (London: Macmillan, 1969), p. 109.

7 Chan, *Source Book*, p. 78.

8 Ibid., p. 152.

9 Ibid., p. 148.

10 Ibid., p. 197.

Chapter 22
Transformations in Chinese Religious History

[1] Holmes Welch, *Taoism: The Parting of the Way* (Boston: Beacon Press, 1966), p. 159.

[2] Michael Saso, *The Teachings of Taoist Master Chuang* (New Haven: Yale University Press, 1978), p. 46.

[3] Wm. Theodore de Bary et al., comps., *Sources of Chinese Tradition*, vol. 1 (New York: Columbia University Press, 1960), pp. 469–470.

Chapter 23
Chinese Worlds of Meaning

[1] Translated in Milton M. Chiu, *The Tao of Chinese Religion* (New York: University Press of America, 1984), pp. 58, 108, 112–113.

[2] D. Howard Smith, *Chinese Religions: From 1000 B.C. to the Present Day* (New York: Holt, Rinehart and Winston, 1968), p. 19.

[3] Wing-tsit Chan, *A Source Book in Chinese Philosophy* (Princeton, NJ: Princeton University Press, 1969), p. 35.

[4] Wing-tsit Chan et al., comps., *The Great Asian Religions: An Anthology* (London: Macmillan, 1969), p. 135.

[5] Translated by James Legge, in Daniel L. Overmyer, *Religions of China* (San Francisco: Harper and Row, 1986), pp. 71–72.

[6] Translated in Chiu, *The Tao*, p. 138.

[7] Chan, *Source Book*, p. 139.

[8] Burton Watson, trans., *The Complete Works of Chuang Tzu* (New York: Columbia University Press, 1968), p. 302.

[9] Chap. 22; Chan, *Source Book*, p. 203.

[10] Wm. Theodore de Bary, et al., comps., *Sources of Chinese Tradition*, vol. I (New York: Columbia University Press, 1960), p. 58.

[11] Chan, *Source Book*, pp. 156–157.

[12] Chap. 6; Chan, *Source Book*, p. 194.

[13] Michael R. Saso, *Taoism and the Rite of Cosmic Renewal* (Pullman: Washington State University Press, 1972), p. 51.

[14] Chan, *Source Book*, p. 638.

[15] Joseph Needham, *Science and Civilisation in China*, vol. II, *History of Scientific Thought* (London: Cambridge University Press, 1956), p. 492.

[16] Quoted in Richard H. Robinson and Willard L. Johnson, *The Buddhist Religion: A Historical Introduction*, 3rd ed. (Belmont, CA: Wadsworth Publishing, 1982), p. 178.

[17] From *San-wu Li-chi*, in N. J. Girardot, *Myth and Meaning in Early Taoism: The Theme of Chaos* (Berkeley: University of California Press, 1983), p. 193.

[18] From *Shu-i Chi*, see Derk Bodde, "Myths of Ancient China," in *Mythologies of the Ancient World*, edited by Samuel Noah Kramer (New York: Doubleday, 1961), p. 383.

[19] From *Tao Yuan*, in Girardot, *Myth and Meaning*, p. 54.

[20] Chan, *Source Book*, p. 160.

[21] *Kuan Tzu* (from the third century B.C.E.), ch. 40, in Chiu, *The Tao*, pp. 147–148.

[22] *Li Yun* III, in ibid., p. 173.

[23] From Liu An (d. 122 B.C.E.), in *Huai-nan Tzu*, in ibid., p. 176.

[24] *Ch'un-ch'ui Fan-lu*, in Chan, *Source Book*, p. 280, and de Bary et al., *Sources of Chinese Tradition*, pp. 163–164.

[25] IIa.6, in de Bary et al., *Sources of Chinese Tradition*, p. 91.

[26] VIa.8, in W. A. C. H. Dobson, *Mencius: A New Translation Arranged and Annotated for the General Reader* (Toronto: University of Toronto Press, 1963), pp. 141–142.

[27] Ch. 23, in de Bary et al., *Sources of Chinese Tradition*, p. 104.

[28] From Yang Hsiung (53 B.C.E.–18 C.E.), in Chan, *Source Book*, p. 289.

[29] Kao Tzu, in *Mencius*, VIa.2, de Bary et al., *Sources of Chinese Tradition*, vol. I, pp. 88–89.

[30] Ch. 8, in Burton Watson, trans., *The Complete Works of Chuang Tzu* (New York: Columbia University Press, 1968), pp. 99–100.

[31] Chan et al., *Great Asian Religions*, p. 209.

[32] Translated by Herbert A. Giles, quoted in Laurence G. Thompson, *The Chinese Way in Religion* (Belmont, CA: Dickenson Publishing Company, 1973), pp. 187, 195.

[33] de Bary et al., *Sources of Chinese Tradition*, p. 22.

[34] Chan, *Source Book*, pp. 86–87.

[35] Ibid., p. 87.

[36] de Bary et al., *Sources of Chinese Tradition*, p. 109.

[37] Ibid., p. 33.

[38] Chan et al., *Great Asian Religions*, p. 110.

[39] Ibid.

[40] Chan, *Source Book*, p. 148.

[41] Ibid., p. 147.

[42] de Bary et al., *Sources of Chinese Tradition*, p. 74.

[43] Ibid., pp. 71–72.

[44] Chang Chung-yuan, trans., *Original Teachings of Ch'an Buddhism: Selected from The Transmission of the Lamp* (New York: Vintage Books, 1971), pp. 116–117.

[45] Chan, *Source Book*, pp. 446–448.

Chapter 24
Worship and the Good Life in China

[1] Ch. 19, in Wm. Theodore de Bary et al., comps., *Sources of Chinese Tradition*, vol. I (New York: Columbia University Press, 1960), p. 109.

[2] Francis L. K. Hsu, *Under the Ancestors' Shadow: Kinship, Personality and Social Mobility in China* (Stanford: Stanford University Press, 1971), pp. 184–192.

[3] John K. Shryock, *The Origin and Development of the State Cult of Confucius* (New York: Paragon Book Reprint Corp., 1966; originally printed 1932), pp. 175–176.

[4] Translated in Laurence G. Thompson, *Chinese Religion: An Introduction*, 3rd ed. (Belmont, CA: Wadsworth, Inc., 1979), p. 83.

[5] Michael R. Saso, *Taoism and the Rite of Cosmic Renewal* (Pullman: Washington State University Press, 1972), pp. 70–72.

[6] Michael Saso, "Orthodoxy and Heterodoxy in Taoist Ritual," in *Religion and Ritual in Chinese Society*, edited by Arthur P. Wolf (Stanford: Stanford University Press, 1974), pp. 329–331.

[7] David K. Jordan, *Gods, Ghosts and Ancestors: Folk Religion in a Taiwanese Village* (Berkeley: University of California Press, 1972), pp. 56–59.

[8] Holmes Welch, *The Practice of Chinese Buddhism, 1900–1950* (Cambridge: Harvard University Press, 1967), pp. 269–301; quotation from p. 274.

[9] Ibid., pp. 53–77.

[10] Margery Wolf, *Women and the Family in Rural Taiwan* (Stanford: Stanford University Press, 1972), pp. 135–136.

[11] Bruce Watson, trans., *Basic Writings of Hsun Tzu* (New York: Columbia University Press, 1967), pp. 117–118.

[12] Osvald Siren, *The Chinese on the Art of Painting: Translations and Comments* (New York: Schocken Books, 1963), pp. 54–56.

[13] de Bary et al., *Sources of Chinese Tradition*, p. 118.

[14] Wing-tsit Chan, *A Source Book in Chinese Philosophy* (Princeton, NJ: Princeton University Press, 1963), p. 226.

[15] de Bary et al., *Sources of Chinese Tradition*, p. 31.

[16] Ch. 10, in Thompson, *Chinese Religion*, p. 40.

[17] Li Chi, X.1, in James Legge, trans., *The Sacred Books of China: Part III, The Li Ki, I-K* (Delhi: Motilal Banarsidass, 1966; orig. published by the Clarendon Press, 1885), pp. 450–451.

[18] 4B.30, in Chan, *Source Book*, p. 77.

[19] Marcel Granet, *The Religion of the Chinese People*, translated by Maurice Freedman (New York: Harper & Row, 1977), pp. 88–89.

[20] Classic of Filiality, ch. 1, in Thompson, *Chinese Religion*, p. 40.

[21] Li Chi, I.1.2, in Legge, *Sacred Books*, pp. 71–72.

[22] Wing-tsit Chan et al., comps., *The Great Asian Religions: An Anthology* (London: Macmillan, 1969), pp. 107–108.

[23] Doctrine of the Mean, ch. 14, in Chan, *Source Book*, p. 101.

[24] Ibid., p. 22.

[25] Holmes Welch, *Taoism: The Parting of the Way* (Boston: Beacon Press, 1966), p. 125.

[26] D. Howard Smith, *Chinese Religions: From 1000 B.C. to the Present Day* (New York: Holt, Rinehart and Winston, 1968), p. 73.

[27] de Bary et al., *Sources of Chinese Tradition*, p. 81.

[28] Chan, *Source Book*, p. 166.

[29] Saso, *Taoism*, pp. 48–51.

[30] de Bary et al., *Sources of Chinese Tradition*, pp. 175–176.

[31] Chan, *Source Book*, pp. 497–498.

[32] Ibid., pp. 731–734.

Chapter 25
Japan: Sacred Story and Historical Context

[1] Nihongi, Bk. 6, 25th yr., translated in Wing-tsit Chan et al., comps., *The Great Asian Religions: An Anthology* (New York: Macmillan, 1969), p. 240.

[2] Nihongi, Bk, 19, 13th yr., in ibid., p. 249.

[3] Ibid., p. 250.

[4] Nihongi, Bk. 22, 12th yr., in ibid., p. 252.

[5] Ibid., p. 279.

Chapter 26
Japanese Worlds of Meaning

[1] Ichiro Hori et al., eds., *Japanese Religion: A Survey by the Agency for Cultural Affairs*, translated by Yoshiya Abe and David Reid (Tokyo: Kodansha International Ltd., 1972), pp. 37–38.

[2] Nihon Shoki, Bk. 5, 7th year, in Wing-tsit Chan et al., *Great Asian Religions: An Anthology* (London: Macmillan, 1969), p. 240.

[3] Yoshito S. Hakeda, trans., *Kukai: Major Works* (New York: Columbia University Press, 1972), p. 93.

[4] Chan et al., *Great Asian Religions*, p. 239.

[5] From the Engi Shiki, ibid., p. 265.

[6] Ibid., pp. 297–298.

[7] Hakeda, *Kukai*, p. 218.

[8] Akutagawa Ryunosuke, "The Spider's Thread," in *Rashomon and Other Stories*, translated by Glenn W. Shaw (Tokyo: Hara Publishing Co., 1964), pp. 164–174.

[9] Chan et al., *Great Asian Religions*, pp. 265–266.

[10] Tsunetsugu Muraoka, *Studies in Shinto Thought*, translated by Delmer Brown and James Araki (Tokyo: Ministry of Education, 1964), p. 37.

[11] A. L. Sadler, *The Ise Daijingu Sankeiki or Diary of a Pilgrim to Ise* (Tokyo: Zaidan Hojin Meiji Seitoku Kinen Gakkai, 1940), pp. 34, 48; quoted in H. Byron Earhart, *Religion in the Japanese Experience: Sources and Interpretations* (Belmont, CA: Dickenson Publishing, 1974), p. 25.

[12] Hakeda, *Kukai*, pp. 230–232.

[13] Ryusaku Tsunoda et al., comps., *Sources of Japanese Tradition*, vol. I (New York: Columbia University Press, 1964), p. 202.

[14] Ibid., p. 211.

[15] Alfred Bloom, *Shinran's Gospel of Pure Grace* (Tucson: University of Arizona Press, 1965), p. 40.

[16] Chan et al., *Great Asian Religions*, p. 287.

[17] Philip B. Yampolsky, trans., *The Zen Master Hakuin: Selected Writings* (New York: Columbia University Press, 1971), pp. 163–164.

[18] Ibid., pp. 135–136.

Chapter 27
Worship and the Good Life in Japan

[1] Norman Waddell and Masao Abe, trans., "Dogen's Fukanzazengi and Shobogenzo zazengi," *The Eastern Buddhist*, NS VI, no. 2 (1973), pp. 122–123.

[2] Yoshito S. Hakeda, trans., *Kukai: Major Works* (New York: Columbia University Press, 1972), p. 91.

[3] Ibid., p. 98.

[4] William R. LaFleur, trans., *Mirror for the Moon: A Selection of Poems by Saigyo (1118–1190)* (New York: New Directions Publishing, 1978), p. 33.

[5] From the *Namboroku*, in *Chado koten zenshu*, Vol. IV, edited by Sen Soshitsu (Kyoto: Tanko Shinsha, 1956–1962), p. 264.

[6] Richard K. Beardsley, John Hall, and Robert E. Ward, *Village Japan* (Chicago: University of Chicago Press, 1969), p. 220.

[7] Floyd Hiatt Ross, *Shinto: The Way of Japan* (Boston: Beacon Press, 1965), p. 155.

[8] Ryusaku Tsunoda et al., comp., *Sources of Japanese Tradition*, vol. II (New York: Columbia University Press, 1964), pp. 42–43.

[9] Sokyo Ono, *The Kami Way* (Tokyo: International Institute for the Study of Religions, 1959), pp. 106–107.

[10] Alfred Bloom, *Shinran's Gospel of Pure Grace* (Tucson: University of Arizona Press, 1965), p. 73.

[11] Wing-tsit Chan et al., comps., *The Great Asian Religions: An Anthology* (London: Macmillan, 1969), p. 300.

[12] Kenji Ueda, "Shinto," in *Japanese Religion: A Survey by the Agency for Cultural Affairs*, edited by Ichiro Hori et al. (Tokyo: Kodansha International Ltd., 1972), pp. 38–41.

[13] Ono, *Kami Way*, p. 82.

BIBLIOGRAPHY

This selection of suggested readings is intended to help students to move toward a deeper understanding of the religions. For more extensive bibliographies and more specialized scholarly works, the student is advised to consult the bibliographies in *The Encyclopedia of Religion* (see asterisk in first section) and in the other works listed here.

PART ONE
UNDERSTANDING THE SACRED PATHS

Basic Dimensions of Religion

Christ, Carol P., and Judith Plaskow, eds. *Womanspirit Rising: A Feminist Reader in Religion.* San Francisco: Harper & Row, 1979.

De Vries, Jan. *The Study of Religion: A Historical Approach.* Translated by Kees W. Bolle. New York: Harcourt, Brace & World, 1967.

Denny, Frederick M., and Rodney L. Taylor, eds. *The Holy Book in Comparative Perspective.* Columbia: University of South Carolina Press, 1985.

*Eliade, Mircea, ed. *The Encyclopedia of Religion.* 15 vols. New York: Macmillan, 1987. An excellent resource for all religions and religious subjects, with up-to-date information and bibliographies, written by a large international team of scholars.

Eliade, Mircea. *Patterns in Comparative Religion.* Translated by Rosemary Shee. Cleveland: World Publishing, 1963.

―――. *The Sacred and the Profane: The Nature of Religion.* Translated by Willard R. Trask. New York: Harcourt, Brace & World, 1959.

Graham, William A. *Beyond the Written Word: Oral Aspects of Scripture in the History of Religion.* New York: Cambridge University Press, 1987.

Hall, T. William, Richard B. Pilgrim, and Ronald R. Cavanagh. *Religion: An Introduction.* San Francisco: Harper & Row, 1985.

Sharma, Arvind, and Katherine Young, eds. *Women in World Religions.* Buffalo: State University of New York Press, 1986.

Slater, Peter. *The Dynamics of Religion: Meaning and Change in Religious Traditions.* San Francisco: Harper & Row, 1978.

Streng, Frederick J. *Understanding Religious Life.* 3rd ed. Belmont, CA: Wadsworth Publishing Company, 1985.

Wach, Joachim. *The Comparative Study of Religions.* Edited by Joseph M. Kitagawa. New York: Columbia University Press, 1958.

Wilson, John. F. *Religion: A Preface.* Englewood Cliffs, NJ: Prentice-Hall, 1982.

Religions of Ancient Peoples

Burkert, Walter. *Greek Religion.* Translated by John Raffan. Cambridge: Harvard University Press, 1985.

Carmody, Denise Lardner. *The Oldest God: Archaic Religion Yesterday and Today.* Nashville: Abingdon Press, 1981.

Eliade, Mircea. *A History of Religious Ideas. Vol. 1: From the Stone Age to the Eleusinian Mysteries. Vol. 2: From Gautama Buddha to the Triumph of Christianity.* Translated by Willard R. Trask. Chicago: University of Chicago Press, 1978, 1982.

Frankfort, Henri. *Ancient Egyptian Religion.* New York: Harper & Row, 1961.

Frankfort, Henri, Mrs. H. W. Frankfort, John A. Wilson, and Thorkild Jacobsen. *Before Philosophy.* Baltimore: Penguin, 1949.

Gimbutas, Marija. *The Goddesses and Gods of Old Europe, 6500–3500 B.C.: Myths and Cult Images.* Berkeley: University of California Press, 1982.

Guthrie, W. K. C. *The Greeks and Their Gods.* Boston: Beacon Press, 1955.

Jacobsen, Thorkild. *The Treasures of Darkness: A History of Mesopotamian Religion.* New Haven: Yale University Press, 1976.

James, E. O. *Prehistoric Religion.* London: Thames and Hudson, 1957.

Kramer, Samuel Noah. *Sumerian Mythology: A Study of Spiritual and Literary Achievement in the Third Millennium B.C.* Rev. ed. New York: Harper & Row, 1961.

Maringer, Johannes. *The Gods of Prehistoric Man.* New York: Knopf, 1960.

Morenz, Siegfried. *Egyptian Religion.* Translated by Ann E. Keep. Ithaca: Cornell University Press, 1973.

Religions of Nonliterate Peoples

Berndt, Ronald M. *Australian Aboriginal Religion.* Leiden: E. J. Brill, 1974.

Carpenter, Edmund. *Eskimo Reality.* New York: Holt, Rinehart & Winston, 1973.

Dorson, Richard M., ed. *African Folklore.* New York: Anchor Books, 1972.

Eliade, Mircea. *Australian Religions.* Ithaca: Cornell University Press, 1973.

———. *Shamanism: Archaic Techniques of Ecstasy.* New York: Pantheon Books, 1964.

Evans-Pritchard, Edward E. *Nuer Religion.* Oxford: Clarendon Press, 1956.

Gill, Sam D. *Beyond "the Primitive": the Religions of Nonliterate Peoples.* Englewood Cliffs, NJ: Prentice-Hall, 1982.

———. *Native American Religions: An Introduction.* Belmont, CA: Wadsworth Publishing Company, 1982.

———. *Native American Traditions: Sources and Interpretations.* Belmont, CA: Wadsworth Publishing Company, 1983.

Hultkrantz, Ake. *Religions of the American Indians.* Translated by Monica Setterwall. Berkeley: University of California Press, 1979.

King, Noel Q. *African Cosmos: An Introduction to Religion in Africa.* Belmont, CA: Wadsworth Publishing Company, 1986.

Lanternari, Vittorio. *The Religions of the Oppressed: A Study of Modern Messianic Cults.* Translated by Lisa Sergio. New York: New American Library, 1965.

Lawson, E. Thomas. *Religions of Africa: Traditions in Transformation.* San Francisco: Harper & Row, 1984.

Ray, Benjamin. *African Religions: Symbol, Ritual, and Community.* Englewood Cliffs, NJ: Prentice-Hall, 1976.

Sullivan, Lawrence E. *Icanchu's Drum: South American Religions, an Orientation to Meaning.* New York: Macmillan, 1988.

Turner, Victor. *The Forest of Symbols: Aspects of Ndembu Ritual.* Ithaca: Cornell University Press, 1967.

Wilson, Bryan R. *Magic and the Millennium: A Sociological Study of Religious Movements of Protest among Tribal and Third-World Peoples.* New York: Harper & Row, 1973.

PART TWO
FAMILIES OF ABRAHAM

General

Peters, F. E. *Children of Abraham: Judaism/Christianity/Islam.* Princeton, NJ: Princeton University Press, 1982.

Judaism

Borowitz, Eugene B. *Choices in Modern Jewish Thought.* New York: Behrman, 1983.

Bulka, Reuven P. *Dimensions of Orthodox Judaism.* New York: KTAV, 1983.

Donin, Hayim. *To Be a Jew: A Guide to Jewish Observance in Contemporary Thought.* New York: Basic Books, 1972.

Encyclopedia Judaica. 16 vols. Jerusalem: Keter Publishing House, 1972.

Greenstein, Howard R. *Judaism—The Eternal Covenant.* Philadelphia: Fortress Press, 1983.

Heschel, Abraham J. *Between God and Man: An Interpretation of Judaism.* Edited by Fritz A. Rothschild. New York: Free Press, 1959.

Heschel, Susannah, ed. *On Being a Jewish Feminist.* New York: Schocken Books, 1983.

Jacobs, Louis. *A Jewish Theology.* New York: Behrman House, 1973.

Kaufmann, Yehezkel. *The Religion of Israel: From Its Beginnings to the Babylonian Exile.* Translated and abridged by Moshe Greenberg. Chicago: University of Chicago Press, 1966.

Levenson, Jon D. *Sinai and Zion: An Entry into the Jewish Bible.* New York: Harper & Row, 1985.

Montefiore, C. G., and H. Loewe, comps. *A Rabbinic Anthology.* New York: Schocken Books, 1974.

Neusner, Jacob. *The Life of Torah: Readings in the Jewish Religious Experience.* Belmont, CA: Dickenson Publishing Company, 1974.

————. *The Way of Torah: An Introduction to Judaism.* 4th ed. Belmont, CA: Dickenson Publishing Company, 1987.

Roth, Cecil. *History of the Jews.* New York: Schocken Books, 1961.

Schauss, Hayyim. *The Jewish Festivals.* Translated by Samuel Jaffe. New York: Schocken Books, 1962.

Scholem, Gershom G. *Major Trends in Jewish Mysticism.* New York: Schocken Books, 1961.

Seltzer, Robert M. *Jewish People, Jewish Thought: the Jewish Experience in History.* New York: Macmillan, 1980.

Steinberg, Milton. *Basic Judaism.* New York: Harcourt, Brace & World, 1947.

Wiesel, Elie. *Souls on Fire: Portraits and Legends of Hasidic Leaders.* Translated by Marian Wiesel. New York: Random House, 1972.

Zborowski, Mark, and Elizabeth Herzog. *Life Is With People.* New York: Schocken Books, 1962.

Christianity

Baly, Denis, and Royal W. Rhodes, *The Faith of Christians: An Introduction to Basic Beliefs.* Philadelphia: Fortress Press, 1984.

Barrett, Charles D. *Understanding the Christian Faith.* Englewood Cliffs, NJ: Prentice-Hall, 1980.

Boff, Leonardo, and Clodovis Boff. Translated by Paul Burns. *Introducing Liberation Theology.* Maryknoll, NY: Orbis Books, 1987.

Brown, Robert McAfee. *The Spirit of Protestantism.* New York: Oxford University Press, 1965.

Chadwick, Owen, ed. *The Pelican History of the Church.* 6 vols. Harmondsworth: Penguin Books, 1960–1970.

Cragg, Kenneth. *The Christ and the Faiths.* Philadelphia: Westminister Press, 1987.

Eckardt, A. Roy. *Jews and Christians: The Contemporary Meeting.* Bloomington: Indiana University Press, 1986.

Fiorenza, Elizabeth Schussler. *In Memory of Her: A Feminist Theological Reconstruction of Christian Origins.* New York: Crossroad, 1983.

Grant, Robert M. *Gods and the One God.* Philadelphia: Westminister Press, 1986.

McKenzie, John. *The Roman Catholic Church.* New York: Doubleday, 1971.

Meyerdorf, John. *The Orthodox Church: Its Past and Its Role in the World Today.* 3rd ed. Crestwood, NY: St. Vladimir's Seminary Press, 1981.

Niebuhr, H. Richard. *Christ and Culture.* New York: Harper Torchbooks, 1956.

Sanders, E. P. *Jesus and Judaism.* Philadelphia: Fortress Press, 1985.

Sloyan, Gerard S. *Jesus in Focus: A Life in Its Setting.* Mystic, CT: Twenty-third Publications, 1983.

Sobrino, Jon. *Christology at the Crossroads.* Maryknoll, NY: Orbis Books, 1978.

Tillich, Paul. *Dynamics of Faith.* New York: Harper & Row, 1957.

Walker, Williston, Richard A. Norris, David W. Lotz, and Robert T. Handy. *A History of the Christian Church.* 4th ed. New York: Scribners, 1985.

Weaver, Mary Jo. *Introduction to Christianity.* Belmont, CA: Wadsworth Publishing Company, 1984.

Welch, Sharon D. *Communities of Resistance and Solidarity: A Feminist Theology of Liberation.* Maryknoll, NY: Orbis Books, 1985.

Wiggins, James B., and Robert S. Ellwood. *Christianity: A Cultural Perspective.* Englewood Cliffs, NJ: Prentice-Hall, 1988.

Islam

Arberry, A. J. *The Koran Interpreted.* New York: Macmillan, 1955.

————. *Sufism: An Account of the Mystics of Islam.* New York: Harper & Row, 1970.

Cragg, Kenneth, and R. Marston Speight. *The House of Islam.* 3rd ed. Belmont, CA: Dickenson Publishing Company, 1987.

————. eds. *Islam From Within: Anthology of a Religion.* Belmont, CA: Wadsworth Publishing Company, 1980.

Denny, Frederick Mathewson. *An Introduction to Islam.* New York: Macmillan, 1985.

Esposito, J. L., ed. *Voices of Resurgent Islam.* New York: Oxford University Press, 1983.

Gibb, H. A. R., J. H. Kramers, E. Levi-Provencal, J. Schacht, B. Lewis, Ch. Pellat, V. L. Menage, and E. van Donzel, eds. *Encyclopaedia of Islam.* New ed. Leiden: E. J. Brill, 1960–.

Guillaume, A., trans. *The Life of Muhammad: A Translation of Ishaq's Sirat Rasul Allah.* London: Oxford University Press, 1955.

Haneef, Suzanne. *What Everyone Should Know About Islam and Muslims.* Des Plaines, IL: Library of Islam, 1985.

Hodgson, Marshall G. *The Venture of Islam: Conscience and History in a World Civilization.* 3 vols. Chicago: University of Chicago Press, 1974.

Holt, P. M., Ann K. S. Lambton, and Bernard Lewis, eds. *The Cambridge History of Islam.* 2 vols. Cambridge: Cambridge University Press, 1970.

Kamal, Ahmed. *The Sacred Journey: Being Pilgrimage to Makkah.* New York: Duell, Sloan and Pearce, 1961.

Mawdudi, Abul A'la. *Towards Understanding Islam.* Translated by Khurshid Ahmad. Plainfield, IN: Muslim Students' Association of the U.S. and Canada, 1980/ 1400 A. H.

Mernissi, Fatima. *Beyond the Veil: Male-Female Dynamics in Modern Muslim Society.* Rev. ed. Bloomington: Indiana University Press, 1987.

Momen, Moojan. *An Introduction to Shi'i Islam: The History and Doctrine of Twelver Shi'ism.* New Haven: Yale University Press, 1985.

Nasr, Seyyed Hossein. *Ideals and Realities of Islam.* Boston: Beacon Press, 1975.

Peters, F. E. *Allah's Commonwealth: A History of the Near East 600–1100 A. D.* New York: Simon and Schuster, 1973.

Rahman, Fazlur. *Islam.* Chicago: University of Chicago Press, 1979.

Savory, R. M., ed. *Introduction to Islamic Civilization.* New York: Cambridge University Press, 1976.

Schimmel, Annemarie. *Mystical Dimensions of Islam.* Chapel Hill: University of North Carolina Press, 1975.

Siddiqi, Abdul-Hamid. *The Life of Muhammad.* Lahore: Islamic Publications, 1975.

Stowasser, Barbara Freyer, ed. *The Islamic Impulse.* Washington, D.C.: Center for Contemporary Arab Studies, Georgetown University, 1987.

Watt, W. Montgomery. *Muhammad: Prophet and Statesman.* London: Oxford University Press, 1961.

PART THREE
RELIGIONS ARISING FROM INDIA

General

Basham, A. L. *The Wonder That Was India: A Survey of the Culture of the Indian Sub-continent Before the Coming of the Muslims.* New York: Grove Press, 1959.

de Bary, Wm. Theodore, Stephen N. Hay, Royal Weiler, and Andrew Yarrow, comps. *Sources of Indian Tradition.* New York: Columbia University Press, 1958.

Koller, John M. *The Indian Way.* New York: Macmillan, 1982.

Nakamura, Hajime. *Ways of Thinking of Eastern Peoples: India-China-Tibet-Japan.* Edited by Philip P. Wiener. Honolulu: East-West Center Press, 1964.

Hinduism

Bharati, Agehananda. *The Tantric Tradition.* New York: Doubleday, 1970.

Bowes, Pratima. *The Hindu Religious Tradition: A Philosophical Approach.* London: Routledge & Kegan Paul, 1976.

Brockington, J. L. *The Sacred Thread: Hinduism in Its Continuity and Diversity.* New York: Columbia University Press, 1981.

Dimmitt, Cornelia, and J. A. B. van Buitenen, trans. *Classical Hindu Mythology: A Reader in the Sanskrit Puranas.* Philadelphia: Temple University Press, 1978.

Dumont, Louis. *Homo Hierarchicus: The Caste System and Its Implications.* London: Paladin, 1972.

Eck, Diana L. *Banaras: City of Light.* Princeton, NJ: Princeton University Press, 1982.

———. *Darshan: Seeing the Divine Image in India.* 2nd ed. Chambersburg, PA: Anima Publications, 1985.

Eliade, Mircea. *Yoga: Immortality and Freedom.* Translated by Willard R. Trask. Princeton, NJ: Princeton University Press, 1970.

Embree, Ainslie T., ed. *The Hindu Religious Tradition: Readings in Oriental Thought.* New York: Random House, 1966.

Hawley, John S. *At Play With Krishna: Pilgrimage Dramas from Brindavan.* Princeton, NJ: Princeton University Press, 1985.

Hawley, John Stratton, and Donna Marie Wulff, eds. *The Divine Consort: Radha and the Goddesses of India.* Boston: Beacon Press, 1986.

Hopkins, Thomas. *The Hindu Religious Tradition.* Belmont, CA: Dickenson Publishing Company, 1971.

Kinsley, David R. *Hindu Goddesses: Visions of the Divine Feminine in the Hindu Religious Tradition*. Berkeley: University of California Press, 1985.

———. *Hinduism: A Cultural Perspective*. Englewood Cliffs, NJ: Prentice-Hall, 1982.

———. *The Sword and the Flute: Kali and Krishna, Dark Visions of the Terrible and the Sublime in Hindu Mythology*. Berkeley: University of California Press, 1977.

Kramrisch, Stella. *The Hindu Temple*. 2 vols. Delhi: Motilal Banarsidass, 1976.

Miller, Barbara Stoler, trans. *The Bhagavad-Gita: Krishna's Counsel in Time of War*. New York: Columbia University Press, 1986.

Nathan, Leonard, and Clinton Seely, trans. *Grace and Mercy in Her Wild Hair: Selected Poems to the Mother Goddess*. Boulder: Great Eastern, 1982.

Nikhilananda, Swami, trans. *The Gospel of Sri Ramakrishna: Originally Recorded in Bengali by M. [Mahendranath Gupta], a Disciple of the Master*. New York: Ramakrishna-Vivekananda Center, 1952.

O'Flaherty, Wendy Doniger. *The Origins of Evil in Hindu Mythology*. Berkeley: University of California Press, 1976.

———, trans. *The Rig Veda: An Anthology*. New York: Penguin Books, 1981.

———. *Shiva: The Erotic Ascetic*. Oxford: Oxford University Press, 1981.

Organ, Troy Wilson. *Hinduism: Its Historical Development*. Woodbury, NY: Barron's Educational Series, 1974.

Ranamjuan, A. K., trans. *Speaking of Shiva*. Baltimore: Penguin Books, Inc., 1973.

Singer, Milton, ed. *Krishna: Myths, Rites, and Attitudes*. Chicago: University of Chicago Press, 1968.

Waghorne, Joanne Punzo and Norman Cutler, eds., in association with Vasudha Narayanan. *Gods of Flesh/Gods of Stone: The Embodiment of Divinity in India*. Chambersburg, PA: Anima Publications, 1987.

Zaehner, R. C. *Hinduism*. London: Oxford University Press, 1962.

Zimmer, Heinrich. *Myths and Symbols in Indian Art and Civilization*. New York: Harper & Row, 1962.

Buddhism

Beyer, Stephen, trans. *The Buddhist Experience: Sources and Interpretations*. Belmont, CA: Dickenson Publishing Company, 1974.

Chen, Kenneth K. S. *Buddhism: the Light of Asia*. Woodbury, NY: Barron's Educational Series, 1968.

Conze, Edward. *Buddhism: Its Essence and Development*. New York: Harper & Row, 1959.

———, ed. *Buddhist Texts Through the Ages*. New York: Harper and Row, 1964.

de Bary, Wm. Theodore, ed. *The Buddhist Tradition in India, China and Japan*. New York: Vintage Books, 1972.

Dumoulin, Heinrich, and John C. Maraldo. *Buddhism in the Modern World*. New York: Macmillan, 1976.

Kalupahana, David J. *Nagarjuna: The Philosophy of the Middle Way*. New York: State University of New York Press, 1986.

Lester, Robert C. *Theravada Buddhism in Southeast Asia*. Ann Arbor: University of Michigan Press, 1973.

Paul, Diana Y. *Women in Buddhism: Images of the Feminine in the Mahayana Tradition*. Berkeley: University of California Press, 1979.

Prebish, Charles S. *American Buddhism*. Belmont, CA: Wadsworth Publishing Company, 1979.

———, ed. *Buddhism: A Modern Perspective*. University Park: Pennsylvania State University Press, 1975.

Rahula, Walpola. *What the Buddha Taught*. Rev. ed. New York: Grove Press, 1974.

Robinson, Richard H., and Willard L. Johnson. *The Buddhist Religion: A Historical Introduction*. 3rd ed. Belmont, CA: Wadsworth Publishing Company, 1982.

Spiro, Melford E. *Buddhist and Society: A Great Tradition and Its Burmese Vicissitudes*. New York: Harper & Row, 1972.

Swearer, Donald K. *Buddhism and Society in Southeast Asia*. Chambersburg, PA: Anima Publishing, 1981.

Takakusu, Junjiro. *The Essentials of Buddhist Philosophy*. 3rd ed. Edited by Wing-tsit Chan and Charles A. Moore. Honolulu: University of Hawaii Press, 1956.

Tambiah, Stanley J. *The Buddhist Saints of the Forest and the Cult of Amulets*. New York: Cambridge University Press, 1984.

Tucci, Giuseppe, *The Religions of Tibet*. Translated by Geoffrey Samuel. Berkeley: University of California Press, 1980.

[See also below under Religions of China and Religions of Japan].

Jainism

Jain, Jyotiprasad. *Religion and Culture of the Jains*. New Delhi: Bharatiya Jnanpith Publications, 1975.

Jaini, Padmanabh. *The Jaina Path of Purification*. Berkeley: University of California Press, 1979.

Sangave, Vilas Adinath. *Jaina Community: A Social Survey*. 2nd, rev. ed. Bombay: Popular Prakashan, 1980.

Sikhism

Cole, W. Owen. *The Guru in Sikhism*. London: Darton, Longman and Todd, 1982.

———— and Piara Singh Sambi. *The Sikhs: Their Religious Beliefs and Practices*. London: Routledge and Kegan Paul, 1978.

McLeod, W. H. *The Evolution of the Sikh Community*. Oxford: Clarendon Press, 1976.

————. *Guru Nanak and the Sikh Religion*. New York: Oxford University Press, 1968.

Singh, Avtar. *Ethics of the Sikhs*. Patiala: Punjabi University, 1970.

Singh, Khushwant. *The Sikhs Today: Their Religion, History, Culture, Customs, and Way of Life*. Rev. ed. New Delhi: Orient Longmans, 1964.

PART FOUR
RELIGIONS OF CHINA AND JAPAN

General

DeVos, George A., and Takao Sofue, eds. *Religion and the Family in East Asia*. Berkeley: University of California Press, 1984.

Dumoulin, Heinrich. *A History of Zen Buddhism*. 2 vols., rev. ed. Translated by James W. Heisig and Paul Knitter. New York: Macmillan, 1987–1988.

Religions of China

Bodde, Derk. *Festivals in Classical China*. Princeton, NJ: Princeton University Press, 1975.

Chan, Wing-tsit. *A Source Book in Chinese Philosophy*. Princeton, NJ: Princeton University Press, 1969.

Ch'en, Kenneth K. S. *The Chinese Transformation of Buddhism*. Princeton, NJ: Princeton University Press, 1973.

Chiu, Milton M. *The Tao of Chinese Religion*. New York: University Press of America, 1984.

Chung-Yuan, Chang, trans. *Original Teachings of Ch'an Buddhism: Selected from The Transmission of the Lamp*. New York: Vintage Press, 1971.

de Bary, Wm. Theodore, Wing-tsit Chan, and Burton Watson, comps. *Sources of Chinese Tradition*. 2 vols. New York: Columbia University Press, 1960.

Eber, Irene, ed. *Confucianism: The Dynamics of Tradition*. New York: Macmillan, 1986.

Girardot, N. J. *Myth and Meaning in Early Taoism: The Theme of Chaos*. Berkeley: University of California Press, 1983.

Hsu, Francis, L. K. *Under the Ancestors' Shadow: Kinship, Personality and Social Mobility in China*. Stanford: Stanford University Press, 1971.

Jochim, Christian. *Chinese Religions: A Cultural Perspective*. Englewood Cliffs, NJ: Prentice-Hall, 1986.

Jordon, David K. *Gods, Ghosts, and Ancestors: Folk Religion in a Taiwanese Village*. Berkeley: University of California Press, 1972.

———— and Daniel K. Overmyer. *The Flying Phoenix: Aspects of Chinese Sectarianism in Taiwan*. Princeton, NJ: Princeton University Press, 1986.

Lagerwey, John. *Taoist Ritual in Chinese Society and History*. New York: Macmillan, 1987.

Maspero, Henri. *Taoism and Chinese Religion*. Translated by Frank A. Kierman. Amherst: University of Massachusetts Press, 1981.

Moore, Charles A., ed. *The Chinese Mind*. Honolulu: University of Hawaii Press, 1967.

Overmyer, Daniel L. *Folk Buddhist Religion: Dissenting Sects in Late Traditional China*. Cambridge: Harvard University Press, 1976.

————. *Religions of China: The World As a Living System*. San Francisco: Harper & Row, 1986.

Saso, Michael. *Taoism and the Rite of Cosmic Renewal*. Pullman: Washington State University Press, 1972.

————. *The Teachings of Taoist Master Chuang*. New Haven: Yale University Press, 1978.

Schwartz, Benjamin I. *The World of Thought in Ancient China*. Cambridge: Belknap Press of Harvard University Press, 1985.

Smith, D. Howard. *Chinese Religions: From 1000 B.C. to the Present Day*. New York: Holt, Rinehart & Winston, 1971.

————. *Confucius*. New York: Scribner's, 1973.

Taylor, Rodney L. *The Way of Heaven: An Introduction to the Confucian Religious Life*. Leiden: E. J. Brill, 1986.

Thompson, Laurence G. *Chinese Religion: an Introduction*. 3rd ed. Belmont, CA: Wadsworth Publishing Company, 1979.

————. *The Chinese Way in Religion*. Belmont, CA: Dickenson Publishing Company, 1973.

Welch, Holmes. *The Practice of Chinese Buddhism, 1900–1950*. Cambridge: Harvard University Press, 1967.

Welch, Holmes, and Anna Seidel. *Facets of Taoism: Essays in Chinese Religion*. New Haven: Yale University Press, 1979.

————. *Taoism: The Parting of the Way*. Boston: Beacon Press, 1966.

Wolf, Arthur P, ed. *Religion and Ritual in Chinese Society*. Stanford: Stanford University Press, 1974.

Wolf, Margery. *Women and the Family in Rural Taiwan*. Stanford: Stanford University Press, 1970.

Wright, Arthur F. *Buddhism in Chinese History*. Stanford: Stanford University Press, 1959.

Yang, C. K. *Religion in Chinese Society*. Berkeley: University of California Press, 1961.

Religions of Japan

Beardsley, Richard K., John Hall, and Robert E. Ward. *Village Japan*. Chicago: University of Chicago Press, 1969.

Bellah, Robert N. *Tokugawa Religion*. Boston: Beacon Press, 1970.

Blacker, Carmen. *The Catalpa Bow: A Study of Shamanistic Practices in Japan*. London: George Allen & Unwin, 1975.

Bloom, Alfred. *Shinran's Gospel of Pure Grace*. Tucson: University of Arizona Press, 1965.

Collcutt, Martin. *Five Mountains: The Rinzai Monastic Institution in Medieval Japan*. Cambridge: Harvard University Press, 1981.

Earhart, H. Byron. *Japanese Religion: Unity and Diversity*. 3rd ed. Belmont, CA: Wadsworth Publishing Company, 1982.

——. *Religion in the Japanese Experience: Sources and Interpretations*. Belmont, CA: Dickenson Publishing Company. 1974.

Ellwood, Robert S., and Richard Pilgrim. *Japanese Religion: A Cultural Perspective*. Englewood Cliffs, NJ: Prentice-Hall, 1985.

Hakeda, Yoshito S., trans. *Kukai: Major Works*. New York: Columbia University Press, 1972.

Hardacre, Helen. *Kurozumikyo and the New Religions of Japan*. Princeton, NJ: Princeton University Press, 1986.

Hoover, Thomas. *Zen Culture*. New York: Vintage Books, 1978.

Hori, Ichiro. *Folk Religion in Japan: Continuity and Change*. Edited by Joseph M. Kitagawa and Allan L. Miller. Chicago: University of Chicago Press, 1968.

Hori, Ichiro, Ikado Fujio, Wakimoto Tsuneya, and Yanagawa Keiichi, eds. *Japanese Religion: A Survey by the Agency for Cultural Affairs*. Translated by Yoshiya Abe and David Reid. Tokyo: Kodansha International., 1972.

Kasulis, T. P. *Zen Action/Zen Person*. Honolulu: University of Hawaii Press, 1981.

Kim, Hee-jin. *Dogen Kigen—Mystical Realist*. Tucson: University of Arizona Press, 1975.

Kitagawa, Joseph M. *On Understanding Japanese Religion*. Princeton, NJ: Princeton University Press, 1987.

——. *Religion in Japanese History*. New York: Columbia University Press, 1966.

LaFleur, William R. *The Karma of Words: Buddhism and the Literary Arts in Medieval Japan*. Berkeley: University of California Press, 1983.

McFarland, H. Neill. *The Rush Hour of the Gods: A Study of New Religious Movements in Japan*. New York: Macmillan, 1967.

Matsunaga, Daigan, and Alicia Matsunaga. *Foundation of Japanese Buddhism*. 2 vols. Los Angeles: Buddhist Books International, 1974.

Muraoka, Tsunetsugu. *Studies in Shinto Thought*. Translated by Delmer Brown and James Araki. Tokyo: Ministry of Education, 1964.

Ono, Sokyo. *Shinto: The Kami Way*. Rutland, VT: Charles E. Tuttle, 1967.

Ross, Floyd Hiatt. *Shinto: The Way of Japan*. Boston: Beacon Press, 1965.

Suzuki, Daisetz T. *Zen and Japanese Culture*. Princeton, NJ: Princeton University Press, 1970.

Suzuki, Shunryu. *Zen Mind, Beginner's Mind*. Tokyo: John Weatherhill, 1970.

Tsunoda, Ryusaku, Wm Theodore de Bary, and Donald Keene, comps. *Sources of Japanese Tradition*. New York: Columbia University Press, 1964.

Varley, H. Paul. *Japanese Culture*. 3rd ed. Honolulu: University of Hawaii Press, 1984.

Yampolsky, Philip B., trans. *The Zen Master Hakuin: Selected Writings*. New York: Columbia University Press, 1971.

Epilogue

Coward, Harold. *Pluralism: Challenge to World Religions*. Maryknoll, NY: Orbis Books, 1985.

Ellwood, Robert S., and Harry B. Partin. *Religious and Spiritual Groups in Modern America*. 2nd ed. Englewood Cliffs, NJ: Prentice-Hall, 1988.

Swidler, Leonard, ed. *Toward a Universal Theology of Religion*. Maryknoll, NY: Orbis Books, 1987.

GLOSSARY

abba Aramaic term for "father" used by Jesus in addressing God.

Abbasids Dynasty of classical Islam, ruling at Baghdad, eighth to thirteenth centuries C.E.

Abu Bakr Companion of the Prophet Muhammad and first caliph.

Adi Granth "Original collection," the sacred scripture of the Sikhs; *see also* **Guru Granth Sahib**.

Advent Season of the Christian church year before the celebration of Christmas.

aesthetic Concerning beauty or artistic perception, important for religious expression.

Agni Vedic god of fire.

ahimsa "Nonviolence," one of the most important Jain principles; also emphasized in Buddhism and Hinduism.

Ainu Nonliterate people living in Hokkaido and islands north of Japan.

Akhnaton King in ancient Egypt who attempted to enforce a form of monotheism of the sun god Aton.

Akitu New Year festival in ancient Babylon.

Al-Ghazli Great thinker (1058–1111 C.E.) who synthesized orthodox thought and Sufism.

'Ali Nephew of the Prophet Muhammad and the fourth caliph.

Allah "The God," Quranic designation for the one God.

Amaterasu Sun kami, ruler of the Plain of High Heaven, ancestress of the Japanese emperors.

Amitabha Buddha of infinite light presiding over the Western paradise. Amida Buddha in Japan.

Analects Compilation of the sayings of Confucius.

ancestor veneration Rituals of worship and respect directed to the ancestral spirits.

Angas Main scriptures of the Jains.

animism Theory proposed by E.B. Tyler that religion originated with people supposing spirits to inhabit all things.

Apache Native Americans of southwestern North America.

Apostles Creed Statement of faith dating from the second century C.E., universally accepted by Christians.

arhant In Buddhism, a perfected saint who has reached nirvana and will be released from samsara at death.

Arianism A teaching advocated by some that Christ was created in time as the Son of God.

Arjan The fourth guru and first Sikh martyr (d. 1606).

Aryans Indo-European people who migrated into India.

Ashoka Great Buddhist king in India (r. ca. 272–236 B.C.E.), the "second founder" of Buddhism.

ashrama A stage of life in Hinduism; also a hermitage or place for meditation.

'Ashura Tenth day of the month of Muharram, day of fasting; sacred to Shi'ites as the day of Husayn's martyrdom.

atman In Hinduism, the soul or self, considered eternal.

atonement Doctrine of how humans are forgiven and reconciled to God through Christ's work.

Augustine Leading theologian in the early Christian church; bishop of Hippo in North Africa.

avatara In Hinduism, descent or incarnation, especially of the great god Vishnu, as in Krishna or Rama.

Ba'al Storm-fertility god of the ancient Canaanites.

Baptism Ritual of initiation into the Christian church through washing with water, viewed as a sacrament by many.

Bar Mitzvah Ceremony in which a thirteen-year-old boy becomes an adult member of the Jewish community.

Bat Mitzvah Equivalent of *Bar Mitzvah* ceremony for girls in Reform and Conservative congregations.

Bear Festival Important festival among bear-hunting people such as the Ainu.

Berith Milah *See* **circumcision.**

Bhagavad Gita Important Hindu scripture containing Krishna's teaching to Arjuna.

bhakti Devotion, self-surrender to one's god, a term used especially in Hinduism.

bhikkhu, bhikkhuni Pali terms for Buddhist monk and nun.

Birthday of the Buddha Important festival celebrated in May (Southeast Asia) or April (China and Japan).

Blessingway Important Navajo rituals that renew the primordial creative actions within life situations today.

Bodh Gaya The place where Siddhartha Gautama attained enlightenment.

Bodhidharma Legendary founder of Ch'an Buddhism in China who supposedly came from India in 470 C.E.

bodhisattva In Buddhist thought, being who is to become fully enlightened; in Mahayana, one who reaches enlightenment but vows to continue rebirths in samsara to assist others.

Brahma Designation for the creator god in Hindu thought.

Brahman Hindu term for ultimate reality; the divine source and pervading essence of the universe.

Brahmanas Ritual commentaries, part of the Vedas.

brahmins Highest ranked, priestly class in Hindu society.

Buddha "Enlightened one."

Bushido "Way of the warrior," the Japanese code of self-discipline for warriors, based on Zen, Shinto, and Neo-Confucian ideals.

Busk Festival at the green corn ripening among the Creek.

butsudan In Japan, Buddhist altar in the home.

Caliph "Deputy," "successor" to the Prophet as leader of Islam.

canon Accepted group of inspired or authoritative writings to be included in the sacred scriptures.

cargo cults Melanesian movements in expectation of the return of the ancestors on great cargo ships, a response to Western influence.

chado *See* **chanoyu.**

Ch'an (Pin-Yin: *Chan*) School of meditation Buddhism in China, influential in the arts; *Zen* in Japan.

Changing Woman Important divine figure among Native Americans of southwestern North America.

chanoyu The art of the Japanese tea ceremony; also called *chado*, "the way of tea."

Chiao Festival Great Taoist festival of cosmic and community renewal.

Ch'ing Ming "Clear and bright" festival; spring festival of visiting and renovating ancestral tombs in China.

Chou Dynasty (Pin-Yin: *Zhou*) Long dynasty (ca. 1123–221 B.C.E.) during which the classics were compiled and Confucianism and Taoism developed.

Christ Greek title meaning "anointed one" from the Hebrew "messiah," applied to Jesus of Nazareth by his followers.

Christology Doctrine about the nature and role of Christ.

Chthonian Gods "Earthy" gods in ancient Greece, associated with fertility and the realm of death.

Chu Hsi (Pin-Yin: *Chu Xi*) Leading thinker of the Neo-Confucian movement (1130–1200 C.E.).

Chuang Tzu (Pin-Yin: *Zhuang Zi*) Important early teacher of Taoism, whose writings have been very influential for the Taoist movement.

Church The community of all Christians; also specific groups, congregations, and buildings used for worship.

circumcision Boys' initiation ritual in many nonliterate societies; also in Judaism and Islam. In Judaism, it ocurrs on the eighth day after birth and is called *berith milah* (covenant of circumcision).

Confirmation A Christian ritual of reaffirming vows taken in Baptism; considered a sacrament by some.

Confucius Teacher whose philosophy of life become dominant in Chinese culture.

Conservative Judaism Movement attempting to adapt Judaism to modern life by using principles of change within the traditional laws; occupies middle ground between Reform and Orthodox Judaism.

Constantine Roman emperor who legalized and promoted Christianity.

cosmic state Perspective in ancient Mesopotamia that the cosmos is governed by great gods of nature.

cosmogonic Related to the creation or founding of the world and of basic human realities.

Council of Nicea First great church council, convened in 325 to settle disputes about the nature of Christ.

Council of Trent Council convened by the pope in 1545 to reform the church and oppose the actions of the Protestants.

Covenant (berith) Relationship between God and Israel, enacted on Mt. Sinai, based on Israel's acceptance of God's Torah.

Creek Native Americans, originally of eastern woodlands of North America.

Crusades Attempts by Christians of Western Europe to recapture the Holy Land by force.

Cultural Revolution The period from 1966–1976 in China during which fanatical Red Guards attempted to destroy all forms of "old" religion and culture.

culture heroes Beings in mythic time who originated important aspects of cultural life.

Daimoku Formula used in Nichiren Buddhist worship: "Praise to the wonderful law of the Lotus Sutra."

Dalai Lama Leader of Tibetan Lamaism.

Dar al-Harb *See* **Dar al-Islam**.

Dar al-Islam "Abode of Islam"; territories of the ummah under Muslim control, whereas the rest of the world is the *Dar al-Harb*, "abode of warfare."

darshana In Hinduism, the ritual act of seeing a sacred image, person, or place.

denomination A church organization consisting of a number of congregations having autonomous structure and usually distinctive teaching, especially within Protestantism.

Dependent Arising (pratitya-samutpada) Central Buddhist teaching that everything is conditioned by something else.

Dharma In Buddhism, truth; the teaching of the Buddha; *dharmas* also refer to the constituents of all phenomena; in Hinduism, the cosmic order, social duty and proper behavior.

dhikr "Remembrance"; ritual in Sufism of spiritual exercises focusing the consciousness on God.

Diaspora The dispersion of Jews away from the land of Israel.

Dietary Law Jewish laws pertaining to the proper preparation, eating, and avoidance of animal food.

Digambara "Sky-clad," renouncing the use of clothing; one of the two major groups among the Jains.

Diksa Initiation ceremony for Jain monks and nuns.

Divali Autumn festival of lights and good fortune in India.

divination Techniques used to read and understand the will of the ancestors or the spiritual forces of the world.

divine kingship Notion in many ancient societies, such as Egypt and Mesopotamia, that the king represents divine power to the human realm.

Djanggawul Australian culture heroes who created the present world in their wanderings in the Dreaming Time.

Docetism Teaching by some in the early church that Christ only appeared to be human.

Dogen Important thinker and founder of Soto Zen in Japan.

Dogon People living in Mali in Africa.

Dreaming Time Mythic Time of the Beginnings in Australian tradition.

Dukkha "Suffering," characteristic of all conditioned reality as stated in the First Noble Truth of Buddhism.

Durga Great Hindu goddess; one of the names of Shiva's consort.

earth-diver myth Creation of the world when an animal dove into the sea to bring up the first mass of earth.

Easter Festival celebrating the resurrection of Christ.

Ecumenical movement Modern movement to achieve understanding, cooperation, and some form of unity between the various branches of Christianity.

Eightfold Path The fundamental path toward nirvana as taught by the Buddha.

Eisai Founder of Rinzai Zen in Japan.

emergence myth Story of original people emerging from lower worlds into the present world, as among the Navajo.

Ennead The group of nine gods headed by the creator Atum, worshiped at Heliopolis in ancient Egypt.

Enuma Elish Epic of creation in ancient Babylon, read during New Year festival.

Epiphany Season after Christmas emphasizing the "showing forth" of Christ to the world.

Eschatology Doctrine about the last things: end of the world, judgment, consummation of God's plan.

Essenes Ascetic Jewish movement around the Dead Sea area from second century B.C.E. to first century C.E.

ethics Thought and study about moral decisions, on the basis of traditions of right and wrong.

Eucharist Principle Christian sacrament, using bread and wine as a reenactment or remembrance of Christ's last supper; also called Mass, Lord's Supper, Divine Liturgy, and Holy Communion.

Exile The Jewish captivity in Babylon, especially the period from the fall of Jerusalem in 586 B.C.E. until the first return to Jerusalem in 538 B.C.E.

Exodus Deliverance of Israelites from Egypt under Moses' leadership.

exorcism Ritual enacted by a priest or spirit medium to drive away demons.

feng shui Geomancy, the Chinese art of reading forces of yin and yang so as to determine the most beneficial location for graves and houses.

filial piety Primary Confucian virtue of respect toward parents and ancestors.

First Council of Buddhism Held at Rajagrha shortly after the Buddha's parinirvana, where, according to tradition, the Buddha's sayings were recited and compiled.

Five Classics The heart of the Confucian scriptures, including the Classic of History (Shu Ching), the Classic of Poetry (Shih Ching), the Classic of Changes (I Ching), the Classic of Rites (Li Ching), and the Spring and Autumn Annals (Ch'un-Ch'iu).

Five Elements Chinese idea of five modes of energy in the universe that mutually influence each other: wood, fire, earth, metal, water.

Five Pillars Required Muslim rituals of serving God: Shahadah (confession), Salat (prayer), Zakat (alms-giving), Sawm (fasting), Hajj (pilgrimage).

Five Precepts The basic moral precepts of Buddhism, to refrain from destroying life, from taking what is not given, from wrongful sexual behavior, from wrongful speech, and from drugs or liquor.

Four Noble Truths Basic teachings presented in the Buddha's first sermon: the truths of suffering, of the cause of suffering, of the overcoming of suffering, and of the path to follow.

Four Sights Sickness, old age, death, and a wandering hermit; seeing these motivated Siddhartha Gautama to seek enlightenment.

free will Ability of humans to make moral choices.

Fundamentalism Holding to the literal inerrancy of scripture and the authority of doctrines derived from it.

Gandhi Leader of the Hindu independence movement, emphasizing spiritual preparation and nonviolent resistance (1869–1948).

Ganesha Son of Shiva, popular elephant-headed Hindu god who overcomes obstacles and brings good fortune.

Gemara Comments on the Mishnah; added to the Mishnah to form the Jewish Talmud.

ghetto Special Jewish quarter in certain European cities.

Ghost Dance Native revival movement among many Native American peoples in the latter part of the nineteenth century.

giri Important Japanese sense of social obligation and duty.

Gnosticism Religious movements in the Hellenistic world that emphasized a special secret knowledge about God and the world.

Gobind Singh The tenth and last Sikh guru, who founded the Khalsa.

Golden Temple Important Sikh gurdwara at Amritsar.

Gospels Writings compiled in the early church relating the story of Jesus' life and death; the four canonical Gospels are Matthew, Mark, Luke, and John.

grace Achievement of spiritual goals as "given" by spiritual powers rather than attained by one's own effort.

Great Commission Commission given to his disciples by Christ to go and "make disciples" of all nations.

Great Mother Feminine sacred being, source of all life and power, worshiped at least as early as late Paleolithic period.

gurdwara Temple and meeting place for Sikhs.

Guru Leader and guide for Sikhs; besides the ten gurus, God and the Adi Granth are also called guru; in Hinduism, a spiritual guide and master.

Guru Granth Sahib "Sacred collection," the sacred scriptures, with the title guru; another name for the Adi Granth.

Hadith A saying or tradition of the Prophet Muhammad transmitted through a trustworthy chain of reporters; the collection of hadiths.

Hagar Mother of Ishmael and ancestress of the Muslims.

Hainuwele Culture hero in Wemale tradition (Ceram Island in Indonesia) from whose body tuberous plants grew.

Hajj Pilgrimage to Mecca.

Halakhah Jewish legal tradition from the Talmud.

Han Dynasty Period in China (from ca. 202 B.C.E. to 220 C.E.) during which Confucianism became the state ideology and cult, Buddhism made its entry, and religious Taoism developed.

Hanukkah Jewish festival of lights in December, celebrating rededication of temple in Maccabean times.

Hasidim Popular mystical and devotional Jewish movement beginning in the seventeenth century in Eastern Europe.

Hebrews Ancestors of the Israelites.

henotheism Dedication to one god while accepting existence of others.

Hidden Christians Christians in Japan who continued their religion secretly after Christianity was outlawed in the mid-seventeenth century.

Hidden Imam In Shi'ism, the last Imam (successor to Muhammad) who disappeared into the state of occultation and will return in the future.

Hijra Emigration of the Prophet and his followers from Mecca to Medina in 622 C.E.

Hinayana "Lesser vehicle," term applied to those Buddhist sects that arose in the first four centuries after the Buddha's death; of these sects, Theravada still survives today.

Holi Popular festival in northern India with carnival atmosphere.

Holocaust An ancient term used in modern times to denote the destruction of Jews and others under the Nazis.

Homo Erectus Human species about 500,000 years ago; lived in communities and probably had common speech.

Homo Sapiens Modern human species, dating back to late Paleolithic period or perhaps to the Neanderthal species.

Honen Founder of Pure Land Buddhism as a separate sect in Japan.

Hopi Native Americans of southwestern North America.

Hsun Tzu (Pin-Yin: *Xun Zi*) Important Confucian thinker (ca. 300–238 B.C.E.) who advocated a realistic understanding of the human inclination toward evil.

Hua-yen A Chinese school of Mahayana Buddhism based on the Garland Sutra.

hunters Peoples who live by hunting and gathering, whose religious ideas are especially associated with animal life.

Husayn Son of 'Ali, killed at Karballah; considered by Shi'ites as a successor to the Prophet Muhammad and a great martyr.

I Ching (Pin-Yin: *Yi Jing*) The Classic of Changes, an ancient Chinese divination manual based on sixty-four hexagrams (each of six unbroken and broken lines).

'Id "Festival" In Islam; the two canonical festivals are *'Id al-adha* (Feast of Sacrifice) during the Hajj month and *'Id al-fitr* (Feast of Breaking the Ramadan Fast).

ihram State of ritual purity and consecration appropriate for entering the sacred precincts of Mecca on the Hajj.

ijma' "Consensus"; for formulating Muslim law consensus among the legal scholars is necessary.

ijtihad Independent legal reasoning in Islam; one who does this is a *mujtahid*.

Imam "Leader," especially in ritual prayer; for Shi'ites, the proper successors to the Prophet are called Imams.

iman "Faith," complete certitude about the truth of Islam.

Impermanence Basic Buddhist doctrine that change is characteristic of everything that arises.

Incarnation "Becoming flesh"; especially the Christian teaching that the eternal Son of God became human in the womb of his mother Mary.

Indra Vedic storm-warrior god.

Indus Valley Civilization Urban-agricultural civilization that flourished in the third millennium B.C.E. and left influences on Hinduism.

Ise Shrine Shrine of Amaterasu, the Japanese Sun Kami.

Ishmael First son of Abraham, ancestor of the Muslims.

isnad The chain of transmitters for a particular hadith in Islam.

Israel "He strives with God"; name given to Jacob and thereafter to the covenant people; name of modern Jewish state.

Izanagi and Izanami The pair of kami who created the world, according to Japanese mythology.

Jade Emperor Supreme god in Chinese popular religion.

jati "Birth"; one's caste or closed social group as determined by birth in India.

jen (Pin-yin: *ren*) Humaneness, an important ideal in Confucianism.

jihad "Striving" for religious perfection and for God's cause, including bearing arms in defense of Islam if necessary.

Jina "Conqueror," Jain idea of one who has reached total liberation; *see also* **Tirthankara**.

Jizo Popular Buddhist divinity in Japan known as the savior of the dead and helper of dead children.

Judgment Day The day on which God will judge all according to their deeds.

justification by faith Christian doctrine that justification before God comes by faith, not by works; emphasized by Protestants.

Ka'bah The cube-shaped stone shrine in the Great Mosque at Mecca, focal point of prayer and pilgrimage.

Kabbalah "Tradition," especially the medieval mystical Jewish tradition.

Kabir A poet (1440–1518), an important predecessor of Guru Nanak, founder of Sikhism.

kafir An unbeliever, in Islamic terms.

Kali Goddess of death and destruction in Hinduism; one of the names of Shiva's consort.

kami Spirits or divinities in Shinto, including mythological beings, powerful and awesome aspects of nature, and important humans.

kamidana Kami altar in the home in Japan.

Kannon Bodhisattva Avalokiteshvara, popular goddess of mercy in Japan. Kuan-Yin in China.

karah parshad Sacred food used in Sikh worship assembly.

Karaites Jewish sect that rejected oral Torah, relying on scripture alone.

karma "Action," law in Hinduism and Buddhism that all deeds and thoughts, according to one's intentions, will have set consequences; Jain idea of subtle form of matter that clings to the soul because of the soul's passion and desire, causing rebirths.

karuna Buddhist ideal of compassion.

kenosis "Emptying out"; ritual separation from evil and pollution.

kevela The highest state of enlightenment, according to Jainism.

Khadija First wife of the Prophet Muhammad.

Khalsa A major military-type group within Sikhism, founded in 1699 by Gobind Singh, the tenth guru, with a special code of discipline.

Kharijites "Seceders," strict moralistic sect of early Islam.

Kingdom of God The rule of God; as proclaimed by Jesus, a present reality, yet to be fully manifested in the future.

kirtan Sikh practice of singing hymns in worship of God.

kirtana In Hinduism, devotional group worship through song and dance.

koan Zen saying or riddle used in meditation.

Kojiki Records of Ancient Matters, earliest writing in Japan, a compilation of stories about the age of the kami and the beginnings of Japan.

kosher "Fit"; anything suitable for use according to Jewish law.

Krishna Avatara of the great Hindu god Vishnu; hero of the Bhagavad Gita and popular god in Vaishnavite devotional movements.

kshatriya The classical warrior class in Hindu society.

Kuan Yin (Pin-yin: *Guan-Yin*) Bodhisattva Avalokiteshvara, widely worshiped in China as a god/goddess of great mercy. Kannon in Japan.

kuei (Pin-yin: *Gui*) Malevolent spirits in Chinese popular thought.

Kukai Great Japanese Buddhist thinker and founder of Shingon.

Lamaism Derived from Lama, "master"; the special form of Buddhism in Tibet.

langar Sikh community kitchen.

Lao Tzu (Pin-yin: *Lao Zi*) Legendary author of the Tao Te Ching and founder of Taoism.

Legalists School of thought in China that emphasized the need for law and order.

Lent Christian season of penitence in preparation for Easter celebration.

li Rites, propriety; the Confucian code of ceremonial behavior.

liminal In ritual, the state between separation (kenosis) and restoration (plerosis).

lingam The phallic pillar that symbolizes the great Hindu god Shiva.

literati Learned Confucian scholars.

liturgy Order of prayer, scripture reading, hymns, and exhortations followed in a worship service.

Lotus Sutra Important early scripture of Mahayana Buddhism.

Lugbara A people of East Africa.

ma'at Ideal of justice and order in ancient Egypt.

Madhyamika Early school of Mahayana Buddhism that emphasized *shunyata* (emptiness).

magic Attempt to control and manipulate forces of spirit and nature.

Mahabharata One of the two great epics of Hinduism.

Mahavairocana the great sun Buddha.

Mahavira In Jainism, the twenty-fourth and last Jina of the present world half-cycle, who lived from 599–527 B.C.E.

Mahayana The "great vehicle," form of Buddhism that arose in India beginning in the second century B.C.E. and eventually spread to East Asia.

Maimonides Great medieval Jewish philosopher (1135–1204 C.E.).

mana Polynesian word for the state in which people, places, or objects are especially filled with sacred power.

mandala Painting of the sacred cosmos used especially in Tantric Buddhist ritual and meditation.

Mandate of Heaven In Chinese religion, the expression of T'ien's moral will, especially in granting prosperity to virtuous rulers and cutting short evil ones.

mantra Sacred word, formula, or verse.

Mao Tse-tung (Pin-yin: *Mao Ze-dong*) Leader (1893–1976) of the Communist movement and of the People's Republic of China.

Marduk God of ancient Babylon city-state.

Marranos Spanish Jews who were outwardly Christianized but who secretly continued Jewish tradition.

Masada Mountain fortress near the Dead Sea where Jewish Zealots made a last stand against the Romans.

master or mistress of animals Divine being, often a prototype of the herd of animals, who protects the herd and also provides boons for humans.

matsuri Shinto festival.

Matteo Ricci First Jesuit missionary to China (1552–1610)

Ma Tsu (Pin-yin: *Ma-zu*) Widely worshiped goddess of Chinese seafarers known as the Queen of Heaven.

maya Appearance, term in India to indicate that which prevents one from seeing truly.

Meiji Restoration Restoration of imperial rule in Japan in 1868.

Mencius Leading thinker after Confucius, whose writings have shaped the Confucian tradition.

Mendelssohn, Moses Jewish Enlightenment thinker (1729–1786).

mendicants Monks and nuns who observe the path of total renunciation.

messiah End-time king, descended from King David, expected to redeem Israel.

microcosm The idea that the world and the human body are miniature replicas of the great sacred cosmos.

mihrab The niche in the mosque wall indicating the direction to Mecca.

minbar The pulpit from which the sermon is given during the Friday prayer in the mosque.

Mishnah Code of Jewish oral law compiled ca. 200 C.E. by Judah the Prince.

mission Motivation in some religions to share the truth and the way to the ideal state with others.

mitzvot Commandments in Judaism; acts in obedience to God's will.

Mogul Great Muslim dynasty in India.

moksha Liberation from bondage to samsara and karma; the goal of Hindu spiritual practice.

monasticism The way of life of monks and nuns, usually celibate, without personal possessions, and dedicated to prayer, study, and service.

monism View that all reality is one unified divine reality.

monotheism Belief in one almighty God, separate from the world.

Moses Leader of Israel in the Exodus from Egypt and the founding of the covenant on Mt. Sinai.

mosque (masjid) The place of communal worship in Islam.

mujtahid *See* Ijtihad.

mulla Persian word for learned Muslim teacher and expounder of the law.

Muslim One who has surrendered to God.

Mu'tazilites School in the classical period of Islam that accepted reason as a primary criterion for establishing beliefs.

Mysteries Secret ritual cults in ancient Greece in which initiates could experience union with a god and promise of life after death.

mysticism Direct inner experience of relationship to the sacred reality, beyond rational thought.

myth Story about sacred beings in the beginning time, telling how existence came to be as it is and providing the pattern for authentic life.

Nagarjuna Important philosopher (ca. 150–250 C.E.) of the Madhyamika school of Buddhism.

Nanak Founder (1469–1539) of Sikhism and the first guru.

Navajo Native American people of southwestern North America.

Ndembu People living in Zambia in Central Africa.

Neanderthal Human species ca. 100,000–35,000 years ago; first clear archaeological evidence of religious activities.

nembutsu Formula of calling on Amida Buddha: "Namu Amida Butsu."

Neo-Confucianism Revival of Confucian thought in the eleventh century C.E., with emphasis on the underlying principle of all things.

Neolithic Period beginning after the last ice age (ca. 10,000 BCE) when planting was discovered and villages and cities founded.

Neo-orthodoxy Modern Protestant theological movement reasserting orthodox tradition about human sinfulness and divine grace.

New Religions New religious movements in Japan, often drawing on and combining aspects of Buddhism, Shinto, and folk religion.

New Year Festival Important annual festival in many societies, a time of purging out the old year and bringing renewal.

Ngaju Dayak Agricultural people living in South Borneo, Indonesia.

Nichiren Japanese Buddhist sect based singlemindedly on the Lotus Sutra, founded by the monk Nichiren.

Nihon Shoki Chronicles of Japan, compiled shortly after the Kojiki and containing stories about the kami and early emperors.

Ninigi Grandson of Amaterasu, sent to earth to begin kami rule on earth, ancestor of first legendary Japanese emperor.

nirvana "Blowing out" the fires of life, liberation from suffering and rebirth, the spiritual goal of Buddhist practice.

No Action (wu-wei) Basic Taoist principle of not doing anything contrary to the flow of nature.

noble person (chun tzu) Ideal Confucian goal, a noble man defined by moral character.

nondualism View that ultimate reality and the phenomenal world are not different.

Norito Ancient Shinto ritual prayers.

No-self (an-atman) The basic Buddhist doctrine that there is no permanent, absolute self.

Obon Festival of the seventh month in Japan welcoming the ancestors.

Old Testament Christian designation for the Hebrew scriptures.

Olorun Supreme god among the Yoruba.

Olympian Gods Powerful gods of ancient Greece ruling from Mt. Olympus.

ordination (upasampada) Important Buddhist ritual marking the beginning of life as a monk or nun.

original sin Christian teaching that the Fall of Adam and Eve represents a basic condition of sinfulness that all humans share.

orisa Divinities in Yoruba belief that control life in the world.

Orthodox Church Term referring to the historic Eastern Christian churches, including the Greek, Russian, Armenian, and other traditions.

Orthodox Judaism Modern movement continuing a strict traditional belief in the binding character of the Torah and Halakhah.

Osiris God of the dead in ancient Egypt, important for the afterlife.

Ottoman Dynasty ruling much of the Muslim world from Istanbul from the fifteenth to the twentieth centuries C.E.

Paleolithic Old Stone Age; in the late Paleolithic period (ca. 50,000 B.C.E.) the modern species of homo sapiens appeared.

P'an Ku In Chinese tradition, mythic primordial person out of whom the whole universe developed.

parables Stories by which Jesus taught his disciples about the Kingdom of God.

parinirvana Full nirvana; complete liberation attained at the death of a Buddha.

Parshva In Jainism, the twenty-third Jina of the present world half-cycle, who lived in the midninth century B.C.E.

Passion Story The climax of each of the four Gospels, telling of the suffering and crucifixion of Jesus.

pastoralists Peoples who live by raising herds of cattle or sheep, whose religious ideas are associated especially with their herds.

Path of Action (karma-marga) The Hindu path toward liberation based on acting according to Dharma, without desire for the fruits of action.

Path of Devotion (bhakti-marga) Hindu path toward liberation based on devotional practices directed toward one's god.

Path of Knowledge (jnana-marga) Hindu path toward liberation based on knowledge, emphasizing meditation.

path of transformation Practice in religion that changes one from the wrong or inadequate state to the ideal state.

Paul Leading apostle who brought the gospel of Christ to non-Jews and whose letters form part of the New Testament.

Pentecost Christian festival approximately seven weeks after Easter, celebrating the coming of the Holy Spirit upon the church.

Pesach (Passover) Jewish spring festival commemorating deliverance from Egypt.

peyote cult Modern Native American revival movement, called the Native American Church, with ceremonial use of peyote (small hallucinogenic cactus).

Pharisees Party in ancient Judaism teaching the oral Torah along with the written Torah, resurrection of the body, and application of the law in everyday life.

Philosophy Humanistic, rational thinking that developed especially in ancient Greece.

Pietism A Christian reaction to the rationalism of the Enlightenment, emphasizing the experience of God's grace and emotional dedication.

plan of salvation Christian idea of God's design for the salvation of the world foretold through prophets and accomplished through Jesus Christ.

planters Peoples who cultivate plants for food and have religious ideas associated especially with vegetation and the fertility of the earth.

plerosis "Filling up"; fulfillment or restoration movement of ritual.

pollution In the Shinto view, anything that hinders life and fertility by causing separation from the kami.

polytheism Belief that many divine powers share in the world's operation.

prehistoric Before written records.

Principle Neo-Confucian concept of the underlying source of all phenomena.

prophecy Belief, especially in Judaism, Christianity, and Islam, that God gives revelation through prophets.

prophets People who spoke God's word and advocated reforms in Israel, especially from the eighth to the fourth centuries B.C.E. In Islam, also the prophet Muhammad.

Protestantism Broad designation in Christianity for the main churches of the Reformation.

puja In Hinduism, ritual worship of the image of a god by offering food, flowers, music, and prayers.

Puranas Late Hindu scriptures that developed from popular theistic devotional movements.

Pure Land Popular Buddhist school that worships Amita Buddha and looks to the Pure Land paradise.

purification Rituals, important in Shinto, to remove pollution and reinstate harmony and communion with the karmi.

Purim Early spring festival in Judaism remembering events of the Book of Esther.

qiyas "Analogy" in legal argumentation and decision making in Islam.

Quran "Recitation," primarily the revelation sent down by God upon the Prophet; the Holy Book.

rabbi "My master"; title for Jewish teacher of the law; spiritual leader of a congregation.

Rabbinic Judaism Designation for Judaism as it developed under the teachers of the oral Torah (Mishnah and Talmud).

Rama Avatara of Vishnu, divine hero of the Ramayana.

Ramanuja Hindu philosopher and advocate of the Vaishnavite bhakti tradition (ca. 1017–1137).

Ramayana Story of Rama, one of the two great epics of Hinduism.

rebirth In the religions of India, belief that after the death of its body the soul takes on another body.

Reconstructionist Judaism Modern movement founded by Mordecai Kaplan (1881–1982), emphasizing Judaism as a civilization.

rectification of names Confucian program for the development of a moral society by properly structuring social relationships.

Reformation Reform movements in the Christian church, especially the reform of the European church through the work of Luther, Calvin, Zwingli, and others.

Reform Judaism Modern movement attempting to conform tradition to conditions of modern life, allowing changes in the Halakhah.

Religious Taoism General term for the variety of Taoist practices related to priests, scriptures, and techniques for prolonging life.

Restraints The Jain vows of nonviolence, not lying, not stealing, refraining from wrong sex, and nonpossession or nonattachment.

Resurrection Rising from the dead; Christ's resurrection as the first fruit of the resurrection of all, in Christian belief.

Rig Veda The earliest and most important collection of Vedic hymns.

rites of passage Rituals connected with the critical changes of life.

Roman Catholic Church The historic Western church as it has continued under the leadership of the pope, the bishop of Rome.

Rosh Hashanah Jewish New Year, first day of Tishri (usually in September); beginning of High Holy Days (which include Yom Kippur).

Sabbath Seventh day of the week, sacred day of rest and study for Jews.

sacrament Christian rituals that convey God's grace, as Baptism and the Eucharist.

sacred story Master story of a religion, providing identity for the adherents.

sacred time Special time of ritual and festival, when mythic events are made present once more.

Sadducees Conservative party of temple priests and sympathizers in ancient Judaism who rejected the oral Torah and the idea of the resurrection.

Safavid Muslim dynasty in Iran.

Salat Required Muslim ritual of prayer five times daily.

salvation Reaching the ideal state of wholeness; "saved" from the wrong state.

Samhitas "Collections" of early Vedic hymns and verses; there are four collections: Rig-Veda, Sama-Veda, Yajur-Veda, and Atharva-Veda.

Samkhya One of the classical schools of Hindu philosophy stressing an absolute distinction between matter and spirit.

samsara The rebirth cycle of existence.

samskaras In Hinduism, rituals performed at the critical changes of life.

samurai The Japanese class of warriors influenced by Zen and Neo-Confucianism.

sandpainting Navajo ceremonial art used in healing rituals.

Sangha The assembly of Buddhist monks, nuns, and laity.

sannyasin One who has renounced the cares and concerns of the world; the fourth stage of life in Hinduism.

Sawm Required Muslim fasting during the month of Ramadan.

School of National Learning Shinto restoration movement during the Tokugawa period.

Shahadah The Muslim formula bearing witness to the unity of God: "I testify that there is no God but God; I testify that Muhammad is His messenger."

Shakti In Hinduism, divine energy, personified as a goddess; wife of a god, especially of Shiva.

Shakyamuni A title of the Buddha: the wise one of the Shakya clan.

shaman, shamaness A person who undergoes special training and can go into trances, communicate with the spiritual world, and bring healing and special benefits.

Shang Ti (Pin-yin: *Shang Di*) Supreme god worshiped by the Shang rulers in ancient China.

Shankara Great philosopher of Advaita (nondual) Vedanta (788–820 C.E.).

Shari'ah Islamic law, based on the Quran and on the sunnah of the Prophet.

Shavuot Jewish Feast of Weeks (Pentecost), commemorating the giving of the Torah on Mt. Sinai.

Shema Statement proclaiming the unity of God, based on Deut. 6:4–9, beginning, "Hear, O Israel, the Lord our God, the Lord is one . . ."

shen In Chinese religion, benevolent and honored spirits, including ancestors.

Shi'ites The "faction" of 'Ali who believe that 'Ali and his descendants are the proper successors of the Prophet Muhammad.

Shingon Esoteric (Tantric) Buddhism in Japan.

Shinran Disciple of Honen and founder of the True Pure Land Buddhist sect in Japan.

Shinto Chinese term (shen tao) used to designate the Japanese "way of the kami."

shirk "Association," Muslim term for the great sin of idolatry or associating something else with God.

Shiva The great ascetic Hindu god symbolized by the lingam; focus of the great Shaivite devotional movement.

Shotoku Prince regent (573–621) who advocated Buddhism as one of the pillars of Japan.

shrine (jinja) In Japan, sacred place because of the presence of a kami; usually has appropriate buildings where a symbol of the kami is housed and where worshipers can consult priests.

Shruti "That which is heard," the eternal truth, that is, the Vedas.

shudras Classical servant class in Hindu society, the fourth class.

shunyata "Emptiness," Mahayana Buddhist teaching that all things are devoid of any substantial or independent reality.

Sikh "Disciple," that is, one who follows the gurus.

Singh Surname taken by men who join the Sikh Khalsa.

Sioux Native American people of the plains of North America.

skandhas "Heaps" or aggregates; the Buddhist teaching that a person is really a changing process of five aggregates.

Smriti "That which is remembered," the tradition, that is, the scriptural writings after the Vedas.

Soka Gakkai Largest new religious movement in Japan, based on Nichiren Buddhism.

Son of Heaven Title of Chinese emperor.

soteriology Theory of salvation.

spirit writing In Chinese religion, writing on a tray of sand or on paper by a spirit who moves the pen.

stupa Memorial Buddhist shrine or reliquary.

Sufi One who follows the mystical path of Islam.

Sukkot Feast of Booths, autumn harvest festival in Judaism.

sun god Divine being manifested through the sun, important especially in ancient Egypt.

Sunna "Custom" or "way of acting," primarily of the Prophet Muhammad; the Prophet's *sunnah* is known through the hadiths.

Sunnites Term for the Muslim majority, those who acknowledge the Quran and the Prophet's sunna as interpreted by the orthodox 'ulama.

supreme god The god with final authority, usually the creator, often associated with the sky.

Susanoo Storm kami in Japanese mythology, unruly brother of Amaterasu.

Svetambara "White clad," accepting the use of clothing; one of the two major Jain groups.

sweat lodge Special lodge among some Native Americans constructed for purification ceremonies.

synagogue Greek term translating Hebrew "house of assembly"; Jewish place for prayer and study.

tabu Polynesian word indicating someone or something is full of sacred power in a volatile, contagious (and therefore potentially harmful) way.

T'ai-p'ing Rebellion Abortive popular movement in the middle nineteenth century in China, based on religious ideas, attempting to change the hierarchical structure of society.

Talmud Jewish "oral Torah," comprised of the Mishnah and Gemara; exists in a Palestinean and a Babylonian version.

Tanakh Hebrew scriptures comprised of Torah (the Pentateuch), Nevi'im (the Prophets), and Ketuvim (the Writings).

Tantrism Movement in Hinduism and Buddhism using initiation, rituals, imagination, and sexual symbolism as spiritual practices leading toward liberation.

Tao (Pin-yin: *Dao*) "Way," Chinese term for the indefinable source of all reality; the way of nature.

Taoist Canon Vast secretive sacred writings produced in religious Taoism.

tao shih Taoist priest.

Tao Te Ching (Pin-yin: *Dao De Jing*) "Classic of the Tao and its Power"; earliest and very influential text of Taoism.

Tathagata Title for the Buddha meaning the "Thus Come One," that is, the perfected one.

Tawhid Muslim term for maintaining the unity of God.

temple Place of worship in many religions.

Tenrikyo The oldest of the existing New Religions in Japan, founded in 1838.

theology Thinking about God and God's work.

Theravada An early Hinayana sect that survives today; term generally used for Buddhism in South and Southeast Asia.

Three Body Teaching Mahayana doctrine of three dimensions of the Buddha: the Dharma Body, the Bliss Body, and the Transformation Body.

Three Pure Ones Designation for highest gods summoned by Taoist priests.

Three Refuges The Buddha, the Dharma, and the Sangha; many Buddhist prayers and declarations begin with the Three Refuge formula.

T'ien (Pin-yin: *Tian*) "Heaven," from ancient times in China considered an ultimate power that rules especially through the moral order.

T'ien-t'ai A school of Mahayana Buddhism in China, based on the Lotus Sutra.

Time of the Beginnings Mythic time when world-fashioning events took place.

Tipataka *See* **Tripataka**

Tirthankara "Ford builder," Jain idea of one who has reached total liberation and shows the way across the ocean of suffering; see also **Jina**.

Torah First five books in the Hebrew scriptures; also the whole of scripture; also the whole corpus of revelation, including oral Torah.

torii Characteristic gateway to the Shinto shrine.

tradition "Passing on" of the sacred story and basic ideas of a religion.

Trinity The Christian doctrine that God is revealed in three persons—Father, Son, and Holy Spirit.

Tripataka (Pali: *Tipataka*) The scriptures of the Pali Canon, meaning "Three Baskets"; they include the Vinaya Pitaka, the Sutra Pitaka, and the Abhidharma Pitaka.

Tsao Chun (Pin-yin: *Zao Jun*) God of the cooking stove in Chinese religion.

T'u Ti Kung (Pin-yin: *Tu Di Gong*) Local earth god in Chinese religion.

Twelvers The largest group within the Muslim Shi'ites; those who hold that there have been twelve Imams.

'ulama The class of learned Muslim legal scholars who study and apply the religious sciences.

Ullambana Buddhist festival in China and Japan worshiping the souls of ancestors and providing for souls temporarily released from purgatory. Called Obon in Japan.

'Umar The third caliph in Islamic history.

Umayyad Dynasty ruling Islam from Damascus from 661–750 C.E.

Ummah A community having a common religion; especially the Muslim community.

understanding "Standing under" another's way of thought and life, comprehending it by reference to one's own experience.

Upanishads Secret teaching; collection of teachings about the self and ultimate reality that makes up the last part of the Vedas.

Uposatha Fortnightly Buddhist holy day when meetings for prayer and meditation are held.

'Uthman The fourth caliph in Islamic history.

vaishyas The classical producer-merchant class in Hindu society.

Vajrayana Diamond Vehicle, the Tantric tradition of Buddhism, represented especially in Tibet.

varna "Color," term for the classes in the classical system of Hindu society.

Varuna Vedic god of the heavens.

Vedanta "End of the Vedas"; influential school of philosophy based especially on the Upanishads.

Vedas Most important scriptures of Hinduism, the Shruti; they consist of the Samhitas, Brahmanas, Aranyakas, and Upanishads.

Vinaya Texts containing rules for Buddhist monastic life and discipline.

Vishnu Great Hindu god manifested in avataras, including Krishna and Rama; focus of the great Vaishnavite devotional movement.

vision quest Native American tradition involving individual purification and several days of fasting and praying in a remote sacred place to attain spiritual powers and direction for life.

Wahhabi Strict reform movement founded in Arabia in the eighteenth century and influential throughout Islam.

wat Monastery complex of buildings in Southeast Asian Buddhism.

way of art In Japan, practice of an art (such as poetry, Noh drama, or the tea ceremony) as a way of self-cultivation.

Wemale Tropical yam planters of West Ceram (Indonesia).

Word of God In Sikh thought, God's presence that reverberates throughout creation, channeled especially through the gurus.

worship Respectful ritual activity in special times, directed toward sacred beings or realities of ultimate value.

Worshipful Ones In Jainism, not gods but beings who can be venerated because they have reached perfection or are well on the way, such as Jinas and masters.

Yahweh Special covenant name of Israel's God as it was probably pronounced; written YHWH in the Hebrew scriptures; at a certain point Jews stopped pronouncing this sacred name and substituted the name Adonai.

yin and yang Chinese idea of polarity of forces in the universe; yin is the passive, earthly force, and yang is the active, heavenly force.

Yoga Techniques of spiritual discipline for overcoming bondage to samsara, often emphasizing breathing and meditation exercises; one of the classical schools of Hindu philosophy.

Yom Kippur Jewish Day of Atonement on the tenth of Tishri, a solemn day of repentance.

yoni A circular sacred image in Hinduism representative of the female reproductive organ, often associated with the lingam.

Yoruba African people living in Nigeria.

Zakat The required Muslim practice of alms-giving or wealth-sharing.

zazen "Sitting in meditation," central practice in Zen.

Zealots Jewish religious party in the Roman period that advocated resistance to Roman occupation.

Zen School of meditation Buddhism in Japan. The two main Zen sects are Rinzai (emphasizing sudden enlightenment) and Soto (emphasizing gradual enlightenment).

Zeus Sovereign over the Olympian gods in ancient Greece.

Zionism Modern movement to secure a Jewish homeland in Palestine.

Zionist churches Independent Christian groups in Africa who have attempted to combine African traditions with Christianity.

ACKNOWLEDGMENTS

TEXT

Verses reprinted with permission of Columbia University Press from *The Bhagavad-Gita: Khrishna's Counsel in Time of War*, translated by Barbara Stoller Miller. Copyright © 1986 Columbia University Press.

Verses reprinted with permission of The University Press of America from Milton Chiu, *The Tao of Chinese Religion*. Copyright © 1984 the University Press of America.

Verses reprinted with permission of Wadsworth Publishing Co., Inc., from Stephen Beyer, *The Buddhist Experience: Sources and Interpretations*. Copyright © 1974 Wadsworth Publishing Co., Inc.

Excerpts reprinted with permission of Macmillan Publishing Co. from *The Koran Interpreted*, translated by A. J. Arberry. Copyright © 1964 George Allen and Unwin Ltd.

Excerpts reprinted with permission of Oxford University Press from *The Life of Muhammed: A Translation of Ishaq's Sirat Ranul Allah*, translated by A. Guillaume. Copyright © 1955 Oxford University Press.

Excerpts reprinted with permission of Wing Tsit Chan, Joseph M. Kitagawa and P. T. Raju from *Great Asian Religions: An Anthology*, by Chan *et al*. Copyright © 1969.

Excerpts reprinted with permission of Oxford University Press from *The Thirteen Principal Upanishads*, translated from the Sanskrit by Robert Ernest Hume. Copyright © 1931 Oxford University Press.

Excerpts reprinted from Bary *et al*, *Sources of Indian Tradition*. Copyright © 1959 Columbia University Press. Used by permission.

Excerpts reprinted with permission of Unwin Hyman Limited from *The Sacred Writings of the Sikhs*, translated by Kushwant Singh. Copyright © 1960 Unwin Hyman Limited.

Excerpts from *Chinese Religions: from 1000 B.C. to the Present Day*, by D. Howard Smith. Copyright © 1968 D. Howard Smith. Reprinted by permission of Henry Holt and Company, Inc.

A Source Book in Chinese Philosophy, translated by Wing-Tsit Chan. Copyright © 1963 Princeton University Press. Scattered excerpts reprinted with permission of Princeton University Press.

Excerpts from Bary *et al*, *Sources of Chinese Tradition*. Copyright © 1960 Columbia University Press. Used by permission.

Excerpts reprinted with permission of Washington State University Press from *Taoism and the Rite of Cosmic Renewal*, by Michael Saso. Copyright © 1972 Washington University Press.

ILLUSTRATIONS

Courtesy of the Japan National Tourist Office: pp. 1, 8, 302, 319, 330, 343, 376–377, 462, 466, 476, 477, 479, 481, 483, 487, 491, 493, 495, 497, 499, 501, 503.

Magnum Photos: pp. 3, 17, 278, 422 © Bruno Barby; pp. 27, 32, 225, Elliott Erwitt, © 1969; p. 30, © Erich Lessing; p. 205, © Leonard Freed; p. 223, © Steele-Perkins; p. 238, photo by Bhupendra Karia; p. 264, 272 © Marc Ribaud; pp. 270, 281, 366, © Marilyn Silverstone; pp. 350, 355, 359 © Alex Webb; pp. 358, 363, 368 © Raghu Rai; p. 432, Rene Burri, © 1967.

Courtesy of the India Tourist Office: pp. 5, 290, 299, 337.

Courtesy of the Israeli Tourist Office: pp. 12, 91, 106, 110, 112, 130, 139, 235.

The Metropolitan Museum of Art: p. 21, Harris Brisbane Dick Fund, 1929; p. 81, purchase, 1871. (71.28); p. 383, Rogers Fund, 1943, (43.25.4).

Courtesy of the United Nations: p. 23.

Courtesy of the Turkish Tourist Office: pp. 28, 36, 187, 211, 217.

Woodfin Camp and Associates: pp. 39, 56 © Jason Laure; p. 67 © Marc and Evelyne Bernheim; p. 352.

Copyright Marcia Keegan: p. 41.

Courtesy of the Department of Library Services, American Museum of Natural History: p. 49, neg. no. 332105; p. 63, neg. no. 124360 (photo by H. C. Meredith); p. 70, neg. no. 124649.

Courtesy of the Southwest Museum, Los Angeles: p. 58.

Photo Researchers, Inc: pp. 74, 99 © Bill Aron; 118 © Hanna W. Schreiber; p. 121 © Sherry Suris; p. 126 © Alice Kandel, 1980; p. 174 © David R. Frazier, 1980; p. 177 © Katrina Thomas; p. 267 © Mary Evans Picture Library; p. 268 © Amy Stromsten, 1982; p. 292 © Bernard Pierre Wolff, 1973; p. 335, 341 © Renee Lynn, 1987; p. 395; p. 398, 410, 436, 459 © Paolo Koch; p. 407 © Robert E. Murowchick, 1984; pp. 415, 428, 440 © Audrey Topping; pp. 438, 448 © Catherine Ursillo; p. 456 © Frederico Arborio Mellas.

Religious News Service: pp. 79, 94, FMB photo by Joanna Pinneo; pp. 82; 102; 107; pp. 115, 119, clarion photo by Reverend Elmo L. Romagosa; pp. 132; 152; 156; 158; pp. 167, 170, photo by Don Rutledge; 172; 180; 182; 185; 244; 251; 306; 308; 316; 318; 322.

The Bettmann Archives: pp. 137, 149, 166, 189, 192, 209, 220, 230, 232, 273, 347, 381, 387, 390, 405, 451.

Copyright Morton Broffman: p.160.

The Asia Society, New York: Mr. and Mrs. John D. Rockefeller 3d: pp. 195, 260, 275, 284, 287, 293, 321, 324, 333, 464.

Courtesy of the Macmillan Publishing Company: p. 208, reprinted by permission from *An Introduction to Islam*, by Frederick Denny. Copyright © 1985 Macmillan.

Courtesy of the Ministry of Information, Saudi Arabia: pp. 228, 233.

New York Public Library Picture Collection: p. 289.

Courtesy of the Cleveland Museum of Art, p. 401, John L. Severance Fund, 64.44.

AP/World Wide Photos: p. 511.

INDEX

Arjuna, 260, 263
Art and religion, 21–23
  Buddhism, 340–342
  Chinese, 450–451
  Christianity, 178–179
  Hinduism, 293–294
  Islam, 235–236
  Jainism, 360
  Japanese Buddhism, 500–502
  Judaism, 122
  nonliterate peoples, 66–67
  Shintoism, 500
  Sikhism, 373
  and specific religion, 23
  types of art forms, 22
  Zen Buddhism, 475, 501
Artha, 298, 299
Aryans, early Hindus, 250–253
Arya Samaj, 266, 300
Asceticism
  Jainism, 357–358
  Sikhs, 367, 369
al-Ash'ari, 202
Ashkenazim, 96, 97
Ashoka, Buddhism, 257, 311, 316, 348
'Ashura, 233–234
Asia
  Buddhism, spread of, 314–317
  East Asian religions, common elements
    of, 378–379
  Southeast Asia, 316–317, 319
  See also Chinese Buddhism; Chinese
    religion; Confucianism; Japanese
    Buddhism; Taoism; Shintoism.
Athanasius, Bishop, 144
Atharva Veda, 252
Atman, 253, 277
Atonement, Christianity, 168
Atsutane, Hirata, 486, 505, 506
Augustine of Hippo, 6, 145
AUM, 280–281
Aurobindo, Sri, 267, 296
Auto da fe (Act of Faith 1481), 96
Avalokiteshvara, 313, 318
Averroes, 202
Avicenna, 202
Axis mundi, 22, 24
al-Azhar, university, 200, 212

Ba'al, versus Yahweh, 103
Babur, 207–208
Babylon, Israelite exile, 89
Baghdad, 198, 200
Banaras, 291
Baptism, Christianity, 176
Bar mitzvah, 121
Barth, Karl, 155
Basho, 475, 502
Basil of Caesarea, 144

Bear Festival, 64
Belur Math, 290
Benedict's Rule, 147
Bernard of Clairvaux, 149
BESHT, 97
Bhagavad Gita, 260, 273–274
  contents of, 260–261
Bhakti, 260, 261, 283–285
  of Shaivites, 285
  of Vaishavites, 283–284
Bible
  New Testament, 131
  Old Testament, 131–132
Birth rituals
  Christianity, 176
  Hinduism, 292
  Islam, 234
  Judaism, 120
  Shintoism, 499
  Sikhism, 372
  See also Prebirth rituals.
Blackheads, Taoism, 404, 453
Black Muslims, 214
Black Stone, 191, 196, 232
Blessings
  Islam, 226
  Judaism, 113
Blessingway ceremonials, 58–59
Bliss Body, Buddha, 325
Bodh Gaya, 306, 307
Bodhidharma, 400
Bodhisattva
  course of, 312–313
  nature of, 313
  vows of, 333, 446
Bohemians, 154
Bon, 317, 318
Book of Common Prayer, The,
  153, 177
Bowing, Buddhism, 336
Boxer Rebellion, 410
Boyhood rituals, 339
  Buddhism, 339
  Hinduism, 292
  Islam, 234
  Judaism, 121
  nonliterate peoples, 65–66
Brahma, 326–327
Brahman, 256–257, 262, 271–272, 277
  nature of, 271
  Nirguna Brahman, 272
  Saguna Brahman, 272
  two levels of, 272
Brahmanas, 253, 255
Brahma Samaj (Society of Brahman),
  265, 266
Brahmin, Vedic sacrifices, 288
Brahmins, class, 294, 295
Breath, in Taoism, 402–403
Brethren of the Common Life, 150

Buddha, 303–309
  death of, 308–309
  Dharma, 307–308
  enlightenment of, 305–307
  Four Noble Truths, 307, 330
  life of, 304–305
  of Mahayana Buddhists, 325–326
  sangha, creation of, 308
  scriptures of, Tripitaka, 309
  as supernatural human, 324–325
  Three Body doctrine, 325
Buddhahood, 325, 328
  path to, 329–334
Buddhaland, 313, 325
Buddha-nature, 332–333
Buddhism
  art and, 340–342
  creation, 326–327
  ethics, 344–347
    Five Precepts as guide, 345–346
    monastic community, 346–347
    practical nature of, 345
    sublime states of meditation,
      344–345
    vegetarianism, 345
  festivals
    birthday of Buddha, 338
    Ullambana festival, 339
  and Hinduism, 307, 312, 316, 326
  historical view
    Ashoka, 309, 311
    bodhisattva, course of, 312–313
    Buddha, story of, 303–309
    communism, effect of, 319
    expansion of, 314–317
    Great Sangha/new sutras, 312
    Madhyamika school, 313–314
    Mahayana, 311–312, 313–314
    revitalization, modern era, 319–320
    Theravada, 311
    Tibetan Buddhism, 317–318
    Vajrayana, 314
    Yogacara school, 314
  holy days, 337–338
    New Year festival, 338
    Rain Retreat, 338–339
    uposatha holy day, 337–338
  human existence, 326–329
    Buddhahood, 328
    clinging, 328
    dependent arising, 322, 327
    impermanence, doctrine of, 327
    karma, 327, 328
    no-self, 328, 343
    rebirth, 329, 332
    wheel of existence, 327, 329, 330
  objects of worship, 337
  prayer, 336
  rituals, 336–337
    basic structure of, 336

Ch'ing Ming festival, 448
Chou era, ancient China, 383–384
  ceremonialism, 384
  decline of, 385–386
  five elements, 384
  I Ching, 384
  religious developments, 383
  yin-yang, 384
Chou Tun-i, 405
Christendom, 147–154
Christianity
  art in, 178–179
  in China, 408–409
  community, 179–181
    church, components of, 179–180
    churches, 180
    congregations, 180
    religious leadership, ministry, 180–181
  creation, 162–163
    and Christ, 162
    as good/right, 162–163
    nature of, 162
  ethics, 181–186
    freedom in approach to, 181–183
    mission in world, 184–186
    Ten Commandments, 183
  God, 159–162
    and evil, 161
    Trinity, 160–161
  historical view
    American Christianity, 154
    Apostles' Creed, 142
    Augustine of Hippo, 145
    Christendom, 147–154
    Christian church, beginning of, 138
    clergy, formation of, 142
    Crusades, 148–149
    Eastern Orthodoxy, 148
    ecumenical councils, 144
    ecumenical movement, 156
    Enlightenment, 154
    fundamentalism, 155
    Gnosticism, 140, 141
    Hellenistic world, gospel and, 140
    Jesus, life/teachings of, 132–138
    Jew/Gentile Christians, 139–140
    Jewish roots, 131–132
    modern theologies, 155–156
    Monasticism, 143–144, 149
    mysticism, 150
    persecution of Christians, 138
    Reformation, 151–154
    Renaissance, 150–151
    Roman era, 142–145
    scholarship, rise of, 149–150
    scientific biblical scholarship, 155
    theological controversy, 144–145
    theological systems, 142
  holy days, 174–176
    Advent, 175

Christmas, 175
  Easter, 175
  Epiphany, 175
  feast days of saints, 176–177
  Lent, season of, 175
  Pentecost, 175
human existence, 162–171
  in Japan, 476
  rituals, 173–174, 176–178
    baptism, 176
    confirmation, 177
    death rituals, 178
    differences in religious groups, 173
    sacraments, 174
    Sunday worship, 173–174
    wedding ritual, 177–178
  salvation, 166–171
    afterlife, 171
    atonement, 168
    faith, 169–171
    and Jesus Christ, 167–169
  sin, 163–166
    consequences of, 165–166
    fall from garden, 163–164
    original sin, 164–165
  worship, daily prayer, 176
Christian Scientists, 154
Christmas, 175
Christological controversy, 144–145
Christology, 140
Chuang Tzu, 391
Chuang Tzu, 424, 427, 433, 457–458
  life/stories of, 391–392
Chu Hsi, 406, 419–420
Circle-worship, 265
Circumcision
  Islam, 234
  Judaism, 120
City of God (Augustine), 145
City-states
  Egyptian, 31, 32
  Greek, 36
  Mesopotamian, 33, 34
Clan, imperial, Japan, 464
Classic of Changes (*I Ching*), 388
Classic of History (*Shu Ching*), 388
Classic of Poetry (*Shih Ching*), 388
Classic of Rites (*Li Ching*), 388, 430, 438, 460
Class system, Hinduism, 294–295
Clement of Alexandria, 131
Clergy, formation of, Christianity, 142
Clinging, human problem, Buddhism, 328
Clovis, King of Franks, 147
Communal identity, nonliterate peoples, 67–68
Communism, effect on Chinese Buddhism, 319, 408, 410
Community, religious identity and, 23–24

Concordat of Worms, 148
Confession, Islam, 229
Confessions (Augustine), 145
Confirmation, 177
Confucianism
  ethics, 453–457
    Doctrine of the Mean, 454–455, 456
    filiality, 454–455
    propriety, 455–456
  heaven, 414–416
    Neo-Confucianists, 415–416
  historical view
    alternative groups and Confucianism, 392, 394
    Analects, 386, 387
    Chang Tsai, 405
    Ch'eng brothers, 406
    Chou Tun-i, 405
    Chu Hsi, 406
    Confucius, life/teachings of, 386–389
    Doctrine of the Mean (*Chung Yung*), 389
    establishment as state ideology, 394
    Five Classics, 388
    Mencius, influence of, 389
    Mind School of Neo-Confucianism, 406
    Neo-Confucianism, 404–406
    Wang Yang-ming, 406
  human existence, 424
  in Japan, 468
  ritual, 430–431
    origins of, 430–431
    purpose of, 388
    varieties of, 430
  transformation, 388–389, 428–431
    propriety, 388, 431
    ritual, 430–431
    study/learning, 429–430
    Tao in, 388
  worship, 439–440
    ancestor worship, 439–440
    community worship, 441
    in home, 439
    state worship, 440–441
Confucius, 386–389
  death of, 387
  disciples of, 389
  life of, 386–387
  teachings of, 387–389
Confusion of the Confusion, The (Ibn Rushd), 202
Confusion of the Philosophers, The (al-Ghazali), 202
Congregations, 180
Conservative Judaism, 99–100
Constantine, Emperor of Rome, 143, 144, 145
Constantinople, fall of, 148